Contents

Foreword

Biological diversity – the variability among living things and the ecosystems they inhabit – is the foundation upon which human civilizations have been built. Its conservation is a prerequisite for sustainable development and, as such, constitutes one of the greatest challenges of the modern era.

The importance of this challenge was universally acknowledged at the Earth Summit, held in Rio de Janeiro in 1992, and through the development of the Convention on Biological Diversity, an international legally binding treaty that now has some 180 Parties. In ratifying the Convention, the Parties have committed themselves, in general terms, to undertaking national and international measures aimed at achieving three explicit objectives: the conservation of biological diversity; the sustainable use of its components; and the equitable sharing of benefits arising out of the utilization of genetic resources.

Since the time of the adoption of the Convention, the Conference of the Parties has met five times and, on each occasion, has, through its decisions, taken steps necessary to translate the general provisions of the Convention into practical action. These measures have included, among other things, the adoption of programmes of work for a number of thematic areas and cross-cutting issues, the issuance of specific guidance for funding of projects through the financial mechanism established under the Convention, and the establishment of ad hoc bodies to focus on the implementation of specific provisions of the Convention, such as those relating to access and benefit-sharing, indigenous knowledge and safety in biotechnology. In the latter instance, this process has led to the adoption of a new legal instrument, the Cartagena Protocol on Biosafety, itself a landmark treaty which provides an international regulatory framework for reconciling the respective needs of free trade and environmental protection with respect to a rapidly growing global industry.

To date, however, these decisions have been available only in separate publications, each covering the work of a particular meeting of the Conference of the Parties. It has therefore been difficult to see their relationship both to each other and to the individual provisions of the Convention. The purpose of this Handbook is to compile them all in a single volume, indicating at the same time how they serve to develop and enlarge upon the general commitments set out in the Convention, and thus providing an accurate and easy guide to the status of each of its provisions.

To this end, the Handbook includes the text of the Convention on Biological Diversity, the Cartagena Protocol on Biosafety and every decision of the Conference of the Parties. It comprehensively explains how the decisions of the Conference of the Parties have developed each and every Article of the Convention. The Handbook also includes other relevant material such as: the Final Act of the Nairobi Conference of Plenipotentiaries for the Adoption of the Agreed Text of the Convention on Biological Diversity; declarations made by Governments upon the adoption, signature and ratification of the Convention; and a current list of Parties to the Convention and the Biosafety Protocol.

An electronic copy of the Handbook, automatically indexed and cross-referenced, with full search facilities is also provided in the accompanying CD-ROM.

I trust that the Handbook will serve as a useful reference guide for those interested in the development of the Convention and the efforts of the international community to protect the world's biological diversity.

Hamdallah Zedan
Executive Secretary
Convention on Biological Diversity

How to use this Handbook

Purpose

This Handbook is intended to provide a reference guide to decisions adopted by the Conference of the Parties (COP) to the Convention on Biological Diversity as well as a guide to ongoing activities in relation to particular Articles and/or thematic areas of the Convention. The structure of the Handbook has been conceived with a view to allowing frequent updates, so as to take into account new decisions of the COP.

Structure

Introduction:	describes the background to the Convention and its institutional arrangements.
Section I:	sets out the full text of the Convention signed by the Contracting Parties in June 1992.
Section II:	sets out the text of the Cartagena Protocol on Biosafety adopted by the COP in January 2000.
Section III:	contains the rules of procedure adopted by the COP and subsidiary bodies.
Section IV:	contains the *modus operandi* of the Subsidiary Body on Scientific, Technical and Technological Advice (SBSTTA).
Section V:	contains the financial rules for the Convention.
Section VI:	provides detailed information on substantive decisions adopted by the COP to date on particular issues (see 'The "guide" to COP decisions' on the following page).
Section VII:	lists the signature and/or ratification dates of the Parties to the Convention.
Section VIII:	contains the declarations made by the Parties upon ratification, accession, acceptance or approval.
Section IX:	sets out the text of the Nairobi Final Act adopted in May 1992.
Section X:	sets out the full text of the decisions of the COP, and recommendations of the SBSTTA that have been specifically endorsed in COP decisions.
Indexes:	allow users to search both for key terms and for particular Articles of the Convention and Protocol, COP decisions and SBSTTA recommendations.

The 'guide' to COP decisions

Section VI presents an overview of COP decisions to date related to specific Articles of the Convention or the thematic work programmes. It provides a brief narrative on how the COP has addressed each Article or thematic area to date. This narrative summary is not intended in any way to replace the text of decisions adopted by the Conference of the Parties, which are reproduced in full in Section X of this Handbook and to which readers should refer. It is intended solely to provide a guide and references to relevant COP decisions so as to enable a user to (i) obtain a brief overview of the COP's consideration of a particular issue, and (ii) find all relevant COP decisions relating to a particular issue. Section VI also provides a listing of specific references to paragraphs of COP decisions which address the Article or thematic area in question, as well as relevant documents officially submitted to meetings of the Convention.

As far as possible, each Article of the Convention and each thematic area has been addressed according to a common format.

Articles or provisions addressed by the COP to date

For the Articles of the Convention addressed by the COP, the format includes the following. Where an Article of the Convention addresses a number of specific issues, these have been addressed separately for ease of reference.

1. **Text of Article**
2. **Notes**

   (i) Terms defined in Article 2
   A list of any relevant definitions found in Article 2 of the Convention.

   (ii) Consideration of the Article by the COP

   (a) Background and status
   A brief summary as to when and how the COP has addressed the Article in question including: decisions adopted; intersessional activities; and current and forthcoming activities.

   (b) COP guidance
   Briefly highlights relevant guidance in COP decisions to the Parties as well as guidance to the financial mechanisms.

3. **References**

   A list of COP decisions or parts thereof of relevance to the Convention provision in question. This list has been divided as follows:

   (i) Decisions on the Article
   Decisions of the COP specifically addressing the Article in question.

   (ii) Guidance to Parties
   Guidance from the COP and requests to the Parties contained in relevant COP decisions, including guidance and requests relating to:

(a) *National action*

(b) *Information and case studies*
Information and case studies to be submitted to the Secretariat or clearing-house mechanism.

(iii) *Financial mechanism and resources*
Decisions of the COP which provide guidance as to the provision of the financial resources from the financial mechanism or other sources to support implementation of the Article in question or related activities. In particular, looking at:

(a) *Guidance to the financial mechanism*

(b) *Other (additional) financial resources*

(iv) *Guidance to the Secretariat*
Indicates activities which the Secretariat has been instructed to undertake in relation to the Article in question.

(v) *Guidance to SBSTTA*
Indicates requests and guidance to SBSTTA regarding advice to the COP and SBSTTA's work programme.

(vi) *Cooperation with other conventions and organizations*
Indicates relevant cooperative and collaborative activities mandated by the COP in relation to the issue in question, as well as requests and statements to other conventions, organisations and processes.

(vii) *Relevant aspects of thematic work programmes*
Indicates aspects of the thematic work programmes and related decisions of relevance to the Article in question.

(viii) *Other relevant decisions*
This is intended to pick up relevant cross-references in other COP decisions.

4. **Declarations**

A list of declarations that were made upon adoption, signature and/or ratification.

5. **Documents**

A list of relevant background and information documents officially submitted to meetings of the COP or its subsidiary bodies.

Articles or provisions not yet addressed by the COP

Some Articles of the Convention have not been addressed by the COP in any detail to date. For these Articles, a simplified format is used, which includes the following:

1. **Text of the Article**

2. **Notes**

(i) *Terms defined in Article 2*
A list of any relevant definitions found in Article 2 of the Convention.

(ii) *Consideration of the Article by the COP*
A brief note on any relevant discussions by the COP and relevant cross-references.

3. **References**

A list of relevant references in COP decisions to date, sub-divided as follows:

(i) Relevant aspects of the thematic work programmes

(ii) Other relevant decisions

Since these Articles have not yet been explicitly addressed by the COP, the references provided represent an attempt to highlight those decisions that have a bearing on the provisions of the Article.

4. **Documents**

Thematic work programmes

The thematic areas are based, as far as possible, on a common format, as follows:

1. **Notes**

(i) Consideration of the thematic area by the COP
Describes the development of the thematic work programme by the COP.

(ii) Elements of the thematic work programme
Highlights the principal elements, objectives and activities of the thematic work programme as set out in the relevant COP decision.

(iii) Implementation of the work programme

2. **List of COP decisions adopted on the thematic area in question**

3. **List of references to that thematic area in other decisions of the COP**

Introduction:
The operation of the Convention on Biological Diversity

The origin of the negotiations for the Convention on Biological Diversity lies in the 1987 Governing Council decision 14/26 of the United Nations Environment Programme (UNEP), which called upon UNEP to convene an Ad Hoc Working Group of Experts on Biological Diversity for the harmonization of existing conventions related to biological diversity. At its first meeting, the Group of Experts agreed on the need to elaborate an internationally binding instrument on biological diversity. In May 1989, another Ad Hoc Working Group of Experts on Biological Diversity was established to prepare an international legal instrument for the conservation and sustainable use of biological diversity, taking into account 'the need to share costs and benefits between developed and developing countries and the ways and means to support innovation by local people'. The Ad Hoc Working Group, which in February 1991 became the Intergovernmental Negotiating Committee (INC), held seven working sessions (five negotiating) which culminated in the adoption of an agreed text of the Convention on Biological Diversity through the Nairobi Final Act of the Conference for the Adoption of the Agreed Text of the Convention on Biological Diversity.

The Convention was opened for signature at the United Nations Conference on Environment and Development (UNCED) in Rio de Janeiro in June 1992. It entered into force on 29 December 1993 and currently has 181 Parties.[1]

The principal objectives of the Convention on Biological Diversity are the conservation and sustainable use of biological diversity, and the fair and equitable sharing of benefits arising from its utilization. The Convention recognizes that the key to maintaining biological diversity depends upon using this diversity in a sustainable manner.

The Convention translates its guiding objectives of conservation, sustainable use and equitable sharing of benefits into binding commitments in its substantive provisions contained in Articles 6 to 20. These articles contain key provisions on, among others: measures for the conservation of biological diversity, both *in situ* and *ex situ*; incentives for the conservation and sustainable use of biological diversity; research and training; public awareness and education; assessing the impacts of projects upon biological diversity; regulating access to genetic resources; access to and transfer of technology; and the provision of financial resources.

In addition to its substantive provisions, the Convention establishes institutional arrangements which provide a mechanism for the further development of, and for monitoring the implementation of, the Convention through meetings, work

1 As at 31 July 2001.

programmes, reviews and negotiations. Three institutions are established by the Convention: the Conference of the Parties (COP), the Subsidiary Body on Scientific, Technical and Technological Advice (SBSTTA) and the Secretariat. In addition, the Convention establishes a financial mechanism, for the provision of financial resources to developing country Parties, and provides for the establishment of a clearing-house mechanism (CHM) for scientific and technical cooperation. Further, the Convention enables the COP to establish additional subsidiary bodies as it deems necessary for the implementation of the Convention.

This chapter provides an overview of the institutions of the Convention on Biological Diversity. It is intended to provide a brief guide to the respective mandates of the various organs established by the Convention, as well as to how they operate and interrelate.[2] It also describes how the programme of work of the Convention has been addressed to date. Detailed information on substantive decisions adopted by the COP to date on particular issues is provided in Section VI of this Handbook.

Institutional arrangements

Conference of the Parties

The governing body of the Convention is the COP, established under Article 23. Its key function is to keep under review the implementation of the Convention and to steer its development. Other important functions of the COP include adoption of the budget, the consideration of national reports, the adoption of protocols or annexes and the development of guidance to the financial mechanism. A list of functions of the COP is set out in Article 23.

To date, there have been five ordinary meetings of the COP, and the next meeting will take place in April 2002 in The Hague, The Netherlands. At the fifth meeting (COP 5), it was decided that ordinary meetings of the COP shall be held every two years. Meetings of the COP are open to all Parties to the Convention, as well as to observers from non-Parties, intergovernmental organizations and non-governmental organizations. In accordance with its rules of procedure, the COP can also hold extraordinary meetings. The first extraordinary meeting of the COP (ExCOP) was held in Cartagena, Colombia, in February 1999, to consider and adopt the first protocol to the Convention, a protocol on biosafety.[3] As agreement on the text of the biosafety protocol was not forthcoming, the first extraordinary meeting of the COP was suspended,[4] and resumed in January 2000 in Montreal, where it concluded its work and adopted the Cartagena Protocol on Biosafety.[5]

The broad scope of the Convention has meant that the COP has been required to deal with a large agenda. The COP has initiated work in a number of areas to elaborate or clarify aspects of the Convention, and has taken some one hundred and seven proce-

2 Further specific information on the institutional arrangements of the Convention can be obtained from Section VI of this Handbook: Article 23 (Conference of the Parties); Article 24 (Secretariat); Article 25 (SBSTTA); Article 18 (paragraph 3 of the clearing-house mechanism); Articles 20, 21 and 39 (Financial mechanism and resources); Article 8 (j) (Traditional knowledge, innovations and practices); Article 15 (Access to genetic resources); and Article 19 (3) (Biosafety).

3 See Section VI of this Handbook: Article 19 (3).

4 Decision EM-I/1.

5 Decision EM-I/3.

dural and substantive decisions to date. At its first meeting (COP 1) in 1994, the COP adopted a programme of work for the years 1995–1997. It reviewed this programme of work at its fourth meeting (COP 4) in 1998, and adopted a programme of work for its fifth to seventh meetings (see 'Programme of work' below).

Subsidiary Body on Scientific, Technical and Technological Advice

Article 25 of the Convention establishes an open-ended intergovernmental scientific advisory body, the SBSTTA, to provide the COP with advice and recommendations on scientific, technical and technological aspects of the implementation of the Convention. Specific functions of SBSTTA include:

- providing scientific and technical assessments of the status of biological diversity;
- preparing scientific and technical assessments of the measures taken to implement the Convention;
- identifying innovative, efficient and state of the art technologies and know how, and advising on how to promote their development;
- providing advice on scientific programmes and international cooperation in research and development; and
- generally responding to scientific, technical and technological and methodological questions asked by the COP.

To date, SBSTTA has held six meetings. The seventh meeting (SBSTTA 7) will be held from 12 to 16 November 2001 in Montreal. It submits its advice to the COP in the form of SBSTTA recommendations. The COP considers SBSTTA's advice on relevant issues before adopting its decisions. In some instances, the COP has explicitly endorsed specific SBSTTA recommendations in whole or in part.[6]

Much discussion relating to the operation of the Convention has related to the need to promote the provision of scientific, technical and technological advice to the COP and to ensure that available expertise in other relevant institutions is utilized. The current *modus operandi* of SBSTTA is set out in annex I to decision IV/16, as amended by paragraph 21 of decision V/20. Additional guidance on the functioning of SBSTTA is given in Part III of decision V/20.[7] SBSTTA's *modus operandi* envisages the use of small groups of experts, in liaison groups, to facilitate the preparation and review of documentation for SBSTTA meetings. It also envisages meetings of ad hoc technical groups of experts on particular issues. COP 5 decided upon terms of reference for three ad hoc technical expert groups on: marine and coastal protected areas; mariculture; and forest biological diversity. It also requested SBSTTA to establish a further ad hoc technical expert group to develop the programme of work adopted on dry and sub-humid lands. Ad hoc technical expert groups are composed from rosters of experts on particular issues drawn up by the Secretariat on the basis of nominations by governments.

---

6 SBSTTA recommendations which have been explicitly endorsed by the COP are reproduced in Section X of this Handbook.
7 See Section IV of this Handbook.

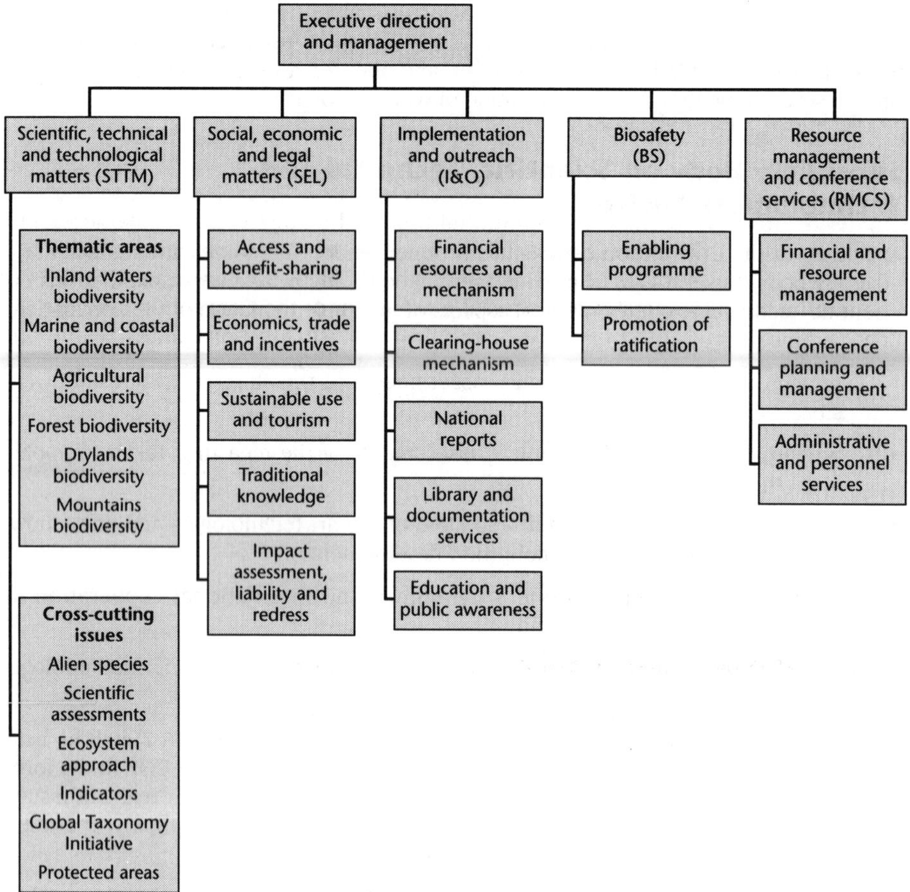

Figure 1 *Programme structure of the Secretariat*

Secretariat

Article 24 establishes a Secretariat whose principal functions are to prepare for and service meetings of the COP and other subsidiary bodies of the Convention and to coordinate with other relevant international bodies. The host institution of the Secretariat is UNEP. The Secretariat is located in Montreal, Canada.

The Secretariat provides administrative support to the COP, SBSTTA and other Convention bodies. It represents the day-to-day focal point of the Convention, organizes all meetings under the Convention and provides background documentation for those meetings. The Secretariat plays a significant role in coordinating the work carried out under the Convention with that of other relevant institutions and conventions, and represents the Convention at meetings of other relevant bodies. The programmatic structure of the Secretariat is described in Figure 1 above.

The Parties to the Convention have established a Trust Fund to meet the costs of administering the Convention, including the costs of the Secretariat. All Parties contribute to the budget of the Convention. The financial rules governing contributions to the Trust

Fund have not yet been finally agreed by the Parties, but in practice contributions are weighted in accordance with the UN scale of assessments.[8]

Financial mechanism

Article 21 establishes a mechanism for the provision of financial resources to developing countries for the purposes of the Convention. In Article 20 developed countries undertake to provide 'new and additional financial resources to enable developing country Parties to meet the agreed full incremental costs' of implementing the obligations of the Convention. Article 39 appointed the Global Environment Facility (GEF) on an interim basis to operate the financial mechanism of the Convention, and the GEF continues to fulfil this function. The financial mechanism functions under the authority and guidance of, and is accountable to, the COP. COP 1 adopted comprehensive guidance for the financial mechanism.[9] This guidance has been refined and augmented at each of the subsequent meetings of the COP.[10] The GEF reports to each meeting of the COP on its implementation of the guidance.

The GEF is managed by a Council which is composed of 32 members representing some 166 Participant states. Projects of the GEF are undertaken by Parties to the Convention and the Implementing Agencies of the GEF: UNEP, the United Nations Development Programme (UNDP) and the World Bank.

Clearing-house mechanism

Paragraph 3 of Article 18 anticipated the establishment of a clearing-house mechanism (CHM) to promote and facilitate technical and scientific cooperation.[11] A pilot phase of the CHM, administered by the Secretariat, was established under decisions I/3 and II/3 of the COP. At the end of 1998, an independent review of the pilot phase of the CHM was initiated.[12] COP 5 supported the implementation of a strategic plan for the CHM[13] and endorsed a longer-term programme of work for the CHM.[14] An informal advisory committee has been established for the CHM.

Additional subsidiary organs

In the course of its consideration of specific issues, the COP has seen fit to establish a number of other subsidiary organs with limited and defined mandates. These include:

- Working Group on Biosafety;[15]
- Expert Panel on Access and Benefit-sharing;[16]
- Working Group on Access and Benefit-sharing;[17]

---

8 The financial rules for the administration of the Trust Fund for the Convention on Biological Diversity, as contained in decision III/1, are set out in Section V of this Handbook.
9 Decision I/2.
10 See Section VI of this Handbook: Articles 20, 21 and 39.
11 See Section VI of this Handbook: Article 18 (3).
12 Decision IV/2, paragraph 10 (k).
13 See document UNEP/CBD/COP/5/INF/2.
14 See decision V/14 and document UNEP/CBD/COP/5/INF/4.
15 See decision II/5 and Section VI of this Handbook: Article 19 (3).
16 See decisions IV/8 and V/26 A–C, and Section VI of this Handbook: Article 15.
17 See decision V/26 A–C and Section VI of this Handbook: Article 15.

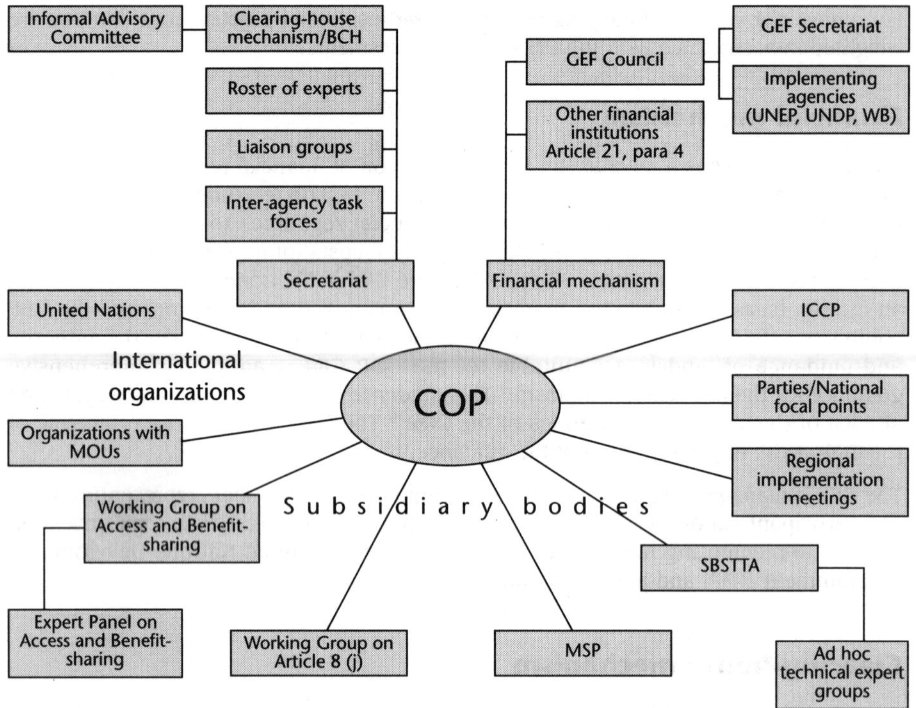

Figure 2 *Institutions of the Convention*

- Working Group on Article 8 (j) and Related Provisions;[18] and
- Intergovernmental Committee for the Cartagena Protocol (ICCP).[19]

These bodies have been established to provide advice and recommendations on specific issues. In each case, the COP has decided the terms of reference of the organ, and has given guidance on its duration and composition.

Other relevant activities

In addition to the formal establishment of subsidiary bodies, over the life of the Convention a wide range of other activities have supported its work. These include:

- workshops and meetings on specific issues organized under the auspices of the Convention, often by the Secretariat in collaboration with one or more sponsoring governments or organizations;
- conferences and other events sponsored by governments or institutions outside the auspices of the Convention but with results being made available at meetings of the COP or SBSTTA (for example, in information documents);
- regional and subregional meetings and activities on implementation of the Convention and by way of preparation for meetings of the COP;

18 See decision IV/9 and Section VI of this Handbook: Article 8 (j).
19 See decision EM-I/3 and 'Cartagena Protocol on Biosafety' later in this chapter.

- initiatives on specific issues, such as the Global Invasive Species Programme and the Global Taxonomy Initiative; and
- information gathering exercises: for example calls for case studies from Parties and institutions for synthesis in COP documents.

How these various institutions and activities relate to one another is illustrated in Figure 2 opposite.

Programme of work

The work of the Convention was initially organized in accordance with a medium-term programme of work which laid out the priorities for work under the Convention from 1995 to 1997.[20] Specifically, the medium-term programme of work set out a schedule for the consideration of particular thematic areas and cross-cutting issues by the COP at its second, third and fourth meetings. It provided for a review of the medium-term programme of work, as well as a broader review of the operations of the COP, to take place at COP 4.

Implementation of the medium-term programme of work saw the evolution of a process for the development of COP decisions and the application of the general principles of the Convention to specific thematic areas and cross-cutting issues. In addition, at its second meeting, the COP decided that the ecosystem approach should be the primary framework of action to be taken under the Convention.[21] This view has been reiterated in subsequent decisions of the COP.[22]

Thematic work programmes

The COP has initiated work on five thematic work programmes, addressing marine and coastal biodiversity, agricultural biodiversity, forest biodiversity, the biodiversity of inland waters, and dry and sub-humid lands. Each thematic programme establishes a vision for, and basic principles to guide, future work; sets out key issues for consideration; identifies potential outputs; and suggests a timetable and means for achieving these outputs. The COP has explicitly directed that the consideration of certain cross-cutting issues should be integrated into the thematic work programmes.[23] Periodic review of the implementation of the work programme by the COP and SBSTTA is provided. It is envisaged that implementation of the work programmes will involve contributions from Parties, the Secretariat, relevant intergovernmental organizations and other organizations.

Cross-cutting issues

Over and above the thematic programmes there are a number of other items on the COP's agenda addressing key cross-cutting issues of relevance to all thematic areas. Essentially these correspond to the issues addressed in the Convention's substantive provisions in Articles 6–20. For example, as indicated in subsequent sections of this

20 Decision I/9; decision II/18; decision III/22.
21 Decision II/8, paragraph 1.
22 See decision IV/1 B and 'Ecosystem approach' in this chapter.
23 See, for example, decision III/18, paragraph 2.

Handbook, work has been initiated on biosafety; access to genetic resources; traditional knowledge, innovations and practices (Article 8 (j)); intellectual property rights; indicators; taxonomy; public education and awareness; incentives; and alien species.

Some cross-cutting initiatives directly support work under thematic programmes, for example the work on indicators. Others are developing discrete products, which in some instances are quite separate from the thematic programmes – for example, the negotiations for a protocol on biosafety. These cross-cutting issues have an important role to play in bringing cohesion to the work of the Convention as they provide the substantive bridges or links between the thematic programmes.

Ecosystem approach[24]

At its fourth meeting, the COP acknowledged that, by virtue of decision II/8, the ecosystem approach has been adopted as a framework for the analysis and implementation of the objectives of the Convention. In effect, the ecosystem approach is the fundamental paradigm for the Convention's activities; a prism through which its activities are to develop. In decision V/6, the COP endorsed a description of the ecosystem approach as well as certain operational guidance, and recommended the application of a number of principles of the ecosystem approach. The principles amount to a strategy for the integrated or holistic management of resources through modern scientific adaptive management practices. Essentially, they require that the process of decision making be transparent and take into account all relevant factors. Collectively the principles are similar to principles associated with strategic environmental assessment methods. The COP recognized that the principles themselves require development and adjustment in light of experience and accordingly encouraged further conceptual elaboration of the ecosystem approach and mandated further work in this area.

Longer-term programme of work; review of operations of the Convention; and the development of a Strategic Plan

At its fourth meeting, the COP reviewed its medium-term programme of work, and considered a longer-term programme of work. COP 4 adopted a programme of work for its fifth to seventh meetings, specifying a thematic area and two cross-cutting issues for in-depth consideration at each of these meetings.[25]

COP 4 reviewed the operations of the Convention to date. Issues discussed included: future periodicity of meetings under the Convention; issues to be addressed at future meetings; and the way in which scientific and technical work under the Convention should be carried out. COP 4 did not reach a conclusion on some aspects of the future operations of the Convention, in particular how to improve preparations for and conduct of future meetings of the COP. It decided to hold an intersessional meeting to consider these issues further.[26] Accordingly, an Intersessional Meeting on the Operations of the Convention (ISOC) was held in June 1999. The ISOC recommended the development of a Strategic Plan for the Convention based on the longer-term programme of work adopted at COP 4.[27] The ISOC recommended that the Strategic Plan be considered and adopted at COP 6.

24 See Section VI of this Handbook.
25 Decision IV/16, annex II.
26 Decision IV/16, paragraph 2.
27 UNEP/CBD/COP/5/4.

COP 5 adopted a further decision on the operations of the Convention, which, *inter alia*, set out a process for the development and adoption of a Strategic Plan for the Convention at COP 6 in 2002. The Strategic Plan is to be based on the longer-term programme of work of the COP and SBSTTA, and is to provide strategic and operational guidance for the implementation of these programmes of work.[28]

COP 5 also adopted certain operational guidance to improve the functioning of the COP and SBSTTA, and provided for a further intersessional meeting to consider, among others, the preparation of the Strategic Plan before COP 6. The meeting on the Strategic Plan will be held in November 2001.

Cooperation with other biodiversity-related conventions, institutions and processes

Given the nature of the issues which the Convention seeks to address, the Convention is heavily dependent for its effectiveness on the actions of Parties and other institutions. The need to develop institutional links with other international bodies, and to develop cooperative relationships with such bodies and hence mechanisms for coordinating these relationships, is fundamental to the implementation of the Convention. At each of its meetings, the COP has reaffirmed the importance it attaches to cooperation and coordination between the CBD and other conventions, institutions and processes of relevance.[29]

Institutional links have been established with a wide range of other bodies. For example, the Convention Secretariat has participated in the Inter-Agency Task Force of the Intergovernmental Panel on Forests and the Inter-Agency Committee on Sustainable Development (IACSD) of the United Nations. Memoranda of Cooperation to provide a framework for developing institutional links and cooperation with other bodies have been concluded between the Convention Secretariat and, inter alia, the secretariats of the Ramsar Convention on Wetlands; the Convention on International Trade in Endangered Species of Fauna and Flora (CITES); the Convention for the Protection of the World Cultural and Natural Heritage; the Convention on Migratory Species; the Intergovernmental Oceanographic Commission, the World Bank, the World Conservation Union (IUCN), the United Nations Conference on Trade and Development (UNCTAD) and the Food and Agriculture Organization of the United Nations (FAO).

The COP has regularly adopted decisions directed towards other processes and has invited them to take an active role in the implementation of aspects of the Convention. For example, the third meeting of the COP invited the Convention on Wetlands of International Importance to cooperate as a lead partner in the implementation of activities under the Convention on Biological Diversity related to inland water biodiversity.[30] The COP subsequently endorsed a joint work plan between the Convention and the Ramsar Convention.[31] The development of a joint work programme with the Convention to Combat Desertification has been requested by the COP in relation to dry and sub-humid lands.

---

28 See decision V/20, part II.

29 See, especially, decisions I/5; II/13; III/21; IV/15 and Section VI of this Handbook: Article 24.

30 Decision III/21, paragraph 7.

31 Decision IV/15, paragraph 2.

Cartagena Protocol on Biosafety

In January 2000, the COP adopted the Cartagena Protocol on Biosafety in accordance with Article 28 of the Convention. The Protocol was negotiated pursuant to Article 19 (3), which required the COP to consider the need for and modalities of a protocol. The COP decided, in decision II/5, to establish the Open-ended Ad Hoc Working Group on Biosafety to negotiate the Protocol. The Working Group held six meetings between July 1996 and February 1999, and submitted its report to the first extraordinary meeting of the COP in February 1999 in Cartagena. The COP was not able to reach consensus on the content of the Protocol at that meeting, and the extraordinary meeting was suspended.[32] Following informal consultations, the extraordinary meeting was resumed in Montreal in January 2000, and the Protocol was adopted on 29 January 2000. It was opened for signature in Nairobi on 15 May 2000. The Protocol has been signed by 103 Parties to the Convention. As of 30 July 2001 there were five Parties to the Protocol. The Protocol will enter into force 90 days after the deposit of the fiftieth instrument of ratification.

Once the Protocol enters into force, the COP to the Convention will serve as the meeting of the Parties to the Protocol, which is the governing body of the Protocol. In order to prepare for the first meeting of the Parties, the COP has established an Intergovernmental Committee for the Cartagena Protocol (ICCP) which is scheduled to meet twice between COP 5 and COP 6. The first meeting was held in Montpellier, France, from 11 to 15 December 2000. The second meeting will be held in Nairobi, Kenya, from 1 to 5 October 2001.

Sources of information

There are many sources of information about the Convention. These include printed materials and worldwide websites. The principal source of information about the Convention is the Convention Secretariat, which is located in Montreal, and the Convention's CHM (administered by the Secretariat). The Secretariat can be contacted at:

World Trade Centre
Suite 300
393 Saint-Jacques Street
Montreal
Quebec
Canada H2Y 1N9
tel: *+1 514 288 2220*
fax: *+1 514 288 6588*
email: *secretariat@biodiv.org*

The Secretariat's website is at *www.biodiv.org*, and includes information on upcoming meetings (including official documentation), as well as background information and links to other useful sources. As well, all technical documents and reports of meetings can be found here. It is also linked to the Convention's CHM (*www.biodiv.org/chm*). National reports of Parties are also available on the website.

---

32 Decision EM-I/1.

Acronyms and abbreviations

AALCC	Asian-African Legal Consultative Committee
ACTS	African Centre for Technology Studies
AVHRR	advanced very high resolution radiometer
BE	Special Voluntary Trust Fund (for additional activities approved by the COP for the biennium 1999–2000)
BSWG	Ad Hoc Working Group on Biosafety
BY	Trust Fund for the Convention
BZ	Special Voluntary Trust Fund (for facilitating participation of Parties in the Convention process for the biennium 1999–2000)
CBD	Convention on Biological Diversity
CCD	Convention to Combat Desertification
CGIAR	Consultative Group on International Agricultural Research
CGRFA	Commission on Genetic Resources for Food and Agriculture
CHM	clearing-house mechanism (CBD)
CITES	Convention on International Trade in Endangered Species of Wild Fauna and Flora
CMS	Convention on the Conservation of Migratory Species of Wild Animals
COP	Conference of the Parties (to the CBD)
COP 1	first meeting of the COP (Nassau, Bahamas, 28 November–9 December, 1994)
COP 2	second meeting of the COP (Jakarta, Indonesia, 6–17 November, 1995)
COP 3	third meeting of the COP (Buenos Aires, Argentina, 4–15 November, 1996)
COP 4	fourth meeting of the COP (Bratislava, Slovak Republic, 4–15 May, 1998)
COP 5	fifth meeting of the COP (Nairobi, Kenya, 15–26 May, 2000)
CSD	Commission on Sustainable Development
CTE	Committee on Trade and Environment (WTO)
EIA	environmental impact assessment
ELCI	Environmental Liaison Centre International
ExCOP	extraordinary meeting of the Conference of the Parties to the Convention
FAO	Food and Agriculture Organization of the United Nations
GBIF	Global Biodiversity Informatics Facility
GEF	Global Environment Facility
GISP	Global Invasive Species Programme
GTI	Global Taxonomy Initiative

GURTs	genetic use restriction technologies
IAC	Informal Advisory Committee
IACSD	Inter-Agency Committee on Sustainable Development (United Nations)
IBPGR	International Board for Plant Genetic Resources (CGIAR)
ICCP	Intergovernmental Committee for the Cartagena Protocol on Biosafety
ICRI	International Coral Reef Initiative
IFF	Intergovernmental Forum on Forests
IMCAM	integrated marine and coastal area management
IMO	International Maritime Organization (United Nations)
INC	Intergovernmental Negotiating Committee
IOC	Intergovernmental Oceanographic Commission
IOCU	International Organization of Consumers Unions
IPF	Intergovernmental Panel on Forests
IPR	intellectual property rights
ISOC	Intersessional Meeting on the Operations of the Convention
IUCN	The World Conservation Union (formerly the International Union for Conservation of Nature and Natural Resources)
LMO	living modified organism
MoU	Memorandum of Understanding
MTPW	medium-term programme of work
NGO	non-governmental organization
NOAA	National Oceanic and Atmospheric Administration (United States)
OECD	Organisation for Economic Co-operation and Development
Op. Obj.	operational objective
Ramsar Convention	Convention on Wetlands of International Importance, especially as Waterfowl Habitat
SADCC	Southern African Development Coordination Conference
SAREC	Department of Research Cooperation (Sida)
SBSTTA	Subsidiary Body on Scientific, Technical and Technological Advice
SBSTTA 1	first meeting of SBSTTA (Paris, France, 4–8 September, 1995)
SBSTTA 2	second meeting of SBSTTA (Montreal, Canada, 2–6 September, 1996)
SBSTTA 3	third meeting of SBSTTA (Montreal, Canada, 1–5 September, 1997)
SBSTTA 4	fourth meeting of SBSTTA (Montreal, Canada, 21–25 June, 1999)
SBSTTA 5	fifth meeting of SBSTTA (Montreal, Canada, 31 January–4 February, 2000)
SCBD	Secretariat of the Convention on Biological Diversity
Sida	Swedish International Development Cooperation Agency
SIDS	small island developing States
TRIPs	Agreement on Trade-related Aspects of Intellectual Property Rights
UNCED	United Nations Conference on Environment and Development
UNCLOS	United Nations Convention on the Law of the Sea
UNCTAD	United Nations Conference on Trade and Development
UNDP	United Nations Development Programme
UNEP	United Nations Environment Programme

UNESCO	United Nations Educational, Scientific and Cultural Organization
UNFF	United Nations Forum on Forests
UNGA	United Nations General Assembly
UNIDO	United Nations Industrial Development Organization
UNSO	United Nations Sudano-Sahelian Office
WHO	World Health Organization
WIPO	World Intellectual Property Organization
WTO	World Trade Organization
WWF	World Wide Fund For Nature *and* World Wildlife Fund (Canada and United States)

Section I

Convention on Biological Diversity

Convention on Biological Diversity

Preamble

The Contracting Parties,

Conscious of the intrinsic value of biological diversity and of the ecological, genetic, social, economic, scientific, educational, cultural, recreational and aesthetic values of biological diversity and its components,

Conscious also of the importance of biological diversity for evolution and for maintaining life sustaining systems of the biosphere,

Affirming that the conservation of biological diversity is a common concern of humankind,

Reaffirming that States have sovereign rights over their own biological resources,

Reaffirming also that States are responsible for conserving their biological diversity and for using their biological resources in a sustainable manner,

Concerned that biological diversity is being significantly reduced by certain human activities,

Aware of the general lack of information and knowledge regarding biological diversity and of the urgent need to develop scientific, technical and institutional capacities to provide the basic understanding upon which to plan and implement appropriate measures,

Noting that it is vital to anticipate, prevent and attack the causes of significant reduction or loss of biological diversity at source,

Noting also that where there is a threat of significant reduction or loss of biological diversity, lack of full scientific certainty should not be used as a reason for postponing measures to avoid or minimize such a threat,

Noting further that the fundamental requirement for the conservation of biological diversity is the *in-situ* conservation of ecosystems and natural habitats and the maintenance and recovery of viable populations of species in their natural surroundings,

Noting further that *ex-situ* measures, preferably in the country of origin, also have an important role to play,

Recognizing the close and traditional dependence of many indigenous and local communities embodying traditional lifestyles on biological resources, and the desirability of sharing equitably benefits arising from the use of traditional knowledge, innovations and practices relevant to the conservation of biological diversity and the sustainable use of its components,

Recognizing also the vital role that women play in the conservation and sustainable use of biological diversity and affirming the need for the full participation of women at all levels of policy-making and implementation for biological diversity conservation,

Stressing the importance of, and the need to promote, international, regional and global cooperation among States and intergovernmental organizations and the non-governmental sector for the conservation of biological diversity and the sustainable use of its components,

Acknowledging that the provision of new and additional financial resources and appropriate access to relevant technologies can be expected to make a substantial difference in the world's ability to address the loss of biological diversity,

Acknowledging further that special provision is required to meet the needs of developing countries, including the provision of new and additional financial resources and appropriate access to relevant technologies,

Noting in this regard the special conditions of the least developed countries and small island States,

Acknowledging that substantial investments are required to conserve biological diversity and that there is the expectation of a broad range of environmental, economic and social benefits from those investments,

Recognizing that economic and social development and poverty eradication are the first and overriding priorities of developing countries,

Aware that conservation and sustainable use of biological diversity is of critical importance for meeting the food, health and other needs of the growing world population, for which purpose access to and sharing of both genetic resources and technologies are essential,

Noting that, ultimately, the conservation and sustainable use of biological diversity will strengthen friendly relations among States and contribute to peace for humankind,

Desiring to enhance and complement existing international arrangements for the conservation of biological diversity and sustainable use of its components, and

Determined to conserve and sustainably use biological diversity for the benefit of present and future generations,

Have agreed as follows:

Article 1: Objectives

The objectives of this Convention, to be pursued in accordance with its relevant provisions, are the conservation of biological diversity, the sustainable use of its components and the fair and equitable sharing of the benefits arising out of the utilization of genetic resources, including by appropriate access to genetic resources and by appropriate transfer of relevant technologies, taking into account all rights over those resources and to technologies, and by appropriate funding.

Article 2: Use of terms

For the purposes of this Convention:

'*Biological diversity*' means the variability among living organisms from all sources including, *inter alia*, terrestrial, marine and other aquatic ecosystems and the ecological complexes of which they are part; this includes diversity within species, between species and of ecosystems.

'*Biological resources*' includes genetic resources, organisms or parts thereof, populations, or any other biotic component of ecosystems with actual or potential use or value for humanity.

'*Biotechnology*' means any technological application that uses biological systems, living organisms, or derivatives thereof, to make or modify products or processes for specific use.

'*Country of origin of genetic resources*' means the country which possesses those genetic resources in *in-situ* conditions.

'*Country providing genetic resources*' means the country supplying genetic resources collected from *in-situ* sources, including populations of both wild and domesticated species, or taken from *ex-situ* sources, which may or may not have originated in that country.

'*Domesticated or cultivated species*' means species in which the evolutionary process has been influenced by humans to meet their needs.

'*Ecosystem*' means a dynamic complex of plant, animal and micro-organism communities and their non-living environment interacting as a functional unit.

'Ex-situ *conservation*' means the conservation of components of biological diversity outside their natural habitats.

'*Genetic material*' means any material of plant, animal, microbial or other origin containing functional units of heredity.

'*Genetic resources*' means genetic material of actual or potential value.

'*Habitat*' means the place or type of site where an organism or population naturally occurs.

'In-situ *conditions*' means conditions where genetic resources exist within ecosystems and natural habitats, and, in the case of domesticated or cultivated species, in the surroundings where they have developed their distinctive properties.

'In-situ *conservation*' means the conservation of ecosystems and natural habitats and the maintenance and recovery of viable populations of species in their natural surroundings and, in the case of domesticated or cultivated species, in the surroundings where they have developed their distinctive properties.

'*Protected area*' means a geographically defined area which is designated or regulated and managed to achieve specific conservation objectives.

'*Regional economic integration organization*' means an organization constituted by sovereign States of a given region, to which its member States have transferred competence in respect of matters governed by this Convention and which has been duly authorized, in accordance with its internal procedures, to sign, ratify, accept, approve or accede to it.

'*Sustainable use*' means the use of components of biological diversity in a way and at a rate that does not lead to the long-term decline of biological diversity, thereby maintaining its potential to meet the needs and aspirations of present and future generations.

'*Technology*' includes biotechnology.

Article 3: Principle

States have, in accordance with the Charter of the United Nations and the principles of international law, the sovereign right to exploit their own resources pursuant to their own environmental policies, and the responsibility to ensure that activities within their jurisdiction or control do not cause damage to the environment of other States or of areas beyond the limits of national jurisdiction.

Article 4: Jurisdictional scope

Subject to the rights of other States, and except as otherwise expressly provided in this Convention, the provisions of this Convention apply, in relation to each Contracting Party:

(a) In the case of components of biological diversity, in areas within the limits of its national jurisdiction; and

(b) In the case of processes and activities, regardless of where their effects occur, carried out under its jurisdiction or control, within the area of its national jurisdiction or beyond the limits of national jurisdiction.

Article 5: Cooperation

Each Contracting Party shall, as far as possible and as appropriate, cooperate with other Contracting Parties, directly or, where appropriate, through competent international organizations, in respect of areas beyond national jurisdiction and on other matters of mutual interest, for the conservation and sustainable use of biological diversity.

Article 6: General measures for conservation and sustainable use

Each Contracting Party shall, in accordance with its particular conditions and capabilities:

(a) Develop national strategies, plans or programmes for the conservation and sustainable use of biological diversity or adapt for this purpose existing strategies, plans or programmes which shall reflect, *inter alia*, the measures set out in this Convention relevant to the Contracting Party concerned; and

(b) Integrate, as far as possible and as appropriate, the conservation and sustainable use of biological diversity into relevant sectoral or cross-sectoral plans, programmes and policies.

Article 7: Identification and monitoring

Each Contracting Party shall, as far as possible and as appropriate, in particular for the purposes of Articles 8 to 10:

(a) Identify components of biological diversity important for its conservation and sustainable use having regard to the indicative list of categories set down in Annex I;

(b) Monitor, through sampling and other techniques, the components of biological diversity identified pursuant to subparagraph (a) above, paying particular attention to those requiring urgent conservation measures and those which offer the greatest potential for sustainable use;

(c) Identify processes and categories of activities which have or are likely to have significant adverse impacts on the conservation and sustainable use of biological diversity, and monitor their effects through sampling and other techniques; and

(d) Maintain and organize, by any mechanism, data derived from identification and monitoring activities pursuant to subparagraphs (a), (b) and (c) above.

Article 8: *In-situ* conservation

Each Contracting Party shall, as far as possible and as appropriate:

(a) Establish a system of protected areas or areas where special measures need to be taken to conserve biological diversity;

(b) Develop, where necessary, guidelines for the selection, establishment and management of protected areas or areas where special measures need to be taken to conserve biological diversity;

(c) Regulate or manage biological resources important for the conservation of biological diversity whether within or outside protected areas, with a view to ensuring their conservation and sustainable use;

(d) Promote the protection of ecosystems, natural habitats and the maintenance of viable populations of species in natural surroundings;

(e) Promote environmentally sound and sustainable development in areas adjacent to protected areas with a view to furthering protection of these areas;

(f) Rehabilitate and restore degraded ecosystems and promote the recovery of threatened species, *inter alia*, through the development and implementation of plans or other management strategies;

(g) Establish or maintain means to regulate, manage or control the risks associated with the use and release of living modified organisms resulting from biotechnology which are likely to have adverse environmental impacts that could affect the conservation and sustainable use of biological diversity, taking also into account the risks to human health;

(h) Prevent the introduction of, control or eradicate those alien species which threaten ecosystems, habitats or species;

(i) Endeavour to provide the conditions needed for compatibility between present uses and the conservation of biological diversity and the sustainable use of its components;

(j) Subject to its national legislation, respect, preserve and maintain knowledge, innovations and practices of indigenous and local communities embodying traditional lifestyles relevant for the conservation and sustainable use of biological diversity and promote their wider application with the approval and involvement of the holders of such knowledge, innovations and practices and encourage the equitable sharing of the benefits arising from the utilization of such knowledge, innovations and practices;

(k) Develop or maintain necessary legislation and/or other regulatory provisions for the protection of threatened species and populations;

(l) Where a significant adverse effect on biological diversity has been determined pursuant to Article 7, regulate or manage the relevant processes and categories of activities; and

(m) Cooperate in providing financial and other support for *in-situ* conservation outlined in subparagraphs (a) to (l) above, particularly to developing countries.

Article 9: *Ex-situ* conservation

Each Contracting Party shall, as far as possible and as appropriate, and predominantly for the purpose of complementing *in-situ* measures:

(a) Adopt measures for the *ex-situ* conservation of components of biological diversity, preferably in the country of origin of such components;

(b) Establish and maintain facilities for *ex-situ* conservation of and research on plants, animals and micro-organisms, preferably in the country of origin of genetic resources;

(c) Adopt measures for the recovery and rehabilitation of threatened species and for their reintroduction into their natural habitats under appropriate conditions;

(d) Regulate and manage collection of biological resources from natural habitats for *ex-situ* conservation purposes so as not to threaten ecosystems and *in-situ* populations of species, except where special temporary *ex-situ* measures are required under subparagraph (c) above; and

(e) Cooperate in providing financial and other support for *ex-situ* conservation outlined in subparagraphs (a) to (d) above and in the establishment and maintenance of *ex-situ* conservation facilities in developing countries.

Article 10: Sustainable use of components of biological diversity

Each Contracting Party shall, as far as possible and as appropriate:

(a) Integrate consideration of the conservation and sustainable use of biological resources into national decision-making;

(b) Adopt measures relating to the use of biological resources to avoid or minimize adverse impacts on biological diversity;

(c) Protect and encourage customary use of biological resources in accordance with traditional cultural practices that are compatible with conservation or sustainable use requirements;

(d) Support local populations to develop and implement remedial action in degraded areas where biological diversity has been reduced; and

(e) Encourage cooperation between its governmental authorities and its private sector in developing methods for sustainable use of biological resources.

Article 11: Incentive measures

Each Contracting Party shall, as far as possible and as appropriate, adopt economically and socially sound measures that act as incentives for the conservation and sustainable use of components of biological diversity.

Article 12: Research and training

The Contracting Parties, taking into account the special needs of developing countries, shall:

(a) Establish and maintain programmes for scientific and technical education and training in measures for the identification, conservation and sustainable use of biological diversity and its components and provide support for such education and training for the specific needs of developing countries;

(b) Promote and encourage research which contributes to the conservation and sustainable use of biological diversity, particularly in developing countries, *inter alia*, in accordance with decisions of the Conference of the Parties taken in consequence of recommendations of the Subsidiary Body on Scientific, Technical and Technological Advice; and

(c) In keeping with the provisions of Articles 16, 18 and 20, promote and cooperate in the use of scientific advances in biological diversity research in developing methods for conservation and sustainable use of biological resources.

Article 13: Public education and awareness

The Contracting Parties shall:

(a) Promote and encourage understanding of the importance of, and the measures required for, the conservation of biological diversity, as well as its propagation through media, and the inclusion of these topics in educational programmes; and

(b) Cooperate, as appropriate, with other States and international organizations in developing educational and public awareness programmes, with respect to conservation and sustainable use of biological diversity.

Article 14: Impact assessment and minimizing adverse impacts

1. Each Contracting Party, as far as possible and as appropriate, shall:

(a) Introduce appropriate procedures requiring environmental impact assessment of its proposed projects that are likely to have significant adverse effects on biological diversity with a view to avoiding or minimizing such effects and, where appropriate, allow for public participation in such procedures;

(b) Introduce appropriate arrangements to ensure that the environmental consequences of its programmes and policies that are likely to have significant adverse impacts on biological diversity are duly taken into account;

(c) Promote, on the basis of reciprocity, notification, exchange of information and consultation on activities under their jurisdiction or control which are likely to significantly affect adversely the biological diversity of other States or areas beyond the limits of national jurisdiction, by encouraging the conclusion of bilateral, regional or multilateral arrangements, as appropriate;

(d) In the case of imminent or grave danger or damage, originating under its jurisdiction or control, to biological diversity within the area under jurisdiction of other States or in areas beyond the limits of national jurisdiction, notify immediately the potentially affected States of such danger or damage, as well as initiate action to prevent or minimize such danger or damage; and

(e) Promote national arrangements for emergency responses to activities or events, whether caused naturally or otherwise, which present a grave and imminent danger to biological diversity and encourage international cooperation to supplement such national efforts and, where appropriate and agreed by the States or regional economic integration organizations concerned, to establish joint contingency plans.

2. The Conference of the Parties shall examine, on the basis of studies to be carried out, the issue of liability and redress, including restoration and compensation, for damage to biological diversity, except where such liability is a purely internal matter.

Article 15: Access to genetic resources

1. Recognizing the sovereign rights of States over their natural resources, the authority to determine access to genetic resources rests with the national governments and is subject to national legislation.

2. Each Contracting Party shall endeavour to create conditions to facilitate access to genetic resources for environmentally sound uses by other Contracting Parties and not to impose restrictions that run counter to the objectives of this Convention.

3. For the purpose of this Convention, the genetic resources being provided by a Contracting Party, as referred to in this Article and Articles 16 and 19, are only those that are provided by Contracting Parties that are countries of origin of such resources or by the Parties that have acquired the genetic resources in accordance with this Convention.

4. Access, where granted, shall be on mutually agreed terms and subject to the provisions of this Article.

5. Access to genetic resources shall be subject to prior informed consent of the Contracting Party providing such resources, unless otherwise determined by that Party.

6. Each Contracting Party shall endeavour to develop and carry out scientific research based on genetic resources provided by other Contracting Parties with the full participation of, and where possible in, such Contracting Parties.

7. Each Contracting Party shall take legislative, administrative or policy measures, as appropriate, and in accordance with Articles 16 and 19 and, where necessary, through the financial mechanism established by Articles 20 and 21 with the aim of sharing in a fair and equitable way the results of research and development and the benefits arising from the commercial and other utilization of genetic resources with the Contracting Party providing such resources. Such sharing shall be upon mutually agreed terms.

Article 16: Access to and transfer of technology

1. Each Contracting Party, recognizing that technology includes biotechnology, and that both access to and transfer of technology among Contracting Parties are essential elements for the attainment of the objectives of this Convention, undertakes subject to the provisions of this Article to provide and/or facilitate access for and transfer to other Contracting Parties of technologies that are relevant to the conservation and sustainable use of biological diversity or make use of genetic resources and do not cause significant damage to the environment.

2. Access to and transfer of technology referred to in paragraph 1 above to developing countries shall be provided and/or facilitated under fair and most favourable terms, including on concessional and preferential terms where mutually agreed, and, where necessary, in accordance with the financial mechanism established by Articles 20 and 21. In the case of technology subject to patents and other intellectual property rights, such access and transfer shall be provided on terms which recognize and are consistent with the adequate and effective protection of intellectual property rights. The application of this paragraph shall be consistent with paragraphs 3, 4 and 5 below.

3. Each Contracting Party shall take legislative, administrative or policy measures, as appropriate, with the aim that Contracting Parties, in particular those that are developing countries, which provide genetic resources are provided access to and transfer of technology which makes use of those resources, on mutually agreed terms, including technology protected by patents and other intellectual property rights, where necessary, through the provisions of Articles 20 and 21 and in accordance with international law and consistent with paragraphs 4 and 5 below.

4. Each Contracting Party shall take legislative, administrative or policy measures, as appropriate, with the aim that the private sector facilitates access to, joint development and transfer of technology referred to in paragraph 1 above for the benefit of both governmental institutions and the private sector of developing countries and in this regard shall abide by the obligations included in paragraphs 1, 2 and 3 above.

5. The Contracting Parties, recognizing that patents and other intellectual property rights may have an influence on the implementation of this Convention, shall cooperate in this regard subject to national legislation and international law in order to ensure that such rights are supportive of and do not run counter to its objectives.

Article 17: Exchange of information

1. The Contracting Parties shall facilitate the exchange of information, from all publicly available sources, relevant to the conservation and sustainable use of biological diversity, taking into account the special needs of developing countries.

2. Such exchange of information shall include exchange of results of technical, scientific and socio-economic research, as well as information on training and surveying programmes, specialized knowledge, indigenous and traditional knowledge as such and in combination with the technologies referred to in Article 16, paragraph 1. It shall also, where feasible, include repatriation of information.

Article 18: Technical and scientific cooperation

1. The Contracting Parties shall promote international technical and scientific cooperation in the field of conservation and sustainable use of biological diversity, where necessary, through the appropriate international and national institutions.

2. Each Contracting Party shall promote technical and scientific cooperation with other Contracting Parties, in particular developing countries, in implementing this Convention, *inter alia*, through the development and implementation of national policies. In promoting such cooperation, special attention should be given to the development and strengthening of national capabilities, by means of human resources development and institution building.

3. The Conference of the Parties, at its first meeting, shall determine how to establish a clearing-house mechanism to promote and facilitate technical and scientific cooperation.

4. The Contracting Parties shall, in accordance with national legislation and policies, encourage and develop methods of cooperation for the development and use of technologies, including indigenous and traditional technologies, in pursuance of the

objectives of this Convention. For this purpose, the Contracting Parties shall also promote cooperation in the training of personnel and exchange of experts.

5. The Contracting Parties shall, subject to mutual agreement, promote the establishment of joint research programmes and joint ventures for the development of technologies relevant to the objectives of this Convention.

Article 19: Handling of biotechnology and distribution of its benefits

1. Each Contracting Party shall take legislative, administrative or policy measures, as appropriate, to provide for the effective participation in biotechnological research activities by those Contracting Parties, especially developing countries, which provide the genetic resources for such research, and where feasible in such Contracting Parties.

2. Each Contracting Party shall take all practicable measures to promote and advance priority access on a fair and equitable basis by Contracting Parties, especially developing countries, to the results and benefits arising from biotechnologies based upon genetic resources provided by those Contracting Parties. Such access shall be on mutually agreed terms.

3. The Parties shall consider the need for and modalities of a protocol setting out appropriate procedures, including, in particular, advance informed agreement, in the field of the safe transfer, handling and use of any living modified organism resulting from biotechnology that may have adverse effect on the conservation and sustainable use of biological diversity.

4. Each Contracting Party shall, directly or by requiring any natural or legal person under its jurisdiction providing the organisms referred to in paragraph 3 above, provide any available information about the use and safety regulations required by that Contracting Party in handling such organisms, as well as any available information on the potential adverse impact of the specific organisms concerned to the Contracting Party into which those organisms are to be introduced.

Article 20: Financial resources

1. Each Contracting Party undertakes to provide, in accordance with its capabilities, financial support and incentives in respect of those national activities which are intended to achieve the objectives of this Convention, in accordance with its national plans, priorities and programmes.

2. The developed country Parties shall provide new and additional financial resources to enable developing country Parties to meet the agreed full incremental costs to them of implementing measures which fulfil the obligations of this Convention and to benefit from its provisions and which costs are agreed between a developing country Party and the institutional structure referred to in Article 21, in accordance with policy, strategy, programme priorities and eligibility criteria and an indicative list of incremental costs established by the Conference of the Parties. Other Parties, including countries undergoing the process of transition to a market economy, may voluntarily assume the obligations of the developed country Parties. For the purpose of this Article, the

Conference of the Parties shall at its first meeting establish a list of developed country Parties and other Parties which voluntarily assume the obligations of the developed country Parties. The Conference of the Parties shall periodically review and if necessary amend the list. Contributions from other countries and sources on a voluntary basis would also be encouraged. The implementation of these commitments shall take into account the need for adequacy, predictability and timely flow of funds and the importance of burden-sharing among the contributing Parties included in the list.

3. The developed country Parties may also provide, and developing country Parties avail themselves of, financial resources related to the implementation of this Convention through bilateral, regional and other multilateral channels.

4. The extent to which developing country Parties will effectively implement their commitments under this Convention will depend on the effective implementation by developed country Parties of their commitments under this Convention related to financial resources and transfer of technology and will take fully into account the fact that economic and social development and eradication of poverty are the first and overriding priorities of the developing country Parties.

5. The Parties shall take full account of the specific needs and special situation of least developed countries in their actions with regard to funding and transfer of technology.

6. The Contracting Parties shall also take into consideration the special conditions resulting from the dependence on, distribution and location of, biological diversity within developing country Parties, in particular small island States.

7. Consideration shall also be given to the special situation of developing countries, including those that are most environmentally vulnerable, such as those with arid and semi-arid zones, coastal and mountainous areas.

Article 21: Financial mechanism

1. There shall be a mechanism for the provision of financial resources to developing country Parties for purposes of this Convention on a grant or concessional basis the essential elements of which are described in this Article. The mechanism shall function under the authority and guidance of, and be accountable to, the Conference of the Parties for purposes of this Convention. The operations of the mechanism shall be carried out by such institutional structure as may be decided upon by the Conference of the Parties at its first meeting. For purposes of this Convention, the Conference of the Parties shall determine the policy, strategy, programme priorities and eligibility criteria relating to the access to and utilization of such resources. The contributions shall be such as to take into account the need for predictability, adequacy and timely flow of funds referred to in Article 20 in accordance with the amount of resources needed to be decided periodically by the Conference of the Parties and the importance of burden-sharing among the contributing Parties included in the list referred to in Article 20, paragraph 2. Voluntary contributions may also be made by the developed country Parties and by other countries and sources. The mechanism shall operate within a democratic and transparent system of governance.

2. Pursuant to the objectives of this Convention, the Conference of the Parties shall at its first meeting determine the policy, strategy and programme priorities, as well as detailed criteria and guidelines for eligibility for access to and utilization of the finan-

cial resources including monitoring and evaluation on a regular basis of such utilization. The Conference of the Parties shall decide on the arrangements to give effect to paragraph 1 above after consultation with the institutional structure entrusted with the operation of the financial mechanism.

3. The Conference of the Parties shall review the effectiveness of the mechanism established under this Article, including the criteria and guidelines referred to in paragraph 2 above, not less than two years after the entry into force of this Convention and thereafter on a regular basis. Based on such review, it shall take appropriate action to improve the effectiveness of the mechanism if necessary.

4. The Contracting Parties shall consider strengthening existing financial institutions to provide financial resources for the conservation and sustainable use of biological diversity.

Article 22: Relationship with other international conventions

1. The provisions of this Convention shall not affect the rights and obligations of any Contracting Party deriving from any existing international agreement, except where the exercise of those rights and obligations would cause a serious damage or threat to biological diversity.

2. Contracting Parties shall implement this Convention with respect to the marine environment consistently with the rights and obligations of States under the law of the sea.

Article 23: Conference of the Parties

1. A Conference of the Parties is hereby established. The first meeting of the Conference of the Parties shall be convened by the Executive Director of the United Nations Environment Programme not later than one year after the entry into force of this Convention. Thereafter, ordinary meetings of the Conference of the Parties shall be held at regular intervals to be determined by the Conference at its first meeting.

2. Extraordinary meetings of the Conference of the Parties shall be held at such other times as may be deemed necessary by the Conference, or at the written request of any Party, provided that, within six months of the request being communicated to them by the Secretariat, it is supported by at least one third of the Parties.

3. The Conference of the Parties shall by consensus agree upon and adopt rules of procedure for itself and for any subsidiary body it may establish, as well as financial rules governing the funding of the Secretariat. At each ordinary meeting, it shall adopt a budget for the financial period until the next ordinary meeting.

4. The Conference of the Parties shall keep under review the implementation of this Convention, and, for this purpose, shall:

(a) Establish the form and the intervals for transmitting the information to be submitted in accordance with Article 26 and consider such information as well as reports submitted by any subsidiary body;

(b) Review scientific, technical and technological advice on biological diversity provided in accordance with Article 25;

(c) Consider and adopt, as required, protocols in accordance with Article 28;

(d) Consider and adopt, as required, in accordance with Articles 29 and 30, amendments to this Convention and its annexes;

(e) Consider amendments to any protocol, as well as to any annexes thereto, and, if so decided, recommend their adoption to the parties to the protocol concerned;

(f) Consider and adopt, as required, in accordance with Article 30, additional annexes to this Convention;

(g) Establish such subsidiary bodies, particularly to provide scientific and technical advice, as are deemed necessary for the implementation of this Convention;

(h) Contact, through the Secretariat, the executive bodies of conventions dealing with matters covered by this Convention with a view to establishing appropriate forms of cooperation with them; and

(i) Consider and undertake any additional action that may be required for the achievement of the purposes of this Convention in the light of experience gained in its operation.

5. The United Nations, its specialized agencies and the International Atomic Energy Agency, as well as any State not Party to this Convention, may be represented as observers at meetings of the Conference of the Parties. Any other body or agency, whether governmental or non-governmental, qualified in fields relating to conservation and sustainable use of biological diversity, which has informed the Secretariat of its wish to be represented as an observer at a meeting of the Conference of the Parties, may be admitted unless at least one third of the Parties present object. The admission and participation of observers shall be subject to the rules of procedure adopted by the Conference of the Parties.

Article 24: Secretariat

1. A secretariat is hereby established. Its functions shall be:

(a) To arrange for and service meetings of the Conference of the Parties provided for in Article 23;

(b) To perform the functions assigned to it by any protocol;

(c) To prepare reports on the execution of its functions under this Convention and present them to the Conference of the Parties;

(d) To coordinate with other relevant international bodies and, in particular to enter into such administrative and contractual arrangements as may be required for the effective discharge of its functions; and

(e) To perform such other functions as may be determined by the Conference of the Parties.

2. At its first ordinary meeting, the Conference of the Parties shall designate the secretariat from amongst those existing competent international organizations which

have signified their willingness to carry out the secretariat functions under this Convention.

Article 25: Subsidiary Body on Scientific, Technical and Technological Advice

1. A subsidiary body for the provision of scientific, technical and technological advice is hereby established to provide the Conference of the Parties and, as appropriate, its other subsidiary bodies with timely advice relating to the implementation of this Convention. This body shall be open to participation by all Parties and shall be multidisciplinary. It shall comprise government representatives competent in the relevant field of expertise. It shall report regularly to the Conference of the Parties on all aspects of its work.

2. Under the authority of and in accordance with guidelines laid down by the Conference of the Parties, and upon its request, this body shall:

(a) Provide scientific and technical assessments of the status of biological diversity;

(b) Prepare scientific and technical assessments of the effects of types of measures taken in accordance with the provisions of this Convention;

(c) Identify innovative, efficient and state-of-the-art technologies and know-how relating to the conservation and sustainable use of biological diversity and advise on the ways and means of promoting development and/or transferring such technologies;

(d) Provide advice on scientific programmes and international cooperation in research and development related to conservation and sustainable use of biological diversity; and

(e) Respond to scientific, technical, technological and methodological questions that the Conference of the Parties and its subsidiary bodies may put to the body.

3. The functions, terms of reference, organization and operation of this body may be further elaborated by the Conference of the Parties.

Article 26: Reports

Each Contracting Party shall, at intervals to be determined by the Conference of the Parties, present to the Conference of the Parties, reports on measures which it has taken for the implementation of the provisions of this Convention and their effectiveness in meeting the objectives of this Convention.

Article 27: Settlement of disputes

1. In the event of a dispute between Contracting Parties concerning the interpretation or application of this Convention, the parties concerned shall seek solution by negotiation.

2. If the parties concerned cannot reach agreement by negotiation, they may jointly seek the good offices of, or request mediation by, a third party.

3. When ratifying, accepting, approving or acceding to this Convention, or at any time thereafter, a State or regional economic integration organization may declare in writing to the Depositary that for a dispute not resolved in accordance with paragraph 1 or paragraph 2 above, it accepts one or both of the following means of dispute settlement as compulsory:

(a) Arbitration in accordance with the procedure laid down in Part 1 of Annex II;

(b) Submission of the dispute to the International Court of Justice.

4. If the parties to the dispute have not, in accordance with paragraph 3 above, accepted the same or any procedure, the dispute shall be submitted to conciliation in accordance with Part 2 of Annex II unless the parties otherwise agree.

5. The provisions of this Article shall apply with respect to any protocol except as otherwise provided in the protocol concerned.

Article 28: Adoption of protocols

1. The Contracting Parties shall cooperate in the formulation and adoption of protocols to this Convention.

2. Protocols shall be adopted at a meeting of the Conference of the Parties.

3. The text of any proposed protocol shall be communicated to the Contracting Parties by the Secretariat at least six months before such a meeting.

Article 29: Amendment of the Convention or protocols

1. Amendments to this Convention may be proposed by any Contracting Party. Amendments to any protocol may be proposed by any Party to that protocol.

2. Amendments to this Convention shall be adopted at a meeting of the Conference of the Parties. Amendments to any protocol shall be adopted at a meeting of the Parties to the protocol in question. The text of any proposed amendment to this Convention or to any protocol, except as may otherwise be provided in such protocol, shall be communicated to the Parties to the instrument in question by the secretariat at least six months before the meeting at which it is proposed for adoption. The secretariat shall also communicate proposed amendments to the signatories to this Convention for information.

3. The Parties shall make every effort to reach agreement on any proposed amendment to this Convention or to any protocol by consensus. If all efforts at consensus have been exhausted, and no agreement reached, the amendment shall as a last resort be adopted by a two-third majority vote of the Parties to the instrument in question present and voting at the meeting, and shall be submitted by the Depositary to all Parties for ratification, acceptance or approval.

4. Ratification, acceptance or approval of amendments shall be notified to the Depositary in writing. Amendments adopted in accordance with paragraph 3 above shall enter into force among Parties having accepted them on the ninetieth day after the deposit of instruments of ratification, acceptance or approval by at least two thirds of the Contracting Parties to this Convention or of the Parties to the protocol concerned, except as may otherwise be provided in such protocol. Thereafter the amendments shall enter into force for any other Party on the ninetieth day after that Party deposits its instrument of ratification, acceptance or approval of the amendments.

5. For the purposes of this Article, 'Parties present and voting' means Parties present and casting an affirmative or negative vote.

Article 30: Adoption and amendment of annexes

1. The annexes to this Convention or to any protocol shall form an integral part of the Convention or of such protocol, as the case may be, and, unless expressly provided otherwise, a reference to this Convention or its protocols constitutes at the same time a reference to any annexes thereto. Such annexes shall be restricted to procedural, scientific, technical and administrative matters.

2. Except as may be otherwise provided in any protocol with respect to its annexes, the following procedure shall apply to the proposal, adoption and entry into force of additional annexes to this Convention or of annexes to any protocol:

(a) Annexes to this Convention or to any protocol shall be proposed and adopted according to the procedure laid down in Article 29;

(b) Any Party that is unable to approve an additional annex to this Convention or an annex to any protocol to which it is Party shall so notify the Depositary, in writing, within one year from the date of the communication of the adoption by the Depositary. The Depositary shall without delay notify all Parties of any such notification received. A Party may at any time withdraw a previous declaration of objection and the annexes shall thereupon enter into force for that Party subject to subparagraph (c) below;

(c) On the expiry of one year from the date of the communication of the adoption by the Depositary, the annex shall enter into force for all Parties to this Convention or to any protocol concerned which have not submitted a notification in accordance with the provisions of subparagraph (b) above.

3. The proposal, adoption and entry into force of amendments to annexes to this Convention or to any protocol shall be subject to the same procedure as for the proposal, adoption and entry into force of annexes to the Convention or annexes to any protocol.

4. If an additional annex or an amendment to an annex is related to an amendment to this Convention or to any protocol, the additional annex or amendment shall not enter into force until such time as the amendment to the Convention or to the protocol concerned enters into force.

Article 31: Right to vote

1. Except as provided for in paragraph 2 below, each Contracting Party to this Convention or to any protocol shall have one vote.

2. Regional economic integration organizations, in matters within their competence, shall exercise their right to vote with a number of votes equal to the number of their member States which are Contracting Parties to this Convention or the relevant protocol. Such organizations shall not exercise their right to vote if their member States exercise theirs, and vice versa.

Article 32: Relationship between this Convention and its protocols

1. A State or a regional economic integration organization may not become a Party to a protocol unless it is, or becomes at the same time, a Contracting Party to this Convention.

2. Decisions under any protocol shall be taken only by the Parties to the protocol concerned. Any Contracting Party that has not ratified, accepted or approved a protocol may participate as an observer in any meeting of the parties to that protocol.

Article 33: Signature

This Convention shall be open for signature at Rio de Janeiro by all States and any regional economic integration organization from 5 June 1992 until 14 June 1992, and at the United Nations Headquarters in New York from 15 June 1992 to 4 June 1993.

Article 34: Ratification, acceptance or approval

1. This Convention and any protocol shall be subject to ratification, acceptance or approval by States and by regional economic integration organizations. Instruments of ratification, acceptance or approval shall be deposited with the Depositary.

2. Any organization referred to in paragraph 1 above which becomes a Contracting Party to this Convention or any protocol without any of its member States being a Contracting Party shall be bound by all the obligations under the Convention or the protocol, as the case may be. In the case of such organizations, one or more of whose member States is a Contracting Party to this Convention or relevant protocol, the organization and its member States shall decide on their respective responsibilities for the performance of their obligations under the Convention or protocol, as the case may be. In such cases, the organization and the member States shall not be entitled to exercise rights under the Convention or relevant protocol concurrently.

3. In their instruments of ratification, acceptance or approval, the organizations referred to in paragraph 1 above shall declare the extent of their competence with respect to the matters governed by the Convention or the relevant protocol. These

organizations shall also inform the Depositary of any relevant modification in the extent of their competence.

Article 35: Accession

1. This Convention and any protocol shall be open for accession by States and by regional economic integration organizations from the date on which the Convention or the protocol concerned is closed for signature. The instruments of accession shall be deposited with the Depositary.

2. In their instruments of accession, the organizations referred to in paragraph 1 above shall declare the extent of their competence with respect to the matters governed by the Convention or the relevant protocol. These organizations shall also inform the Depositary of any relevant modification in the extent of their competence.

3. The provisions of Article 34, paragraph 2, shall apply to regional economic integration organizations which accede to this Convention or any protocol.

Article 36: Entry into force

1. This Convention shall enter into force on the ninetieth day after the date of deposit of the thirtieth instrument of ratification, acceptance, approval or accession.

2. Any protocol shall enter into force on the ninetieth day after the date of deposit of the number of instruments of ratification, acceptance, approval or accession, specified in that protocol, has been deposited.

3. For each Contracting Party which ratifies, accepts or approves this Convention or accedes thereto after the deposit of the thirtieth instrument of ratification, acceptance, approval or accession, it shall enter into force on the ninetieth day after the date of deposit by such Contracting Party of its instrument of ratification, acceptance, approval or accession.

4. Any protocol, except as otherwise provided in such protocol, shall enter into force for a Contracting Party that ratifies, accepts or approves that protocol or accedes thereto after its entry into force pursuant to paragraph 2 above, on the ninetieth day after the date on which that Contracting Party deposits its instrument of ratification, acceptance, approval or accession, or on the date on which this Convention enters into force for that Contracting Party, whichever shall be the later.

5. For the purposes of paragraphs 1 and 2 above, any instrument deposited by a regional economic integration organization shall not be counted as additional to those deposited by member States of such organization.

Article 37: Reservations

No reservations may be made to this Convention.

Article 38: Withdrawals

1. At any time after two years from the date on which this Convention has entered into force for a Contracting Party, that Contracting Party may withdraw from the Convention by giving written notification to the Depositary.

2. Any such withdrawal shall take place upon expiry of one year after the date of its receipt by the Depositary, or on such later date as may be specified in the notification of the withdrawal.

3. Any Contracting Party which withdraws from this Convention shall be considered as also having withdrawn from any protocol to which it is party.

Article 39: Financial interim arrangements

Provided that it has been fully restructured in accordance with the requirements of Article 21, the Global Environment Facility of the United Nations Development Programme, the United Nations Environment Programme and the International Bank for Reconstruction and Development shall be the institutional structure referred to in Article 21 on an interim basis, for the period between the entry into force of this Convention and the first meeting of the Conference of the Parties or until the Conference of the Parties decides which institutional structure will be designated in accordance with Article 21.

Article 40: Secretariat interim arrangements

The secretariat to be provided by the Executive Director of the United Nations Environment Programme shall be the secretariat referred to in Article 24, paragraph 2, on an interim basis for the period between the entry into force of this Convention and the first meeting of the Conference of the Parties.

Article 41: Depositary

The Secretary-General of the United Nations shall assume the functions of Depositary of this Convention and any protocols.

Article 42: Authentic texts

The original of this Convention, of which the Arabic, Chinese, English, French, Russian and Spanish texts are equally authentic, shall be deposited with the Secretary-General of the United Nations.

IN WITNESS WHEREOF the undersigned, being duly authorized to that effect, have signed this Convention.

Done at Rio de Janeiro on this fifth day of June, one thousand nine hundred and ninety-two.

Annex I: Identification and monitoring

1. Ecosystems and habitats: containing high diversity, large numbers of endemic or threatened species, or wilderness; required by migratory species; of social, economic, cultural or scientific importance; or, which are representative, unique or associated with key evolutionary or other biological processes;

2. Species and communities which are: threatened; wild relatives of domesticated or cultivated species; of medicinal, agricultural or other economic value; or social, scientific or cultural importance; or importance for research into the conservation and sustainable use of biological diversity, such as indicator species; and

3. Described genomes and genes of social, scientific or economic importance.

Annex II: Arbitration and conciliation

Part 1: Arbitration

Article 1

The claimant party shall notify the secretariat that the parties are referring a dispute to arbitration pursuant to Article 27. The notification shall state the subject-matter of arbitration and include, in particular, the articles of the Convention or the protocol, the interpretation or application of which are at issue. If the parties do not agree on the subject matter of the dispute before the President of the tribunal is designated, the arbitral tribunal shall determine the subject matter. The secretariat shall forward the information thus received to all Contracting Parties to this Convention or to the protocol concerned.

Article 2

1. In disputes between two parties, the arbitral tribunal shall consist of three members. Each of the parties to the dispute shall appoint an arbitrator and the two arbitrators so appointed shall designate by common agreement the third arbitrator who shall be the President of the tribunal. The latter shall not be a national of one of the parties to the dispute, nor have his or her usual place of residence in the territory of one of these parties, nor be employed by any of them, nor have dealt with the case in any other capacity.

2. In disputes between more than two parties, parties in the same interest shall appoint one arbitrator jointly by agreement.

3. Any vacancy shall be filled in the manner prescribed for the initial appointment.

Article 3

1. If the President of the arbitral tribunal has not been designated within two months of the appointment of the second arbitrator, the Secretary-General of the United Nations shall, at the request of a party, designate the President within a further two-month period.

2. If one of the parties to the dispute does not appoint an arbitrator within two months of receipt of the request, the other party may inform the Secretary-General who shall make the designation within a further two-month period.

Article 4

The arbitral tribunal shall render its decisions in accordance with the provisions of this Convention, any protocols concerned, and international law.

Article 5

Unless the parties to the dispute otherwise agree, the arbitral tribunal shall determine its own rules of procedure.

Article 6

The arbitral tribunal may, at the request of one of the parties, recommend essential interim measures of protection.

Article 7

The parties to the dispute shall facilitate the work of the arbitral tribunal and, in particular, using all means at their disposal, shall:

(a) Provide it with all relevant documents, information and facilities; and

(b) Enable it, when necessary, to call witnesses or experts and receive their evidence.

Article 8

The parties and the arbitrators are under an obligation to protect the confidentiality of any information they receive in confidence during the proceedings of the arbitral tribunal.

Article 9

Unless the arbitral tribunal determines otherwise because of the particular circumstances of the case, the costs of the tribunal shall be borne by the parties to the dispute in equal shares. The tribunal shall keep a record of all its costs, and shall furnish a final statement thereof to the parties.

Article 10

Any Contracting Party that has an interest of a legal nature in the subject-matter of the dispute which may be affected by the decision in the case, may intervene in the proceedings with the consent of the tribunal.

Article 11

The tribunal may hear and determine counterclaims arising directly out of the subject-matter of the dispute.

Article 12

Decisions both on procedure and substance of the arbitral tribunal shall be taken by a majority vote of its members.

Article 13

If one of the parties to the dispute does not appear before the arbitral tribunal or fails to defend its case, the other party may request the tribunal to continue the proceedings and to make its award. Absence of a party or a failure of a party to defend its case shall not constitute a bar to the proceedings. Before rendering its final decision, the arbitral tribunal must satisfy itself that the claim is well founded in fact and law.

Article 14

The tribunal shall render its final decision within five months of the date on which it is fully constituted unless it finds it necessary to extend the time-limit for a period which should not exceed five more months.

Article 15

The final decision of the arbitral tribunal shall be confined to the subject-matter of the dispute and shall state the reasons on which it is based. It shall contain the names of the members who have participated and the date of the final decision. Any member of the tribunal may attach a separate or dissenting opinion to the final decision.

Article 16

The award shall be binding on the parties to the dispute. It shall be without appeal unless the parties to the dispute have agreed in advance to an appellate procedure.

Article 17

Any controversy which may arise between the parties to the dispute as regards the interpretation or manner of implementation of the final decision may be submitted by either party for decision to the arbitral tribunal which rendered it.

Part 2: Conciliation

Article 1

A conciliation commission shall be created upon the request of one of the parties to the dispute. The commission shall, unless the parties otherwise agree, be composed of five members, two appointed by each Party concerned and a President chosen jointly by those members.

Article 2

In disputes between more than two parties, parties in the same interest shall appoint their members of the commission jointly by agreement. Where two or more parties have separate interests or there is a disagreement as to whether they are of the same interest, they shall appoint their members separately.

Article 3

If any appointments by the parties are not made within two months of the date of the request to create a conciliation commission, the Secretary-General of the United Nations shall, if asked to do so by the party that made the request, make those appointments within a further two-month period.

Article 4

If a President of the conciliation commission has not been chosen within two months of the last of the members of the commission being appointed, the Secretary-General of the United Nations shall, if asked to do so by a party, designate a President within a further two-month period.

Article 5

The conciliation commission shall take its decisions by majority vote of its members. It shall, unless the parties to the dispute otherwise agree, determine its own procedure. It shall render a proposal for resolution of the dispute, which the parties shall consider in good faith.

Article 6

A disagreement as to whether the conciliation commission has competence shall be decided by the commission.

Section II

Cartagena Protocol on Biosafety to the Convention on Biological Diversity

(Annex to decision EM-I/3)

Cartagena Protocol on Biosafety

The Parties to this Protocol,

Being Parties to the Convention on Biological Diversity, hereinafter referred to as 'the Convention',

Recalling Article 19, paragraphs 3 and 4, and Articles 8 (g) and 17 of the Convention,

Recalling also decision II/5 of 17 November 1995 of the Conference of the Parties to the Convention to develop a Protocol on biosafety, specifically focusing on transboundary movement of any living modified organism resulting from modern biotechnology that may have adverse effect on the conservation and sustainable use of biological diversity, setting out for consideration, in particular, appropriate procedures for advance informed agreement,

Reaffirming the precautionary approach contained in Principle 15 of the Rio Declaration on Environment and Development,

Aware of the rapid expansion of modern biotechnology and the growing public concern over its potential adverse effects on biological diversity, taking also into account risks to human health,

Recognizing that modern biotechnology has great potential for human well-being if developed and used with adequate safety measures for the environment and human health,

Recognizing also the crucial importance to humankind of centres of origin and centres of genetic diversity,

Taking into account the limited capabilities of many countries, particularly developing countries, to cope with the nature and scale of known and potential risks associated with living modified organisms,

Recognizing that trade and environment agreements should be mutually supportive with a view to achieving sustainable development,

Emphasizing that this Protocol shall not be interpreted as implying a change in the rights and obligations of a Party under any existing international agreements,

Understanding that the above recital is not intended to subordinate this Protocol to other international agreements,

Have agreed as follows:

Article 1: Objective

In accordance with the precautionary approach contained in Principle 15 of the Rio Declaration on Environment and Development, the objective of this Protocol is to contribute to ensuring an adequate level of protection in the field of the safe transfer, handling and use of living modified organisms resulting from modern biotechnology that may have adverse effects on the conservation and sustainable use of biological diversity, taking also into account risks to human health, and specifically focusing on transboundary movements.

Article 2: General provisions

1. Each Party shall take necessary and appropriate legal, administrative and other measures to implement its obligations under this Protocol.

2. The Parties shall ensure that the development, handling, transport, use, transfer and release of any living modified organisms are undertaken in a manner that prevents or reduces the risks to biological diversity, taking also into account risks to human health.

3. Nothing in this Protocol shall affect in any way the sovereignty of States over their territorial sea established in accordance with international law, and the sovereign rights and the jurisdiction which States have in their exclusive economic zones and their continental shelves in accordance with international law, and the exercise by ships and aircraft of all States of navigational rights and freedoms as provided for in international law and as reflected in relevant international instruments.

4. Nothing in this Protocol shall be interpreted as restricting the right of a Party to take action that is more protective of the conservation and sustainable use of biological diversity than that called for in this Protocol, provided that such action is consistent with the objective and the provisions of this Protocol and is in accordance with that Party's other obligations under international law.

5. The Parties are encouraged to take into account, as appropriate, available expertise, instruments and work undertaken in international forums with competence in the area of risks to human health.

Article 3: Use of terms

For the purposes of this Protocol:

(a) 'Conference of the Parties' means the Conference of the Parties to the Convention;

(b) 'Contained use' means any operation, undertaken within a facility, installation or other physical structure, which involves living modified organisms that are controlled by specific measures that effectively limit their contact with, and their impact on, the external environment;

(c) 'Export' means intentional transboundary movement from one Party to another Party;

(d) 'Exporter' means any legal or natural person, under the jurisdiction of the Party of export, who arranges for a living modified organism to be exported;

(e) 'Import' means intentional transboundary movement into one Party from another Party;

(f) 'Importer' means any legal or natural person, under the jurisdiction of the Party of import, who arranges for a living modified organism to be imported;

(g) 'Living modified organism' means any living organism that possesses a novel combination of genetic material obtained through the use of modern biotechnology;

(h) 'Living organism' means any biological entity capable of transferring or replicating genetic material, including sterile organisms, viruses and viroids;

(i) 'Modern biotechnology' means the application of:

a. *In vitro* nucleic acid techniques, including recombinant deoxyribonucleic acid (DNA) and direct injection of nucleic acid into cells or organelles, or

b. Fusion of cells beyond the taxonomic family, that overcome natural physiological reproductive or recombination barriers and that are not techniques used in traditional breeding and selection;

(j) 'Regional economic integration organization' means an organization constituted by sovereign States of a given region, to which its member States have transferred competence in respect of matters governed by this Protocol and which has been duly authorized, in accordance with its internal procedures, to sign, ratify, accept, approve or accede to it;

(k) 'Transboundary movement' means the movement of a living modified organism from one Party to another Party, save that for the purposes of Articles 17 and 24 transboundary movement extends to movement between Parties and non-Parties.

Article 4: Scope

This Protocol shall apply to the transboundary movement, transit, handling and use of all living modified organisms that may have adverse effects on the conservation and sustainable use of biological diversity, taking also into account risks to human health.

Article 5: Pharmaceuticals

Notwithstanding Article 4 and without prejudice to any right of a Party to subject all living modified organisms to risk assessment prior to the making of decisions on import, this Protocol shall not apply to the transboundary movement of living modified organisms which are pharmaceuticals for humans that are addressed by other relevant international agreements or organizations.

Article 6: Transit and contained use

1. Notwithstanding Article 4 and without prejudice to any right of a Party of transit to regulate the transport of living modified organisms through its territory and make available to the Biosafety Clearing-House, any decision of that Party, subject to Article 2, paragraph 3, regarding the transit through its territory of a specific living modified organism, the provisions of this Protocol with respect to the advance informed agreement procedure shall not apply to living modified organisms in transit.

2. Notwithstanding Article 4 and without prejudice to any right of a Party to subject all living modified organisms to risk assessment prior to decisions on import and to set standards for contained use within its jurisdiction, the provisions of this Protocol with respect to the advance informed agreement procedure shall not apply to the transboundary movement of living modified organisms destined for contained use undertaken in accordance with the standards of the Party of import.

Article 7: Application of the advance informed agreement procedure

1. Subject to Articles 5 and 6, the advance informed agreement procedure in Articles 8 to 10 and 12 shall apply prior to the first intentional transboundary movement of living modified organisms for intentional introduction into the environment of the Party of import.

2. 'Intentional introduction into the environment' in paragraph 1 above, does not refer to living modified organisms intended for direct use as food or feed, or for processing.

3. Article 11 shall apply prior to the first transboundary movement of living modified organisms intended for direct use as food or feed, or for processing.

4. The advance informed agreement procedure shall not apply to the intentional transboundary movement of living modified organisms identified in a decision of the Conference of the Parties serving as the meeting of the Parties to this Protocol as being not likely to have adverse effects on the conservation and sustainable use of biological diversity, taking also into account risks to human health.

Article 8: Notification

1. The Party of export shall notify, or require the exporter to ensure notification to, in writing, the competent national authority of the Party of import prior to the intentional transboundary movement of a living modified organism that falls within the scope of Article 7, paragraph 1. The notification shall contain, at a minimum, the information specified in Annex I.

2. The Party of export shall ensure that there is a legal requirement for the accuracy of information provided by the exporter.

Article 9: Acknowledgement of receipt of notification

1. The Party of import shall acknowledge receipt of the notification, in writing, to the notifier within ninety days of its receipt.

2. The acknowledgement shall state:

   (a) The date of receipt of the notification;

   (b) Whether the notification, prima facie, contains the information referred to in Article 8;

   (c) Whether to proceed according to the domestic regulatory framework of the Party of import or according to the procedure specified in Article 10.

3. The domestic regulatory framework referred to in paragraph 2 (c) above, shall be consistent with this Protocol.

4. A failure by the Party of import to acknowledge receipt of a notification shall not imply its consent to an intentional transboundary movement.

Article 10: Decision procedure

1. Decisions taken by the Party of import shall be in accordance with Article 15.

2. The Party of import shall, within the period of time referred to in Article 9, inform the notifier, in writing, whether the intentional transboundary movement may proceed:

   (a) Only after the Party of import has given its written consent; or

   (b) After no less than ninety days without a subsequent written consent.

3. Within two hundred and seventy days of the date of receipt of notification, the Party of import shall communicate, in writing, to the notifier and to the Biosafety Clearing-House the decision referred to in paragraph 2 (a) above:

   (a) Approving the import, with or without conditions, including how the decision will apply to subsequent imports of the same living modified organism;

   (b) Prohibiting the import;

   (c) Requesting additional relevant information in accordance with its domestic regulatory framework or Annex I; in calculating the time within which the Party of import is to respond, the number of days it has to wait for additional relevant information shall not be taken into account; or

   (d) Informing the notifier that the period specified in this paragraph is extended by a defined period of time.

4. Except in a case in which consent is unconditional, a decision under paragraph 3 above, shall set out the reasons on which it is based.

5. A failure by the Party of import to communicate its decision within two hundred and seventy days of the date of receipt of the notification shall not imply its consent to an intentional transboundary movement.

6. Lack of scientific certainty due to insufficient relevant scientific information and knowledge regarding the extent of the potential adverse effects of a living modified organism on the conservation and sustainable use of biological diversity in the Party of import, taking also into account risks to human health, shall not prevent that Party from taking a decision, as appropriate, with regard to the import of the living modified organism in question as referred to in paragraph 3 above, in order to avoid or minimize such potential adverse effects.

7. The Conference of the Parties serving as the meeting of the Parties shall, at its first meeting, decide upon appropriate procedures and mechanisms to facilitate decision-making by Parties of import.

Article 11: Procedure for living modified organisms intended for direct use as food or feed, or for processing

1. A Party that makes a final decision regarding domestic use, including placing on the market, of a living modified organism that may be subject to transboundary movement for direct use as food or feed, or for processing shall, within fifteen days of making that decision, inform the Parties through the Biosafety Clearing-House. This information shall contain, at a minimum, the information specified in Annex II. The Party shall provide a copy of the information, in writing, to the national focal point of each Party that informs the Secretariat in advance that it does not have access to the Biosafety Clearing-House. This provision shall not apply to decisions regarding field trials.

2. The Party making a decision under paragraph 1 above, shall ensure that there is a legal requirement for the accuracy of information provided by the applicant.

3. Any Party may request additional information from the authority identified in paragraph (b) of Annex II.

4. A Party may take a decision on the import of living modified organisms intended for direct use as food or feed, or for processing, under its domestic regulatory framework that is consistent with the objective of this Protocol.

5. Each Party shall make available to the Biosafety Clearing-House copies of any national laws, regulations and guidelines applicable to the import of living modified organisms intended for direct use as food or feed, or for processing, if available.

6. A developing country Party or a Party with an economy in transition may, in the absence of the domestic regulatory framework referred to in paragraph 4 above, and in exercise of its domestic jurisdiction, declare through the Biosafety Clearing-House that its decision prior to the first import of a living modified organism intended for direct use as food or feed, or for processing, on which information has been provided under paragraph 1 above, will be taken according to the following:

(a) A risk assessment undertaken in accordance with Annex III; and

(b) A decision made within a predictable timeframe, not exceeding two hundred and seventy days.

7. Failure by a Party to communicate its decision according to paragraph 6 above, shall not imply its consent or refusal to the import of a living modified organism intended for direct use as food or feed, or for processing, unless otherwise specified by the Party.

8. Lack of scientific certainty due to insufficient relevant scientific information and knowledge regarding the extent of the potential adverse effects of a living modified organism on the conservation and sustainable use of biological diversity in the Party of import, taking also into account risks to human health, shall not prevent that Party from taking a decision, as appropriate, with regard to the import of that living modified organism intended for direct use as food or feed, or for processing, in order to avoid or minimize such potential adverse effects.

9. A Party may indicate its needs for financial and technical assistance and capacity-building with respect to living modified organisms intended for direct use as food or feed, or for processing. Parties shall cooperate to meet these needs in accordance with Articles 22 and 28.

Article 12: Review of decisions

1. A Party of import may, at any time, in light of new scientific information on potential adverse effects on the conservation and sustainable use of biological diversity, taking also into account the risks to human health, review and change a decision regarding an intentional transboundary movement. In such case, the Party shall, within thirty days, inform any notifier that has previously notified movements of the living modified organism referred to in such decision, as well as the Biosafety Clearing-House, and shall set out the reasons for its decision.

2. A Party of export or a notifier may request the Party of import to review a decision it has made in respect of it under Article 10 where the Party of export or the notifier considers that:

(a) A change in circumstances has occurred that may influence the outcome of the risk assessment upon which the decision was based; or

(b) Additional relevant scientific or technical information has become available.

3. The Party of import shall respond in writing to such a request within ninety days and set out the reasons for its decision.

4. The Party of import may, at its discretion, require a risk assessment for subsequent imports.

Article 13: Simplified procedure

1. A Party of import may, provided that adequate measures are applied to ensure the safe intentional transboundary movement of living modified organisms in accordance with the objective of this Protocol, specify in advance to the Biosafety Clearing-House:

(a) Cases in which intentional transboundary movement to it may take place at the same time as the movement is notified to the Party of import; and

(b) Imports of living modified organisms to it to be exempted from the advance informed agreement procedure.

Notifications under subparagraph (a) above, may apply to subsequent similar movements to the same Party.

2. The information relating to an intentional transboundary movement that is to be provided in the notifications referred to in paragraph 1 (a) above, shall be the information specified in Annex I.

Article 14: Bilateral, regional and multilateral agreements and arrangements

1. Parties may enter into bilateral, regional and multilateral agreements and arrangements regarding intentional transboundary movements of living modified organisms, consistent with the objective of this Protocol and provided that such agreements and arrangements do not result in a lower level of protection than that provided for by the Protocol.

2. The Parties shall inform each other, through the Biosafety Clearing-House, of any such bilateral, regional and multilateral agreements and arrangements that they have entered into before or after the date of entry into force of this Protocol.

3. The provisions of this Protocol shall not affect intentional transboundary movements that take place pursuant to such agreements and arrangements as between the parties to those agreements or arrangements.

4. Any Party may determine that its domestic regulations shall apply with respect to specific imports to it and shall notify the Biosafety Clearing-House of its decision.

Article 15: Risk assessment

1. Risk assessments undertaken pursuant to this Protocol shall be carried out in a scientifically sound manner, in accordance with Annex III and taking into account recognized risk assessment techniques. Such risk assessments shall be based, at a minimum, on information provided in accordance with Article 8 and other available scientific evidence in order to identify and evaluate the possible adverse effects of living modified organisms on the conservation and sustainable use of biological diversity, taking also into account risks to human health.

2. The Party of import shall ensure that risk assessments are carried out for decisions taken under Article 10. It may require the exporter to carry out the risk assessment.

3. The cost of risk assessment shall be borne by the notifier if the Party of import so requires.

Article 16: Risk management

1. The Parties shall, taking into account Article 8 (g) of the Convention, establish and maintain appropriate mechanisms, measures and strategies to regulate, manage and control risks identified in the risk assessment provisions of this Protocol associated with the use, handling and transboundary movement of living modified organisms.

2. Measures based on risk assessment shall be imposed to the extent necessary to prevent adverse effects of the living modified organism on the conservation and sustainable use of biological diversity, taking also into account risks to human health, within the territory of the Party of import.

3. Each Party shall take appropriate measures to prevent unintentional transboundary movements of living modified organisms, including such measures as requiring a risk assessment to be carried out prior to the first release of a living modified organism.

4. Without prejudice to paragraph 2 above, each Party shall endeavour to ensure that any living modified organism, whether imported or locally developed, has undergone an appropriate period of observation that is commensurate with its life-cycle or generation time before it is put to its intended use.

5. Parties shall cooperate with a view to:

(a) Identifying living modified organisms or specific traits of living modified organisms that may have adverse effects on the conservation and sustainable use of biological diversity, taking also into account risks to human health; and

(b) Taking appropriate measures regarding the treatment of such living modified organisms or specific traits.

Article 17: Unintentional transboundary movements and emergency measures

1. Each Party shall take appropriate measures to notify affected or potentially affected States, the Biosafety Clearing-House and, where appropriate, relevant international organizations, when it knows of an occurrence under its jurisdiction resulting in a release that leads, or may lead, to an unintentional transboundary movement of a living modified organism that is likely to have significant adverse effects on the conservation and sustainable use of biological diversity, taking also into account risks to human health in such States. The notification shall be provided as soon as the Party knows of the above situation.

2. Each Party shall, no later than the date of entry into force of this Protocol for it, make available to the Biosafety Clearing-House the relevant details setting out its point of contact for the purposes of receiving notifications under this Article.

3. Any notification arising from paragraph 1 above, should include:

(a) Available relevant information on the estimated quantities and relevant characteristics and/or traits of the living modified organism;

(b) Information on the circumstances and estimated date of the release, and on the use of the living modified organism in the originating Party;

(c) Any available information about the possible adverse effects on the conservation and sustainable use of biological diversity, taking also into account risks to human health, as well as available information about possible risk management measures;

(d) Any other relevant information; and

(e) A point of contact for further information.

4. In order to minimize any significant adverse effects on the conservation and sustainable use of biological diversity, taking also into account risks to human health, each Party, under whose jurisdiction the release of the living modified organism referred to in paragraph 1 above, occurs, shall immediately consult the affected or potentially affected States to enable them to determine appropriate responses and initiate necessary action, including emergency measures.

Article 18: Handling, transport, packaging and identification

1. In order to avoid adverse effects on the conservation and sustainable use of biological diversity, taking also into account risks to human health, each Party shall take necessary measures to require that living modified organisms that are subject to intentional transboundary movement within the scope of this Protocol are handled, packaged and transported under conditions of safety, taking into consideration relevant international rules and standards.

2. Each Party shall take measures to require that documentation accompanying:

(a) Living modified organisms that are intended for direct use as food or feed, or for processing, clearly identifies that they 'may contain' living modified organisms and are not intended for intentional introduction into the environment, as well as a contact point for further information. The Conference of the Parties serving as the meeting of the Parties to this Protocol shall take a decision on the detailed requirements for this purpose, including specification of their identity and any unique identification, no later than two years after the date of entry into force of this Protocol;

(b) Living modified organisms that are destined for contained use clearly identifies them as living modified organisms; and specifies any requirements for the safe handling, storage, transport and use, the contact point for further information, including the name and address of the individual and institution to whom the living modified organisms are consigned; and

(c) Living modified organisms that are intended for intentional introduction into the environment of the Party of import and any other living modified organisms within the scope of the Protocol, clearly identifies them as living modified organisms; specifies the identity and relevant traits and/or characteristics, any requirements for the safe handling, storage, transport and use, the contact point for further information and, as appropriate, the name and address of the importer and exporter; and contains a declaration that the movement is in conformity with the requirements of this Protocol applicable to the exporter.

3. The Conference of the Parties serving as the meeting of the Parties to this Protocol shall consider the need for and modalities of developing standards with regard to

identification, handling, packaging and transport practices, in consultation with other relevant international bodies.

Article 19: Competent national authorities and national focal points

1. Each Party shall designate one national focal point to be responsible on its behalf for liaison with the Secretariat. Each Party shall also designate one or more competent national authorities, which shall be responsible for performing the administrative functions required by this Protocol and which shall be authorized to act on its behalf with respect to those functions. A Party may designate a single entity to fulfil the functions of both focal point and competent national authority.

2. Each Party shall, no later than the date of entry into force of this Protocol for it, notify the Secretariat of the names and addresses of its focal point and its competent national authority or authorities. Where a Party designates more than one competent national authority, it shall convey to the Secretariat, with its notification thereof, relevant information on the respective responsibilities of those authorities. Where applicable, such information shall, at a minimum, specify which competent authority is responsible for which type of living modified organism. Each Party shall forthwith notify the Secretariat of any changes in the designation of its national focal point or in the name and address or responsibilities of its competent national authority or authorities.

3. The Secretariat shall forthwith inform the Parties of the notifications it receives under paragraph 2 above, and shall also make such information available through the Biosafety Clearing-House.

Article 20: Information sharing and the Biosafety Clearing-House

1. A Biosafety Clearing-House is hereby established as part of the clearing-house mechanism under Article 18, paragraph 3, of the Convention, in order to:

(a) Facilitate the exchange of scientific, technical, environmental and legal information on, and experience with, living modified organisms; and

(b) Assist Parties to implement the Protocol, taking into account the special needs of developing country Parties, in particular the least developed and small island developing States among them, and countries with economies in transition as well as countries that are centres of origin and centres of genetic diversity.

2. The Biosafety Clearing-House shall serve as a means through which information is made available for the purposes of paragraph 1 above. It shall provide access to information made available by the Parties relevant to the implementation of the Protocol. It shall also provide access, where possible, to other international biosafety information exchange mechanisms.

3. Without prejudice to the protection of confidential information, each Party shall make available to the Biosafety Clearing-House any information required to be made available to the Biosafety Clearing-House under this Protocol, and:

(a) Any existing laws, regulations and guidelines for implementation of the Protocol, as well as information required by the Parties for the advance informed agreement procedure;

(b) Any bilateral, regional and multilateral agreements and arrangements;

(c) Summaries of its risk assessments or environmental reviews of living modified organisms generated by its regulatory process, and carried out in accordance with Article 15, including, where appropriate, relevant information regarding products thereof, namely, processed materials that are of living modified organism origin, containing detectable novel combinations of replicable genetic material obtained through the use of modern biotechnology;

(d) Its final decisions regarding the importation or release of living modified organisms; and

(e) Reports submitted by it pursuant to Article 33, including those on implementation of the advance informed agreement procedure.

4. The modalities of the operation of the Biosafety Clearing-House, including reports on its activities, shall be considered and decided upon by the Conference of the Parties serving as the meeting of the Parties to this Protocol at its first meeting, and kept under review thereafter.

Article 21: Confidential information

1. The Party of import shall permit the notifier to identify information submitted under the procedures of this Protocol or required by the Party of import as part of the advance informed agreement procedure of the Protocol that is to be treated as confidential. Justification shall be given in such cases upon request.

2. The Party of import shall consult the notifier if it decides that information identified by the notifier as confidential does not qualify for such treatment and shall, prior to any disclosure, inform the notifier of its decision, providing reasons on request, as well as an opportunity for consultation and for an internal review of the decision prior to disclosure.

3. Each Party shall protect confidential information received under this Protocol, including any confidential information received in the context of the advance informed agreement procedure of the Protocol. Each Party shall ensure that it has procedures to protect such information and shall protect the confidentiality of such information in a manner no less favourable than its treatment of confidential information in connection with domestically produced living modified organisms.

4. The Party of import shall not use such information for a commercial purpose, except with the written consent of the notifier.

5. If a notifier withdraws or has withdrawn a notification, the Party of import shall respect the confidentiality of commercial and industrial information, including research and development information as well as information on which the Party and the notifier disagree as to its confidentiality.

6. Without prejudice to paragraph 5 above, the following information shall not be considered confidential:

(a) The name and address of the notifier;

(b) A general description of the living modified organism or organisms;

(c) A summary of the risk assessment of the effects on the conservation and sustainable use of biological diversity, taking also into account risks to human health; and

(d) Any methods and plans for emergency response.

Article 22: Capacity-building

1. The Parties shall cooperate in the development and/or strengthening of human resources and institutional capacities in biosafety, including biotechnology to the extent that it is required for biosafety, for the purpose of the effective implementation of this Protocol, in developing country Parties, in particular the least developed and small island developing States among them, and in Parties with economies in transition, including through existing global, regional, subregional and national institutions and organizations and, as appropriate, through facilitating private sector involvement.

2. For the purposes of implementing paragraph 1 above, in relation to cooperation, the needs of developing country Parties, in particular the least developed and small island developing States among them, for financial resources and access to and transfer of technology and know-how in accordance with the relevant provisions of the Convention, shall be taken fully into account for capacity-building in biosafety. Cooperation in capacity-building shall, subject to the different situation, capabilities and requirements of each Party, include scientific and technical training in the proper and safe management of biotechnology, and in the use of risk assessment and risk management for biosafety, and the enhancement of technological and institutional capacities in biosafety. The needs of Parties with economies in transition shall also be taken fully into account for such capacity-building in biosafety.

Article 23: Public awareness and participation

1. The Parties shall:

(a) Promote and facilitate public awareness, education and participation concerning the safe transfer, handling and use of living modified organisms in relation to the conservation and sustainable use of biological diversity, taking also into account risks to human health. In doing so, the Parties shall cooperate, as appropriate, with other States and international bodies;

(b) Endeavour to ensure that public awareness and education encompass access to information on living modified organisms identified in accordance with this Protocol that may be imported.

2. The Parties shall, in accordance with their respective laws and regulations, consult the public in the decision-making process regarding living modified organisms and shall make the results of such decisions available to the public, while respecting confidential information in accordance with Article 21.

3. Each Party shall endeavour to inform its public about the means of public access to the Biosafety Clearing-House.

Article 24: Non-Parties

1. Transboundary movements of living modified organisms between Parties and non-Parties shall be consistent with the objective of this Protocol. The Parties may enter into bilateral, regional and multilateral agreements and arrangements with non-Parties regarding such transboundary movements.

2. The Parties shall encourage non-Parties to adhere to this Protocol and to contribute appropriate information to the Biosafety Clearing-House on living modified organisms released in, or moved into or out of, areas within their national jurisdictions.

Article 25: Illegal transboundary movements

1. Each Party shall adopt appropriate domestic measures aimed at preventing and, if appropriate, penalizing transboundary movements of living modified organisms carried out in contravention of its domestic measures to implement this Protocol. Such movements shall be deemed illegal transboundary movements.

2. In the case of an illegal transboundary movement, the affected Party may request the Party of origin to dispose, at its own expense, of the living modified organism in question by repatriation or destruction, as appropriate.

3. Each Party shall make available to the Biosafety Clearing-House information concerning cases of illegal transboundary movements pertaining to it.

Article 26: Socio-economic considerations

1. The Parties, in reaching a decision on import under this Protocol or under its domestic measures implementing the Protocol, may take into account, consistent with their international obligations, socio-economic considerations arising from the impact of living modified organisms on the conservation and sustainable use of biological diversity, especially with regard to the value of biological diversity to indigenous and local communities.

2. The Parties are encouraged to cooperate on research and information exchange on any socio-economic impacts of living modified organisms, especially on indigenous and local communities.

Article 27: Liability and redress

The Conference of the Parties serving as the meeting of the Parties to this Protocol shall, at its first meeting, adopt a process with respect to the appropriate elaboration of international rules and procedures in the field of liability and redress for damage resulting from transboundary movements of living modified organisms, analysing and taking due account of the ongoing processes in international law on these matters, and shall endeavour to complete this process within four years.

Article 28: Financial mechanism and resources

1. In considering financial resources for the implementation of this Protocol, the Parties shall take into account the provisions of Article 20 of the Convention.

2. The financial mechanism established in Article 21 of the Convention shall, through the institutional structure entrusted with its operation, be the financial mechanism for this Protocol.

3. Regarding the capacity-building referred to in Article 22 of this Protocol, the Conference of the Parties serving as the meeting of the Parties to this Protocol, in providing guidance with respect to the financial mechanism referred to in paragraph 2 above, for consideration by the Conference of the Parties, shall take into account the need for financial resources by developing country Parties, in particular the least developed and the small island developing States among them.

4. In the context of paragraph 1 above, the Parties shall also take into account the needs of the developing country Parties, in particular the least developed and the small island developing States among them, and of the Parties with economies in transition, in their efforts to identify and implement their capacity-building requirements for the purposes of the implementation of this Protocol.

5. The guidance to the financial mechanism of the Convention in relevant decisions of the Conference of the Parties, including those agreed before the adoption of this Protocol, shall apply, *mutatis mutandis*, to the provisions of this Article.

6. The developed country Parties may also provide, and the developing country Parties and the Parties with economies in transition avail themselves of, financial and technological resources for the implementation of the provisions of this Protocol through bilateral, regional and multilateral channels.

Article 29: Conference of the Parties serving as the meeting of the Parties to this Protocol

1. The Conference of the Parties shall serve as the meeting of the Parties to this Protocol.

2. Parties to the Convention that are not Parties to this Protocol may participate as observers in the proceedings of any meeting of the Conference of the Parties serving as the meeting of the Parties to this Protocol. When the Conference of the Parties serves as the meeting of the Parties to this Protocol, decisions under this Protocol shall be taken only by those that are Parties to it.

3. When the Conference of the Parties serves as the meeting of the Parties to this Protocol, any member of the bureau of the Conference of the Parties representing a Party to the Convention but, at that time, not a Party to this Protocol, shall be substituted by a member to be elected by and from among the Parties to this Protocol.

4. The Conference of the Parties serving as the meeting of the Parties to this Protocol shall keep under regular review the implementation of this Protocol and shall make, within its mandate, the decisions necessary to promote its effective implementation. It shall perform the functions assigned to it by this Protocol and shall:

(a) Make recommendations on any matters necessary for the implementation of this Protocol;

(b) Establish such subsidiary bodies as are deemed necessary for the implementation of this Protocol;

(c) Seek and utilize, where appropriate, the services and cooperation of, and information provided by, competent international organizations and intergovernmental and non-governmental bodies;

(d) Establish the form and the intervals for transmitting the information to be submitted in accordance with Article 33 of this Protocol and consider such information as well as reports submitted by any subsidiary body;

(e) Consider and adopt, as required, amendments to this Protocol and its annexes, as well as any additional annexes to this Protocol, that are deemed necessary for the implementation of this Protocol; and

(f) Exercise such other functions as may be required for the implementation of this Protocol.

5. The rules of procedure of the Conference of the Parties and financial rules of the Convention shall be applied, *mutatis mutandis*, under this Protocol, except as may be otherwise decided by consensus by the Conference of the Parties serving as the meeting of the Parties to this Protocol.

6. The first meeting of the Conference of the Parties serving as the meeting of the Parties to this Protocol shall be convened by the Secretariat in conjunction with the first meeting of the Conference of the Parties that is scheduled after the date of the entry into force of this Protocol. Subsequent ordinary meetings of the Conference of the Parties serving as the meeting of the Parties to this Protocol shall be held in conjunction with ordinary meetings of the Conference of the Parties, unless otherwise decided by the Conference of the Parties serving as the meeting of the Parties to this Protocol.

7. Extraordinary meetings of the Conference of the Parties serving as the meeting of the Parties to this Protocol shall be held at such other times as may be deemed necessary by the Conference of the Parties serving as the meeting of the Parties to this Protocol, or at the written request of any Party, provided that, within six months of the request being communicated to the Parties by the Secretariat, it is supported by at least one third of the Parties.

8. The United Nations, its specialized agencies and the International Atomic Energy Agency, as well as any State member thereof or observers thereto not party to the Convention, may be represented as observers at meetings of the Conference of the Parties serving as the meeting of the Parties to this Protocol. Any body or agency, whether national or international, governmental or non-governmental, that is qualified in matters covered by this Protocol and that has informed the Secretariat of its wish to be represented at a meeting of the Conference of the Parties serving as a meeting of the Parties to this Protocol as an observer, may be so admitted, unless at least one third of the Parties present object. Except as otherwise provided in this Article, the admission and participation of observers shall be subject to the rules of procedure, as referred to in paragraph 5 above.

Article 30: Subsidiary bodies

1. Any subsidiary body established by or under the Convention may, upon a decision by the Conference of the Parties serving as the meeting of the Parties to this Protocol, serve the Protocol, in which case the meeting of the Parties shall specify which functions that body shall exercise.

2. Parties to the Convention that are not Parties to this Protocol may participate as observers in the proceedings of any meeting of any such subsidiary bodies. When a subsidiary body of the Convention serves as a subsidiary body to this Protocol, decisions under the Protocol shall be taken only by the Parties to the Protocol.

3. When a subsidiary body of the Convention exercises its functions with regard to matters concerning this Protocol, any member of the bureau of that subsidiary body representing a Party to the Convention but, at that time, not a Party to the Protocol, shall be substituted by a member to be elected by and from among the Parties to the Protocol.

Article 31: Secretariat

1. The Secretariat established by Article 24 of the Convention shall serve as the secretariat to this Protocol.

2. Article 24, paragraph 1, of the Convention on the functions of the Secretariat shall apply, *mutatis mutandis*, to this Protocol.

3. To the extent that they are distinct, the costs of the secretariat services for this Protocol shall be met by the Parties hereto. The Conference of the Parties serving as the meeting of the Parties to this Protocol shall, at its first meeting, decide on the necessary budgetary arrangements to this end.

Article 32: Relationship with the Convention

Except as otherwise provided in this Protocol, the provisions of the Convention relating to its protocols shall apply to this Protocol.

Article 33: Monitoring and reporting

Each Party shall monitor the implementation of its obligations under this Protocol, and shall, at intervals to be determined by the Conference of the Parties serving as the meeting of the Parties to this Protocol, report to the Conference of the Parties serving as the meeting of the Parties to this Protocol on measures that it has taken to implement the Protocol.

Article 34: Compliance

The Conference of the Parties serving as the meeting of the Parties to this Protocol shall, at its first meeting, consider and approve cooperative procedures and institutional mechanisms to promote compliance with the provisions of this Protocol and to address cases of non-compliance. These procedures and mechanisms shall include provisions to offer advice or assistance, where appropriate. They shall be separate from, and without prejudice to, the dispute settlement procedures and mechanisms established by Article 27 of the Convention.

Article 35: Assessment and review

The Conference of the Parties serving as the meeting of the Parties to this Protocol shall undertake, five years after the entry into force of this Protocol and at least every five years thereafter, an evaluation of the effectiveness of the Protocol, including an assessment of its procedures and annexes.

Article 36: Signature

This Protocol shall be open for signature at the United Nations Office at Nairobi by States and regional economic integration organizations from 15 to 26 May 2000, and at United Nations Headquarters in New York from 5 June 2000 to 4 June 2001.

Article 37: Entry into force

1. This Protocol shall enter into force on the ninetieth day after the date of deposit of the fiftieth instrument of ratification, acceptance, approval or accession by States or regional economic integration organizations that are Parties to the Convention.

2. This Protocol shall enter into force for a State or regional economic integration organization that ratifies, accepts or approves this Protocol or accedes thereto after its entry into force pursuant to paragraph 1 above, on the ninetieth day after the date on which that State or regional economic integration organization deposits its instrument of ratification, acceptance, approval or accession, or on the date on which the Convention enters into force for that State or regional economic integration organization, whichever shall be the later.

3. For the purposes of paragraphs 1 and 2 above, any instrument deposited by a regional economic integration organization shall not be counted as additional to those deposited by member States of such organization.

Article 38: Reservations

No reservations may be made to this Protocol.

Article 39: Withdrawal

1. At any time after two years from the date on which this Protocol has entered into force for a Party, that Party may withdraw from the Protocol by giving written notification to the Depositary.

2. Any such withdrawal shall take place upon expiry of one year after the date of its receipt by the Depositary, or on such later date as may be specified in the notification of the withdrawal.

Article 40: Authentic texts

The original of this Protocol, of which the Arabic, Chinese, English, French, Russian and Spanish texts are equally authentic, shall be deposited with the Secretary-General of the United Nations.

IN WITNESS WHEREOF the undersigned, being duly authorized to that effect, have signed this Protocol.

DONE at Montreal on this twenty-ninth day of January, two thousand.

Annex I: Information required in notifications under Articles 8, 10 and 13

(a) Name, address and contact details of the exporter.

(b) Name, address and contact details of the importer.

(c) Name and identity of the living modified organism, as well as the domestic classification, if any, of the biosafety level of the living modified organism in the State of export.

(d) Intended date or dates of the transboundary movement, if known.

(e) Taxonomic status, common name, point of collection or acquisition, and characteristics of recipient organism or parental organisms related to biosafety.

(f) Centres of origin and centres of genetic diversity, if known, of the recipient organism and/or the parental organisms and a description of the habitats where the organisms may persist or proliferate.

(g) Taxonomic status, common name, point of collection or acquisition, and characteristics of the donor organism or organisms related to biosafety.

(h) Description of the nucleic acid or the modification introduced, the technique used, and the resulting characteristics of the living modified organism.

(i) Intended use of the living modified organism or products thereof, namely, processed materials that are of living modified organism origin, containing detectable novel combinations of replicable genetic material obtained through the use of modern biotechnology.

(j) Quantity or volume of the living modified organism to be transferred.

(k) A previous and existing risk assessment report consistent with Annex III.

(l) Suggested methods for the safe handling, storage, transport and use, including packaging, labelling, documentation, disposal and contingency procedures, where appropriate.

(m) Regulatory status of the living modified organism within the State of export (for example, whether it is prohibited in the State of export, whether there are other restrictions, or whether it has been approved for general release) and, if the living modified organism is banned in the State of export, the reason or reasons for the ban.

(n) Result and purpose of any notification by the exporter to other States regarding the living modified organism to be transferred.

(o) A declaration that the above-mentioned information is factually correct.

Annex II: Information required concerning living modified organisms intended for direct use as food or feed, or for processing under Article 11

(a) The name and contact details of the applicant for a decision for domestic use.

(b) The name and contact details of the authority responsible for the decision.

(c) Name and identity of the living modified organism.

(d) Description of the gene modification, the technique used, and the resulting characteristics of the living modified organism.

(e) Any unique identification of the living modified organism.

(f) Taxonomic status, common name, point of collection or acquisition, and characteristics of recipient organism or parental organisms related to biosafety.

(g) Centres of origin and centres of genetic diversity, if known, of the recipient organism and/or the parental organisms and a description of the habitats where the organisms may persist or proliferate.

(h) Taxonomic status, common name, point of collection or acquisition, and characteristics of the donor organism or organisms related to biosafety.

(i) Approved uses of the living modified organism.

(j) A risk assessment report consistent with Annex III.

(k) Suggested methods for the safe handling, storage, transport and use, including packaging, labelling, documentation, disposal and contingency procedures, where appropriate.

Annex III: Risk assessment

Objective

1. The objective of risk assessment, under this Protocol, is to identify and evaluate the potential adverse effects of living modified organisms on the conservation and sustainable use of biological diversity in the likely potential receiving environment, taking also into account risks to human health.

Use of risk assessment

2. Risk assessment is, *inter alia*, used by competent authorities to make informed decisions regarding living modified organisms.

General principles

3. Risk assessment should be carried out in a scientifically sound and transparent manner, and can take into account expert advice of, and guidelines developed by, relevant international organizations.

4. Lack of scientific knowledge or scientific consensus should not necessarily be interpreted as indicating a particular level of risk, an absence of risk, or an acceptable risk.

5. Risks associated with living modified organisms or products thereof, namely, processed materials that are of living modified organism origin, containing detectable novel combinations of replicable genetic material obtained through the use of modern biotechnology, should be considered in the context of the risks posed by the non-modified recipients or parental organisms in the likely potential receiving environment.

6. Risk assessment should be carried out on a case-by-case basis. The required information may vary in nature and level of detail from case to case, depending on the living modified organism concerned, its intended use and the likely potential receiving environment.

Methodology

7. The process of risk assessment may on the one hand give rise to a need for further information about specific subjects, which may be identified and requested during the assessment process, while on the other hand information on other subjects may not be relevant in some instances.

8. To fulfil its objective, risk assessment entails, as appropriate, the following steps:

(a) An identification of any novel genotypic and phenotypic characteristics associated with the living modified organism that may have adverse effects on biological diversity in the likely potential receiving environment, taking also into account risks to human health;

(b) An evaluation of the likelihood of these adverse effects being realized, taking into account the level and kind of exposure of the likely potential receiving environment to the living modified organism;

(c) An evaluation of the consequences should these adverse effects be realized;

(d) An estimation of the overall risk posed by the living modified organism based on the evaluation of the likelihood and consequences of the identified adverse effects being realized;

(e) A recommendation as to whether or not the risks are acceptable or manageable, including, where necessary, identification of strategies to manage these risks; and

(f) Where there is uncertainty regarding the level of risk, it may be addressed by requesting further information on the specific issues of concern or by implementing appropriate risk management strategies and/or monitoring the living modified organism in the receiving environment.

Points to consider

9. Depending on the case, risk assessment takes into account the relevant technical and scientific details regarding the characteristics of the following subjects:

(a) *Recipient organism or parental organisms.* The biological characteristics of the recipient organism or parental organisms, including information on taxonomic status, common name, origin, centres of origin and centres of genetic diversity, if known, and a description of the habitat where the organisms may persist or proliferate;

(b) *Donor organism or organisms.* Taxonomic status and common name, source, and the relevant biological characteristics of the donor organisms;

(c) *Vector.* Characteristics of the vector, including its identity, if any, and its source or origin, and its host range;

(d) *Insert or inserts and/or characteristics of modification.* Genetic characteristics of the inserted nucleic acid and the function it specifies, and/or characteristics of the modification introduced;

(e) *Living modified organism.* Identity of the living modified organism, and the differences between the biological characteristics of the living modified organism and those of the recipient organism or parental organisms;

(f) *Detection and identification of the living modified organism.* Suggested detection and identification methods and their specificity, sensitivity and reliability;

(g) *Information relating to the intended use.* Information relating to the intended use of the living modified organism, including new or changed use compared to the recipient organism or parental organisms; and

(h) *Receiving environment.* Information on the location, geographical, climatic and ecological characteristics, including relevant information on biological diversity and centres of origin of the likely potential receiving environment.

Section III

Rules of procedure for meetings of the Conference of the Parties to the Convention on Biological Diversity

(Annex to decision I/1, as amended by decision V/20)

Rules of procedure

Purposes

Rule 1

These rules of procedure shall apply to any meeting of the Conference of the Parties to the Convention on Biological Diversity convened in accordance with article 23 of the Convention.

Definitions

Rule 2

For the purposes of these rules:

(a) 'Convention' means the Convention on Biological Diversity adopted in Nairobi on 22 May 1992 and opened for signature in Rio de Janeiro on 5 June 1992;

(b) 'Parties' means Parties to the Convention;

(c) 'Conference of the Parties' means the Conference of the Parties established in accordance with article 23 of the Convention;

(d) 'Meeting' means any ordinary or extraordinary meeting of the Conference of the Parties convened in accordance with article 23 of the Convention;

(e) 'Regional economic integration organization' has the same meaning as that assigned to it in article 2 of the Convention;

(f) 'President' means the President elected in accordance with rule 21, paragraph 1, of the present rules of procedure;

(g) 'Secretariat' means the Secretariat established under article 24 of the Convention;

(h) 'Subsidiary bodies' includes committees and working groups.

Place of meetings

Rule 3

The meetings of the Conference of the Parties shall take place at the seat of the Secretariat, unless the Conference of the Parties decides otherwise or other appropriate arrangements are made by the Secretariat in consultation with the Parties.

Dates of meetings

Rule 4

1. Ordinary meetings of the Conference of the Parties shall be held every two years. The Conference of the Parties shall from time to time review the periodicity of its ordinary meetings in the light of the progress achieved in the implementation of the Convention.

2. At each ordinary meeting, the Conference of the Parties shall decide on the date and duration of the next ordinary meeting.

3. Extraordinary meetings of the Conference of the Parties shall be convened at such times as may be deemed necessary by the Conference of the Parties, or at the written request of any Party, provided that, within six months of the request being communicated to them by the Secretariat, it is supported by at least one third of the Parties.

4. In the case of an extraordinary meeting convened at the written request of a Party, it shall be convened not more than ninety days after the date at which the request is supported by at least one third of the Parties in accordance with paragraph 3 of this rule.

Rule 5

The Secretariat shall notify all Parties of the dates and venue of a meeting at least two months before the meeting is due to commence.

Observers

Rule 6

1. The Secretariat shall notify the United Nations, its specialized agencies and the International Atomic Energy Agency as well as any State not Party to the Convention of meetings of the Conference of the Parties so that they may be represented as observers.

2. Such observers may, upon invitation of the President, participate without the right to vote in the proceedings of any meeting unless at least one third of the Parties present at the meeting object.

Rule 7

1. The Secretariat shall notify any body or agency, whether governmental or non-governmental, qualified in fields relating to the conservation and sustainable use of biological diversity, which has informed the Secretariat of its wish to be represented, of meetings of the Conference of the Parties so that they may be represented as observers unless at least one third of the Parties present at the meeting object.

2. Such observers may, upon invitation of the President, participate without the right to vote in the proceedings of any meeting in matters of direct concern to the body or agency they represent unless at least one third of the Parties present at the meeting object.

Agenda

Rule 8

In agreement with the President, the Secretariat shall prepare the provisional agenda of each meeting.

Rule 9

The provisional agenda of each ordinary meeting shall include, as appropriate:

(a) Items arising from the articles of the Convention, including those specified in article 23 of the Convention;

(b) Items the inclusion of which has been decided at a previous meeting;

(c) Items referred to in rule 15 of the present rules of procedure;

(d) Any item proposed by a Party and received by the Secretariat before the provisional agenda is produced;

(e) The proposed budget as well as all questions pertaining to the accounts and financial arrangements.

Rule 10

The provisional agenda, together with supporting documents, for each ordinary meeting shall be distributed in the official languages by the Secretariat to the Parties at least six weeks before the opening of the meeting.

Rule 11

The Secretariat shall, in agreement with the President, include any item which is proposed by a Party and has been received by the Secretariat after the provisional agenda has been produced, but before the opening of the meeting, in a supplementary provisional agenda.

Rule 12

The Conference of the Parties shall examine the provisional agenda together with any supplementary provisional agenda. When adopting the agenda, it may add, delete, defer or amend items. Only items which are considered by the Conference of the Parties to be urgent and important may be added to the agenda.

Rule 13

The provisional agenda for an extraordinary meeting shall consist only of those items proposed for consideration in the request for the holding of the extraordinary meeting. It shall be distributed to the Parties at the same time as the invitation to the extraordinary meeting.

Rule 14

The Secretariat shall report to the Conference of the Parties on the administrative and financial implications of all substantive agenda items submitted to the meeting, before they are considered by it. Unless the Conference of the Parties decides otherwise, no such item shall be considered until at least forty-eight hours after the Conference of the Parties has received the Secretariat's report on the administrative and financial implications.

Rule 15

Any item of the agenda of an ordinary meeting, consideration of which has not been completed at the meeting, shall be included automatically in the agenda of the next ordinary meeting, unless otherwise decided by the Conference of the Parties.

Representation and credentials

Rule 16

Each Party participating in a meeting shall be represented by a delegation consisting of a head of delegation and such other accredited representatives, alternate representatives and advisers as it may require.

Rule 17

A representative may be designated as an alternate head of delegation. An alternate representative or an adviser may act as a representative upon designation by the head of delegation.

Rule 18

The credentials of representatives and the names of alternate representatives and advisers shall be submitted to the Executive Secretary of the Conference of the Parties or the representative of the Executive Secretary if possible not later than twenty-four hours after the opening of the meeting. Any later change in the composition of the delegation shall also be submitted to the Executive Secretary or the representative of the Executive Secretary. The credentials shall be issued either by the Head of State or Government or by the Minister for Foreign Affairs or, in the case of a regional economic integration organization, by the competent authority of that organization.

Rule 19

The Bureau of any meeting shall examine the credentials and submit its report to the Conference of the Parties for decision.

Rule 20

Pending a decision of the Conference of the Parties upon their credentials, representatives shall be entitled to participate provisionally in the meeting.

Officers

Rule 21

1. At the commencement of the first session of each ordinary meeting a President and ten Vice-Presidents, one of whom shall act as Rapporteur, are to be elected from among the representatives of the Parties. They shall serve as the bureau of the Conference of the Parties. The term of office of the President shall commence straight away and the terms of office of the Vice-Presidents shall commence upon the closure of the meeting at which they are elected. In electing its Bureau, the Conference of the Parties shall have due regard to the principle of equitable geographical representation of the Small Island Developing States. The offices of President and Rapporteur of the meeting of the Conference of the Parties shall normally be subject to rotation among the five groups of States referred to in section I, paragraph 1, of General Assembly resolution 2997 (XXVII) of 15 December 1972, by which the United Nations Environment Programme was established.

2. The President shall remain in office until a new President is elected at the commencement of the next ordinary meeting and the Vice-Presidents shall remain in office until the closure of the next ordinary meeting. They shall serve as the bureau of any extraordinary meeting held during their term of office and provide guidance to the Secretariat with regard to preparations for, and conduct of, meetings of the Conference of the Parties. No officer may be re-elected for a third consecutive term.

3. The President shall participate in the meeting in that capacity and shall not at the same time exercise the rights of a representative of a Party. The Party concerned shall designate another representative who shall be entitled to represent the Party in the meeting and to exercise the right to vote.

Rule 22

1. In addition to exercising the powers conferred upon the President elsewhere by these rules, the President shall declare the opening and closing of the meeting, preside at the sessions of the meeting, ensure the observance of these rules, accord the right to speak, put questions to the vote and announce decisions. The President shall rule on points of order and, subject to these rules, shall have complete control of the proceedings and over the maintenance of order thereat.

2. The President may propose to the Conference of the Parties the closure of the list of speakers, a limitation on the time to be allowed to speakers and on the number of times each representative may speak on a question, the adjournment or the closure of the debate and the suspension or the adjournment of a session.

3. The President, in the exercise of the functions of that office, remains under the authority of the Conference of the Parties.

Rule 23

The President, if temporarily absent from a session or any part thereof, shall designate a Vice-President to act as President. A Vice-President acting as President shall have the same powers and duties as the President.

Rule 24

If an officer of the Bureau resigns or is otherwise unable to complete the assigned term of office or to perform the functions of the office, a representative of the same Party shall be named by the Party concerned to replace the said officer for the remainder of that officer's mandate.

Rule 25

At the first session of each ordinary meeting, the President of the previous ordinary meeting, or in the absence of the President, a Vice-President, shall preside until the Conference of the Parties has elected a new President.

Subsidiary bodies

Rule 26

1. In addition to the subsidiary body on scientific, technical and technological advice established under article 25 of the Convention, the Conference of the Parties may establish other subsidiary bodies. It may also establish committees and working groups if it deems it necessary for the implementation of the Convention. Where appropriate, meetings of subsidiary bodies shall be held in conjunction with meetings of the Conference of the Parties.

2. The Conference of the Parties may decide that any such subsidiary bodies may meet in the period between ordinary meetings.

3. Unless otherwise decided by the Conference of the Parties, the chairperson for each such subsidiary body shall be elected by the Conference of the Parties. The Conference of the Parties shall determine the matters to be considered by each such subsidiary body and may authorize the President, upon the request of the chairperson of a subsidiary body, to make adjustments to the allocation of work.

4. Subject to paragraph 3 of this rule, each subsidiary body shall elect its own officers.

5. Unless otherwise decided by the Conference of the Parties, these rules shall apply mutatis mutandis to the proceedings of subsidiary bodies, except that:

(a) A majority of the Parties designated by the Conference of the Parties to take part in the subsidiary body shall constitute a quorum, but in the event of the subsidiary body being open-ended, one quarter of the Parties shall constitute a quorum;

(b) The chairperson of a subsidiary body may exercise the right to vote; and

(c) Decisions of subsidiary bodies shall be taken by a majority of the Parties present and voting, except that the reconsideration of a proposal or of an amendment to a proposal shall require the majority established by rule 38.

Secretariat

Rule 27

1. The head of the Secretariat of the Convention shall be the Executive Secretary of the Conference of the Parties. The Executive Secretary or the representative of the Executive Secretary shall act in that capacity in all meetings of the Conference of the Parties and of subsidiary bodies.

2. The Executive Secretary shall provide and direct the staff required by the Conference of the Parties or subsidiary bodies.

Rule 28

The Secretariat shall, in accordance with these rules:

(a) Arrange for interpretation at the meeting;

(b) Receive, translate, reproduce and distribute the documents of the meeting;

(c) Publish and circulate the official documents of the meeting;

(d) Make and arrange for keeping of sound recordings of the meeting;

(e) Arrange for the custody and preservation of the documents of the meeting; and

(f) Generally perform all other work that the Conference of the Parties may require.

Conduct of business

Rule 29

1. Sessions of the Conference of the Parties shall be held in public, unless the Conference of the Parties decides otherwise.

2. Sessions of subsidiary bodies shall be held in public unless the subsidiary body concerned decides otherwise.

Rule 30

The President may declare a session of the meeting open and permit the debate to proceed if at least one third of the Parties to the Convention are present and have any decisions taken when representatives of at least two thirds of the Parties are present.

Rule 31

1. No one may speak at a session of the Conference of the Parties without having previously obtained the permission of the President. Subject to rules 32, 33, 34 and 36, the President shall call upon speakers in the order in which they signify their desire to speak. The Secretariat shall maintain a list of speakers. The President may call a speaker to order if the speaker's remarks are not relevant to the subject under discussion.

2. The Conference of the Parties may, on a proposal from the President or from any Party, limit the time allowed to each speaker and the number of times each representative may speak on a question. Before a decision is taken, two representatives may speak in favour of and two against a proposal to set such limits. When the debate is limited and a speaker exceeds the allotted time, the President shall call the speaker to order without delay.

Rule 32

The chairperson or rapporteur of a subsidiary body may be accorded precedence for the purpose of explaining the conclusions arrived at by that subsidiary body.

Rule 33

During the discussion of any matter, a representative may at any time raise a point of order which shall be decided immediately by the President in accordance with these rules. A representative may appeal against the ruling of the President. The appeal shall be put to the vote immediately and the ruling shall stand unless overruled by a majority of the Parties present and voting. A representative may not, in raising a point of order, speak on the substance of the matter under discussion.

Rule 34

Any motion calling for a decision on the competence of the Conference of the Parties to discuss any matter or to adopt a proposal or an amendment to a proposal submitted to it shall be put to the vote before the matter is discussed or a vote is taken on the proposal or amendment in question.

Rule 35

Proposals and amendments to proposals shall normally be introduced in writing by the Parties and handed to the Secretariat, which shall circulate copies to delegations. As a general rule, no proposal shall be discussed or put to the vote at any session unless copies of it, translated into the official languages of the Conference of the Parties, have been circulated to delegations not later than the day preceding the session. Nevertheless, the President may, in exceptional circumstances and in cases of urgency, permit the discussion and consideration of proposals, amendments to proposals or of procedural motions even though these proposals, amendments or motions have not been circulated or have been circulated only the same day or have not been translated into all the official languages of the Conference of the Parties.

Rule 36

1. Subject to rule 33, the following motions shall have precedence, in the order indicated below, over all other proposals or motions:

(a) To suspend a session;

(b) To adjourn a session;

(c) To adjourn the debate on the question under discussion; and

(d) For the closure of the debate on the question under discussion.

2. Permission to speak on a motion falling within (a) to (d) above shall be granted only to the proposer and, in addition, to one speaker in favour of and two against the motion, after which it shall be put immediately to the vote.

Rule 37

A proposal or motion may be withdrawn by its proposer at any time before voting on it has begun, provided that the motion has not been amended. A proposal or motion withdrawn may be reintroduced by any other Party.

Rule 38

When a proposal has been adopted or rejected, it may not be reconsidered at the same meeting, unless the Conference of the Parties, by a two-thirds majority of the Parties present and voting, decides in favour of reconsideration. Permission to speak on a motion to reconsider shall be accorded only to the mover and one other supporter, after which it shall be put immediately to the vote.

Voting

Rule 39

1. Except as provided for in paragraph 2 of this rule, each Party shall have one vote.

2. Regional economic integration organizations, in matters within their competence, shall exercise their right to vote with a number of votes equal to the number of their member States which are Parties. Such organizations shall not exercise their right to vote if their member States exercise theirs, and vice versa.

Rule 40

[1. The Parties shall make every effort to reach agreement on all matters of substance by consensus. If all efforts to reach consensus have been exhausted and no agreement reached, the decision [except a decision under paragraph 1 or 2 of article 21 of the Convention] shall, as a last resort, be taken by a two-thirds majority vote of the Parties present and voting, unless otherwise provided by the Convention, the financial rules referred to in paragraph 3 of article 23 of the Convention, or the present rules of procedure. [Decisions of the Parties under paragraphs 1 and 2 of article 21 of the Convention shall be taken by consensus.]]

2. Decisions of the Conference of the Parties on matters of procedure shall be taken by a majority vote of the Parties present and voting.

3. If the question arises whether a matter is one of procedural or substantive nature, the President shall rule on the question. An appeal against this ruling shall be put to the vote immediately and the President's ruling shall stand unless overruled by a majority of the Parties present and voting.

4. If on matters other than elections a vote is equally divided, a second vote shall be taken. If this vote is also equally divided, the proposal shall be regarded as rejected.

5. For the purposes of these rules, the phrase "Parties present and voting" means Parties present at the session at which voting takes place and casting an affirmative or negative vote. Parties abstaining from voting shall be considered as not voting.

Rule 41

If two or more proposals relate to the same question, the Conference of the Parties, unless it decides otherwise, shall vote on the proposals in the order in which they have been submitted. The Conference of the Parties may, after each vote on a proposal, decide whether to vote on the next proposal.

Rule 42

Any representative may request that any parts of a proposal or of an amendment to a proposal be voted on separately. The President shall allow the request unless a Party objects. If objection is made to the request for division, the President shall permit two representatives to speak, one in favour of and the other against the motion, after which it shall be put immediately to the vote.

Rule 43

If the motion referred to in rule 42 is adopted, those parts of a proposal or of an amendment to a proposal which are approved shall then be put to the vote as a whole. If all the operative parts of a proposal or amendment have been rejected the proposal or amendment shall be considered to have been rejected as a whole.

Rule 44

A motion is considered to be an amendment to a proposal if it merely adds to, deletes from, or revises parts of that proposal. An amendment shall be voted on before the proposal to which it relates is put to the vote, and if the amendment is adopted, the amended proposal shall then be voted on.

Rule 45

If two or more amendments are moved to a proposal, the Conference of the Parties shall first vote on the amendment furthest removed in substance from the original proposal, then on the amendment next furthest removed therefrom, and so on, until all amendments have been put to the vote. The President shall determine the order of voting on the amendments under this rule.

Rule 46

Voting, except for election, shall normally be by show of hands. A roll-call vote shall be taken if one is requested by any Party. It shall be taken in the English alphabetical order of the names of the Parties participating in the meeting, beginning with the Party whose name is drawn by lot by the President. However, if at any time a Party requests a secret ballot, that shall be the method of voting on the issue in question.

Rule 47

The vote of each Party participating in a roll-call vote shall be recorded in the relevant documents of the meeting.

Rule 48

After the President has announced the beginning of voting, no representative shall interrupt the voting except on a point of order in connection with the actual conduct of the voting. The President may permit the Parties to explain their votes, either before or after the voting. The President may limit the time to be allowed for such explanations. The President shall not permit proposers of proposals or of amendments to proposals to explain their vote on their own proposals or amendments, except if they have been amended.

Rule 49

All elections shall be held by secret ballot, unless otherwise decided by the Conference of the Parties.

Rule 50

1. If, when one person or one delegation is to be elected, no candidate obtains in the first ballot a majority of the votes cast by the Parties present and voting, a second ballot restricted to the two candidates obtaining the largest number of votes shall be taken. If in the second ballot the votes are equally divided, the President shall decide between the candidates by drawing lots.

2. In the case of a tie in the first ballot among three or more candidates obtaining the largest number of votes, a second ballot shall be held. If a tie results among more than two candidates, the number shall be reduced to two by lot and the balloting, restricted to them, shall continue in accordance with the procedure set forth in paragraph 1 of this rule.

Rule 51

1. When two or more elective places are to be filled at one time under the same conditions, those candidates, not exceeding the number of such places, obtaining in the first ballot the largest number of votes and a majority of the votes cast by the Parties present and voting shall be deemed elected.

2. If the number of candidates obtaining such majority is less than the number of persons or delegations to be elected, there shall be additional ballots to fill the remaining places, the voting being restricted to the candidates obtaining the greatest number of votes in the previous ballot, to a number not more than twice the places remaining to be filled, provided that, after the third inconclusive ballot, votes may be cast for any eligible person or delegation.

3. If three such unrestricted ballots are inconclusive, the next three ballots shall be restricted to the candidates who obtained the greatest number of votes in the third of the unrestricted ballots, to a number not more than twice the places remaining to be filled, and the following three ballots thereafter shall be unrestricted, and so on until all the places have been filled.

Languages

Rule 52

The official and working languages of the Conference of the Parties shall be those of the United Nations Organization.

Rule 53

1. Statements made in an official language shall be interpreted into the other official languages.

2. A representative of a Party may speak in a language other than an official language, if the Party provides for interpretation into one such official language.

Rule 54

Official documents of the meetings shall be drawn up in one of the official languages and translated into the other official languages.

Sound records of the meetings

Rule 55

Sound records of the meetings of the Conference of the Parties, and whenever possible of its subsidiary bodies, shall be kept by the Secretariat in accordance with the practice of the United Nations.

Amendments to rules of procedure

Rule 56

These rules of procedure may be amended by consensus by the Conference of the Parties.

Overriding authority of the Convention

Rule 57

In the event of any conflict between any provision of these rules and any provision of the Convention, the Convention shall prevail.

Documents

UNEP/CBD/COP/1/2 Draft rules of procedure for meeting of the Conference of the Parties to the Convention on Biological Diversity

UNEP/CBD/COP/2/4 Pending issues arising from the first meeting of the Conference of the Parties

UNEP/CBD/COP/3/2 Pending issues arising from the second meeting of the Conference of the Parties

UNEP/CBD/COP/4/3 Pending issues arising from the third meeting of the Conference of the Parties

Section IV

Modus operandi of the Subsidiary Body on Scientific, Technical and Technological Advice

(Annex I to decision IV/16 and section III of decision V/20)

Modus operandi

I Functions

1. The functions of the Subsidiary Body on Scientific, Technical and Technological Advice are those contained in Article 25 of the Convention. Accordingly, the Subsidiary Body on Scientific, Technical and Technological Advice will fulfil its mandate under the authority of, and in accordance with, guidance laid down by the Conference of the Parties, and upon its request.

2. Pursuant to Article 25, paragraph 3, of the Convention, the functions, terms of reference, organization and operation of the Subsidiary Body on Scientific, Technical and Technological Advice may be further elaborated, for approval by the Conference of the Parties.

II Rules of procedure

3. The rules of procedure for meetings of the Conference of the Parties to the Convention on Biological Diversity shall apply, in accordance with rule 26, paragraph 5, *mutatis mutandis*, to the proceedings of the Subsidiary Body on Scientific, Technical and Technological Advice. Therefore, rule 18, on credentials, will not apply.

4. In accordance with rule 52, the official and working languages of the Subsidiary Body on Scientific, Technical and Technological Advice will be those of the United Nations Organization. The proceedings of the Subsidiary Body on Scientific, Technical and Technological Advice will be carried out in the working languages of the Conference of the Parties.

5. In order to facilitate continuity in the work of the Subsidiary Body on Scientific, Technical and Technological Advice and taking into account the technical and scientific character of the input of the Subsidiary Body, the terms of office of members of its Bureau will be two years. At each meeting of the Subsidiary Body on Scientific, Technical and Technological Advice one of the two regional representatives shall be elected in order to achieve staggered terms of office. The members of the Bureau of the Subsidiary Body will take office at the end of the meeting at which they are elected.

6. The Chairman of the Subsidiary Body on Scientific, Technical and Technological Advice, elected at an ordinary meeting of the Conference of the Parties, shall take office from the end of the next ordinary meeting of the Subsidiary Body on Scientific, Technical and Technological Advice and remain in office until his/her successor takes office. As a general rule the chairmanship of the Subsidiary Body shall rotate among United Nations regional groups. Candidates for the Chair of the Subsidiary Body should be recognized experts, qualified in the field of biological diversity and experienced in the process of the Convention and the Subsidiary Body on Scientific, Technical and Technological Advice.

III Frequency and timing of meetings of the Subsidiary Body on Scientific, Technical and Technological Advice

7. The Subsidiary Body on Scientific, Technical and Technological Advice shall meet at intervals to be determined by the Conference of the Parties and sufficiently in advance of each regular meeting of the Conference of the Parties, for a duration to be determined by the Conference of the Parties which should not normally exceed five days. The number and length of the meetings and activities of the Subsidiary Body on Scientific, Technical and Technological Advice and its organs should be reflected in the budget adopted by the Conference of the Parties or other sources of extra budgetary funding.

IV Documentation

8. The documentation prepared for meetings will be distributed three months before the meeting in the working languages of the Subsidiary Body on Scientific, Technical and Technological Advice, will be concrete, focused draft technical reports and will include proposed conclusions and recommendations for consideration of the Subsidiary Body on Scientific, Technical and Technological Advice.

9. To facilitate the preparation of documentation, and in order to avoid duplication of efforts and ensure the use of available scientific, technical and technological competence available within international and regional organizations, including non-governmental organizations and scientific unions and societies, qualified in fields relating to conservation and sustainable use of biodiversity, the Executive Secretary may establish, in consultation with the Chairman and the other members of the Bureau of the Subsidiary Body, liaison groups, as appropriate. Such liaison groups will depend on the resources available.

V Organization of work during the meetings

10. Each meeting of the Subsidiary Body on Scientific, Technical and Technological Advice will propose to the Conference of the Parties, in light of the programme of work for the Conference of the Parties and the Subsidiary Body, a particular theme as the focus of work for the following meeting of the Subsidiary Body.

11. Two open-ended sessional working groups of the Subsidiary Body on Scientific, Technical and Technological Advice could be established and operate simultaneously during meetings of the Subsidiary Body. They shall be established on the basis of well-defined terms of reference, and will be open to all Parties and observers. The financial implications of these arrangements should be reflected in the budget of the Convention.

VI Ad hoc technical expert group meetings

12. A limited number of ad hoc technical expert groups on specific priority issues on the programme of work of the Subsidiary Body on Scientific, Technical and Technological Advice may be established, as required, for a limited duration. The establishment of such ad hoc technical expert groups would be guided by the following elements:

(a) The ad hoc technical expert groups should draw on the existing knowledge and competence available within, and liaise with, international, regional and national organizations, including non-governmental organizations and the scientific community in fields relevant to this Convention;

(b) The Executive Secretary will nominate scientific and technical experts drawn from the roster for the ad hoc technical expert groups in consultation with the Bureau of the Subsidiary Body on Scientific, Technical and Technological Advice. The ad hoc technical expert groups shall be composed of no more than fifteen experts competent in the relevant field of expertise, with due regard to geographical representation and to the special conditions of least-developed countries and small island developing States;

(c) Within the available budgetary resources, the Subsidiary Body on Scientific, Technical and Technological Advice will determine the exact duration and specific terms of reference when establishing such expert groups under the guidance of the Conference of the Parties;

(d) Expert groups will be encouraged to use innovative means of communication and to minimize the need for face-to-face meetings;

(e) The ad hoc technical expert groups may also convene meetings parallel to the proceedings of the Subsidiary Body on Scientific, Technical and Technological Advice;

(f) Reports produced by the ad hoc technical expert groups should, as a general rule, be submitted for peer review;

(g) All efforts will be made to provide adequate voluntary financial assistance for the participation of experts in the expert groups from developing countries and countries with economies in transition Parties; and

(h) The number of ad hoc technical expert groups active each year will be limited to the minimum necessary and will depend on the amount of resources designated to the Subsidiary Body by the Conference of the Parties in its budget or on the availability of extra-budgetary resources.

VII Contribution of non-governmental organizations

13. The scientific and technical contribution of non-governmental organizations to the fulfilment of the mandate of the Subsidiary Body will be strongly encouraged in accordance with the relevant provisions of the Convention and the rules of procedure for meetings of the Conference of the Parties.

VIII Cooperation with other relevant bodies

14. The Subsidiary Body on Scientific, Technical and Technological Advice shall cooperate with other relevant international, regional and national organizations, under the guidance of the Convention of the Parties, thus building upon the vast experience and knowledge available.

15. In this context, the Subsidiary Body on Scientific, Technical and Technological Advice emphasizes the importance of research to further increase available knowledge and reduce uncertainties, and recommends that the Conference of the Parties consider this issue in relation to the financial resources required for the effective implementation of the Convention.

IX Regional and subregional preparatory meetings

16. Regional and subregional meetings for the preparation of regular meetings of the Subsidiary Body on Scientific, Technical and Technological Advice may be organized as appropriate for specific items. The possibility of combining such meetings with other scientific regional meetings, in order to make maximum use of available resources, should be considered. The convening of such regional and subregional meetings will be subject to the availability of voluntary financial contributions.

17. The Subsidiary Body on Scientific, Technical and Technological Advice should, in the fulfilment of its mandate, draw upon the contributions of the existing regional and subregional intergovernmental organizations or initiatives.

X Focal points

18. A list of focal points and focal persons to the Subsidiary Body on Scientific, Technical and Technological Advice shall be established and regularly updated by the Executive Secretary, on the basis of information provided by Parties and other relevant regional, subregional and intergovernmental organizations.

XI Roster of experts

19. Rosters of experts in the relevant fields of the Convention will be compiled by the Executive Secretary on the basis of input from Parties and, as appropriate, from other countries and relevant bodies. The rosters will be administered by the Executive Secretary in an efficient, effective and transparent manner. The Executive Secretary together with the national focal points and relevant bodies, will regularly update the rosters of experts, including the information on each expert. The information on the rosters will be made accessible through the clearing-house mechanism, save to the extent that an expert objects to information concerning him/her being released.

20. The Executive Secretary as well as the ad hoc technical expert groups and liaison groups referred to above, should make full use of such rosters of experts, *inter alia*, through the type of consultations as described in paragraph 21 below. The Executive Secretary will inform Parties, at least one month prior to the convening of a meeting of experts, of the details of the meeting and of the experts invited.

21. The experts on the rosters are invited to make available, upon request of the Executive Secretary, Parties or other countries and relevant bodies, their specific expertise in order to contribute to the further development of the scientific, technical and technological issues of the work programme of the Convention on Biological Diversity. Such requests could entail, *inter alia*, peer reviews, questionnaires, clarifications or examinations of scientific, technological and technical issues, specific contributions to the compilation of documents, participation in global and regional workshops and assisting in connecting the Convention-process to international, regional and national scientific, technical and technological processes.

Decision V/20: Operations of the Convention

III Operations of the Subsidiary Body on Scientific, Technical and Technological Advice

The Conference of the Parties,

17. *Decides* that meetings of the Subsidiary Body on Scientific Technical and Technological Advice should take place every year;

18. *Decides* that the Chair of the Subsidiary Body on Scientific, Technical and Technological Advice or other members of the Bureau authorized by him or her may represent the Subsidiary Body at meetings of the scientific bodies of other conventions and relevant biological-diversity-related conventions, institutions and processes;

19. *Encourages* the Bureau of the Subsidiary Body on Scientific, Technical and Technological Advice to hold meetings with equivalent bodies of other relevant biological-diversity-related conventions, institutions and processes;

20. *Recognizes* that in certain cases it will be appropriate for the Subsidiary Body on Scientific, Technical and Technological Advice to make recommendations that include options or alternatives;

...

22. *Confirms* that the Subsidiary Body on Scientific, Technical and Technological Advice, within the available budgetary resources for matters related to its mandate, may make requests to the Executive Secretary and utilize the clearing-house mechanism, and other appropriate means, to assist in the preparation of its meetings;

...

24. *Decides* that the guidance to the Subsidiary Body on Scientific, Technical and Technological Advice contained in specific decisions of a meeting of the Conference of the Parties should take into account the need for a coherent and realistic programme of work for the Subsidiary Body, including the identification of priority issues, allowing flexibility in timing, and agrees that the Subsidiary Body on Scientific, Technical and Technological Advice may, if necessary, adjust the timing of its consideration of issues;

25. *Recognizes* that there is a need to improve the quality of the scientific, technical and technological advice provided to the Conference of the Parties, and to undertake sound scientific and technical assessments, including in-depth assessments of the state of knowledge on issues critical for the implementation of the Convention;

26. *Requests* the Subsidiary Body on Scientific, Technical and Technological Advice to continue to improve the way it conducts its scientific, technical and technological work in order to improve the quality of its advice to the Conference of the Parties;

27. *Decides* that, in its scientific, technical and technological work and, in particular, scientific assessments, the Convention should make use of existing programmes and activities of the Convention or of other bodies and of expertise made available by Parties;

28. *Notes* the report of the brainstorming meeting on scientific assessment (UNEP/CBD/COP/5/INF/1), and refers it to the Subsidiary Body on Scientific, Technical and Technological Advice for consideration and, where appropriate, use in its work;

29. *Requests* the Subsidiary Body on Scientific, Technical and Technological Advice:

(a) To identify and, where needed, further develop, procedures and methods to undertake or participate in scientific assessments, or make use of existing ones, taking into account considerations of participation, effectiveness and costs;

(b) To undertake a limited number of pilot scientific assessment projects, in preparation for the sixth meeting of the Conference of the Parties, and to invite, among others, the Millennium Ecosystem Assessment to work closely together with the Subsidiary Body in this area; and to facilitate and support the implementation of these projects; and, at an appropriate stage, to carry out an evaluation of them;

(c) To develop further its methodologies for scientific assessment, and to provide advice to Parties on scientific assessment design and implementation;

(d) To identify and regularly update, within the context of its programme of work, assessment priorities and information needs;

(e) To review the implementation of decision II/1 relating to the Global Biodiversity Outlook and provide the results of that review to the Conference of the Parties at its sixth meeting, together with advice on means to enhance implementation and/or any desirable amendments to the decision;

30. *Notes* the proposed uniform methodology for the use of the roster of experts, set out in annex I to recommendation V/14 of the Subsidiary Body on Scientific, Technical and Technological Advice, and refers this to the Subsidiary Body and the Executive Secretary for consideration and, where appropriate, use in their work;

31. *Encourages* Parties, other Governments and relevant bodies when nominating their experts for inclusion in the roster to consider:

(a) Gender balance;

(b) Involvement of indigenous people and members of local communities;

(c) Range of relevant disciplines and expertise, including, *inter alia*, biological, legal, social and economic sciences, and traditional knowledge;

Section V

Financial rules for the administration of the Trust Fund for the Convention on Biological Diversity

(Annex I to decision I/6, as amended by decision III/1)

Financial rules[1]

1. The Conference of the Parties to the Convention shall designate an organization (hereinafter referred to as the Trustee) which shall establish and manage the Trust Fund for the Convention on Biological Diversity (hereinafter referred to as the Trust Fund) in accordance with these rules.

2. The Trust Fund shall be used for funding the administration of the Convention including the functions of the Secretariat.

3. The Trust Fund shall be financed from:

(a) Contributions made by Parties to the Convention based on the scale set forth in the Appendix to the budget;

(b) Additional contributions made by such Parties;

(c) Contributions from States not Parties to the Convention, as well as governmental, intergovernmental and non-governmental organizations, and other sources.

4. It is for the Conference of the Parties to determine the scale referred to in paragraph 3 (a) above. The scale is to be based on the United Nations scale of assessments for the apportionment of the expenses of the United Nations [adjusted to provide that no developing country Party shall be required to pay more than any developed country Party]. This scale of assessments shall apply unless amended by the Conference of the Parties. The contributions referred to in paragraph 3 (a) shall be due on 1 January of each calendar year.

5. All contributions shall be paid in United States dollars or its equivalent in a convertible currency and into a bank account to be specified by the Trustee. In conversion of currencies into United States dollars, the United Nations operational rate of exchange shall be used.

6. Accounting records shall be kept in such currency or currencies as the Trustee deems necessary.

7. (a) Budget proposals expressed in United States dollars covering the expenditure and income from contributions referred to in paragraph 3 (a) above shall be prepared by the head of the Secretariat (hereinafter referred to as the Executive Secretary) for periods of two calendar years at the minimum. At least 90 days before the date fixed for the opening of each ordinary meeting of the Conference of the Parties,

1 References should also be made to the administrative arrangements between UNEP and the SCBD as contained in document UNEP/CBD/COP/4/23 and endorsed in decision IV/17 and the various decisions on the budget: decisions I/6, II/20, III/24, IV/17 and V/22.

these budget proposals shall be dispatched by the Executive Secretary to all Parties to the Convention.

(b) The budget shall, in accordance with Rule 16, be approved by the Conference of the Parties and, if necessary, be revised at an ordinary or extraordinary meeting of the Parties.

8. Contributions referred to in paragraphs 3 (b) and (c) shall be used in accordance with any terms and conditions agreed between the Executive Secretary and the respective contributor. At each ordinary meeting of the Conference of the Parties, the Executive Secretary shall present a report on contributions received and expected as well as their sources, amounts, purposes and conditions.

9. The Executive Secretary may commit resources against the Trust Fund only if such commitments are covered by contributions already received. In the event that the Trustee anticipates that there might be a shortfall in resources over the financial period as a whole, it shall notify the Executive Secretary, who shall adjust the budget so that expenditures are at all times fully covered by contributions received.

10. The Trustee, on the advice of the Executive Secretary, may make transfers from one budget line to another within the budget in accordance with the Financial Regulations and Rules of the United Nations.

11. Contributions referred to in paragraph 3 (a) above from States and regional economic integration organizations that become Parties to the Convention after the beginning of a financial period shall be made *pro rata temporis* for the balance of that financial period. Consequent adjustments shall be made at the end of each financial period for other Parties.

12. Contributions not immediately required for the purposes of the Trust Fund shall be invested and any interest so earned shall be credited to the Trust Fund.

13. It is for the Conference of the Parties and the Trustee to agree on an administrative support charge to be paid to the Trustee.

14. At the end of each calendar year, the Trustee shall transfer any balance to the following calendar year and submit to the Conference of the Parties, through the Executive Secretary, the certified and audited accounts for that year as soon as practicable. The Trust Fund shall be subjected to the internal and external auditing procedure of the United Nations as laid down in its Financial Regulations and Rules of the United Nations.

15. In the event that the Conference of the Parties decides to terminate the Trust Fund, a notification to that effect shall be presented to the Trustee at least six months before the date of termination selected by the Conference of the Parties. The Conference of the Parties shall decide, in consultation with the Trustee, on the distribution of any unspent balance after all liquidation expenses have been met.

[16A. The Parties shall reach agreement by consensus on:

(a) The scale and any subsequent revision to it;

(b) The budget.]

[16B. The Parties shall make every effort to reach agreement on the budget by consensus. If all efforts to reach consensus on the budget have been exhausted and no agreement has been reached, the budget shall, as a last resort, be adopted by a [two-thirds] [four-fifths] majority vote of the Parties present and voting representing a [two-thirds] [four-fifths] majority vote of the developing country Parties present and voting and a [two-thirds] [four-fifths] majority vote of the other Parties present and voting.]

17. Any amendments to these rules shall be adopted by the Conference of the Parties by consensus.

Section VI

Guide to the decisions of the Conference of the Parties

Articles of the Convention on Biological Diversity

Preamble

The Contracting Parties,

Conscious of the intrinsic value of biological diversity and of the ecological, genetic, social, economic, scientific, educational, cultural, recreational and aesthetic values of biological diversity and its components,

Conscious also of the importance of biological diversity for evolution and for maintaining life sustaining systems of the biosphere,

Affirming that the conservation of biological diversity is a common concern of humankind,

Reaffirming that States have sovereign rights over their own biological resources,

Reaffirming also that States are responsible for conserving their biological diversity and for using their biological resources in a sustainable manner,

Concerned that biological diversity is being significantly reduced by certain human activities,

Aware of the general lack of information and knowledge regarding biological diversity and of the urgent need to develop scientific, technical and institutional capacities to provide the basic understanding upon which to plan and implement appropriate measures,

Noting that it is vital to anticipate, prevent and attack the causes of significant reduction or loss of biological diversity at source,

Noting also that where there is a threat of significant reduction or loss of biological diversity, lack of full scientific certainty should not be used as a reason for postponing measures to avoid or minimize such a threat,

Noting further that the fundamental requirement for the conservation of biological diversity is the *in-situ* conservation of ecosystems and natural habitats and the maintenance and recovery of viable populations of species in their natural surroundings,

Noting further that *ex-situ* measures, preferably in the country of origin, also have an important role to play,

Recognizing the close and traditional dependence of many indigenous and local communities embodying traditional lifestyles on biological resources, and the desirability of sharing equitably benefits arising from the use of traditional knowledge, innovations and practices relevant to the conservation of biological diversity and the sustainable use of its components,

Recognizing also the vital role that women play in the conservation and sustainable use of biological diversity and affirming the need for the full participation of women at all levels of policy-making and implementation for biological diversity conservation,

Stressing the importance of, and the need to promote, international, regional and global cooperation among States and intergovernmental organizations and the non-governmental sector for the conservation of biological diversity and the sustainable use of its components,

Acknowledging that the provision of new and additional financial resources and appropriate access to relevant technologies can be expected to make a substantial difference in the world's ability to address the loss of biological diversity,

Acknowledging further that special provision is required to meet the needs of developing countries, including the provision of new and additional financial resources and appropriate access to relevant technologies,

Noting in this regard the special conditions of the least developed countries and small island States,

Acknowledging that substantial investments are required to conserve biological diversity and that there is the expectation of a broad range of environmental, economic and social benefits from those investments,

Recognizing that economic and social development and poverty eradication are the first and overriding priorities of developing countries,

Aware that conservation and sustainable use of biological diversity is of critical importance for meeting the food, health and other needs of the growing world population, for which purpose access to and sharing of both genetic resources and technologies are essential,

Noting that, ultimately, the conservation and sustainable use of biological diversity will strengthen friendly relations among States and contribute to peace for humankind,

Desiring to enhance and complement existing international arrangements for the conservation of biological diversity and sustainable use of its components, and

Determined to conserve and sustainably use biological diversity for the benefit of present and future generations,

Have agreed as follows:

Notes

Terms defined in Article 2

'Biological diversity', 'biological resources', 'ecosystem', 'genetic resources', 'habitat', '*in situ* conservation', 'sustainable use' and 'technology'.

Article 1: Objectives

The objectives of this Convention, to be pursued in accordance with its relevant provisions, are the conservation of biological diversity, the sustainable use of its components and the fair and equitable sharing of the benefits arising out of the utilization of genetic resources, including by appropriate access to genetic resources and by appropriate transfer of relevant technologies, taking into account all rights over those resources and to technologies, and by appropriate funding.

Notes

Terms defined in Article 2

'Biological diversity', 'sustainable use', 'genetic resources' and 'technology'.

References

Many COP decisions make explicit reference to one or all of the Convention's objectives. These decisions have not been listed separately here.

Article 2: Use of terms

For the purposes of this Convention:

'*Biological diversity*' means the variability among living organisms from all sources including, *inter alia*, terrestrial, marine and other aquatic ecosystems and the ecological complexes of which they are part; this includes diversity within species, between species and of ecosystems.

'*Biological resources*' includes genetic resources, organisms or parts thereof, populations, or any other biotic component of ecosystems with actual or potential use or value for humanity.

'*Biotechnology*' means any technological application that uses biological systems, living organisms, or derivatives thereof, to make or modify products or processes for specific use.

'*Country of origin of genetic resources*' means the country which possesses those genetic resources in *in-situ* conditions.

'*Country providing genetic resources*' means the country supplying genetic resources collected from *in-situ* sources, including populations of both wild and domesticated species, or taken from *ex-situ* sources, which may or may not have originated in that country.

'*Domesticated or cultivated species*' means species in which the evolutionary process has been influenced by humans to meet their needs.

'*Ecosystem*' means a dynamic complex of plant, animal and micro-organism communities and their non-living environment interacting as a functional unit.

'Ex-situ *conservation*' means the conservation of components of biological diversity outside their natural habitats.

'*Genetic material*' means any material of plant, animal, microbial or other origin containing functional units of heredity.

'*Genetic resources*' means genetic material of actual or potential value.

'*Habitat*' means the place or type of site where an organism or population naturally occurs.

'In-situ *conditions*' means conditions where genetic resources exist within ecosystems and natural habitats, and, in the case of domesticated or cultivated species, in the surroundings where they have developed their distinctive properties.

'In-situ *conservation*' means the conservation of ecosystems and natural habitats and the maintenance and recovery of viable populations of species in their natural surroundings and, in the case of domesticated or cultivated species, in the surroundings where they have developed their distinctive properties.

'*Protected area*' means a geographically defined area which is designated or regulated and managed to achieve specific conservation objectives.

'*Regional economic integration organization*' means an organization constituted by sovereign States of a given region, to which its member States have transferred competence in respect of matters governed by this Convention and which has been duly authorized, in accordance with its internal procedures, to sign, ratify, accept, approve or accede to it.

'*Sustainable use*' means the use of components of biological diversity in a way and at a rate that does not lead to the long-term decline of biological diversity, thereby maintaining its potential to meet the needs and aspirations of present and future generations.

'*Technology*' includes biotechnology.

Notes

Terms defined in Article 2

Cross-references to terms defined in Article 2 are given as appropriate under the specific articles and thematic areas dealt with in this section of the Handbook

Consideration of Article 2 by the COP

COP 2 confirmed that the human genetic resources are not included within the framework of the Convention [*decision II/11, paragraph 2*].

References

Declarations

Argentina (adoption) and Peru (adoption)

Article 3: Principle

States have, in accordance with the Charter of the United Nations and the principles of international law, the sovereign right to exploit their own resources pursuant to their own environmental policies, and the responsibility to ensure that activities within their jurisdiction or control do not cause damage to the environment of other States or of areas beyond the limits of national jurisdiction.

Notes

Consideration of Article 3 by the COP

The COP has made only one specific reference to Article 3 in its decisions, noted below.

References

Other relevant decisions

Decision V/8, annex I, Guiding principle 4 (Alien species)

Declarations

Colombia (adoption), France (signature), Sudan (ratification) and UK (signature and ratification)

Article 4: Jurisdictional scope

Subject to the rights of other States, and except as otherwise expressly provided in this Convention, the provisions of this Convention apply, in relation to each Contracting Party:

(a) In the case of components of biological diversity, in areas within the limits of its national jurisdiction; and

(b) In the case of processes and activities, regardless of where their effects occur, carried out under its jurisdiction or control, within the area of its national jurisdiction or beyond the limits of national jurisdiction.

Notes

Terms defined in Article 2

'Biological diversity'.

Consideration of Article 4 by the COP

To date, the COP has not specifically addressed this article. Although, the COP did reaffirm that human genetic resources are not included within the framework of the Convention [*decision II/11, paragraph 2*]. Also note that upon ratification, Chile declared that certain exotic species were not within the scope of the Convention.

Article 5: Cooperation

Each Contracting Party shall, as far as possible and as appropriate, cooperate with other Contracting Parties, directly or, where appropriate, through competent international organizations, in respect of areas beyond national jurisdiction and on other matters of mutual interest, for the conservation and sustainable use of biological diversity.

Notes

Terms defined in Article 2

'Biological diversity' and 'sustainable use'.

Consideration of Article 5 by the COP

To date, the COP has not explicitly addressed this article. However, it has made a number of references to bilateral and regional cooperation between Parties in its decisions, particularly at COP 5. The list of references below includes *only* references to cooperation between Parties (directly or, where appropriate, through competent international organizations) in respect of areas beyond national jurisdiction or on other matters of mutual interest. It does not include COP decisions on cooperation with other biodiversity-related conventions, processes and organizations, which are addressed in the guide to Article 24 later in this section of the Handbook.

References

Relevant aspects of thematic work programmes

Decision IV/4, paragraph 7 (b), annex I, A, paragraph 9 (k), 18 (Inland water)
Decision IV/5, annex, paragraph 11 (Marine and coastal)
Decision IV/7, annex, paragraph 15 (Forest)
Decision V/23, paragraph 3; annex I, II, part B, Activity 8 (d) (Dry and sub-humid lands)

Other relevant decisions

Decision II/7, paragraph 2 (Consideration of Articles 6 and 8)
Decision III/9, paragraph 1 (Implementation of Articles 6 and 8)
Decision IV/1 D, annex, paragraph 9 (Taxonomy)
Decision IV/15, paragraph 6 (Cooperation)
Decision V/6, paragraph 7; C, paragraph 12 (Ecosystem approach)
Decision V/7, paragraph 2 (Identification, monitoring and assessment, indicators)
Decision V/8, paragraph 7; annex I, B, Guiding principle 9; annex II, paragraph 4 (a) (Alien species)
Decision V/20, paragraphs 33, 40 (Operations of the Convention)

Article 6: General measures for conservation and sustainable use

Each Contracting Party shall, in accordance with its particular conditions and capabilities:

(a) Develop national strategies, plans or programmes for the conservation and sustainable use of biological diversity or adapt for this purpose existing strategies, plans or programmes which shall reflect, *inter alia*, the measures set out in this Convention relevant to the Contracting Party concerned; and

(b) Integrate, as far as possible and as appropriate, the conservation and sustainable use of biological diversity into relevant sectoral or cross-sectoral plans, programmes and policies.

Editors' note:

Implementation of Article 6 (b), in particular with respect to procedures for mainstreaming, is closely linked to development and implementation of Articles 10 (a) and 14.1.

Notes

Terms defined in Article 2

'Biological diversity'and 'sustainable use'.

Consideration of Article 6 by the COP

Background and status

As part of its medium-term programme of work, the COP decided to address Article 6 for the first time at COP 2 [*decision I/9*], where it adopted decision II/7 entitled 'Consideration of Articles 6 and 8 of the Convention'. It urged exchange of information and sharing of experiences on implementation of Article 6 and 8, and asked the Secretariat to make such information and experiences available through the clearing-house mechanism (CHM) [*decision II/7, paragraphs 1, 3*]. COP 3 adopted decision III/9 on Implementation of Articles 6 and 8 of the Convention.

COP guidance

Guidance to Parties

The COP has provided specific additional guidance to Parties in relation to Article 6. For example, it has encouraged Parties, *inter alia*, to:

- take into account guidelines such as those provided in *National Biodiversity Planning* published by UNEP, World Resources Institute and IUCN,[1] when preparing and implementing their national strategies and action plans to collaborate with relevant organizations [*decision II/7, paragraph 5*];
- include in their national plans, strategies or legislation measures for *in situ* and *ex situ* conservation; sectoral integration of biodiversity considerations; and equitable sharing of benefits from the use of genetic resources [*decision III/9, paragraph 2*];
- set measurable targets to achieve biodiversity conservation and sustainable use objectives [*decision III/9, paragraph 5*]; and
- ensure that the conservation and sustainable use of wetlands, and of migratory species and their habitats, are fully incorporated into national strategies, programmes and plans [*decision III/21, paragraph 8*].

The COP has also requested Parties to integrate elements of all the thematic work programmes into their national strategies and sectoral plans, and has also stressed the need for cross-border coordination of national strategies and the importance of regional and international cooperation for implementation of Article 6 [*decision II/7, paragraph 2; decision III/9, paragraph 1*]. Implementation of Article 6 was the focus of the first national reports by Parties, submitted in accordance with Article 26 [*decision II/17, paragraph 3*].

Financial mechanism and resources

COP 2 emphasized the importance of capacity-building and the availability of adequate financial resources, and requested the financial mechanism to facilitate urgent implementation of Article 6 (and Article 8) by making resources available to developing countries in a flexible and expeditious manner [*decision II/6, paragraph 5; decision II/7, paragraph 6*].

Accordingly, the Global Environment Facility (GEF) provides funding for enabling activities. The GEF Operational Strategy defines enabling activities in biodiversity as:

> *'[Activities] that prepare the foundation to design and implement effective response measures to achieve Convention objectives. They will assist recipient countries to develop national strategies, plans or programs referred to in Article 6 of the Convention on Biological Diversity, and to identify components of biodiversity together with processes and activities likely to have significant adverse impacts on conservation and sustainable use of biodiversity pursuant to Article 7 of the Convention on Biological Diversity. They will normally involve the review and assessment of information and will assist a recipient country to gain a better understanding of the nature and scope of its biodiversity assets and issues as well as a clearer sense of the options for*

1 Miller, K R and Lanou, SM (1995) *National Biodiversity Planning: Guidelines Based on Early Experiences Around the World*, World Resources Institute/UNEP/ IUCN, Washington, DC

the sustainable management and conservation of biodiversity. Enabling activities include supporting country-driven activities for taking stock of or inventorying biodiversity based on national programs and relying on studies, without new primary research; identifying options and establishing priorities to conserve and sustainably use biodiversity; preparing and developing biodiversity planning exercises, such as national strategies, action plans and sectoral plans; and disseminating of information through national communications to the Convention on Biological Diversity'

How this goal is operationalized is laid out in the GEF's *Operational Criteria for Enabling Activities: Biodiversity*.[2] In response to the emphasis that the COP placed on capacity-building needs and identifying those needs, the GEF Council revised the operational criteria at its 13th meeting (see *Guidelines for Additional Funding of Biodiversity Enabling Activities (Expedited Procedures)*, GEF, issued in February 2000).[3] These were revised again in October 2000 in the light of guidance from COP 5 (see *Revised Guidelines for Additional Funding of Biodiversity Enabling Activities (Expedited Procedures)*),[4] in particular, to support the production of the second national report of Parties.

References

Decisions on Article 6

Decision II/7 (Consideration of Articles 6 and 8)
Decision III/9 (Implementation of Articles 6 and 8)

Guidance to Parties

National action

Decision II/7, paragraph 5 (Consideration of Articles 6 and 8)
Decision II/10, paragraph 3 (Marine and coastal)
Decision III/9, paragraphs 1–3, 5, 6 (Implementation of Articles 6 and 8)
Decision III/11, paragraphs 15, 16 (Agriculture)
Decision III/18, paragraph 4 (Incentive measures)
Decision III/21, paragraph 8 (Cooperation)
Decision IV/1 A–D, annex, paragraph 11 (j) (Taxonomy)
Decision IV/1 C, paragraph 4 (Alien species)
Decision IV/4, paragraph 5; annex I, paragraph 9 (a) (Inland water)
Decision IV/5, annex, B, paragraph 10 (Marine and coastal)
Decision IV/10 B, paragraph 1 (a) (Public education and awareness)
Decision V/4, paragraph 8 (Forest)
Decision V/5, annex, B, programme element 4 (Agriculture)
Decision V/6, annex, C, paragraph 12 (Ecosystem approach)
Decision V/8, paragraph 6; annex I, C, Guiding principle 11, paragraph 2 (Alien species)

---

2 GEF (2000) *Operational Criteria for Enabling Activities: Biodiversity*, Global Environment Facility, Washington, DC

3 GEF (February 2000) *Guidelines for Additional Funding of Biodiversity Enabling Activities (Expedited Procedures)*, Global Environment Facility, Washington, DC

4 GEF (October 2000) *Revised Guidelines for Additional Funding of Biodiversity Enabling Activities (Expedited Procedures)*, Global Environment Facility, Washington, DC

Decision V/17, paragraph 6 (Education and public awareness)
Decision V/18, I, paragraph 2 (a) (Impact assessment, liability and redress)
Decision V/26 A, paragraph 3 (Access to genetic resources)

Information and case studies

Decision II/7, paragraph 1 (Consideration of Articles 6 and 8)

Financial mechanism and resources

Guidance to the financial mechanism

Decision I/2, annex I, paragraph 4 (b) (Financial mechanism and resources)
Decision II/6, paragraph 5 (Financial mechanism and resources)
Decision II/7, paragraph 6 (Consideration of Articles 6 and 8)
Decision III/8, annex, paragraph 5.1 (d) (Memorandum of Understanding between the COP and the GEF Council)
Decision III/9, paragraph 4 (Implementation of Articles 6 and 8)
Decision IV/4, paragraph 6 (Inland water)
Decision IV/13, paragraph 3 (Additional guidance to the financial mechanism)
Decision V/13, paragraph 2 (n) (Further guidance to the financial mechanism)

Other financial resources

Decision V/11, paragraph 11 (Additional financial resources)

Guidance to the Secretariat

Decision II/7, paragraphs 3, 4, 7 (Consideration of Articles 6 and 8)
Decision III/9, paragraph 7 (Implementation of Articles 6 and 8)
Decision III/14, paragraph 10 (Implementation of Article 8 (j))
Decision IV/2, paragraph 5 (a) (Clearing-house mechanism)
Decision IV/15, paragraph 6 (Cooperation)

Cooperation with other conventions and organizations

Decision III/21, paragraph 8 (Cooperation)
Decision IV/5, annex, C, operational objectives 1.1, 1.2 (Marine and coastal)
Decision IV/7, annex, II, paragraphs 19, 20 (Forest)
Decision IV/15, paragraph 6 (Cooperation)
Decision V/19, paragraph 10 (National reports)
Decision V/23, annex I, B, Activity 8 (e) (Dry and sub-humid lands)

Relevant aspects of thematic work programmes

Decision II/9, annex, paragraph 10 (Forest – Statement to IPF)
Decision II/10, paragraph 3 (Marine and coastal)
Decision III/11, paragraphs 14–16 (Agriculture)
Decision III/12, paragraph 6 (b); annex, paragraph (b) (Forest)
Decision IV/7, annex, paragraphs 3 (a), 11–13, 18–20, 37 (Forest)
Decision IV/4, paragraphs 5, 6; annex I, A, paragraph 9 (a) (Inland water)
Decision IV/5, annex, B, paragraph 10; C, operational objectives 1.1, 1.2 (Marine and coastal)

Decision V/2, paragraph 8 (Inland water)
Decision V/4, paragraph 8 (Forest)
Decision V/5, annex, A, paragraphs 3 (a), 4; annex, B, programme element 3, Activity 3.3; programme element 4 (Agriculture)
Decision V/23, annex I, I, paragraph 2 (f); annex I, II, part B, Activity 8, paragraph (e) (Dry and sub-humid lands)

Other relevant decisions

Decision II/17, paragraph 3 (National reports)
Decision III/10, paragraph 5 (Identification, monitoring and assessment)
Decision III/19, annex, C, paragraph 24 (b) (Statement to UNGA Special Session)
Decision IV/14, annex, paragraph 3 (National reports)
Decision V/15, paragraph 2 (e) (Incentive measures)
Decision V/20, paragraph 38 (c) (Operations of the Convention)

Declarations

Denmark (ratification), Finland (ratification), Norway and Sweden (adoption)

Documents

UNEP/CBD/COP/2/12 Consideration of Articles 6 and 8 of the Convention
UNEP/CBD/COP/3/11 Implementation of Articles 6 and 8
UNEP/CBD/SBSTTA/1/4 Alternative ways and means to start the process of considering the components of biological diversity particularly those under threat and the identification of action which could be taken under the Convention (priority item)

Article 7: Identification and monitoring

Each Contracting Party shall, as far as possible and as appropriate, in particular for the purposes of Articles 8 to 10;

(a) Identify components of biological diversity important for its conservation and sustainable use having regard to the indicative list of categories set down in Annex I

(b) Monitor, through sampling and other techniques, the components of biological diversity identified pursuant to subparagraph (a) above, paying particular attention to those requiring urgent conservation measures and those which offer the greatest potential for sustainable use;

(c) Identify processes and categories of activities which have or are likely to have significant adverse impacts on the conservation and sustainable use of biological diversity, and monitor their effects through sampling and other techniques; and

(d) Maintain and organize, by any mechanism, data derived from identification and monitoring activities pursuant to subparagraphs (a), (b) and (c) above.

Editors' note:

This section deals first with the COP's consideration of Article 7. It then goes on to address the issues of indicators and taxonomy. See also Annex I to the Convention.

Notes

Terms defined in Article 2

'Biological diversity' and 'sustainable use'.

Consideration of Article 7 by the COP

Background and status

COP 2 considered, in a preliminary fashion, components of biological diversity particularly under threat. It endorsed paragraphs 2, 4 and 5 of recommendation I/3 of SBSTTA [*decision II/8, paragraph 2*] and stressed that it was essential to identify the driving forces determining the status and trends of components of biological diversity [*decision II/8, paragraph 3*].

COP 3 considered options for implementing Article 7 in its discussion on identification, monitoring and assessment. It endorsed SBSTTA recommendation II/1 which provided general advice and identified a number of priority tasks, and proposed specific recommendations. The SBSTTA recommendation advocated a two-track approach to assessment and indicator development: in the short-term assessment of reasonably well-known sectors and components of biological diversity should be carried out, while at the same time longer-term programmes should be developed involving research and capacity-building in areas needing advances in knowledge. It also proposed that indicators, assessment and monitoring should be considered together as a standing item on the agenda of SBSTTA [*decision III/10*].

Discussion of Article 7 at COP 4 was essentially confined to deliberations on SBSTTA's recommendations on indicators, assessments and monitoring [*decision IV/1 A*] and on the work programmes for agricultural [*decision IV/6*], inland water [*decision IV/4*], forest [*decision IV/7*] and marine and coastal [*decision IV/5*] biological diversity. Part of the programme of work on dry and sub-humid lands established at COP 5 concerns assessments [*decision V/23, annex I; annex II, part A*].

COP 5 requested the Executive Secretary to carry out pending activities set out in decision IV/1 A [*decision V/7, paragraph 1*].

COP guidance

Guidance to Parties

The COP has urged Parties to develop innovative methods of implementing Article 7 as a high priority. It has recommended that Parties consider a step-by-step approach to this, beginning with rapid implementation of Article 7 (a) and (c) [*decision III/10, paragraphs 1, 6*]. It has also called on Parties to cooperate on a voluntary pilot project to demonstrate the use of successful assessment and indicator methodologies [*decision III/10, paragraph 6*] and to prepare, where appropriate, reports on experiences on the application of assessment methodologies and results of assessments [*decision III/10, paragraph 7*].

With regard to the identification of threats to biological diversity (Article 7 (c)), in its consideration of incentive measures (see the guide to Article 11 later in this section of the Handbook), the COP encouraged Parties, Governments and relevant organizations to identify underlying threats as a first step towards formulating incentive measures [*decision IV/10 A, paragraph 1 (c)*]. It further urged them to identify perverse incentives that had negative effects on biological diversity [*decision IV/10 A, paragraph 1 (f)*]. States have also been urged to undertake appropriate research and monitoring of alien invasive species and long-term monitoring and assessment of the impacts of tourism on biological diversity [*decisions V/8, annex I, A, Guiding principle 5; decision V/25, paragraph 4 (c)*].

The work programme on inland water biological diversity makes several specific recommendations to Parties relevant to Article 7, including the preparation of indicative lists of inland water ecosystems using the criteria set out in Annex I of the Convention [*decision IV/4, annex I, A, paragraphs 9 (e), 12*].

Financial mechanism and resources

COP 3 requested the financial mechanism to provide financial resources to developing countries in order to address the need for capacity-building, including taxonomy, to enable them to develop and carry out an initial assessment for designing, implementing and monitoring programmes in accordance with Article 7, taking into account the special needs of small island States [*decision III/5, paragraph 2 (b); decision III/10, paragraph 10*]. COP 3 also decided that the GEF should provide adequate and timely financial support for activities under the forest work programme relevant to Article 7 [*decision III/13, paragraph 4*]. This call was reiterated at COP 4 [*decision IV/7, paragraph 6*]. COP 5 urged the GEF to fund, *inter alia*, projects that enable countries to strengthen capabilities to develop monitoring programmes and suitable indicators for biological diversity, and for the implementation of capacity-building measures for the assessment and monitoring of inland water biological diversity [*decision V/13, paragraph 2 (j), (n)*].

Guidance to SBSTTA

In decision IV/1 A, the COP encouraged SBSTTA to further cooperate with DIVERSITAS and with other relevant organizations and institutions on issues such as the scientific research that should be undertaken, *inter alia*, for the effective implementation of Article 7 [*decision IV/1 A, paragraphs 5, 6*]. COP 5 requested SBSTTA to carry out a number of activities to develop and improve its methodologies for scientific assessment, including a limited number of pilot scientific assessment projects in preparation for COP 6 and in close cooperation with the Millennium Ecosystem Assessment[5] [*decision V/20, III paragraph 29; decision V/21, paragraph 10*].

In annex I to decision IV/4, which set out a work programme on inland water biological diversity, the COP requested SBSTTA, *inter alia*, to develop and disseminate regional guidelines for rapid assessment of inland water biological diversity, paying special attention to early cooperation with small island States and States within which there were inland water ecosystems suffering from ecological disaster [*decision IV/4, annex I, A, paragraphs 6, 7, 8 (b)*]. It further requested SBSTTA to work jointly with the Scientific and Technical Review Panel of the Ramsar Convention to achieve desirable conver-

5 The Millennium Ecosystem Assessment was launched by the United Nations in June 2001. Organized and supported by an array of governments, United Nations agencies and leading scientific organizations, it is intended to bring the best available information and knowledge on ecosystem goods and services to bear on policy and management decisions

gence between approaches on criteria and classification of inland water ecosystems between the two conventions [*decision IV/4, annex I, B, paragraph 12*].

References

Decisions on Article 7

Decision II/8 (Components of biological diversity particularly under threat)
Decision III/10 (see also SBSTTA recommendations II/1 and II/2) (Identification, monitoring and assessment)
Decision IV/1 A (see also SBSTTA recommendation III/5) (Report and recommendations of the third meeting of SBSTTA)
Decision IV/1 D (Taxonomy)
Decision V/7 (Identification, monitoring and assessment, and indicators)

Guidance to Parties

National action

Decision III/10, paragraphs 1, 4, and 6 (Identification, monitoring and assessment)
Decision III/11, paragraphs 9, 15 (a) (g) (m) (n), 16 (Agriculture)
Decision IV/4, paragraph 5; annex I, A, paragraph 9 (e), annex I, B, paragraphs 12, 13; annex I, C, paragraph 14 (Inland water)
Decision IV/10 A, paragraph 1 (b) (f) (Incentive measures)
Decision V/8, annex I, A, Guiding principle 5 (Alien species)
Decision V/25, paragraph 4 (c) (Biological diversity and tourism)

Information and case studies

Decision III/10, paragraphs 6, 7 (Identification, monitoring and assessment)

Financial mechanism and resources

Guidance to the financial mechanism

Decision I/2, annex I, paragraph 4 (c), (d) (Financial mechanism and resources)
Decision III/5, paragraph 2 (b) (Additional guidance to the financial mechanism)
Decision III/10, paragraph 10 (Identification, monitoring and assessment)
Decision IV/7, paragraph 6 (Forest)
Decision IV/13, paragraph 4 (Additional guidance to the financial mechanism)
Decision V/13, paragraph 2 (j), (n) (Further guidance to the financial mechanism)

Guidance to the Secretariat

Decision III/12, paragraph 6 (d) (Forest)
Decision III/14, paragraph 10 (Implementation of Article 8 (j))
Decision IV/4, annex I, B, paragraph 12 (Inland water)
Decision IV/5, annex, C, operational objectives 1.3, 2.1 (Marine and coastal)
Decision V/7, paragraph 2 (Identification, monitoring and assessment, and indicators)
Decision V/8, paragraph 14 (f) (Alien species)
Decision V/14, annex II, paragraph (h) (Clearing-house mechanism)

Decision V/21, paragraph 7 (Cooperation)

Guidance to SBSTTA

Decision III/10, paragraph 9 (Identification, monitoring and assessment)
Decision III/12, paragraph 10 (Forest)
Decision IV/1 A, paragraph 6 (Report and recommendations of the third meeting of SBSTTA)
Decision IV/4, annex I, A, paragraphs 5–8; annex I, B, paragraph 12 (Inland water)
Decision IV/6, paragraph 11 (Agriculture)
Decision V/21, paragraph 10 (Cooperation)

Cooperation with other conventions and organizations

Decision IV/1 A, paragraphs 5, 6 (Report and recommendations of the third meeting of SBSTTA)
Decision IV/4, annex I, B, paragraph 12 (Inland water)
Decision IV/5, annex, C, operational objective 2.1 (Marine and coastal)
Decision V/2, paragraph 7 (Inland water)
Decision V/8, paragraph 14 (f) (Alien species)
Decision V/21, paragraphs 7, 10 (Cooperation)

Relevant aspects of thematic work programmes

Decision II/9, annex, paragraphs 12, 15, 17 (Forest – Statement to IPF)
Decision III/11, paragraphs 9, 15 (a), (g), (m), (n), 16 (Agriculture)
Decision III/12, paragraphs 6 (d), 10; annex, paragraphs (b), (c) (Forest)
Decision IV/4, paragraphs 1, 5; annex I, paragraphs 6, 7, 8 (a), (b), 9 (e), 12, 14, 15, 19, 20 (Inland water)
Decision IV/5, annex, C, operational objectives 1.3, 2.1 (Marine and coastal)
Decision IV/6, paragraphs 6, 11 (Agriculture)
Decision IV/7, paragraph 6; annex, paragraphs 33, 35, 38, 40–49 (Forest)
Decision V/2, paragraphs 3, 7, 8 (Inland water)
Decision V/3, I, paragraphs 6 (b), 8, 13; II, paragraph 10; III, paragraph 13; annex, A, C (Marine and coastal)
Decision V/4, paragraphs 12, 14, 15; annex, paragraph 2 (a) (Forest)
Decision V/5, paragraphs 15 (a), 26; annex, A, paragraph 5, B, programme elements 1.4, 2.1 (c) (Agriculture)
Decision V/23, paragraphs 5, 7 (a); annex I, II, part A (Dry and sub-humid lands)

Other relevant decisions

Decision V/16, annex, III, element 3, task 13 (Article 8 (j) and related provisions)
Decision V/25, paragraph 1 (b) (Biological diversity and tourism)

Indicators

Notes

Consideration of indicators by the COP

Background and status

The COP first addressed the issue of indicators of biological diversity at its second meeting, when it endorsed paragraph 4 of SBSTTA recommendation I/3 [*decision II/8*], which stated:

> *'There is a need for each party to start assessing the effectiveness of measures taken under the Convention. However, methods for assessing the effectiveness of measures to conserve or sustainably use biological diversity should be reviewed. The use of indicators of biological diversity and the status of its components is particularly time- and cost-effective. Several indicators are currently being used and developed. They should be reviewed and their use promoted'.*

In response to this endorsement, SBSTTA 2 reviewed indicators for assessing the effectiveness of measures taken under the Convention. COP 3 endorsed SBSTTA's resulting recommendation II/1 [*decision II/10*]. This recommendation dealt with, *inter alia*, the review and promotion of indicators of biological diversity and made a number of general observations on indicator development and use. It advocated a two-track approach: in the short-term, use should be made of indicators known to be operational, while in areas needing advances in knowledge longer-term programmes involving research and capacity-building should be developed [*decision III/10, paragraph 2; SBSTTA recommendation II/1, paragraphs 9, 19*].

Among the priority tasks identified in SBSTTA recommendation II/1 was the development of a core set of indicators for national reports and of indicators in thematic areas important to the Convention, particularly coastal and marine ecosystems, agricultural biological diversity, forests and freshwater ecosystems [*SBSTTA recommendation II/1, paragraphs 7, 12*].

The Executive Secretary was requested to produce, in consultation with a liaison or expert group: a guideline report to assist Parties, particularly in preparation of national reports, containing, *inter alia*, information on indicators and monitoring techniques; a listing of current approaches to indicator development and recommendations for a preliminary core set of indicators of biological diversity, particularly those related to threats; and a list of options for capacity-building in developing countries in the application of guidelines and indicators for subsequent national reports [*SBSTTA recommendation II/1, paragraph 23*]. Accordingly, the Executive Secretary convened a liaison group, which met in Wageningen, the Netherlands, 30 May–2 June 1997. The report and recommendations of this group were considered by SBSTTA 3, resulting in recommendation III/5. The annex to this recommendation contained a preliminary outline of work under the two-track approach, to be undertaken chiefly by the Secretariat and liaison group.

COP 4 endorsed SBSTTA recommendation III/5 and requested the Executive Secretary to undertake the work outlined in the annex in accordance with the guidance contained in that recommendation, for consideration at SBSTTA 4, noting also that further work on indicators should take account of the development of the ecosystem approach [*decision*

IV/1 A, paragraphs 3, 4]. Recommendation III/5 stressed that the primary role of indicators in this context should be as a tool for management of biological diversity at local and national level and assessing the implementation of the Convention, but also recognized that they may have a wider role and further stressed that in future the development of regional and global indicators would be necessary to address specific aspects of the world's biological diversity [*SBSTTA recommendation III/5, paragraphs 2, 3*].

COP 5 repeated its request to the Executive Secretary to carry out the programme of work on indicators approved in decision IV/1 A and to present a report on this to COP 6 [*decision V/7, paragraphs 1, 5*].

COP guidance

Guidance to Parties

COP 3 urged Parties to identify indicators of biological diversity as a high priority [*decision III/10, paragraph 1*]. It also called on Parties to cooperate on a voluntary pilot project to demonstrate the use of successful assessment and indicator methodologies [*decision III/10, paragraph 6*]. COP 4 further urged Parties to share relevant experience through the CHM and other means and to include in their future national reports specific reference to indicator development activities and their capacity to implement indicators [*decision IV/1 A, paragraph 3, SBSTTA recommendation III/5, paragraph 7 (g)*].

COP 3 also encouraged Parties to develop national strategies, programmes and plans that, *inter alia*, study, use and/or develop, and promote the application of indicators to monitor the impacts of agricultural development on biological diversity [*decision III/11, paragraph 15 (m)*]. COP 5 invited Parties and Governments to identify indicators and incentive measures for sectors relevant to the conservation and sustainable use of biological diversity [*decision V/24, paragraph 4*]. It also called on Parties and Governments to increase regional cooperation in the field of indicators and invited Parties, Governments and organizations to assist in capacity-building by other Parties for development and use of indicators [*decision V/7, paragraphs 2, 4*].

Financial mechanism and resources

COP 5 urged the GEF to fund projects that enable countries to strengthen capabilities to develop monitoring programmes and suitable indicators for biological diversity [*decision V/13, paragraph 2 (j)*].

References

Decisions on indicators

Decision III/10 (Identification, monitoring and assessment)
Decision V/7 (Identification, monitoring and assessment, and indicators)

Guidance to Parties

National action

Decision II/17, annex, paragraph (j) (National reports)
Decision III/10, paragraphs 1, 6; (Identification, monitoring and assessment)
Decision III/11, paragraph 15 (m) (Agriculture)

Decision V/7, paragraphs 2, 4 (Identification, monitoring and assessment, and indicators)
Decision V/24, paragraph 4 (Sustainable use)

Information and case studies

Decision IV/1 A, paragraph 3 (see also SBSTTA recommendation III/5, paragraph 7 (g)) (Report and recommendations of the third meeting of SBSTTA)
Decision IV/14, annex, paragraph 3 (National reports)

Financial mechanism and resources

Guidance to the financial mechanism

Decision V/13, paragraph 2 (j) (Further guidance to the financial mechanism)

Other financial resources

Decision V/7, paragraph 4 (Identification, monitoring and assessment, and indicators)

Guidance to the Secretariat

Decision III/10, paragraph 2 (see also SBSTTA recommendation III/5, paragraph 17) (Identification, monitoring and assessment)
Decision IV/1 A, paragraph 3 (see also SBSTTA recommendation III/5, paragraphs 4, 7 (b), (c), (d), (e)) (Report and recommendations of the third meeting of SBSTTA)
Decision IV/5, annex, C, operational objective 1.3 (Marine and coastal)
Decision V/4, paragraph 15 (Forest)
Decision V/7, paragraphs 1, 5 (Identification, monitoring and assessment, and indicators)

Guidance to SBSTTA

Decision III/10, paragraph 2 (see also SBSTTA recommendation II/1, paragraphs 20, 26) (Identification, monitoring and assessment)
Decision IV/15, annex, C, operational objective 1.3 (Marine and coastal)
Decision V/3, II, paragraph 10 (Marine and coastal)
Decision V/7, paragraph 5 (Identification, monitoring and assessment, and indicators)

Cooperation with other conventions and organizations

Decision V/4, paragraph 15 (Forest)
Decision V/21, paragraph 7 (Cooperation)

Relevant aspects of thematic work programmes

Decision II/9, annex, paragraph 15 (Forest – Statement to IPF)
Decision III/11, paragraph 15 (m) (Agriculture)
Decision III/12, paragraphs 6 (d), 10 (a); annex, first paragraph (c), second paragraph (a) (Forest)
Decision IV/4, annex I, paragraph 9 (e) (ii), 15 (Inland water)
Decision IV/5, annex, C, operational objective 1.3 (Marine and coastal)
Decision IV/6, paragraph 6 (Agriculture)

Decision IV/7, annex, II, paragraphs 40–48 (Forest)
Decision V/3, II, paragraph 10 (Marine and coastal)
Decision V/5, annex, A, paragraph 3 (c); annex, B, programme element 1, Activity 1.5 (a) (Agriculture)
Decision V/23, paragraph 7 (a); annex I, II, A, Activity 3 (Dry and sub-humid lands)

Other relevant decisions

Decision II/8, paragraph 2 (see also SBSTTA recommendation I/3, paragraphs 2, 4, 5) (Components of biological diversity particularly under threat)
Decision III/10, paragraphs 2, 6 (Identification, monitoring and assessment)
Decision IV/1 A, paragraphs 3, 4 (see also SBSTTA recommendation III/5) (Report and recommendations of the third meeting of SBSTTA)
Decision V/25, paragraph 4 (c) (g) (Biological diversity and tourism)

Taxonomy

Notes

Consideration of taxonomy by the COP

Background and status

COP 2 asked SBSTTA to address the issue of the lack of taxonomists needed for the national implementation of the Convention, and to advise the COP [*decision II/8 paragraph 7*]. COP 3 endorsed the resulting recommendation of SBSTTA (recommendation II/2), concerning practical approaches for capacity-building for taxonomy [*decision III/10, paragraph 3*]. The COP requested the financial mechanism to provide financial resources for capacity building, including taxonomy [*decision III/10, paragraph 10* and see below]. SBSTTA recommended that national institutions and regional and subregional networks be established or strengthened and linkages enhanced with taxonomic institutions in developing and developed countries. It emphasized the importance of training and noted that consideration should be given to information needs and capacity-building specifically for bioprospecting, habitat conservation, sustainable agriculture and the sustainable use of biological resources, particularly in countries of origin [*SBSTTA recommendation II/2, paragraph 1*].

COP 4 launched a Global Taxonomy Initiative and set out suggestions for action on taxonomy [*decision IV/1 D, annex*]. The annex to decision IV/1 D stressed that the Global Taxonomy Initiative should occur on the basis of country-driven projects at the national, regional and subregional levels and contains, *inter alia*, a detailed series of recommendations for action addressed to Parties concerning its implementation, dealing mainly with: maintenance, coordination and development of taxonomic institutions; priority-setting; training; and exchange and dissemination of information. COP 5 reviewed the implementation of the initiative and established the Global Taxonomy Initiative coordination mechanism [*decision V/9*]. In addition to the coordination mechanism, the Global Taxonomy Initiative comprises national focal points, a series of regional meetings, a liaison group, a group of experts and a roster of experts.

COP guidance

The COP has made recommendations for national taxonomic needs assessments and creation of employment opportunities for taxonomists [*decision III/10, paragraph 3; SBSTTA recommendation II/2, paragraphs 4, 5*].

Government members of the OECD have been advised that they should endorse and support recommendations from the OECD Megascience Forum's Biodiversity Informatics Subgroup, regarding the development of a Global Biodiversity Informatics Facility (GBIF) [*decision IV/1 A–D, annex, paragraph 9*].

Financial mechanism and resources

The COP has requested the GEF to provide technical resources for country driven activities within the context of its operational programmes to participate in a Global Taxonomy Initiative. Such projects should take into the account the elements of the suggestions for action that focus on capacity-building in countries of origin and increasing dissemination of information worldwide, for example by the production and distribution of regional taxonomic guides [*decision III/10, paragraph 3, decision IV/13, paragraph 2*].

Development of guidelines and programme priorities for funding should also take into account specific needs for capacity-building in taxonomy to serve areas such as bio-prospecting, habitat conservation and the sustainable use of biological diversity. Such support should recognize the need for adequate, long-term housing of collections and records and long-term research [*decision III/10, paragraph 3; see also SBSTTA recommendation II/2, paragraph 3*] and should take into account elements of the Suggestions for Action contained in the annex to decision IV/1 D [*decision IV/13, paragraph 2; decision IV/1 D, paragraph 9*].

COP 4 requested the GEF to report at COP 5 on the work already under way in response to decision III/10 [*decision IV/1 D, paragraph 1*].

Thematic work programmes

The importance of taxonomy and of capacity-building for taxonomy has been stressed in the work programmes on agricultural biological diversity (particularly with respect to pollinators), inland water biological diversity, marine and coastal biological diversity, and forest biological diversity [*decision IV/4, annex I, paragraph 16*; *decision IV/5, annex, paragraph 6*; *decision IV/7, annex, paragraphs 42, 44; decision V/3, paragraph 6 (e); decision V/5, paragraph 15 (b)*].

References

Decisions on taxonomy

Decision IV/1 D; annex (Taxonomy)
Decision V/9 (Global Taxonomy Initiative)

Guidance to Parties

Decision III/10, paragraph 3 (see also SBSTTA recommendation II/2) (Identification, monitoring and assessment)
Decision IV/1 D, annex, paragraphs 2–9, 11 (Taxonomy)
Decision V/9, paragraphs 2, 4, 6 (Global Taxonomy Initiative)

Financial mechanism and resources

Guidance to the financial mechanism

Decision III/5, paragraph 2 (b) (Additional guidance to the financial mechanism)
Decision III/10, paragraph 3 (see also SBSTTA recommendation II/2, paragraph 10) (Identification, monitoring and assessment)
Decision IV/1 D, paragraphs 1, 9 (Taxonomy)
Decision IV/13, paragraphs 2, 4 (Additional guidance to the financial mechanism)
Decision V/9, paragraph 6 (Global Taxonomy Initiative)
Decision V/13, paragraph 2 (k) (Further guidance to the financial mechanism)

Guidance to the Secretariat

Decision IV/1 D, annex, paragraph 10 (Taxonomy)
Decision V/9, paragraph 3; annex (Global Taxonomy Initiative)

Guidance to SBSTTA

Decision II/8, paragraph 7 (Components of biodiversity particularly under threat)
Decision IV/1, D, paragraph 3 (Taxonomy)
Decision V/9, annex (Global Taxonomy Initiative)

Cooperation with other conventions and organizations

Decision IV/1 D, paragraph 5 (Taxonomy)
Decision V/8, paragraph 14 (g) (Alien species)
Decision V/21, paragraph 7 (Cooperation)

Relevant aspects of thematic work programmes

Decision III/12, annex, second paragraph (a) (Forest)
Decision IV/4, paragraph 5; annex I, paragraphs 16, 21 (Inland water)
Decision IV/5, annex, B, paragraph 6; C, operational objective 6.2 (Marine and coastal)
Decision IV/7, annex, paragraphs 42, 44 (Forest)
Decision V/3, paragraph 6 (e) (Marine and coastal)
Decision V/5, paragraph 15 (b); annex, A, paragraph 3 (c) (Agriculture)

Other relevant decisions

Decision V/8, annex I, B, Guiding principle 8 (Alien species)
Decision V/16, annex, III, element 3, task 13 (Article 8 (j) and related provisions)

Documents

UNEP/CBD/COP/3/12 Options for Implementing Article 7
UNEP/CBD/COP/3/13 Assessments of biological diversity and methodologies for future assessments
UNEP/CBD/COP/4/Inf.18 Recommendations on Scientific Research that should be Undertaken to Achieve the Implementation of Articles 7, 8, 9, 10 and 14 of the Convention on Biological Diversity, Mexico City, March 1998
UNEP/CBD/COP/5/12 Progress report on crosscutting issues

UNEP/CBD/SBSTTA/1/4 Alternative ways and means to start the process of considering the components of biological diversity particularly those under threat and the identification of action which could be taken under the Convention (priority item)
UNEP/CBD/SBSTTA/2/2 Assessment of biological diversity and methodologies for future assessments
UNEP/CBD/SBSTTA/2/3 Identification, monitoring and assessments of components of biological diversity and processes which have adverse impacts.
UNEP/CBD/SBSTTA/2/4 Review and promotion of indicators of biological diversity
UNEP/CBD/SBSTTA/2/5 Practical approaches for capacity building for taxonomy
UNEP/CBD/SBSTTA/2/Inf.9 Submissions received by the Secretariat concerning identification, monitoring and assessment of biological diversity
UNEP/CBD/SBSTTA/3/7 Identification and monitoring of components of biological diversity of inland water ecosystems (consideration of Article 7 and elaboration of terms in Annex I of the Convention)
UNEP/CBD/SBSTTA/3/9 Recommendations for a core set of indicators on biological diversity
UNEP/CBD/SBSTTA/3/Inf.11 Implementation of Article 7: report of the meeting of a liaison group on biological diversity indicators
UNEP/CBD/SBSTTA/3/Inf.13 Recommendations on a core set of indicators of biological diversity: background document prepared by the liaison group
UNEP/CBD/SBSTTA/3/Inf.14 Exploring biodiversity indicators and targets under the Convention on Biological Diversity
UNEP/CBD/SBSTTA/4/6 and 6/Corr.1 Further advancement of the Global Taxonomy Initiative
UNEP/CBD/SBSTTA/5/4 Review of the Global Taxonomy Initiative
UNEP/CBD/SBSTTA/5/12 Development of indicators of biological diversity

Article 8: *In-situ* conservation

Each Contracting Party shall, as far as possible and as appropriate:

(a) Establish a system of protected areas or areas where special measures need to be taken to conserve biological diversity;

(b) Develop, where necessary, guidelines for the selection, establishment and management of protected areas or areas where special measures need to be taken to conserve biological diversity;

(c) Regulate or manage biological resources important for the conservation of biological diversity whether within or outside protected areas, with a view to ensuring their conservation and sustainable use;

(d) Promote the protection of ecosystems, natural habitats and the maintenance of viable populations of species in natural surroundings;

(e) Promote environmentally sound and sustainable development in areas adjacent to protected areas with a view to furthering protection of these areas;

(f) Rehabilitate and restore degraded ecosystems and promote the recovery of threatened species, *inter alia*, through the development and implementation of plans or other management strategies;

(g) Establish or maintain means to regulate, manage or control the risks associated with the use and release of living modified organisms resulting from biotechnology which are likely to have adverse environmental impacts that could affect the conservation and sustainable use of biological diversity, taking also into account the risks to human health;

(h) Prevent the introduction of, control or eradicate those alien species which threaten ecosystems, habitats or species;

(i) Endeavour to provide the conditions needed for compatibility between present uses and the conservation of biological diversity and the sustainable use of its components;

(j) Subject to its national legislation, respect, preserve and maintain knowledge, innovations and practices of indigenous and local communities embodying traditional lifestyles relevant for the conservation and sustainable use of biological diversity and promote their wider application with the approval and involvement of the holders of such knowledge, innovations and practices and encourage the equitable sharing of the benefits arising from the utilization of such knowledge, innovations and practices;

(k) Develop or maintain necessary legislation and/or other regulatory provisions for the protection of threatened species and populations;

(l) Where a significant adverse effect on biological diversity has been determined pursuant to Article 7, regulate or manage the relevant processes and categories of activities; and

(m) Cooperate in providing financial and other support for *in-situ* conservation outlined in subparagraphs (a) to (l) above, particularly to developing countries.

Editors' note:

Article 8 covers a very wide range of issues linked to in situ *conservation of biological diversity. As its work has developed, the COP has begun to address a number of these issues separately, as well as within the context of the thematic work programmes and cross-cutting issues. Each of the issues is treated separately below, and an overview is provided of general deliberations concerning Article 8. The major issues identified are:*

- *protected areas (paragraphs a–c);*
- *protection of ecosystems, habitats and viable populations (paragraph d);*
- *buffer zones (paragraph e);*
- *ecosystem restoration and species recovery plans (paragraph f);*
- *biosafety (paragraph g);*
- *alien species (paragraph h);*
- *traditional knowledge, innovations and practices (paragraph j and related provisions); and*
- *mitigation of threats (paragraph l).*

Consideration of Article 8 is closely linked to consideration of almost all of the other substantive articles of the Convention, and in particular Article 7 (and Annex I). Reference should also be made to the guide to Article 7 in this section.

Notes

Terms defined in Article 2

'Biological diversity', 'biological resources', 'biotechnology', 'ecosystem', 'habitat', '*in situ* conservation', 'protected area', and 'sustainable use'.

Consideration of Article 8 by the COP

Background and status

The COP considered Article 8 at its second and third meetings and has now adopted two decisions on the article, in each case addressing it together with Article 6 [*decision II/7 and decision III/9*].

Decision II/7 dealt with the need for exchange of information and capacity-building. Decision III/9 again stressed the importance of dissemination of information and recommended the development of a thematic approach in the further compilation and dissemination of information, emphasizing methodologies to evaluate and mitigate threats to biological diversity, alien species and protected areas, as well as suppression or mitigation of perverse incentives (see Article 11) [*decision III/9, paragraph 9*].

The COP has asked the Executive Secretary to make available through the CHM information based on national experience and drawn from national reports on the implementation of Article 8 [*decision II/7, paragraph 3*]. The Executive Secretary has also been asked to compile and disseminate information on the implementation of Article 8, based both on national experiences and experiences of relevant organizations and to prepare suggestions on how the sharing of information might be enhanced, in particular by involving relevant organizations in a more regular and systematic fashion [*decision II/7, paragraph 4, decision III/9, paragraph 7*].

The COP has made frequent references to *in situ* conservation and sustainable use of biological diversity in its decisions, particularly in the thematic work programmes.

COP guidance

Guidance to Parties

The COP has stressed the importance of regional and international cooperation in the implementation of Article 8 and has urged Parties to exchange relevant information and share experiences [*decision II/7, paragraphs 1, 2*]. It has also urged Parties to include measures for *in situ* conservation of biological diversity in their national plans, strategies and legislation [*decision III/9, paragraph 2,* and see *Article 6*].

The COP has made reference to *in situ* conservation as it relates to forest biological diversity in decisions II/9 [*annex, paragraph 13*] and IV/7 [annex, *paragraphs 54, 55*], as it relates to dry and sub-humid lands in decision V/23 [*annex I, II, part B, paragraph 9; Activity 7 (f)*], as it relates to Article 8 (j) in decisions III/14 [*paragraph 10*] and V/16 [*annex, III, element 3, task 13*], and as it relates to access to genetic resources in decision V/26 A [*paragraph 11*]. In decision III/10 it stressed that timely implementation of Article 8 should not necessarily wait on the implementation of Article 7 [*decision III/10, paragraph 5*].

Financial mechanism and resources

COP 2 requested the financial mechanism to facilitate urgent implementation of Article 8 by funding projects in a flexible and expeditious manner [*decision II/7, paragraph 6*]. COP 3 requested the mechanism to make resources available to allow urgent incorporation of measures for *in situ* conservation of biological diversity in the national plans, strategies and legislation [*decision III/9, paragraph 4*].

References

Decisions on Article 8

Decision II/7 (Consideration of Articles 6 and 8)
Decision III/9 (Implementation of Articles 6 and 8)

Guidance to Parties

National action

Decision II/7, paragraph 2 (Consideration of Articles 6 and 8)
Decision III/9, paragraphs 2, 6 (Implementation of Articles 6 and 8)
Decision III/10, paragraph 5 (Identification, monitoring and assessment)

Information and case studies

Decision II/7, paragraphs 1, 9 (Consideration of Articles 6 and 8)

Financial mechanism and resources

Guidance to the financial mechanism

Decision I/2, annex I, paragraph 4 (c) (d) (Financial mechanism and resources)
Decision II/7, paragraph 6 (Consideration of Articles 6 and 8)
Decision III/9, paragraph 4 (Implementation of Articles 6 and 8)

Guidance to the Secretariat

Decision II/7, paragraphs 3, 4, 7 (Consideration of Articles 6 and 8)
Decision III/9, paragraphs 7, 8 (Implementation of Articles 6 and 8)
Decision III/14, paragraph 10 (Implementation of Article 8 (j))

Cooperation with other conventions and organizations

Decision II/9, annex, paragraph 13 (Forest – Statement to IPF)
Decision IV/1 A, paragraph 5 (Report and recommendations of the third meeting of SBSTTA)

Relevant aspects of thematic work programmes

Decision II/9, annex, paragraph 13 (Forest – Statement to IPF)
Decision IV/7, annex, paragraphs 54, 55 (Forest)
Decision V/5, paragraph 26; annex, B, programme element 4, Activity 4.4 (Agriculture)
Decision V/23, annex I, II, part B, paragraph 9; Activity 7 (f) (Dry and sub-humid lands)

Other relevant decisions

Decision V/6 (Ecosystem approach)
Decision V/10 (Global strategy for plant conservation)
Decision V/16, annex, III, element 3, task 13 (Article 8 (j) and related provisions)
Decision V/26 A, paragraph 11 (Access to genetic resources)

Declarations

France (adoption)

Documents

UNEP/CBD/COP/2/12 Consideration of Articles 6 and 8 of the Convention
UNEP/CBD/COP/3/11 Implementation of Articles 6 and 8
UNEP/CBD/COP/3/30 Cooperation between the Convention on Wetlands of International Importance, Especially as Waterfowl Habitat and the Convention on Biological Diversity
UNEP/CBD/COP/4/13 Cooperation with other agreements, institutions and processes relevant to *in-situ* conservation
UNEP/CBD/COP/4/Inf.18 Recommendations on Scientific Research that should be Undertaken to Achieve the Implementation of Articles 7, 8, 9, 10 and 14 of the Convention on Biological Diversity, Mexico City, March 1998
UNEP/CBD/COP/4/Inf.22 Linkages and Coordination between the Convention on the Conservation of Migratory Species of Wild Animals (Bonn Convention or CMS) and the Convention on Biological Diversity (CBD)

Protected areas (Article 8 (a–c))

Each Contracting Party shall, as far as possible and as appropriate:

(a) Establish a system of protected areas or areas where special measures need to be taken to conserve biological diversity;

(b) Develop, where necessary, guidelines for the selection, establishment and management of protected areas or areas where special measures need to be taken to conserve biological diversity;

(c) Regulate or manage biological resources important for the conservation of biological diversity whether within or outside protected areas, with a view to ensuring their conservation and sustainable use;

Notes

Terms defined in Article 2

'Biological diversity', 'biological resources', 'protected area', and 'sustainable use'.

Consideration of Article 8 (a–c) by the COP

Background and status

The COP has decided that protected areas should be one of three items for in-depth consideration at COP 7 [*decision IV/16, annex* II], and has recommended protected areas as one of four specific themes for the compilation and dissemination of information on the implementation of Articles 6 and 8 [*decision III/9, paragraph 9*]. The COP has encouraged the Executive Secretary to develop relationships with other processes with a view to fostering good management practices in areas such as: methods and approaches to deal with protected areas; ecosystem and bioregional approaches to protected area management and sustainable use of biological diversity; mechanisms to enhance stakeholder involvement; methods for developing systems plans and integrating biological diversity considerations into sectoral strategies and plans; and transboundary protected areas [*decision IV/15, paragraph 6*].

The COP has also emphasized the importance of protected areas in the work programmes on forest biological diversity, marine and coastal biological diversity, inland water biological diversity and biological diversity of dry and sub-humid lands.

The COP has decided that one of the eight objectives of the work programme on forest biological diversity should be 'to identify the contribution of networks of protected areas to the conservation and sustainable use of forest biological diversity' [*decision IV/7, annex, paragraph 3 (h)*]. This is addressed in programme area 1 of the work programme, on holistic and intersectoral ecosystem approaches, and programme area 4, on further research and technical priorities [*decision IV/7, annex, paragraphs 17,* 52]. In its statements to the Intergovernmental Panel on Forests (IPF), the COP has also emphasized the importance of the establishment and management of protected areas, and noted that this should be integrated in national forest and land-use plans [*decision II/9, annex, paragraph 13, decision III/12, annex, paragraph (b), (f)*].

Marine and coastal protected areas are identified as one of the five key programme elements under the work programme on marine and coastal biological diversity. The COP noted that protected areas should be integrated into wider strategies for preventing adverse effects to marine and coastal ecosystems from external activities [*decision IV/5, annex, paragraph 1 and part C, programme element 3*]. The COP has also established Ad Hoc Technical Expert Groups on Marine and Coastal Protected Areas and on Mariculture, which are to advise on priorities for action under the programme element in time for SBSTTA 8 and COP 7 in 2004 [*decision V/3, paragraph 15*].

The work plan for inland water biological diversity adopted by the COP includes as part of SBSTTA's work plan the compilation of case studies on watershed, catchment and river basin management, synthesis of lessons and dissemination of information. It states that one of the areas where SBSTTA should concentrate its efforts is the use of protected areas and their management strategies for conservation and sustainable use of inland water ecosystems [*decision IV/4, annex I, paragraph 8 (c) (vii)*].

The use and establishment of additional protected areas is identified as one of the necessary targeted actions for the implementation of the work programme on dry and sub-humid lands [*decision V/23, annex I, II, part B, Activity 7 (a)*].

References

Guidance to Parties

National action

Decision V/3, I, paragraph 6 (d); annex, C (Marine and coastal)
Decision V/4, paragraph 10 (Forest)

Information and case studies

Decision III/9, paragraph 9 (Implementation of Articles 6 and 8)
Decision IV/5, annex, C, operational objective 3.1 (Marine and coastal)
Decision IV/15, paragraph 14 (f) (Cooperation)

Financial mechanism and resources

Other financial resources

Decision IV/5, annex, C, operational objective 3.1, paragraph (e) and 'Budgetary implications' (Marine and coastal)

Guidance to the Secretariat

Decision IV/5, C, programme element 3 (Marine and coastal)
Decision IV/15, paragraph 6 (Cooperation)
Decision V/21, paragraph 7 (Cooperation)
Decision V/25, paragraph 2 (Biological diversity and tourism)

Guidance to SBSTTA

Decision IV/4, annex I, paragraph 8 (c) (vii) (Inland water)
Decision V/3 III paragraph 13 (Marine and coastal)

Cooperation with other conventions and organizations

Decision II/9, annex, paragraph 13 (Forest – Statement to IPF)
Decision III/12, annex, paragraphs (a), (f) (Forest)
Decision IV/5, annex, C, programme element 3 (Marine and coastal)
Decision IV/15, paragraph 6 (Cooperation)
Decision V/21, paragraph 7 (Cooperation)
Decision V/25, paragraph 2 (Biological diversity and tourism)

Relevant aspects of thematic work programmes

Decision II/9, annex, paragraph 13 (Forest – Statement to IPF)
Decision II/10, annex I, paragraph (iv) (Marine and coastal)
Decision III/12, annex, paragraphs (a), (f) (Forest)

Decision IV/4, annex I, paragraph 8 (c) (iii) (Inland water)
Decision IV/5, annex, A, paragraph 1; annex, C, programme element 3 (Marine and coastal)
Decision IV/7, annex, paragraph 3 (h), 17, and 52 (Forest)
Decision V/3 I, paragraph 6 (d), III paragraph 13; annex C (Marine and coastal)
Decision V/4, paragraph 10; annex, 2 (b) (i) (Forest)
Decision V/23, annex I, II, part B, Activity 7 (a) (Dry and sub-humid lands)

Other relevant decisions

Decision IV/16, annex II (Institutional matters and programme of work)

Protection of ecosystems, natural habitats and the maintenance of viable populations of species in natural surroundings (Article 8 (d))

> Each Contracting Party shall, as far as possible and as appropriate:
>
> (d) Promote the protection of ecosystems, natural habitats and the maintenance of viable populations of species in natural surroundings;

Notes

Terms defined in Article 2

'ecosystem' and 'habitat'.

Consideration of Article 8 (d) by the COP

Most consideration of this issue is implicitly included in the discussion of protected areas above. However, some explicit reference has been made under discussion of marine and coastal biological diversity and in the work programmes for inland water biological diversity, forest biological diversity and dry and sub-humid lands. General references to conservation of biological diversity have not been dealt with here. Reference should also be made to the COP's consideration of the ecosystem approach (see guide in this section of the Handbook).

With respect to marine and coastal biological diversity, the COP has noted that conservation measures for living marine resources should emphasize the protection of ecosystem functioning in addition to protecting specific stocks [*decision II/10, annex I, paragraph (iv)*]. In the work programme on dry and sub-humid lands, one of the identified targeted activities is the sustainable management of dry and sub-humid land production systems [*decision V/23, annex I, II, part B, Activity 7 (d)*]. Identification of new measures and ways to improve the conservation of forest biological diversity in and outside protected areas forms part of the terms of reference of the Ad Hoc Technical Working Group on Forest Biological Diversity established in decision V/4 to assist with implementation of the work programme [*decision V/4, annex, 2 (b) (i)*].

Parties have been recommended by the COP to encourage the adoption of integrated land and watershed management approaches for the protection, use, planning and management of inland water ecosystems [*decision IV/4, annex I, paragraph 9 (a) (i)*].

References

Relevant aspects of thematic work programmes

Decision II/10, annex I, paragraph (iv) (Marine and coastal)
Decision IV/4, annex I, paragraph 9 (a) (i) (Inland water)
Decision V/4, annex, 2 (b) (i) (Forest)
Decision V/23, annex I, II, part B, Activity 7 (d) (Dry and sub-humid lands)

Other relevant decisions

Decision V/6, annex, B (Ecosystem approach)

Declarations

Algeria and Niger (adoption)

Buffer zones (Article 8 (e))

> Each Contracting Party shall, as far as possible and as appropriate:
>
> (e) Promote environmentally sound and sustainable development in areas adjacent to protected areas with a view to furthering protection of these areas;

Notes

Terms defined in Article 2

'protected area'.

Consideration of Article 8 (e) by the COP

The COP has only explicitly referred to buffer zones in its consideration of forest biological diversity. Programme area 4 of the work programme on forest biological diversity adopted by the COP, on research and technological priorities, identified as a research component the reduction in gaps in knowledge in the areas of habitat fragmentation and population viability, to include mitigation options such as ecological corridors and buffer zones [*decision IV/7, annex, paragraph 53*].

References

Relevant aspects of thematic work programmes

Decision IV/7, annex, paragraph 53 (Forest)

Rehabilitation and restoration of degraded ecosystems and recovery of threatened species (Article 8 (f))

> Each Contracting Party shall, as far as possible and as appropriate:
>
> (f) Rehabilitate and restore degraded ecosystems and promote the recovery of threatened species, *inter alia*, through the development and implementation of plans or other management strategies;

Notes

Terms defined in Article 2

'ecosystem'.

Consideration of Article 8 (f) by the COP

Background and status

COP 3 requested Parties to take action to restore habitats [*decision III/9, paragraph 6*]. The COP has also referred to habitat restoration in each of the thematic work programmes. Restoration is a major focus of the International Initiative for the Conservation and Sustainable Use of Pollinators (established as a cross-cutting initiative within the work programme on agricultural biological diversity) and is one of the targeted actions in response to identified needs in the work programme on dry and sub-humid lands [*decision V/5, paragraphs 15 (d), 16–18; decision V/23, annex I, II, part B, Activity 7 (b) and 'Ways and means'*].

COP guidance

Guidance to Parties

The COP has encouraged Parties to strengthen capacities for restoration of forests, as part of the implementation of the work programme on forest biological diversity [*decision V/4, paragraph 10*].

With respect to inland water biological diversity, the COP has recommended that Parties encourage the adoption of integrated watershed, catchment and river basin management strategies to restore or improve the biological diversity and other functions and values of inland water ecosystems [*decision IV/4, annex I, paragraph 9 (a) (ii)*]. It has also recommended that Parties encourage the development of preventative strategies to avoid degradation and promote restoration of inland water ecosystems [*decision IV/4, annex I, paragraph 9 (b) (ii)*].

The COP has recommended that Parties raise awareness of the possible problems and costs associated with the deliberate or accidental introduction of alien species and genotypes that adversely affect aquatic biological diversity. Policies and guidelines should be developed to rehabilitate sites where possible [*decision IV/4, annex I, paragraph 9 (h)* and see alien species (Article 8 (h)) below].

The COP has encouraged Parties to develop national strategies, programmes and plans that encourage the development of technologies and farming practices that increase productivity and arrest degradation as well as reclaim, rehabilitate, restore and enhance biological diversity [*decision III/11, paragraph 15 (e)*].

Guidance to the Secretariat

Operational objective 1.2 of the work programme on marine and coastal biological diversity, concerning integrated marine and coastal area management (IMCAM), includes as one of its activities the promotion of restoration of areas important for reproduction and other important habitats for marine living resources [*decision IV/5, annex, C, operational objective 1.2, paragraph (c)*]. Operational objective 1.3 concerns identification of key habitats for marine living resources on a regional basis, and the pursuit of restoration of degraded habitats, including coral reef systems [*decision IV/5, annex, C, operational objective 1.3, paragraph (c) and 'Ways and means'*]. These activities are to be carried out by the Executive Secretary in collaboration with relevant organizations [*decision IV/5, annex, C, operational objectives 1.2, 1.3, 'Ways and means'*].

Guidance to SBSTTA

In the work programme on inland water biological diversity, the work plan for SBSTTA includes the compilation and dissemination of case studies on restoration and rehabilitation of degraded inland water ecosystems [*decision IV/4, annex I, paragraph 8 (c) (iv)*].[6]

References

Guidance to Parties

National action

Decision III/9, paragraph 6 (Implementation of Articles 6 and 8)
Decision III/11, paragraphs 15 (e), 17 (b) (Agriculture)
Decision IV/4, annex I, paragraph 9 (a) (ii), (b) (ii), (h) (Inland water)
Decision V/4, paragraph 10 (Forest)

Information and case studies

Decision V/5, paragraph 18 (Agriculture)

Guidance to the Secretariat

Decision IV/5, annex, C, operational objectives 1.2, 1.3 (Marine and coastal)
Decision V/5, paragraph 15, 16, 18 (Agriculture)

6 This decision drew attention to section II.4.b. *Rehabilitation and restoration of ecosystems* in document UNEP/CBD/COP/4/Inf.8 concerning co-operation between the Convention on Biological Diversity and the Convention on Wetlands.

Guidance to SBSTTA

Decision IV/4, annex I, paragraph 8 (c) (iv) (Inland water)
Decision V/5, paragraphs 15, 18 (Agriculture)

Cooperation with other conventions and organizations

Decision IV/4, annex I, paragraph 8 (c) (iv) (Inland water)
Decision IV/5, annex, C, operational objectives 1.2, 1.3, 'Ways and means' (Marine and coastal)
Decision V/5, paragraphs 15, 17 (Agriculture)

Relevant aspects of thematic work programmes

Decision III/11, paragraphs 15 (e), 17 (b) (Agriculture)
Decision IV/4, annex I, paragraphs 8 (c) (iv), 9 (a) (ii), (h) (Inland water)
Decision IV/5, annex, C, operational objectives 1.2, 1.3 (Marine and coastal)
Decision V/4, paragraph 10; annex, 2 (b) (iv) (Forest)
Decision V/5, paragraphs 15 (d), 16–18 (Agriculture)
Decision V/23, annex I, II, part B, Activity 7 (b) (Dry and sub-humid lands)

Declarations

Algeria and Niger (adoption)

Biosafety (Article 8 (g))

> Each Contracting Party shall, as far as possible and as appropriate:
>
> (g) Establish or maintain means to regulate, manage or control the risks associated with the use and release of living modified organisms resulting from biotechnology which are likely to have adverse environmental impacts that could affect the conservation and sustainable use of biological diversity, taking also into account the risks to human health;

Editors' note:

For the COP's consideration of a protocol on biosafety, see the guide to Article 19.3 later in this section of the Handbook.

Notes

Terms defined in Article 2

'biological diversity', 'biotechnology', and 'sustainable use'.

Consideration of Article 8 (g) by the COP

Virtually all the COP's deliberations on biosafety have concerned Article 19 (3) and the need for and modalities of a Protocol on biosafety, which is discussed under Article 19 below. It has, however, also referred to genetically modified organisms with respect to inland water biological diversity [*decision IV/4, annex I, paragraph 9 (h)*] and capacity-building, including for the implementation of the UNEP International Technical Guidelines on Safety in Biotechnology [*decision III/5, paragraph 2 (a)*].

The COP has recommended that Parties raise awareness of the possible problems and costs associated with the deliberate or accidental introduction of genetically modified organisms which adversely affect aquatic biological diversity. Policies and guidelines should be developed to prevent and control such introductions and to rehabilitate sites where possible [*decision IV/4, annex I, paragraph 9 (h)*]. The COP has also recalled Article 8 (g) in asking Parties to carry out assessments on ecological, social and economic effects of genetic use restriction technologies (GURTs) [*decision V/5, part III, paragraph 25*].

The COP has stated that the GEF should provide financial resources for capacity-building in biosafety, including for the implementation by developing countries of the UNEP International Technical Guidelines on Safety in Biotechnology [*decision III/5, paragraph 2 (a)*].

References

Guidance to Parties

National action

Decision IV/4, annex I, paragraph 9 (h) (Inland water)

Information and case studies

Decision V/5, III, paragraph 25 (Agriculture)

Financial mechanism and resources

Guidance to the financial mechanism

Decision III/5, paragraph 2 (a) (Additional guidance to the financial mechanism)

Relevant aspects of thematic work programmes

Decision IV/4, annex I, paragraph 9 (h) (Inland water)
Decision V/5, III, paragraph 25 (Agriculture)

Other relevant decisions

See guide to Article 19 (3) below and Cartagena Protocol on Biosafety.

Alien species (Article 8 (h))

> Each Contracting Party shall, as far as possible and as appropriate:
>
> (h) Prevent the introduction of, control or eradicate those alien species which threaten ecosystems, habitats or species;

Notes

Terms defined in Article 2

'ecosystem' and 'habitat'.

Consideration of Article 8 (h) by the COP

Background and status

The COP has referred to alien species in a number of decisions, most importantly decision IV/1 C and decision V/8. In decision IV/1 C, the COP decided that alien species were a cross-cutting issue within the Convention, and recognized the particular importance of geographically and evolutionarily isolated ecosystems such as small islands when considering it [*decision IV/10 C, paragraph 1*]. It asked SBSTTA to report on alien species to COP 5 and to examine the Global Invasive Species Programme (GISP) with a view to developing proposals for further action under the Convention on this issue [*decision IV/1 C, paragraph 2*].

SBSTTA considered alien species at both its fourth and fifth meetings. It recommended a format for case studies and proposed that the COP adopt a set of guiding principles on introduction of alien species [*SBSTTA recommendations IV/4 and V/4*]. COP 5 adopted a modified version of these guiding principles [*decision V/8, paragraph 1, annex*]. It urged Parties, Governments and relevant organizations to apply the guiding principles on an interim basis, noting that the definition of many of the terms was not yet settled. It also called for case studies to be submitted. The COP stressed the importance of the GISP, calling on the latter to develop a second phase of its activities and urged financial support for the GISP [decision V/8, paragraphs 13, *17]*.

COP 4 decided that alien species would be one of three priority issues for COP 6 [*decision IV/16, annex II*]. COP 5 decided that it would consider at COP 6 further options for implementing Article 8 (h), including the possibility of developing an international instrument [*decision V/8, paragraph 16]*. SBSTTA also addressed alien species again at its sixth meeting. A roster of experts has also been established. A series of liaison group meetings and regional meetings are also being organized to assist with preparations for COP 6.

In the work programme on forest biological diversity, alien species serve as a focus of attention under programme area 2 ('Comprehensive analysis of the ways in which human activities, in particular forest-management practices, influence biological diversity and assessment of ways to minimize or mitigate negative influences') and programme area 4 ('Further research and technological priorities') [*decision IV/7, annex, paragraphs 32, 35, 51*].

The COP has also identified alien species as one of five programme elements in the work programme on marine and coastal biological diversity [*decision IV/5, annex, programme element 5*], and specifically addressed alien species in part A of the work programme on inland water biological diversity [*decision IV/4, annex I, paragraph 8 (c) (vi)*].

COP guidance

Guidance to Parties

The COP has invited Parties to develop country-driven projects at both national and supra-national levels to address alien species, and to incorporate the issue into their biodiversity strategies and action plans [*decision IV/1 C, paragraphs 3, 4*]. Parties have been urged to carry out a number of actions regarding alien species, including application of the interim guiding principles contained in annex I of decision V/8, undertaking of case studies, development of mechanisms for transboundary, regional and multilateral cooperation, and development of education, training and public-awareness measures [*decision V/8, paragraphs 1, 3, 5–9, 12*].

The COP has made a number of specific recommendations on these issues as they apply to alien species in inland water ecosystems [*decision IV/4, annex I, paragraph 9 (e) (iv), 9 (h)*].

Financial mechanism and resources

The COP has stated that the GEF should provide adequate and timely support for country-driven projects at national, regional and subregional levels addressing the issue of alien species in accordance with decision IV/1 C [*decision IV/13, paragraph 1*]. It also requested the GEF and other bodies to provide support to enable the GISP to fulfil the tasks outlined in decision V/8 [*decision V/8, paragraph 17; decision V/13, paragraph 2 (m)*].

Guidance to the Secretariat

The COP has requested the Executive Secretary to carry out a number of activities regarding alien species in collaboration with a range of other international bodies. These include dissemination of case studies and comments, assisting Parties in activities concerned with alien species and preparation of a paper outlining progress to date, existing measures and future options for work on alien species for consideration by SBSTTA 6 [*decision V/8, paragraphs 4, 5, 11, 14, 15*]. The Executive Secretary or Secretariat is identified as the major actor in the implementation of programme element 5, on alien species, of the work programme on marine and coastal biological diversity [*decision IV/5, annex, Programme area 5*].

References

Decisions on Article 8 (h)

Decision IV/1 C (Alien species)
Decision V/8 (Alien species)

Guidance to Parties

National action

Decision IV/1 C, paragraphs 3, 4 (Alien species)
Decision IV/4, annex I, paragraph 9 (e) (iv), 9 (h) (Inland water)
Decision V/8, paragraphs 1, 6–9 (Alien species)
Decision V/18 I, paragraph 1 (a) (Impact assessment, liability and redress)
Decision V/23, annex I, II, part B, Activity 7 (c) (Dry and sub-humid lands)

Information and case studies

Decision V/8, paragraphs 3, 5, 7, 12 (Alien species)
Decision V/19, paragraph 8 (National reports)

Financial mechanism and resources

Guidance to the financial mechanism

Decision IV/13, paragraph 1 (Additional guidance to the financial mechanism)
Decision V/8, paragraph 17 (Alien species)
Decision V/13, paragraph 2 (m) (Further guidance to the financial mechanism)

Other financial resources

Decision V/8, paragraph 17 (Alien species)

Guidance to the Secretariat

Decision IV/5, annex, Programme area 5 (Marine and coastal)
Decision V/3, IV, paragraph 14 (Marine and coastal)
Decision V/8, paragraphs 4, 5, 11, 14, 15 (Alien species)

Guidance to SBSTTA

Decision IV/1 C, paragraphs 2, 5, 6 (Alien species)
Decision IV/4, annex I, paragraph 8 (c) (vi) (Inland water)
Decision V/2, paragraph 5 (Inland water)

Cooperation with other conventions and organizations

Decision III/9, paragraph 10 (Implementation of Articles 6 and 8)
Decision IV/1 C, paragraph 6 (Alien species)
Decision IV/5, annex, Programme area 5 (Marine and coastal)
Decision V/8, paragraphs 1, 3, 6, 8, 10–15 (Alien species)
Decision V/23, annex I, II, part B, Activity 7 (c) (Dry and sub-humid lands)

Relevant aspects of thematic work programmes

Decision II/10, annex I, paragraph (xi) (Marine and coastal)
Decision IV/4, annex I, paragraphs 8 (c) (vi), 9 (h) (Inland water)
Decision IV/5, annex, programme element 5 (Marine and coastal)
Decision IV/7, annex, paragraphs 32, 35, 51 (Forest)
Decision V/2, paragraph 5 (Inland water)

Decision V/3, IV, paragraph 14 (Marine and coastal)
Decision V/5, annex, A, paragraph 3 (c); annex, B, programme element 2, Activity 2.1 (d) (Agriculture)
Decision V/23, annex I, II, part B, Activity 7 (c) (Dry and sub-humid lands)

Other relevant decisions

Decision III/9, paragraph 9 (c) (Implementation of Articles 6 and 8)
Decision IV/16, annex II (Institutional matters and programme of work)

Documents

UNEP/CBD/COP/5/INF/9 Gaps in existing or proposed legal instruments, guidelines and procedures to counteract the introduction of and the adverse effects exerted by alien species and genotypes that threaten ecosystems, habitats or species
UNEP/CBD/COP/5/INF/32 Alien Species that Threaten Ecosystems, Habitats or Species (Implementation of Decision IV/1 C), Including the question of Global Plant Conservation
UNEP/CBD/COP/5/INF/33 Invasive Species in Eastern Africa
UNEP/CBD/SBSTTA/4/8 Development of guiding principles for the prevention of impacts of alien species by identifying priority areas of work on isolated ecosystems and by evaluating and giving recommendations for the further development of the Global Invasive Species Programme, with a view to cooperation
UNEP/CBD/SBSTTA/5/5 Alien Species: guiding principles for the prevention, introduction and mitigation of impacts

Traditional knowledge, innovations and practices of indigenous and local communities (Article 8 (j) and related provisions)

Article 8 (j) (*In-situ* conservation)

Each Contracting Party shall, as far as possible and as appropriate [...]

(j) subject to its national legislation, respect, preserve and maintain knowledge, innovations and practices of indigenous and local communities embodying traditional lifestyles relevant for the conservation and sustainable use of biological diversity and promote their wider application with the approval and involvement of the holders of such knowledge, innovations and practices and encourage the equitable sharing of the benefits arising from the utilization of such knowledge, innovations and practices; [...]

Article 10 (c) (Sustainable use of components of biological diversity)

Each Contracting Party shall, as far as possible and as appropriate: [...]

c) Protect and encourage customary use of biological resources in accordance with traditional cultural practices that are compatible with conservation or sustainable use requirements;

Article 17 (2) (Exchange of information)

2. Such exchange of information shall include exchange of results of technical, scientific and socio-economic research, as well as information on training and surveying programmes, specialised knowledge, indigenous and traditional knowledge as such and in combination with the technologies referred to in Article 16, paragraph 1. It shall also, where feasible, include repatriation of information.

Article 18 (4) (Technical and scientific cooperation)

4. The Contracting Parties shall, in accordance with national legislation and policies, encourage and develop methods of cooperation for the development and use of technologies, including indigenous and traditional technologies, in pursuance of the objectives of this Convention. For this purpose, the Contracting Parties shall also promote cooperation in the training of personnel and exchange of experts.

Editors' note:

The COP's consideration of Article 8 (j) is closely linked to its consideration of a number of other provisions of the Convention, in particular Articles 10 (c), 15, 16, 17 (2), 18 (4) and 19, and also to the thematic work programmes on marine and coastal, agricultural, inland water and forest biological diversity, and biodiversity of dry and sub-humid lands. Reference should therefore also be made to the guides on these articles and themes elsewhere in this section of the Handbook. Decisions explicitly addressing Article 8 (j) and related provisions are addressed below, as are references in other decisions relating to traditional knowledge, innovations and practices of local and indigenous communities.

Article 8 (j) and most of the relevant COP decisions discussed below refer to 'indigenous and local communities embodying traditional lifestyles relevant for the conservation and sustainable use of biological diversity'. By way of abbreviation only, the term 'indigenous and local communities' is used throughout.

Notes

Terms defined in Article 2

'Biological diversity', '*in situ* conservation', 'sustainable use', and 'technology'.

Consideration of Article 8 (j) and related provisions by the COP

Background and status

As part of its first medium-term programme of work, the COP decided to address knowledge, innovations and practices of indigenous and local communities and implementation of Article 8 (j) at its third meeting [*decision I/9 and decision II/18*]. However, the issues of traditional knowledge, innovations and practices of indigenous and local communities have also arisen frequently in COP discussions on intellectual property rights (IPRs), access to genetic resources and benefit-sharing and forest biological diversity.

COP 3 adopted decision III/14 on implementation of Article 8 (j) which set in motion a process for consideration of further work in this area. As part of this process, the COP agreed upon the need for a workshop to advise the COP on the possibility of developing a work plan on Article 8 (j) and related provisions, and to examine the need for an intersessional working group or subsidiary body to consider the role of traditional knowledge, innovations and practices relevant to the conservation and sustainable use of biological diversity [*decision III/14, annex, paragraph 1 (g)*].

The Workshop on Traditional Knowledge and Biological Diversity was held in Madrid, Spain, in November 1997 and prepared a report for COP 4 [see document UNEP/CBD/COP/4/10/Add.1]. The report contained recommendations for elements of a work plan.

In decision IV/9, COP 4 decided to establish an Ad Hoc Open-ended Inter-sessional Working Group to address the implementation of Article 8 (j) and related provisions [*decision IV/9, paragraph 1*]. The mandate of this Working Group is to:

(a) provide advice as a priority on the application and development of legal and other appropriate forms of protection for the knowledge, innovations and practices of indigenous and local communities embodying traditional lifestyles relevant to the conservation and sustainable use of biological diversity;

(b) provide the COP with advice relating to the implementation of Article 8 (j) and related provisions, in particular on the development and implementation of a programme of work at national and international levels;

(c) to develop a programme of work, based on the structure of the elements proposed in the Madrid workshop report [see *decision IV/9, annex*];

(d) identify those objectives falling within the scope of the Convention; to recommend priorities taking into account the programme of work of the COP, such as the equitable sharing of benefits; to identify for which work-plan objectives and activities advice should be directed to the COP and which should be directed to SBSTTA; to recommend which of the work-plan objectives and activities should be referred to other international bodies or processes; and to identify opportunities for collaboration and coordination with other international bodies or processes with the aim of fostering synergy and avoiding duplication of work; and

(e) provide advice to the COP on measures to strengthen cooperation at the international level among indigenous and local communities embodying traditional lifestyles relevant to the conservation and sustainable use of biological diversity and make proposals on the strengthening of mechanisms that support such cooperation [*decision IV/9, paragraph 1*].

The Working Group held its first meeting in Seville, Spain, in March 2000, and provided a report to COP 5 [see document UNEP/CBD/COP/5/5]. Based on the recommendation of the Working Group, the COP adopted a programme of work on Article 8 (j) and related provisions [*decision V/16, paragraphs 1, 2*]. The programme of work is divided into two phases according to the priority assigned to the tasks. The mandate of the Working Group was extended to undertake specific tasks under the programme of work, to review progress on its implementation, and to make recommendations for further actions [*decision V/16, paragraph 9*]. The work programme comprises seven elements, based on those identified at the Madrid workshop, as follows:

Element 1: Participatory mechanisms for indigenous and local communities.

Element 2: Status and trends in relation to Article 8 (j) and related provisions.

Element 3: Traditional cultural practices for conservation and sustainable use.

Element 4: Equitable sharing of benefits.

Element 5: Exchange and dissemination of information.

Element 6: Monitoring elements.

Element 7: Legal elements.

For each element a range of specific tasks to be undertaken by the Parties, the Secretariat and/or the Working Group is identified [*decision V/16, annex*]. Among the tasks of the Working Group is the elaboration of a number of sets of guidelines, including:

- Guidelines for the development of mechanisms, legislation or other initiatives to ensure benefit-sharing and prior informed consent [*decision V/16, annex, II, element 4, task 7*].
- Guidelines or recommendations for the conduct of cultural, environmental and social impact assessments regarding proposed developments on sacred sites and on lands or waters occupied or used by indigenous and local communities [*decision V/16, annex, II, element 6, task 9*].
- Guidelines to assist Parties and Governments in the development of legislation or other mechanisms to implement Article 8 (j) [*decision V/16, annex, II, element 7, task 12*].
- Guidelines for the respect, preservation and maintenance of traditional knowledge, innovations and practices and their wider application in accordance with Article 8 (j) [*decision V/16, annex, III, element 3, task 6*].
- Guiding principles and standards to strengthen the use of traditional knowledge and other knowledge for the conservation and sustainable use of biodiversity [*decision V/16, annex, III, element 3, task 13*].
- Guidelines and proposals for national incentive schemes for indigenous and local communities to preserve and maintain their traditional knowledge [*decision V/16, annex, III, element 3, task 14*].
- Guidelines to facilitate the repatriation of information in accordance with Article 17 (2) [*decision V/16, annex, III, element 3, task 15*].
- Standards and guidelines for the reporting and prevention of unlawful appropriation of traditional knowledge and related genetic resources [*decision V/16, annex, III, element 6, task 10*].

The Working Group is due to hold its second meeting in February 2002 in Montreal, Canada.

Participation of indigenous and local communities in the operations of the Convention at the national and international level

In a number of its decisions related to Article 8 (j) and related provisions, the COP has addressed the involvement and participation of indigenous and local communities in the operation and implementation of the Convention. A key objective of the work programme on Article 8 (j) and related provisions adopted at COP 5 is the full and effective participation of indigenous and local communities at all stages and levels of its implementation [*decision V/16, annex, I, paragraph 1*].

The COP has encouraged Parties to include representatives of indigenous and local communities in their delegations for the Working Group, and to promote consultations among indigenous and local communities on issues to be dealt with in the Working Group [*decision IV/9, paragraphs 3, 4, 12; decision V/16, paragraphs 5, 18*]. The COP has also decided that the Panel of Experts on Access and Benefit-sharing and the Ad Hoc Open-ended Working Group on Access and Benefit-sharing (see the guide to Article 15 later in this section of the Handbook) should include representatives of indigenous and local communities [*decision IV/8, paragraph 3; decision V/26 A, paragraph 11*].

COP guidance

Guidance to Parties

The COP has provided guidance to Parties relating to the implementation of Article 8 (j) and related provisions both in its decisions addressing this article, and also in decisions on other articles and thematic areas. It has requested those Parties that have not yet done so to develop national legislation and corresponding strategies for the implementation of Article 8 (j) in consultation with representatives of their indigenous and local communities [*decision III/14, paragraph 1*].

In a number of its decisions, the COP has called for information and case studies relating to the implementation of Article 8 (j) and related provisions. Decision III/14 urged Parties to supply information about the implementation of Article 8 (j) and related provisions and to include such information in national reports [*decision III/14, paragraph 2*]. The COP also invited Governments, international agencies, research institutions, representatives of indigenous and local communities and non-governmental organizations (NGOs), to submit case studies to the Executive Secretary on measures taken to develop and implement the Convention's provisions relating to indigenous and local communities [*decision III/14, paragraph 3*]. COP 4 reiterated a call for case studies on aspects of implementation of Article 8 (j) as background information for the Ad Hoc Open-ended Inter-sessional Working Group established under decision IV/9 [*decision IV/9, paragraph 10; decision V/16, paragraph 15*]. Case studies submitted to the Secretariat pursuant to these requests are to be disseminated through the CHM, as well as transmitted to the World Intellectual Property Organization (WIPO) [*decision IV/9, paragraph 15*].

The COP has called upon Parties:

- to integrate biological diversity concerns into education strategies, recognizing the particular needs of indigenous and local communities [*decision IV/10 B, paragraph 1 (d)*];

- where necessary, to illustrate and translate the provisions of the Convention into the respective local languages to promote public education and awareness-raising of relevant sectors, including local communities [*decision IV/10 B, paragraph 4*].

Financial mechanism and resources

The COP has decided that the financial mechanism should provide support, *inter alia,* for the implementation of priority activities identified in the programme of work on Article 8 (j) [*decision V/13, paragraph 2 (i)*]. COP 3 also requested the financial mechanism to examine support for capacity-building projects for indigenous and local communities [*decision III/14, paragraph 5; decision III/5, paragraph 5*].

Relationship with other agreements and processes

The COP has repeatedly emphasized that further work is required to help develop a common appreciation of the relationship between IPRs, the World Trade Organization (WTO) Agreement on Trade-related Aspects of Intellectual Property Rights (TRIPs Agreement) and the CBD [*decision IV/15, paragraph 10*]. A particularly important aspect of this relationship is the use of IPRs with respect to the implementation of Article 8 (j) and related provisions. The COP has transmitted its decisions to the WTO, and has invited the WTO to explore the interrelationship between the CBD and the TRIPs Agreement [*decision V/16, paragraph 14; decision V/26 B, paragraph 2*]. The COP has also sought to initiate cooperation with WIPO on this issue. For example, the Secretariat has been asked to transmit compilations of case studies submitted to it on implementation of Article 8 (j) to WIPO [*decision IV/9, paragraph 15*]. The COP invited WIPO to take into account the lifestyles and traditional systems of access and use of the knowledge, technologies and practices of indigenous and local communities in its work [*decision IV/9, paragraph 16*].

Article 8 (j) and forest biological diversity are closely related. The Executive Secretary, at the request of the COP, has acted as the focal point for traditional knowledge in the United Nations processes on forests [ie *decision II/9, paragraph 2 (a)*]. Many elements of the work programme on forest biological diversity relate to Article 8 (j) and related provisions. The objectives of the work programme include to:

> (d) identify traditional forest systems of conservation and sustainable use of forest biological diversity and to promote the wider application, use and role of traditional forest-related knowledge in sustainable forest management ...; and
>
> (e) identify mechanisms that facilitate the financing of activities for the conservation, incorporation of traditional knowledge and sustainable use of forest biological diversity...
>
> [*decision IV/7, annex, paragraphs 3 (d), (e)*].

Among the activities to be carried out under the work programme are:

- the development of methodologies to advance the integration of traditional forest-related knowledge into sustainable forest management [*decision IV/7, annex, paragraph 14*];
- the improvement of dissemination of research results and synthesis of reports of the best available scientific and traditional knowledge on key forest biological diversity issues [*decision IV/7, annex, paragraph 34*].

In addition, proposed outcomes of elements of the work programme include:

- [...] an enhanced understanding of the role of traditional knowledge in ecosystem management to minimize or mitigate negative influences, and to promote the positive effects [*decision IV/7, annex, paragraph 38*];
- an expansion of research capacity to develop and assess options incorporating the applications of traditional knowledge to minimize or mitigate negative influences, and to promote the positive effects [*decision IV/7, annex, paragraph 39*].

Other thematic work programmes also address Article 8 (j) and related provisions. For example, the work programme on marine and coastal biological diversity is to use and draw upon scientific, technical and technological knowledge of local and indigenous communities [*decision IV/5, annex, paragraph 9; decision II/10, annex II, paragraph 3 (d)*].

In relation to agricultural biological diversity, the COP has encouraged Parties to develop national strategies, programmes and plans which empower their indigenous and local communities and build their capacity for *in situ* management of agricultural biological diversity [*decision III/11, paragraph 15 (f)*]. The COP has also emphasized the importance for the conservation and sustainable use of agricultural biological diversity of respecting the knowledge, innovations and practices deriving from traditional farming systems and to this end requested the Executive Secretary to discuss with indigenous and local communities the impact of the use of GURTs and Farmers' Rights [*decision V/5, paragraph 29*].

References

Decisions on Article 8 (j) and related provisions

Decision III/14 (Implementation of Article 8 (j))
Decision IV/9 (Implementation of Article 8 (j) and related provisions)
Decision V/16 (Article 8 (j) and related provisions)

Guidance to Parties

National action

Decision III/11, paragraph 15 (f) (Agriculture)
Decision III/14, paragraph 1 (Implementation of Article 8 (j))
Decision IV/4, annex I, paragraphs 9 (l), 14 (Inland water)
Decision IV/9, paragraph 13 (Implementation of Article 8 (j) and related provisions)
Decision IV/10 B, paragraphs 1 (d), 4 (Public education and awareness)
Decision V/4, paragraphs 9, 10 (Forest)
Decision V/5, annex, B, programme element 3, Activities 3.1 – 3.4, 3.6 (Agriculture)
Decision V/6, annex, B, Principle 11 (Ecosystem approach)
Decision V/16, paragraphs 3, 4, 10, 12, 16; annex, II, element 1, tasks 1, 2, 4 (Article 8 (j) and related provisions)
Decision V/18 I, paragraph 1 (d) (Impact assessment, liability and redress)
Decision V/24, paragraph 6 (Sustainable use)
Decision V/25, paragraph 4 (a), (b), (g), (h), (i) (Biological diversity and tourism)
Decision V/26 A, paragraph 4 (c), (d) (Access to genetic resources)

Information and case studies

Decision III/14, paragraphs 2, 3 (Implementation of Article 8 (j))
Decision III/17, paragraph 1 (Intellectual property rights)
Decision IV/9, paragraphs 10, 15 (Implementation of Article 8 (j) and related provisions)
Decision V/16, paragraphs 12 (f), 13, 15; annex, II, element 2, task 5 (Article 8 (j) and related provisions)

Financial mechanism and resources

Guidance to the financial mechanism

Decision I/2, annex I, paragraph 4 (j) (Financial mechanism and resources)
Decision III/5, paragraph 5 (Additional guidance to the financial mechanism)
Decision III/14, paragraph 5 (Implementation of Article 8 (j))
Decision IV/8, paragraph 4 (d) (Access and benefit-sharing)
Decision V/13, paragraph 2 (i) (Further guidance to the financial mechanism)

Other financial resources

Decision IV/7, annex, paragraph 3 (e) (Forest)
Decision V/16, paragraphs 7, 20; annex, IV (Article 8 (j) and related provisions)

Guidance to the Secretariat

Decision II/9, paragraph 2 (a) (Forest – Statement to IPF)
Decision II/10, annex II, paragraph 3 (d) (Marine and coastal)
Decision II/12, paragraphs b, c (Intellectual property rights)
Decision III/12, paragraph 6 (e) (Forest)
Decision III/14, paragraphs 4, 6, 9–11 (Implementation of Article 8 (j))
Decision IV/2, paragraph 10 (b) (Clearing-house mechanism)
Decision IV/5, annex, C, operational objective 1.2, paragraph (h); operational objective 2.1, paragraph (e) (Marine and coastal)
Decision IV/9, paragraphs 11, 14, 15, 17 (Implementation of Article 8 (j) and related provisions)
Decision IV/10 C, paragraph 7 (Impact assessment and minimizing adverse effects)
Decision V/3, paragraph 11 (Marine and coastal)
Decision V/4, paragraphs 5, 15 (Forest)
Decision V/5, III, paragraph 29 (Agriculture)
Decision V/8, paragraph 14 (c) (Alien species)
Decision V/16, paragraphs 8, 10, 19 (a); annex, II, element 2, task 5; element 6, task 17; annex, IV (Article 8 (j) and related provisions)
Decision V/17, paragraph 7 (a) (Education and public awareness)
Decision V/24, paragraph 1 (Sustainable use)

Guidance to SBSTTA

Decision IV/9, paragraph 7 (Implementation of Article 8 (j) and related provisions)
Decision V/18, I, paragraph 4 (Impact assessment, liability and redress)

Cooperation with other conventions and organizations

Decision II/9, annex, paragraphs 8, 16, 17 (Forest – Statement to IPF)

Decision III/17, paragraph 8 (Intellectual property rights)
Decision III/19, annex, paragraphs 10 (iii), 18, 19 (e), 20 (i), 24 (d) (Statement to UNGA Special Session)
Decision IV/9, paragraphs 14, 16, 17 (Implementation of Article 8 (j) and related provisions)
Decision IV/15, paragraphs 9–11, 14 (c) (Cooperation)
Decision V/8, paragraph 14 (c) (Alien species)
Decision V/16, paragraph 14 (Article 8 (j) and related provisions)

Relevant aspects of thematic work programmes

Decision II/9, paragraph 2 (a); annex, paragraphs 8, 16, 17 (Forest – Statement to IPF)
Decision II/10, annex II, paragraph 3 (d) (Marine and coastal)
Decision III/11, paragraph 15 (f) (Agriculture)
Decision III/12, paragraph 6 (e) (Forest)
Decision IV/4, annex I, paragraphs 9 (1), 14 (Inland water)
Decision IV/5, annex, B, paragraph 9; C, operational objective 1.2, paragraph (h); operational objective 2.1, paragraph (e) (Marine and coastal)
Decision IV/6, paragraph 1 (see also SBSTTA recommendation III/4, paragraph 7) (Agriculture)
Decision IV/7, annex, paragraphs 3 (d), (e), 14, 15, 21, 30, 34, 38, 39 (Forest)
Decision V/2, paragraph 8 (Inland water)
Decision V/3, paragraph 11 (Marine and coastal)
Decision V/4, paragraphs 5–7, 9, 10, 15; annex, 2 (b) (v) (Forest)
Decision V/5, paragraphs 5, 29; annex, A, paragraphs 3 (c), 4; annex, B, programme element 1, activity 1.3; programme element 2, activity 2.2 (c) (ii); Activities 2.3; 3.1; 3.2; 3.3, 3.4, 3.6 (Agriculture)
Decision V/23, annex I, I, paragraph 3; annex I, II, part A, paragraph 6, Activity 6; part B, Activity 8, paragraphs (a), (b) (Dry and sub-humid lands)

Other relevant decisions

Decision IV/1 D, paragraph 8 (Taxonomy)
Decision IV/8, paragraph 3 (Access and benefit-sharing)
Decision IV/10 C, paragraph 1 (Impact assessment and minimizing adverse effects)
Decision V/15, paragraph 4 (Incentive measures)
Decision V/20, III, paragraph 31 (b), (c) (Operations of the Convention)
Decision V/26 A, paragraphs 11, 12, 14, 15 (e); B, paragraph 1 (Access to genetic resources)
Decision V/26 B, paragraph 1 (Intellectual property rights)

Declarations

Colombia (adoption), Malawi (adoption) and Peru (adoption)

Documents

UNEP/CBD/COP/3/19 Implementation of Article 8 (j)
UNEP/CBD/COP/3/Inf.3 Submissions received by the Executive Secretary concerning knowledge, innovations and practices of indigenous and local communities

UNEP/CBD/COP/4/10 Implementation of Article 8 (j) and related provisions
UNEP/CBD/COP/5/5 Report of the Ad Hoc Working Group on Article 8 (j) and related provisions
UNEP/CBD/SBSTTA/2/7 Knowledge, innovations and practices of indigenous and local communities
UNEP/CBD/SBSTTA/2/Inf.3 Traditional forest-related knowledge and the Convention on Biological Diversity
UNEP/CBD/SBSTTA/2/Inf.8 Submissions received by the Secretariat concerning knowledge, innovations and practices of indigenous and local communities
UNEP/CBD/TKBD/1/1/Rev.1 Provisional Agenda
UNEP/CBD/TKBD/1/1/Add.1 Annotated Provisional Agenda
UNEP/CBD/TKBD/1/2 Traditional Knowledge and Biological Diversity
UNEP/CBD/TKBD/1/3 Report of the Workshop on Traditional Knowledge and Biological Diversity
UNEP/CBD/WG8J/1/1 Provisional agenda
UNEP/CBD/WG8J/1/1/Add.1 Annotated provisional agenda
UNEP/CBD/WG8J/1/2 Legal and other appropriate forms of protection for the Knowledge, Innovations and Practices of Indigenous and local communities embodying traditional lifestyles relevant for the conservation and sustainable use of Biological Diversity
UNEP/CBD/WG8J/1/3 Proposed Programme of Work on the implementation of Article 8 (j) and Related Provisions of the Convention on Biological Diversity at National and International Levels
UNEP/CBD/WG8J/1/4 International Cooperation among indigenous and local communities
UNEP/CBD/WG8J/1/Inf.1 Indicative List of Activities that could be carried out under the tasks identified in the programme of work on Article 8 (j) and related provisions of the Convention on Biological Diversity
UNEP/CBD/WG8J/1/Inf.2 Synthesis of case studies and relevant information on Article 8 (j) and related provisions of the Convention on Biological Diversity
UNEP/CBD/WG8J/1/Inf.3 Briefing Note from the Spanish and Colombian Governments on Protected Areas and Indigenous Peoples
UNEP/CBD/WG8J/1/Inf.4 Report of the International Conference on Indigenous and Scientific Knowledge on the Sustainable Use of Plants
UNEP/CBD/WG8J/1/Inf.5 The outcome of the Intergovernmental Forum on Forests (IFF) relevant to the Ad-hoc Open-ended Inter-sessional Working Group on Article 8 (j) and Related Provisions of the Convention on Biological Diversity

Mitigation of threats (Article 8 (l))

Each Contracting Party shall, as far as possible and as appropriate:

(l) Where a significant adverse effect on biological diversity has been determined pursuant to Article 7, regulate or manage the relevant processes and categories of activities;

Editors' note:

Readers should also refer to the guides to Articles 7 (c), 10 (b) and 14 (l) in this section of the Handbook

Notes

Terms defined in Article 2

'biological diversity'.

Consideration of Article 8 (l) by the COP

Background and status

This aspect of Article 8 is linked to Articles 7 (c), 10 (b) and 14 (l) of the Convention. While the COP has not specifically addressed Article 8 (l), it has recommended methodologies to evaluate and mitigate threats to biological diversity as one of four specific themes for the compilation and dissemination of information on the implementation of Articles 6 and 8 [*decision III/9, paragraph 9 (a)*].

In programme area 2 of the work programme on forest biological diversity, research is intended to promote four activities, one of which is to provide options to minimize or mitigate negative, and to promote positive, human influences on forest biological diversity [*decision IV/7, annex, paragraph 31*]. COP 5 drew attention to the potential impacts of climate change, uncontrolled forest fires and harvesting of non-timber forest resources on forest biological diversity, and asked SBSTTA to consider these issues [*decision V/4, paragraphs 11, 12, 14*].

One of the activities under the work programme on marine and coastal biological diversity is to promote identification of key habitats for marine living resources on a regional basis, with a view to further developing policies for action to prevent physical alteration and destruction of these habitats, including, *inter alia,* coral reef systems. This work is to be carried out by the Executive Secretary and SBSTTA in collaboration with relevant organizations [*decision IV/5, annex, C, operational objective 1.3, paragraph (c)*].

COP guidance

Guidance to Parties

COP 5 encouraged Parties to include mitigation measures in environmental impact assessment (EIA) [*decision V/18, part I, paragraph 2 (b)*]. It also stressed the importance of minimizing risks to biological diversity in its consideration of biological diversity and tourism [*decision V/25, paragraph 4 (b)*].

The COP has urged Parties to take appropriate actions to mitigate impacts upon marine and coastal biological diversity [*decision IV/5, II, paragraph 4*].

The COP has encouraged Parties to develop national strategies, programmes and plans which, *inter alia*, encourage the consideration of introducing necessary measures and/or legislation to encourage appropriate use of and discourage excessive dependence on agro-chemicals with a view to reducing negative impacts on biological diversity [*decision III/11, paragraph 15 (l)*]. It has also urged Parties and Governments to identify ways to address the potential impacts of GURTs on agricultural biological diversity [*decision V/5, paragraph 26*].

References

Guidance to Parties

National action

Decision III/11, paragraph 15 (l) (Agriculture)
Decision IV/5, II, paragraph 4 (Marine and coastal)
Decision V/5, paragraph 26 (Agriculture)
Decision V/18, I, paragraph 2 (b) (Impact assessment, liability and redress)
Decision V/25, paragraph 4 (b) (Biological diversity and tourism)

Financial mechanism and resources

Guidance to the financial mechanism

Decision IV/13, paragraph 4 (Additional guidance to the financial mechanism)

Guidance to the Secretariat

Decision IV/5, annex, C, operational objective 1.3, paragraph (c) (Marine and coastal)
Decision V/4, paragraph 15 (Forest)

Guidance to SBSTTA

Decision IV/5, annex, C, operational objective 1.3, paragraph (c) (Marine and coastal)
Decision V/4, paragraphs 11, 12, 14 (Forest)

Cooperation with other conventions and organizations

Decision IV/5, annex, C, operational objective 1.3, paragraph (c) (Marine and coastal)
Decision V/3, I, paragraph 5 (Marine and coastal)
Decision V/4, paragraphs 11, 15 (Forest)

Relevant aspects of thematic work programmes

Decision III/11, paragraph 15 (l) (Agriculture)
Decision IV/5, II, paragraph 4; annex, C, operational objective 1.3, paragraph (c) (Marine and coastal)
Decision IV/7, annex, paragraph 31 (Forest)
Decision V/3, I, paragraph 5 (coral reefs) (Marine and coastal)
Decision V/4, paragraphs 11, 12, 14, 15; annex, paragraph 2 (b) (ii) (Forest)
Decision V/5, paragraph 26; annex, A paragraph 2 (a), B, Activity 2.3 (Agriculture)

Other relevant decisions

Decision V/6, (Ecosystem approach)
Decision V/8, paragraph 15 (a); annex I, D, Guiding principles 12–15 (Alien species)

Article 9: *Ex-situ* conservation

Each Contracting Party shall, as far as possible and as appropriate, and predominantly for the purpose of complementing *in-situ* measures:

(a) Adopt measures for the *ex-situ* conservation of components of biological diversity, preferably in the country of origin of such components;

(b) Establish and maintain facilities for *ex-situ* conservation of and research on plants, animals and micro-organisms, preferably in the country of origin of genetic resources;

(c) Adopt measures for the recovery and rehabilitation of threatened species and for their reintroduction into their natural habitats under appropriate conditions;

(d) Regulate and manage collection of biological resources from natural habitats for *ex-situ* conservation purposes so as not to threaten ecosystems and *in-situ* populations of species, except where special temporary *ex-situ* measures are required under subparagraph (c) above; and

(e) Cooperate in providing financial and other support for *ex-situ* conservation outlined in subparagraphs (a) to (d) above and in the establishment and maintenance of *ex-situ* conservation facilities in developing countries.

Editors' note:

COP decisions on taxonomy are addressed in the guide to Article 7 earlier in this section of the Handbook. COP decisions relating to access to ex situ *collections not acquired in accordance with the Convention are addressed in the guide to Article 15. See also agricultural biodiversity, in particular references to the State of the World's Plant Genetic Resources for Food and Agriculture. Although the COP has not addressed recovery and rehabilitation of threatened species (Article 9 (c)) in detail, the COP's deliberations regarding Article 8 (f) are relevant here.*

Notes

Terms defined in Article 2

'Biological diversity', 'biological resources', 'country of origin of genetic resources', 'ecosystem', '*ex situ* conservation' and 'habitat'.

Consideration of Article 9 by the COP

Background and status

COP 1 decided to address models and mechanisms for linkages between *in situ* and *ex situ* conservation at COP 4 [*decision I/9*]. However, this item was not considered at the latter meeting. To date, the COP has not specifically considered Article 9 on *ex situ* conservation. Some issues of relevance have nevertheless arisen in its consideration of other items on its agenda. At present, the programme of work adopted by the COP for its sixth and seventh meetings does not provide for the specific consideration of Article 9 [*decision IV/16, paragraph 16, annex II*].

In decision III/10, the COP recommended to Parties that they explore ways to make taxonomic information housed in collections worldwide readily available, in particular, to countries of origin (see also Article 17) [*decision III/10, paragraph 8*]. The COP has subsequently adopted two wide-ranging decisions on taxonomy, which include a number of elements of relevance to *ex situ* collections. Decision IV/1 D and decision V/9 are addressed in the guide to Article 7 earlier in this section of the Handbook.

The COP has initiated an information-gathering exercise as part of its work on access to genetic resources and benefit-sharing, on *ex situ* collections acquired prior to the entry into force of the Convention and not addressed by the Commission on Plant Genetic Resources for Food and Agriculture. COP 5 invited Parties, Governments and other organizations to provide capacity-building and technology development and transfer for the maintenance and utilization of *ex situ* collections [*decision V/26 C, paragraph 4*].

COP welcomed contributions provided by a DIVERSITAS Working Group of Experts containing recommendations on scientific research that should be undertaken for the effective implementation of, *inter alia*, Article 9 of the Convention, and transmitted them to SBSTTA for further consideration and use [*decision IV/1 A, paragraphs 5, 6*].[7]

Responding to a call from organizations housing *ex situ* collections, including the XVI International Botanical Congress for the development of a Global Strategy for Plant Conservation, COP 5 decided to consider at COP 6 a global strategy for plant conservation. To prepare for this matter the COP requested SBSTTA to consider the development of such a strategy [*decision V/10, paragraphs 3, 4*].

References

Relevant aspects of thematic work programmes

Decision III/11, annex 2, paragraph 3 (Agriculture)
Decision IV/4, annex I, paragraph 9 (f) (iv) (Inland water)
Decision V/5, paragraph 26; annex, B, programme element 4, Activity 4.4 (Agriculture)
Decision V/23, annex I, II, part B, paragraph 9; Activity 7 (f) (Dry and sub-humid lands)

Other relevant decisions

Decision III/10, paragraph 8 (Identification, monitoring and assessment)
Decision IV/1 A, paragraphs 5, 6 (Report and recommendations of the third meeting of SBSTTA)
Decision IV/1 D, annex (Taxonomy)
Decision V/10 (Global strategy for plant conservation)
Decision V/26 A, paragraph 11 (Access to genetic resources)
Decision V/26 C, paragraph 4 (*Ex situ* collections)

Documents

UNEP/CBD/COP/4/Inf.18 Recommendations on Scientific Research that should be undertaken to achieve the Implementation of Articles 7, 8, 9, 10 and 14 of the

7 The DIVERSITAS recommendations were contained in document UNEP/CBD/COP/4/Inf.18, and reprinted in *A Programme for Change: Decision from the Fourth Meeting of the Conference of the Parties to the Convention on Biological Diversity* (UNEP, 1998). The DIVERSITAS experts meeting was held in Mexico City in March 1998.

Convention on Biological Diversity, Mexico City, March 1998
UNEP/CBD/COP/5/INF/32 The Gran Canaria Declaration

Article 10: Sustainable use of components of biological diversity

Each Contracting Party shall, as far as possible and as appropriate:

(a) Integrate consideration of the conservation and sustainable use of biological resources into national decision-making;

(b) Adopt measures relating to the use of biological resources to avoid or minimize adverse impacts on biological diversity;

(c) Protect and encourage customary use of biological resources in accordance with traditional cultural practices that are compatible with conservation or sustainable use requirements;

(d) Support local populations to develop and implement remedial action in degraded areas where biological diversity has been reduced; and

(e) Encourage co-operation between its governmental authorities and its private sector in developing methods for sustainable use of biological resources.

Editors' note:

As well as being the subject of Article 10, the sustainable use of the components of biological diversity is also one of the three objectives of the Convention (Article 1). In addition it is referred to either as sustainable use of biological diversity, of the components of biological diversity or of biological resources in Articles 5, 6, 7, 8, 11, 12, 13, 16, 17, 18, 19, 21, 25 and Annex I of the Convention. General references to sustainable use as they pertain to these parts of the Convention are not included here.

The specific provisions of Article 10 are also in each case closely linked to provisions in other articles of the Convention. In particular, Article 10 (a) is closely related to Article 6 (b), Article 10 (b) to Article 8 (i) and Article 8 (l), Article 10 (c) to Article 8 (j), and Article 10 (d) to Article 8 (f). The reader is referred to these for further detail.

Notes

Terms defined in Article 2

'Biological diversity', 'biological resources' and 'sustainable use'.

Consideration of Article 10 by the COP

Background and status

COP 4 decided to consider sustainable use, including tourism at COP 5 [*decision IV/16, annex* II]. COP 5 considered sustainable use as a cross-cutting issue [*decision V/24*] and considered the relationship between biological diversity and tourism within the context of sustainable use [*decision V/25,* see below]. References to sustainable use or sustainable management of biological resources have also been made in each of the thematic work programmes.

COP 5 asked the Executive Secretary to invite organizations involved in sustainable-use initiatives and others to compile and disseminate case studies on best practice and lessons learned from the use of biological diversity under the thematic areas of the Convention. It also asked the Executive Secretary to adapt the process being used to develop the ecosystem approach and apply it to relevant work on sustainable use and to develop appropriate guidance to assist Parties and Governments. The Executive Secretary has been asked to assemble practical principles, operational guidelines and instruments, and guidance specific to sectors and biomes, to assist Parties to achieve sustainable use of biological diversity. A progress report on this is to be submitted to SBSTTA before COP 6 [*decision V/24, paragraphs 1–4*].

COP guidance

COP 5 invited Parties to identify indicators and incentive measures for sectors relevant to the conservation and sustainable use of biodiversity. It also invited Parties to explore mechanisms to involve the private sector and indigenous and local communities in initiatives on the sustainable use of biological diversity. It further invited Parties, Governments and organizations to assist other Parties in capacity-building to implement sustainable-use practices [*decision V/24, paragraphs 4–6*].

The COP has also given guidance to Parties on sustainable management of biological resources in each of the thematic work programmes [for example, *decision IV/4, annex I, paragraph 9 (f); decision II/10, paragraph 3; decision III/11, paragraph 15 (f); decision V/23, annex I, II, part B, Activity 9 (b, c, d)*].

Tourism

The COP decided to consider the relationship between tourism and biological diversity at its fifth meeting. By way of preparation, the COP asked Parties to submit information on sustainable tourism and biological diversity for the Executive Secretary to use as a base for inputs to the Commission on Sustainable Development (CSD) [*decision IV/15, paragraphs 14, 16*].

SBSTTA 4 considered the interlinkages between tourism and biological diversity at length. It prepared an assessment that discussed both the potential benefits of tourism for conservation of biological diversity and sustainable use of its components and its possible adverse impacts. This assessment, with very minor modifications, was adopted by COP 5 as the annex to decision V/25.

The COP also noted that the United Nations General Assembly (UNGA) had proclaimed 2002 as the International Year of Ecotourism and accepted an invitation to participate in the international work programme on sustainable tourism development under the CSD, in particular with a view to contributing to international guidelines on sustainable tourism development in areas important for biological diversity. The COP transmitted its assessment of the interlinkages between biodiversity and tourism to the CSD and recommended to governments, the tourism industry and relevant international organizations, especially the World Trade Organization, that they use the assessment as the basis for their policies, programmes and activities in the field of sustainable tourism [*decision V/25, paragraphs 3, 4*]. It encouraged submission of case studies to enable sharing of knowledge, experience and best practice through the CHM [*decision V/25, paragraph 5*]. The COP also requested the Executive Secretary to convene a workshop to prepare a proposal for the contribution on the international guidelines [*decision V/25, paragraph 2*].

References

Decisions on Article 10

Decision V/24 (Sustainable use)
Decision V/25 (Biological diversity and tourism)

Guidance to Parties

National action

Decision II/10, paragraph 3 (Marine and coastal)
Decision III/11, paragraph 15 (f) (Agriculture)
Decision III/18, paragraph 4 (Incentive measures)
Decision IV/4, annex I, paragraph 9 (f) (Inland water)
Decision V/4, paragraph 10 (Forest)
Decision V/18, I, paragraph 1 (a) (Impact assessment, liability and redress)
Decision V/23, annex I, II, part B, Activity 9 (b, c, d) (Dry and sub-humid lands)
Decision V/24, paragraphs 4–7 (Sustainable use)
Decision V/25, paragraphs 4, 7 (Biological diversity and tourism)

Information and case studies

Decision IV/6, paragraph 6 (Agriculture)
Decision IV/9, paragraphs 10 (c), 15 (Implementation of Article 8 (j) and related provisions)
Decision IV/15, paragraph 14 (Cooperation)
Decision V/23, annex I, II, part B, Activity 9 (b, c, d) and 'Ways and means', (c) (Dry and sub-humid lands)
Decision V/24, paragraph 7 (Sustainable use)
Decision V/25, paragraph 5 (Biological diversity and tourism)

Financial mechanism and resources

Other financial resources

Decision V/24, paragraph 5 (Sustainable use)

Guidance to the Secretariat

Decision III/14, paragraph 10 (Implementation of Article 8 (j))
Decision IV/15, paragraph 16 (Cooperation)
Decision V/21, paragraph 7 (Cooperation)
Decision V/23, annex I, II, part B, Activity 9 (b, c, d) and 'Ways and means' (Dry and sub-humid lands)
Decision V/24, paragraphs 1–3 (Sustainable use)
Decision V/25, paragraphs 2, 6 (Biological diversity and tourism)

Guidance to SBSTTA

Decision IV/1 A, paragraph 6 (Report and recommendations of the third meeting of SBSTTA)
Decision IV/15, paragraph 14 (f) (Cooperation)
Decision V/3, paragraph 13 (Marine and coastal)
Decision V/4, paragraph 14 (Forest)
Decision V/25, paragraphs 5, 6 (Biological diversity and tourism)

Cooperation with other conventions and organizations

Decision I/8, annex (Statement to CSD)
Decision IV/1 A, paragraphs 5, 6 (Report and recommendations of the third meeting of SBSTTA)
Decision IV/15, paragraphs 14, 16 (Cooperation)
Decision V/21, paragraph 7 (Cooperation)
Decision V/23, annex I, II, part B, Activity 9 (b, c, d) (Dry and sub-humid lands)
Decision V/24, paragraphs 1–3, 5, 6 (Sustainable use)
Decision V/25, paragraphs 2–7 (Biological diversity and tourism)

Relevant aspects of thematic work programmes

Decision II/9, annex, paragraphs 8, 12 (Forest – Statement to IPF)
Decision II/10, paragraph 3; annex I, paragraph (vii); annex II, paragraph 4 (Marine and coastal)
Decision III/11, paragraph 15 (f) (Agriculture)
Decision III/12, annex, paragraph (g) (Forest)
Decision IV/4, annex I, paragraphs 9 (f), 17 (Inland water)
Decision IV/5, annex, C, operational objective 2.1 (Marine and coastal)
Decision IV/7, annex (Forest)
Decision V/4, paragraphs 10, 14; annex, paragraph 2 (a), (b) (Forest)
Decision V/5, annex, A, paragraph 3 (a) (Agriculture)
Decision V/23, annex I, II, part B, Activity 9 (b) (c) (d) (Dry and sub-humid lands)

Other relevant decisions

Decision IV/9, paragraph 1 (c); annex, C (Implementation of Article 8 (j) and related provisions)
Decision IV/16, annex II (Institutional matters and programme of work).

Documents

UNEP/CBD/COP/5/INF/13 Tourism and the sustainable use of biological diversity: A survey of ongoing international initiatives
UNEP/CBD/COP/5/INF/35 International Workshop: Case Studies on Sustainable Tourism and Biodiversity
UNEP/CBD/COP/4/Inf.18 Recommendations on Scientific Research that should be Undertaken to Achieve the Implementation of Articles 7, 8, 9, 10 and 14 of the Convention on Biological Diversity, Mexico City, March 1998
UNEP/CBD/COP/4/Inf.21 Biological Diversity and Sustainable Tourism: Preparation of Global Guidelines

UNEP/CBD/COP/5/13 Progress report on the mechanisms for implementation
UNEP/CBD/COP/5/20 Sustainable use, including tourism
UNEP/CBD/SBSTTA/4/11 Development of approaches and practices for the sustainable use of biological resources, including tourism
UNEP/CBD/SBSTTA/4/Inf.9 Sustainable Tourism as a Development Option – Practical Guides for Local Planners, Developers and Decision Makers, Submitted by the German Federal Ministry for Economic Co-operation and Development
UNEP/CBD/SBSTTA/5/13 Sustainable use of the components of biological diversity: identification of sectoral activities that could adopt biodiversity-friendly practices and technologies

Article 11: Incentive measures

> Each Contracting Party shall, as far as possible and as appropriate, adopt economically and socially sound measures that act as incentives for the conservation and sustainable use of components of biological diversity.

Notes

Terms defined in Article 2

'Biological diversity' and 'sustainable use'.

Consideration of Article 11 by the COP

Background and status

The COP has adopted three decisions on incentive measures: decision III/18; decision IV/10 A;[8] and decision V/15. The issue of incentive measures has been closely linked to the question of the economic and other valuation of biological diversity. SBSTTA 2 considered the question of economic valuation of biological diversity, particularly in relation to access to genetic resources [*SBSTTA recommendation II/9*].

In decision III/18, the COP endorsed SBSTTA's recommendation on economic valuation of biological diversity. It also resolved that incentive measures should be integrated into the sectoral and thematic items of its work programme, and requested SBSTTA to provide scientific, technical and technological advice to the COP on the implementation of Article 11 in the relevant thematic areas. In the decisions adopted at its third and fourth meetings, the COP extended its consideration of incentive measures beyond economic valuation of biological diversity to 'market and non-market values of biological diversity' [*decision III/18, paragraph 4*] and 'economic, social, cultural and ethical valuation' [*decision IV/10 A, paragraph 1 (c)*].

8 Decision IV/10, entitled *Measures for Implementing the CBD* is divided into three parts. Parts B and C of decision IV/10 address Article 13 and Article 14, respectively, and are dealt with in the corresponding sections of this Handbook.

COP 3 and COP 4 encouraged Parties, Governments and relevant organizations to submit case studies on the design and implementation of incentive measures. A number of case studies have been submitted to date.[9] The COP has also asked Parties to include information on incentive measures in their second national reports, submitted under Article 26 [*decision IV/10 A, paragraph 2*].

At COP 5, a programme of work on incentive measures was established in order to support Parties in developing practical policies and projects and to develop practical guidelines to the financial mechanism for effective support and prioritization of these policies and projects [*decision V/15, paragraph 1*]. The programme of work is to result in:

(a) The assessment of representative existing incentive measures, review of case studies, identification of new opportunities for incentive measures, and dissemination of information through the CHM and other means.

(b) The development of methods to promote information on biodiversity in consumer decisions.

(c) The assessment, as appropriate, of the values of biodiversity.

(d) A consideration of biodiversity concerns in liability schemes.

(e) The creation of incentives for integration of biodiversity concerns in all sectors.

[*decision V/15, paragraph 2*]

In the first phase of the programme of work the COP requested the Secretariat to gather information on incentives measures (positive and negative) and to elaborate proposals for the design and implementation of incentive measures for consideration by SBSTTA at its sixth or seventh meetings and by COP 6 [*decision V/15, paragraph 3*]. This issue is now due to be considered at SBSTTA 7 in November 2001.

COP guidance

Guidance to Parties

The COP has addressed guidance to the Parties on the design and implementation of incentive measures. For example, Parties have been encouraged to:

- review existing policies to identify and promote incentives for the conservation and sustainable use of components of biological diversity [*decision III/18, paragraph 3*];
- ensure adequate incorporation of market and non-market values of biodiversity into plans, policies and programmes, including national accounting systems and investment strategies [*decision III/18, paragraph 4*];
- develop training and capacity-building programmes and promote private sector initiatives in this area [*decision III/18, paragraph 5*];
- incorporate biodiversity considerations into impact assessments [*decision III/18, paragraph 6*].

9 A number of the case studies can be found on the CHM website and in the following documents: UNEP/CBD/COP/3/Inf.36 and UNEP/CBD/COP/4/18.

COP 4 issued further specific guidance to the Parties (as well as to Governments and relevant organizations), including to:

- promote the design and implementation of appropriate incentive measures;
- identify threats to biological diversity and underlying causes of reduction or loss of biological diversity and relevant actors, as a step in the formulation of incentive measures;
- develop supportive legal and policy frameworks for the design and implementation of incentive measures;
- carry out participatory consultative processes at the relevant level to define incentive measures to address the identified underlying causes of biodiversity reduction or loss and unsustainable use;
- identify perverse incentives and consider the removal or mitigation of their negative effects on biological diversity; and
- undertake value addition and enhancement of naturally occurring genetic resources, based on the participatory approach.

  [*decision IV/10 A, paragraph 1*]

The COP has also adopted specific guidance to Parties relating to incentive measures on a wide range of matters including: the thematic work programmes (see, for example, inland waters *decision IV/4, annex I, paragraph 9 (f), (m)* and agriculture *decision III/11, paragraph 15 (b), (c), (d)* respectively).

The COP has recommended that in relation to Articles 6 and 8 consideration should be given to ways to suppress and mitigate perverse or negative incentives having a deleterious effect on biodiversity [*decision III/9, paragraph 9 (b)*].

Parties have also been urged to explore ways and means by which incentive measures promoted through the 1997 Kyoto Protocol on Climate Change can support the objectives of the Convention [*decision V/15, paragraph 6*].

Financial mechanism and resources

Incentive measures were identified as a programme priority for the financial mechanism at COP 1 [*decision I/2, annex I, III, paragraph 4 (i)*]. Decision III/5 reconfirmed the importance of the GEF's support for incentive measures [*decision III/5, paragraph 3*]. The request to the financial mechanism to provide support for the implementation of incentive measures (including the capacity-building necessary for their design and implementation) was reiterated at COP 4 and COP 5 [*decision IV/13, paragraph 7; decision V/13, paragraph 2 (h)*].

References

Decisions on Article 11

Decision III/18 (see also SBSTTA recommendation II/9) (Incentive measures)
Decision IV/10 A (Incentive measures)
Decision V/15 (Incentive measures)

Guidance to Parties

National action

Decision III/11, paragraph 15 (b), (c), (d) (Agriculture)
Decision III/18, paragraphs 1 (see also SBSTTA recommendation II/9, paragraph 3), 3–6 (Incentive measures)
Decision IV/4, annex I, paragraph 9 (f), (m) (Inland water)
Decision IV/10 A, paragraph 1 (Incentive measures)
Decision V/4, paragraph 13 (Forest)
Decision V/6, annex, B, Principle 4; annex, C, paragraph 9 (Ecosystem approach)
Decision V/11, paragraph 16 (Additional financial resources)
Decision V/15, paragraph 6 (Incentive measures)
Decision V/24, paragraph 4 (Sustainable use)
Decision V/25, paragraph 4 (a), (d), (g) (Biological diversity and tourism)

Information and case studies

Decision III/14, paragraphs 2, 3 (Implementation of Article 8 (j))
Decision III/18, paragraph 7 (Incentive measures)
Decision IV/6, paragraph 6 (Agriculture)
Decision IV/10 A, paragraphs 1 (g), 2 (Incentive measures)
Decision IV/10 C, paragraph 1 (f) (Impact assessment and minimizing adverse effects)
Decision V/24, paragraph 7 (Sustainable use)

Financial mechanism and resources

Guidance to the financial mechanism

Decision I/2, annex I, paragraph 4 (i) (Financial mechanism and resources)
Decision III/5, paragraph 3 (Additional guidance to the financial mechanism)
Decision IV/8, paragraph 4 (b) (Access and benefit-sharing)
Decision IV/10 A, paragraph 3 (Incentive measures)
Decision IV/13, paragraph 7, 8 (b) (Additional guidance to the financial mechanism)
Decision V/13, paragraph 2 (h) (Further guidance to the financial mechanism)

Other financial resources

Decision V/11, paragraph 16 (Additional financial resources)

Guidance to the Secretariat

Decision III/14, paragraph 10 (Implementation of Article 8 (j))
Decision III/18, paragraphs 7–9 (Incentive measures)
Decision IV/10 A, paragraph 5 (Incentive measures)
Decision V/15, paragraphs 3, 5 (Incentive measures)

Guidance to SBSTTA

Decision III/18, paragraph 10 (Incentive measures)
Decision IV/4, annex I, paragraph 8 (d) (Inland water)
Decision V/3, paragraph 13 (Marine and coastal)
Decision V/15, paragraph 3 (c) (Incentive measures)

Cooperation with other conventions and organizations

Decision III/18, paragraph 9 (Incentive measures)
Decision IV/6, paragraph 6 (Agriculture)
Decision IV/10 A, paragraphs 4, 5 (b) (Incentive measures)
Decision V/15, paragraphs 3, 5, 6 (Incentive measures)
Decision V/21, paragraph 3 (Cooperation)

Relevant aspects of thematic work programmes

Decision II/10, annex I, paragraph (vii) (Marine and coastal)
Decision III/11, paragraph 15 (b), (c), (d) (Agriculture)
Decision IV/4, annex I, paragraphs 8 (d), 9 (f), (m) (Inland water)
Decision IV/5, annex, C, operational objective 3.2, Activity (c) (Marine and coastal)
Decision IV/6, paragraph 6 (Agriculture)
Decision IV/7, annex, paragraph 56 (Forest)
Decision V/3, paragraph 13 (Marine and coastal)
Decision V/4, paragraph 13 (Forest)
Decision V/5, paragraphs 5, 15 (c); annex, B, programme element 2, Activity 2.2 (c); programme element 3, Activity 3.4 (Agriculture)
Decision V/23, annex I, II, part B, paragraph 11; Activity 7 (g), Activity 9 (Dry and sub-humid lands)

Other relevant decisions

Decision III/9, paragraph 9 (b) (Implementation of Articles 6 and 8)
Decision IV/8, annex, paragraph 6 (Access and benefit-sharing)
Decision V/16, annex, III, element 3, task 14 (Article 8 (j) and related provisions)
Decision V/26 A, paragraph 12 (Access to genetic resources)

Documents

UNEP/CBD/COP/3/24 Sharing of experiences on incentive measures for conservation and sustainable use
UNEP/CBD/COP/4/18 Design and implementation of incentive measures
UNEP/CBD/COP/4/Inf.25 Benefit Sharing Case Studies: *Aristocladus korupensis* and *Prunus africana* (submission by UNEP)
UNEP/CBD/COP/5/13 Progress report on the mechanisms for implementation
UNEP/CBD/COP/5/15 Further analysis of the design and implementation of incentive measures
UNEP/CBD/SBSTTA/2/13 Economic valuation of biological diversity
UNEP/CBD/SBSTTA/3/Inf.17 Incentive measures to promote the conservation and the sustainable use of biodiversity: A framework for case studies (OCDE/GD(97)125, submitted by OECD)

Article 12: Research and training

> The Contracting Parties, taking into account the special needs of developing countries, shall:
>
> (a) Establish and maintain programmes for scientific and technical education and training in measures for the identification, conservation and sustainable use of biological diversity and its components and provide support for such education and training for the specific needs of developing countries;
>
> (b) Promote and encourage research which contributes to the conservation and sustainable use of biological diversity, particularly in developing countries, *inter alia*, in accordance with decisions of the Conference of the Parties taken in consequence of recommendations of the Subsidiary Body on Scientific, Technical and Technological Advice; and
>
> (c) In keeping with the provisions of Articles 16, 18 and 20, promote and cooperate in the use of scientific advances in biological diversity research in developing methods for conservation and sustainable use of biological resources.

Notes

Terms defined in Article 2

'Biological diversity', 'biological resources', and 'sustainable use'.

Consideration of Article 12 by the COP

The COP has not so far addressed the issue of research and training under Article 12 as a separate agenda item. However, references to research and training are included in numerous COP decisions. A preliminary attempt has been made to list these references below. Readers should also refer to the guides to Articles 13, 16 and 18, below in this section of the Handbook.

A DIVERSITAS group of experts put forward at COP 4 a set of recommendations on scientific research that should be undertaken for the effective implementation of Articles 7, 8, 9, 10 and 14 of the Convention.[10] The COP welcomed this contribution and decided to transmit the recommendations to SBSTTA for further consideration [*decision IV/1 A, paragraphs 5, 6*].

References

Relevant aspects of thematic work programmes

Research

Decision II/9, annex, paragraph 15 (Forest – Statement to IPF)

10 UNEP/CBD/COP/4/Inf.18.

Decision II/10, annex I, paragraph (v) (Marine and coastal)
Decision III/11, paragraph 15, (i), (j), (k) (Agriculture)
Decision III/12, paragraphs 5, 6, 9, 10, annex (Forest)
Decision IV/4, paragraph 7 (c), annex I, paragraph 1, 9 (d), (m) (iv) (Inland water)
Decision IV/5, annex, B, paragraph 5; C, operational objectives 1.3, 3.1, 3.2 (Marine and coastal)
Decision IV/7, annex, paragraphs1, 2, 11–56 (Forest)
Decision V/3, paragraph 6 (f); annex, A, B (Marine and coastal)
Decision V/4, annex, paragraph 1 (Forest)
Decision V/5, paragraph 25; annex, B, programme element 3.1 (Agriculture)
Decision V/23, annex I, II, part A, paragraph 7 (b); B, Activity 7 (k) (Dry and sub-humid lands)

Training

Decision II/9, annex, paragraph 15 (Forest – Statement to IPF)
Decision IV/5, annex, C, Operational objective 1.3 (Marine and coastal)
Decision V/5, annex, B, programme element 2.2 (c) (vi). 3.1 (Agriculture)
Decision V/23, annex I, II, part B, Activity 7 (i) (Dry and sub-humid lands)

Other relevant decisions

Research

Decision II/3, paragraph 5 (a) (Clearing-house mechanism)
Decision III/5, paragraph 6 (a) (Additional guidance to the financial mechanism)
Decision III/15, paragraph 1 (c) (Access to genetic resources)
Decision IV/1 A, paragraphs 5, 6 (Report and recommendations of the third meeting of SBSTTA)
Decision IV/1 D, annex, paragraph 11 (d) (Taxonomy)
Decision IV/8, paragraph 4 (d) (Access and benefit-sharing)
Decision IV/10 A, paragraph 4 (b) (Incentive measures)
Decision IV/13, paragraph 8 (d) (Additional guidance to the financial mechanism)
Decision IV/14, annex, paragraph 3 (National reports)
Decision IV/16, annex I, paragraph 15 (Institutional matters and programme of work)
Decision V/8, annex I, A, Guiding principle 5 (Alien species)
Decision V/14, annex I, paragraph (g) (iii) (Clearing-house mechanism)

Training

Decision II/3, paragraph 5 (a) (i), (c) (Clearing-house mechanism)
Decision III/5, paragraph 2 (d) (i) (Additional guidance to the financial mechanism)
Decision III/18, paragraph 5 (Incentive measures)
Decision IV/1 D, paragraph 7, annex, paragraphs 3, 5, 11 (Taxonomy)
Decision IV/2, paragraph 9 (c), 10 (b) (Clearing-house mechanism)
Decision IV/10 B, paragraph 6 (Public education and awareness)
Decision IV/13, paragraph 5 (b) (Additional guidance to the financial mechanism)
Decision V/7, paragraph 4 (a) (Identification, monitoring and assessment, and indicators)
Decision V/8, annex I, B, Guiding principle 9 (c) (Alien species)
Decision V/14, annex I, paragraph (g) (v) (Clearing-house mechanism)
Decision V/18 I, paragraph 1 (e) (Impact assessment, liability and redress)
Decision V/25, paragraph 4 (f) (Biological diversity and tourism)

Article 13: Public education and awareness

The Contracting Parties shall:

(a) Promote and encourage understanding of the importance of, and the measures required for, the conservation of biological diversity, as well as its propagation through media, and the inclusion of these topics in educational programmes; and

(b) Cooperate, as appropriate, with other States and international organizations in developing educational and public awareness programmes, with respect to conservation and sustainable use of biological diversity.

Notes

Terms defined in Article 2

'Biological diversity' and 'sustainable use'.

Consideration of Article 13 by the COP

Background and status

The COP addressed Article 13 for the first time at its fourth meeting, under the agenda item Measures for Implementing the Convention. Public education and awareness is addressed in decision IV/10 B[11] and subsequently in decision V/17.

COP 4 decided that public education and awareness issues will be integrated into and become an integral component of all sectoral and thematic items under the programme of work of the Convention [*decision IV/10 B, paragraph 5*]. This approach was reiterated at COP 5 [*decision V/17, paragraph 5*].

COP 4 invited UNESCO to consider launching a global initiative on biodiversity education, training and public awareness, and requested the Executive Secretary to explore the feasibility of such an initiative and report to COP 5 on progress [*decision IV/10 B, paragraph 6*]. COP 5 requested the Executive Secretary, in cooperation with UNESCO, to convene a Consultative Working Group of Experts to identify priority activities for the proposed global initiative on biological diversity education and public awareness. The Working Group is to take into account priorities developed by the COP and priorities identified in the Strategic Plan which is to be prepared for the Convention.[12] The first meeting of the CBD/UNESCO Consultative Working Group of Experts was held in Paris, France in July 2000. The report of that meeting is document UNEP/CBD/GEEPA/1/3. The second meeting was held in November 2000 in Bergen, Norway. The report of that meeting is document UNEP/CBD/GEEPA/2/3. The Executive Secretary is to report to COP 6 on progress in developing the global initiative [*decision V/17, paragraph 7 (d)*].

11 Parts A and C of decision IV/10 address Article 11 and Article 14 respectively, and are dealt with in the corresponding sections of this Handbook.
12 See the guide to Article 23 in this section of the Handbook.

COP guidance

The COP has urged Parties to place special emphasis on Article 13 in the development of their national strategies and action plans. It has also urged Parties to:

- promote education on biodiversity through relevant institutions including NGOs;
- allocate resources for the use of education and communication instruments;
- allocate appropriate resources for the strategic use of education and communication instruments at each phase of policy formulation, planning, implementation and evaluation;
- integrate biodiversity concerns into education strategies; and
- support relevant initiatives by major groups which foster stakeholder participation in biodiversity conservation and sustainable use.

  [*decision IV/10 B, paragraph 1*]

The COP has encouraged Parties to make use of the media to promote public education and awareness about the importance of and appropriate methods for the conservation and sustainable use of biodiversity. Where necessary, provisions of the Convention should be illustrated and translated into local languages [*decision IV/10 B, paragraphs 3, 4*].

The COP has recognized the importance of public awareness and education in relation to each of the thematic work programmes and has urged Parties to strengthen education and awareness programmes in relation to agricultural biological diversity, inland water biological diversity and marine and coastal biological diversity. Although the COP has noted that the implementation of forest conservation and sustainable use policies depends, *inter alia*, on the level of public awareness and policies outside the forest sector [*decision III/12, preamble*], and that attention needs to be paid to the further raising of public awareness and the understanding of the importance of biological diversity through educational programmes and information [*decision III/19, paragraph 24 (a)*], public awareness and education does not appear to be explicitly addressed in the work programme on forest biological diversity adopted in decision IV/7 of the COP.

In relation to Article 8 (j) and related provisions, the COP has urged Parties, *inter alia,* to use means of communication other than internet, including newspapers, bulletins and radio, and increasing the use of local languages [*decision V/16, paragraph 12 (e)*].

Parties have been urged by the COP to propose projects to the financial mechanism which promote measures for implementing Article 13 [*decision IV/10 B, paragraph* 9].

References

Decisions on Article 13

Decision IV/10 B (Public education and awareness)
Decision V/17 (Education and public awareness)

Guidance to Parties

National action

Decision III/11, paragraph 13 (Agriculture)

Decision IV/4, annex I, paragraph 9 (i) (Inland water)
Decision IV/10 B, paragraphs 1, 3, 4, 8, 9 (Public education and awareness)
Decision V/3, I, paragraph 6 (c) (Marine and coastal)
Decision V/5, paragraph 10; annex, B, Programe element 3, Activity 3.5; Programme element 4, Activity 4.3 (Agriculture)
Decision V/8, paragraph 9; annex I, A, Guiding principle 6 (Alien species)
Decision V/14, annex I, paragraph (i) (Clearing-house mechanism)
Decision V/16, paragraph 12 (e) (Article 8 (j) and related provisions)
Decision V/17, paragraph 6 (Education and public awareness)
Decision V/18, I, paragraph 1 (e) (Impact assessment, liability and redress)
Decision V/25, paragraph 4 (f) (Biological diversity and tourism)

Information and case studies

Decision IV/10 B, paragraph 2 (Public education and awareness)

Financial mechanism and resources

Guidance to the financial mechanism

Decision IV/10 B, paragraph 9 (Public education and awareness)
Decision V/13, paragraph 2 (l) (Further guidance to the financial mechanism)

Other financial resources

Decision IV/10 B, paragraph 8 (Public education and awareness)

Guidance to the Secretariat

Decision IV/5, annex, C, operational objectives 1.2 (g), 3.2 (d) (Marine and coastal)
Decision IV/10 B, paragraph 6 (Public education and awareness)
Decision V/17, paragraphs 2, 7 (Education and public awareness)
Decision V/21, paragraphs 7-9 (Cooperation)

Cooperation with other conventions and organizations

Decision II/9, annex, paragraph 14 (Forest – Statement to IPF)
Decision IV/10 B, paragraphs 6, 7 (Public education and awareness)
Decision V/17, paragraphs 2, 4 (Education and public awareness)
Decision V/21, paragraph 7, 9 (Coöperation)

Relevant aspects of thematic work programmes

Decision II/9, annex, paragraph 14 (Forest – Statement to IPF)
Decision III/11, paragraph 13 (Agriculture)
Decision IV/4, annex I, paragraph 9 (i) (Inland water)
Decision IV/5, annex, C, operational objectives 1.2 (g), 3.2 (d) (Marine and coastal)
Decision IV/7, annex, paragraph 29 (Forest)
Decision V/2, paragraph 8 (Inland water)
Decision V/3, I, paragraph 6 (c); annex, B (Marine and coastal)
Decision V/5, paragraph 10; annex, B, programme elements 3.5; 4.3 (Agriculture)
Decision V/23, annex I, II, part B, Activity 7 (i) (Dry and sub-humid lands)

Other relevant decisions

Decision III/19, annex, paragraph 24 (a) (Statement to UNGA Special Session)

Documents

UNEP/CBD/COP/4/19 Public education and awareness: implementation of Article 13
UNEP/CBD/COP/4/Inf.15 Education, Training and Public Awareness on Biological Diversity – An additional contribution by UNESCO on Agenda Item 15.2
UNEP/CBD/COP/5/13 Progress report on the mechanisms for implementation
UNEP/CBD/GEEPA/1/1 Report of the CBD-UNESCO Consultative Group of Experts on Biological Diversity Education and Public Awareness on the Work of its First Meeting

Article 14: Impact assessment and minimizing adverse impacts

1. Each Contracting Party, as far as possible and as appropriate, shall:

(a) Introduce appropriate procedures requiring environmental impact assessment of its proposed projects that are likely to have significant adverse effects on biological diversity with a view to avoiding or minimizing such effects and, where appropriate, allow for public participation in such procedures;

(b) Introduce appropriate arrangements to ensure that the environmental consequences of its programmes and policies that are likely to have significant adverse impacts on biological diversity are duly taken into account;

(c) Promote, on the basis of reciprocity, notification, exchange of information and consultation on activities under their jurisdiction or control which are likely to significantly affect adversely the biological diversity of other States or areas beyond the limits of national jurisdiction, by encouraging the conclusion of bilateral, regional or multilateral arrangements, as appropriate;

(d) In the case of imminent or grave danger or damage, originating under its jurisdiction or control, to biological diversity within the area under jurisdiction of other States or in areas beyond the limits of national jurisdiction, notify immediately the potentially affected States of such danger or damage, as well as initiate action to prevent or minimize such danger or damage; and

(e) Promote national arrangements for emergency responses to activities or events, whether caused naturally or otherwise, which present a grave and imminent danger to biological diversity and encourage international cooperation to supplement such national efforts and, where appropriate and agreed by the States or regional economic integration organizations concerned, to establish joint contingency plans.

2. The Conference of the Parties shall examine, on the basis of studies to be carried out, the issue of liability and redress, including restoration and compensation, for damage to biological diversity, except where such liability is a purely internal matter.

Editors' note:

The notes below address Article 14 (1) and Article 14 (2) separately. Article 14 (1) is related to Articles 7 (c), 8 (l) and 10 (b). COP decisions explicitly addressing Article 14 (1) are considered below, along with other decisions that address procedures for EIA of projects, policies and programmes. Decisions regarding scientific assessment for the COP or other bodies of the Convention are addressed in the guide to Article 7.

Identification by Parties of processes and categories of activities that have or are likely to have significant adverse impacts on the conservation and sustainable use of biological diversity is addressed in the guide to Article 7 (c). The management and regulation by Parties of such activities, once identified, are addressed in the guide to Article 8 (l). The adoption of measures relating to use of biological resources to avoid or minimize adverse impacts on biological diversity is addressed in the guide to Article 10 (b). Readers should therefore also refer to guidance on these articles above in this section of the Handbook.

Notes

Terms defined in Article 2

'Biological diversity' and 'regional economic integration organization'.

Consideration of Article 14 by the COP

Background and status

The COP has adopted two decisions on Article 14: decision IV/10 C[13] and decision V/18. Relevant references in other decisions relate principally to Article 14 (1). Article 14 (1), which contains provisions on impact assessment, is addressed below, followed by Article 14 (2) on liability and redress for damage to biological diversity.

Impact assessment (Article 14 (1))

Background and status

COP 4 asked for information on:

- Impact assessments that consider environmental effects and interrelated socio-economic aspects relevant to biological diversity.
- Strategic environmental assessments.
- Reports relating to existing legislation on EIA.
- Reports and case studies relating to EIA in the thematic areas, including in respect of activities with transboundary implications.

  [*decision IV/10 C, paragraph 1*]

The COP requested the Secretariat to prepare a synthesis report based on these submissions for the consideration of SBSTTA [*decision IV/10 C, paragraph 2*]. It also asked

13 Decision IV/10, which is divided into three parts, is entitled *Measures for Implementing the CBD*. Part A of Decision IV/10 is on incentive measures and Part B on public awareness.

SBSTTA to identify actions to promote implementation of Article 14 and to consider whether there was a need to develop guidelines on the incorporation of biodiversity considerations into EIA. SBSTTA 4 considered this issue and submitted recommendation IV/6 to COP 5. COP 5 requested SBSTTA to develop guidelines for incorporating biodiversity-related issues in legislation and/or processes on strategic EIA with a view to completing this work by COP 6 [*decision V/18, paragraph 4*]. This issue will be considered at SBSTTA 7.

COP 5 also reiterated the call for information and case studies on impact assessment, and requested the Executive Secretary to disseminate case studies and existing guidelines, procedures and provisions for EIA through, *inter alia*, the CHM [*decision V/18, paragraphs 3, 5*].

The COP has recommended that appropriate issues related to EIA should be integrated into, and become an integral component of, relevant sectoral and thematic items under its programme of work [*decision IV/10 C, paragraph 4*].

COP guidance

COP 5 invited Parties, Governments and other organizations to take certain actions at the national level to address biodiversity concerns in EIA [*decision V/18, paragraph 1*]. The COP has also emphasized the need to ensure involvement of interested and affected stakeholders in all stages of the assessment process, including indigenous and local communities embodying traditional lifestyles and NGOs [*decision IV/10 C, paragraph 7; decision V/18, paragraph 1 (d)*]. Parties have also been encouraged to assess not only impacts of individual projects, but also their cumulative and global effects through strategic environmental assessment, incorporating biodiversity considerations at the decision-making and/or environmental planning level [*decision V/18, paragraph 2 (a)*].

Guidance to Parties related to EIAs has been included in the work programmes on inland water biological diversity and agricultural biological diversity [*decision IV/4, annex I, paragraph 9 (g); decision III/11, paragraphs 9, 15 (g)*]. As part of the marine and coastal biodiversity work programme the consequences of mariculture for marine and coastal biodiversity will be assessed and techniques to minimize adverse impacts promoted [*decision IV/5, annex, programme element 4*]. Another element of the work programme on marine and coastal biological diversity is to achieve better understanding of the causes of introduction of alien species and genotypes and the impacts of such introductions on biological diversity [*decision IV/5, annex, programme element 5, operational objective 5.1*]. The work programme on forest biological diversity, adopted at COP 4, includes reference to some activities of relevance to Article 14 (1). For example, the work programme is to promote activities to assemble management experiences and information to provide for the sharing of approaches and tools that lead to improved forest practices with regard to forest biological diversity [*decision IV/7, annex, paragraph 30*].

Liability and redress (Article 14 (2))

Background and status

COP 4 invited submissions on national and international measures on: liability and redress applicable to damage to biodiversity; and information on experiences in implementation, as well as information on access by foreign citizens to national courts in cases of transboundary harm [*decision IV/10 C, paragraph 8*]. At the request of the COP the Secretariat prepared a synthesis report based on these submissions for COP 5 [see document UNEP/CBD/COP/5/16, *decision IV/10 C, paragraph 10*].

The call for information was renewed at COP 5, and the Secretariat was asked to update the synthesis report, based on submissions as well as developments in other international fora [*decision V/18, paragraphs 6, 7*]. At COP 5 France offered to organize a workshop on liability and redress in the context of the Convention. This workshop was held on 13–15 July 2001 in Paris. COP 6 is due to consider a process for reviewing Article 14 (2), including the establishment of an ad hoc technical expert group, taking into account the outcome of the workshop and the consideration of these issues within the framework of the Cartagena Protocol on Biosafety[14] [*decision V/18, paragraph 9*].

References

Decisions on Article 14

Decision IV/10 C (Impact assessment and minimizing adverse effects)
Decision V/18 (Impact assessment, liability and redress)

Guidance to Parties

National action

Decision III/11, paragraphs 9, 15 (g) (Agriculture)
Decision III/18, paragraph 6 (Incentive measures)
Decision IV/4, annex I, paragraph 9 (e), (g) (Inland water)
Decision V/5, paragraph 23 (Agriculture)
Decision V/8, annex I, Guiding principles 7, 10, 11 (Alien species)
Decision V/18, paragraphs 1, 2 (Impact assessment, liability and redress)
Decision V/25, paragraph 4 (g) (Biological diversity and tourism)

Information and case studies

Decision IV/10 C, paragraphs 1, 8 (Impact assessment and minimizing adverse effects)
Decision V/18, paragraphs 3, 6 (Impact assessment, liability and redress)

Guidance to the Secretariat

Decision IV/10 C, paragraphs 2, 5, 6, 10 (Impact assessment and minimizing adverse effects)
Decision V/18, paragraphs 5, 7 (Impact assessment, liability and redress)

Guidance to SBSTTA

Decision IV/4, annex I, paragraph 8 (c) (iii) (Inland water)
Decision IV/5, annex, programme element 4 (Marine and coastal)
Decision IV/10 C, paragraph 3 (Impact assessment and minimizing adverse effects)
Decision V/2, paragraph 5 (Inland water)
Decision V/18, paragraph 4 (Impact assessment, liability and redress)

Cooperation with other conventions and organizations

Decision II/9, annex, paragraph 10 (Forest – Statement to IPF)
Decision IV/10 C, paragraph 6 (Impact assessment and minimizing adverse effects)

14 See Article 27, Cartagena Protocol on Biosafety.

Decision V/8, paragraph 10 (Alien species)
Decision V/18, paragraph 4 (Impact assessment, liability and redress)

Relevant aspects of thematic work programmes

Decision II/9, annex, paragraph 10 (Forest – Statement to IPF)
Decision III/11, paragraphs 9, 15 (g) (Agriculture)
Decision IV/4, annex I, paragraphs 8 (c) (iii), 9 (e), (g) and 20 (Inland water)
Decision IV/5, annex, programme element 4 (Marine and coastal)
Decision IV/7, annex, paragraphs 30, 31, 51 (Forest)
Decision V/2, paragraph 5 (Inland water)
Decision V/5, paragraph 23; annex, B paragraph 2.2 (b) (Agriculture)

Other relevant decisions

Decision IV/1 A, paragraph 5 (Report and recommendations of the third meeting of SBSTTA)
Decision V/15, paragraph 2 (d) (Incentive measures) (Article 14 (2))
Decision V/16, annex, II, element 6, task 9; annex, III, element 3, task 13 (Article 8 (j) and related provisions)

Declarations

India (adoption) and USA (adoption)

Documents

UNEP/CBD/COP/4/20 Impact assessment and minimizing adverse effects: implementation of Article 14
UNEP/CBD/COP/4/Inf.18 Recommendations on Scientific Research that should be Undertaken to Achieve the Implementation of Articles 7, 8, 9, 10 and 14 of the Convention on Biological Diversity, Mexico City, March 1998
UNEP/CBD/COP/5/13 Progress report on the mechanisms for implementation
UNEP/CBD/COP/5/16 Impact Assessment, Liability, and Redress (Article 14)
UNEP/CBD/SBSTTA/4/10 Synthesis of reports and case-studies relating to environmental impact assessment

Article 15: Access to genetic resources

1. Recognizing the sovereign rights of States over their natural resources, the authority to determine access to genetic resources rests with the national governments and is subject to national legislation.
2. Each Contracting Party shall endeavour to create conditions to facilitate access to genetic resources for environmentally sound uses by other Contracting Parties and not to impose restrictions that run counter to the objectives of this Convention.
3. For the purpose of this Convention, the genetic resources being provided by a Contracting Party, as referred to in this Article and Articles 16 and 19, are only

those that are provided by Contracting Parties that are countries of origin of such resources or by the Parties that have acquired the genetic resources in accordance with this Convention.

4. Access, where granted, shall be on mutually agreed terms and subject to the provisions of this Article.

5. Access to genetic resources shall be subject to prior informed consent of the Contracting Party providing such resources, unless otherwise determined by that party.

6. Each Contracting Party shall endeavour to develop and carry out scientific research based on genetic resources provided by other Contracting Parties with the full participation of, and where possible in, such Contracting Parties.

7. Each Contracting Party shall take legislative, administrative or policy measures, as appropriate, and in accordance with Articles 16 and 19 and, where necessary, through the financial mechanism established by Articles 20 and 21 with the aim of sharing in a fair and equitable way the results of research and development and the benefits arising from the commercial and other utilization of genetic resources with the Contracting Party providing such resources. Such sharing shall be upon mutually agreed terms.

Editors' note:

The COP's consideration of Article 15 is closely linked to its consideration of a number of other issues, in particular Articles 8 (j), 11, 16, 17, 18 and 19, and also to the thematic work programmes, particularly that on agricultural biological diversity. Reference should therefore also be made to the guides on these articles and themes elsewhere in this section of the Handbook.

Notes

Terms defined in Article 2

'Country of origin of genetic resources', 'country providing genetic resources', 'genetic material' and 'genetic resources'.

The COP has reaffirmed that human genetic resources are not included within the framework of the Convention [*Decision II/11, paragraph 2*].

Consideration of Article 15 by the COP

Background and status

COP 1 decided to address the question of access to genetic resources at COP 2 and COP 3, and the question of benefit-sharing at COP 4. It also decided to consider the Convention's relationship with the FAO Global System for Plant Genetic Resources for Food and Agriculture at COP 2 [*decision I/9*]. At COP 4, a programme of work for COP 5 to COP 7 was adopted, under which access to genetic resources would be addressed at COP 5, and benefit-sharing at COP 6 [*decision IV/16*].

To date, the COP has adopted four decisions specifically on access to genetic resources: decisions II/11, III/15, IV/8 and V/26. In addition, a number of decisions have been adopted relating to the FAO Global System for the Conservation of Plant Genetic Resources for Food and Agriculture.

The initial focus of the COP in relation to Article 15 was on promoting the development of relevant measures, gathering information on national and regional approaches to regulating access to genetic resources, and disseminating this information. Thus, the COP has called on Parties to submit information on national legislative, administrative and policy measures to implement Article 15 to the CBD Secretariat [*decisions II/11, paragraph 3 and III/15, paragraph 1*] and requested the Executive Secretary to compile surveys and summaries of this information [*decisions II/11, III/15 and IV/8*].[15] COP 5 noted that there is a particular need for more information regarding:

- User institutions.
- The market for genetic resources.
- Non-monetary benefits.
- New and emerging mechanisms for benefit-sharing.
- Incentive measures.
- Clarification of definitions.
- *Sui generis* systems.
- 'Intermediaries'.

[*decision V/26 A, paragraph 12*]

COP 4 decided to establish a panel of experts to develop a common understanding of basic concepts and to explore all options for access and benefit-sharing on mutually agreed terms, including guiding principles, guidelines, and codes of best practice for access and benefit-sharing arrangements [*decision IV/8, paragraph 3*].

The first meeting of the Panel of Experts on Access and Benefit-sharing was held in October 1999. The Inter-sessional Meeting on the Operations of the Convention (ISOC) in June 1999 considered options for access and benefit-sharing mechanisms and made recommendations for future work as well and provided some preliminary advice to guide the work of the Panel [*decision IV/8, paragraph 1*]. COP 5 considered both the report of the Panel (contained in document UNEP/CBD/COP/5/8) and recommendations 2, 3 and 4 of ISOC. It decided to reconvene the Panel to conduct further work on outstanding issues from COP 1, especially:

(a) Assessment of user and provider experience in access to genetic resources and benefit-sharing and study of complementary options.

(b) Identification of approaches to involvement of stakeholders in access to genetic resources and benefit-sharing processes.

[*decision V/26 A, paragraph 10*]

15 These surveys are contained in documents UNEP/CBD/COP/2/13; UNEP/CBD/COP/3/20; UNEP/CBD/COP/4/21; UNEP/CBD/COP/4/22; UNEP/CBD/COP/4/23; and UNEP/CBD/COP/4/Inf.7. Copies of case studies are also available on the CHM website.

COP 5 also decided to establish an Ad Hoc Open-ended Working Group on Access and Benefit-sharing to develop guidelines and other approaches for consideration by COP 6, and to assist Parties and stakeholders in addressing a list of elements relevant to access and benefit-sharing. The elements listed are: terms for prior informed consent and mutually agreed terms; roles, responsibilities and participation of stakeholders; relevant aspects relating to *in situ* and *ex situ* conservation and sustainable use; mechanisms for benefit-sharing, for example through technology transfer and joint research and development; and means to ensure the respect, preservation and maintenance of knowledge, innovations and practices of indigenous and local communities. The Working Group is open to all stakeholders [*decision V/26 A, paragraph 11*].

The Panel held its second meeting in March 2001 in Montreal. The first meeting of the Working Group will be held in Bonn, Germany, in October 2001.

The Ad Hoc Open-ended Inter-sessional Working Group on the implementation of Article 8 (j) and related provisions, established under decision IV/9, will also consider issues of relevance to access to genetic resources from the perspective of Article 8 (j) [*decision IV/9, annex; decision V/16, annex;* see the guide to Article 8 (j) in this section of the Handbook]. For example, at its first meeting the Working Group reaffirmed the importance of *sui generis* systems. The Working Group is due to meet for the second time in February 2002.

The COP has acknowledged that there are close links between provisions of the Convention on access and benefit-sharing and the WTO in particular with respect to IPRs and benefit-sharing. The COP has requested the Executive Secretary to cooperate with the WTO through the WTO's Committee on Trade and Environment to explore the extent to which there may be linkages between Article 15 and relevant articles of the TRIPs Agreement[16] [*decision III/15, paragraph 8*]. It has also emphasized that further work is needed to help develop a common appreciation of the relationship between the TRIPs Agreement and the Convention with regard to, *inter alia*, the fair and equitable sharing of benefits arising out of the use of genetic resources [*decision III/17, paragraph 8; decision IV/15, paragraph 10 and decision V/26 B*]. The COP's consideration of this issue is addressed in the guide to Article 16 in this section of the Handbook.

COP 2 requested the Secretariat to consult with the United Nations Office for Ocean Affairs and the Law of the Sea to undertake a study on the relationship between the Convention and the United Nations Convention on the Law of the Sea with regard to the conservation and sustainable use of genetic resources on the deep seabed. The study was prepared for SBSTTA with a view to it considering the scientific, technical and technological issues relating to bioprospecting of genetic resources on the deep seabed [*decision II/10, paragraph 12*]. An information document (UNEP/CBD/COP/5/Inf.7) was prepared by the Executive Secretary, and COP 5 requested SBSTTA to analyse and provide advice on scientific, technical and technological matters related to the issue of marine and coastal genetic resources [*decision V/3, paragraph 12*].

Issues of access to genetic resources and benefit-sharing have been incorporated to some extent into the thematic work programmes adopted by the COP (see list of references below). Article 15 is also related to the COP's work on incentive measures under Article 11, and particularly closely linked to the consideration of traditional knowledge (Article 8 (j) and related provisions), and IPRs. The COP has adopted a number of

16 Decision III/17 (Intellectual Property Rights) requested the Executive Secretary to apply for observer status in the WTO Committee on Trade and Environment.

decisions on these issues, of particular relevance to benefit-sharing, for example: decisions III/14, IV/9, and V/16 (Traditional knowledge); and decisions II/12 and III/17 (Intellectual property rights).

COP guidance

Guidance to Parties

The COP has encouraged Governments to explore, develop and implement guidelines and practices, in collaboration with relevant stakeholders, to ensure benefit-sharing [*decision III/15, paragraph 5*], and to include in their national plans or strategies and legislation measures for the equitable sharing of benefits arising out of the use of genetic resources [*decision III/9, paragraph 2 (c)*]. The COP has also urged recipient countries to adopt measures to support efforts made by provider countries to ensure that access to genetic resources is subject to Articles 15, 16 and 19 of the Convention [*decision V/26 A, paragraph 4 (c)*].

The COP has requested Parties to identify and communicate to the Secretariat details of their focal points and competent national authorities responsible for granting access to genetic resources [*decision III/15, paragraph 6; decision V/26 A, paragraph 2*].

Financial mechanism and resources

Guidance to the financial mechanism on this issue has been adopted in decision III/5, decision IV/8[17] and decision V/13. The COP urged the GEF to support capacity-building for the development and implementation of measures and guidance on access to genetic resources [*decision III/5, paragraph 4*]. It also requested the Secretariats of the Convention and the GEF to collaborate in preparing a proposal on the means to address fair and equitable sharing of benefits arising out of genetic resources, including assistance to developing country Parties, for consideration at COP 4 [*decision III/5, paragraph 7*].

The COP has also invited support from Governments, regional economic integration organizations, international, regional and national organizations, and private sector to support and implement capacity-building programmes to promote the development and implementation of measures on access to genetic resources, and efforts by Parties and Governments to develop and promote measures which facilitate the distribution of benefits arising from the use of genetic resources on mutually agreed terms [*decision III/15, paragraph 3; decision IV/8, paragraph 5*].

COP 5 noted the following four key capacity-building needs:

1. Assessment and inventory of biological resources as well as information management.
2. Contract negotiation skills.
3. Legal drafting skills for development of access and benefit-sharing measures.
4. Means for the protection of traditional knowledge associated with genetic resources. [decision V/26 A, paragraph 14]

17 See also decision IV/13.

Specific issues arising under Article 15

Decisions on, or related to, access to genetic resources and benefit-sharing make frequent references to the FAO International Undertaking on Plant Genetic Resources and to the question of genetic resources in *ex situ* collections. These references are addressed here. Decisions relating to other FAO activities, and the Global System for Plant Genetic Resources for Food and Agriculture are addressed in the guide to agricultural biological diversity under Thematic work programmes later in this section of this Handbook.

(a) FAO International Undertaking on Plant Genetic Resources for Food and Agriculture

Resolution 3 of the Nairobi Final Act on the adoption of the Convention, recognized the need to:

> *'seek solutions to outstanding matters concerning plant genetic resources within the Global System for the Conservation and Sustainable Use of Plant Genetic Resources for Food and Sustainable Agriculture, in particular (a) access to* ex situ *collections not acquired in accordance with this Convention; and (b) the question of farmers' rights.'*

Resolution 7/93 of the FAO Conference by way of response to Resolution 3, recognized the importance and urgency of revising the International Undertaking in harmony with the CBD, on a step-by-step basis, starting with the integration of the Undertaking and its annexes. It requested the Director General of the FAO to provide a forum for negotiations for the adaptation of the International Undertaking in harmony with the Convention; for consideration of the issue of access to plant genetic resources on mutually agreed terms, including *ex situ* collections not addressed by the Convention; and for the issue of realization of Farmers' Rights.

Negotiations for revision of the International Undertaking are ongoing and are scheduled to be completed in 2001. The COP has urged Governments and regional economic integration organizations to finalize the negotiation for the adaptation of the International Undertaking on Plant Genetic Resources for Food and Agriculture, in harmony with the CBD, in particular, providing solutions to access to *ex situ* collections not acquired in accordance with the Convention [*decision III/15, paragraph 7; decision V/26 A, paragraph 8*]. The COP has also affirmed its willingness to consider a decision by the FAO Conference that the revised Undertaking should take the form of a legally binding instrument with strong links to the Convention [*decision III/11, paragraph 18; decision V/26 A, paragraph 8*]. It has called upon Parties to coordinate their positions in both forums [*decision V/26 A, paragraph 8*].

The COP recognized that several issues require further work in the context of the FAO Global System, in particular: 'financing; the realization of Farmers' Rights as discussed in the Global Plan of Action; as well as terms of technology transfer to developing countries and access and benefit-sharing arrangements, in accordance with relevant provisions of the Convention' [*decision III/11, paragraph 19*].

(b) Ex situ *collections of genetic resources*

Article 15 (3) excludes from the Convention's provisions on access to genetic resources and benefit-sharing, those resources which were collected prior to the entry into force of the Convention for a particular Party, by providing that the genetic resources referred to in Articles 15, 16 and 19 are 'only those that are provided by Contracting Parties that are countries of origin of such resources or by the Parties that have acquired the genetic resources in accordance with this Convention'.

As noted above, *ex situ* collections of genetic resources covered by the FAO Global System for Plant Genetic Resources for Food and Agriculture are being considered in the context of the revision of the International Undertaking. In addition, the COP has begun to raise the question of whether and, if so, how, pre-existing *ex situ* collections of genetic resources, other than those under the FAO Global System, might be treated under the Convention, with due regard to the provisions of the Convention. COP 4 requested the Executive Secretary to invite information from Parties and relevant organizations in time for ISOC on *ex situ* collections which were acquired prior to the entry into force of the CBD and which are *not* addressed by the Commission on Genetic Resources for the FAO [*decision IV/8, paragraph 2*]. This issue was addressed again in decision V/26 C, in which the COP decided to continue the information-gathering exercise, and requested the Executive Secretary to report again on this issue at COP 6.

References

Decisions on Article 15

Decision II/11 (Access to genetic resources)
Decision III/15 (Access to genetic resources)
Decision IV/8 (Access and benefit-sharing)
Decision V/26 A (Access to genetic resources)
Decision V/26 C (*Ex situ* collections)

Guidance to Parties

National action

Decision III/9, paragraph 2 (c) (Implementation of Articles 6 and 8)
Decision III/15, paragraphs 5, 6 (Access to genetic resources)
Decision IV/6, paragraph 6 (Agriculture)
Decision V/5, annex, B, programme element 3, Activity 3.4 (Agriculture)
Decision V/26 A, paragraphs 1, 4 (a), (c), (d), 6, 7; C, paragraph 4 (Access to genetic resources)

Information and case studies

Decision II/11, paragraph 3 (Access to genetic resources)
Decision III/15, paragraphs 1, 4 (Access to genetic resources)
Decision III/17, paragraph 1 (b), (d) (Intellectual property rights)
Decision IV/8, paragraph 2 (Access and benefit-sharing)
Decision V/26 A, paragraphs 2, 15 (a) (Access to genetic resources)

Financial mechanism and resources

Guidance to the financial mechanism

Decision III/5, paragraph 4 (Additional guidance to the financial mechanism)
Decision III/15, paragraph 3 (Access to genetic resources)

Decision IV/8, paragraph 4 (Access and benefit-sharing)
Decision IV/13, paragraph 8 (Additional guidance to the financial mechanism)
Decision V/13, paragraph 2 (g) (Further guidance to the financial mechanism)

Other financial resources

Decision III/15, paragraph 3 (Access to genetic resources)
Decision IV/8, paragraph 5 (Access and benefit-sharing)

Guidance to the Secretariat

Decision II/10, paragraph 12 (Marine and coastal)
Decision II/11, paragraphs 1, 4 (Access to genetic resources)
Decision II/12, paragraph (c) (Intellectual property rights)
Decision III/5, paragraph 7 (Additional guidance to the financial mechanism)
Decision III/14, paragraph 10 (a) (Implementation of Article 8 (j))
Decision III/15, paragraphs 2, 8, 9 (Access to genetic resources)
Decision IV/8, paragraphs 2, 6 (Access and benefit-sharing)
Decision V/5, paragraph 29 (Agriculture)
Decision V/26 A, paragraphs 13, 15 (b), (c), (f); C, paragraphs 2, 5 (Access to genetic resources)

Guidance to SBSTTA

Decision II/8, paragraph 7 (Components of biological diversity particularly under threat)
Decision II/10, paragraph 12 (Marine and coastal)
Decision IV/4, annex I, paragraph 8 (c) (v) (Inland water)
Decision V/3, paragraph 12 (Marine and coastal)

Cooperation with other conventions and organizations

Decision II/9, annex, paragraph 9 (Forest – Statement to IPF)
Decision II/10, paragraph 12 (Marine and coastal)
Decision II/15, paragraph 2 (1) (FAO Global System)
Decision II/16, annex, paragraphs 8 (h), 9 (Statement to FAO International Technical Conference)
Decision III/5, paragraph 7 (Additional guidance to the financial mechanism)
Decision III/11, paragraphs 18, 19 (Agriculture)
Decision III/15, paragraphs 8, 9 (Access to genetic resources)
Decision IV/6, paragraph 6 (Agriculture)
Decision V/16, paragraph 14 (Article 8 (j) and related provisions)
Decision V/26 A, paragraphs 8, 15 (c), (d), (e); part C, paragraph 3 (Access to genetic resources)

Relevant aspects of thematic work programmes

Decision II/9, annex, paragraph 9 (Forest – Statement to IPF)
Decision II/10, paragraph 12 (Marine and coastal)
Decision III/11, paragraphs 1, 18, 19 (Agriculture)
Decision IV/4, annex I, paragraph 8 (c) (v) (Inland water)
Decision IV/5, annex, C, programme element 2, operational objective 2.2 (Marine and coastal)

Decision IV/6, paragraph 6 (Agriculture)
Decision V/3, paragraph 12 (Marine and coastal)
Decision V/5, paragraph 29; annex, A, paragraphs 2 (c), 3 (b), 4; annex, B, programme element 2, Activity 2.2 (c) (iv); programme element 3, Activity 3.4 (Agriculture)
Decision V/23, annex I, II, part B, Activity 9 (e) (Dry and sub-humid lands)

Other relevant decisions

Decision III/17, paragraph 8 (Intellectual property rights)
Decision III/19, annex, paragraph 24 (c) (Statement to UNGA Special Session)
Decision IV/9, paragraphs 1 (d), 10 (e); annex (Implementation of Article 8 (j) and related provisions)
Decision IV/16, paragraph 2 (Institutional matters and the programme of work)
Decision V/16, paragraph 5; annex, II, element 1, task 2; element 4, task 7 (Article 8 (j) and related provisions)
Decision V/19, paragraph 8 (National reports)

Declarations

Malawi (adoption) and Switzerland (signature)

Documents

UNEP/CBD/COP/2/13 Access to genetic resources and benefit-sharing: Legislation, administrative and policy information
UNEP/CBD/COP/2/18 FAO Global System for Plant Genetic Resources for Food and Agriculture
UNEP/CBD/COP/3/15 Progress under the Food and Agriculture Organization's Global System for the Conservation and Utilization of Plant Genetic Resources for Food and Agriculture
UNEP/CBD/COP/3/20 Access to genetic resources
UNEP/CBD/COP/3/22 The impact of intellectual property rights systems on the conservation and sustainable use of biodiversity and on the equitable sharing of benefits from its use
UNEP/CBD/COP/3/23 The Convention on Biological Diversity and the Agreement on Trade-related Aspects of Intellectual Property Rights (TRIPS): Relationships and synergies
UNEP/CBD/COP/3/Inf.5 Submissions received by the Executive Secretary concerning the possible influence that intellectual property rights may have on the implementation of the Convention
UNEP/CBD/COP/4/21 Measures to promote and advance the distribution of benefits from biotechnology in accordance with Article 19
UNEP/CBD/COP/4/22 Addressing the fair and equitable sharing of benefits arising out of genetic resources: options for assistance to developing countries Party to the CBD
UNEP/CBDCOP/4/23 Review of national, regional and sectoral measures and guidelines for the implementation of Article 15
UNEP/CBD/COP/4/Inf.7 Synthesis of case studies on benefit-sharing
UNEP/CBD/COP/4/Inf.10 Report of the international workshop 'Best Practices' for Access to Genetic Resources, Cordoba, 16–17 January 1998
UNEP/CBD/COP/4/Inf.16 Access to Genetic Resources and Means for Fair and Equitable Benefit Sharing – A Case Study, April 1998

UNEP/CBD/COP/4/Inf.20 Report of the Fourth Extraordinary Session of the Commission on Genetic Resources for Food and Agriculture, Rome, 1–5 December 1997
UNEP/CBD/COP/4/Inf.25 Benefit Sharing Case Studies: *Ancistrocladus korupensis* and *Prunus africana*. Submission by UNEP
UNEP/CBD/COP/5/8 Report of the Panel of Experts on Access and Benefit-Sharing
UNEP/CBD/COP/5/21 Access to genetic resources
UNEP/CBD/SBSTTA/2/15 Bio-prospecting of genetic resources of the deep seabed

Article 16: Access to and transfer of technology

1. Each Contracting Party, recognizing that technology includes biotechnology, and that both access to and transfer of technology among Contracting Parties are essential elements for the attainment of the objectives of this Convention, undertakes subject to the provisions of this Article to provide and/or facilitate access for and transfer to other Contracting Parties of technologies that are relevant to the conservation and sustainable use of biological diversity or make use of genetic resources and do not cause significant damage to the environment.

2. Access to and transfer of technology referred to in paragraph 1 above to developing countries shall be provided and/or facilitated under fair and most favourable terms, including on concessional and preferential terms where mutually agreed, and, where necessary, in accordance with the financial mechanism established by Articles 20 and 21. In the case of technology subject to patents and other intellectual property rights, such access and transfer shall be provided on terms which recognize and are consistent with the adequate and effective protection of intellectual property rights. The application of this paragraph shall be consistent with paragraphs 3, 4 and 5 below.

3. Each Contracting Party shall take legislative, administrative or policy measures, as appropriate, with the aim that Contracting Parties, in particular those that are developing countries, which provide genetic resources, are provided access to and transfer of technology which makes use of those resources, on mutually agreed terms, including technology protected by patents and other intellectual property rights, where necessary, through the provisions of Articles 20 and 21 and in accordance with international law and consistent with paragraphs 4 and 5 below.

4. Each Contracting Party shall take legislative, administrative or policy measures, as appropriate, with the aim that the private sector facilitates access to, joint development and transfer of technology referred to in paragraph 1 above for the benefit of both governmental institutions and the private sector of developing countries and in this regard shall abide by the obligations included in paragraphs 1, 2 and 3 above.

5. The Contracting Parties, recognizing that patents and other intellectual property rights may have an influence on the implementation of this Convention, shall co-operate in this regard subject to national legislation and international law in order to ensure that such rights are supportive of and do not run counter to its objectives.

Editors' note:

The issues addressed in Article 16 are linked to other articles of the Convention, in particular Articles 8 (j), 12, 15, 17, 18, 19, 20 and 21, and also to the thematic work programmes. Reference should also be made to the guides on those articles elsewhere in this section of the Handbook.

Notes

Terms defined in Article 2

'Biological diversity', 'biotechnology', 'genetic resources' and 'technology'.

Consideration of Article 16 by the COP

As part of its medium-term programme of work, the COP decided to consider access to and transfer and development of technology, as envisaged in Articles 16 and 18 of the Convention, at COP 2 and COP 3. It requested SBSTTA to consider and provide advice on this issue. It also decided that it would consider at COP 2, in relation to access to genetic resources, information related to IPRs as provided under Article 16, as well as access to and transfer of technology that makes use of genetic resources.

The COP's practice to date has been to address (i) access to and transfer of technology, and (ii) IPRs in separate decisions. These issues are therefore addressed separately below.

Access to and transfer of technology

Background and status

COP 2 took note of SBSTTA recommendation I/4 [*decision II/4, paragraph 1*], and asked SBSTTA to submit a detailed report to COP 3 [*decision II/, paragraph 4*].

COP 3 took note of SBSTTA recommendation II/3 [*decision III/16, paragraph 1*], and endorsed the recommendation that SBSTTA conduct its work on technology transfer within sectoral themes related to the priority issues under its programme of work as set out in SBSTTA recommendation II/12 [*decision III/16, paragraph 3*]. The COP noted that the issue of technology would be addressed at its fourth meeting, focusing especially on matters related to benefit-sharing and measures to promote and advance the distribution of benefits from biotechnology in accordance with Article 19 [*decision III/6, paragraph 2*].

The COP has emphasized the importance of technology transfer in the achievement of each of the three objectives of the Convention [*decision III/16, paragraph 4*]. In its Statement to the Special Session of the UNGA, the COP recognized that attention needs to be paid, *inter alia*, to the transfer of and access to technologies relevant to the Convention [*decision III/19, annex, paragraph 24 (e)*].

As part of the long-term programme of work, COP 4 decided that transfer of technology and technology cooperation will be addressed at COP 7. Related issues of access to genetic resources and benefit-sharing were to be addressed at COP 5 and COP 6, respectively [*decision IV/16, paragraph 16; annex II*].

Technology transfer is referred to in the COP's decisions on the thematic work programmes on agricultural biological diversity, inland water biological diversity, and forest biological diversity [*decision III/11, paragraphs 1 (f), 8; decision IV/6, paragraph 1; and decision IV/7, annex, paragraph 3 (g) respectively*]. Several elements of the forest biodiversity work programme make explicit reference to Article 16 [eg, *decision IV/7, paragraphs 7 (d), 15, 28*]. The work programmes on inland water biodiversity and agricultural biological diversity provide that the CHM should be used to promote and facilitate the development and transfer of relevant technology [*decision IV/4, annex I, paragraph 5; decision III/11, paragraph 8; decision IV/6, paragraph 1*].

COP guidance

The COP has adopted little direct guidance to Parties relating to action at the national level on access to and transfer of technology, although some relevant guidance was adopted at COP 5 in decisions primarily addressing other issues [see list of references below].

Article 16 is among the programme priorities for financial resources adopted by COP 1 [*decision I/2, annex I, paragraph 4 (f)*].

References

Decisions on access to and transfer of technology

Decision II/4 (Access to, and transfer and development of technology)
Decision III/16 (Access to, and transfer and development of technology)

Guidance to the Parties

National action

Decision IV/1 D, annex, paragraph 3 (Taxonomy)
Decision IV/4, annex I, paragraph 9 (c) (Inland water)
Decision V/8, annex I, B, Guiding principle 9 (c) (Alien species)
Decision V/14, annex I, paragraph (g) (ii) (Clearing-house mechanism)
Decision V/24, paragraph 5 (d) (Sustainable use)
Decision V/26 A, paragraph 4 (a), (c) (Access to genetic resources)
Decision V/26 C, paragraph 4 (*Ex situ* collections)

Information and case studies

Decision II/4, paragraph 3 (Access to, and transfer and development of technology)

Financial mechanism and resources

Guidance to the financial mechanism

Decision I/2, annex I, paragraph 4 (f) (Financial mechanism and resources)
Decision IV/2, paragraph 9 (c) (Clearing-house mechanism)

Guidance to the Secretariat

Decision II/3, paragraph 5 (a) (iii) (Clearing-house mechanism)

Decision II/4, paragraphs 2, 3 (Access to, and transfer and development of technology)
Decision II/10, annex II, paragraph 3 (c) (Marine and coastal)
Decision III/14, paragraph 10 (a) (Implementation of Article 8 (j))
Decision IV/2, paragraph 10 (e) (Clearing-house mechanism)
Decision V/14, annex II, paragraph (f) (Clearing-house mechanism)

Guidance to SBSTTA

Decision II/4, paragraph 4 (Access to, and transfer and development of technology)
Decision III/16, paragraph 3 (Access to, and transfer and development of technology)

Cooperation with other conventions and organizations

Decision III/11, paragraph 19 (Agriculture)
Decision III/19, annex, paragraph 24 (e) (Statement to UNGA Special Session)

Relevant aspects of the thematic programmes

Decision II/10, annex II, paragraph 3 (c) (Marine and coastal)
Decision III/11, paragraphs 1 (f), 8, 19; annex 3 (Agriculture)
Decision IV/4, annex I, paragraphs 5, 9 (c) (Inland water)
Decision IV/6, paragraph 1 (see also SBSTTA recommendation III/4, paragraph 11) (Agriculture)
Decision IV/7, annex, paragraphs 3 (g), 7 (d), 15, 28 (Forest)
Decision V/4, annex, paragraph 2 (c) (Forest)

Other relevant decisions

Decision II/5, annex, paragraph 5 (d) (Consideration of the need for and modalities of a protocol for the safe transfer, handling and use of LMOs)
Decision IV/8, annex, paragraph 4 (Access and benefit-sharing)
Decision IV/16, annex II (Institutional matters and programme of work)
Decision V/4, annex, paragraph 2 (c) (Forest)
Decision V/20, paragraph 32 (Operations of the Convention)
Decision V/26 A, paragraph 11 (Access to genetic resources)

Intellectual property rights

Background and status

Decisions of the COP with respect to IPRs have focused on gathering information on the impacts of IPRs on the objectives of the Convention, and on exploring the relationship between the provisions of the Convention and the WTO TRIPs Agreement.

COP 2 adopted decision II/12 on IPRs. It requested the Executive Secretary to liaise with the WTO, and to undertake a preliminary study of the impacts of IPR systems on the conservation and sustainable use of biological diversity and the equitable sharing of benefits derived from its use in order to gain a better understanding of the implications of Article 16 (5) of the Convention.

COP 3 called for case studies on the impacts of IPRs on the achievement of the Convention's objectives [*decision III/17, paragraph 1*]. It also addressed the relationship and cooperation between the Convention, the WTO and WIPO.

In decision IV/15, the COP again addressed the relationship between the Convention and the WTO agreements, including the TRIPs Agreement [*decision IV/15, paragraph 9*]. The COP has emphasized that further work is required to help develop a common appreciation of the relationship between IPRs and the relevant provisions of the TRIPs Agreement and the CBD, in particular on issues relating to technology transfer [*decision III/17, paragraph 8; decision IV/15, paragraph 10*]. COP 4 stressed the need to ensure consistency in implementing the CBD and the WTO agreements, including the TRIPs Agreement. It invited the WTO to consider how to achieve these objectives in the light of Article 16 (5) of the Convention, taking into account the planned review of Article 27 (3) (b) of the TRIPs Agreement in 1999 [*decision IV/15, paragraph 9*]. It requested ISOC to consider this issue [*decision IV/8, paragraph 1*]. Based on the recommendations of the Panel of Experts on Access and Benefit-sharing and ISOC, COP 5 addressed IPRs in decision V/26 B. It reaffirmed the importance of *sui generis* and other systems for the protection of traditional knowledge, and invited the WTO to acknowledge relevant provisions of the Convention and to explore the interrelationship between relevant provisions of TRIPs Agreement and of the Convention [*decision V/26 B, paragraphs 1, 2*]. The COP also renewed its request to the Executive Secretary to apply for observer status in the TRIPs Council of the WTO [*decision V/26 B, paragraph 4*].

With respect to the role of IPRs in implementing access and benefit-sharing arrangements the COP noted that the Panel of Experts was not able to come to any conclusions, although it had identified a number of specific issues that require further study. These include: the effectiveness of IPRs (relative to other measures) with respect to reinforcing prior informed consent; the role of IPRs in protecting traditional knowledge; and the scope of IPRs and their impact on the legitimate interests of other stakeholders. The COP called for information on these issues to be provided to the Secretariat, which is to use this information as the basis for a report on this issue for the Ad Hoc Open-ended Working Group on Access and Benefit-sharing [*decision V/26 A, paragraph 15*]. The Working Group is due to meet in October 2001 in Bonn, Germany, and will report to COP 6.

The COP further invited relevant organizations, including WIPO and UPOV, to analyse and take account of the relationship between IPRs and the provisions of the Convention in their work [*decision V/26 A, paragraph 15 (d), (e)*].

References

Decisions on intellectual property rights

Decision II/12 (Intellectual property rights)
Decision III/17 (Intellectual property rights)
Decision V/26 B (Intellectual property rights)

Guidance to the Parties

Information and case studies

Decision III/17, paragraph 1 (Intellectual property rights)
Decision IV/9, paragraphs 10 (b), 15 (Implementation of Article 8 (j) and related provisions)

Guidance to the Secretariat

Decision II/12 (Intellectual property rights)
Decision III/14, paragraph 10 (a) (Implementation of Article 8 (j))
Decision III/15, paragraph 8 (Access to genetic resources)
Decision III/17, paragraphs 3, 4, 6 (Intellectual property rights)
Decision IV/9, paragraphs 15, 17 (Implementation of Article 8 (j) and related provisions)
Decision IV/15, paragraph 11 (Cooperation)
Decision V/26 B, paragraphs 3, 4 (Intellectual property rights)

Cooperation with other conventions and organizations

Decision II/12, paragraph 1 (a) (Intellectual property rights)
Decision III/15, paragraph 8 (Access to genetic resources)
Decision III/17, paragraphs 3–6 (Intellectual property rights)
Decision IV/15, paragraphs 9,–11 (Cooperation)
Decision V/26 B, paragraphs 2, 3, 4 (Intellectual property rights)

Relevant aspects of the thematic programmes

Decision V/5, annex, B, programme element 2, Activity 2.2 (c) (iv) (Agriculture)

Other relevant decisions

Decision IV/8, annex, paragraph 4 (Access and benefit-sharing)
Decision V/16, annex, II, element 7, tasks 11 and 12 (Article 8 (j) and related provisions)
Decision V/26 A, paragraph 15 (Access to genetic resources)

Declarations

European Community (ratification), France (ratification), Ireland (ratification), Liechtenstein (ratification), Malaysia (adoption), Switzerland (signature and ratification) and USA (adoption)

Documents

UNEP/CBD/COP/2/17 Intellectual property rights and transfer of technology which makes use of genetic resources
UNEP/CBD/COP/3/21 Promoting and facilitating access to and transfer and development of technology
UNEP/CBD/COP/3/22 The impact of intellectual property rights systems on the conservation and sustainable use of biological diversity and on the equitable sharing of benefits for its use (a preliminary study)
UNEP/CBD/COP/3/23 The Convention on Biological Diversity and the Agreement on Trade-related Aspects of Intellectual Property Rights (TRIPs): Relationships and synergies
UNEP/CBD/COP/3/Inf.4 Submissions received by the Executive Secretary concerning ways and means to promote and facilitate access to and transfer and development of technology
UNEP/CBD/COP/3/Inf.5 Submissions received by the Executive Secretary concerning the possible influence that intellectual property rights may have on the implementation of the Convention

UNEP/CBD/COP/4/22 Addressing the fair and equitable sharing of benefits arising out of genetic resources: Options for assistance to developing country Parties to the CBD
UNEP/CBD/COP/4/Inf.7 Synthesis of case studies on benefit-sharing
UNEP/CBD/COP/5/4 Report of the Inter-Sessional Meeting on the Operations of the Convention
UNEP/CBD/COP/5/8 Report of the Panel of Experts on Access and Benefit Sharing
UNEP/CBD/SBSTTA/1/5 Ways and means to promote and facilitate access to, and transfer and development of technologies as envisaged in Articles 16 and 18 of the Convention
UNEP/CBD/SBSTTA/2/6 Ways and means to promote and facilitate access to, and transfer and development of technology, including biotechnology
UNEP/CBD/SBSTTA/2/Inf.2 Submissions received by the Secretariat concerning the transfer and development of technologies

Article 17: Exchange of information

1. The Contracting Parties shall facilitate the exchange of information, from all publicly available sources, relevant to the conservation and sustainable use of biological diversity, taking into account the special needs of developing countries.

2. Such exchange of information shall include exchange of results of technical, scientific and socio-economic research, as well as information on training and surveying programmes, specialized knowledge, indigenous and traditional knowledge as such and in combination with the technologies referred to in Article 16, paragraph 1. It shall also, where feasible, include repatriation of information.

Notes

Terms defined in Article 2

'Biological diversity', 'sustainable use' and 'technology'.

Consideration of Article 17 by the COP

Background and status

To date, the COP has not specifically addressed Article 17. However, gathering and exchange of information has formed an important component of the COP's work and the COP has made numerous references to exchange of information in its decisions on other articles and thematic areas. These have included, in particular, requests to Parties and others to submit case studies or other information to the Secretariat for dissemination through the CHM and/or to provide inputs to background documentation for the COP. Most of the references set out below relate to such requests. Readers should refer to the parts of the guides on particular articles and thematic areas in this section of the Handbook entitled 'Information and case studies'. Readers should also refer to the guides on the CHM (Article 18 (3)), access to and transfer of technology (Article 16), and national reports (Article 26) in this section.

References to information on indigenous and traditional knowledge are addressed in the guide to Article 8 (j) and related provisions.

COP guidance

The COP has referred to repatriation of information in a number of its decisions. COP 3 recommended that Parties explore ways to make taxonomic information housed in collections worldwide readily available, in particular to countries of origin [*decision III/10, paragraph 8*]. In decision IV/1 D, on the Global Taxonomy Initiative, the COP suggested that Parties should report on measures adopted to make information housed in collections available to countries of origin [*decision IV/1 D, annex, paragraph 7, decision V/14, annex I, paragraph (g) (iv)*].

In the second phase of its work programme, the Ad Hoc Open-ended Inter-sessional Working Group on Article 8 (j) and related provisions is to develop guidelines to facilitate the repatriation of information, including cultural property, in order to facilitate the recovery of traditional knowledge of biological diversity [*decision V/16, annex, III, element 3, task 15*]. The information-gathering exercise on *ex situ* collections acquired prior to the entry into force of the Convention is to gather information on, *inter alia*, policies relating to repatriation of information and of duplicates of germplasm samples [*decision V/26 C, annex I, paragraph 4*].

References

Relevant aspects of thematic work programmes

Decision II/10, annex I, paragraph (iii) (Marine and coastal)
Decision III/11, paragraphs 1 (e) (f), 4, 10, 11 (Agriculture)
Decision IV/4, annex I, paragraphs 5, 8 (c) (Inland water)
Decision IV/5, annex, C, Operational objectives 2.1 (b), 3.2 (c), 4 (b), 5.1 (a) (c), 5.2, 5.3 (b), 6.1, 6.2 (Marine and coastal)
Decision IV/6, paragraph 3; 4; 5 (Agriculture)
Decision IV/7, annex, paragraph 7 (d), 16, 17, 30, 34, 35, 37 (Forest)
Decision V/3, paragraph 7 (Marine and coastal)
Decision V/4, paragraph 7 (Forest)
Decision V/5, paragraphs 5, 9, 18, 22, 23, 25; annex, B, programme elements 1.5 (c); 2.1; 3.6 (Agriculture)
Decision V/23, annex I, II, part A, paragraphs 5, 7 (c), (d); part A, Activity 6; part B, Activity 7 (j) (Dry and sub-humid lands)

Other relevant decisions

Decision II/1, paragraph 4 (see also SBSTTA recommendation I/6) (Report of the first meeting of SBSTTA)
Decision II/2 (Publication and distribution of scientific and technical information)
Decision II/3, paragraph 5 (a) (Clearing-house mechanism)
Decision II/7, paragraphs 1, 4 (Consideration of Articles 6 and 8)
Decision II/11, paragraph 3 (Access to genetic resources)
Decision II/12, paragraph (c) (Intellectual property rights)
Decision III/4, paragraph 7 (Clearing-house mechanism)
Decision III/9, paragraphs 7, 9 (Implementation of Articles 6 and 8)

Decision III/10, paragraphs 7, 8 (Identification, monitoring and assessment)
Decision III/14, paragraphs 2, 3 (Implementation of Article 8 (j))
Decision III/15, paragraphs 1, 2, 4 (Access to genetic resources)
Decision III/17, paragraph 1 (Intellectual property rights)
Decision III/18, paragraph 7 (Incentive measures)
Decision IV/1 D, paragraphs 6, 8; annex, paragraphs 1, 6, 7, 9, 10, 11 (Taxonomy)
Decision IV/2, paragraph 10 (e) (Clearing-house mechanism)
Decision IV/8, paragraphs 2, 6 (Access and benefit-sharing)
Decision IV/9, paragraphs 10, 15; annex, paragraph E (Implementation of Article 8 (j) and related provisions)
Decision IV/10 A, paragraph 1 (g) (Incentive measures)
Decision IV/10 B, paragraph 2 (Public awareness and education)
Decision IV/10 C, paragraphs 1, 8 (Impact assessment and minimizing adverse effects)
Decision IV/15, paragraphs 14, 15 (Cooperation)
Decision V/6, paragraph 3; B, Principle 11 (Ecosystem approach)
Decision V/7, paragraphs 2, 4 (c) (Identification, monitoring and assessment and indicators)
Decision V/8, paragraphs 2, 3, 4, 7, 12; annex I, B, Guiding principle 8; annex II (Alien species)
Decision V/9, paragraph 2 (d) (Global Taxonomy Initiative)
Decision V/14, annex I, paragraph (g) (iv); annex II, paragraph (h) (Clearing-house mechanism)
Decision V/15, paragraphs 2 (a), 3 (a), (b) (Incentive measures)
Decision V/16, paragraphs 12 (f), 13, 15, 19; annex, II, element 1, task 4 (d); annex, III, element 3, task 15, element 5, task 16 (Article 8 (j) and related provisions)
Decision V/18, I, paragraph 5 (Impact assessment, liability and redress)
Decision V/20, paragraph 32 (Operations of the Convention)
Decision V/24, paragraphs 1, 5 (d) (Sustainable use)
Decision V/25, paragraphs 4 (f), 5 (Biological diversity and tourism)
Decision V/26 A, paragraph 13 (Access to genetic resources)
Decision V/26 C; annex I, paragraph 4 (*Ex situ* collections)

Article 18: Technical and scientific cooperation

Editors' note:

*The COP has adopted a number of specific decisions on, and issued specific instructions to, the CHM provided for under paragraph 3 of Article 18. The CHM (Article 18 (3)) is therefore addressed separately below. However, the development of the CHM is an integral part of implementation of Article 18 on technical and scientific information. In its Statement to the Special Session of the UNGA, the COP noted that a number of articles of the Convention address the issues of technical and scientific cooperation and capacity-building, in which the CHM will play a key role [*decision III/19, annex, paragraph 14*]. The specific consideration of the CHM by the COP has been dealt with separately here simply for ease of reference.*

Aspects of Article 18 (4) related to indigenous and traditional knowledge are addressed in the guide to Article 8 (j) and related provisions.

Capacity-building (Article 18 (1), (2), (4) and (5))

1. The Contracting Parties shall promote international technical and scientific co-operation in the field of conservation and sustainable use of biological diversity, where necessary, through the appropriate international and national institutions.

2. Each Contracting Party shall promote technical and scientific cooperation with other Contracting Parties, in particular developing countries, in implementing this Convention, *inter alia*, through the development and implementation of national policies. In promoting such cooperation, special attention should be given to the development and strengthening of national capabilities, by means of human resources development and institution building.

3. [For paragraph 3 of Article 18, see below]

4. The Contracting Parties shall, in accordance with national legislation and policies, encourage and develop methods of cooperation for the development and use of technologies, including indigenous and traditional technologies, in pursuance of the objectives of this Convention. For this purpose, the Contracting Parties shall also promote cooperation in the training of personnel and exchange of experts.

5. The Contracting Parties shall, subject to mutual agreement, promote the establishment of joint research programmes and joint ventures for the development of technologies relevant to the objectives of this Convention.

Notes

Terms defined in Article 2

'Biological diversity', 'sustainable use' and 'technology'.

Consideration of Article 18 (1), (2), (4) and (5) by the COP

Background and status

Aside from its consideration of the CHM, the COP has not as yet addressed the issue of technical and scientific cooperation as a separate agenda item. However, the issue of technical and scientific cooperation, and the related issue of capacity-building, has been referred to frequently in COP decisions.

In its decision on the medium-term programme of work for 1996–1997, COP 2 noted that treatment of the items on the programme of work should reflect the importance of capacity-building as one of the elements of successful Convention implementation [*decision II/18, annex, paragraph 4*].

References

Note: Most of the references listed below are references in COP decisions to capacity-building.

Decisions on Article 18 (1), (2), (4) and (5)

Except in relation to the CHM (see below), the COP has not adopted any decisions specifically on Article 18.

Guidance to Parties

National action

Decision III/18, paragraph 5 (Incentive measures)
Decision V/3, paragraph 6 (e) (Marine and coastal)
Decision V/4, paragraph 10 (Forest)
Decision V/5, paragraphs 9, 23 (Agriculture)
Decision V/6, paragraph 3; annex, C, paragraphs 9, 10 (Ecosystem approach)
Decision V/7, paragraph 4 (Identification, monitoring and assessment and indicators)
Decision V/8, annex I, B, Guiding principle 9 (c) (Alien species)
Decision V/9, paragraph 2 (b), (d) (Global Taxonomy Initiative)
Decision V/16, paragraph 12 (a), (b), (c), (d); annex, II, element 1, task 1 (Article 8 (j) and related provisions)
Decision V/17, paragraph 6 (Education and public awareness)
Decision V/24, paragraph 5 (Sustainable use)
Decision V/25, paragraphs 4 (f), 7 (Biological diversity and tourism)
Decision V/26 C, paragraph 4 (*Ex situ* collections)

Financial mechanism and resources

Guidance to the financial mechanism

Decision I/2, annex I, paragraph 4 (e), (h) (Financial mechanism and resources)
Decision II/3, paragraph 9 (Clearing-house mechanism)
Decision II/6, paragraph 11 (Financial mechanism and resources)
Decision II/7, paragraph 6 (Consideration of Articles 6 and 8)
Decision III/5, paragraphs 2 (a), (b), (d) (i), 4, 5 (Additional guidance to the financial mechanism)
Decision III/10, paragraph 10 (Identification, monitoring and assessment)
Decision III/14, paragraph 5 (Implementation of Article 8 (j))
Decision III/15, paragraph 3 (Access to genetic resources)
Decision III/20, paragraph 2 (b), (c) (Issues related to biosafety)
Decision IV/1 D, paragraph 7 (Taxonomy)
Decision IV/2, paragraph 9 (b) (c) (Clearing-house mechanism)
Decision IV/6, paragraph 12 (Agriculture)
Decision IV/8, paragraph 4 (a), (c) (Access and benefit-sharing)
Decision IV/10 A, paragraph 3 (Incentive measures)
Decision IV/13, paragraphs 4, 5, 7, 8 (Additional guidance to the financial mechanism)
Decision V/13, paragraphs 1, 2 (d), (j), (k), (l), (n) (Further guidance to the financial mechanism)

Other financial resources

Decision III/4, paragraphs 4, 5 (Clearing-house mechanism)
Decision III/15, paragraph 3 (Access to genetic resources)
Decision IV/6, paragraph 12 (Agriculture)
Decision V/5, paragraph 9 (Agriculture)

Decision V/6, paragraph 6 (Ecosystem approach)
Decision V/11, paragraph 11 (Additional financial resources)
Decision V/23, paragraph 11 (Dry and sub-humid lands)

Guidance to the Secretariat

Decision II/3, paragraphs 3, 5 (a) (i) (Clearing-house mechanism)
Decision II/4, paragraph 2 (Access to, and transfer and development of technology)
Decision II/10, annex II, paragraph 3 (c) (Marine and coastal)
Decision III/17, paragraph 3 (Intellectual property rights)
Decision IV/5, annex, C, operational objectives 1.2 (e); 2.1 (e); 5.2 (d) (Marine and coastal)
Decision V/9, paragraph 3 (b) (Global Taxonomy Initiative)
Decision V/14, annex II, paragraph (d) (Clearing-house mechanism)

Guidance to SBSTTA

Decision IV/1 D, paragraph 3 (Taxonomy)
Decision V/3, paragraph 13 (Marine and coastal)
Decision V/18, I, paragraph 4 (Impact assessment, liability and redress)

Cooperation with other conventions and organizations

Decision II/16, annex, paragraph 8 (e) (Statement to FAO International Technical Conference)
Decision III/17, paragraph 3 (Intellectual property rights)
Decision IV/5, annex, C, operational objectives 2.1 (e); 5.2 (d) (Marine and coastal)
Decision V/19, paragraph 10 (National reports)

Relevant aspects of thematic work programmes

Decision II/10, annex II, paragraph 3 (c) (Marine and coastal)
Decision IV/5, annex, C, operational objectives 1.2 (e), 2.1 (e), 5.2 (d) (Marine and coastal)
Decision IV/6, paragraph 12 (Agriculture)
Decision IV/7, annex, paragraphs 1, 47 (Forest)
Decision V/2, paragraph 8 (Inland water)
Decision V/3, paragraph 6 (e), 13; annex, B (Marine and coastal)
Decision V/4, paragraph 10 (Forest)
Decision V/5, paragraphs 5, 9, 23; annex, B, programme elements 2.2 (c) (vi), 3 (Agriculture)
Decision V/23, paragraph 11; annex I, II, part A, paragraph 7 (d); part B, Activity 7 (k) (Dry and sub-humid lands)

Other relevant decisions

Decision II/8, paragraph 5 (Components of biological diversity particularly under threat)
Decision II/18, annex, paragraphs 4, 7.5 (Medium-term programme of work)
Decision III/10, paragraphs 2, 3, 10 (see also SBSTTA recommendations II/1 and II/2) (Identification, monitoring and assessment)

ARTICLE 18 (1), (2), (4) AND (5)

Decision III/19, annex, paragraph 14 (Statement to UNGA Special Session)
Decision III/20, paragraph 2 (Issues related to biosafety)
Decision IV/1 A, paragraph 3 (see also SBSTTA recommendation III/5, paragraph 7 (h)) (Report and recommendations of the third meeting of SBSTTA)
Decision IV/1 D, paragraph 2 (Taxonomy)
Decision V/7, paragraph 3 (Identification, monitoring and assessment and indicators)
Decision V/20, paragraph 32 (Operations of the Convention)
Decision V/26 A, paragraphs 11, 14 (Access to genetic resources)

Documents

UNEP/CBD/COP/3/21 Promoting and facilitating access to and transfer and development of technology
UNEP/CBD/COP/3/22 Intellectual property rights
UNEP/CBD/COP/3/Inf.4 Submissions received by the Executive Secretary concerning ways and means to promote and facilitate access to and transfer and development of technology
UNEP/CBD/COP/3/Inf.5 Submissions received by the Executive Secretary concerning the possible influence that intellectual property rights may have on the implementation of the Convention
UNEP/CBD/COP/4/22 Means to address the fair and equitable sharing of benefits
UNEP/CBD/COP/4/Inf.7 Synthesis of case studies on benefit-sharing
UNEP/CBD/COP/5/4 Report of the Inter-Sessional Meeting on the Operations of the Convention
UNEP/CBD/COP/5/8 Report of the Panel of Experts on Access and Benefit-Sharing
UNEP/CBD/SBSTTA/1/5 Ways and means to promote and facilitate access to, and transfer and development of technologies as envisaged in Articles 16 and 18 of the Convention (priority item)
UNEP/CBD/SBSTTA/2/6 Ways and means to promote and facilitate access to, and transfer and development of technology, including biotechnology
UNEP/CBD/SBSTTA/2/Inf.2 Submissions received by the Secretariat concerning the transfer and development of technologies

Clearing-house mechanism (Article 18 (3))

3. The Conference of the Parties, at its first meeting, shall determine how to establish a clearing-house mechanism to promote and facilitate technical and scientific cooperation.

Notes

Consideration of Article 18 (3) by the COP

Background and status

As part of its first medium-term programme of work, the COP decided to consider the CHM as a standing item on its agenda [*decision I/9*]. COP 1 decided that a CHM should be established to promote and facilitate technical and scientific cooperation. It also decided that the activities of the CHM should be funded through the regular budget of the Convention as well as from voluntary contributions [*decision I/3, paragraph 2*].

COP 2 decided that establishment of the CHM should start with a pilot phase for 1996–1997, the implementation of which would be reviewed at COP 3 [*decision II/3, paragraph 4*]. The COP subsequently decided [*decision III/4, paragraph 1*] to extend the pilot phase until December 1998. The COP has given certain specific guidance as to the nature and content of the CHM [*decision II/3, paragraph 4; decision III/4, paragraphs 6, 7; decision IV/2, paragraphs 5–7*] and decided that the Secretariat should act as a focal point [*decision II/3, paragraph 5; decision IV/2, paragraph 10 (b)*].

The CHM is assisted in its functioning by an Informal Advisory Committee (IAC), constituted and coordinated by the Executive Secretary. The IAC is to guide and integrate the development of pilot phase activities and endeavour to ensure that all Parties can participate in the CHM [*decision III/4, paragraph 10; decision IV/2, paragraph 10 (c)*]. COP 5 clarified the objectives of the IAC [*decision V/14, paragraph 7*]. The continuation and mandate of the IAC, as well as operational procedures, will be reviewed at COP 7 [*decision V/14, paragraph 9*].

Four CHM regional workshops and two expert meetings were held in 1997 and 1998. The regional workshops were held in October 1997 in Colombia for the Latin American and Caribbean region and in Hungary for the Central and Eastern European region, in December 1997 in Malaysia for the Asian region and in March 1998 in Kenya for the African region. The expert meetings were held in June 1997 in Germany and in July 1998 in Italy. Their purpose was to attain a clear definition of national and regional level scientific and technical information needs and priorities, as well as modalities to deliver information and evaluate national capacities for the implementation of the Convention. Their main recommendation was that a global strategic plan was required for implementation of the CHM.

In 1999 an independent review of the pilot phase of the CHM was undertaken for SBSTTA [*decision IV/2, paragraph 10*]. The review process identified key achievements of the pilot phase and also developed a strategic plan and longer-term programme of work for the CHM. SBSTTA 5 considered the review and the longer-term programme of work and submitted recommendation V/2, which was subsequently considered by COP 5. At its fifth meeting the COP:

- noted the report of the independent review of the pilot phase (document UNEP/CBD/COP/5/Inf.2);
- endorsed a longer-term programme of work for the CHM (contained in document UNEP/CBD/COP/5/Inf.4); and
- supported the implementation of a strategic plan for the CHM, which will become a component of the Strategic Plan for the Convention (document UNEP/CBD/COP/5/Inf.3) (see the guide to Article 23 later in this section of the Handbook).

[*decision V/14, paragraphs 1, 2, 4, 5*]

The strategic plan proposed three goals to guide the further development of the CHM, as follows:

1. Cooperation – the promotion and facilitation of scientific and technical cooperation.

2. Information exchange – the development of a global mechanism for exchanging and integrating information on biodiversity.
3. Network development – the development of the CHM focal points and their partners.

COP 5 also set out measures and activities to be undertaken in relation to the development of the CHM by: (a) Parties and Governments at the national level; and (b) the Secretariat in consultation with the IAC [*decision V/14, annexes I and II*].

The COP has highlighted the importance of cooperation with other organizations in the development of the CHM. It invited all organizations to cooperate as active partners in the operation of the CHM [*decision II/3, paragraph 8*], and welcomed the offer of the FAO to link its information systems to the CHM [*decision II/16, paragraph 2*]. COP 4 instructed the Executive Secretary to improve synergy with regard to information exchange with other biodiversity related conventions and ongoing information initiatives [*decision IV/2, paragraph 10 (g)*].

The COP has given substantial guidance, both in its decisions on the CHM and in decisions on thematic areas and other articles, on the types of information which should be made available through the CHM. This guidance is listed in the references below under the heading 'Information to be disseminated through the CHM'. In some cases the COP has requested Parties to make information available through the CHM directly; in other cases Parties have been requested to make information available to the Secretariat for dissemination through the CHM.

The Executive Secretary, in consultation with the IAC, has been asked to monitor and review the operation of the CHM and report to COP 6 on any recommended adjustments to its operation or to the strategic plan [*decision V/14, paragraph 3*].

COP guidance

Guidance to Parties

The COP has adopted certain guidance to Parties with regard to the development of the CHM. COP 2 called on Parties that had not already done so to designate their national focal point for the CHM [*decision II/3, paragraph 7*]. As of 19 July 2001 there are 143 CHM national focal points (110 of which have email and 50 of which have websites). COP 4, *inter alia*:

- recommended that each Party organize an appropriate multidisciplinary national CHM steering committee or working group [*decision IV/2, paragraph 3*];
- recommended that in building up the content of information in the CHM at the national, subregional and regional level, the following be included: country profiles; biodiversity strategies and action plans; appropriate legislation; scientific and technological information; and financial sources [*decision IV/2, paragraph 5 (a)*]; and
- requested Parties to link their national CHMs to the Secretariat CHM via the internet where possible [*decision IV/2, paragraph 6*].

As noted above, annex I to decision V/14 contains further specific guidance to Parties with regard to the development of the CHM.

Financial mechanism and resources

COP 3 requested the financial mechanism to support capacity-building in developing countries, including training in information system technologies, and country-driven pilot projects to enable developing countries to begin to implement the main features of the pilot phase of the CHM [*decision III/4, paragraph 2*]. It also requested the financial mechanism to implement its revised operational criteria for enabling activities in relation to the CHM to give effect to these activities [*decision III/4, paragraph 3*]. Further guidance to the financial mechanism was adopted by COP 4 and COP 5 [*decision IV/2, paragraph 9, decision IV/13, paragraph 5; decision V/13, paragraph 2 (f)*].

The COP has requested Governments and other bilateral and multilateral funding institutions to provide funding for capacity-building for the implementation of the CHM. It has further requested Governments and financial, scientific and technical institutions to facilitate, including through funding, regional workshops to identify needs and priorities and modalities for implementation of the CHM [*decision III/4, paragraphs 4, 5; decision IV/2, paragraph 1*].

References

Decisions on Article 18 (3)

Decision I/3 (Clearing-house mechanism)
Decision II/3 (Clearing-house mechanism)
Decision III/4 (Clearing-house mechanism)
Decision IV/2 (Clearing-house mechanism)
Decision V/14 (Clearing-house mechanism)

Financial mechanism and resources

Guidance to the financial mechanism

Decision II/3, paragraph 9 (Clearing-house mechanism)
Decision II/6, paragraph 11 (Financial mechanism and resources)
Decision III/4, paragraphs 2, 3 (Clearing-house mechanism)
Decision III/5, paragraph 2 (d) (Additional guidance to the financial mechanism)
Decision IV/2, paragraph 9 (Clearing-house mechanism)
Decision IV/7, paragraph 6 (Forest)
Decision IV/13, paragraph 5 (Additional guidance to the financial mechanism)
Decision V/13, paragraph 2 (f) (Further guidance to the financial mechanism)

Additional financial resources

Decision III/4, paragraphs 4, 5 (Clearing-house mechanism)
Decision IV/2, paragraph 1 (Clearing-house mechanism)

Cooperation with other conventions and organizations

Decision I/8, annex, paragraph 13 (Statement to CSD)
Decision II/3, paragraphs 3, 4 (g), (h), 5 (a), 8 (Clearing-house mechanism)
Decision II/16, paragraph 2 (Statement to FAO International Technical Conference)
Decision III/4, paragraph 13 (Clearing-house mechanism)

Decision III/19, annex, paragraph 14 (Statement to UNGA Special Session)
Decision IV/2, paragraph 10 (g) (Clearing-house mechanism)
Decision IV/8, paragraph 6 (a) (Access and benefit-sharing)
Decision V/14, paragraph 7 (e); annex II, paragraph (c) (Clearing-house mechanism)

Information to be disseminated through the CHM

Decision II/7, paragraph 3 (Consideration of Articles 6 and 8)
Decision II/17, paragraph 10 (National reports)
Decision III/10, paragraph 7 (Identification, monitoring and assessment)
Decision III/11, paragraph 10 (Agriculture)
Decision III/15, paragraph 2 (b) (Access to genetic resources)
Decision III/17, paragraph 1 (Intellectual property rights)
Decision III/18, paragraph 7 (Incentive measures)
Decision IV/1 A, paragraph 3 (see also SBSTTA recommendation III/5, paragraph 7 (g)) (Report and recommendations of the third meeting of SBSTTA)
Decision IV/2, paragraph 5 (Clearing-house mechanism)
Decision IV/4, annex I, paragraphs 5, 8 (c) (Inland water)
Decision IV/5, annex, C, operational objectives 1.3 (e), 3.2 (c), 5.3 (b), 6.1 (c), 6.2 (b) (Marine and coastal)
Decision IV/7, annex, paragraph 37 (Forest)
Decision IV/8, paragraph 6 (Access and benefit-sharing)
Decision IV/9, paragraph 15 (Implementation of Article 8 (j) and related provisions)
Decision IV/10 A, paragraph 5 (a) (Incentive measures)
Decision IV/10 B, paragraph 2 (Public awareness and education)
Decision IV/10 C, paragraph 5 (Impact assessment and minimizing adverse effects)
Decision IV/16, annex I, paragraph 19 (Institutional matters and programme of work)
Decision V/2, paragraph 6 (Inland water)
Decision V/3, paragraphs 7, 11 (Marine and coastal)
Decision V/5, paragraphs 18, 22, 23, 25, 27; annex, B, programme element 1.5 (c) (Agriculture)
Decision V/6, paragraph 3 (Ecosystem approach)
Decision V/8, paragraphs 4, 12; annex I, B, Guiding principle 8 (Alien species)
Decision V/11, paragraph 1 (Additional financial resources)
Decision V/14, annex I, paragraph (g) (Clearing-house mechanism)
Decision V/15, paragraph 2 (a) (Incentive measures)
Decision V/18, I, paragraph 5 (d) (Impact assessment, liability and redress)
Decision V/19, paragraphs 5, 9 (a) (National reports)
Decision V/20, paragraph 34 (Operations of the Convention)
Decision V/23, paragraph 10 (Dry and sub-humid lands)
Decision V/24, paragraph 1 (Sustainable use)
Decision V/25, paragraph 5 (Biological diversity and tourism)
Decision V/26 A, paragraph 13 (Access to genetic resources)

Relevant aspects of thematic work programmes

Decision II/10, annex II, paragraph 3 (e) (Marine and coastal)
Decision III/11, paragraphs 8, 10, 13 (Agriculture)
Decision IV/4, annex I, paragraph 5, 8 (c) (Inland water)
Decision IV/5, annex, C, operational objectives 1.3 (e), 3.2 (c), 5.3 (b), 6.1 (c), 6.2 (Marine and coastal)

Decision IV/7, paragraph 6; annex, paragraphs 7, 18, 37 (Forest)
Decision V/2, paragraph 6 (Inland water)
Decision V/3, paragraphs 7, 11 (Marine and coastal)
Decision V/5, paragraphs 18, 22, 23, 25, 27; annex, B, programme element 1.5 (c) (Agriculture)
Decision V/23, paragraph 10 (Dry and sub-humid lands)

Other relevant decisions

Decision I/9, annex, paragraph 2.5 (Medium-term programme of work)
Decision II/4, paragraph 2 (Access to, and transfer and development of technology)
Decision II/18, annex, paragraph 2.5 (Medium-term programme of work)
Decision IV/1 D, annex, paragraph 10 (Taxonomy)
Decision V/9, annex (Global Taxonomy Initiative)
Decision V/16, paragraph 19 (a); annex, II, element 5, task 8 (Article 8 (j) and related provisions)
Decision V/17, paragraph 7 (a), (b) (Education and public awareness)
Decision V/20, III, paragraph 22, IV, paragraph 32 (Operations of the Convention)

Documents

UNEP/CBD/COP/1/8 Clearing-house mechanism for technical and scientific cooperation
UNEP/CBD/COP/2/6 Clearing-house mechanism
UNEP/CBD/COP/3/4 Report on the assessment and review of the operation of the clearing-house mechanism
UNEP/CBD/COP/4/8 Implementation of the pilot phase of the clearing-house mechanism
UNEP/CBD/COP/4/Inf.6 Reports of the regional workshops on the clearing-house mechanism
UNEP/CBD/COP/5/13 Progress report on the mechanisms for implementation
UNEP/CBD/COP/5/Inf.2 Report of the independent review of the pilot phase of the clearing-house mechanism
UNEP/CBD/COP/5/Inf.3 Clearing-house mechanism's Strategic Plan
UNEP/CBD/COP/5/Inf.4 Clearing-house mechanism's longer-term programme of work
UNEP/CBD/SBSTTA/2/9 Role of the clearing-house mechanism in facilitating and promoting technical and scientific cooperation in research and development
UNEP/CBD/SBSTTA/3/3 Report on the implementation of the pilot phase of the clearing-house mechanism in facilitating and promoting technical and scientific cooperation
UNEP/CBD/SBSTTA/3/Inf.12 Report on the International Expert Meeting on Building the Clearing-house (June 1997, Germany)
UNEP/CBD/SBSTTA/5/3 Pilot phase of the clearing-house mechanism

Article 19: Handling of biotechnology and distribution of its benefits

Participating in biotechnological research and promoting access to the results and benefits (Article 19 (1) and (2))

1. Each Contracting Party shall take legislative, administrative or policy measures, as appropriate, to provide for the effective participation in biotechnological research activities by those Contracting Parties, especially developing countries, which provide the genetic resources for such research, and where feasible in such Contracting Parties.

2. Each Contracting Party shall take all practicable measures to promote and advance priority access on a fair and equitable basis by Contracting Parties, especially developing countries, to the results and benefits arising from biotechnologies based upon genetic resources provided by those Contracting Parties. Such access shall be on mutually agreed terms.

...

[For paragraphs 3 and 4 of Article 19, see below]

Editors' note:

Article 19, paragraphs 1 and 2, are closely linked to other provisions of the Convention, particularly Articles 8 (j), 15, 16 and 18. Readers should make reference to the guides on these articles above in this section of the Handbook.

Article 19, paragraphs (3) and (4) are addressed separately under the heading 'Consideration of the need for and modalities of a protocol on biosafety'.

Notes

Terms defined in Article 2

'Biotechnology' and 'genetic resources'.

Consideration of Article 19 (1) and (2) by the COP

Background and status

As part of its first medium-term programme of work, the COP decided to consider measures to promote and advance the distribution of benefits from biotechnology in accordance with Article 19 at COP 4 [*decision I/9, decision II/18*]. COP 3 noted that the issue of technology would be dealt with at COP 4 in the context of agenda items on matters related to benefit-sharing will be considered at COP 6, and technology transfer and technology cooperation at COP 7 [*decision IV/16, annex II*].

Issues related to Article 19 have been considered in the context of COP 4 and COP 5 discussions on access and benefit-sharing. At its first meeting the Panel of Experts on

Access and Benefit-sharing considered options for access and benefit-sharing, including mutually agreed terms on benefit-sharing, IPRs and technology transfer [*decision IV/8, paragraph 3; annex; see guide to Article 15*]. The most relevant conclusions for Article 19 were those relating to benefit-sharing options (part b, paragraphs 74–90, document UNEP/CBD/COP/5/8). These issues were considered further at the second meeting of the Panel of Experts in March 2001 and will be addressed in the Ad Hoc Open-ended Working Group on Access and Benefit-sharing which will meet for the first time in October 2001. Readers should also refer to the guide to Article 15 for further detail on these discussions.

Decision V/26 A urged Parties to pay particular attention to their obligations under Articles 15, 16 and 19 of the Convention and requested them to report to the COP on measures taken to this effect [*decision V/26 A, paragraph 4 (a)*].

References

See references in the guides to Articles 15 and 16 earlier in this section of the Handbook.

Documents

UNEP/CBD/COP/3/21 Promoting and facilitating access to and transfer and development of technology
UNEP/CBD/COP/3/22 Intellectual property rights
UNEP/CBD/COP/3/Inf.4 Submissions received by the Executive Secretary concerning ways and means to promote and facilitate access to and transfer and development of technology
UNEP/CBD/COP/4/21 Measures to promote and advance the distribution of benefits from biotechnology in accordance with Article 19
UNEP/CBD/COP/4/22 Means to address the fair and equitable sharing of benefits
UNEP/CBD/COP/4/Inf.7 Synthesis of case studies on benefit-sharing

Consideration of the need for and modalities of a protocol on biosafety (Article 19 (3) and (4))

...

3. The Parties shall consider the need for and modalities of a protocol setting out appropriate procedures, including, in particular, advance informed agreement, in the field of the safe transfer, handling and use of any living modified organism resulting from biotechnology that may have adverse effect on the conservation and sustainable use of biological diversity.

4. Each Contracting Party shall, directly or by requiring any natural or legal person under its jurisdiction providing the organisms referred to in paragraph 3 above, provide any available information about the use and safety regulations required by that Contracting Party in handling such organisms, as well as any available information on the potential adverse impact of the specific organisms concerned to the Contracting Party into which those organisms are to be introduced.

Notes

Terms defined in Article 2

'Biological diversity', 'biotechnology', and 'sustainable use'.

Consideration of Article 19 (3) and (4) by the COP

Background and status: The Cartagena Protocol on Biosafety

COP 1 decided to establish an Open-ended Ad Hoc Group of Experts, nominated by Governments, to consider the need for and modalities of a protocol under Article 19 (3) [*decision I/9, paragraph 3*]. It also decided that the Secretariat would establish a panel of 15 government-nominated experts to prepare a background document for the meeting of the Open-ended Ad Hoc Group of Experts [*decision I/9, paragraph 7*]. The expert panel met in Cairo from 1 to 5 May 1995. The Open-ended Ad Hoc Group of Experts met in Madrid from 24 to 28 July 1995 and presented a report to COP 2.[18]

Having considered the report of the Open-ended Ad Hoc Group of Experts, COP 2 adopted decision II/5 by which it established the Open-ended Ad Hoc Working Group, commonly referred to as the Biosafety Working Group (BSWG), under the COP to develop a draft protocol on biosafety [*decision II/5, paragraphs 1, 2*]. Terms of reference for the BSWG were set out in annex to decision II/5. The terms of reference indicated, *inter alia*, that the BSWG should endeavour to complete its work in 1998.

The BSWG met six times between July 1996 and February 1999:

Aarhus, Denmark, 22–26 July 1996

Montreal, Canada, 12–16 May 1997

Montreal, Canada, 13–17 October 1997

Montreal, Canada, 5–13 February 1998

Montreal, Canada, 17–28 August 1998

Cartagena, Colombia, 14–22 February 1999

In 1996, the BSWG presented a report to COP 3, which adopted certain decisions relating to the Bureau of the BSWG and future meetings [*decision III/20*]. COP 3 endorsed SBSTTA recommendation II/5, in particular the realization of activities to promote the application of the UNEP International Technical Guidelines for Safety in Biotechnology and the importance of funding for capacity-building in biosafety. In this regard, the COP requested the financial mechanism to provide financial resources to developing country Parties for capacity-building in biosafety [*decision III/20, paragraph 2; decision III/5, paragraph 2 (a)*]. The COP also noted that guidelines on biosafety, including the UNEP guidelines, may be used as an interim mechanism during the development of the protocol and to complement it after its completion for the purposes of facilitating the development of national capacities to assess and manage risks, establish adequate information systems and develop expert human resources in biotechnology [*decision II/5 preamble; decision III/20, paragraph 2; see also SBSTTA recommendation II/5, paragraph 2*].

18 UNEP/CBD/COP/2/7.

The BSWG held three further meetings between COP 3 and COP 4. COP 4 considered the report of the fourth meeting of the BSWG, and accepted the recommendation in the report that the BSWG should hold two further meetings to complete its work, and that the final meeting should be convened not later than February 1999 [*decision IV/3, paragraph 1*]. It also decided that an extraordinary meeting of the COP would be held in February 1999 to address all matters relating to the adoption of the protocol on biosafety and preparation for the first meeting of the Parties to the protocol [*decision IV/3, paragraphs 3, 4*].

The first extraordinary meeting of the COP was held from 22 to 23 February 1999 in Cartagena, Colombia, immediately after the sixth meeting of the BSWG. Since a number of issues remained unresolved, the COP decided that its extraordinary meeting should be suspended, to be resumed as soon as practicable, and in any event, no later than COP 5 [*decision EM-I/1, paragraphs 1, 2*]. The COP decided that the protocol would be called the Cartagena Protocol on Biosafety to the Convention on Biological Diversity [*decision EM-1/1, paragraph 3*].

Informal consultations on the protocol were held in Montreal in July 1999, in Vienna from 15 to 19 September 1999, and in Montreal in January 2000. The resumed session of the extraordinary meeting of the COP was held in Montreal from 24 to 28 January 2000, (following further informal consultations from 20 to 22 January 2000) and the Cartagena Protocol on Biosafety was adopted on 29 January 2000 [*decision EM-3/1*]. The text of the Protocol is reproduced in Section II of this Handbook.

The Protocol was opened for signature on 15 May 2000 in Nairobi, Kenya, on the occasion of COP 5. It remained open for signature in Nairobi until 26 May 2000. Thereafter, it was open for signature at United Nations Headquarters in New York from 5 June 2000 to 4 June 2001. Only Parties to the Convention may become Parties to the Cartagena Protocol on Biosafety. As of 23 July 2001, 103 Parties have signed the protocol, and 5 have ratified it.

The Protocol will enter into force on the 90th day after the deposit of the fiftieth instrument of ratification, acceptance, approval or accession.

In decision EM-I/3, the COP established an Open-ended Ad Hoc Intergovernmental Committee for the Cartagena Protocol (ICCP) to undertake the preparations necessary for the first meeting of the Parties. Parties and other States were requested to designate a focal point for the ICCP and inform the Secretariat [*decision EM-I/3, paragraph 11*]. The COP appointed the Chair of the ICCP, Ambassador Philemon Yang (Cameroon) [*decision EM-3, paragraph 8*].

COP 5 adopted decision V/1 which endorsed a work plan for the ICCP over two meetings [*decision V/1, paragraph 1; annex*]. The first meeting of the ICCP took place from 11 to 15 December 2000 in Montpellier, France. The second meeting is scheduled for 1 to 5 October 2001 in Nairobi, Kenya.

The extraordinary meeting of the COP requested the Executive Secretary to commence preparatory work on the functioning of the Biosafety Clearing-House referred to in Article 20 of the Protocol [*decision EM-I/3, paragraph 13*]. In accordance with paragraph 3 of decision V/1, the Secretariat convened a meeting of technical experts in Montreal from 11 to 13 September 2000. The report of this meeting was submitted to the first meeting of the ICCP (document UNEP/CBD/ICCP/1/3). The COP further decided to establish a regionally balanced roster of experts, nominated by Governments, in fields relevant to risk assessment and risk management related to the Protocol, to, *inter alia,* provide advice and support, as appropriate and upon request, to developing country Parties and Parties with economies in transition [*decision EM-I/3, paragraph 14*].

COP 5 welcomed the decision of the GEF Council to request the GEF Secretariat, in consultation with the GEF Implementing Agencies and the CBD Secretariat to develop an initial strategy for assisting countries to prepare for the entry into force of the biosafety protocol [*decision V/13, paragraph 1*]. It has also emphasized the importance of financial support for capacity-building for implementation of the Protocol [*decision V/11, paragraph 11*].

Further information on the content and development of the Protocol, together with documentation for the meetings of the ICCP, is available on the Convention website.

References

Decisions on Article 19 (3) and (4)

Decision I/9, paragraphs 3–8 (Medium-term programme of work)
Decision II/5 (Consideration of the need for and modalities of a protocol for the safe transfer, handling and use of LMOs)
Decision III/20 (Issues related to biosafety)
Decision IV/3 (Issues related to biosafety)
Decision EM-I/1 (Decision on the continuation of the first extraordinary meeting of the COP)
Decision EM-I/3 (Adoption of the Cartagena Protocol and interim arrangements)
Decision V/1 (Work plan of the ICCP)

Other relevant decisions

Decision II/10, annex I, paragraph (xi) (Marine and coastal)
Decision III/5, paragraph 2 (Additional guidance to the financial mechanism)
Decision III/19, paragraph 13 (Statement to UNGA Special Session)
Decision IV/10 C, paragraph 11 (Impact assessment and minimizing adverse effects)
Decision V/11, paragraph 11 (Additional financial resources)
Decision V/13, paragraph 1 (Further guidance to the financial mechanism)
Decision V/18, II, paragraph 9 (Impact assessment, liability and redress)

Declarations

Malaysia (adoption) and Peru (adoption)

Documents

UNEP/CBD/COP/1/4 Report of the First Meeting of the Open-ended Ad Hoc Working Group on Biosafety
UNEP/CBD/COP/2/7 Report of the Open-ended Expert Group on Biosafety
UNEP/CBD/COP/3/26 Report of the first meeting of the Open-ended Ad Hoc Working Group on Biosafety
UNEP/CBD/COP/3/27 Report on the Elaboration of a Protocol on Biosafety
UNEP/CBD/COP/3/28 UNEP International Technical Guidelines for Safety in Biotechnology

UNEP/CBD/COP/4/9 Issues related to biosafety
UNEP/CBD/ExCOP/1/1/Rev.1 Provisional agenda
UNEP/CBD/ExCOP/1/1/Rev.2 Provisional revised agenda
UNEP/CBD/ExCOP/1/1/Add.1/Rev.1 Annotated provisional agenda
UNEP/CBD/ExCOP/1/1/Rev.2/Add.1 Annotations to the provisional revised agenda
UNEP/CBD/ExCOP/1/2 Report of the Sixth Meeting of the Open-ended Ad-Hoc Working Group on Biosafety
UNEP/CBD/ExCOP/1/L.2/Rev.1 Draft Report of the Extraordinary Meeting of the Conference of the Parties for the Adoption of the Protocol on Biosafety to the Convention on Biological Diversity
UNEP/CBD/ExCOP/1/3 Report of the Extraordinary Meeting of the Conference of the Parties for the Adoption of the Protocol on Biosafety to the Convention on Biological Diversity
UNEP/CBD/ExCOP/1/Inf.1 Documentation containing draft text of the Protocol for the resumed session: explanatory note by the Secretariat
UNEP/CBD/ExCOP/1/Inf.2 Aide-memoire: Chairman's summary of informal consultations held in Montreal on 1 July 1999
UNEP/CBD/ExCOP/1/Inf.3 Chairman's summary of informal consultations held in Vienna from 15 to 19 September 1999
UNEP/CBD/COP/5/6 Report on the status of the Biosafety Protocol
UNEP/CBD/SBSTTA/2/8 Capacity-building in biosafety for developing countries
UNEP/CBD/BSWG1/1 Provisional Agenda
UNEP/CBD/BSWG1/1/Add.1 Annotated Provisional Agenda
UNEP/CBD/BSWG/1/Add.2 Provisional Organization of work
UNEP/CBD/BSWG/1/2 Terms of reference of the Open-ended Ad Hoc Working Group on Biosafety
UNEP/CBD/BSWG/1/3 Note by Secretariat (Elaboration of the terms of reference of the Open-ended Ad Hoc Working Group on Biosafety
UNEP/CBD/BSWG/1/4 (UNEP/CBD/COP/2/7) Report of the First Meeting of the Open-ended Ad Hoc Working Group on Biosafety
UNEP/CBD/BSWG/2/1 Provisional agenda
UNEP/CBD/BSWG/2/1/Add.1 Annotations to the provisional agenda
UNEP/CBD/BSWG/2/2 Compilation of views of Governments on the contents of the future protocol
UNEP/CBD/BSWG/2/3 Background document on existing international agreements related to Biosafety
UNEP/CBD/BSWG/2/4 Potential socio-economic effects of biotechnology: a bibliography
UNEP/CBD/BSWG/2/5 Glossary of terms relevant to a biosafety protocol: results of a preliminary survey
UNEP/CBD/BSWG/2/6 Report of the Second Meeting of the Open-ended Ad Hoc Working Group on Biosafety
UNEP/CBD/BSWG/2/Inf.1 Submission of individual Governments/regional groups on the contents of future protocol
UNEP/CBD/BSWG/3/1 Provisional Agenda
UNEP/CBD/BSWG/3/1/Add.1 Annotated Provisional Agenda
UNEP/CBD/BSWG/3/2 Chairman's review of items addressed by country submission at BSWG/2
UNEP/CBD/BSWG/3/3 Compilation of government submissions of draft text on selected items
UNEP/CBD/BSWG/3/4 Compilation of draft text prepared by the Secretariat on selected items

UNEP/CBD/BSWG/3/5 Government submissions
UNEP/CBD/BSWG/3/6 Report of the Third Meeting of the Open-ended Ad Hoc Working Group on Biosafety
UNEP/CBD/BSWG/3/Inf.1 Compilation of definitions and terms relevant to a biosafety protocol
UNEP/CBD/BSWG/3/Inf.2 Background document on existing international agreements related to Biosafety
UNEP/CBD/BSWG/3/Inf.3 Study on existing international information sharing systems
UNEP/CBD/BSWG/4/1 Provisional Agenda
UNEP/CBD/BSWG/4/1/Add.1 Annotated Provisional Agenda
UNEP/CBD/BSWG/4/2 Compilation of Government Submissions of Draft text on Selected Items: Articles 1, 1 bis and 23–27
UNEP/CBD/BSWG/4/3 Compilation of Government Submissions of Draft text on Items Other than Articles 1, 1 bis and 23–27
UNEP/CBD/BSWG/4/4 Report of the Fourth Meeting of the Open-ended Ad Hoc Working Group on Biosafety
UNEP/CBD/BSWG/4/Inf.1 Chairman's Note on Articles 3–10 and 12–14
UNEP/CBD/BSWG/4/Inf.1/Add.1 Chairman's Note on Article 11
UNEP/CBD/BSWG/4/Inf.2 Chairman's Note on Articles 1, 1 bis and 15–27
UNEP/CBD/BSWG/4/Inf.3 Preamble
UNEP/CBD/BSWG/4/Inf.4 Implementation Mechanisms for Information Sharing under a Protocol on Biosafety under the Convention on Biological Diversity
UNEP/CBD/BSWG/4/Inf.5 The Consolidated Text from the Third Meeting of the Open-Ended Ad Hoc Working Group on Biosafety
UNEP/CBD/BSWG/4/Inf.8 Chairman's Note on Articles 28–43
UNEP/CBD/BSWG/5/1 Provisional Agenda
UNEP/CBD/BSWG/5/1/Add.1 Annotated Provisional Agenda
UNEP/CBD/BSWG/5/2 Compilation of New Government Submissions of Draft Text
UNEP/CBD/BSWG/5/3 Report of the Fifth Meeting of the Open-ended Ad Hoc Working Group on Biosafety
UNEP/CBD/BSWG/5/Inf.1 Revised Consolidated Text of the Draft Articles
UNEP/CBD/BSWG/5/Inf.2 Government Submissions
UNEP/CBD/BSWG/5/Inf.2/Add.1 Georgia – Comments on the Revised Consolidated Text of the Draft Articles
UNEP/CBD/BSWG/5/Inf.3 Term 'Products Thereof'
UNEP/CBD/BSWG/5/Inf.4 Submission from the Government of Vietnam
UNEP/CBD/BSWG/6/1 Provisional Agenda
UNEP/CBD/BSWG/6/1/Add.1 Annotated Provisional Agenda
UNEP/CBD/BSWG/6/2 Draft Negotiating Text
UNEP/CBD/BSWG/6/2/Rev.1 Draft Negotiating Text (English only)
UNEP/CBD/BSWG/6/3 Clusters Analysis
UNEP/CBD/BSWG/6/4 Preparation of the Draft Negotiating Text of the Protocol on Biosafety
UNEP/CBD/BSWG/6/5 Development of a Legally Binding Instrument
UNEP/CBD/BSWG/6/6 Report: Meeting of the Extended Bureau of the Open-ended Ad-Hoc Working Group on Biosafety, Montreal (21–22 October 1998)
UNEP/CBD/BSWG/6/7 Transshipment
UNEP/CBD/BSWG/6/8 Overview and Annotated Draft Negotiating Text of the Protocol on Biosafety
UNEP/CBD/BSWG/6/Inf.1 (UNEP/CBD/BSWG/5/2) Compilation of New Government Submissions of Draft Text (structured by Article)

UNEP/CBD/BSWG/6/Inf.2 Government Submissions on the Preamble and Annexes (submitted prior to BSWG5)

UNEP/CBD/BSWG/6/Inf.3 Proposition of the Government of Chile: Settlement of Disputes

UNEP/CBD/BSWG/6/Inf.4 Resolutions on Biodiversity and the Environment (ACP-EU Joint Assembly, 24 Sept. 1998, Brussels, Belgium)

UNEP/CBD/BSWG/6/Inf.5 Comments by the United Nations Economic and Social Council's Committee of Experts on the Transport of Dangerous Goods on the Draft Protocol on Biosafety

UNEP/CBD/BSWG/6/Inf.6 Remarks submitted by Slovenia

UNEP/CBD/BSWG/6/Inf.7 Remarks submitted by the Office International des Épizooties

UNEP/CBD/BSWG/6/Inf.8 Note by the Co-Chairs of Contact Group I: Programme of Work

UNEP/CBD/BSWG/6/Inf.9 Note from the Co-Chairs of Contact Group II to the Extended Bureau

UNEP/CBD/ICCP/1/1 Provisional Agenda

UNEP/CBD/ICCP/1/1/ADD1 Annotations to the Provisional Agenda

UNEP/CBD/ICCP/1/2 Report of the Executive Secretary on inter-sessional work requested by EXCOP (decisions EM-I/3, paragraphs 11–14) and COP 5 (decision V/1, paragraph 3)

UNEP/CBD/ICCP/1/3 Information-Sharing (Art. 20, Art. 19) Outcome of the Meeting of Technical Experts on the Biosafety Clearing-House

UNEP/CBD/ICCP/1/3/ADD1 Information Sharing (Art. 20, Art. 19) Outcome of the Meeting of Technical Experts on the BCH – Addendum: Estimate of resources for the pilot phase of the Biosafety Clearing-House

UNEP/CBD/ICCP/1/4 Capacity Building (Art. 22, Art. 28)

UNEP/CBD/ICCP/1/5 Decision-Making Procedures (Art. 10, paragraph 7) Facilitating decision-making by Parties of import

UNEP/CBD/ICCP/1/6 Handling, Transport, Packaging and Identification (Art. 18)

UNEP/CBD/ICCP/1/7 Compliance (Art. 34) Development of compliance procedures and mechanisms under the Cartagena Protocol on Biosafety

UNEP/CBD/ICCP/1/8 Future Work of the Intergovernmental Committee for the Cartagena Protocol on Biosafety

UNEP/CBD/ICCP/1/Inf.1 Biosafety Capacity-Building: Completed, Ongoing and Planned Projects/Programmes

Articles 20, 21 and 39: Financial resources, financial mechanism and financial interim arrangements

Article 20: Financial resources

1. Each Contracting Party undertakes to provide, in accordance with its capabilities, financial support and incentives in respect of those national activities which are intended to achieve the objectives of this Convention, in accordance with its national plans, priorities and programmes.

2. The developed country Parties shall provide new and additional financial resources to enable developing country Parties to meet the agreed full incremental costs to them of implementing measures which fulfil the obligations of this

Convention and to benefit from its provisions and which costs are agreed between a developing country Party and the institutional structure referred to in Article 21, in accordance with policy, strategy, programme priorities and eligibility criteria and an indicative list of incremental costs established by the Conference of the Parties. Other Parties, including countries undergoing the process of transition to a market economy, may voluntarily assume the obligations of the developed country Parties. For the purpose of this Article, the Conference of the Parties shall at its first meeting establish a list of developed country Parties and other Parties which voluntarily assume the obligations of the developed country Parties. The Conference of the Parties shall periodically review and if necessary amend the list. Contributions from other countries and sources on a voluntary basis would also be encouraged. The implementation of these commitments shall take into account the need for adequacy, predictability and timely flow of funds and the importance of burden-sharing among the contributing Parties included in the list.

3. The developed country Parties may also provide, and developing country Parties avail themselves of, financial resources related to the implementation of this Convention through bilateral, regional and other multilateral channels.

4. The extent to which developing country Parties will effectively implement their commitments under this Convention will depend on the effective implementation by developed country Parties of their commitments under this Convention related to financial resources and transfer of technology and will take fully into account the fact that economic and social development and eradication of poverty are the first and overriding priorities of the developing country Parties.

5. The Parties shall take full account of the specific needs and special situation of least developed countries in their actions with regard to funding and transfer of technology.

6. The Contracting Parties shall also take into consideration the special conditions resulting from the dependence on, distribution and location of, biological diversity within developing country Parties, in particular small island States.

7. Consideration shall also be given to the special situation of developing countries, including those that are most environmentally vulnerable, such as those with arid and semi-arid zones, coastal and mountainous areas.

Article 21: Financial mechanism

1. There shall be a mechanism for the provision of financial resources to developing country Parties for purposes of this Convention on a grant or concessional basis, the essential elements of which are described in this Article. The mechanism shall function under the authority and guidance of, and be accountable to, the Conference of the Parties for purposes of this Convention. The operations of the mechanism shall be carried out by such institutional structure as may be decided upon by the Conference of the Parties at its first meeting. For purposes of this Convention, the Conference of the Parties shall determine the policy, strategy, programme priorities

and eligibility criteria relating to the access to and utilization of such resources. The contributions shall be such as to take into account the need for predictability, adequacy and timely flow of funds referred to in Article 20 in accordance with the amount of resources needed to be decided periodically by the Conference of the Parties and the importance of burden-sharing among the contributing Parties included in the list referred to in Article 20, paragraph 2. Voluntary contributions may also be made by the developed country Parties and by other countries and sources. The mechanism shall operate within a democratic and transparent system of governance.

2. Pursuant to the objectives of this Convention, the Conference of the Parties shall at its first meeting determine the policy, strategy and programme priorities, as well as detailed criteria and guidelines for eligibility for access to and utilization of the financial resources including monitoring and evaluation on a regular basis of such utilization. The Conference of the Parties shall decide on the arrangements to give effect to paragraph 1 above after consultation with the institutional structure entrusted with the operation of the financial mechanism.

3. The Conference of the Parties shall review the effectiveness of the mechanism established under this Article, including the criteria and guidelines referred to in paragraph 2 above, not less than two years after the entry into force of this Convention and thereafter on a regular basis. Based on such review, it shall take appropriate action to improve the effectiveness of the mechanism if necessary.

4. The Contracting Parties shall consider strengthening existing financial institutions to provide financial resources for the conservation and sustainable use of biological diversity.

Article 39: Financial interim arrangements

Provided that it has been fully restructured in accordance with the requirements of Article 21, the Global Environment Facility of the United Nations Development Programme, the United Nations Environment Programme and the International Bank for Reconstruction and Development shall be the institutional structure referred to in Article 21 on an interim basis, for the period between the entry into force of this Convention and the first meeting of the Conference of the Parties or until the Conference of the Parties decides which institutional structure will be designated in accordance with Article 21.

Notes

Terms defined in Article 2

'Biological diversity', 'sustainable use' and 'technology'.

Consideration of Articles 20, 21 and 39 by the COP

The provisions of Articles 20, 21, and 39 are closely linked. They are therefore addressed together below.

Background and status

At COP 1 and COP 2, one decision was adopted on financial mechanism and resources. However, the practice since COP 2 has been to address in separate decisions: (i) the financial mechanism and resources provided through the financial mechanism in accordance with Article 20 (2) and Article 21; and (ii) other financial resources and financial institutions related to the implementation of the Convention which are *not* provided through the financial mechanism (such as resources from bilateral, regional or multilateral funding agencies). An attempt has been made to reflect this approach below, and address in turn:

(a) The financial mechanism and financial resources provided through the financial mechanism.

(b) Other financial resources, which have been termed 'additional financial resources' in relevant COP decisions.

(c) Financial support for national activities to achieve the Convention's objectives (Article 20 (1)).

Financial mechanism

Editors' note:

Further information on GEF programmes and activities referred to here are available in GEF publications and on the GEF website at http://www.gefweb.com

As part of its medium-term programme of work, the COP has considered the financial mechanism and resources as a standing item on its agenda [*decision I/9, decision II/18*].

A number of specific issues have arisen in relation to paragraph 2 of Article 20 and paragraphs 1–3 of Article 21. These include:

- (i) Designation of the institutional structure operating the financial mechanism
- (ii) Memorandum of Understanding (MoU) between the COP and the GEF Council
- (iii) Policy, strategy, programme priorities and eligibility criteria
- (iv) Additional guidance to the financial mechanism
- (v) Review of effectiveness of the financial mechanism
- (vi) Parties assuming the obligations of developed country Parties under Article 20 (2)

These are addressed separately below.

Designation of the institutional structure operating the financial mechanism

Article 39 of the Convention makes provision for financial interim arrangements. COP 1 and COP 2 decided that the restructured GEF would continue to serve as the institutional structure to operate the financial mechanism on an interim basis, in accordance with Article 39 [*decision I/2, paragraph 2 and decision II/6, paragraph 1*]. This issue is further addressed in the MoU between the COP and the GEF Council, adopted COP 3 (see below) [*decision III/8, annex*].

Memorandum of Understanding between the COP and the GEF Council

Elaboration and adoption of the Memorandum of Understanding

In relation to arrangements for the relationship between the COP and the GEF, the COP authorized the Secretariat, on its behalf, to consult with the restructured GEF on the content of an MoU [*decision I/2, paragraph 4*].

COP 2 took note of a draft MoU prepared jointly by the Convention Secretariat and the GEF Secretariat, and requested the Convention Secretariat to continue consultations and submit a revised draft to COP 3 [*decision II/6, paragraph 4*]. A revised MoU was presented to COP 3, and the COP adopted the MoU as contained in the annex to decision III/8 [*decision III/8, paragraph 1*]. The COP requested the Executive Secretary to transmit decision III/8 to the GEF Council [*decision III/8, paragraph 2*]. The GEF Council also adopted the MoU at its meeting in May 1997. In accordance with the terms of the MoU, the MoU is now in effect between the COP and the GEF Council [*MoU, decision III/8, annex, paragraph 10.1*].

Content of the Memorandum of Understanding[19]

The MoU states that its purpose is to make provision for the relationship between the COP and the GEF Council in order to give effect to the provisions of Article 21 (1) of the Convention and paragraph 26 of the GEF Instrument[20] and, on an interim basis, in accordance with Article 39 of the Convention [*MoU, decision III/8, annex, paragraph 1*]. Broadly, the MoU provides for:

- Communication of guidance, and any revisions to guidance, from the COP to the GEF on the following matters:
  - (a) policy and strategy;
  - (b) programme priorities;
  - (c) eligibility criteria;
  - (d) an indicative list of incremental costs;
  - (e) a list of developed country Parties and other Parties which voluntarily assume the obligations of developed country Parties;
  - (f) any other matter relating to Article 21, including periodic determination of the amount of resources needed.
- Submission of a report by the GEF Council to each ordinary meeting of the COP, with specific information on the application and implementation of COP guidance.
- Monitoring and evaluation.
- Determination of funding requirements.

19 Readers should refer to the full text of the MoU in the annex to Decision III/8.
20 Instrument for the Establishment of the Restructured Global Environment Facility, 1994.

- Reciprocal representation of the GEF at meetings of the COP and of the Convention at meetings of the GEF.
- Cooperation between the Convention Secretariat and the Secretariat of the GEF.

Policy, strategy, programme priorities and eligibility criteria

COP 1 adopted the policy, strategy, programme priorities and eligibility criteria for access to and utilization of financial resources, as provided in paragraphs 1 and 2 of Article 21. These are annexed to decision I/2. The COP also adopted interim guidelines for monitoring and evaluation of the utilization of financial resources, as provided in paragraph 2 of Article 21. These are contained in annex III to decision I/2. The COP instructed the GEF to take prompt measures to support programmes, projects and activities consistent with the policy, strategy, programme priorities and eligibility criteria.

In October 1995, the GEF Council approved the Operational Strategy of the GEF. The GEF has developed four operational programmes for biodiversity:

1 Arid and semi-arid zone ecosystems.
2 Coastal, marine and freshwater ecosystems.
3 Forest ecosystems.
4 Mountain ecosystems.

The COP has requested the GEF to fully incorporate guidance from the COP on an ongoing basis, into the further development of the Operational Strategy and programmes to ensure that the objectives of the Convention are addressed[21] [*decision II/6, paragraph 6*]. It has also asked the GEF to take steps to expedite the project preparation and approval process with a view to implementing fully the guidance set out in annex I to decision I/2 [*decision II/6, paragraph 7*].

Additional guidance to the financial mechanism

The COP has given additional guidance to the financial mechanism in a number of its decisions. Since COP 3, the practice of the COP has been to consolidate such additional guidance in a COP decision entitled 'Additional guidance to the financial mechanism' [*see decision III/5; decision IV/13; decision V/13*]. Some attempt to consolidate guidance to the financial mechanism was also made in decision II/6 [*decision II/6, paragraph 11*]. In addition, guidance given to the financial mechanism in respect of specific issues, articles or thematic areas of the Convention is sometimes also reflected in the decisions on those issues.

The COP has requested the financial mechanism to facilitate urgent implementation of Article 6 of the Convention and to make financial resources available to developing country Parties to assist in the preparation of national reports under Article 26 of the Convention [*decision II/6, paragraphs 5, 11; decision II/7, paragraph 6; decision II/17, paragraph 12; decision IV/13, paragraph 6; decision IV/14, paragraph 5*]. Accordingly, the GEF has provided funding for Enabling Activities.[22]

21 With regard to additional guidance to the GEF, see below. See also the guides in this section of this Handbook related to specific articles and thematic areas under the heading 'Guidance to the financial mechanism'.

22 See GEF *Operational Criteria for Enabling Activities: Biodiversity* and *Revised Guidelines for Additional Funding of Biodiversity Enabling Activities (Expedited Procedures)* (October 2000). See also the guide to Article 6 in this section of the Handbook.

The COP has also given guidance as to GEF procedures and as to public participation. For example, as noted above (see 'Policy, strategy, programme priorities and eligibility criteria'), the COP has further requested the GEF to take steps to expedite the project preparation and approval process with a view to implementing fully the guidance set out in annex I to decision I/2 [*decision II/6, paragraph 7*]. The COP has also recommended that the GEF explore the possibility of promoting diverse forms of public involvement and more effective collaboration between tiers of government and civil society, including feasibility of a programme for medium-sized projects [*decision II/6, paragraph 10*].

Where the Convention Secretariat includes in pre-session documentation suggestions for further guidance to the financial mechanism on a specific issue, the COP has now asked that the Secretariat addresses the relationship between existing guidance given to the financial mechanism and the proposed new guidance [*decision IV/11, paragraph 4*].

COP 5 welcomed the decision of the GEF Council to develop an initial strategy for assisting countries to prepare for the entry into force of the Cartagena Protocol on Biosafety [*decision V/13, paragraph 1*].

Review of effectiveness of the financial mechanism

Article 21 (3) provides that the COP shall first review the effectiveness of the financial mechanism not less than two years after the entry into force of the Convention. In accordance with paragraph 3 of Article 21, the COP requested the Secretariat to present to it a report on the financial mechanism so that it could adopt decisions on the timetable and nature of the review of the financial mechanism [*decision I/2, paragraph 6*].

COP 2 decided to review the effectiveness of the financial mechanism at COP 4, and thereafter every three years [*decision II/6, paragraph 2*]. The Executive Secretary was asked to develop guidelines for the review [*decision II/6, paragraph 3*]. Guidelines for the review were adopted at COP 3 [*decision III/7, annex*]. COP 3 also decided that the review of effectiveness should be conducted under the authority of the COP, and that based on the results of the review, the COP would take appropriate action to improve the effectiveness of the mechanism if necessary [*decision III/17, paragraphs 2, 3*].

COP 4 adopted a decision on the review of the effectiveness of the financial mechanism [*decision IV/11*], in which it asked the GEF to take action identified in an annex to the decision with a view to improving effectiveness, and to report to COP 5 on action taken.

COP 5 determined the terms of reference for the second review of the financial mechanism [*decision V/12*], which will be conducted in time for COP 6. The second review will cover all operational programmes of the financial mechanism relevant to the Convention, during the period from November 1996 to June 2001. The terms of reference for the review are set out in the annex to decision V/12. Parties, countries and stakeholders have been invited to communicate their views on the effectiveness and efficiency of the financial mechanism during the period under review by 30 September 2001. The Secretariat issued a call for tenders for an independent evaluator to conduct the review.

Parties assuming the obligations of developed country Parties under Article 20 (2)

In relation to the provision of new and additional financial resources by developed country Parties, Article 20 (2) provides, *inter alia*, that other Parties, including countries undergoing the process of transition to market economy, may voluntarily assume the obligations of the developed country Parties. It further provides that, for the purpose of

Article 20, the COP shall at its first meeting establish a list of developed country Parties and other Parties which voluntarily assume the obligations of developed country Parties, and that the COP shall periodically review and, if necessary, amend the list. Accordingly, COP 1 adopted such a list. This is contained in annex II to decision I/2. To date, the COP has not reviewed or amended this list.

Additional financial resources

In addition to the provision of financial resources through the financial mechanism, the Convention also provides that developed country Parties may also provide, and developing country Parties avail themselves of, financial resources related to the implementation of the Convention through bilateral, regional and multilateral channels (*Article 20 (3)*). It further provides that the Parties shall consider strengthening existing financial institutions to provide financial resources for the conservation and sustainable use of biological diversity (*Article 21 (4)*).

The COP has adopted a number of decisions that call upon Parties, Governments, international organizations and/or bilateral, regional and multilateral donors to provide support for activities to implement the Convention. References to these decisions are listed below under the sub-heading 'Additional financial resources'.

COP 1 requested the Secretariat to provide to COP 2 a study on the availability of financial resources additional to those provided through the financial mechanism, and on ways and means of mobilizing and channelling these resources in support of the Convention's objectives [*decision I/2, paragraph 7*]. In decision II/6, the COP requested the Executive Secretary to explore this issue further and to study characteristics specific to biodiversity activities to allow the COP to make suggestions to funding institutions on how to make their activities in the area of biodiversity more supportive of the Convention [*decision II/6, paragraph 9*]. COP 3 adopted decision III/6 entitled 'Additional financial resources'. In this decision, it urged all funding institutions, including bilateral and multilateral donors, as well as regional funding institutions and NGOs, to make their activities more supportive of the Convention. It requested the Executive Secretary to explore ways of collaborating with funding institutions to facilitate these efforts, and invited institutions to provide information to the Secretariat on their relevant activities [*decision III/6, paragraphs 2, 5*].

The COP has also urged developed country Parties to cooperate in the development of standardized information on their financial support for the objectives of the Convention, and where possible to submit this in their national reports [*decision III/6, paragraph 4; decision IV/14, paragraph 4*].

For COP 5, the Executive Secretary was asked to prepare a report on additional financial resources, including proposals for monitoring financial support for the Convention; possible collaboration with relevant organizations; exploring possibilities for additional financial support for elements of the longer-term programme of work, and examining issues related to private sector support for implementation of the Convention.

COP 5 adopted decision V/11 on Additional Financial Resources. This decision, *inter alia*, urges reporting on financial support to biodiversity by Parties, as well as funding institutions, United Nations bodies, intergovernmental organizations and NGOs [*decision V/11, paragraphs 4, 5*]. It also requests the Secretariat to further develop a database on biodiversity-related funding information. The COP invited the GEF to assist the Convention Secretariat, in collaboration with other institutions, to convene a workshop on financing for biodiversity to share knowledge and experience among funding institutions and to explore the potential of the GEF as a funding catalyst [*decision V/11, paragraph 2*]. This workshop was held on 16–17 July 2001 in Cuba.

Decision V/11 also urged developed country Parties to promote support for implementation of the Convention in the funding policy of their bilateral funding institutions and those of regional and multilateral funding institutions [*decision V/11, paragraph 9*].

COP 6 will consider implementation of decision V/11.

Financial support and incentives for national activities (Article 20 (1))

Under Article 20 (1), each Party undertakes to provide, in accordance with its capabilities, financial support and incentives in respect of those national activities intended to achieve the objectives of the Convention in accordance with its national plans, priorities and programmes. In decision III/11, in relation to agricultural biological diversity, the COP drew the attention of Parties to this provision in the context of support and incentives for the conservation and sustainable use of biological diversity important to agriculture [*decision III/11, paragraph 21*].

COP 5 urged Parties to promote the consideration of tax exemptions in national taxation systems for biodiversity-related donations [*decision V/11, paragraph 16*].

References

Decisions on Articles 20, 21 and 39

Financial mechanism

Decision I/2 (Financial mechanism and resources)
Decision II/6 (Financial mechanism and resources)
Decision III/5 (Additional guidance to the financial mechanism)
Decision III/7 (Guidelines for the review of the effectiveness of the financial mechanism)
Decision III/8 (Memorandum of Understanding between the COP and the GEF Council)
Decision IV/11 (Review of the effectiveness of the financial mechanism)
Decision IV/13 (Additional guidance to the financial mechanism)
Decision V/12 (Second review of the financial mechanism)
Decision V/13 (Further guidance to the financial mechanism)

Additional financial resources

Decision I/2, paragraph 7 (Financial mechanism and resources)
Decision II/6, paragraph 9 (Financial mechanism and resources)
Decision III/6 (Additional financial resources)
Decision IV/12 (Additional financial resources)
Decision V/11 (Additional financial resources)

Relevant aspects of thematic work programmes

Financial mechanism

Decision II/10, paragraph 11 (Marine and coastal)
Decision III/11, paragraph 22 (Agriculture)

Decision IV/4, paragraphs 6, 7; annex I, paragraph 10 (Inland water)
Decision IV/6, paragraphs 12, 13 (Agriculture)
Decision IV/7, paragraphs 5, 6, 8 (Forest)
Decision V/5, paragraph 18 (Agriculture)

Additional financial resources

Decision II/10, paragraph 11 (Marine and coastal)
Decision III/11, paragraphs 21, 22 (Agriculture)
Decision IV/4, annex I, paragraph 11 (Inland water)
Decision IV/5, III (Marine and coastal)
Decision IV/6, paragraphs 4, 12 (Agriculture)
Decision IV/7, paragraph 5 (Forest)
Decision V/3, annex, D (Marine and coastal)
Decision V/5, paragraph 9 (Agriculture)
Decision V/23, paragraphs 3, 11 (Dry and sub-humid lands)

Other relevant decisions

Financial mechanism

Decision II/3, paragraph 9 (Clearing-house mechanism)
Decision II/7, paragraph 6 (Consideration of Articles 6 and 8)
Decision II/17, paragraph 12 (National reports)
Decision III/4, paragraphs 2, 3 (Clearing-house mechanism)
Decision III/9, paragraph 4 (Implementation of Articles 6 and 8)
Decision III/10, paragraph 10 (Identification, monitoring and assessment)
Decision III/14, paragraph 5 (Implementation of Article 8 (j))
Decision III/15, paragraph 3 (Access to genetic resources)
Decision III/19, annex, paragraphs 16, 17 (Statement to UNGA Special Session)
Decision III/20, paragraph 2 (c) (Issues related to biosafety)
Decision III/21, paragraph 12 (Cooperation)
Decision IV/1 C, paragraph 3 (Alien species)
Decision IV/1 D, paragraphs 1, 9 (Taxonomy)
Decision IV/2, paragraph 9 (Clearing-house mechanism)
Decision IV/8, paragraph 4 (Access and benefit-sharing)
Decision IV/9, paragraph 13 (Implementation of Article 8 (j) and related provisions)
Decision IV/10 A, paragraph 3 (Incentive measures)
Decision IV/10 B, paragraph 9 (Public education and awareness)
Decision IV/14, paragraph 5 (National reports)
Decision V/8, paragraph 17 (Alien species)
Decision V/9, paragraph 6 (Global Taxonomy Initiative)
Decision V/11, paragraph 2 (Additional financial resources)
Decision V/20, I, paragraph 8 (Operations of the Convention)

Additional financial resources

Decision III/4, paragraph 4 (Clearing-house mechanism)
Decision III/15, paragraph 3 (Access to genetic resources)
Decision III/19, annex, paragraph 15 (Statement to UNGA Special Session)
Decision IV/2, paragraph 1 (Clearing-house mechanism)
Decision IV/10 B, paragraph 8 (Public education and awareness)

Decision IV/14, paragraph 4 (National reports)
Decision V/6, paragraph 6 (Ecosystem approach)
Decision V/8, paragraph 17 (Alien species)
Decision V/14, I, paragraph (g) (i) (Clearing-house mechanism)
Decision V/16, paragraphs 7, 19 (b), 20 (Article 8 (j) and related provisions)

Declarations

Australia et al (adoption), Denmark et al (adoption), France (signature and ratification), India (adoption), Italy (ratification), Malaysia (adoption), Saudi Arabia (adoption), Switzerland (signature), UK (signature and ratification) and USA (adoption),

Documents

UNEP/CBD/COP/1/5 Policy, strategy, programme priorities and eligibility criteria regarding access to and utilization of financial resources
UNEP/CBD/COP/1/6 Institutional structure to operate the financial mechanism under the Convention
UNEP/CBD/COP/1/7 List of developed country Parties and other Parties which voluntarily assume the obligations of developed country Parties
UNEP/CBD/COP/2/8 Report of the Global Environment Facility
UNEP/CBD/COP/2/9 Report of the Secretariat on the financial mechanism under the Convention
UNEP/CBD/COP/2/10 Study on the availability of additional financial resources
UNEP/CBD/COP/2/11 Memorandum of understanding between the COP and the GEF
UNEP/CBD/COP/3/5 Report of Global Environment Facility
UNEP/CBD/COP/3/6 Report of the Executive Secretary on financial resources and mechanism UNEP/CBD/COP/3/7 Characteristics specific to biological diversity and suggestions to funding institutions on how to make their activities more supportive of the Convention
UNEP/CBD/COP/3/8 Review of the effectiveness of the financial mechanism under the Convention
UNEP/CBD/COP/3/9 Designation of the institutional structure to operate the financial mechanism
UNEP/CBD/COP/3/10 Memorandum of Understanding between the Conference of the Parties and the Council of the Global Environment Facility
UNEP/CBD/COP/3/34 Date and venue of the fourth meeting of the Conference of the Parties
UNEP/CBD/COP/3/Inf.1 Submissions received by the Executive Secretary concerning guidelines for the review of the effectiveness of the financial mechanism
UNEP/CBD/COP/3/Inf.2 Submissions received by the Executive Secretary concerning the 'Draft Memorandum of Understanding Between the Conference of the Parties to the Convention on Biological Diversity and the Council of the Global Environment Facility, regarding the Institutional Structure Operating the Financial Mechanism of the Convention'
UNEP/CBD/COP/4/15 Report on the activities of the Global Environment Facility
UNEP/CBD/COP/4/16 Review of the effectiveness of the financial mechanism.
UNEP/CBD/COP/4/17 Additional financial resources
UNEP/CBD/COP/4/Inf.23 Review of the Effectiveness of the Financial Mechanism – Information Received at the Secretariat

UNEP/CBD/COP/5/7 Report of the Global Environment Facility
UNEP/CBD/COP/5/13 Progress report on the mechanisms for implementation
UNEP/CBD/COP/5/14 Additional Financial Resources

Article 22: Relationship with other international conventions

1. The provisions of this Convention shall not affect the rights and obligations of any Contracting Party deriving from any existing agreement, except where the exercise of those rights and obligations would cause a serious threat to biological diversity.

2. Contracting Parties shall implement this Convention with respect to the marine environment consistently with the rights and obligations of States under the law of the sea.

Notes

Terms defined in Article 2

'Biological diversity'.

Consideration of Article 22 by the COP

Background and status

The COP has not explicitly addressed Article 22 to date. It has, however, taken a wide range of decisions which have some bearing on the relationship between the provisions of the Convention and other existing agreements. Most of these decisions are referenced under the heading 'Cooperation' in the guides on each article and the thematic work programme in this section of the Handbook. For example, with respect to the relationship between the Convention and the TRIPs Agreement, see the guide to Article 16, including references under the sub-headings 'Consideration of Article 16 by the COP' and 'Cooperation with other conventions and organizations'; and decision V/26 B.

COP 2 requested the Executive Secretary, in consultation with the United Nations Office for Ocean Affairs and the Law of the Sea, to undertake a study on the relationship between the Convention and the United Nations Convention on the Law of the Sea with regard to the conservation and sustainable use of genetic resources on the deep seabed [*decision II/10, paragraph 12*]. COP 5 had before it an information document on marine and coastal genetic resources and bioprospecting (see Document UNEP/CBD/COP/V/Inf.7). It took note of this work and asked SBSTTA to analyse and provide advice on scientific, technical and technological matters related to the issue of marine and coastal genetic resources [*decision V/3, paragraph* 12].

References

Declarations

Argentina (ratification), Chile (adoption), Colombia (ratification), India (adoption), Papua New Guinea (ratification) and USA (adoption)

Article 23: Conference of the Parties

1. A Conference of the Parties is hereby established. The first meeting of the Conference of the Parties shall be convened by the Executive Director of the United Nations Environment Programme not later than one year after the entry into force of this Convention. Thereafter, ordinary meetings of the Conference of the Parties shall be held at regular intervals to be determined by the Conference at its first meeting.

2. Extraordinary meetings of the Conference of the Parties shall be held at such other times as may be deemed necessary by the Conference, or at the written request of any Party, provided that, within six months of the request being communicated to them by the Secretariat, it is supported by at least one third of the Parties.

3. The Conference of the Parties shall by consensus agree upon and adopt rules of procedure for itself and for any subsidiary body it may establish, as well as financial rules governing the funding of the Secretariat. At each ordinary meeting, it shall adopt a budget for the financial period until the next ordinary meeting.

4. The Conference of the Parties shall keep under review the implementation of this Convention, and, for this purpose, shall:

(a) Establish the form and the intervals for transmitting the information to be submitted in accordance with Article 26 and consider such information as well as reports submitted by any subsidiary body;

(b) Review scientific, technical and technological advice on biological diversity provided in accordance with Article 25;

(c) Consider and adopt, as required, protocols in accordance with Article 28;

(d) Consider and adopt, as required, in accordance with Articles 29 and 30, amendments to this Convention and its annexes;

(e) Consider amendments to any protocol, as well as to any annexes thereto, and, if so decided, recommend their adoption to the parties to the protocol concerned;

(f) Consider and adopt, as required, in accordance with Article 30, additional annexes to this Convention;

(g) Establish such subsidiary bodies, particularly to provide scientific and technical advice, as are deemed necessary for the implementation of this Convention;

(h) Contact, through the Secretariat, the executive bodies of conventions dealing with matters covered by this Convention with a view to establishing appropriate forms of cooperation with them; and

> (i) Consider and undertake any additional action that may be required for the achievement of the purposes of this Convention in the light of experience gained in its operation.
>
> 5. The United Nations, its specialized agencies and the International Atomic Energy Agency, as well as any State not Party to this Convention, may be represented as observers at meetings of the Conference of the Parties. Any other body or agency, whether governmental or non-governmental, qualified in fields relating to conservation and sustainable use of biological diversity, which has informed the Secretariat of its wish to be represented as an observer at a meeting of the Conference of the Parties, may be admitted unless at least one third of the Parties present object. The admission and participation of observers shall be subject to the rules of procedure adopted by the Conference of the Parties.

Notes

Terms defined in Article 2

'biological diversity' and 'sustainable use'.

Meetings of the COP

To date, five ordinary meetings of the COP have been held:

1 Nassau, Bahamas, 28 November–9 December 1994.

2 Jakarta, Indonesia, 6–17 November 1995.

3 Buenos Aires, Argentina, 4–15 November 1996.

4 Bratislava, Slovakia, 4–15 May 1998.

5 Nairobi, Kenya, 15–26 May 2000.

COP 6 will be held in The Hague, the Netherlands, in April 2002. One extraordinary meeting of the COP has also been held, for the adoption of the Cartagena Protocol on Biosafety (see the guide to Article 19 (3)). The extraordinary meeting was held in two sessions, in Cartagena, Colombia, from 22 to 23 February 1999, and in Montreal, Canada, from 24 to 28 January 2000 [*decision EM-I/1, paragraphs 1, 2*].

COP 5 decided that ordinary meetings of the COP shall be held every two years, and adopted an amendment to the rules of procedure to this effect [*decision V/20, paragraph 1*].

Budget

The administrative costs of the COP, its subsidiary bodies – SBSTTA, the Ad Hoc Open-ended Inter-sessional Working Group on Article 8 (j), the Panel of Experts on Access and Benefit-sharing and the Convention Secretariat are met through a biennial budget adopted by the COP at each meeting. Contributions to this budget are made each year by Parties on the basis of an indicative scale of assessments for the apportionment of the expenses, based on the United Nations scale. The current budget is for the biennium 2001–2002 [*decision V/22*].

Rules of procedure and financial rules

Rules of procedure

In decision I/1, COP 1 adopted the rules of procedure contained in the annex to that decision, with the exception of paragraph 1 of rule 40 (which relates to voting on matters of substance). For ease of reference the rules of procedure (as amended at COP 5, see below) have been reproduced separately in Section III of this Handbook.

COP 3, COP 4 and COP 5 considered paragraph 1 of rule 40 further, under the agenda item 'Pending issues'. On each occasion, the COP decided to invite the President to conduct informal consultations with a view to considering this matter at its next meeting. As a result there is still no rule of voting with respect to substantive decisions of the COP.

COP 5 adopted decision V/20 on the operations of the Convention, which included a number of decisions relating to the functioning of future meetings [*decision V/20 I*] and certain formal amendments to its rules of procedure. The formal amendments addressed:

- Periodicity of COP meetings [decision V/20 I, paragraph 1].
- Term of office of the COP Bureau [decision V/20 I, paragraph 5 (a), (b)].
- Presidency of the COP [decision V/20 I, paragraph 5 (c)].

Financial rules

COP 1 adopted the Financial Rules for the Administration of the Trust Fund for the Convention on Biological Diversity, which are annexed to decision I/6, to apply in conjunction with the general procedures governing the operations of the Fund of UNEP and the Financial Regulations and Rules of the United Nations. It designated UNEP as the Trustee of the Trust Fund for the Convention. For ease of reference the financial rules have been reproduced separately in Section V of this Handbook.

Paragraphs 4 and 16 of the financial rules adopted at COP 1 contained text that remained in square brackets. At COP 2, these paragraphs were transmitted to COP 3 for further consideration [*decision II/20, paragraphs 11, 12*]. COP 3 considered paragraphs 4 and 16 of the financial rules and transmitted them to COP 4 for further consideration [*decision III/1, paragraphs 1, 2*], having made certain amendments to paragraph 4 [*decision III/1, paragraph 1; annex*]. However, elements of paragraphs 4 and 16 remain in square brackets. The latest version of the financial rules is contained in the appendix to decision III/1 and reproduced in Section V of this Handbook. No decision was taken on this issue at COP 4 or COP 5.

Review of operations of the Convention

As part of its first medium-term programme of work, the COP decided to review the operations of the COP and subsidiary organs and to consider a longer-term programme of work at COP 4 [*decision I/9, decision II/18, decision III/22, paragraph 2*]. Accordingly, COP 4 considered these issues and adopted decision IV/16. It decided to hold an inter-sessional meeting to consider possible arrangements to improve preparations for and conduct of the meetings of the COP, taking into account proposals made at COP 4, and to consider the results at COP 5 [*decision IV/16, paragraphs 2, 4*]. Decision IV/16 also gave certain specific guidance to the Executive Secretary, Parties and SBSTTA in relation to improving preparations for COP meetings;[23] and adopted a programme of work for the period between COP 4 and COP 7.

In accordance with decision IV/16, an ISOC was held in Montreal in June 1999.[24] The recommendations of the ISOC were considered at COP 5, which adopted decision V/20 on the operations of the Convention. As noted above, this incorporated certain decisions and clarifications of the working methods of the COP, as well as certain formal adjustments to the COP's rules of procedure [*decision V/20 I*].

COP 5 decided that it was necessary to enhance the review and facilitation of implementation of the Convention [*decision V/20 V, paragraph 37*]. It decided to hold another inter-sessional meeting, to assist with preparations for COP 6. This meeting will be held in November 2001 and will consider the Strategic Plan (see below), national reports and means to support implementation of the Convention, in particular priority actions in national biodiversity strategies and action plans. COP 6 will review the role of inter-sessional processes in enhancing implementation of the Convention [*decision V/20 V, paragraph 39*]. COP 5 also decided to enhance the functions of subregional and regional processes in preparing for COP meetings and in promoting regional, subregional and national implementation of the Convention [*decision V/20 V, paragraph 40;* see also *decision V/20 IV, paragraph 33*].

Strategic Plan

In decision V/20, the COP decided to prepare a Strategic Plan for the Convention with a view to adopting the Strategic Plan at COP 6. The Strategic Plan will initially cover the period 2002–2010. It will be based upon the longer-term programme of work of the COP and of SBSTTA, and is to provide strategic and operational guidance for implementation of these programmes of work [*decision V/20 II, paragraphs 10, 11*].

The Strategic Plan is to be developed by the Executive Secretary through a participatory process incorporating views of Parties, the COP Bureau, SBSTTA and other relevant subsidiary bodies, as well as other interested countries and organizations [*decision V/20 II, paragraph 16*]. Operational goals in the Strategic Plan are to relate to: the thematic work programmes; cross-cutting issues and initiatives; and the implementation of the provisions of the Convention. Within each of these goals, the Plan is to identify: planned activities; expected products, timing of activities and products; relevant actors and mechanisms; and financial, human-resources and other capacity-requirements [*decision V/20 II, paragraphs 13, 15*].

Development of the Strategic Plan is now underway, and views have been invited from Parties and other countries and organizations. Preparation of the Strategic Plan will be considered at the inter-sessional meeting in November 2001 [*decision V/20 V, paragraph 38 (a)*].

References

Decisions on Article 23

Decision V/20 I (Operations of the Convention)

23 In relation to the decisions of the COP related to the *modus operandi* of SBSTTA, see the guide to Article 25 in this section of the Handbook.
24 The report of the meeting is contained in UNEP/CBD/COP/5/4.

Note: Only those decisions specifically relating to the provisions of Article 23 and the functioning of the COP are listed below. The headings are provided for ease of reference only.

Date and venue of COP meetings (Article 23 (1) and (2))

Decision II/21 (Date and venue of COP 3)
Decision III/25 (Date and venue of COP 4)
Decision IV/16, paragraph 1 (Institutional matters and the programme of work)
Decision IV/18 (Date and venue of COP 5)
Decision V/29 (Date and venue of COP 6)

Financing and budget (Article 23 (3))

Decision I/6 Parts I and II (Financing of and budget for the Convention)
Decision II/20 (Financing of and budget for the Convention)
Decision III/24 (Budget of the Trust Fund for the Convention on Biological Diversity)
Decision IV/17 (Programme budget for the biennium 1999–2000)
Decision V/22 (Budget for the programme of work for the biennium 2001–2002)

Rules of procedure and financial rules (Article 23 (3))

[For decisions relating to the *modus operandi* of SBSTTA, see the guide to Article 25 later in this section of the Handbook]

Decision I/1 (Rules of procedure for the COP)
Decision I/6 Parts I and II (Financing of and budget for the Convention)
Decision I/10, paragraph 6 (Location of the Secretariat)
Decision III/1 (Pending issues arising from the work of the second meeting of the COP)
Decision IV/16 (Institutional matters and the programme of work)
Decision EM-I/3, II, paragraph 7 (Adoption of the Cartagena Protocol and interim arrangements)
Decision V/1, annex, B, paragraph 5 (Work plan of the ICCP)
Decision V/20, I (Operations of the Convention)

Programme of work

Decision I/9 (Medium-term programme of work)
Decision II/18 (Medium-term programme of work of the COP for 1996–1997)
Decision III/22 (Medium-term programme of work for 1996–1997)
Decision IV/16 (Institutional matters and the programme of work)

Strategic plan

Decision V/14, paragraph 4 (Clearing-house mechanism)
Decision V/20, II; V, paragraph 38 (a) (Operations of the Convention)

Establishment of subsidiary bodies (Article 23 (4) (g))

Decision I/9, paragraphs 3, 7 (Medium-term programme of work)
Decision II/5, paragraph 2 (Consideration of the need for and modalities of a protocol for the safe transfer, handling and use of LMOs)
Decision IV/8, paragraph 3 (Access and benefit-sharing)
Decision IV/9, paragraph 1 (Implementation of Article 8 (j) and related provisions)

Decision IV/16 (Institutional matters and programme of work)
Decision EM-I/3, II (Adoption of the Cartagena Protocol and programme of work)
Decision V/3, paragraph 15; (see also SBSTTA recommendation V/14, annex II) (Marine and coastal)
Decision V/4, paragraph 4; annex (Forest)
Decisions V/23, paragraph 7 (Dryland and sub-humid lands)
Decision V/26 A, paragraphs 10, 11 (Access to genetic resources)

Requests for voluntary funding for Convention meetings

Decision I/9, paragraph 8 (Medium-term programme of work)
Decision I/11, paragraph 2 (Preparations for COP 2)
Decision II/22, paragraph 2 (Regional and subregional meetings)
Decision III/14, paragraph 12 (Implementation of Article 8 (j))
Decision III/26, paragraph 2 (Regional and subregional meetings)
Decision IV/3, paragraph 7 (Issues related to biosafety)
Decision EM-I/3, IV, paragraph 18 (Adoption of the Cartagena Protocol and interim arrangements)
Decision V/1, paragraph 3 (Work plan of the ICCP)
Decision V/22, paragraphs 16, 17; Tables 3, 4 (Budget for the programme of work for the biennium 2001–2002)

Documents

UNEP/CBD/COP/1/1 Provisional agenda
UNEP/CBD/COP/1/1/Add.1 Annotated provisional agenda
UNEP/CBD/COP/1/10 Draft Financial Rules governing the funding of the Secretariat of the Convention on Biological Diversity
UNEP/CBD/COP/1/13 Medium-term programme of work on the Conference of the Parties
UNEP/CBD/COP/1/14 Budget for the Secretariat of the Convention
UNEP/CBD/COP/2/1 Provisional agenda
UNEP/CBD/COP/2/1/Add.1/Rev.1 Annotated provisional agenda
UNEP/CBD/COP/2/3 and 3/Add.1 Proposed Budget for the Convention
UNEP/CBD/COP/2/4 Pending issues arising from COP 1
UNEP/CBD/COP/3/1 Provisional agenda
UNEP/CBD/COP/3/1/Add.1 Annotated provisional agenda
UNEP/CBD/COP/3/2 Pending issues arising from the second meeting of the Conference of the Parties
UNEP/CBD/COP/3/31 Medium-term programme of work of the Conference of the Parties for 1996–1997
UNEP/CBD/COP/3/33 Proposed budget of the trust for the Convention on Biological Diversity
UNEP/CBD/COP/4/3 Pending issues arising from the work of the third meeting of the Conference of the Parties
UNEP/CBD/COP/4/1 Provisional agenda and annotations, including suggestions for the organization of work
UNEP/CBD/COP/4/14 Synthesis of views on the operations of the Convention.
UNEP/CBD/COP/4/25 Proposed budget for the Trust Fund of the Convention
UNEP/CBD/COP/4/25/Add.1 Proposed Supplementary Budget for the Activities Related to the Biosafety Protocol
UNEP/CBD/COP/4/Inf.2 Review of the operations of the Convention: Submission by the Government of the United Kingdom

UNEP/CBD/COP/4/Inf.12 Programme Budget of the Convention for the Biennium 1999–2000: Programmes of Work
UNEP/CBD/COP/5/1 Provisional agenda
UNEP/CBD/COP/5/1/Add.1 Annotated provisional agenda
UNEP/CBD/COP/5/4 Report of the inter-sessional meeting on the operations of the Convention
UNEP/CBD/COP/5/17 Operations of the Convention
UNEP/CBD/COP/5/18 Proposed Budget for the Programme of Work for the biennium 2001–2002

Article 24: Secretariat

1. A secretariat is hereby established. Its functions shall be:

(a) To arrange for and service meetings of the Conference of the Parties provided for in Article 23;

(b) To perform the functions assigned to it by any protocol;

(c) To prepare reports on the execution of its functions under this Convention and present them to the Conference of the Parties

(d) To coordinate with other relevant international bodies and, in particular, to enter into such administrative and contractual arrangements as may be required for the effective discharge of its functions; and

(e) To perform such other functions as may be determined by the Conference of the Parties.

2. At its first ordinary meeting, the Conference of the Parties shall designate the secretariat from amongst those existing competent international organizations which have signified their willingness to carry out the secretariat functions under this Convention.

Editors' note:

With regard to staffing of the Secretariat, reference should also be made to decisions of the COP on the financing and budget of the Convention (see the guide to Article 23 above). See also Article 40 on Secretariat interim arrangements.

Notes

Consideration of Article 24 by the COP

Background and status

Designation of the Secretariat and administrative arrangements

COP 1 designated UNEP to carry out the functions of the Secretariat while ensuring its autonomy to discharge the functions referred to in Article 24 [*decision I/4, paragraph 1*]. The COP welcomed the willingness demonstrated by international organizations to support and cooperate with the Secretariat, and requested the Executive Secretary to coordinate with those organizations with a view to entering into arrangements to make effective such offers [*decision I/5, paragraphs 1, 2*].

In decision III/23, the COP invited the Executive Director of UNEP and the Executive Secretary of the Convention to develop procedures with regard to the functioning of the Secretariat to clarify and make more effective their respective roles and responsibilities [*decision III/23, paragraph 1*]. COP 4 endorsed the administrative arrangements between UNEP and the Secretariat and requested the Executive Secretary to report regularly to the COP, through its Bureau, on their implementation [*decision IV/17, paragraph 1*].[25]

The COP has instructed the Executive Secretary to enter into direct administrative and contractual arrangements with Parties and organizations in response to offers of human resources and other support to the Secretariat to ensure effective discharge of the functions of the Secretariat [*decision V/22, paragraph 20*].

Location of the Secretariat

COP 1 decided to consider the location of the Secretariat at COP 2, and decided upon a procedure for taking the decision on this issue [*decision I/10, paragraphs 1, 6*]. COP 2 decided to accept the offer of the Government of Canada to host the Secretariat in Montreal [*decision II/19, paragraph 2*].

References

Decisions on Article 24

Decision I/4 (Selection of a competent international organization to carry out the functions of the Secretariat)
Decision I/5 (Support to the Secretariat by international organizations)
Decision I/10 (Location of the Secretariat)
Decision II/19 (Location of the Secretariat)
Decision III/23 (Administrative matters)
Decision IV/17, paragraph 1 (Programme budget for the biennium 1999–2000)
Decision V/22, paragraph 20 (Budget for the programme of work for the biennium 2001–2002)

Cooperation with other biodiversity-related conventions, processes and organizations

Consideration of cooperation with other biodiversity-related conventions, processes and organizations by the COP

Background and status

COP 1 decided to consider as a standing item on its agenda the relationship of the Convention with the CSD and biodiversity-related conventions, other international agreements, institutions and processes of relevance [*decision I/9*].

25 The administrative arrangements are contained in annex III to document UNEP/CBD/COP/4/24 and are reproduced in Section X.

The COP has consistently recognized the importance of cooperation and synergy with other conventions and organizations. COP 2 stressed the need to make implementation of the Convention and activities of other international and regional conventions mutually supportive, and the need to avoid unnecessary duplication of activities [*decision II/13, paragraphs 2, 3*]. The COP has requested the Executive Secretary, on behalf of the COP, to consider matters of liaison, cooperation and collaboration as a key responsibility [*decision IV/15, paragraph 4*]. It has requested the Executive Secretary to coordinate with Secretariats of other biodiversity-related conventions, institutions and processes with a view to, *inter alia*, facilitating exchange of information, exploring harmonization or efficiencies of reporting requirements, exploring the possibility of coordinating work programmes [*decision II/13, paragraph 4; decision III/21, paragraph 3; decision IV/15, paragraph 5*].

In the light of this request, the Secretariat has entered into Memoranda of Cooperation with a number of relevant conventions and institutions, such as:

- Centre for International Forestry Research For Scientific and Technical Cooperation.
- Convention on International Trade in Endangered Species of Wild Fauna and Flora.
- Convention on the Conservation of Migratory Species of Wild Animals.
- Convention on Wetlands of International Importance, especially as Waterfowl Habitat (Ramsar Convention).
- Intergovernmental Oceanographic Commission.
- Pan-European Biological and Landscape Diversity Strategy.
- United Nations Conference on Trade and Development.
- United Nations Educational, Scientific and Cultural Organization.
- World Conservation Union.

This approach has been endorsed by the COP [*decision III/21, paragraph 2; decision IV/15, paragraph 3*]. The Secretariat has also participated in a project on harmonizing reporting requirements of biodiversity-related conventions and has developed joint work programmes [eg *decision IV/15, paragraph 5*; *decision V/19, paragraph 9 (c)*].

While the COP has adopted decisions on cooperation at each of its meetings since COP 1, it has also made frequent references to cooperation with other conventions and organizations in its decisions on specific articles, cross-cutting issues and thematic areas.[26] The COP has endorsed a joint programme of work with the Ramsar Convention [*decision IV/15, paragraph 1; decision V/21, paragraph 4*], and has requested the Executive Secretary to collaborate, *inter alia*, with:

- the Secretariat of the Convention to Combat Desertification on a joint work programme to support the Convention's programme on biodiversity of dry and sub-humid lands [*decision V/23, paragraph 8*];

26 See references below, and the guides in this section of this Handbook on specific articles under the sub-heading 'Cooperation with other conventions and organizations'.

- the Secretariat of the Convention on Migratory Species to develop a proposal on how migratory species could be integrated into the CBD work programme [*decision V/21, paragraph 7*];
- the FAO in the development and implementation of the work programme on agricultural biological diversity [*decision V/5, paragraph 6*]; and
- the Millennium Ecosystem Assessment with the view to facilitate and support the undertaking of a number of pilot scientific assessments for SBSTTA [*decision V/20, III, paragraph 29 (b); decision V/21, paragraphs 10, 11*].

In addition to cooperation at the inter-secretariat level, the COP has made inputs to other relevant processes through statements adopted by way of COP decisions and transmitted via the Secretariat to the body concerned [*eg decision I/8; decision II/9; decision II/16; decision III/19*]. It has also invited the governing bodies of other conventions related to biological diversity to consider their possible contribution to the implementation of the objectives of the Convention [*decision II/13, paragraph 5; decision III/21, paragraph 9*].

The COP has emphasized the importance of cooperation at the scientific and technical level [*decision III/2, paragraph 5; decision II/6, paragraph 8; decision IV/16, annex I, paragraph 14; decision V/20, II, paragraph 19; decision V/21, paragraph 1*].

In relation to action at the national level, the COP has also called on national focal points of biodiversity-related conventions to cooperate on implementation and to avoid duplication of effort [*decision III/21, paragraph 10*].

References

Decisions pertaining to cooperation with other conventions, organizations and processes

Decision II/13 (Cooperation)
Decision II/14 (Intergovernmental workshop on cooperation)
Decision III/21 (Cooperation)
Decision IV/15 (Cooperation)
Decision V/21 (Cooperation)

Relevant aspects of thematic work programmes

Decision II/9, paragraphs 1, 2, 4; annex (Forest – Statement to IPF)
Decision II/10, paragraphs 4, 5, 10, 12, 13; annex I, paragraphs (vi) (viii) (xi); annex II, paragraphs 2 (c), 3 (b) (Marine and coastal)
Decision III/11, paragraphs 1–3, 7, 14, 19, 20, 23, 24 (Agriculture)
Decision III/12, paragraphs 1–7; annex (Forest)
Decision III/13, paragraph 1 (Terrestrial)
Decision IV/4, paragraphs 2–4, 8 (b), (c); annex I, paragraphs 1–4, 12, 13 (Inland water)
Decision IV/5, I, paragraph 4; II, paragraphs 2, 3; annex, B, paragraphs 7, 11, 12, 14; C, operational objectives 1.3, 2.1, 3.1, 3.2, 5.1, 6.1 (Marine and coastal)
Decision IV/6, paragraphs 2 (b), 7–10 (Agriculture)
Decision IV/7, paragraphs 2, 4, 9, 11, 13; annex, paragraphs 3 (f), 8, 9, 18, 22, 23, 40, 45, 48, 49, 50 (Forest)
Decision V/2, paragraphs 2, 7 (Inland water)

Decision V/3, paragraphs 4, 5, 6 (b), 17, 18; annex, C (Marine and coastal)
Decision V/4, paragraphs 3, 6, 7, 11, 13, 15–20 (Forest)
Decision V/5, paragraphs 2, 4, 6, 10–12, 14, 16, 17, 20–22, 29; annex, A, paragraph 3 (b), (d); B, Activity 1.1 (Agriculture)
Decision V/23, paragraphs 6, 8, 9; annex I, I, paragraph 2 (c); annex I, II, part A, paragraph 7 (a); part B, Activity 7 (l) (m); III, paragraph 12 (b) (Dry and sub-humid lands)

Other relevant decisions

Decision I/5 (Support to the Secretariat by international organizations)
Decision I/7, paragraph 1 (d) (SBSTTA)
Decision I/8 (Statement to CSD)
Decision II/3, paragraphs 2, 3, 4 (g) (h), 8 (Clearing-house mechanism)
Decision II/6, paragraph 8 (Financial mechanism and resources)
Decision II/7, paragraph 5 (Consideration of Articles 6 and 8)
Decision II/12, paragraphs (a), (c) (Intellectual property rights)
Decision II/15 (FAO Global System)
Decision II/16 (Statement to FAO International Technical Conference)
Decision II/17, paragraph 13 (National reports)
Decision III/9, paragraphs 7, 8 (Implementation of Articles 6 and 8)
Decision III/14, paragraph 4; annex, paragraph 2 (a) (Implementation of Article 8 (j))
Decision III/15, paragraphs 7–9 (Access to genetic resources)
Decision III/17, paragraphs 1 (f), 2–8; annex (Intellectual property rights)
Decision III/18, paragraph 9 (Incentive measures)
Decision III/19 (Statement to UNGA Special Session)
Decision III/20, paragraph 2 (a) (Issues related to biosafety)
Decision IV/1 A, paragraphs 5, 6 (Report and recommendations of the third meeting of SBSTTA)
Decision IV/1 C, paragraph 6 (Alien species)
Decision IV/1 D, paragraph 5; annex, paragraphs 9, 10 (Taxonomy)
Decision IV/2, paragraph 10 (g) (Clearing-house mechanism)
Decision IV/9, paragraphs 14–17 (Implementation of Article 8 (j) and related provisions)
Decision IV/10 A, paragraph 5 (b) (Incentive measures)
Decision IV/10 B, paragraph 6; 7 (Public education and awareness)
Decision IV/10 C, paragraph 6 (Impact assessment and minimizing adverse effects)
Decision IV/12, paragraph (b) (Additional financial resources)
Decision V/7, paragraphs 1, 2, 4 (Identification, monitoring and assessment, and indicators)
Decision V/8, paragraphs 5, 10–15 (Alien species)
Decision V/9, paragraph 5; annex (Global Taxonomy Initiative)
Decision V/10, paragraphs 2, 5 (Global strategy for plant conservation)
Decision V/11, paragraphs 2, 5, 7, 8, 15 (Additional financial resources)
Decision V/14, paragraph 7 (e); annex I, paragraph (k); annex II, paragraph (c) (Clearing-house mechanism)
Decision V/15, paragraphs 3, 5, 6 (Incentive measures)
Decision V/16, paragraph 14; annex, IV (Article 8 (j) and related provisions)
Decision V/17, paragraphs 2, 4 (Education and public awareness)
Decision V/18, I, paragraph 4; II, paragraph 6 (Impact assessment, liability and redress)
Decision V/19, paragraphs 9 (c), 10 (National reports)
Decision V/20, III, paragraphs 18, 19, 27, 29 (b) (Operations of the Convention)

ARTICLE 24

Decision V/24, paragraphs 1, 3 (Sustainable use)
Decision V/25, paragraphs 2–4, 6, 7 (Biological diversity and tourism)
Decision V/26 A, paragraphs 8, 15 (c), (d), (e) (Access to genetic resources)
Decision V/26 B, paragraphs 2-4 (Intellectual property rights)
Decision V/27 (Contribution to ten-year review of UNCED)

Documents

UNEP/CBD/COP/1/9 Selection of a competent international organization to carry out the functions of the Secretariat of the Convention

UNEP/CBD/COP/1/12 Preparation of the participation of the Convention on Biological Diversity in the third session of the Commission on Sustainable Development

UNEP/CBD/COP/2/2/Rev.1 Location of the Secretariat

UNEP/CBD/COP/2/15 and 15/Corr.1 Report on the administration of the Convention

UNEP/CBD/COP/3/25 Submission to the Special Session of the General Assembly to review implementation of Agenda 21

UNEP/CBD/COP/3/29 Cooperation with other biodiversity-related conventions and processes

UNEP/CBD/COP/3/30 Cooperation between the Convention on Wetlands of International Importance, Especially as Waterfowl Habitat and the Convention on Biological Diversity

UNEP/CBD/COP/3/32 Report of the Executive Secretary on the administration of the Convention

UNEP/CBD/COP/4/12 Implications of the outcome of the Special Session of the General Assembly

UNEP/CBD/COP/4/13 Cooperation with other agreements, institutions and processes relevant to in-situ conservation

UNEP/CBD/COP/4/24 Administration of Convention

UNEP/CBD/COP/4/Inf.8 Cooperation with the Convention on Wetlands

UNEP/CBD/COP/4/Inf.13 Report of the Pan-European Biological and Landscape Diversity Strategy to the Fourth Meeting of the Conference of the Parties

UNEP/CBD/COP/4/Inf.14 Outcome of the Special Session of the General Assembly (A/RES/S-19/2, 28 June 1997)

UNEP/CBD/COP/5/9 Report of the Executive Secretary on the administration of the Convention and budget for the Trust Fund of the Convention

UNEP/CBD/SBSTTA/2/12 Future programme of work for terrestrial biological diversity in light of the outcome of the third session of the Commission on Sustainable Development

UNEP/CBD/SBSTTA/5/2 Cooperation with other bodies

UNEP/CBD/COP/4/Inf.22 Linkages and Coordination between the Convention on the Conservation of Migratory Species of Wild Animals (Bonn Convention or CMS) and the Convention on Biological Diversity (CBD)

Article 25: Subsidiary Body on Scientific, Technical and Technological Advice

1. A subsidiary body for the provision of scientific, technical and technological advice is hereby established to provide the Conference of the Parties and, as appropriate, its other subsidiary bodies with timely advice relating to the implementation of this Convention. This body shall be open to participation by all Parties and shall be multidisciplinary. It shall comprise government representatives competent in the relevant field of expertise. It shall report regularly to the Conference of the Parties on all aspects of its work.

2. Under the authority of and in accordance with guidelines laid down by the Conference of the Parties, and upon its request, this body shall:

(a) Provide scientific and technical assessments of the status of biological diversity;

(b) Prepare scientific and technical assessments of the effects of types of measures taken in accordance with the provisions of this Convention;

(c) Identify innovative, efficient and state-of-the-art technologies and know-how relating to the conservation and sustainable use of biological diversity and advise on the ways and means of promoting development and/or transferring such technologies;

(d) Provide advice on scientific programmes and international cooperation in research and development related to conservation and sustainable use of biological diversity; and

(e) Respond to scientific, technical, technological and methodological questions that the Conference of the Parties and its subsidiary bodies may put to the body.

3. The functions, terms of reference, organization and operation of this body may be further elaborated by the Conference of the Parties.

Editors' note:

Only the functioning of SBSTTA is addressed here. COP requests for specific advice from SBSTTA have not been listed separately – see list of references headed 'Guidance to SBSTTA' in the guides on specific thematic work programmes and articles in this section of the Handbook.

Notes

Terms defined in Article 2

'Biological diversity', 'sustainable use' and 'technology'.

Meetings of SBSTTA

To date, SBSTTA has held six meetings:

1 Paris, France, 4–8 September 1995.

2 Montreal, Canada, 2–6 September 1996.

3 Montreal, Canada, 1–5 September 1997.

4 Montreal, Canada, 21–25 June 1999.

5 Montreal, Canada, 31 January–4 February 2000.

6 Montreal, Canada, 12–16 March 2001.

An organizational meeting of SBSTTA was held at COP 1 in 1994 (see annex VI, UNEP/CBD/COP/1/17).

SBSTTA 7 will be held in Montreal from 12 to 16 November 2001.

Modus operandi of SBSTTA

Readers should consult the text of the *modus operandi* of SBSTTA, as adopted and subsequently amended by the COP, which is reproduced in Section IV of this Handbook.

In accordance with rule 26, paragraph 5, of the rules of procedure, unless otherwise decided by the COP, the rules of procedure of the COP [*decision I/1, annex*] apply *mutatis mutandis* to the proceedings of subsidiary bodies (subject to exceptions specified in rule 26 (5)).

Consideration of Article 25 by the COP

Background and status

COP 1 decided that the *modus operandi* of SBSTTA should be considered at SBSTTA 1 [*decision I/7, paragraph 1 (d)*]. COP 2 endorsed recommendation I/1 of SBSTTA on the *modus operandi*, and requested SBSTTA to keep this under review with a view to improving its functioning on the basis of experience gained [*decision II/1, paragraphs 2, 3*]. SBSTTA 2 reviewed its *modus operandi* and, in recommendation II/11, advised certain revisions. COP 3 noted this recommendation and decided to consider it further at COP 4 as part of the longer-term review of the programme of work and the operations of the COP and subsidiary organs [*decision III/2, paragraph 2*]. In decision IV/16, COP 4 adopted a revised *modus operandi* of SBSTTA [*decision IV/16, paragraph 11; annex I*].

In decision V/20, the COP adopted further conclusions relating to improving the operations of SBSTTA. It decided that meetings of SBSTTA should take place every year (so that there will be two meetings of SBSTTA between each ordinary meeting of the COP) [*decision V/20 III, paragraph 17*]. It adopted a further amendment to the *modus operandi* of SBSTTA, to allow SBSTTA to establish ad hoc technical expert groups and adopt terms of reference for them under the guidance of the COP [*decision V/20 III, paragraph 21*].

COP 5 recognized that there is a need to improve the quality of scientific, technical and technological advice provided to the COP, and to undertake sound scientific and technical assessments on issues critical for implementation of the Convention. It requested SBSTTA to continue to improve the way it conducts its work [*decision V/20 III, paragraphs 25, 26*], and asked SBSTTA to identify and develop methods to undertake or participate in scientific assessments, and to identify and regularly update assessment priorities and information needs [*decision V/20 III, paragraph 29*]. COP 6 will make an assessment of the recommendations made to it by SBSTTA with a view to providing guidance to SBSTTA on ways to improve its inputs [*decision V/20 III, paragraph 23*].

Following the COP's request in decision IV/16, SBSTTA made recommendations to COP 5 on terms of reference for ad hoc technical expert groups on thematic areas [*decision IV/16, paragraph 21*]. In its decisions on certain thematic areas, COP 5 approved terms of reference for ad hoc technical expert groups to assist SBSTTA on:

- Marine and coastal protected areas [*decision V/3, paragraph 15*].
- Mariculture [*decision V/3, paragraph 15*].
- Forest biological diversity [*decision V/4, paragraphs 4–6*].
- Biodiversity of dry and sub-humid lands [*decision V/23, paragraph 7*].

The COP has also established a roster of experts in the following areas:

- Access and benefit-sharing.
- Agricultural biodiversity.
- Dry and sub-humid lands.
- Forest biological diversity.
- Global Taxonomy Initiative.
- Biodiversity indicators.
- Marine and coastal biodiversity.
- Inland waters.
- Biosafety.

The experts on these rosters have been invited to make available upon request their specific expertise in order to contribute to the development of issues of the work programme of the Convention. It is anticipated that such request may take the form of peer reviews, questionnaires, clarifications or examinations of issues, specific contributions to the compilation of documents, participation in workshops and assisting in connecting the Convention process to other relevant processes (see *modus operandi* reproduced in Section IV of this Handbook).

Cooperation with other bodies

As part of the *modus operandi* of SBSTTA, the COP has encouraged the development of cooperative arrangements at the scientific and technical level with appropriate biodiversity-related conventions and institutions through SBSTTA [*decision III/21, paragraph 5*]. With regard to the financial mechanism, the COP requested reciprocal representation at meetings of SBSTTA and the Scientific and Technical Advisory Panel of the GEF [*decision II/6, paragraph 8*]. COP 5 decided that the Chair of SBSTTA or other members of the SBSTTA Bureau authorized by the Chair, may represent SBSTTA at meetings of scientific bodies of other conventions and relevant biodiversity-related conventions, institutions and processes [*decision V/20 III, paragraph 18*]. It further encouraged the SBSTTA Bureau to hold meetings with equivalent bodies of other biodiversity-related conventions, institutions and processes [*decision V/20 III, paragraph 19*].

ARTICLE 25

References

Decisions on Article 25

Decision I/7 (SBSTTA)
Decision II/1 (Report of the first meeting of SBSTTA)
Decision II/2 (Publication and distribution of scientific and technical information)
Decision III/2 (Report and recommendations of the second meeting of SBSTTA)
Decision III/3 (Use of languages in meetings of SBSTTA)
Decision IV/1 A (Report and recommendations of the third meeting of SBSTTA)
Decision IV/16, paragraphs 11-15, 20-21; annex I (Institutional matters and the programme of work)
Decision V/20, III (Operations of the Convention)

Relevant aspects of thematic work programmes

Decision V/3, paragraphs 15, 16 (Marine and coastal)
Decision V/4, paragraphs 4–6; annex (Forest)
Decision V/23, paragraph 7 (Dry and sub-humid lands)

Documents

UNEP/CBD/COP/1/1 Provisional agenda
UNEP/CBD/COP/1/1/Add.1 Annotated provisional agenda
UNEP/CBD/COP/1/11 Subsidiary Body on Scientific, Technical and Technological Advice
UNEP/CBD/COP/1/16 Report of the Open-ended Intergovernmental Meeting of Scientific Experts on Biological Diversity, including the agenda for scientific and technological research
UNEP/CBD/COP/2/1/Rev.1 Provisional agenda
UNEP/CBD/COP/2/1/Add.1/Rev.1 Annotated provisional agenda
UNEP/CBD/COP/2/5 Report of the first meeting of SBSTTA
UNEP/CBD/COP/3/1 Provisional agenda
UNEP/CBD/COP/3/1/Add.1 Annotated provisional agenda
UNEP/CBD/COP/3/3 Report of the second meeting of the Subsidiary Body on Scientific, Technical and Technological Advice
UNEP/CBD/COP/4/1/Rev.1 Provisional agenda
UNEP/CBD/COP/4/1/Add.1 Annotated provisional agenda
UNEP/CBD/COP/4/2 Report of the third meeting of the Subsidiary Body on Scientific, Technical and Technological Advice
UNEP/CBD/COP/5/1 Provisional agenda
UNEP/CBD/COP/5/1/Add.1 Annotated provisional agenda
UNEP/CBD/COP/5/2 Report of the fourth meeting of the Subsidiary Body on Scientific, Technical and Technological Advice
UNEP/CBD/COP/5/3 Report of the fifth meeting of the Subsidiary Body on Scientific, Technical and Technological Advice
UNEP/CBD/SBSTTA/1/2 Matters related to the *modus operandi* of the SBSTTA
UNEP/CBD/SBSTTA/1/3 Programme of work of the SBSTTA for 1995–1997
UNEP/CBD/SBSTTA/1/Inf.1 Written submissions by Governments and international organizations on the *modus operandi* of the SBSTTA
UNEP/CBD/SBSTTA/2/16 *Modus Operandi* of the Subsidiary Body on Scientific, Technical and Technological Advice

UNEP/CBD/SBSTTA/2/17 Review of the medium-term programme of work of the Subsidiary Body on Scientific, Technical and Technological Advice, 1995–1997
UNEP/CBD/SBSTTA/3/10 Overall assessment of the Subsidiary Body on Scientific, Technical and Technological Advice
UNEP/CBD/SBSTTA/4/5 Terms of reference for the ad hoc technical expert groups
UNEP/CBD/SBSTTA/5/15 Ad hoc technical expert groups: Terms of reference, and rosters of experts and proposal on a uniform methodology for their use

Article 26: Reports

Each Contracting Party shall, at intervals to be determined by the Conference of the Parties, present to the Conference of the Parties, reports on measures which it has taken for the implementation of the provisions of this Convention and their effectiveness in meeting the objectives of this Convention.

Notes

Consideration of Article 26 by the COP

Background and status

Article 26 requires the Parties to present reports to the COP on measures taken to implement the Convention and the effectiveness of those measures in meeting the Convention's objectives. Article 23 (4) (a) of the Convention requires the COP to establish the form and intervals for the transmission of information under Article 26 and to consider such information.

The COP decided to address the form and intervals for national reports at COP 2 [*decision I/9*]. It was therefore decided that SBSTTA 1 should consider, as a priority item, what kind of scientific and technical information should be contained in national reports under Article 26 [*decision I/7, annex, paragraph 5.5.1*]. SBSTTA subsequently submitted recommendation I/5.

COP 2 adopted decision II/17 on the form and intervals of national reports by Parties which provided that first national reports should be submitted by COP 4 in 1997 (*paragraph 4*), and preferably by 30 June 1997 (*paragraph 11*), and that these should focus on measures taken for the implementation of Article 6 of the Convention (*paragraph 3*). The deadline for submission of first national reports was subsequently extended to 1 January 1998 [*decision III/9, paragraph 11*]. An annex to decision II/17 sets out suggested guidelines for national reporting on Article 6.

With regard to the consideration of information in national reports, the COP requested the Secretariat to prepare a synthesis of information contained in national reports and other relevant information for consideration of the COP [*decision II/17, paragraph 9*].

By the end of COP 4, 107 national reports had been received in final or draft form. COP 4 adopted a further decision on national reports, which welcomed the number of first national reports received so far and urged those Parties which had not yet done so to submit their reports by 31 December 1998 [*decision IV/14, paragraph 1*]. It also requested the Secretariat to prepare for SBSTTA a revised version of the synthesis of information contained in national reports [*decision IV/14, paragraph 2*]. The COP requested SBSTTA to consider the Secretariat's synthesis report and to provide COP 5 with advice as to the form and intervals of subsequent national reports by Parties [*decision IV/14, paragraph 3*]. SBSTTA's advice was to cover:

- the nature of information needed from Parties in order to assess the state of implementation of the Convention;
- recommendations on improving the reporting process (through guidance on format, style, length and treatment) with a view to ensuring comparability between reports; and
- identification of ways and means to further facilitate national implementation of the Convention.

SBSTTA 5 considered guidelines for future national reporting that had been developed by the Secretariat through a pilot project, carried out with the collaboration of a number of Parties, to identify a methodology for assessing the state of implementation of the Convention, and adopted recommendation V/13. COP 5 endorsed a format for future national reports (contained in annex I to document UNEP/CBD/COP/5/13/Add.2), and asked the Secretariat to further develop this format and make it available to Parties by 30 September 2000 [*decision V/19, paragraphs 2, 3*]. Accordingly, the Secretariat revised the format for national reporting and made it available to Parties on 11 September 2000. The format is also available on the Convention website. In accordance with decision V/19, second national reports are to be submitted by 15 May 2001 in both hard copy and electronic format. Thereafter, reports are to be submitted for consideration at alternate ordinary meetings of the COP [*decision V/19, paragraph 5*]. The COP recommended that Parties prepare their national reports through a consultative process involving all relevant stakeholders [*decision V/19, paragraph 6*].

COP 5 also invited Parties to prepare detailed thematic reports on items due to be considered in depth at future COP meetings. For COP 6, reports on forest ecosystems, alien species and benefit-sharing are invited. Formats for these detailed reports have also been prepared by the Secretariat and made available to Parties. The formats are also on the Convention website. Deadlines for the submissions of these detailed reports are given in decision V/19 [*decision V/19, paragraph 8*].

In addition to its specific decisions on national reports, the COP has issued guidance to Parties in other decisions as to further information to be included in national reports on particular issues. These references are listed below under the heading 'Guidance to Parties'. Such guidance has now been incorporated into the guidelines for the second national reports.

Following the guidance of the COP, support for the preparation of national reports by developing country Parties has been provided through the financial mechanism [*decision II/17, paragraph 12; decision II/6, paragraph 11; decision IV/13, paragraph 6; decision IV/14, paragraph 5; decision V/13, paragraph 2 (e)*].

The COP has devoted some attention to the possibility of harmonizing reporting requirements of the Convention and other biodiversity-related conventions. In this regard, the Executive Secretary has been asked to coordinate with secretariats of other biodiversity-related conventions with a view to, *inter alia*, exploring the possibility of harmonizing reporting requirements [*decision II/13, paragraph 4 (b); decision III/21, paragraph 3; decision IV/15, paragraph 5 (b)*].

References

Decisions on Article 26

Decision II/17 (National reports)
Decision IV/14 (National reports)
Decision V/19 (National reports)

Guidance to Parties

Decision II/8, paragraph 6 (i) (Components of biological diversity particularly under threat)
Decision II/17, paragraphs 3, 4, 6, 11, 13; annex (National reports)
Decision III/6 (Additional financial resources)
Decision III/9, paragraphs 3, 11 (Implementation of Articles 6 and 8)
Decision III/14, paragraph 2 (Implementation of Article 8 (j))
Decision IV/1 A, paragraph 3 (see also SBSTTA recommendation III/5, 7 (g)) (Report and recommendations of the third meeting of SBSTTA)
Decision IV/2, paragraph 2 (Clearing-house mechanism)
Decision IV/10 A, paragraph 2 (Incentive measures)
Decision IV/10 C, paragraph 9 (Impact assessment and minimizing adverse effects)
Decision IV/14, paragraphs 1, 4 (National reports)
Decision V/2, paragraph 3 (Inland water)
Decision V/4, paragraph 7 (Forest)
Decision V/11, paragraphs 4, 14 (Additional financial resources)
Decision V/18, I, paragraph 3 (Impact assessment, liability and redress)
Decision V/19, paragraphs 5–8 (National reports)
Decision V/23, annex I, III, paragraph 12 (a) (Dry and sub-humid lands)

Financial mechanism and resources

Guidance to the financial mechanism

Decision II/6, paragraph 11 (Financial mechanism and resources)
Decision II/17, paragraph 12 (National reports)
Decision III/9, paragraph 4 (Implementation of Articles 6 and 8)
Decision IV/13, paragraph 6 (Additional guidance to the financial mechanism)
Decision IV/14, paragraph 5 (National reports)
Decision V/13, paragraph 2 (e) (Further guidance to the financial mechanism)

Guidance to the Secretariat

Decision II/7, paragraph 3 (Consideration of Articles 6 and 8)
Decision II/10, annex II, paragraph 3 (e) (Marine and coastal)
Decision II/13, paragraph 4 (b) (Cooperation)
Decision II/17, paragraphs 9, 10 (National reports)
Decision III/21, paragraph 3 (Cooperation)
Decision IV/1 A, paragraph 3 (see also SBSTTA recommendation III/5, annex) (Report and recommendations of the third meeting of SBSTTA)
Decision IV/5, annex, C, operational objective 5.3 (Marine and coastal)
Decision IV/7, paragraph 10 (Forest)
Decision IV/14, paragraph 2 (National reports)

Decision IV/15, paragraph 5 (b) (Cooperation)
Decision V/14, annex II paragraph (h) (Clearing-house mechanism)
Decision V/16, annex, III, element 6, task 17 (Article 8 (j) and related provisions)
Decision V/19, paragraphs 3, 9 (National reports)
Decision V/20, IV, paragraph 36 (Operations of the Convention)

Guidance to SBSTTA

Decision I/7, annex, paragraph 5.5.1 (SBSTTA)
Decision II/17, paragraph 8 (National reports)
Decision IV/14, paragraph 3; annex (National reports)

Cooperation with other conventions and organizations

Decision II/13, paragraph 4 (b) (Cooperation)
Decision III/21, paragraph 3 (Cooperation)
Decision IV/15, paragraph 5 (b) (Cooperation)
Decision V/19, paragraph 10 (National reports)

Relevant aspects of thematic work programmes

Decision II/10, annex II, paragraph 3 (e) (Marine and coastal)
Decision IV/5, annex, C, operational objective 5.3 (Marine and coastal)
Decision IV/7, paragraph 10 (Forest)
Decision V/2, paragraph 3 (Inland water)
Decision V/4, paragraph 7 (Forest)
Decision V/23, annex I, III, paragraph 12 (a) (Dry and sub-humid lands)

Other relevant decisions

Decision III/10, paragraph 2 (see also SBSTTA recommendation II/1, paragraph 5) (Identification, monitoring and assessment)
Decision V/20 V, paragraph 38 (b) (Operations of the Convention)

Documents

UNEP/CBD/COP/2/14 Form and intervals of national reports by Parties
UNEP/CBD/COP/4/11 Synthesis of information contained in national reports on the implementation of the Convention
UNEP/CBD/COP/5/13 Progress report on the mechanisms for implementation
UNEP/CBD/COP/5/13/Add.2 Progress report on the mechanisms for implementation: National Reporting (Article 26)
UNEP/CBD/SBSTTA/1/6 Scientific and technical information to be contained in national reports of Parties
UNEP/CBD/SBSTTA/3/Inf.15 Strengthening the first set of national reports under the Convention on Biological Diversity: A discussion paper on indicators, targets and other types of information
UNEP/CBD/SBSTTA/3/Inf.16 Further guidelines for the preparation of national reports
UNEP/CBD/SBSTTA/5/14 Establishment of guidelines for the second national reports, including indicators and incentive measures

Article 27: Settlement of disputes

1. In the event of a dispute between Contracting Parties concerning the interpretation or application of this Convention, the parties concerned shall seek solution by negotiation.

2. If the parties concerned cannot reach agreement by negotiation, they may jointly seek the good offices of, or request mediation by, a third party.

3. When ratifying, accepting, approving or acceding to this Convention, or at any time thereafter, a State or regional economic integration organization may declare in writing to the Depositary that for a dispute not resolved in accordance with paragraph 1 or paragraph 2 above, it accepts one or both of the following means of dispute settlement as compulsory:

   (a) Arbitration in accordance with the procedure laid down in Part 1 of Annex II;

   (b) Submission of the dispute to the International Court of Justice.

4. If the parties to the dispute have not, in accordance with paragraph 3 above, accepted the same or any procedure, the dispute shall be submitted to conciliation in accordance with Part 2 of Annex II unless the parties otherwise agree.

5. The provisions of this Article shall apply with respect to any protocol except as otherwise provided in the protocol concerned.

Notes

See also Annex II of the Convention: Arbitration and conciliation.

According to Article 32 of the Cartagena Protocol on Biosafety:

> *'Except as otherwise provided in this Protocol, the provisions of the Convention relating to its Protocols shall apply to this Protocol.'*

Since the Biosafety Protocol contains no special provisions on the settlement of disputes, then pursuant to Article 32 of the Protocol and Article 27 (5) of the Convention, the provisions of Article 27 of the Convention also apply to the settlement of disputes under the Protocol.

Terms defined in Article 2

'Regional economic integration organization'.

References

Declarations

Austria (ratification), Cuba (ratification), Georgia (ratification) and Latvia (ratification)

Article 28: Adoption of protocols

1. The Contracting Parties shall cooperate in the formulation and adoption of protocols to this Convention.

2. Protocols shall be adopted at a meeting of the Conference of the Parties.

3. The text of any proposed protocol shall be communicated to the Contracting Parties by the Secretariat at least six months before such a meeting.

Notes

The Cartagena Protocol on Biosafety was adopted by the COP on 29 January 2000. See the guide to Article 19 (3), earlier in this section.

Article 29: Amendment of the Convention or protocols

1. Amendments to this Convention may be proposed by any Contracting Party. Amendments to any protocol may be proposed by any party to that protocol.

2. Amendments to this Convention shall be adopted at a meeting of the Conference of the Parties. Amendments to any protocol shall be adopted at a meeting of the Parties to the protocol in question. The text of any proposed amendment to this Convention or to any protocol, except as may otherwise be provided in such protocol, shall be communicated to the parties to the instrument in question by the secretariat at least six months before the meeting at which it is proposed for adoption. The secretariat shall also communicate proposed amendments to the signatories to this Convention for information.

3. The parties shall make every effort to reach agreement on any proposed amendment to this Convention or to any protocol by consensus. If all efforts at consensus have been exhausted, and no agreement reached, the amendment shall as a last resort be adopted by a two-thirds majority vote of the parties to the instrument in question present and voting at the meeting, and shall be submitted by the Depositary to all parties for ratification, acceptance or approval.

4. Ratification, acceptance or approval of amendments shall be notified to the Depositary in writing. Amendments adopted in accordance with paragraph 3 above shall enter into force among parties having accepted them on the ninetieth day after the deposit of instruments of ratification, acceptance or approval by at least two-thirds of the Contracting Parties to this Convention or of the parties of the protocol concerned, except as may otherwise be provided in such protocol. Thereafter the amendments shall enter into force for any other party on the ninetieth day after that party deposits its instrument of ratification, acceptance or approval of the amendments.

5. For the purposes of this Article, 'Parties present and voting' means parties present and casting an affirmative or negative vote.

Notes

To date no amendments have been proposed to the Convention.

According to Article 32 of the Cartagena Protocol on Biosafety:

> *'Except as otherwise provided in this Protocol, the provisions of the Convention relating to its Protocols shall apply to this Protocol.'*

Since the Biosafety Protocol contains no special provisions on amendment of the Protocol, the provisions of Article 29 of the Convention apply to the amendment of the Protocol.

Article 30: Adoption and amendment of annexes

1. The annexes of this Convention or to any protocol shall form an integral part of the Convention or of such protocol, as the case may be, and, unless expressly provided otherwise, a reference to this Convention or its protocols constitutes at the same time a reference to any annexes thereto. Such annexes shall be restricted to procedural, scientific, technical and administrative matters.

2. Except as may be otherwise provided in any protocol with respect to its annexes, the following procedure shall apply to the proposal, adoption and entry into force of additional annexes to this Convention or of annexes to any protocol:

   (a) Annexes to this Convention or to any protocol shall be proposed and adopted according to the procedure laid down in Article 29.

   (b) Any party that is unable to approve an additional annex to this Convention or an annex to any protocol to which it is party shall so notify the Depositary, in writing, within one year from the date of the communication of the adoption by the Depositary. The Depositary shall without delay notify all parties of any such notification received. A Party may at any time withdraw a previous declaration of objection and the annexes shall thereupon enter into force for that party subject to subparagraph (c) below.

   (c) On the expiry of one year from the date of the communication of the adoption by the Depositary, the annex shall enter into force for all parties to this Convention or to any protocol concerned which have not submitted a notification in accordance with the provisions of subparagraph (b) above.

3. The proposal, adoption and entry into force of amendments to annexes to this Convention or to any protocol shall be subject to the same procedure as for the proposal, adoption and entry into force of annexes to the Convention or annexes to the protocol.

4. If an additional annex or amendment to an annex is related to an amendment to this Convention or to any protocol, the additional annex or amendment shall not enter into force until such time as the amendment to the Convention or to the protocol concerned enters into force.

Notes

To date no new annexes have been adopted, nor have any amendments been adopted to the existing annexes of the Convention.

According to Article 32 of the Cartagena Protocol on Biosafety:

> *'Except as otherwise provided in this Protocol, the provisions of the Convention relating to its Protocols shall apply to this Protocol.'*

Since the Biosafety Protocol contains no special provisions on the adoption and amendment of annexes, the provisions of Article 30 of the Convention apply to the adoption and amendment of annexes to the Protocol.

Article 31: Right to vote

1. Except as provided for in paragraph 2 below, each Contracting Party to this Convention or to any protocol shall have one vote.

2. Regional economic integration organizations, in matters within their competence, shall exercise their right to vote with a number of votes equal to the number of their member states which are Contracting Parties to this Convention or the relevant protocol. Such organizations shall not exercise their right to vote if their member states exercise theirs, and vice versa.

Notes

The provisions of Article 31 of the Convention also apply to the right to vote under the Protocol.

Terms defined in Article 2

'Regional economic integration organization'.

Article 32: Relationship between this Convention and its protocols

1. A state or regional economic integration organization may not become a party to a protocol unless it is, or becomes at the same time, a Contracting Party to this Convention.

2. Decisions under any protocol shall be taken only by parties to the protocol concerned. Any Contracting Party that has not ratified, accepted or approved a protocol may participate as an observer in any meeting of the parties to that protocol.

Notes

In accordance with paragraph 2 of Article 32, the Cartagena Protocol on Biosafety provides in its Article 29, paragraph 2, that Parties to the Convention that are not Parties to the Protocol may participate as observers in the proceedings of any meeting of the COP serving as the meeting of the Parties to the Protocol. It also provides that when the COP serves as the meeting of the Parties to the Protocol, decisions under the Protocol shall be taken only by those that are Parties to it.

Terms defined in Article 2

'Regional economic integration organization'.

Article 33: Signature

> This convention shall be open for signature at Rio de Janeiro by all States and any regional economic integration organization from 5 June 1992 until 14 June 1992, and at the United Nations Headquarters in New York from 15 June 1992 to 4 June 1993.

Notes

The Convention was signed by 157 States between 5 June 1992 and 14 June 1992 in Rio de Janeiro. It was signed by 11 States between 15 June 1992 and 4 June 1993 at United Nations headquarters in New York.[27]

Terms defined in Article 2

'Regional economic integration organization'.

References

Declarations

Denmark (ratification), Finland (ratification), Norway (adoption) and Sweden (ratification)

27 For ratification status to date, see Section VII of this Handbook.

Article 34: Ratification, acceptance or approval

1. This Convention and any protocol shall be subject to ratification, acceptance or approval by States and by regional economic integration organizations. Instruments of ratification, acceptance or approval shall be deposited with the Depositary.

2. Any organization referred to in paragraph 1 above which becomes a Contracting party to this Convention or any protocol without any of its member States being a Contracting party shall be bound by all the obligations under the Convention or the protocol, as the case may be. In the case of such organizations, one or more of whose member States is a Contracting Party to this Convention or relevant protocol, the organization and its member States shall decide on their respective responsibilities for the performance of their obligations under the Convention or protocol, as the case may be. In such cases, the organization and the member States shall not be entitled to exercise rights under the Convention or relevant protocol concurrently.

3. In their instruments of ratification, acceptance or approval, the organization referred to in paragraph 1 above shall declare the extent of their competence with respect to the matters governed by the Convention or the relevant protocol. These organizations shall also inform the Depositary of any relevant modification in the extent of their competence.

Notes

As of 31 July 2001, 180 States and one regional economic integration organization have become Parties to the Convention.

Terms defined in Article 2

'Regional economic integration organization'.

Article 35: Accession

1. This Convention and any protocol shall be open for accession by States and by regional economic integration organizations from the date on which the Convention and any protocol concerned is closed for signature. The instruments of accession shall be deposited with the Depositary.

2. In their instruments of accession, the organizations referred to in paragraph 1 above shall declare the extent of their competence with respect to the matters governed by the Convention or the relevant protocol. These organizations shall also inform the Depositary of any relevant modification in the extent of their competence.

3. The provisions of Article 34, paragraph 2, shall apply to regional economic integration organizations which accede to this Convention or any protocol.

Notes

Since the Convention was closed for signature 30 States have acceded to the Convention.[28]

Since the Biosafety Protocol contains no special provisions on accession, the provisions of Article 35 of the Convention also apply to accession under the Protocol.

Terms defined in Article 2

'Regional economic integration organization'.

Article 36: Entry into force

1. This Convention shall enter into force on the ninetieth day after the date of deposit of the thirtieth instrument of ratification, acceptance, approval or accession.

2. Any protocol shall enter into force on the ninetieth day after the date of deposit of the number of instruments of ratification, acceptance, approval or accession, specified in that protocol, has been deposited.

3. For each Contracting Party which ratifies, accepts or approves this Convention or accedes thereto after the deposit of the thirtieth instrument of ratification, acceptance, approval or accession, it shall enter into force on the ninetieth day after the date of deposit by such Contracting Party of its instrument of ratification, acceptance, approval or accession.

4. Any protocol, except as otherwise provided in such protocol, shall enter into force for a Contracting party that ratifies, accepts or approves that protocol or acceded thereto after its entry into force pursuant to paragraph 2 above, on the ninetieth day after the date on which that Contracting Party deposits its instrument of ratification, acceptance, approval or accession, or on the date on which this Convention enters into force for that Contracting Party, whichever shall be the later.

5. For the purposes of paragraphs 1 and 2 above, any instrument deposited by a regional economic integration organization shall not be counted as additional to those deposited by member States of such organization.

Notes

The Convention entered into force, in accordance with Article 36, paragraph 1, on 29 December 1993.[29]

Terms defined in Article 2

'Regional economic integration organization'.

28 For ratification status to date, see Section VII of this Handbook.
29 For ratification status to date, see Section VII of this Handbook.

Article 37: Reservations

No reservations may be made to this Convention.

Article 38: Withdrawals

1. At any time after two years from the date on which this Convention has entered into force for a Contracting Party, that Contracting party may withdraw from the Convention by giving written notification to the Depositary.

2. Any such withdrawal shall take place upon expiry of one year after the date of its receipt by the Depositary, or on such later date as may be specified in the notification of the withdrawal.

3. Any Contracting Party which withdraws from this Convention shall be considered as also having withdrawn from any protocol to which it is party.

Notes

No Contracting Parties have withdrawn from the Convention.

Article 40: Secretariat interim arrangements

The secretariat to be provided by the Executive Director of the United Nations Environment Programme shall be the secretariat referred to in Article 24, paragraph 2, on an interim basis for the period between the entry into force of this Convention and the first meeting of the Conference of the Parties.

Notes

See the guide to Article 24 earlier in this section of the Handbook.

Article 41: Depositary

The Secretary-General of the United Nations shall assume the functions of Depositary of this Convention and any Protocols.

Article 42: Authentic texts

The original of this Convention, of which the Arabic, Chinese, English, French, Russian and Spanish texts are equally authentic, shall be deposited with the Secretary-General of the United Nations.

Annex I: Identification and monitoring

1. Ecosystems and habitats: containing high diversity, large numbers of endemic or threatened species, or wilderness; required by migratory species; of social, economic, cultural or scientific importance; or, which are representative, unique or associated with key evolutionary or other biological processes;

2. Species and communities which are: threatened; wild relatives of domesticated or cultivated species; of medicinal, agricultural or other economic value; or social, scientific or cultural importance; or importance for research into the conservation and sustainable use of biological diversity, such as indicator species; and Described genomes and genes of social, scientific or economic importance.

Notes

See the guide to Article 7 earlier in this section of the Handbook.

Annex II: Arbitration and conciliation

Part 1 ARBITRATION

Article 1

The claimant party shall notify the secretariat that the parties are referring a dispute to arbitration pursuant to Article 27. The notification shall state the subject-matter of arbitration and include, in particular, the articles of the Convention or the protocol, the interpretation or application of which are at issue. If the parties do not agree on the subject matter of the dispute before the President of the tribunal is designated, the arbitral tribunal shall determine the subject matter. The secretariat shall forward the information thus received to all Contracting Parties to this Convention or to the protocol concerned.

Article 2

1. In disputes between two parties, the arbitral tribunal shall consist of three members. Each of the parties to the dispute shall appoint an arbitrator and the two

arbitrators so appointed shall designate by common agreement the third arbitrator who shall be the President of the tribunal. The latter shall not be a national of one of the parties to the dispute, nor have his or her usual place of residence in the territory of one of these parties, nor be employed by any of them, nor have dealt with the case in any other capacity.

2. In disputes between more than two parties, parties in the same interest shall appoint one arbitrator jointly by agreement.

3. Any vacancy shall be filled in the manner prescribed for the initial appointment.

Article 3

1. If the President of the arbitral tribunal has not been designated within two months of the appointment of the second arbitrator, the Secretary-General of the United Nations shall, at the request of a party, designate the President within a further two-month period.

2. If one of the parties to the dispute does not appoint an arbitrator within two months of receipt of the request, the other party may inform the Secretary-General who shall make the designation within a further two-month period.

Article 4

The arbitral tribunal shall render its decisions in accordance with the provisions of this Convention, any protocols concerned, and international law.

Article 5

Unless the parties to the dispute otherwise agree, the arbitral tribunal shall determine its own rules of procedure.

Article 6

The arbitral tribunal may, at the request of one of the parties, recommend essential interim measures of protection.

Article 7

The parties to the dispute shall facilitate the work of the arbitral tribunal and, in particular, using all means at their disposal, shall:

(a) Provide it with all relevant documents, information and facilities; and

(b) Enable it, when necessary, to call witnesses or experts and receive their evidence.

Article 8

The parties and the arbitrators are under an obligation to protect the confidentiality of any information they receive in confidence during the proceedings of the arbitral tribunal.

Article 9

Unless the arbitral tribunal determines otherwise because of the particular circumstances of the case, the costs of the tribunal shall be borne by the parties to the dispute in equal shares. The tribunal shall keep a record of all its costs, and shall furnish a final statement thereof to the parties.

Article 10

Any Contracting Party that has an interest of a legal nature in the subject-matter of the dispute which may be affected by the decision in the case, may intervene in the proceedings with the consent of the tribunal.

Article 11

The tribunal may hear and determine counterclaims arising directly out of the subject-matter of the dispute.

Article 12

Decisions both on procedure and substance of the arbitral tribunal shall be taken by a majority vote of its members.

Article 13

If one of the parties to the dispute does not appear before the arbitral tribunal or fails to defend its case, the other party may request the tribunal to continue the proceedings and to make its award. Absence of a party or a failure of a party to defend its case shall not constitute a bar to the proceedings. Before rendering its final decision, the arbitral tribunal must satisfy itself that the claim is well founded in fact and law.

Article 14

The tribunal shall render its final decision within five months of the date on which it is fully constituted unless it finds it necessary to extend the time-limit for a period which should not exceed five more months.

Article 15

The final decision of the arbitral tribunal shall be confined to the subject-matter of the dispute and shall state the reasons on which it is based. It shall contain the names of the members who have participated and the date of the final decision. Any member of the tribunal may attach a separate or dissenting opinion to the final decision.

Article 16

The award shall be binding on the parties to the dispute. It shall be without appeal unless the parties to the dispute have agreed in advance to an appellate procedure.

Article 17

Any controversy which may arise between the parties to the dispute as regards the interpretation or manner of implementation of the final decision may be submitted by either party for decision to the arbitral tribunal which rendered it.

Part 2 CONCILIATION

Article 1

A conciliation commission shall be created upon the request of one of the parties to the dispute. The commission shall, unless the parties otherwise agree, be composed of five members, two appointed by each Party concerned and a President chosen jointly by those members.

Article 2

In disputes between more than two parties, parties in the same interest shall appoint their members of the commission jointly by agreement. Where two or more parties have separate interests or there is a disagreement as to whether they are of the same interest, they shall appoint their members separately.

Article 3

If any appointments by the parties are not made within two months of the date of the request to create a conciliation commission, the Secretary-General of the United Nations shall, if asked to do so by the party that made the request, make those appointments within a further two-month period.

Article 4

If a President of the conciliation commission has not been chosen within two months of the last of the members of the commission being appointed, the Secretary-General of the United Nations shall, if asked to do so by a party, designate a President within a further two-month period.

Article 5

The conciliation commission shall take its decisions by majority vote of its members. It shall, unless the parties to the dispute otherwise agree, determine its own procedure. It shall render a proposal for resolution of the dispute, which the parties shall consider in good faith.

Article 6

A disagreement as to whether the conciliation commission has competence shall be decided by the commission.

Notes

See Article 27 above.

Thematic work programmes

Forest biological diversity

Notes

Consideration of forest biological diversity by the COP

Background and status

COP 1 requested SBSTTA to consider the ways and means in which the COP could start the process of considering the components of biological diversity, particularly those under threat, and to identify the action which could be taken under the Convention [*decision I/7, annex, paragraph 5.1.1*]. In its consideration of this agenda item, SBSTTA 1 noted, *inter alia*, the establishment of the IPF and recommended that the COP consider whether an input into the IPF process would be desirable [*SBSTTA recommendation I/3, paragraph 8*]. SBSTTA 1 further suggested the main elements to be considered.

COP 2 adopted a statement from the Convention to the IPF on biological diversity and forests [*decision II/9, paragraph 1, annex*]. It also requested the Executive Secretary to produce a background document on the links between forests and biological diversity, in order to consider at COP 3 whether further input into the IPF process was required [*decision II/9, paragraph 2 (b)*]. The COP also requested the Executive Secretary to provide advice and information on the relationship between indigenous and local communities and forests as invited by the Inter-Agency Task Force of the IPF [*decision II/9, paragraph 2 (a)*].

SBSTTA 2 recommended that the COP ask the Executive Secretary to explore ways and means to cooperate with the IPF with a view to developing common priorities for further consideration at SBSSTA 3, taking into account certain research and technical priorities identified by SBSTTA [*SBSTTA recommendation II/8, paragraph 2*]. It also recommended certain additional inputs to the IPF. COP 3 endorsed recommendation II/8 of SBSTTA regarding further input to the IPF [*decision III/12, paragraph 2; annex*].

COP 3 also requested the Secretariat to develop a focused work programme on forest biological diversity, in accordance with certain guidance provided in that decision [*decision III/12, paragraph 6*]. In developing the work programme, the Executive Secretary was asked to work closely with IPF and other relevant institutions. Parties to the Convention were encouraged to assist with the development of the work programme [*decision III/12, paragraph 7*], and SBSTTA was asked to advise on the draft work programme and report back to COP 4 in May 1998 [*decision III/12, paragraph 9*].

COP 3 further directed SBSTTA, in the light of the proposed work programme and the research and technical priorities it had identified in recommendation II/8, to advance its scientific, technical and technological consideration of forest biological diversity by initially focusing on development of criteria and indicators for the conservation of biological diversity and analysing the ways in which human activities, in particular forest management practices, influence biological diversity and assessment of ways to minimize or mitigate negative influences [*decision III/12, paragraph 10*].

In order to be able to draw effectively upon the active assistance of all Parties (as requested in paragraph 7 of decision III/12), the Secretariat has established a roster of experts on forest biological diversity. Drawing on the roster of experts, the Secretariat convened a meeting of a liaison group on forest biological diversity in Helsinki from 25 to 28 May 1997, on the invitation of the Government of Finland. The liaison group identified a number of potential elements for a work programme on forest biological diversity.

SBSTTA 3 considered a draft work programme on forest biological diversity and the report of the liaison group meeting, and submitted recommendation III/3 to COP 4.

COP 4 endorsed a work programme on forest biological diversity [*decision IV/7, paragraph 1, annex*]. It urged Parties, countries, international and regional organizations, major groups and other relevant bodies to collaborate in carrying out the task identified in the work programme [*decision IV/7, paragraph 2*]. COP 5 reviewed implementation of the work programme and called for its further implementation by Parties, relevant organizations and the Executive Secretary [*decision V/4*]. It also called for the Executive Secretary to contribute to the work of the United Nations Forum on Forests [*decision V/4, paragraph 3*].

Elements of the work programme on forest biological diversity

The work programme on forest biological diversity reflects a rolling three-year planning horizon in three phases [*decision IV/7, annex, paragraph 4*]. It is subject to periodic review and interim reports are due after each three-year phase to assess implementation [*decision IV/7, annex, paragraphs 5, 6*]. Decision IV/7 states that the work programme is action-oriented, demand-driven, needs-driven and flexible enough to reflect and respond to changing conditions, including, but not limited to, the outcome and priorities to be identified by the Intergovernmental Forum on Forests (IFF) [*decision IV/7, annex, paragraph 2*].

The elements of the first three-year phase of the work programme are:

- Holistic and inter-sectoral ecosystem approaches that integrate the conservation and sustainable use of biological diversity, taking account of social and cultural and economic considerations.
- Comprehensive analysis of the ways in which human activities, in particular forest-management practices, influence biological diversity and assessment of ways to minimize or mitigate negative influences.
- Methodologies necessary to advance the elaboration and implementation of criteria and indicators for forest biological diversity.
- Further research and technological priorities identified in the recommendation II/8 of SBSTTA as well as issues identified in the review and planning process under the work programme.

The COP has further noted in its decisions that work on the following issues should be incorporated into the thematic work programmes, including that for forest biological diversity; alien species; incentive measures; implementation of Article 8 (j); public education and awareness; and impact assessment [*decision V/8, paragraph 10; decision V/15, paragraph 4; decision V/16, paragraph 8; decision V/17, paragraph 5; decision V/18 part I, paragraph 1 (a)*].

Implementation of the work programme

The COP has urged the GEF to give high priority to the allocation of resources to activities that advance the objectives of the Convention in respect of forest biological diversity [*decision IV/7, paragraph 5, decision V/13, paragraph 2 (b) (iii)*]. It has provided some specific guidance to the GEF on financial support for activities relating to the work programme on forest biological diversity [*decision IV/7, paragraph 6; decision IV/13, paragraph 4*] and has urged Parties to propose projects that promote the implementation of the work programme [*decision IV/7, paragraph 7*]. The COP also requested the financial mechanism to consider the operational objectives of the work programme as guidance for funding in the field of forest biological diversity, and to assist in implementation of the work programme at the national, regional and subregional level [*decision IV/7, paragraph 8*].

In its long-term programme of work the COP decided that forests would form one of the three priority themes for COP 6 [*decision IV/16, annex I*]. COP 5 decided that COP 6 should consider expanding the focus of the programme from research to practical action. It also called on Parties to take a number of practical steps to address urgently the conservation and sustainable use of forest biological diversity, noting that such work should contribute to the future work of the United Nations Forum on Forests [*decision V/4, paragraphs 1–3, 7–10, 13*]. The COP further invited Parties to submit a detailed report on forest ecosystems to the Executive Secretary for consideration at COP 6 [*decision V/19, paragraph 8*].

COP 5 established an ad hoc technical expert group on forest biological diversity to:

- (i) provide advice on scientific programmes and international cooperation in research and development;
- (ii) carry out a review of available information on status, trends and threats to forest biological diversity;
- (iii) identify options and suggest priority actions for the conservation and sustainable use of forest biological diversity; and
- (iv) identify innovative, efficient and state-of-art technologies and know-how. [*decision V/4, paragraphs 4–6; annex*].

COP 5 asked SBSTTA for advice on a number of relevant matters, including the impacts of climate change, human-induced uncontrolled forest fires and harvesting of non-timber forest products on forest biological diversity [decision V/4, paragraphs 11, 12, 14]. Forests will be the focus of the work of SBSTTA 7. The Ad Hoc Technical Experts group on Forests met for the first time in Montreal from 27 November to 1 December 2000, and for the second time from 23 to 27 April 2001 in Edinburgh, UK.

References

Decisions on forest biological diversity

Decision II/9 (Forest – Statement to IPF)
Decision III/12 (Forest)
Decision IV/7 (Forest)
Decision V/4 (Forest)

Guidance to Parties

National action

Decision II/9, paragraph 3 (Forest – Statement to IPF)
Decision III/11, paragraph 15 (e) (h) (Agriculture)
Decision IV/7, paragraphs 2, 3, 5, 7; annex, paragraphs 7, 8, 18, 20, 45 (Forest)
Decision V/4, paragraphs 1, 3, 8–10, 13 (Forest)

Information and case studies

Decision IV/7, annex, paragraphs 16, 35, 37 (Forest)
Decision V/4, paragraph 7 (Forest)
Decision V/19, paragraph 8 (National reports)

Financial mechanism and resources

Guidance to the financial mechanism

Decision IV/7, paragraphs 5–8 (Forest)
Decision IV/13, paragraph 4 (Additional guidance to the financial mechanism)
Decision V/13, paragraph 2 (b) (iii) (Further guidance to the financial mechanism)

Other financial resources

Decision IV/7, paragraph 5 (Forest)

Guidance to the Secretariat

Decision II/9, paragraph 2 (Forest – Statement to IPF)
Decision III/12, paragraphs 2, 5–8; annex (see also SBSTTA recommendation II/8, paragraph 2) (Forest)
Decision IV/7, paragraphs 9–11, 13; annex, paragraphs 18, 37 (Forest)
Decision V/4, paragraphs 5, 6, 15, 17, 20 (Forest)

Guidance to SBSTTA

Decision I/7, annex, paragraph 5.1.1 (SBSTTA)
Decision III/12, paragraphs 9, 10 (Forest)
Decision IV/7, paragraph 12 (Forest)
Decision V/4, paragraphs 4, 11, 12, 14, 18 (Forest)

Cooperation with other conventions and organizations

Decision I/8, annex, paragraph 15 (Statement to CSD)

Decision II/9 (Forest – Statement to IPF)
Decision III/12, paragraphs 1–5, 7; annex (Forest)
Decision III/19, annex, paragraph 12 (Statement to UNGA Special Session)
Decision IV/7, paragraphs 4, 9, 11, 13; annex, paragraphs 7–9, 18–20, 22, 36, 45, 49, 50 (Forest)
Decision V/4, paragraphs 3, 6, 7, 11, 13, 15–20 (Forest)
Decision V/21, paragraph 3 (Cooperation)

Other relevant decisions

Decision III/10, paragraph 2 (see also SBSTTA recommendation II/1, paragraphs 14, 22) (Identification, monitoring and assessment)
Decision IV/16, annex II (Institutional matters and programme of work)
Decision V/5, annex, A, paragraph 3 (c) (Agriculture)
Decision V/8, paragraph 10 (Alien species)
Decision V/15, paragraph 4 (Incentive measures)
Decision V/16, paragraph 8 (Article 8 (j) and related provisions)
Decision V/17, paragraph 5 (Education and public awareness)
Decision V/18, I, paragraph 1 (a) (Impact assessment, liability and redress)

Documents

UNEP/CBD/COP/3/16 Forests and biological diversity
UNEP/CBD/COP/3/17 Communication of the Secretariat of the Intergovernmental Panel on Forests on progress on issues relevant to forests and biological diversity
UNEP/CBD/COP/4/7 Draft programme of work on forest biological diversity.
UNEP/CBD/COP/4/Inf.11 Submissions by Governments on the Proposed Programme of Work on Forest Biological Diversity
UNEP/CBD/COP/5/Inf.18 Status of forest biological diversity: Summary of information from national reports
UNEP/CBD/COP/5/Inf.22 Report of the Global Workshop to Address the Underlying Causes of Deforestation and Forest Degradation
UNEP/CBD/SBSTTA/2/11 Biological diversity in forests
UNEP/CBD/SBSTTA/2/Inf.5 Submissions received by the Secretariat concerning forests and biological diversity
UNEP/CBD/SBSTTA/2/Inf.6 Submission by the Government of Sweden on forests and biological diversity
UNEP/CBD/SBSTTA/2/Inf.7 Submission by the Government of Finland on forests and biological diversity
UNEP/CBD/SBSTTA/3/5 Draft programme of work for forest biological diversity
UNEP/CBD/SBSTTA/3/Inf.5 Report of Meeting of the Liaison Group on Forest Biological Diversity
UNEP/CBD/SBSTTA/4/3 Progress report on the implementation of programmes of work on thematic areas
UNEP/CBD/SBSTTA/5/8 Forest biological diversity: Status and trends and identification of options for conservation and sustainable use

Inland water biological diversity

Notes

Consideration of inland water biological diversity by the COP

Background and status

The COP decided to assess the status and trends of the biodiversity of inland water ecosystems and identify options for conservation and sustainable use at COP 4 [*decision II/18*].

In decision III/10, on identification, monitoring and assessment, the COP instructed SBSTTA to provide scientific advice and further guidance, through its thematic work on ecosystems, to assist the national implementation of Annex I of the Convention, using the elaboration of terms set out in paragraphs 12–29 of document UNEP/CBD/COP/3/12 (see the guide to Article 7 earlier in this section of the Handbook). Accordingly, SBSTTA 3 considered this issue within the context of inland water biological diversity, and submitted recommendation III/1 to the COP.

COP 3 also decided to invite the Ramsar Convention to cooperate as a lead partner in the implementation of activities under the Convention related to wetlands. It requested the Executive Secretary to seek inputs from the Ramsar Convention in preparation of documentation concerning the status and trends of inland water ecosystems for consideration by COP 4 [*decision III/21, paragraph 7 (a) (ii)*]. The Secretariat has signed a Memorandum of Cooperation with the Ramsar Convention Bureau, which has been endorsed by the COP [*decision III/21, paragraph 2*]. At COP 4, the Ramsar Bureau put forward a proposal for a joint work plan on wetlands (document UNEP/CBD/COP/4/Inf. 8), which has also been endorsed by the COP [*decision IV/15, paragraph 2*]. COP 5 endorsed a further joint work programme with the Ramsar Convention (document UNEP/CBD/SBSTTA/5/Inf.12) [*decision V/2, paragraph 2*].

On the basis of SBSTTA recommendation III/1, with modifications, COP 4 adopted a work programme on biological diversity of inland water ecosystems [*decision IV/4, paragraph 1*]. In addition to the programme of work, decision IV/4 also contains certain other guidance regarding inland water biological diversity addressed to Parties and Governments, the financial mechanism, SBSTTA and the Secretariat.

Elements of the work programme on inland water biological diversity

The programme of work adopted under decision IV/4 is set out in annex I to the decision and addresses the following areas:

A. Assessment of the status and trends of the biological diversity of inland water ecosystems and identification of options for conservation and sustainable use.

B. Provision of scientific advice and further guidance to assist in the national elaboration of Annex I of the Convention (as pertaining to inland water ecosystems).

C. Review of methodologies for assessment of biological diversity (as pertaining to inland water ecosystems).

D. The urgency of needed action on taxonomy.

The COP has requested the Executive Secretary to facilitate the programme of work [*decision IV/4, paragraph 10*]. It has also requested SBSTTA to undertake activities to implement the programme of work, and to report on progress to COP 5 [*decision IV/4, paragraph 8*]. Annex II to decision IV/4 sets out a possible time-frame for the work programme of SBSTTA in this area.

The COP noted that while the implementation of the programme of work is subject to the availability of financial resources, particular attention should be given to early progress in the development of rapid assessment methodologies especially in relation to small island States [*decision IV/4, paragraph 11*].

COP guidance

Guidance to Parties

The work programme in annex I to decision IV/4 contains a number of specific recommendations to Parties [*decision IV/4, annex I, paragraphs 9, 12–20*].[30]

The COP has urged Parties when requesting support from the financial mechanism to give priority to certain projects related to inland water ecosystems [*decision IV/4, paragraph 7*]. It has also urged Parties to integrate elements of the work programme addressing inland water ecosystems into their national and sectoral plans and to implement these as soon as possible.

COP 5 further encouraged Parties to address the lack of information on inland water biological diversity and to include this information in their national reports and urged capacity-building measures for developing and implementing national and sectoral plans for the conservation and sustainable use of inland water ecosystems [*decision V/2, paragraphs 3, 8*].

Financial mechanism and resources

COP 4 requested the financial mechanism, in the context of implementing national biodiversity strategies and action plans, to provide support to eligible projects that help Parties develop and implement plans for the conservation and sustainable use of inland water biological diversity [*decision IV/4, paragraph 6*]. This call was repeated at COP 5 [*decision V/13, paragraph 2 (n)*].

The COP invited all relevant organizations to support efforts by Parties and Governments to implement national and sectoral plans for the conservation and sustainable use of the biological diversity of inland water ecosystems [*decision IV/4, paragraph 9*].

Cooperation with other conventions and processes

As noted above, COP 4 encouraged the implementation of the joint work plan with the Ramsar Convention proposed by the Ramsar Bureau as a framework for enhanced cooperation [*decision IV/4, paragraph 4*]. As part of the implementation of the work programme, the COP has requested SBSTTA to pursue cooperation with the Scientific and Technical Review Panel of the Ramsar Convention [*decision IV/4, paragraph 8 (c)*].

30 Recommendations to the Parties contained in the work programme [*decision IV/4, annex, paragraph 9*] which relate to specific articles of the Convention are addressed in the sections of the Handbook dealing with those articles.

The COP welcomed the recommendations of the CSD on strategic approaches to freshwater management. It urged Parties and Governments to include information on biological diversity of inland waters in their voluntary communications and reports to the CSD, and to consider inland water biological diversity in the agenda of subsequent CSD meetings to further the recommendations [*decision IV/4, paragraph 2*].

Implementation of the work programme

COP 5 took note of some of the obstacles to implementing the work plan set out in a note provided to SBSTTA 5 by the Executive Secretary (UNEP/CBD/SBSTTA/5/6) and asked the Executive Secretary to report further before COP 7. Information on the implementation of the work programme is to be disseminated through the CHM [*decision V/2, paragraphs 1, 6*].

COP 5 asked SBSTTA to consider the recommendations in the report of the World Commission on Dams and to advise COP 6 how these might be taken into consideration in the work plan on inland water biological diversity. It also asked SBSTTA to provide further advice on elaboration and refinement of the work programme by COP 7, and invited relevant organizations to contribute to the assessment of inland water biological diversity [*decision V/2, paragraphs 4, 5, 7*].

The COP has further noted in its decisions that work on the following issues should be incorporated into the thematic work programmes, including that for inland water biological diversity; alien species; incentive measures; implementation of Article 8 (j); and public education and awareness; and impact assessment [*decision V/8, paragraph 10; decision V/15, paragraph 4; decision V/16, paragraph 8; decision V/17, paragraph 5; decision V/18 I, paragraph 1 (a)*].

References

Decisions on inland water biological diversity

Decision IV/4 (Inland water)
Decision V/2 (Inland water)

Guidance to Parties

National action

Decision IV/4, paragraphs 3, 5, 7; annex I, paragraphs 9, 12–20 (Inland water)
Decision V/2, paragraph 3 (Inland water)

Financial mechanism and resources

Guidance to the financial mechanism

Decision IV/4, paragraph 6; annex I, paragraph 10 (Inland water)
Decision IV/13, paragraph 3 (Additional guidance to the financial mechanism)
Decision V/13, paragraph 2 (n) (Further guidance to the financial mechanism)

Other financial resources

Decision IV/4, paragraph 9; annex I, paragraph 11 (Inland water)

Guidance to the Secretariat

Decision III/21, paragraph 7 (Cooperation)
Decision IV/4, paragraph 10; annex I, paragraphs 1, 2, 4–7, 12, 21; annex II (Inland water)
Decision IV/5, paragraph 4 (Marine and coastal)
Decision V/21, paragraph 5 (Cooperation)
Decision V/25, paragraph 2 (Biological diversity and tourism)

Guidance to SBSTTA

Decision III/13, paragraph 2 (Terrestrial)
Decision IV/4, paragraph 8; annex I, paragraphs 6, 7, 8, 12; annex II (Inland water)
Decision V/21, paragraph 5 (Cooperation)

Cooperation with other conventions and organizations

Decision III/21, paragraphs 1, 7 (Cooperation)
Decision IV/4, paragraphs 2, 3, 4, 8; annex I, paragraphs 1–4, 12, 13, 18; annex II (Inland water)
Decision IV/5, paragraph 4 (Marine and coastal)
Decision IV/15, paragraph 2 (Cooperation)
Decision V/21, paragraphs 4, 5 (Cooperation)
Decision V/23, annex I, II, part B, Activity 7 (l) (Dry and sub-humid lands)
Decision V/25, paragraph 2 (Biological diversity and tourism)

Other relevant decisions

Decision II/18, annex, paragraph 7.6 (Medium-term programme of work)
Decision III/10, paragraph 2 (see also SBSTTA recommendation II/1, paragraphs 12, 22) (Identification, monitoring and assessment)
Decision III/11, paragraph 15 (h) (Agriculture)
Decision III/19, annex, paragraph 20 (a) (Statement to UNGA Special Session)
Decision III/22, appendix, paragraph 7.6.1 (Medium-term programme of work)
Decision V/5, annex, A, paragraph 3 (c) (Agriculture)
Decision V/8, paragraph 10 (Alien species)
Decision V/15, paragraph 4 (Incentive measures)
Decision V/16, paragraph 8 (Article 8 (j) and related provisions)
Decision V/17, paragraph 5 (Education and public awareness)
Decision V/18, I, paragraph 1 (a) (Impact assessment, liability and redress)
Decision V/23, annex I, II, part A, Activity 2; part B, Activity 7 (e) (l) (Dry and sub-humid lands)

Documents

UNEP/CBD/COP/4/4 Status and trends of the biological diversity of inland water ecosystems and options for conservation and sustainable use
UNEP/CBD/COP/5/10 Progress report on the implementation of programmes of work on inland water ecosystems, marine and coastal, and forest biological diversity.
UNEP/CBD/SBSTTA/3/2 Biological diversity of inland waters
UNEP/CBD/SBSTTA/3/8 Methodologies for the assessment of biological diversity in inland water ecosystems

UNEP/CBD/SBSTTA/3/Inf.4 Institutions related to inland waters biological diversity
UNEP/CBD/SBSTTA/3/Inf.18 Workshop on freshwater biodiversity, Selbu, Norway, 5–7 June, 1997 (Draft report) (submitted by organizing institutes in Norway and Sweden)
UNEP/CBD/SBSTTA/3/Inf.26 Biodiversity of inland waters workshop
UNEP/CBD/SBSTTA/4/3 Progress report on the implementation of programmes of work on thematic areas
UNEP/CBD/SBSTTA/5/6 Inland waters biological diversity: Ways and means to implement the work programme

Agricultural biological diversity

Editors' note:

The COP's consideration of agricultural biological diversity is linked to a number of items on the COP's agenda, including access to genetic resources and benefit-sharing. Decisions on agricultural biological diversity make frequent references to the FAO International Undertaking on Plant Genetic Resources. These references are addressed in the guide to Article 15 earlier in this section of the Handbook. Decisions relating to other FAO activities and the Global System for Plant Genetic Resources for Food and Agriculture are addressed below.

Notes

Consideration of agricultural biological diversity by the COP

Background and status

As part of its first medium-term programme of work, the COP decided to consider agricultural biological diversity at COP 3 [*decision I/9*]. It has also addressed issues relevant to agricultural biological diversity in its consideration of other items on its medium-term programme of work, including the relationship with the FAO Global System for Plant Genetic Resources for Food and Agriculture, and access to genetic resources (see the guide to Article 15 earlier in this section of the Handbook).

Guide to decisions

COP 2 adopted a statement for transmission to the International Technical Conference on the Conservation and Utilization of Plant Genetic Resources for Food and Agriculture in June 1996 [*decision II/16, annex*].

SBSTTA 2 considered agricultural biological diversity and submitted recommendation II/7 to the COP. COP 3 adopted decision III/11, on conservation and sustainable use of agricultural biological diversity, which, *inter alia*, decided to establish a multi-year programme of activities on agricultural biological diversity. The aims of the work programme should be to promote:

- the positive effects and mitigate the negative impacts of agricultural practices on biological diversity in agro-ecosystems and their interface with other ecosystems;
- the conservation and sustainable use of genetic resources of actual or potential value for food and agriculture; and
- the fair and equitable sharing of benefits arising out of the utilization of genetic resources [*decision III/1, paragraph 1*].

The decision requested the Secretariat and FAO, in close collaboration with other relevant organizations, to identify and assess relevant ongoing national and international activities and instruments [*decision III/11, paragraph 2; annex 2*]. The results of this assessment were to be reported back through SBSTTA, which at its third meeting, reviewed progress to date in initiating the multi-year work programme, and submitted recommendation III/4 to the COP. In decision IV/6, the COP endorsed recommendation III/4, and requested that SBSTTA develop and provide to COP 5, advice and recommendations as to the development of the multi-year programme of work [*decision IV/6, paragraph 7*].

The advice and recommendations of SBSTTA were provided in recommendation V/9. COP 5 adopted a programme of work to further implement decision III/11 [*decision V/5, paragraph 3*].

Much of the work on agricultural biological diversity under the Convention to date has been undertaken in cooperation with the FAO. In addition, the COP has welcomed the contribution that the Global Plan of Action for the Conservation and Sustainable Utilization of Plant Genetic Resources provides to the implementation of the Convention and has endorsed its priorities and policy recommendations, while recognizing the need for further work in the context of the FAO Global System [*decision III/11, paragraph 19*]. The COP has also expressed support for the Global Strategy for the Management of Farm Animal Genetic Resources under the FAO [*decision III/11, paragraph 20*]. The COP has asked the FAO and other relevant organizations to support implementation of the work programme [*decision V/5, paragraph 6*].

The COP has recommended collaboration and consultation with the WTO in developing a better appreciation of the relationship between trade and agricultural biological diversity [*decision III/11, paragraph 24*]. The COP has requested the Executive Secretary to apply for observer status in the WTO Committee on Agriculture [*decision IV/6, paragraph 9*]. Parties have been encouraged to support this application [*decision V/5, paragraph 14*]. The Executive Secretary was requested to report to the COP on the impact of trade liberalization on the conservation and sustainable use of agricultural biological diversity in consultation with, *inter alia*, the WTO [*decision IV/6, paragraph 10*].

Elements of the work programme on agricultural biological diversity

The programme comprises four mutually reinforcing programme elements:

1. Assessments: to provide a comprehensive analysis of status and trends of the world's agricultural biodiversity and of their underlying causes, as well of local knowledge of its management.

2. Adaptive management: to identify management practices, technologies and policies that promote the positive and mitigate the negative impacts of agriculture on biodiversity, and enhance productivity and the capacity to sustain livelihoods, by expanding knowledge, understanding and awareness of the multiple goods and services provided by the different levels and functions of agricultural biodiversity.

3. Capacity-building: to strengthen the capacities of farmers, indigenous and local communities and their organizations and other stakeholders, to manage sustainably agricultural biodiversity so as to increase their benefits, and to promote awareness and responsible action.

4. Mainstreaming: to support the development of national plans or strategies for the conservation and sustainable use of agricultural biodiversity and to promote their mainstreaming and integration in sectoral and cross-sectoral plans and programmes [*decision V/15, annex B*].

For each of these, an operational objective, rationale, set of activities, ways and means and timing of expected outputs are provided.

The COP has recognized the contribution of farmers, indigenous and local communities to the conservation and sustainable use of agricultural biodiversity and the importance of agricultural biodiversity to their livelihoods, emphasizes the importance of their participation in the implementation of the programme of work [*decision V/5, paragraph 5*].

COP 5 further noted that work on the following issues should be incorporated into the thematic work programmes, including that for agricultural biological diversity; incentive measures; implementation of Article 8 (j); public education and awareness; and impact assessment [*decision V/15, paragraph 4; decision V/16, paragraph 8; decision V/17, paragraph 5; decision V/18, part I, paragraph 1 (a)*].

COP guidance

Guidance to Parties

The COP has adopted certain policy guidance to Parties in its decisions on this issue and has also called upon Parties to provide information and case studies on particular issues.

In relation to national action, decision III/11 encourages Parties to develop national strategies, programmes and plans which address agricultural biological diversity, and provides specific guidance related to agricultural biological diversity which Parties are encouraged to incorporate into those strategies, programmes and plans [*decision III/11, paragraph 15*]. Parties are also encouraged to address specific aspects of plant, animal and microbial genetic resources [*decision III/11, paragraph 16*]. The COP has also given guidance related to agricultural practices [*decision III/11, paragraph 17*] as well as indicators, public awareness and incentives [*decision III/11, paragraphs 9, 13, 21*].

A central part of the work programme has been the call for a range of information from Parties and others. For example, the COP has asked Parties for case studies on topics such as GURTs, adaptive management practices, pollinators and soil biota. A list of topics is provided in decision V/5 [*decision V/5, annex, B, programme element 2, Activity 2.1*].

Financial mechanism and resources

The COP has requested the GEF to give priority to supporting efforts for the conservation and sustainable use of biological diversity important for agriculture [*decision III/11, paragraph 22*]. COP 5 requested the GEF to support the implementation of the programme of work on agricultural biodiversity [*decision V/13, paragraph 2 (b)*]. The COP has drawn the attention of international funding agencies, including the financial mechanism, to the need to support capacity-building in the development and implementation of the work programme on agricultural biological diversity [*decision IV/6, paragraph 12; decision V/5, paragraph 9*]. It has also requested the GEF to provide support for the International Initiative for the Conservation and Sustainable Use of Pollinators [*decision V/5/13, paragraph 2 (c)*].

International Initiative for the Conservation and Sustainable Use of Pollinators

COP 5 also established an International Initiative for the Conservation and Sustainable Use of Pollinators as a cross-cutting initiative within the agricultural work programme. It requested the Executive Secretary to invite the FAO to facilitate and coordinate the initiative in cooperation with other relevant organizations who were invited to support actions in Parties and countries subject to pollinator decline. The Executive Secretary, SBSTTA and the financial mechanism were asked to support the Initiative and Parties and Governments were asked to collaborate and compile case studies and pilot projects and to report to COP 6, when the initiative will be reviewed [*decision V/5, paragraphs 15–18*].

Genetic use restriction technologies (GURTs)

The COP considered GURTS at COP 4 [*decision IV/6, paragraph 11*] and at COP 5. COP 5 decided to continue work on GURTs under each of the four elements of the programme of work. It invited relevant organizations to study further the implications for biological diversity of such technologies, and asked them to inform COP 6 of initiatives in this area. It recommended that such technologies should not be approved for field testing by Parties until appropriate scientific data to justify such testing were available. It also urged Parties to carry out scientific studies of such technologies and their impacts and to disseminate the results through the CHM. It further encouraged them to identify ways and means of addressing these impacts, including the possible need for national regulations. The Executive Secretary has been asked to prepare a report on the status of GURTs based on information provided by Parties and organizations for the consideration of SBSTTA 7. The Executive Secretary was also asked to prepare a report for COP 6 on the implications of such technologies for the implementation of Article 8 (j) [*decision V/5, paragraphs 19–29*].

References

Decisions on agricultural biological diversity

Decision III/11 (Agriculture)
Decision IV/6 (see also SBSTTA recommendation III/4) (Agriculture)
Decision V/5 (Agriculture)

Guidance to Parties

National action

Decision III/11, paragraphs 9, 13, 15–17, 21 (Agriculture)
Decision IV/6, paragraph 11 (Agriculture)
Decision V/5, paragraphs 4, 9, 10, 12–14, 23, 24, 26, 27; annex, B, (Agriculture)

Information and case studies

Decision III/11, paragraphs 4–6, 10, 11; annex 2; annex 3 (Agriculture)
Decision IV/6, paragraphs 4–6 (Agriculture)
Decision V/5, paragraphs 25, 27; annex, B, programme element 2, (Agriculture)

Financial mechanism and resources

Guidance to the financial mechanism

Decision III/5, paragraph 2 (c) (Additional guidance to the financial mechanism)
Decision III/11, paragraph 22 (Agriculture)
Decision IV/6, paragraph 12 (Agriculture)
Decision V/5, paragraph 18 (Agriculture)
Decision V/13, paragraph 2 (b) (i), 2 (c) (Further guidance to the financial mechanism)

Other financial resources

Decision III/11, paragraph 22 (Agriculture)
Decision V/5, paragraph 9; annex, B, programme element 3, 'Ways and means' (Agriculture)

Guidance to the Secretariat

Decision III/11, paragraphs 2, 7, 8, 10; annex 2 (Agriculture)
Decision IV/6, paragraph 1 (see also SBSTTA recommendation III/4, paragraph 11) (Agriculture)
Decision V/5, paragraphs 6–8, 16, 28, 29; annex, B, programme element 2 (Agriculture)

Guidance to SBSTTA

Decision III/11, paragraphs 2, 12 (Agriculture)
Decision IV/6, paragraph 7 (Agriculture)
Decision V/5, paragraphs 16, 18, 19, 28; annex, B, programme element 2 (Agriculture)

Cooperation with other conventions and organizations

Decision II/15 (FAO Global System)
Decision II/16 (Statement to FAO International Technical Conference)
Decision III/11, paragraphs 2–20, 24; annex 2 (Agriculture)
Decision III/19, annex, paragraph 12 (Statement to UNGA Special Session)
Decision IV/6, paragraphs 9, 10 (Agriculture)
Decision V/5, paragraphs 2, 6, 11–14, 16, 17, 20, 21, 22, 29, programme element 1, 'Ways and means', programme element 4, 'Ways and means' (Agriculture)

Other relevant decisions

Decision I/9, annex, paragraph 6.3 (Medium-term programme of work)
Decision III/10, paragraph 2, (see also SBSTTA recommendation II/1, paragraphs 13, 14, 22) (Identification, monitoring and assessment)
Decision V/15, paragraph 4 (Incentive measures)
Decision V/16, paragraph 8 (Article 8(j) and related provisions)
Decision V/17, paragraph 5 (Education and public awareness)
Decision V/18, I, paragraph 1 (a) (Impact assessment, liability and redress)

Documents

UNEP/CBD/COP/2/18 FAO Global System for Plant Genetic Resources for Food and Agriculture

UNEP/CBD/COP/3/14 Consideration of agricultural biological diversity under the Convention on Biological Diversity

UNEP/CBD/COP/3/15 Report on the Food and Agriculture Organization's Global System for the Conservation and Utilization of Plant Genetic Resources for Food and Agriculture

UNEP/CBD/COP/4/6 Ongoing instruments and activities on agricultural biodiversity.

UNEP/CBD/COP/4/Inf.17 Inter-agency Consultation on Wild Plant Genetic Resources of Interest for Food and Agriculture, Paris, February 1998

UNEP/CBD/COP/4/Inf.20 Report of the Fourth Extraordinary Session of the Commission on Genetic Resources for Food and Agriculture, Rome, 1–5 December 1997

UNEP/CBD/COP/4/Inf.24 Sharing the Benefits of Agricultural Biodiversity

UNEP/CBD/COP/5/11 Review of Programme of Work: Phase I and adoption of multi-year Programme of Work

UNEP/CBD/COP/5/Inf.10 Summaries of case-studies on soil biota, pollinators and landscape diversity, and of coverage of agricultural biodiversity in national reports

UNEP/CBD/COP/5/Inf.11 Agricultural biological diversity: Review of phase I of the programme of work and adoption of multi-year programme of work: The ecosystem approach: Towards its application to agricultural biological diversity

UNEP/CBD/COP/5/Inf.12 Agricultural biological diversity: Report on the negotiations for the revision of the International Undertaking on Plant Genetic Resources

UNEP/CBD/SBSTTA/1/7 Contribution to the preparation for the forthcoming International Technical Conference on the Conservation and Utilization of Plant Genetic Resources for Food and Agriculture in 1996

UNEP/CBD/SBSTTA/2/10 Agricultural biological diversity

UNEP/CBD/SBSTTA/2/Inf.15 FAO Global System for the Conservation and Utilization of Plant Genetic Resources for Food and Agriculture; report of the Fourth International Technical Conference on the Conservation on the Conservation and Utilization of Plant Genetic Resources for Food and Agriculture (Leipzig, Germany, 17–23 June 1996)

UNEP/CBD/SBSTTA/3/6 Review of ongoing activities on agricultural biological diversity

UNEP/CBD/SBSTTA/3/Inf.6 Reports from international organizations on policies, programmes, and activities on agricultural biological diversity (CGRFA-7/97/7 Parts I, II, III and Add. 1, submitted by FAO)

UNEP/CBD/SBSTTA/3/Inf.7 Report from FAO on its policies, programmes, and activities on agricultural biological diversity and progress report on the Global System for the Conservation and Sustainable Use of Plant Genetic Resources for Food and Agriculture (CGRFA-7/97/8.1 and 8.2 and CGRFA-7/97/3, submitted by FAO)

UNEP/CBD/SBSTTA/3/Inf.8 Report of Seventh Session of Commission on Genetic Resources for Food and Agriculture, May 1997 (CGRFA-7/97 REP, submitted by FAO)

UNEP/CBD/SBSTTA/3/Inf.9 Compilation of contributions on agricultural biological diversity received from parties

UNEP/CBD/SBSTTA/3/Inf.10 Report of the Joint FAO-CBD Secretariat Technical Consultations and Technical Workshop (June 1997, Rome)

UNEP/CBD/SBSTTA/4/3 Progress report on the implementation of programmes of work on thematic areas

UNEP/CBD/SBSTTA/4/9/Rev.1 Consequences of the use of the new technology for the control of plant gene expression for the conservation and sustainable use of biological diversity

UNEP/CBD/SBSTTA/4/Inf.3 Supplementary information to SBSTTA/4/9/Rev.1 Consequences of the Use of the New Technology for the Control of Plant Gene Expression for the Conservation and Sustainable Use of Biological Diversity

UNEP/CBD/SBSTTA/5/10 Agricultural biological diversity: Assessment of ongoing activities and priorities for a programme of work

UNEP/CBD/SBSTTA/5/Inf.10 Agricultural biological diversity: Assessment of ongoing activities and instruments

Marine and coastal biological diversity

Notes

Consideration of marine and coastal biological diversity by the COP

Background and status

The COP identified marine and coastal biological diversity as an early priority. COP 1 requested SBSTTA to advise on scientific, technical and technological aspects of the conservation and sustainable use of marine and coastal biological diversity [*decision I/7, annex, paragraph 5.5.3*].

Accordingly, SBSTTA 1 submitted recommendation I/8 to COP 2 on scientific, technical and technological aspects of the conservation and sustainable use of marine and coastal biological diversity.

COP 2 subsequently adopted decision II/10 on the conservation and sustainable use of marine and coastal biological diversity, supporting some of SBSTTA's recommendations, subject to additional conclusions by the COP (as set out in annex I to decision II/10). Decision II/10 provided certain guidance on the process to be used to develop a work programme on marine and coastal biological diversity, and on key substantive elements of the work programme. It also provided some guidance to the Parties in relation to marine and coastal biological diversity, and on cooperation with related conventions and relevant international and regional organizations. It also requested the Executive Secretary to prepare for SBSTTA a study on the bio-prospecting of genetic resources of the deep seabed in consultation with the secretariat of the UNCLOS [*decision II/10, paragraph 12*].

Also at COP 2, the Ministerial Statement on the Implementation of the Convention on Biological Diversity referred to the new global consensus on the importance of marine and coastal biological diversity as the 'Jakarta Mandate on Marine and Coastal Biological Diversity'. The Ministerial Statement reaffirmed the critical need for the COP to address the conservation and sustainable use of marine and coastal biological diversity, and urged Parties to initiate immediate action to implement COP decisions on this issue [*Jakarta Ministerial Statement*].

Decision II/10 instructed the Executive Secretary to provide to SBSTTA, in accordance with annex II to the decision, advice and options for recommendations to COP in further elaborating the recommendations of SBSTTA [*decision II/10, paragraph 7*]. This annex required the Executive Secretary to produce annual reports to SBSTTA on this issue. It also required the Executive Secretary to establish a roster of experts on marine and coastal biological diversity.

In accordance with decision II/10, the Executive Secretary established a roster of experts on marine and coastal biological diversity, on the basis of country input; and, drawing from the roster of experts, convened the First Meeting of the Group of Experts on Marine and Coastal Biological Diversity (Jakarta, March 1997). The outcome of this meeting provided the basis for the elaboration by the Executive Secretary of a draft three-year programme of work on marine and coastal biological diversity. This programme of work was considered and amended by SBSTTA 3 [*SBSTTA recommendation III/2*].

Based on the recommendations of SBSTTA, COP 4 adopted decision IV/5 on the conservation and sustainable use of marine and coastal biological diversity. Decision IV/5 contains, in an annex, the programme of work arising from decision II/10 [*decision IV/5, I, annex*]. It also specifically addresses the issue of coral bleaching, and related biodiversity loss, and the special needs and considerations of small island developing States in implementation of the work programme [*decision IV/5, II, III*].

Elements of the work programme on marine and coastal biological diversity

Five key thematic issues were identified in the Jakarta Mandate. These issues are reflected in the programme elements of the work programme adopted in decision IV/5. The operational objectives set out in the work programme are highlighted here. Readers should refer to the annex to decision IV/5 for the full text of the work programme, which sets out specific activities and timeframes for the achievement of these objectives.

Programme element 1. Integrated marine and coastal area management (IMCAM)

Operational objectives

1.1 reviewing existing instruments related to IMCAM;

1.2 promoting the development and implementation of IMCAM at the local, national and regional level;

1.3 developing guidelines for ecosystem evaluation and assessment (including indicators).

Programme element 2. Marine and coastal living resources[31]

Operational objectives

2.1 promoting ecosystem approaches to the sustainable use of marine and coastal living resources;

2.2 making available to Parties information on marine and coastal genetic resources, including bioprospecting.

Programme element 3. Marine and coastal protected areas

Operational objectives

3.1 facilitating research and monitoring activities on the value and effects of marine

31 The work element on coral reefs is to be integrated into this programme element [*decision V/3, paragraph 1, part I*].

and coastal protected areas or similarly restricted areas on sustainable use of marine and coastal living resources;

3.2 developing criteria for the establishment and management of marine and coastal protected areas.

Programme element 4. Mariculture

Operational objectives

4.1 assessing the consequences of mariculture for marine and coastal biological diversity and promoting techniques to minimize adverse impacts.

Programme element 5. Alien species and genotypes

Operational objectives

5.1 achieving better understanding of the causes and impacts of introductions of alien species and genotypes;

5.2 identifying gaps in existing or proposed legal instruments, guidelines and procedures and collecting information on national and international actions;

5.3 establishing an 'incident list' of introductions.

Programme element 6. General

Operational objectives

6.1 assembling a database of initiatives on programme elements, particularly integrated marine and coastal area management;

6.2 developing a database of experts from the Roster of Experts and other sources for the development and implementation of national policies on marine and coastal biological diversity.

Activities relating to the six programme elements are to be carried out through a variety of activities, coordinated by the Secretariat, and involving collaborative linkages and the use of experts.

Implementation of the work progarmme

COP 5 reviewed progress in the implementation of the work programme, encouraging the Executive Secretary and SBSTTA to complete the implementation of decision IV/5 as soon as possible. It also added a work element on coral reefs, specifically on coral bleaching, to be integrated into programme element 2 ('Marine and coastal living resources'), with a minimum three-year time schedule. It further endorsed the results of the Expert Consultation on Coral Bleaching, held in Manila from 11 to 13 October 1999, which are included as an annex to the decision. The annex contains priority areas for action on coral bleaching under four headings: information-gathering; capacity-building; policy development/implementation; and financing.

COP 5 also made suggestions for further action in each of the existing programme elements and approved the terms of reference and duration of work specified for the Ad

Hoc Technical Expert Groups on Marine and Coastal Protected Areas and on Mariculture as contained in annex II to recommendation V/14 of SBSTTA, with slight modifications [*decision V/3, paragraph 15*]. It invited UNESCO to continue its strong involvement with the work programme and asked the Executive Secretary to coordinate with the secretariats of the regional seas conventions and action plans with a view to exploring further collaboration, including the development of joint work programmes [*decision V/3, paragraphs 17, 18*].

COP 5 further noted in the relevant decisions that work on the following issues should be incorporated into the thematic work programmes, including that for marine and coastal biological diversity; incentive measures; implementation of Article 8 (j); public education and awareness; and impact assessment [*decision V/15, paragraph 4; decision V/16, paragraph 8; decision V/17, paragraph 5; decision V/18, I, paragraph 1 (a)*].

The COP has urged Parties when requesting assistance through the financial mechanism to propose projects that promote implementation of the programme of work on marine and coastal biological diversity [*decision IV/5 I, paragraph 3*]. It has also urged Parties, countries, relevant organizations and donor agencies to contribute to the implementation of specific elements of the work programme [*decision IV/5 I, paragraph 2*].

References

Decisions on marine and coastal biological diversity

Decision II/10 (Marine and coastal)
Decision IV/5 (Marine and coastal)
Decision V/3 (Marine and coastal)

Guidance to Parties

National action

Decision II/10, paragraphs 2, 4 (Marine and coastal)
Decision III/11, paragraph 15 (h) (Agriculture)
Decision IV/5, I, paragraphs 2, 3; II, paragraph 4; III; annex, paragraphs 10, 13 (Marine and coastal)
Decision V/3, paragraphs 4, 6 (Marine and coastal)
Decision V/25, paragraph 7 (Biological diversity and tourism)

Information and case studies

Decision V/3, paragraph 7 (Marine and coastal)

Financial mechanism and resources

Guidance to the financial mechanism

Decision I/2, annex I, paragraph 4 (k) (Financial mechanism and resources)
Decision II/10, paragraph 11 (Marine and coastal)
Decision V/13, paragraph 2 (d) (Further guidance to the financial mechanism)

Other financial resources

Decision II/10, paragraph 11 (Marine and coastal)
Decision IV/5, I, paragraph 2 (Marine and coastal)

Guidance to the Secretariat

Decision II/10, paragraphs 7, 8, 12; annex II (Marine and coastal)
Decision IV/5, I, paragraph 4, II, paragraph 2; annex A, paragraphs 1, 8, 13, C[32] (Marine and coastal)
Decision V/3, paragraphs 1, 4, 7, 10, 11, 14, 16–18 (Marine and coastal)
Decision V/21, paragraph 3 (Cooperation)
Decision V/25, paragraph 2 (Biological diversity and tourism)

Guidance to SBSTTA

Decision I/7, annex, paragraph 5.5.3 (SBSTTA)
Decision II/10, paragraph 14 (Marine and coastal)
Decision IV/5, II, paragraph 1[33] (Marine and coastal)
Decision V/3, paragraphs 1, 8, 10, 12, 13 (Marine and coastal)

Cooperation with other conventions and organizations

Decision II/10, paragraphs 4, 5, 10, 12, 13; annex II, paragraphs 2 (c), 3 (b) (Marine and coastal)
Decision III/19, annex, paragraphs 10, 11 (Statement to UNGA Special Session)
Decision IV/5, I, paragraph 4; II, paragraphs 2, 3; annex, paragraphs 7, 11, 12, 14, C[34] (Marine and coastal)
Decision V/3, paragraphs 5–7, 17, 18 (Marine and coastal)
Decision V/21, paragraph 3 (Cooperation)
Decision V/25, paragraph 2 (Biological diversity and tourism)

Other relevant decisions

Decision I/9, annex, paragraph 5.3.1 (Medium-term programme of work)
Decision III/10, paragraph 2 (see also SBSTTA recommendation II/1, paragraphs 12, 14, 22) (Identification, monitoring and assessment)
Decision III/18, paragraph 1 (see also SBSTTA recommendation II/9, paragraph 2) (Incentive measures)
Decision V/5, annex, A, paragraph 3 (c) (Agriculture)
Decision V/8, paragraph 10 (Alien species)
Decision V/15, paragraph 4 (Incentive measures)
Decision V/16, paragraph 8 (Article 8 (j) and related provisions)
Decision V/17, paragraph 5 (Education and public awareness)
Decision V/18, I, paragraph 1 (a) (Impact assessment, liability and redress)

---

32 All activities in the work programme are to be carried out primarily by the Executive Secretary or Secretariat. See text of the decision for details.
33 SBSTTA is to participate in activities under the following operational objectives listed in part C of the annex: 1.3, 3.1, 3.2, 4, 5.1.
34 Activities under the following operational objectives listed in part C of the annex are to be carried out by the Executive Secretary in cooperation with other relevant organizations: 1.1, 1.2, 1.3, 2.1, 3.1, 5.1, 5.2, 6.2.

Documents

UNEP/CBD/COP/4/5 Implementation of the programme of work on marine and coastal biological diversity
UNEP/CBD/COP/5/Inf.6 Review of existing instruments relevant to integrated marine and coastal area management and their implications for the implementation of the Convention
UNEP/CBD/COP/5/Inf.7 Information on marine and coastal genetic resources, including bioprospecting
UNEP/CBD/COP/5/Inf.8 Criteria for the selection of marine and coastal protected areas
UNEP/CBD/SBSTTA/1/8 Scientific, technical and technological aspects of the conservation and sustainable use of coastal and marine biological diversity
UNEP/CBD/SBSTTA/2/14 Report by the Executive Secretary on marine and biological diversity
UNEP/CBD/SBSTTA/2/Inf.4 Submissions received by the Secretariat concerning the conservation and sustainable use of marine and coastal biological diversity
UNEP/CBD/SBSTTA/2/15 Bioprospecting of Genetic Resources of the Deep Sea-Bed
UNEP/CBD/SBSTTA/3/4 Conservation sustainable use of marine and coastal biological diversity
UNEP/CBD/SBSTTA/3/Inf.1 Report of the First Meeting of Experts on Marine and Coastal Biological Diversity
UNEP/CBD/SBSTTA/4/3 Progress report on the implementation of programmes of work on thematic areas
UNEP/CBD/SBSTTA/5/7 Marine and coastal biological diversity: Consideration of implementation tools for the programme of work, and analysis of coral bleaching

Dry and sub-humid lands

Notes

Consideration of dry and sub-humid lands by the COP

Background and status

Dryland ecosystems were first considered by COP 3 under the agenda item 'Terrestrial biological diversity' [*decision III/13*]. COP 4 decided that one of the items for in-depth consideration at COP 5 would be dryland, Mediterranean, arid, semi-arid, grassland and savannah ecosystems [*decision IV/16, annex II*]. Accordingly, SBSTTA 4 considered an assessment of status and trends, and options for conservation and sustainable use, of these ecosystems. As a result of recommendation IV/3 arising from this meeting, SBSTTA 5 considered options for the development of a programme of work and submitted recommendation V/8. This invited the COP to establish a work programme, the proposed first phase of which was included as an annex to the recommendation. The COP adopted a modified version of this work programme, noting that the programme could be referred to as the programme on 'dry and sub-humid lands' [*decision V/23, paragraphs 1, 2*]. The COP then urged Parties and organizations and others to implement the programme and to support its activities [*decision V/23, paragraphs 3, 11*].

SBSTTA was asked to establish an ad hoc technical group of experts charged with a series of tasks relevant to the work programme [*decision V/23, paragraph 7*]. The

Executive Secretary was asked to review the programme of work, taking into account the suggestions of the expert group, and identify expected outcomes, in close collaboration with the Secretariat of the Convention to Combat Desertification (CCD) and other relevant bodies. The findings were to be presented to SBSTTA [*decision V/23, paragraph 6*]. The COP also asked the Executive Secretary to develop a joint work programme with the CCD and collaborate with it and other relevant bodies in the establishment of a roster of experts [*decision V/23, paragraphs 8, 9*]. Possible elements of a joint work programme between the secretariats of the two conventions were set out in an information document prepared for COP 5 (document UNEP/CBD/COP/5/Inf.15).

SBSTTA has been asked asked to review periodically the status and trends of biological diversity of dry and sub-humid lands on the basis of outputs from the work programme and make recommendations for the further modification of the work programme in light of this [*decision V/23, paragraph 5*].

The GEF has been asked to fund projects which implement the work programme through the development, review and implementation of its operational programmes, in particular the operational programme on arid and semi-arid ecosystems [*decision V/13, paragraph 2 (b) (ii)*].

Elements of the work programme on dry and sub-humid lands

The programme is divided into two parts, 'assessments' and 'targeted actions in response to identified needs', to be implemented in parallel [*decision V/23, annex I, II, paragraph 4*].

Under assessments, six activities are identified, all concerning assessments in dry and sub-humid lands:

1. Assessment of the status and trends of biological diversity.
2. Identification of specific areas of value for biological diversity, with reference to the criteria in Annex I to the Convention.
3. Further development of indicators.
4. Building knowledge on ecological, physical and social processes.
5. Identification of local and global benefits derived from biological diversity.
6. Identification and dissemination of best management practices, including knowledge, innovation and practices of indigenous and local communities [*decision V/23, annex I, II, part A, Activities 1–6*].

These activities are to be carried out through: consolidation of information from existing sources; targeted research; multidisciplinary and interdisciplinary case studies on management practices, carried out primarily by national and regional institutions; dissemination of information; and capacity-building [*decision V/23, annex I, II, part A, paragraph 7*].

Under targeted actions, three clusters of activities are identified:

1 Promotion of specific measures for the conservation and sustainable use of biological diversity, through for example, use and establishment of additional protected areas, appropriate management and sustainable use of water resources and management of invasive alien species.

2 Promotion of responsible resource management, at appropriate levels, applying the ecosystem approach, through an enabling policy environment.

3 Support for sustainable livelihoods, through diversifying sources of income, promotion of sustainable harvesting, including of wildlife, and exploring innovative sustainable use of biological diversity [*decision V/23, annex I, II, Activities 7–9*].

These activities are to be carried out through capacity-building, particularly at national and local levels, establishment of an international network of designated demonstration sites, case studies on successful management, partnerships between relevant stakeholders, and enhanced interaction between the work programmes of this Convention and the Convention to Combat Desertification [*decision V/23, annex I, II, part B, 'Ways and means'*].

Parties and other bodies have been asked to report on implementation through appropriate sections in their national reports to the Convention, and in reports made in the context of the Convention to Combat Desertification and other relevant conventions. SBSTTA is to review such reports and make recommendations for further prioritization and refinement of the work programme [*decision V/23, annex I, III, paragraphs 12, 13*].

Annex II of decision V/23 contained an indicative list of levels of implementation of the various activities identified in the programme of work.

The COP further noted in its relevant decisions that work on the following issues should be incorporated into the thematic work programmes, including that for dry and sub-humid lands; alien species; incentive measures; implementation of Article 8 (j); public education and awareness; and impact assessment [*decision V/8, paragraph 10; decision V/15, paragraph 4; decision V/16, paragraph 8; decision V/17, paragraph 5; decision V/18 I, paragraph 1 (a)*].

References

Decisions on dry and sub-humid lands

Decision V/23 (Dry and sub-humid lands)

Guidance to Parties

National action

Decision V/23, paragraph 3; annex I, II, part A, paragraphs 7 (b), (d); part B, (a),(b),(d),(f), (Dry and sub-humid lands)

Information and case studies

Decision V/23, annex I, II, part A, paragraph 7 (c), (d); annex I, III, paragraph 12 (Dry and sub-humid lands)

Financial mechanism and resources

Guidance to the financial mechanism

Decision I/2, annex I, paragraph (4) (k) (Financial mechanism and resources)

Decision V/13, paragraph 2 (b) (ii) (Further guidance to the financial mechanism)

Other financial resources

Decision V/23, paragraph 3; annex I, II, part B, paragraph (a) (Dry and sub-humid lands)

Guidance to the Secretariat

Decision III/13, paragraph 1 (a) and 1 (c) (Terrestrial)
Decision V/23, paragraphs 6, 8–10; annex I, II, part A, paragraph 7 (a); part B, paragraph 5 (d) (e) (Dry and sub-humid lands)

Guidance to SBSTTA

Decision V/23, paragraphs 5, 7; annex I, III, paragraph 13 (Dry and sub-humid lands)

Cooperation with other conventions and organizations

Decision III/13, paragraph 1 (a) (Terrestrial)
Decision V/21, paragraph 3 (Cooperation)
Decision V/23, paragraphs 3, 6, 8, 9; annex I, I, paragraph 2 (c), (f); annex I, II, part A, paragraph 7 (a), (b), (c); part B, Activity 7 (l), (m), paragraphs (a), (d), (e), (f); annex I, III paragraph 12 (b) (Dry and sub-humid lands)

Other relevant decisions

Decision IV/16, annex II (Institutional matters and programme of work)
Decision V/5, annex, A, paragraph 3 (c) (Agriculture)
Decision V/8, paragraph 10 (Alien species)
Decision V/15, paragraph 4 (Incentive measures)
Decision V/16, paragraph 8 (Article 8 (j) and related provisions)
Decision V/17, paragraph 5 (Education and public awareness)
Decision V/18, I, paragraph 1 (a) (Impact assessment, liability and redress)

Documents

UNEP/CBD/COP/5/19 Options for Conservation and Sustainable Use of Biological Diversity in Dryland, Mediterranean, Arid, Semi-Arid, Grassland and Savannah Ecosystems
UNEP/CBD/COP/5/Inf.15 Consideration of Options for Conservation and Sustainable use of Biological Diversity in Dryland, Mediterranean, arid, semi-arid, grassland and Savannah Ecosystems
UNEP/CBD/SBSTTA/4/7 Assessment of the Status and Trends and Options for Conservation and Sustainable Use of Terrestrial Biological Diversity: Dryland, Mediterranean, Arid, Semi-Arid, Grassland and Savannah Ecosystems
UNEP/CBD/SBSTTA/5/9 Biological Diversity of Dryland, Mediterranean, Arid, Semi-Arid, Grassland and Savannah Ecosystems: Options for the Development of a Programme of Work

Ecosystem approach

Terms defined in Article 2

'Ecosystem'.

Consideration of the ecosystem approach by the COP

COP 2 decided that the ecosystem approach should be the primary framework of action to be taken under the Convention [*decision II/8, paragraph 1*].

In deliberations on the ecosystem approach, it was apparent that there were a wide variety of views as to what exactly it entails. In 1998, the Executive Secretary and the Governments of Malawi and the Netherlands organized a workshop with a view to encouraging clarification of the approach. The results of the workshop were presented to COP 4 in document UNEP/CBD/COP/4/Inf.9.

COP 4 noted the results of the Malawi workshop, and asked SBSTTA to develop principles and other guidance on the ecosystem approach, taking into consideration the results of the workshop [*decision IV/1B, paragraph 2*]. On the basis of a note prepared by the Executive Secretary (UNEP/CBD/SBSTTA/5/11), SBSTTA submitted recommendation V/10 to the COP. This contained a description of the ecosystem approach, a set of 12 guiding principles in its application and five points of operational guidance. With minor modifications, this formed the annex to decision V/6, in which the COP endorsed a description and twelve principles of the ecosystem approach, and points of operational guidance, and recommended application of the principles as reflecting the present level of common understanding. It also encouraged further conceptual elaboration and practical verification [*decision V/6, paragraph 1*].

The approach adopted by the COP is based on modern techniques of integrated management. The description of the ecosystem approach stresses that, as defined under the Convention, an ecosystem can be a functional unit at any spatial scale. It also observes that humans are an integral part of many ecosystems, and notes that, because of the often unpredictable nature of ecosystem responses and our incomplete understanding of ecosystem functioning, application of the ecosystem approach will require adaptive management techniques. It further states that the ecosystem approach does not preclude other management and conservation approaches, such as protected areas and single-species conservation programmes, but could rather integrate all these approaches to deal with complex situations [*decision V/6, annex, A*]. The five specific points of operational guidance are:

1. Focus on functional relationships and processes within ecosystems.
2. Enhance benefit-sharing.
3. Use adaptive management practices.
4. Carry out management actions at the scale appropriate for the issue being addressed, with decentralization to lowest level, as appropriate.
5. Ensure intersectoral cooperation [*decision V/6, annex, C*].

The COP called on Parties, and other relevant organizations to apply the approach, encouraging in particular regional cooperation, the identification of case studies and implementation of pilot projects, and the provision of technical and financial support for capacity-building [*decision V/6, paragraphs 2, 3, 6, 7*]. It asked the Executive Secretary to prepare a synthesis of case studies and lessons learned for presentation to SBSTTA before COP 7 and asked SBSTTA to review the principles and guidelines of the ecosystem approach, to prepare guidelines for its implementation and to review its incorporation into the various work programmes. This work is to be carried out before COP 7 [*decision V/6, paragraphs 4, 5*]. The COP also decided that the GEF should fund projects utilizing the ecosystem approach in accordance with decision V/6 [*decision V/13, paragraph 2 (a)*].

References

Decisions on the ecosystem approach

Decision IV/1 B (Ecosystem approach)
Decision V/6 (Ecosystem approach)

Guidance to Parties

National action

Decision IV/4, paragraph 7 (b) (Inland water)
Decision V/4, paragraphs 3, 8 (Forest)
Decision V/6, paragraphs 2, 6, 7 (Ecosystem approach)
Decision V/8, paragraph 8; annex I, Guiding principle 3 (Alien species)
Decision V/16, annex, II, task 2 (Article 8 (j) and related provisions)
Decision V/25, paragraph 4 (b) (Biological diversity and tourism)

Information and case studies

Decision V/6, paragraph 3 (Ecosystem approach)
Decision V/18, I, paragraph 5 (b) (Impact assessment, liability and redress)

Financial mechanism and resources

Guidance to the financial mechanism

Decision V/13, paragraph 2 (a) (Further guidance to the financial mechanism)

Other financial resources

Decision V/6, paragraph 6 (Ecosystem approach)

Guidance to the Secretariat

Decision V/6, paragraph 4 (Ecosystem approach)
Decision V/7, paragraph 1 (b) (Identification, monitoring and assessment, and indicators)
Decision V/18, I, paragraph 5 (b) (Impact assessment, liability and redress)
Decision V/21, paragraph 7 (Cooperation)
Decision V/24, paragraphs 2, 3 (Sustainable use)

Guidance to SBSTTA

Decision IV/1 B, paragraph 2 (Ecosystem approach)
Decision V/6, paragraph 5 (Ecosystem approach)

Cooperation with other conventions and organizations

Decision V/6, paragraphs 2, 3, 6 (Ecosystem approach)
Decision V/8, paragraph 8 (Alien species)
Decision V/21, paragraph 7 (Cooperation)
Decision V/24, paragraph 3 (Sustainable use)

Relevant aspects of thematic work programmes

Decision IV/4, paragraph 7 (b) (Inland water)
Decision IV/5, annex, B, paragraph 2; annex C, operational objective 2.1 (Marine and coastal)
Decision IV/7, annex I, paragraph 3 (b); annex II, paragraphs 11-27 (Forest)
Decision V/3, paragraph 9 (Marine and coastal)
Decision V/4, paragraphs 3, 8 (Forest)
Decision V/5, annex, A, paragraph 4 (Agriculture)
Decision V/23, annex I, paragraph 3; Annex I, II, Part b, Activity 8 (Dry and sub-humid lands)

Other relevant decisions

Decision II/8, paragraph 1 (Components of biological diversity particularly under threat)
Decision III/18, paragraph 1 (see also SBSTTA recommendation I/9, paragraph 2) (Incentive measures)
Decision V/16, annex, I, paragraph 4; III, element 3, task 13 (Article 8 (j) and related provisions)

Documents

UNEP/CBD/COP/3/Inf.34 An ecosystem approach to the management of northern coniferous forests
UNEP/CBD/COP/4/Inf.9 Report of the Workshop on the Ecosystem Approach
UNEP/CBD/COP/5/12 Progress Report on Cross-Cutting Issues
UNEP/CBD/COP/5/Inf.11 The ecosystem approach: Towards its application to agricultural biodiversity
UNEP/CBD/COP/5/Inf.27 Ecosystem Approach: Adoption of Principles (Implementation of Decision IV/1 B)
UNEP/CBD/SBSTTA/5/11 Item 4.2.1 of the Provisional Agenda Ecosystem Approach: Further Conceptual Elaboration

Section VII

Status of signature, ratification, accession, acceptance and approval – Convention on Biological Diversity *and* Cartagena Protocol on Biosafety

Status of signature, ratification, accession, acceptance and approval

	CONVENTION ON BIOLOGICAL DIVERSITY	CARTAGENA PROTOCOL ON BIOSAFETY
OPENED FOR SIGNATURE:	5 June 1992, Rio de Janeiro	15 May 2001, Nairobi
ENTRY INTO FORCE:	29 December 1993	–
STATUS:	Signatories: 168 Parties: 181	103 5

	Convention on Biological Diversity		*Cartagena Protocol on Biosafety*	
State/Regional economic integration organization	*Signature*	*Party**	*Signature*	*Party**
Afghanistan	12/06/1992			
Albania		05/01/1994 acs		
Algeria	13/06/1992	14/08/1995 rtf	25/05/2000	
Andorra				
Angola	12/06/1992	01/04/1998 rtf		
Antigua and Barbuda	05/06/1992	09/03/1993 rtf	24/05/2000	
Argentina	12/06/1992	22/11/1994 rtf	24/05/2000	
Armenia	13/06/1992	14/05/1993 acs		
Australia	05/06/1992	18/06/1993 rtf		
Austria	13/06/1992	18/08/1994 rtf	24/05/2000	
Azerbaijan	12/06/1992	03/08/2000 apv		
Bahamas	12/06/1992	02/09/1993 rtf	24/05/2000	
Bahrain	09/06/1992	30/08/1996 rtf		
Bangladesh	05/06/1992	03/05/1994 rtf	24/05/2000	
Barbados	12/06/1992	10/12/1993 rtf		
Belarus	11/06/1992	08/09/1993 rtf		
Belgium	05/06/1992	22/11/1996 rtf	24/05/2000	
Belize	13/06/1992	30/12/1993 rtf		
Benin	13/06/1992	30/06/1994 rtf	24/05/2000	
Bhutan	11/06/1992	25/08/1995 rtf		
Bolivia	13/06/1992	03/10/1994 rtf	24/05/2000	

Bosnia and Herzegovina				
Botswana	08/06/1992	12/10/1995 rtf	01/06/2001	
Brazil	05/06/1992	28/02/1994 rtf		
Brunei Darussalam				
Bulgaria	12/06/1992	17/04/1996 rtf	24/05/2000	13/10/2000 rtf
Burkina Faso	12/06/1992	02/09/1993 rtf	24/05/2000	
Burundi	11/06/1992	15/04/1997 rtf		
Cambodia		09/02/1995 acs		
Cameroon	14/06/1992	19/10/1994 rtf	09/02/2001	
Canada	11/06/1992	04/12/1992 rtf	19/04/2001	
Cape Verde	12/06/1992	29/03/1995 rtf		
Central African Republic	13/06/1992	15/03/1995 rtf	24/05/2000	
Chad	12/06/1992	07/06/1994 rtf	24/05/2000	
Chile	13/06/1992	09/09/1994 rtf	24/05/2000	
China	11/06/1992	05/01/1993 rtf	08/08/2000	
Colombia	12/06/1992	28/11/1994 rtf	24/05/2000	
Comoros	11/06/1992	29/09/1994 rtf		
Congo	11/06/1992	01/08/1996 rtf	21/11/2000	
Cook Islands	12/06/1992	20/04/1993 rtf	21/05/2001	
Costa Rica	13/06/1992	26/08/1994 rtf	24/05/2000	
Côte d'Ivoire	10/06/1992	29/11/1994 rtf		
Croatia	11/06/1992	07/10/1996 rtf	08/09/2000	
Cuba	12/06/1992	08/03/1994 rtf	24/05/2000	
Cyprus	12/06/1992	10/07/1996 rtf		
Czech Republic	04/06/1993	03/12/1993 apv	24/05/2000	
Democratic People's Republic of Korea	11/06/1992	26/10/1994 apv	20/04/2001	
Democratic Republic of the Congo	11/06/1992	03/12/1994 rtf		
Denmark	12/06/1992	21/12/1993 rtf	24/05/2000	
Djibouti	13/06/1992	01/09/1994 rtf		
Dominica		06/04/1994 rtf		
Dominican Republic	13/06/1992	25/11/1996 rtf		
Ecuador	09/06/1992	23/02/1993 rtf	24/05/2000	
Egypt	09/06/1992	02/06/1994 rtf	20/12/2000	
El Salvador	13/06/1992	08/09/1994 rtf	24/05/2000	
Equatorial Guinea		06/12/1994 acs		
Eritrea		21/03/1996 acs		
Estonia	12/06/1992	27/07/1994 rtf	06/09/2000	
Ethiopia	10/06/1992	05/04/1994 rtf	24/05/2000	
European Community	13/06/1992	21/12/1993 apv	24/05/2000	
Fiji	09/10/1992	25/02/1993 rtf	02/05/2001	05/06/2001 rtf
Finland	05/06/1992	27/07/1994 acs	24/05/2000	
Former Yugoslav Republic of Macedonia		02/12/1997 acs	26/07/2000	
France	13/06/1992	01/07/1994 rtf	24/05/2000	
Gabon	12/06/1992	14/03/1997 rtf		

Gambia	12/06/1992	10/06/1994 rtf	24/05/2000
Georgia		02/06/1994 acs	
Germany	12/06/1992	21/12/1993 rtf	24/05/2000
Ghana	12/06/1992	29/08/1994 rtf	
Greece	12/06/1992	04/08/1994 rtf	24/05/2000
Grenada	03/12/1992	11/08/1994 rtf	24/05/2000
Guatemala	13/06/1992	10/07/1995 rtf	
Guinea	12/06/1992	07/05/1993 rtf	24/05/2000
Guinea Bissau	12/06/1992	27/10/1995 rtf	
Guyana	13/06/1992	29/08/1994 rtf	
Haiti	13/06/1992	25/09/1996 rtf	24/05/2000
Holy See			
Honduras	13/06/1992	31/07/1995 rtf	24/05/2000
Hungary	13/06/1992	24/02/1994 rtf	24/05/2000
Iceland	10/06/1992	12/09/1994 rtf	01/06/2001
India	05/06/1992	18/02/1994 rtf	23/01/2001
Indonesia	05/06/1992	23/08/1994 rtf	24/05/2000
Iran (Islamic Republic of)	14/06/1992	06/08/1996 rtf	23/04/2001
Iraq			
Ireland	13/06/1992	22/03/1996 rtf	24/05/2000
Israel	11/06/1992	07/08/1995 rtf	
Italy	05/06/1992	15/04/1994 rtf	24/05/2000
Jamaica	11/06/1992	06/01/1995 rtf	04/06/2001
Japan	13/06/1992	28/05/1993 acs	
Jordan	11/06/1992	12/11/1993 rtf	11/10/2000
Kazakhstan	09/06/1992	06/09/1994 rtf	
Kenya	11/06/1992	26/07/1994 rtf	15/05/2000
Kiribati		16/08/1994 acs	07/09/2000
Kuwait	09/06/1992		
Kyrgyzstan		06/08/1996 acs	
Lao People's Democratic Republic		20/09/1996 acs	
Latvia	11/06/1992	14/12/1995 rtf	
Lebanon	12/06/1992	15/12/1994 rtf	
Lesotho	11/06/1992	10/01/1995 rtf	
Liberia	12/06/1992	08/11/2000 rtf	
Libyan Arab Jamahiriya	29/06/1992	12/07/2001 rtf	
Liechtenstein	05/06/1992	19/11/1997 rtf	
Lithuania	11/06/1992	01/02/1996 rtf	24/05/2000
Luxembourg	09/06/1992	09/05/1994 rtf	11/07/2000
Madagascar	08/06/1992	04/03/1996 rtf	14/09/2000
Malawi	10/06/1992	02/02/1994 rtf	24/05/2000
Malaysia	12/06/1992	24/06/1994 rtf	24/05/2000
Maldives	12/06/1992	09/11/1992 rtf	
Mali	30/09/1992	29/03/1995 rtf	04/04/2001
Malta	12/06/1992	29/12/2000 rtf	
Marshall Islands	12/06/1992	08/10/1992 rtf	
Mauritania	12/06/1992	16/08/1996 rtf	

Mauritius	10/06/1992	04/09/1992 rtf		
Mexico	13/06/1992	11/03/1993 rtf	24/05/2000	
Micronesia (Federated States of)	12/06/1992	20/06/1994 rtf		
Monaco	11/06/1992	20/11/1992 rtf	24/05/2000	
Mongolia	12/06/1992	30/09/1993 rtf		
Morocco	13/06/1992	21/08/1995 rtf	25/05/2000	
Mozambique	12/06/1992	25/08/1995 rtf	24/05/2000	
Myanmar	11/06/1992	25/11/1994 rtf	11/05/2001	
Namibia	12/06/1992	16/05/1997 rtf	24/05/2000	
Nauru	05/06/1992	11/11/1993 rtf		
Nepal	12/06/1992	23/11/1993 rtf	02/03/2001	
The Netherlands[1]	05/06/1992	12/07/1994 acs	24/05/2000	
New Zealand	12/06/1992	16/09/1993 rtf	24/05/2000	
Nicaragua	13/06/1992	20/11/1995 rtf	26/05/2000	
Niger	11/06/1992	25/07/1995 rtf	24/05/2000	
Nigeria	13/06/1992	29/08/1994 rtf	24/05/2000	
Niue		28/02/1996 acs		
Norway	09/06/1992	09/07/1993 rtf	24/05/2000	10/05/2001 rtf
Oman	10/06/1992	08/02/1995 rtf		
Pakistan	05/06/1992	26/07/1994 rtf	04/06/2001	
Palau		06/01/1999 acs	29/05/2001	
Panama	13/06/1992	17/01/1995 rtf	11/05/2001	
Papua New Guinea	13/06/1992	16/03/1993 rtf		
Paraguay	12/06/1992	24/02/1994 rtf	03/05/2001	
Peru	12/06/1992	07/06/1993 rtf	24/05/2000	
Philippines	12/06/1992	08/10/1993 rtf	24/05/2000	
Poland	05/06/1992	18/01/1996 rtf	24/05/2000	
Portugal[2]	13/06/1992	21/12/1993 rtf	24/05/2000	
Qatar	11/06/1992	21/08/1996 rtf		
Republic of Korea	13/06/1992	03/10/1994 rtf	06/09/2000	
Republic of Moldova	05/06/1992	20/10/1995 rtf	14/02/2001	
Romania	05/06/1992	17/08/1994 rtf	11/10/2000	
Russian Federation	13/06/1992	05/04/1995 rtf		
Rwanda	10/06/1992	29/05/1996 rtf	24/05/2000	
Saint Kitts and Nevis	12/06/1992	07/01/1993 rtf		23/05/2001 acs
Saint Lucia		28/07/1993 acs		
Saint Vincent and the Grenadines		03/06/1996 acs		
Samoa	12/06/1992	09/02/1994 rtf	24/05/2000	
San Marino	10/06/1992	28/10/1994 rtf		
Sao Tome and Principe	12/06/1992	29/09/1999 rtf		
Saudi Arabia				
Senegal	13/06/1992	17/10/1994 rtf	31/10/2000	
Seychelles	10/06/1992	22/09/1992 rtf	23/01/2001	
Sierra Leone		12/12/1994 acs		
Singapore	12/06/1992	21/12/1995 rtf		
Slovak Republic	19/05/1993	25/08/1994 apv	24/05/2000	
Slovenia	13/06/1992	09/07/1996 rtf	24/05/2000	

Solomon Islands	13/06/1992	03/10/1995 rtf		
Somalia				
South Africa	04/06/1993	02/11/1995 rtf		
Spain	13/06/1992	21/12/1993 rtf	24/05/2000	
Sri Lanka	10/06/1992	23/03/1994 rtf	24/05/2000	
Sudan	09/06/1992	30/10/1995 rtf		
Suriname	13/06/1992	12/01/1996 rtf		
Swaziland	12/06/1992	09/11/1994 rtf		
Sweden	08/06/1992	16/12/1993 rtf	24/05/2000	
Switzerland	12/06/1992	21/11/1994 rtf	24/05/2000	
Syrian Arab Republic	03/05/1993	04/01/1996 rtf		
Tajikistan		29/10/1997 acs		
Thailand	12/06/1992			
Togo	12/06/1992	04/10/1995 acs	24/05/2000	
Tonga		19/05/1998 acs		
Trinidad and Tobago	11/06/1992	01/08/1996 rtf		05/10/2000 acs
Tunisia	13/06/1992	15/07/1993 rtf	19/04/2001	
Turkey	11/06/1992	14/02/1997 rtf	24/05/2000	
Turkmenistan		18/09/1996 acs		
Tuvalu	08/06/1992			
Uganda	12/06/1992	08/09/1993 rtf	24/05/2000	
Ukraine	11/06/1992	07/02/1995 rtf		
United Arab Emirates	11/06/1992	10/02/2000 rtf		
United Kingdom of Great Britain and Northern Ireland[3]	12/06/1992	03/06/1994 rtf	24/05/2000	
United Republic of Tanzania	12/06/1992	08/03/1996 rtf		
United States of America	04/06/1993			
Uruguay	09/06/1992	05/11/1993 rtf	01/06/2001	
Uzbekistan		19/07/1995 acs		
Vanuatu	09/06/1992	25/03/1993 rtf		
Venezuela	12/06/1992	13/09/1994 rtf	24/05/2000	
Viet Nam	28/05/1993	16/11/1994 rtf		
Yemen	12/06/1992	21/02/1996 rtf		
Yugoslavia	08/06/1992			
Zambia	11/06/1992	28/05/1993 rtf		
Zimbabwe	12/06/1992	11/11/1994 rtf	04/06/2001	

Notes: * rtf = ratification; acs = accession; acp = acceptance; apv = approval.

1 On 4 June 1999: for the Netherlands Antilles and Aruba.

2 On 28 June 1999, the Government of Portugal informed the Secretary-General that the Convention would also apply to Macau.

3 In respect of the United Kingdom of Great Britain and Northern Ireland, the Bailiwick of Jersey, the British Virgin Islands, the Cayman Islands, Gibraltar, St. Helena and St. Helena Dependencies.

Section VIII

Declarations

Declarations[1]

Australia, Austria, Belgium, Canada, Denmark, Finland, France, Germany, Greece, Italy, Japan, Malta, Netherlands, New Zealand, Portugal, Spain, Switzerland, United Kingdom, and United States

Upon adoption:

Declaration:

Australia, Austria, Belgium, Canada, Denmark, Finland, France, Germany, Greece, Italy, Japan, Malta, Netherlands, New Zealand, Portugal, Spain, Switzerland, the United Kingdom and the United States of America state their understanding that the decision to be taken by the Conference of the Parties under Article 21, paragraph 1, of the Convention refers to the 'amount of resources needed' by the financial mechanism, not to the extent or nature and form of the contributions of the Contracting Parties.

Denmark, Finland, Sweden and Norway

Upon adoption:

Declaration:

1. The Nordic countries stress that concept and idea of national action plans for the conservation and sustainable use of biological diversity is an important implementation tool to fulfil the obligations under the Convention. Without strong national commitments, the Convention will not achieve its objectives.

2. The Nordic countries would also like to stress the special obligations of developed countries to contribute financially and technologically to enable developing countries to fulfil their obligations under the Convention. The highly different socio-economic conditions and the enormous differences in the amount of biological diversity found in various countries, must be taken into account. A fair international burden sharing according to each country's means and needs is therefore absolutely crucial for the ultimate achievement of the objectives of the Convention.

1 Unless otherwise indicated, the declarations were made upon ratification, accession, acceptance or approval.

3. The Nordic countries will continue full participation in and contribution to the work for conservation and sustainable use of biological diversity worldwide. The Nordic countries urge all countries of the world to sign the Convention in Rio de Janeiro and to ratify it as soon as possible.

Algeria and Niger

Upon adoption:

Declaration:

1. The Saharo-Sahelian region hosts several species of wild animals. Currently, the is little information and knowledge on the status and distribution of these rare and endangered species.

2. Some of these species such as the addax, the algazel oryx, the maned moufflon, the dam gazelle and the slender-horned gazelle are considered to be disappearing.

3. In this light, it appears necessary to take an initiative to protect them.

4. With this in mind, Algeria and the Niger are proposing to hold a seminar on the protection of Saharo-Sahelian fauna with a view to considering the possibility of adopting a protocol on the subject.

5. The countries that may be interested are those that share the arid and semi-arid areas of West and North Africa.

6. This protocol of agreement would be of great importance for the conservation of biological diversity and could offer prospects for cooperation among the States concerned through regional projects.

Argentina

Declaration:

The Argentine Government considers that this Convention represents a step forward in that it establishes among its objectives the sustainable use of biological diversity. Likewise, the definitions contained in article 2 and other provisions of the Convention indicate that the terms 'genetic resources', 'biological resources' and 'biological material' do not include the human genome. In accordance with the commitments entered into in the Convention, the Argentine Nation will pass legislation on the conditions of access to biological resources and the ownership of future rights and benefits arising from them. The Convention is fully consistent with the principles established in the 'Agreement on trade-related aspects of intellectual property rights', including trade in counterfeit goods, contained in the Final Act of the Uruguay Round of GATT.

Austria

Declaration:

The Republic of Austria declares in accordance with article 27, paragraph 3 of the Convention that it accepts both of the means of dispute settlement mentioned in this paragraph as compulsory in relation to any Party accepting an obligation concerning one or both of these means of dispute settlement.

Chile

Upon adoption:

Declaration:

The delegation of Chile wishes to state that its agreement to Article 22, on the relationship with other international conventions, was based on a desire not to block the existing consensus, although it would have preferred that the Article did not appear in this Convention. The Government of Chile hopes that the content and scope of this Article will be thoroughly studied within the framework of the Conference of the Parties.

Declaration:

The Government of Chile, on ratifying the Convention on Biological Diversity of 1992, wishes to place on record that the pine tree and other species that the country exploits as one of its forestry resources are considered exotic and are not taken to fall within the scope of the Convention.

Colombia

Upon adoption:

Declaration:

1. A thorough review of the text we are adopting today by a consensus to which Colombia was party reveals areas on which we must confirm and specify our position, with a view to strengthening the Convention in the near future and making it more useful with respect to the concerns of developing countries such as our own.

2. First, with respect to the principle laid down in the third article of the Convention, our country shares its spirit but interprets the text to mean that no country shall be responsible for activities carried out beyond the control of its Government, within its national jurisdiction, which cause damage to the environment of other States or of areas beyond the limits of national jurisdiction.

3. Secondly, our country welcomes the full recognition within the Convention of the knowledge, innovations and practices of indigenous communities, but considers that such communities must be fully guaranteed participation in the benefits arising from the use of such knowledge, innovations and practices and not only that such participation should be encouraged, as the text of Convention rather weakly states. We therefore believe a future instrument under the Convention should endeavour to improve on this point.

4. Furthermore, Colombia questions the inclusion in the Convention of an article laying down the relationship with other international treaties, since this matter falls under the Vienna Convention on the Law of Treaties and also because the Article refers to another legal instrument that has still not entered into force.

Cuba

Declaration:

The Government of the Republic of Cuba declares, with respect to article 27 of the Convention on Biological Diversity, that as far as the Republic of Cuba is concerned, disputes that arise between Parties concerning the interpretation or application of this international legal instrument shall be settled by negotiation through the diplomatic channel or, failing that, by arbitration in accordance with the procedure laid down in Annex II on arbitration of the Convention.

European Community

Declaration:

Within their respective competence, the European Community and its Member States wish to reaffirm the importance they attach to transfers of technology and to biotechnology in order to ensure the conservation and sustainable use of biological diversity. The compliance with intellectual property rights constitutes an essential element for the implementation of policies for technology transfer and co-investment.

For the European Community and its member States, transfers of technology and access to biotechnology, as defined in the text of the Convention on Biological Diversity, will be carried out in accordance with article 16 of the said Convention and in compliance with the principles and rules of protection of intellectual property, in particular multilateral and bilateral agreements signed or negotiated by the Contracting Parties to this Convention.

The European Community and its Member States will encourage the use of the financial mechanism established by the Convention to promote the voluntary transfer of intellectual property rights held by European operators, in particular as regards the granting of licences, through normal commercial mechanisms and decisions, while ensuring adequate and effective protection of property rights.

France

Upon adoption:

Declaration:

1. France expected practical and sound provisions to strengthen the conservation of biodiversity. Such provisions are few and too vague. In this respect, it seemed to stand to reason to include a provision existing in several conventions (World Heritage and Biosphere Reserve of UNESCO, Ramsar, CITES) in a convention on biological diversity:

we refer to global lists. France regrets that the manner in which the text of the Convention was adopted did not allow it to make a compromise proposal on the question of the global approach to biological diversity.

2. The difference of outlook on the part of some delegations towards a provision that France regarded as essential, together with the way in which the text of the Convention under-values the scientific approach, force France to refrain from initialling the Final Act of the Conference.

Upon signature:

Declaration:

With reference to article 3, that it interprets that article as a guiding principle to be taken into account in the implementation of the Convention;

With reference to article 21, paragraph 1, that the decision taken periodically by the Conference of the Parties concerns the 'amount of resources needed' and that no provision of the Convention authorizes the Conference of the Parties to take decisions concerning the amount, nature or frequency of the contributions from Parties to the Convention.

Upon ratification:

Declaration:

With reference to article 3, that it interprets that article as a guiding principle to be taken into account in the implementation of the Convention;

The French Republic reaffirms its belief in the importance of the transfer of technology and biotechnology in guaranteeing the protection and long-term utilization of biological diversity. Respect for intellectual property rights is an essential element of the implementation of policies for technology transfer and co-investment.

The French Republic affirms that the transfer of technology and access to biotechnology, as defined in the Convention on Biological Diversity, will be implemented according to article 16 of that Convention and with respect for the principles and rules concerning the protection of intellectual property, including multilateral agreements signed or negotiated by the Contracting parties to the present Convention.

The French Republic will encourage recourse to the financial mechanism established by the Convention for the purpose of promoting the voluntary transfer of intellectual property rights under French ownership, *inter alia*, as regards the granting of licences, by traditional commercial decisions and mechanisms while ensuring the appropriate and effective protection of property rights.

With reference to article 21, paragraph 1, the French Republic considers that the decision taken periodically by the Conference of the Parties concerns the 'amount of resources needed' and that no provision of the Convention authorizes the Conference of the Parties to take decisions concerning the amount, nature or frequency of the contributions from Parties to the Convention.

Georgia

Declaration:

The Republic of Georgia will use both means for dispute settlement referred to in the Convention:

1. Arbitral consideration in accordance with the procedure given in the enclosure II, Part I.

2. Submitting of disputes to the International Court.

India

Upon adoption:

Declaration:

1. The Government of India is of the view that the issue of liability and compensation for damage to biological diversity, referred to in Article 14, paragraph 2, of the Convention, is not a priority area of work to be addressed by the Conference of the Parties. There is lack of clarity as regards the subject matter and the scope of the studies referred to in that Article. It also believes that the focus of the studies referred to and relating to liability and compensation should be on subjects such as biotechnology products, the environmental impacts or effects of genetically modified organisms, and acid rain.

2. As regards Article 22, paragraph 1, of the Convention, it is the clear understanding of the Government of India that the reference to 'any existing international agreement' means 'any existing international agreement compatible with the conservation and sustainable use of biological diversity'.

3. It is also the understanding of the Government of India that the 'institutional structure' referred to in Article 39 of the Convention and the 'mechanism' referred to in Article 21 are identical. Moreover, the phrase 'Provided that it has been fully restructured in accordance with the requirements of Article 21' implies that for the Global Environment Facility to be the interim institutional structure as per Article 39 would require that it shall (a) function under the authority and guidance of, and be accountable to, the Conference of the Parties; (b) operate within a democratic and transparent system of governance; and (c) have universal membership.

Ireland

Declaration:

Ireland wishes to reaffirm the importance it attaches to transfers of technology and to biotechnology in order to ensure the conservation and sustainable use of biological diversity. The compliance with intellectual property rights constitutes an essential element for the implementation of policies for technology transfer and co-investment.

For Ireland, transfers of technology and access to biotechnology, as defined in the text of the Convention on Biological Diversity and in compliance with the principles and rules of protection of intellectual property, in particular multilateral and bilateral agreements signed or negotiated by the contracting parties to this Convention.

Ireland will encourage the use of the financial mechanism established by the Convention to promote the voluntary transfer of intellectual property rights held by Irish operators, in particular as regards the granting of licences, through normal commercial mechanisms and decisions, while ensuring adequate and effective protection of property rights.

Italy

Declaration made upon signature and confirmed upon ratification:

The Italian Government [...] declares its understanding that the decision to be taken by the the Conference of the Parties under article 21.1 of the Convention refers to the 'amount of resources needed' by the financial mechanism, not to the extent or nature and form of the contributions of the Contracting Parties.

Latvia

Declaration:

The Republic of Latvia declares in accordance with article 27 paragraph 3 of the Convention that it accepts both the means of dispute settlement mentioned in this paragraph as compulsory.

Liechtenstein

Declaration:

The Principality of Liechtenstein wishes to reaffirm the importance it attaches to transfers of technology and to biotechnology in order to ensure the conservation and sustainable use of biological diversity. The compliance with intellectual property rights constitutes an essential element for the implementation of policies for technology transfer and co-investment.

For the Principality of Liechtenstein, transfers of technology and access to biotechnology, as defined in the text of the [said] Convention, will be carried out in accordance with article 16 of the said Convention and in compliance with the principles and rules of protection of intellectual property, in particular multilateral and bilateral agreements signed or negotiated by the Contracting Parties to this Convention.

The Principality of Liechtenstein will encourage the use of the financial mechanism established by the Convention to promote the voluntary transfer of intellectual property rights held by Liechtenstein operators, in particular as regards the granting of licenses, through normal commercial mechanisms and decisions, which ensuring adequate and effective protection of property rights.

Malawi

Upon adoption:

Declaration:

1. Malawi will sign the Convention on Biological Diversity because she strongly believes that this instrument will save the ever-declining conservation and sustainable utilization of biological diversity, especially in the developing countries. We feel that the mechanisms that have been developed in the various articles of this Convention, namely, access to and transfer of relevant technologies, provision of new and additional financial resources to developing countries, and fair and equitable sharing of the benefits arising out of the utilization of genetic resources will achieve the underlying aims of the Convention.

2. Malawi attaches great importance to the protection and sustainable use of all forms of biological resources. We agree with the policy of involving the public in the protection of the country's biological resources, especially those communities living near protected areas (national parks and forest reserves) where a number of conservation economic activities have been initiated.

3. Malawi endorses the sovereign right of each State to exploit its own biological resources in accordance with its policies, but each Contracting Party as a State has a responsibility for the conservation and sustainable use of its biological resources.

Malaysia

Upon adoption:

Declaration:

1. My delegation wishes to state that the terms of transfer of technology referred to in Article 16, paragraph 2, do not fully reflect the position of my country which requires that such transfer should be specifically on concessional and preferential terms.

2. Our reservation on Article 39, on financial interim arrangements, are recorded in the draft report of the sixth plenary meeting in document UNEP/Bio.Div/N7-INC.5/L.1/Add.3 and reads as follows:

> *'The Malaysian delegation always maintained that we do not see any role for the GEF in this Convention. It has always been our clear position that the Convention should have its own specific funds, called the Biological Diversity Fund. In view of that, we wish to express our reservations in the strongest terms that the GEF has been accepted into the draft Convention, even on an interim basis. As we all know, in spite of our best efforts and intentions, these interim measures have the habit of becoming permanent features.'*

3. While concurring with the consensus on Article 19 of the Convention dealing with handling of biotechnology and distribution of its benefits, the delegation of Malaysia understands the term 'living modified organisms' to mean 'genetically modified organisms'.

Papua New Guinea

Declaration:

The Government of the Independent State of Papua New Guinea declares its understanding that ratification of the Convention shall in no way constitute a renunciation of any rights under International Law concerning State responsibility for the adverse effects of Biological Diversity as derogating from the principles of general International Law.

Peru

Upon adoption:

Declaration:

1. Article 2 lacks a definition of the term 'conservation of biological diversity', which should cover the preservation or integral protection, maintenance, sustainable use and recovery of its components.

2. In Article 19, paragraph 3, there is no express mention of the human being within the scope of this paragraph, that is, the protection of the human being from the adverse effects that may be produced by living organisms modified by biotechnology.

3. In paragraph (j) of Article 8 (*In-situ* conservation), the equitable distribution of the benefits should be stipulated, with a change in the word 'encourage'.

Saudi Arabia

Upon adoption:

Declaration:

1. The delegation of my country would like to extend its congratulations and thanks to your Excellency, the Executive Director, the Bureau, the secretariat and to our colleagues in the INC, for what they have achieved. We would like also to extend our thanks to the Kenyan Government for its hospitality.

2. Due to the fact that the weekend in my country is on Thursday and Friday, it was very difficult for me to communicate the changes made, particularly on Article 21 of the Convention, to my Government. Hence, I could not manage to obtain instructions from it. Therefore, I would like to put the following on record.

3. My acceptance to adopt the text of this Convention to be open for signature in Rio de Janeiro is my sole personal responsibility. However, this does not imply that the Government of Saudi Arabia would not sign the Convention.

Sudan

Understanding:

'With respect to the principle stipulated in Article 3, the Government of the Sudan agrees with the spirit of the article and interprets it to mean that no state is responsible for acts that take place outside its control event if they fall within its judicial jurisdiction and may cause damage to the environment of other states or of areas beyond the limits of national judicial jurisdiction.'

'The Sudan also sees as regards Article 14 (2), that the issue of liability and redress for damage to biological diversity should not form a priority to be tackled by the Agreement as there is ambiguity regarding the essence and scope of the studies to be carried out, in accordance with the above-mentioned article. The Sudan further believes that any such studies on liability and redress should shift towards effects of areas such as biotechnology products, environmental impacts, genetically modified organisms and acid rains.'

Switzerland

Upon signature:

Declaration:

The Swiss Government wishes to emphasize particularly the progress made in establishing standard terms for cooperation between States in a very important field: research activities and activities for the transfer of technology relevant to resources from third countries.

The important provisions in question create a platform for even closer cooperation with public research bodies or institutions in Switzerland and for the transfer of technologies available to governmental or public bodies, particularly universities and various publicly-funded research and development centres.

It is our understanding that genetic resources acquired under the procedure specified in article 15 and developed by private research institutions will be the subject of programmes of cooperation, joint research and the transfer of technology which will respect the principles and rules for the protection of intellectual property.

These principles and rules are essential for research and private investment, in particular in the latest technologies, such as modern biotechnology which requires substantial financial outlays. On the basis of this interpretation, the Swiss Government wishes to indicate that it is ready, at the opportune time, to take the appropriate general policy measures, particularly under articles 16 and 19, with a view to promoting and encouraging cooperation, on a contractual basis, between Swiss firms and the private firms and governmental bodies of other Contracting Parties.

With regard to financial cooperation, Switzerland interprets the provisions of articles 20 and 21 as follows: the resources to be committed and the management system will have regard, in an equitable manner, to the needs and interests of the developing countries and to the possibilities and interests of the developed countries.

Upon ratification:

Declaration:

Switzerland wishes to reaffirm the importance it attaches to transfers of technology and to biotechnology in order to ensure the conservation and sustainable use of biological diversity The compliance with intellectual property rights constitutes an essential element for the implementation of policies for technology transfer and co-investment.

For Switzerland, transfers of technology and access to biotechnology, as defined in the text of the Convention on Biological Diversity, will be carried out in accordance with article 16 of the said Convention and in compliance with the principles and rules of protection of intellectual property, in particular multilateral and bilateral agreements signed or negotiated by the Contracting Parties to this Convention.

Switzerland will encourage the use of the financial mechanism established by the Convention to promote the voluntary transfer of intellectual property rights held by Swiss operators, in particular as regards the granting of licences, through normal commercial mechanisms and decisions, while ensuring adequate and effective protection of property rights.

Syrian Arab Republic

Upon signature:

Declaration:

It is being understood that the signing of this Convention shall not constitute recognition of Israel or leading to any intercourse with it.

United Kingdom of Great Britain and Northern Ireland

Declaration made upon signature and confirmed upon ratification:

The Government of the United Kingdom of Great Britain and Northern Ireland declare their understanding that article 3 of the Convention sets out a guiding principle to be taken into account in the implementation of the Convention.

The Government of the United Kingdom of Great Britain and Northern Ireland also declare their understanding that the decisions to be taken by the Conference of the Parties under paragraph 1 of article 21 concern 'the amount of resources needed' by the financial mechanism, and that nothing in article 20 or 21 authorises the Conference of the Parties to take decisions concerning the amount, nature, frequency or size of the contributions of the Parties under the Convention.

United States of America

Upon adoption:

Declaration:

1. In signing the Final Act, the United States recognizes that this negotiation has drawn to a close.

2. The United States strongly supports the conservation of biodiversity and, as is known, was an original proponent of a convention on this important subject. We continue to view international cooperation in this area as extremely desirable.

3. It is deeply regrettable to us that – whether because of the haste with which we have completed our work or the result of substantive disagreement – a number of issues of serious concern in the United States have not been adequately addressed in the course of this negotiation. As a result, in our view, the text is seriously flawed in a number of important respects.

4. As a matter of substance, we find particularly unsatisfactory the text's treatment of intellectual property rights; finances, including, importantly, the role of the Global Environment Facility (GEF); technology transfer and biotechnology.

5. In addition, we are disappointed with the development of issues related to environmental impact assessments, the legal relationship between this Convention and other international agreements, and the scope of obligations with respect to the marine environment.

6. Procedurally, we believe that the hasty and disjointed approach to the preparation of this Convention has deprived delegations of the ability to consider the text as a whole before adoption. Further, it has not resulted in a text that reflects well on the international treaty-making process in the environmental field.

Section IX

Nairobi Final Act of the Conference for the Adoption of the Agreed Text of the Convention on Biological Diversity

Nairobi Final Act

1. The Conference for the Adoption of the Agreed Text of the Convention on Biological Diversity was convened by the Executive Director of the United Nations Environment Programme (UNEP) pursuant to decision 15/34, adopted by the Governing Council of UNEP on 25 May 1989, which, *inter alia*:

> '6. *Authorizes the Executive Director, on the basis of the final report of the Ad Hoc Working Group of Legal and Technical Experts, to convene, in consultation with Governments and within available resources, an ad hoc working group of legal and technical experts with a mandate to negotiate an international legal instrument for the conservation of the biological diversity of the planet;*
>
> '...
>
> '8. *Requests the Executive Director, subject to the availability of resources, to expedite the work of the ad hoc working groups as a matter of urgency with the aim of having the proposed new international legal instrument ready for adoption as soon as possible;*'

2. The Conference for the Adoption of the Agreed Text of the Convention on Biological Diversity met at UNEP Headquarters, Nairobi, at the kind invitation of the Government of Kenya on 22 May 1992.

3. All States were invited to participate in the Conference. The following States accepted the invitation and participated in the Conference:

> Algeria, Argentina, Australia, Austria, Bahamas, Bangladesh, Barbados, Belgium, Bhutan, Botswana, Brazil, Bulgaria, Burkina Faso, Burundi, Cameroon, Canada, Central African Republic, Chile, China, Colombia, Comoros, Congo, Costa Rica, Cote D'Ivoire, Cuba, Czechoslovakia, Denmark, Djibouti, Ecuador, Egypt, Equatorial Guinea, Ethiopia, Finland, France, Gambia, Germany, Ghana, Greece, Guinea, Guinea-Bissau, Guyana, Hungary, India, Indonesia, Iran (Islamic Republic of), Ireland, Italy, Japan, Jordan, Kenya, Lesotho, Libyan Arab Jamahiriya, Madagascar, Malawi, Malaysia, Maldives, Malta, Mauritius, Mexico, Morocco, Mongolia, Mozambique, Myanmar, Netherlands, New Zealand, Niger, Nigeria, Norway, Oman, Pakistan, Papua New Guinea, Peru, Philippines, Poland, Portugal, Republic of Korea, Romania, Russian Federation, Rwanda, Sao Tome and Principe, Saudi Arabia, Senegal, Seychelles, Spain, Sri Lanka, Sudan, Sweden, Switzerland, Thailand, Turkey, Uganda, United Kingdom of Great Britain and Northern Ireland, United Republic of Tanzania, United States of America, Uruguay, Venezuela, Yemen, Yugoslavia, Zaire, Zambia and Zimbabwe.

4. The European Economic Community also participated.

5. Observers from the following United Nations bodies, specialized agencies, intergovernmental and non-governmental organizations also attended the Conference:

> Secretariat of the United Nations Conference on Environment and Development (UNCED), United Nations Environment Programme/CMS Secretariat, United Nations Sudano-Sahelian Office (UNSO), United Nations Centre for Human Settlements (Habitat), Food and Agriculture Organization of the United Nations (FAO), United Nations Educational Scientific and Cultural Organization (UNESCO), World Bank, International Board for Plant Genetic Resources (IBPGR), Regional Gene Bank of the Southern African Development Coordination Conference (SADCC), African Centre for Technology Studies (ACTS), Asian-African Legal Consultative Committee (AALCC), Defenders of Wildlife, Environmental Liaison Centre International (ELCI), Friends World Committee for Consultation (QUAKERS), Greenpeace International, International Organization of Consumers Unions (IOCU), South Pacific Regional Environment Programme, World Conservation Monitoring Centre, World Conservation Union (IUCN), World Resources Institute (WRI) and World Wide Fund For Nature (WWF).

6. The Conference had been preceded by three meetings of technical experts and seven negotiating sessions, held between November 1988 and May 1992. Pursuant to Governing Council decision 14/26 of 17 June 1987, the Ad Hoc Working Group of Experts on Biological Diversity was established and held three sessions between November 1988 and July 1990. On the basis of the final report of the Ad Hoc Working Group of Experts, the Governing Council, pursuant to decision 15/34 of 25 May 1989, established the Ad Hoc Working Group of Legal and Technical Experts, with a mandate to negotiate an international legal instrument for the conservation and rational use of biological diversity. The Ad Hoc Working Group held two negotiating sessions in Nairobi in November 1990 and in February/March 1991. By decision 16/42 of 31 May 1991, the Governing Council of UNEP renamed the Ad Hoc Working Group of Legal and Technical Experts on Biological Diversity the 'Intergovernmental Negotiating Committee (INC) for a Convention on Biological Diversity', which held the following meetings: the third negotiating session/first session of INC in Madrid, Spain, from 24 June to 3 July 1991; the fourth negotiating session/second session of INC in Nairobi, Kenya, from 23 September to 2 October 1991; the fifth negotiating session/third session of INC in Geneva, Switzerland, from 25 November to 4 December 1991; the sixth negotiating session/fourth session of INC in Nairobi, Kenya, from 6 to 15 February 1992; and the final negotiating session in Nairobi, Kenya, from 11 to 22 May 1992.

7. The Conference was formally opened by Dr. Mostafa K. Tolba, the Executive Director of UNEP. In the course of the Conference, statements were made by Central African Republic, Uruguay, Nigeria, United Republic of Tanzania, Malaysia, Norway (on behalf of the Nordic countries), Sweden, Uganda, Germany, Indonesia, Spain, Ethiopia, Venezuela, Guinea-Bissau, Lesotho, Burundi, Portugal (on behalf of the European Community and its member States), Colombia, Costa Rica, Algeria, Denmark, Russian Federation (on behalf of the Group of Eastern European States), Ghana, Kenya, the Food and Agriculture Organization of the United Nations, and the World Conservation Union.

8. Dr. Mostafa K. Tolba served as Secretary-General of the Conference and Ms. Iwona Rummel-Bulska (UNEP) served as Executive Secretary.

9. The Bureau of the INC continued as the Bureau of the Conference and comprised the following members:

Chairman:	H.E. Mr. V. Sanchez	(Chile)
Vice-Chairmen:	Mr. V. Koester	(Denmark)
	Mr. J. Muliro	(Kenya)
	Mr. G. Zavarzin	(Russian Federation)
Rapporteur:	Mr. J. Hussain	(Pakistan)

10. The Conference adopted the following agenda:

1. *Opening of the Conference.*
2. *Bureau of the Conference.*
3. *Adoption of the agenda.*
4. *Organization of the work of the Conference.*
5. *Credentials of representatives:*
   (a) *Appointment of the Credentials Committee;*
   (b) *Report of the Credentials Committee.*
6. *Adoption of the agreed text of the Convention.*
7. *Adoption of resolutions.*
8. *Adoption of the Final Act of the Conference.*
9. *Signature of Final Act.*
10. *Closure of the Conference.*

11. The Conference decided that the rules of procedure adopted by the Ad Hoc Working Group of Legal and Technical Experts at its session from 25 February to 6 March 1991 (UNEP/Bio.Div/WG.2/2/5) would apply *mutatis mutandis* for the work of the Conference.

12. The Conference decided that its Bureau would execute the functions of the Credentials Committee.

13. The main document which was before the Conference for adoption was the draft Convention on Biological Diversity (UNEP/Bio.Div/CONF/L.2).

14. In addition, the Conference had before it a number of draft resolutions for its consideration and adoption.

15. The Conference approved the recommendation of its Credentials Committee that the credentials of the representatives of the participating States as listed in paragraph 3 should be recognized as being in order.

16. The Conference, on 22 May 1992, adopted the agreed text of the Convention on Biological Diversity. The Convention, which is appended to this Final Act, will be open for signature during the Plenipotentiary Conference on the Convention on Biological Diversity, convened at the time of the United Nations Conference on Environment and Development (UNCED) in Rio de Janeiro, on 5 June 1992 and will remain open for signature at Rio de Janeiro from 5 June 1992 to 14 June 1992, and at United Nations Headquarters in New York from 15 June 1992 to 4 June 1993.

17. The Conference also adopted four resolutions, the texts of which are attached to this Final Act.

18. At the time of the adoption of this Final Act, several States made declarations, the texts of which are attached to this Final Act.

IN WITNESS WHEREOF the representatives have signed this Final Act.

DONE in Nairobi this twenty-second day of May one thousand nine hundred and ninety-two in one original in the Arabic, Chinese, English, French, Russian and Spanish languages, each language version being equally authentic. The original text will be deposited with the Secretary-General of the United Nations.

Resolutions adopted by the Conference for the Adoption of the Agreed Text of the Convention on Biological Diversity

Resolution 1: Interim financial arrangements

The Conference,

Having agreed upon and adopted the text of the Convention on Biological Diversity at Nairobi on 22 May 1992,

Considering that preparations should be made during the period between the opening of the Convention for signature and its entry into force for early and effective implementation of the relevant provisions of the Convention once it has entered into force,

Noting that financial support and a financial mechanism during the period between opening of the Convention for signature and its entry into force are necessary for the early and effective operation of the Convention,

1. *Invites* the Global Environment Facility of the United Nations Development Programme, the United Nations Environment Programme and the International Bank for Reconstruction and Development to undertake the operation of the financial mechanism in accordance with Article 21 on an interim basis for the period between the opening of the Convention for signature and its entry into force and, for the purposes of Article 39, until the first meeting of the Conference of the Parties to the Convention;

2. *Calls upon* the United Nations Development Programme, the International Bank for Reconstruction and Development, the regional development banks, the United Nations Environment Programme and other United Nations bodies and agencies such as the Food and Agriculture Organization of the United Nations and the United Nations Educational, Scientific and Cultural Organization to provide financial and other resources for the provisional implementation of the Convention on Biological Diversity on an interim basis for the period between the opening of the Convention for signature and its entry into force and for the purposes of Article 39, until the first meeting of the Conference of the Parties.

Adopted on 22 May 1992

Resolution 2: International cooperation for the conservation of biological diversity and the sustainable use of its components pending the entry into force of the Convention on Biological Diversity

The Conference,

Having agreed upon and adopted the text of the Convention on Biological Diversity at Nairobi on 22 May 1992,

Noting that preparations are required for an early and effective operation of the Convention once it has entered into force,

Noting further that, in the interim arrangements, involvement in the negotiations of all Governments, particularly those that participated in the Conference for the Adoption of the Agreed Text of the Convention on Biological Diversity, is desirable,

Noting with appreciation the work so far undertaken under the auspices of the United Nations Environment Programme in the first set of country studies conducted with national, bilateral and multilateral support,

Recognizing the ongoing joint programmes of the United Nations Environment Programme and other organizations that have mobilized the involvement, in each region, of all sectors to explore options for the conservation of biological diversity and the sustainable use of its components,

Further recognizing that the preparation of biological diversity country studies is the first systematic attempt to assist countries in establishing baseline information on their biological diversity and is the basis for national action programmes on conservation of biological diversity and the sustainable use of its components,

1. *Calls upon* all States and regional economic integration organizations entitled to consider signing the Convention during the United Nations Conference on Environment and Development in Rio de Janeiro or at the earliest subsequent opportunity and thereafter to consider the ratification, acceptance, approval of or accession to the Convention;

2. *Invites* the Governing Council of the United Nations Environment Programme to consider requesting the Executive Director of the Programme to convene meetings of an Intergovernmental Committee on the Convention on Biological Diversity starting in 1993, to consider the following issues:

(a) Assistance to Governments, upon request, in further work in the preparation of country studies in recognition of their importance in the development of their national biological diversity strategy and action plans, *inter alia*:

- (i) To identify components of biological diversity of importance for its conservation and the sustainable use of its components including the collection and evaluation of data needed for effective monitoring of those components;
- (ii) To identify processes and activities which have or are likely to have an adverse impact on biological diversity;
- (iii) To evaluate the potential economic implications of the conservation of biological diversity and the sustainable use of biological and genetic resources and to ascribe values to biological and genetic resources;

(iv) To suggest priority action for the conservation of biological diversity and the sustainable use of its components;

(v) To review and, where appropriate, suggest revision of the draft guidelines for country studies on biological diversity;

(vi) To identify modalities for providing support to countries, in particular developing countries, undertaking studies;

(b) Organization of the preparation of an agenda for scientific and technological research on conservation of biological diversity and the sustainable use of its components, including possible institutional arrangements *ad interim* for scientific cooperation among Governments for the early implementation of the provisions of the Convention on Biological Diversity before it has entered into force;

(c) Consideration of the need for and modalities of a protocol setting out appropriate procedures including, in particular, advance informed agreement, in the field of the safe transfer, handling and use of any living modified organism resulting from biotechnology that may have adverse effect on the conservation and sustainable use of biological diversity;

(d) Modalities for the transfer of technologies, in particular to developing countries, relevant to the conservation of biological diversity and the sustainable use of its components, as well as technical cooperation in support of national capacity-building in those areas;

(e) Provision of policy guidance to the institutional structure invited to undertake the operation of the financial mechanism in accordance with Article 21 of the Convention on an interim basis for the period between the opening of the Convention for signature and its entry into force;

(f) Modalities for bringing into early effect the provisions of Article 21;

(g) Development of the policy, strategy and programme priorities, as well as detailed criteria and guidelines for eligibility for access to and utilization of the financial resources, including monitoring and evaluation on a regular basis of such utilization;

(h) Financial implications of and relevant arrangements in support of international cooperative action before the entry into force of the Convention, including voluntary contributions in cash and kind required for the operation of an interim secretariat and the meetings of the Intergovernmental Committee on the Convention on Biological Diversity;

(i) Other preparations for the first meeting of the Conference of the Parties to the Convention;

3. *Further requests* the Executive Director of the United Nations Environment Programme to provide the secretariat on an interim basis until the Convention has entered into force and also requests the Executive Director to seek the full and active involvement of the Food and Agriculture Organization of the United Nations and the United Nations Educational, Scientific and Cultural Organization in the establishment and operations of the Interim Secretariat, as well as full cooperation with the secretariats of relevant conventions and agreements and the Consultative Group on International Agricultural Research, the World Conservation Union and other relevant international organizations, taking into account relevant decisions of the United Nations Conference on Environment and Development.

4. *Invites* the Food and Agriculture Organization of the United Nations and the United Nations Educational, Scientific and Cultural Organization to provide full support to the establishment and operations of the interim secretariat;

5. *Also requests* the Executive Director of the United Nations Environment Programme to contribute to the financing of the costs of the preparations for and the holding of the meetings, subject to the availability of resources in the Environment Fund;

6. *Invites* Governments to contribute generously to the functioning of the interim secretariat and the successful conduct of the meetings of the Intergovernmental Committee on the Convention on Biological Diversity and to assist financially with a view to ensuring full and effective participation of developing countries;

7. *Further invites* Governments to inform the meetings of national action taken for the conservation of biological diversity and the sustainable use of its components consistent with the provisions of the Convention and pending its entry into force;

8. *Also invites* the secretariats of major international and regional environmental conventions, agreements and organizations to provide information to the Intergovernmental Committee on their activities, and the Secretary-General of the United Nations to provide the relevant sections of Agenda 21 that will be adopted at the United Nations Conference on Environment and Development in Rio de Janeiro.

Adopted on 22 May 1992

Resolution 3: The interrelationship between the Convention on Biological Diversity and the promotion of sustainable agriculture

The Conference,

Having agreed upon and adopted the text of the Convention on Biological Diversity at Nairobi on 22 May 1992,

Recognizing the basic and continuing needs for sufficient food, shelter, clothing, fuel, ornamental plants and medicinal products for peoples of the world,

Emphasizing that the Convention on Biological Diversity stresses the conservation and sustainable use of biological resources,

Recognizing the benefits from the care and improvement by the peoples of the world of animal, plant and microbial genetic resources to supply those basic needs and from the institutional research on and development of those genetic resources,

Recalling that broadly-based consultations in international organizations and forums have studied, debated and achieved consensus on urgent action for the security and sustainable use of plant genetic resources for food and agriculture,

Noting that the Preparatory Committee of the United Nations Conference on Environment and Development has recommended that policies and programmes of priority for *in situ*, on-farm and *ex-situ* conservation and sustainable use of plant genetic resources for food and sustainable agriculture, integrated into strategies and programmes for sustainable agriculture, should be adopted not later than the year 2000 and that such national action should include *inter alia*:

(a) Preparation of plans or programmes of priority action on conservation and sustainable use of plant genetic resources for food and sustainable agriculture based, as appropriate, on country studies on plant genetic resources for food and sustainable agriculture;

(b) Promotion of crop diversification in agricultural systems where appropriate, including new plants with potential value as food crops;

(c) Promotion of utilization of, as well as research on, poorly known but potentially useful plants and crops, where appropriate;

(d) Strengthening of national capabilities for utilization of plant genetic resources for food and sustainable agriculture, plant breeding and seed production capabilities, both by specialized institutions and farmers' communities;

(e) The completion of the first regeneration and safe duplication of existing ex-situ collections on a world-wide basis as soon as possible; and

(f) The establishment of *ex-situ* base collection networks,

Noting further that the Preparatory Committee for the United Nations Conference on Environment and Development has recommended:

(a) The strengthening of the Global System for the Conservation and Sustainable Use of Plant Genetic Resources for Food and Sustainable Agriculture operated by the Food and Agriculture Organization of the United Nations in close cooperation with the International Board for Plant Genetic Resources, the Consultative Group on International Agricultural Research and other relevant organizations;

(b) The promotion of the Fourth International Technical Conference on the Conservation and Sustainable Use of Plant Genetic Resources for Food and Sustainable Agriculture in 1994 to adopt the first State-of-the-World Report and the first Global Plan of Action on the Conservation and Sustainable Use of Plant Genetic Resources for Food and Sustainable Agriculture; and

(c) The adjustment of the Global System for the Conservation and Sustainable Use of Plant Genetic Resources for Food and Sustainable Agriculture in line with the outcome of the negotiations on a Convention on Biological Diversity,

Recalling the agreement in the Preparatory Committee for the United Nations Conference on Environment and Development on provisions regarding conservation and utilization of animal genetic resources for sustainable agriculture,

1. *Confirms* the great importance of the provisions of the Convention on Biological Diversity for the conservation and utilization of genetic resources for food and agriculture;

2. *Urges* that ways and means should be explored to develop complementarity and cooperation between the Convention on Biological Diversity and the Global System for the Conservation and Sustainable Use of Plant Genetic Resources for Food and Sustainable Agriculture;

3. *Recognizes* the need for the provision of support to the implementation of all activities agreed upon in the programme area on conservation and sustainable utilization of plant genetic resources for food and sustainable agriculture and in the programme area on conservation and utilization of animal genetic resources for sustainable agriculture in the Agenda 21 proposed to be adopted at the United Nations Conference on Environment and Development in Rio de Janeiro;

4. *Further recognizes* the need to seek solutions to outstanding matters concerning plant genetic resources within the Global System for the Conservation and Sustainable Use of Plant Genetic Resources for Food and Sustainable Agriculture, in particular:

(a) Access to *ex-situ* collections not acquired in accordance with this Convention; and

(b) The question of farmers' rights.

Adopted on 22 May 1992

Resolution 4: Tribute to the Government of the Republic of Kenya

The Conference,

Having met in Nairobi on 22 May 1992 at the gracious invitation of the Government of the Republic of Kenya,

Deeply appreciative of the courtesy and hospitality extended by the Government of the Republic of Kenya and the City of Nairobi to the members of the delegations, observers and the secretariat attending the Conference,

1. *Expresses its sincere gratitude* to the Government of the Republic of Kenya, to the authorities of the City of Nairobi and, through them, to the Kenyan people for the cordial welcome which they accorded to the Conference and to those associated with its work and for their contribution to the success of the Conference;

2. *Decides*, as a further sign of appreciation, to call the Final Act of the Conference the 'Nairobi Final Act'.

Adopted on 22 May 1992

Section X

Decisions of the Conference of the Parties

(with relevant SBSTTA recommendations)

Decisions adopted by the first meeting of the Conference of the Parties

Nassau, Bahamas, 28 November–9 December 1994

Decision I/1: Rules of procedure for the Conference of the Parties

The Conference of the Parties,

Decides to adopt the rules of procedures of the Conference contained in the annex[1] to this decision, with the exception of paragraph 1 of rule 40.

Decision I/2: Financial resources and mechanism

The Conference of the Parties,

1. *Decides* to adopt the policy, strategy, programme priorities and eligibility criteria for access to and utilization of financial resources contained in annex I to this decision, and the list of developed country Parties and other Parties which voluntarily assume the obligations of developed country Parties contained in annex II to this decision;

2. *Decides also* that the restructured Global Environment Facility (GEF) shall continue to serve as the institutional structure to operate the financial mechanism under the Convention on an interim basis, in accordance with Article 39 of the Convention;

3. *Decides* to instruct the restructured Global Environment Facility to take prompt measures to support programmes, projects and activities consistent with the policy, strategy, programme priorities and eligibility criteria for access to and utilization of financial resources contained in annex I to this decision;

4. *Authorizes* the Secretariat, on behalf of the Conference of the Parties (COP) and taking account of the views of participants in the first meeting of the Conference of the Parties, which should be provided in writing by 1 February 1995, to consult with the restructured Global Environment Facility on the content of a memorandum of understanding which should be formally considered at the second meeting of the Conference of the Parties;

1 The rules of procedure are reproduced in Section III of this Handbook.

5. *Decides*, pending the adoption of the memorandum of understanding, to adopt the interim guidelines for monitoring and evaluation of the utilization of financial resources by the restructured Global Environment Facility contained in annex III to this decision;

6. *Requests* the Secretariat to present to the Conference of the Parties at its second meeting, a report on the financial mechanism, in order that decisions can be adopted by the Conference of the Parties at its second meeting, on the timetable and nature of the review required in Article 21, paragraph 3 of the Convention;

7. *Requests also* the Secretariat to present to the Conference of the Parties at its second meeting, a study on the availability of financial resources additional to those provided through the restructured Global Environment Facility, and on the ways and means for mobilizing and channeling these resources in support of the objectives of the Convention, taking into account the views expressed by participants on the subject at the Conference of the Parties at its first meeting;

8. *Further requests* the Secretariat to include items on the agenda of the Conference of the Parties at its second meeting, which would enable the latter to review the financial resources and, bearing in mind Article 39 of the Convention, to take a decision at that meeting on which institutional structure shall be designated in accordance with Article 21 of the Convention.

Annex I: Policy, strategy, programme priorities and eligibility criteria for access to and utilization of financial resources

I Policy and strategy

Financial resources should be allocated to projects that fulfil the eligibility criteria and are endorsed and promoted by the Parties concerned. Projects should contribute to the extent possible to build cooperation at the sub-regional, regional and international levels in the implementation of the Convention. Projects should promote utilization of local and regional expertise. The institutional structure should over time assist all eligible countries to fulfil their obligations under the Convention. Policy and strategy may be revised, as necessary, by the Conference of the Parties.

II Eligibility criteria

Only developing countries that are Parties to the Convention are eligible to receive funding upon the entry into force of the Convention for them. In accordance with the provisions of the Convention, projects that seek to meet the objectives of conservation of biological diversity and sustainable use of its components are eligible for financial support from the institutional structure.

III Programme priorities

1. The conservation of biological diversity and sustainable use of its components is one

of the key elements in achieving sustainable development and therefore contribute to combating poverty.

2. All the actions contemplated in the Convention will have to be carried out at the national and international level, as appropriate. However, for the purpose of giving direction to the interim structure operating the financial mechanism, a list of programme priorities is given in paragraph 4 below. The list may be revised by the Conference of the Parties, as necessary.

3. Programme priorities should promote utilization of regional and local expertise and be flexible to accommodate national priorities and regional needs within the aims of the Convention.

4. The programme priorities are as follows:

(a) Projects and programmes that have national priority status and that fulfil the obligations of the Convention;

(b) Development of integrated national strategies, plans or programmes for the conservation of biological diversity and sustainable use of its components in accordance with Article 6 of the Convention;

(c) Strengthening conservation, management and sustainable use of ecosystems and habitats identified by national Governments in accordance with Article 7 of the Convention;

(d) Identification and monitoring of wild and domesticated biodiversity components, in particular those under threat, and implementation of measures for their conservation and sustainable use;

(e) Capacity-building, including human resources development and institutional development and/or strengthening, to facilitate the preparation and/or implementation of national strategies, plans for priority programmes and activities for conservation of biological diversity and sustainable use of its components;

(f) In accordance with Article 16 of the Convention, and to meet the objectives of conservation of biological diversity and sustainable use of its components, projects which promote access to, transfer of and cooperation for joint development of technology;

(g) Projects that promote the sustainability of project benefits; that offer a potential contribution to experience in the conservation of biological diversity and sustainable use of its components which may have application elsewhere; and that encourage scientific excellence;

(h) Activities that provide access to other international, national and/or private sector funds and scientific and technical cooperation;

(i) Innovative measures, including in the field of economic incentives, aiming at conservation of biological diversity and/or sustainable use of its components, including those which assist developing countries to address situations where opportunity costs are incurred by local communities and to identify ways and means by which these can be compensated, in accordance with Article 11 of the Convention;

(j) Projects that strengthen the involvement of local and indigenous people in the conservation of biological diversity and sustainable use of its components;

(k) Projects that promote the conservation and sustainable use of biological diversity of coastal and marine resources under threat. Also, projects which promote the conservation of biological diversity and sustainable use of its components in other environmentally vulnerable areas such as arid and semi-arid and mountainous areas;

(l) Projects that promote the conservation and/or sustainable use of endemic species;

(m) Projects aimed at the conservation of biological diversity and sustainable use of its components which integrate social dimensions including those related to poverty.

Annex II: List of developed country Parties and other Parties which voluntarily assume the obligations of developed country Parties

A List of developed country Parties

Australia
Austria
Canada
Denmark
Finland
France
Germany
Greece
Iceland
Italy
Japan
Luxembourg
Monaco
Netherlands
New Zealand
Norway
Portugal
Spain
Sweden
Switzerland
United Kingdom of Great Britain and Northern Ireland

B List of Parties which voluntarily assume the obligations of developed country Parties

Annex III: Interim guidelines for monitoring and evaluation of utilization of financial resources by the restructured GEF

1. The Conference of the Parties (COP) to the Convention on Biological Diversity decides to instruct the restructured GEF to prepare and submit through the Convention Secretariat an annual report on its operations in support of the Convention.

2. The report should include specific information on how it has applied the guidance and decisions of the COP in its work related to the Convention. This report should be of a substantive nature and incorporate the programme of future activities of the restructured GEF in the areas covered by the Convention and an analysis of how the restructured GEF, in its operations, implemented the policy, strategy, programme priorities and eligibility criteria related to the Convention which have been adopted by the COP.

3. In particular, the report should provide information on the following:

(a) A synthesis of the different projects under implementation;

(b) A list of project proposals submitted by eligible Parties, for funding, reporting on their approval status;

(c) A review of the project activities approved by the restructured GEF and their outcomes, including information on funding and progress in implementation.

4. In order to meet the requirements of accountability to the COP, reports submitted by the restructured GEF should cover all its activities carried out in implementing the Convention, whether decisions on such activities are made by the GEF Council or by the implementing agencies. To this end, it shall make arrangements with such bodies as might be necessary regarding disclosure of information.

Decision I/3: Clearing-house mechanism for technical and scientific cooperation

The Conference of the Parties,

1. *Decides* to implement the provisions of Article 18, paragraph 3, of the Convention on the establishment of a clearing-house mechanism to promote and facilitate technical and scientific cooperation, operating under the authority of the Conference of the Parties;

2. *Decides also* that the activities of the clearing-house mechanism to promote and facilitate technical and scientific cooperation should be funded from the regular budget of the Secretariat as well as from voluntary contributions, subject to decisions to be taken by the Conference of the Parties at its second meeting, in the light of the study referred to in paragraph 3 of the present decision;

3. *Requests* the Secretariat to prepare, and report back to the Conference of the Parties at its second meeting on, a comprehensive study, according to Article 18 of the Convention, containing concrete costed recommendations to assist the Conference of the Parties in the establishment of the clearing-house mechanism to promote and facilitate technical and scientific cooperation, taking fully into account the views expressed at its first meeting and submitted to the Secretariat in writing before the end of February 1995, as well as the need to draw on all relevant existing institutional structures;

4. *Decides also* to include an item on this issue on the agenda of the second meeting of the Conference of the Parties.

Decision I/4: Selection of a competent international organization to carry out the functions of the Secretariat of the Convention

The Conference of the Parties,

1. *Designates* the United Nations Environment Programme to carry out the functions of the Secretariat of the Convention while ensuring its autonomy to discharge the functions referred to in Article 24;

2. *Decides* that the functions of the Secretariat shall be carried out by the Secretariat that was provided for under Article 40 of the Convention, until such time as the staff of the Secretariat have been appointed;

3. *Requests* the Executive Director of the United Nations Environment Programme to select the Executive Secretary of the Secretariat for the Convention in consultation with the Bureau of the Conference of the Parties.

Decision I/5: Support to the Secretariat by international organizations

The Conference of the Parties,

1. *Welcomes* the willingness demonstrated by international organizations to support and cooperate with the Secretariat for the effective discharge of its functions, and in particular the concrete offers made by the Food and Agriculture Organization of the United Nations and the United Nations Educational, Scientific and Cultural Organization, including by secondment of staff;

2. *Requests* the Executive Secretary to coordinate with those organizations with a view to entering into such administrative and contractual arrangements as may be required to make effective those offers, as provided for in Article 24.1 (d) of the Convention;

3. *Invites* other competent organizations which wish to do so to make further proposals to the Secretariat in this regard;

4. *Requests* the Executive Secretary to contact the Secretariats of conventions dealing with matters covered by this Convention with a view to establishing appropriate forms of cooperation between this Convention and those conventions and report to the Conference of the Parties on this issue, as provided for in Article 23.4 (h) of the Convention.

Decision I/6: Financing of and budget for the Convention

Part I

The Conference of the Parties,

1. *Adopts* the Financial Rules for the Administration of the Trust Fund for the Convention on Biological Diversity, which are attached as annex I to this decision, to apply in conjunction with the general procedures governing the operations of the Fund of the United Nations Environment Programme and the Financial Regulations and Rules of the United Nations;

2. *Designates* the United Nations Environment Programme as the Trustee of the Trust Fund for the Convention on Biological Diversity;

3. *Decides* that the Trust Fund shall be established for an initial period of two years, beginning on 1 January 1995 and ending on 31 December 1996;

4. *Adopts* the budget for 1995, which is attached as annex II to this decision;

5. *Urges* all the Parties to pay promptly their contributions to the Trust Fund, based on the scale set forth in the appendix to the budget;

6. *Requests* the Parties and States not Parties to the Convention, as well as governmental, intergovernmental and non-governmental organizations and other sources, to contribute to the Trust Fund;

7. *Requests* the Executive Director of the United Nations Environment Programme to ensure, by advances, that the 1995 budget of the Convention is financed until such time as sufficient contributions have been paid in 1995 to allow for the functioning of the Secretariat;

8. *Takes note* of the indicative budget for 1996, also attached as annex II to this decision, and directs the Secretariat to prepare an indicative budget that would provide for implementing the remainder of the medium-term programme of work;

9. *Directs* the Secretariat to consider carefully all offers of support from other organizations and to cooperate with them with a view to making the most effective use of the competencies and resources available.

Part II

The Conference of the Parties,

1. *Adopts* for 1995 the scale for contributions contained in the Appendix to the budget (annex II), based on the United Nations scale of assessments for the apportionment of the expenses of the United Nations adjusted to provide that no one contribution shall exceed 25 per cent of the total and that no contribution from a least developed country Party shall exceed 0.01 per cent of the total. The contribution referred to in paragraph 3 (a) of the Financial Rules shall be due 1 January 1995;

2. *Being aware* that a comprehensive review of all aspects of scale methodology is to be presented to the General Assembly of the United Nations at its fiftieth session, requests the Secretariat to make it available, as well as information related to scale methodology in other international organizations and information provided by Governments to assist the second meeting of the Conference of the Parties in its consideration of this matter;

3. *Decides* to transfer to the next meeting of the Conference of the Parties, for further consideration, paragraph 4 of the Financial Rules contained in annex I of the present decision;

4. *Also decides* to transmit paragraph 16 of the Financial Rules to the second meeting of the Conference of the Parties for further consideration;

5. *Decides* that at its second meeting it will agree upon and adopt a Financial Rule governing the determination of the scale, taking account of paragraphs 2 and 3 above, and a Financial Rule governing decision-making under the Financial Rules, taking into account paragraph 4 above.

Annex I:
Financial rules for the administration of the Trust Fund for the Convention on Biological Diversity[2]

ꟼ ꟼ ꟼ

Annex II:
Proposed budget for 1995 and indicative budget for 1996

Description of functions	*Inputs*	*Costs (US$ thousands) 1995*	*1996*
1 Executive direction and management			
	Executive Secretary D-2	182	192
	Fund Management/Administration Officer P-4[1]	0	0
	Special Assistant to the Executive Secretary P-2	91	96
	Administrative Assistant G-6/G-7	96	100
	Senior Secretary G-5/G-6	88	92
Subtotal 1		*457*	*480*
2 Intergovernmental processes and cooperative arrangements			
	Principal Officer D-1	172	181
	Secretary G-4/G-5	80	84
	Consultants	30	21
	Informal expert consultations	30	32
	Servicing of COP meeting (6 languages, 10 working days, 2 working groups)	750	800
	Travel of COP Bureau (10 people, four-day meeting, once a year)	40	42
	Travel of staff to COP (1995 – Geneva)	0	100
Subtotal 2		*1102*	*1260*
2.1 Financial mechanism and economic analysis			
	Programme Officer – Financial instruments P-4	137	144
	Consultants	50	0
Subtotal 2.1		*187*	*144*
2.2 Legal advice and support			
	Programme Officer – Lawyer P-4	137	144
	Secretary G-4/G-5	80	84
	Consultants	60	63
Subtotal 2.2		*277*	*291*

2 The financial rules for the administration of the Trust Fund for the Convention on Biological Diversity are reproduced in Section V of this Handbook.

3 Scientific, technical and technological matters			
	Principal Officer D-1	172	181
	Programme Officer P-4	137	144
	Programme Officer P-4[2]	0	0
	Programme Officer P-4[3]	0	0
	Secretary G-4/G-5	80	84
	Secretary G-4/G-5	80	84
	Travel of staff to SBSTTA (1995 – Paris)	30	78
	Servicing of SBSTTA meeting (6 languages, 5 working days, 1 working group)[4]	350	368
	Travel of SBSTTA Bureau	30	32
	Travel of SBSTTA Panels	0	68
	Consultants	65	70
Subtotal 3		*944*	*1109*
4 Information management and communication			
4.1 Information access, storage and retrieval			
	Programme Officer – Information P-2	91	96
	Data base operator/Library assistant G-4/G-5	80	84
	Clerk G-2/G-3	60	63
	Library acquisitions	15	10
Subtotal 4.1		*246*	*253*
4.2 Communication			
	Programme Officer – Communication P-2[1]	0	0
	Communication plan and promotion materials	100	105
Subtotal 4.2		*100*	*105*
4.3 Clearing-house mechanism			
	Programme Officer – Clearing-house P-4	0	144
	Secretary G-3/G-4	0	74
	Consultants	100	121
Subtotal 4.3		*100*	*239*
5 Common costs			
5.1 Travel of staff	Travel general	180	190
Subtotal 5.1		*180*	*190*
5.2 Equipment			
	Equipment, general	130	150
Subtotal 5.2		*130*	*150*
5.3 Premises	Rent[5]	0	0
	Security services	0	0
	Building maintenance	0	0
	Utilities (gas, electricity, etc)	30	32
	Insurance	5	5
Subtotal 5.3		*35*	*37*
5.4 Miscellaneous	Temporary assistance and overtime	80	84
	Communications (phone, fax, email, etc)	170	180
	Recruitment costs/travel on interviews	40	80
	Relocation of staff and removal expenses	80	80

	Other	5	5
	Hospitality	20	20
Subtotal 5.4		*395*	*449*
Subtotal 1 to 5		*4153*	*4707*
6 Contingencies (2% subtotal 1 to 5)		**83**	**94**
Subtotal 1 to 6		*4236*	*4801*
7 Administrative support charge (13%)		**551**	**624**
Secretariat administrative budget total (1 to 7)		**4787**	**5425**

1 Expected to be provided by UNEP at an estimated cost of US$228,000 in 1995 and US$240,000 in 1996.
2 Expected to be provided by FAO at an estimated cost of US$137,000 in 1995 and US$144,000 in 1996.
3 Expected to be provided by UNESCO at an estimated cost of US$137,000 in 1995 and US$144,000 in 1996.
4 The number of languages and working groups will be reviewed at COP 2.
5 Paragraph (a) of the Agreement between the Government of Switzerland and the United Nations Environment Programme concerning the Interim Secretariat on Biological Diversity, states that the Government of Switzerland 'will provide accommodation for the Interim Secretariat at least twelve months after the first meeting of the contracting parties' (UNEP/CBD/IC/2/20). It is also expected that the host Government will make a similar offer for 1996.

Appendix to annex II: Scale for 1995 contributions to the Trust Fund for the Convention on Biological Diversity

Party	*United Nations scale of assessments 1995*[1] (%)	*Scale for the Trust Fund with 25 per cent ceiling and no least developed country Party paying more than 0.01%* (%)	*Contributions as per 6 December 1994* (US$)
Albania	0.01	0.02	752
Antigua & Barbuda	0.01	0.02	752
Argentina	0.48	0.75	36,118
Armenia	0.08	0.13	6,020
Australia	1.46	2.29	109,860
Austria	0.85	1.34	63,959
Bahamas	0.02	0.03	1,505
Bangladesh	0.01	0.01	479
Barbados	0.01	0.02	752
Belarus	0.37	0.58	27,841
Belize	0.01	0.02	752
Benin	0.01	0.01	479

Bolivia	0.01	0.02	752
Brazil	1.62	2.55	121,899
Burkina Faso	0.01	0.01	479
Cameroon	0.01	0.02	752
Canada	3.07	4.83	231,006
Chad	0.01	0.01	479
Chile	0.08	0.13	6,020
China	0.72	1.13	54,177
Colombia	0.11	0.17	8,277
Comoros	0.01	0.01	479
Cook Islands	0.01	0.02	752
Costa Rica	0.01	0.02	752
Côte d'Ivoire	0.01	0.02	752
Cuba	0.07	0.11	5,267
Czech Republic	0.32	0.50	24,079
Democratic People's Republic of Korea	0.04	0.06	3,010
Denmark	0.70	1.10	52,672
Djibouti	0.01	0.01	479
Dominica	0.01	0.02	752
Ecuador	0.02	0.03	1,505
Egypt	0.07	0.11	5,267
El Salvador	0.01	0.02	752
Equatorial Guinea	0.01	0.01	479
Estonia	0.05	0.08	3,762
Ethiopia	0.01	0.01	479
European Community		2.50	119,675
Fiji	0.01	0.02	752
Finland	0.61	0.96	45,900
France	6.32	9.93	475,557
Gambia	0.01	0.01	479
Georgia	0.16	0.25	12,039
Germany	8.94	14.05	672,703
Ghana	0.01	0.02	752
Greece	0.37	0.58	27,841
Grenada	0.01	0.02	752
Guinea	0.01	0.01	479
Guyana	0.01	0.02	752
Hungary	0.15	0.24	11,287
Iceland	0.03	0.05	2,257
India	0.31	0.49	23,326
Indonesia	0.14	0.22	10,534
Italy	4.79	7.53	360,430
Japan	13.95	21.93	1,049,687
Jordan	0.01	0.02	752
Kazakhstan	0.26	0.41	19,564
Kenya	0.01	0.02	752
Kiribati	0.01	0.01	479
Luxembourg	0.07	0.11	5,267
Malawi	0.01	0.01	479
Malaysia	0.14	0.22	10,534

Maldives	0.01	0.01	479
Marshall Islands	0.01	0.02	752
Mauritius	0.01	0.02	752
Mexico	0.78	1.23	58,692
Micronesia (Federated States of)	0.01	0.02	752
Monaco	0.01	0.02	752
Mongolia	0.01	0.02	752
Myanmar	0.01	0.01	479
Nauru	0.01	0.02	752
Nepal	0.01	0.01	479
Netherlands	1.58	2.48	118,889
New Zealand	0.24	0.38	18,059
Nigeria	0.16	0.25	12,039
Norway	0.55	0.86	41,386
Pakistan	0.06	0.09	4,515
Papua New Guinea	0.01	0.02	752
Paraguay	0.01	0.02	752
Peru	0.06	0.09	4,515
Philippines	0.06	0.09	4,515
Portugal	0.24	0.38	18,059
Republic of Korea	0.80	1.26	60,197
Romania	0.15	0.24	11,287
Saint Kitts and Nevis	0.01	0.02	752
Saint Lucia	0.01	0.02	752
Samoa	0.01	0.01	479
San Marino	0.01	0.02	752
Senegal	0.01	0.02	752
Seychelles	0.01	0.02	752
Slovakia	0.10	0.16	7,525
Spain	2.24	3.52	168,552
Sri Lanka	0.01	0.02	752
Swaziland	0.01	0.02	752
Sweden	1.22	1.92	91,801
Switzerland	1.21	1.90	91,048
Tunisia	0.03	0.05	2,257
Uganda	0.01	0.01	479
United Kingdom of Great Britain and Northern Ireland	5.27	8.28	396,548
Uruguay	0.04	0.06	3,010
Vanuatu	0.01	0.01	479
Venezuela	0.40	0.63	30,099
Viet Nam	0.01	0.02	752
Zaire	0.01	0.01	479
Zambia	0.01	0.01	479
Zimbabwe	0.01	0.02	752
	62.10	**100.00**	**4,787,000**

1 United Nations Report of the Committee on Contributions, Supplement No. 11 (A/49/11).

DECISION I/6

Decision I/7: Subsidiary Body on Scientific, Technical and Technological Advice

The Conference of the Parties,

1. *Decides:*

(a) That the Subsidiary Body on Scientific, Technical and Technological Advice (SBSTTA) shall operate in accordance with the terms of reference as given in Article 25, paragraphs 1 and 2, until further elaborated by the Conference of the Parties;

(b) That SBSTTA shall report to the Conference of the Parties at each of its ordinary meetings;

(c) That SBSTTA shall meet sufficiently in advance of each meeting of the Conference of the Parties to enable its report to be considered by Parties in their preparation for the meeting of the Conference of the Parties;

(d) That, at its first ordinary meeting, SBSTTA shall consider its *modus operandi*, taking fully into account all views expressed on this matter at the first meeting of the Conference of the Parties and submitted to the Secretariat in writing by the end of February 1995, as well as the need to draw on relevant existing institutional structures;

2. *Requests* SBSTTA to prepare a proposal for a medium-term programme of work based on the priorities set in the programme of work of the Conference of the Parties and on Article 25 and submit it to the Conference of the Parties at its second meeting;

3. *Decides also* that it will decide, at each of its meetings, on which topics advice is required for the implementation of the Convention, taking into account its medium-term work programme and SBSTTA's remit as outlined in Article 25;

4. *Decides further* that the first meeting of SBSTTA shall be held at the headquarters of UNESCO in Paris from 4 to 8 September 1995 to consider the attached provisional agenda.

Annex:
First meeting of the Subsidiary Body on Scientific, Technical and Technological Advice (SBSTTA)

Draft provisional agenda

1. Opening of the meeting.
2. Organizational matters:
   - 2.1 Election of officers;
   - 2.2 Adoption of the agenda;
   - 2.3 Organization of work.
3. Matters related to the *modus operandi* of SBSTTA.

4. Programme of work of SBSTTA for 1995–1997.

5. Matters on which advice from SBSTTA is required by the second meeting of the Conference of the Parties.

5.1 Provision of scientific and technical assessments of the status of biological diversity (Article 25, paragraph 2 (a));

5.1.1 Alternative ways and means in which the Conference of the Parties could start the process of considering the components of biological diversity particularly those under threat and the identification of action which could be taken under the Convention (priority item);

5.2 Preparation of scientific and technical assessments of the effects of types of measures taken in accordance with the provisions of the Convention (Article 25, paragraph 2 (b));

5.3 Identification of innovative, efficient and state-of-the-art technologies and know-how relating to the conservation and sustainable use of biological diversity and provision of advice on the ways and means of promoting development and/or transferring such technologies (Article 25, paragraph 2 (c));

5.3.1 Ways and means to promote and facilitate access to, and transfer and development of technologies as envisaged in Articles 16 and 18 of the Convention (priority item);

5.4 Provision of advice on scientific programmes and international cooperation in research and development related to conservation and sustainable use of biological diversity (Article 25, paragraph 2 (d));

5.5 Scientific, technical, technological and methodological questions that the Conference of the Parties and its subsidiary bodies may put to the body (Article 25, paragraph 2 (e));

5.5.1 What kind of scientific and technical information should be contained in national reports on measures taken for the implementation of the provisions of the Convention and their effectiveness in meeting the objectives of the Convention? (priority item);

5.5.2 How can the Convention on Biological Diversity contribute to the preparation for the forthcoming International Technical Conference on the Conservation and Utilization of Plant Genetic Resources for Food and Agriculture in 1996?

5.5.3 Provision of advice on the scientific, technical and technological aspects of the conservation and sustainable use of coastal and marine biological diversity (also taking into account the other provisions in Article 25, paragraph 2) (priority item).

6. Draft provisional agenda of the second meeting of SBSTTA.

7. Date and venue of the second meeting.

8. Other matters.

9. Adoption of the report.

10. Closure of the meeting.

DECISION I/7

Decision I/8: Preparation of the participation of the Convention on Biological Diversity in the third session of the Commission on Sustainable Development

The Conference of the Parties,

Decides to invite its President to transmit the statement contained in the annex to this decision to the high-level segment of the Commission on Sustainable Development at its third session.

Annex:
Statement from the Conference of the Parties to the Convention on Biological Diversity to the Commission on Sustainable Development at its third session

1. The planet's essential goods, ecological functions and services depend on the variety and variability of genes, species, populations and ecosystems. If humanity is to have a future on this earth, biological diversity must be conserved so that these functions and services are maintained. The current decline in biodiversity is largely the result of human activity and represents a serious threat to human development. Despite efforts to conserve the world's biological diversity, its depletion has continued. The entry into force of the Convention provides an international framework through which to address this depletion which causes threats to ecosystems that are vital for the sustenance of human societies in all countries. By becoming Parties to the Convention, Governments have committed themselves to the conservation of biological diversity, the sustainable use of its components, and the fair and equitable sharing of the benefits arising out of the utilization of genetic resources.

2. The Convention on Biological Diversity is the primary international legal instrument for advancing the conservation of biological diversity, the sustainable use of its components and the fair and equitable sharing of benefits arising out of the use of genetic resources while recognizing the important role of other conventions to the objectives of the Convention.

3. The Convention was opened for signature during the United Nations Conference on Environment and Development in Rio de Janeiro. Since then the Convention has received 168 signatures. It entered into force on 29 December 1993, and has been ratified or acceded to by 105 States and the European Community at the time of the first meeting of the Conference of the Parties.

4. The Conference of the Parties to the Convention on Biological Diversity held its first meeting at Nassau, from 28 November to 9 December 1994, at which it took a number of decisions and adopted a medium-term programme of work for the period 1995 to 1997. These are attached to this statement for the information of the Commission on Sustainable Development.

5. The above information is conveyed to the Commission on Sustainable Development in the light of the recommendation contained in paragraph 38.13 (f) of Agenda 21.

6. The Conference of the Parties is vested with the responsibility of implementing the provisions of the Convention on Biological Diversity, of reviewing the further development of matters relating to the conservation of biological diversity, the sustainable use of its components, and the fair and equitable sharing of benefits arising from the use of genetic resources and where appropriate, of bringing these within the purview of the Convention. In this context, the Conference of the Parties seeks to establish links with other bodies and processes relevant to biodiversity issues with a view to promoting coherent and urgent attention to these issues.

7. The Conference of the Parties attaches importance to the development of a substantive relationship with the Commission on Sustainable Development, given the Commission's responsibilities in respect of Agenda 21 and the complementarity of its mandate with that of the Conference of the Parties to the Convention on Biological Diversity.

8. At its first meeting, the Conference of the Parties was pervaded by a sense of urgency and an awareness of the magnitude of the task before it. The Conference of the Parties appeals to the Commission on Sustainable Development to make all efforts in its own right to advance the concerns of the Convention on Biological Diversity.

9. The Convention leaves no doubt that biological diversity is a cross-cutting issue. The provisions of the Convention are of the utmost relevance to the issues to be reviewed by the Commission at its third session; to the planning and management of land resources, combating deforestation, managing fragile ecosystems and promoting sustainable agriculture and rural development. Many aspects of the programme areas to be considered by the Commission, their bases for action, objectives, activities, and means of implementation correspond to the objectives and provisions of the Convention.

10. The Convention ushers in a new era concerning access to genetic resources which is subject to the provisions of Article 15 of the Convention and is characterized by a fair and equitable sharing of the benefits arising out of the use of such resources.

11. The Conference of the Parties was informed of the ongoing negotiations under the auspices of the FAO to bring the International Undertaking on Plant Genetic Resources for Food and Agriculture in harmony with the Convention on Biological Diversity. The Conference of the Parties recognizes this process and hopes that these negotiations will come to a meaningful conclusion. The Commission on Sustainable Development may wish to convey this message to the FAO and to advise it on the intention of the Conference of the Parties to consider the issue of access to genetic resources at its second and third meetings. In this regard, it would be desirable to coordinate efforts carried out in both fora in order to collaborate and to avoid overlapping in the respective fields of competence of the FAO and the Convention on Biological Diversity.

12. The provisions of the Convention are also relevant to the cross-sectoral cluster and should be considered by the Commission on Sustainable Development when it reviews critical elements of sustainability as indicated in Agenda 21. The Conference of the Parties notes in particular the relevance of the following cross-sectoral issues on the agenda of the third session of the Commission on Sustainable Development: Chapters 3 Combating poverty; 5 Demographic dynamics and sustainability; 8 Integrating environment and development in decision-making; 16 Environmentally sound management of biotechnology; 23–32 Roles of major groups; 33 Financial resources and mechanisms; 34 Transfer of technology; 35 Science for sustainable development; and 40 Information for decision-making.

DECISION I/8

13. The Conference of the Parties wishes to inform the Commission on Sustainable Development of its intention to take immediate action to: 1) undertake work on biosafety, establishing an ad hoc working group to consider the needs for and modalities of a protocol to the Convention on this issue; 2) establish a clearing-house mechanism to promote technical and scientific cooperation; 3) facilitate the establishment of the subsidiary body on scientific, technical and technological advice and 4) undertake work relevant to biodiversity related Conventions, other institutional agreements and processes of relevance. The Conference of the Parties would be willing to coordinate and collaborate with other United Nations bodies on further work in these four areas. It would also be desirable that future work on the protection of traditional knowledge and practices of indigenous and local communities relevant to conservation and sustainable use should be coordinated with the relevant bodies.

14. Given the complementarity of their respective mandates, the Conference of the Parties is convinced it can make a major contribution to the implementation of Agenda 21. Article 23.4 (i) calls upon the Conference of the Parties to consider and undertake any additional action that may be required for the achievement of the purposes of the Convention. Implementation of the Convention will be facilitated by the Conference of the Parties and the Commission on Sustainable Development jointly exploring ways in which any additional issues identified can be further developed within the organizing framework of the Convention.

15. Biological diversity is of great importance for the ecosystem function of forests. The Conference of the Parties emphasizes the importance of conservation, management and sustainable use of forests for achieving the objectives of the Convention and encourages further consideration by the Commission on Sustainable Development on the implementation of the Non-Legally Binding Authoritative Statement of Principles for a Global Consensus on the Management, Conservation and Sustainable Development of all Types of Forests. The Conference of the Parties to the Convention on Biological Diversity stands ready to make its own contribution to that process consistent with its role in developing measures to achieve the objectives of the Convention with respect to forests. The Conference of the Parties would welcome a dialogue with the Commission on Sustainable Development and seek dialogue and cooperation with other relevant international organizations on the issue of forests.

16. Desertification is associated with land degradation and entails the loss of biological diversity. The Conference of the Parties to the Convention on Biological Diversity will explore the ways in which it can cooperate with the Conference of the Parties to the Convention to Combat Desertification to the extent that their mandates are complementary.

17. The Conference of the Parties invites the Commission on Sustainable Development to:

(a) Urge States that have not yet done so to become Parties to the Convention;

(b) Consider the biodiversity issue in the light of the three interrelated objectives of the Convention;

(c) Approach the subject of biodiversity as a multisectoral issue which is relevant to virtually all of its concerns;

(d) Urge Governments to recognize the mutually supportive relationship between biodiversity and sustainable development;

(e) Encourage Governments to improve coordination among departments at the national level in order to more effectively implement measures for the conservation of biological diversity and the sustainable use of its components, given the cross-cutting nature of these issues;

(f) Consider the sectoral issues to be addressed at its 1995 session in the context of their close interrelationship with biodiversity;

(g) Urge States to work cooperatively to address the subject of poverty in the context of its close interrelationship with biodiversity;

(h) Stress to Governments the advantages deriving from coordination between its work, that of the Convention on Biological Diversity, and that of other conventions, intergovernmental bodies and fora concerned with the conservation of biological diversity and the sustainable use of its components.

18. Given the views and proposals outlined above, the Conference of the Parties believes that the Commission on Sustainable Development and the Convention on Biological Diversity should establish links, through their respective organs and mechanisms, to facilitate a collaborative approach to issues of mutual concern. To this end, the Conference of the Parties will regularly consider the issues to be addressed by the Commission at its future meetings.

19. The Conference of the Parties to the Convention on Biological Diversity hopes that this statement will be helpful to the Commission on Sustainable Development.

20. The Conference of the Parties to the Convention on Biological Diversity reaffirms its commitment to caring for the earth and its people.

Decision I/9: Medium-term programme of work of the Conference of the Parties

The Conference of the Parties,

1. *Decides* to adopt the medium-term programme of work for the period 1995 to 1997 contained in the annex to the present decision;

2. *Also decides* to review at its next meeting the medium-term programme of work in light of the progress achieved in the implementation of the Convention.

Taking into account that the Parties share the deep concern and interest about the need for the safe transfer, handling and use of all living modified organisms resulting from biotechnology to avoid adverse effects on the conservation and sustainable use of biological diversity,

3. *Also decides* to establish an open-ended ad hoc group of experts nominated by Governments without undue delay to consider the need for and modalities of a protocol setting out appropriate procedures, including, in particular, advance informed agreement, in the field of the safe transfer, handling and use of any living modified organism resulting from biotechnology that may have adverse effect on the conservation and sustainable use of biological diversity;

4. *Also decides* that the open-ended ad hoc group of experts nominated by Governments shall hold one meeting of one week's duration during 1995 with a view to presenting its report to the Conference of the Parties.

5. *Decides* that the open-ended group of experts nominated by Governments will consider, as appropriate, existing knowledge, experience and legislation in the field of biosafety, including the views of the Parties, subregional, regional and international organizations, with a view to presenting a report for the consideration of the second meeting of the Conference of the Parties, so as to enable the Conference of the Parties to reach an informed decision as to the need for and modalities of a protocol.

6. *Requests* the Secretariat to submit to the open-ended ad hoc group of experts nominated by Governments relevant information on these matters in sufficient time to facilitate the discussions of the open-ended ad hoc group of experts.

7. *Decides* that, in order to prepare for the work of the open-ended ad hoc group of experts nominated by Governments, the Secretariat shall establish a panel of 15 experts nominated by Governments, with an equitable geographical representation, in consultation with the Bureau of the COP, assisted by UNIDO, UNEP, FAO and WHO, to prepare a background document to be submitted to the open-ended ad hoc group of experts nominated by Governments based on a consideration, as appropriate, of existing knowledge and experience on risk assessment and management, and guidelines and/or legislation already prepared by the Parties, other Governments and by national and competent subregional, regional and international organizations.

8. *Calls upon* the international community, particularly the developed countries and non-governmental sectors, to contribute voluntary funds to assist the open-ended ad hoc group of experts nominated by Governments to discharge its mandate effectively.

Annex:
Medium-term programme of work of the Conference of the Parties 1995–1997

1. The medium-term programme of work will be constructed on the basis of standing and rolling issues.

2. Standing items will include *inter alia*:

2.1 Matters relating to the financial mechanism, including report from the interim institutional structure entrusted with its operation;

2.2 Report from the Secretariat on the administration of the Convention and budget for the Secretariat;

2.3 Report from, instructions to and consideration of recommendations from the Subsidiary Body on Scientific, Technical and Technological Advice (SBSTTA);

2.4 Reports by Parties on implementation of the Convention;

2.5 Report on, assessment and review of the operation of the clearing-house mechanism;

2.6 Relationship of the Convention on Biological Diversity with the Commission on Sustainable Development and biodiversity related conventions, other international agreements, institutions and processes of relevance.

3. The other issues and derived activities necessary to implement the Convention should be treated on a year-by-year agenda, on the understanding that these relevant

rotating issues will be developed and continually treated in accordance with the decisions of the Conference of the Parties by the SBSTTA and any eventual working groups appointed by the Conference of the Parties. The year-by-year agenda has to be flexible.

4. Treatment of the Work Programme items should also reflect the importance of capacity-building as one of the elements of successful Convention implementation. The Work Programme should always reflect a balance among the Convention's objectives as set forth in Article 1.

5. In 1995, the second meeting of the Conference of the Parties may consider, *inter alia*, the following items:[3]

5.1 General measures for conservation and sustainable use

5.1.1 To provide information and share experiences on the implementation of Article 6.

5.2 Conservation of biological diversity

5.2.1 Preliminary consideration of components of biological diversity particularly under threat and action which could be taken under the Convention;

5.2.2 To provide information and share experiences on measures for implementing Article 8.

5.3 Conservation and sustainable use of coastal and marine biological diversity

5.3.1 To consider coastal and marine biological diversity within the context of the Convention's three objectives and its provisions.

5.4 Access to genetic resources

5.4.1 To compile existing legislation, administrative and policy information on access to genetic resources and the equitable sharing of benefits derived from their use;

5.4.2 To compile information provided by Governments as well as relevant reports from appropriate international organizations regarding policy, legislative, or administrative measures related to intellectual property rights as provided in Article 16 of the Convention and to access to and transfer of technology that makes use of genetic resources.

5.5 Issues relating to technology

5.5.1 To consider ways to promote and facilitate access to and transfer and development of technology, as envisaged by Articles 16 and 18 of the Convention.

5.6 Handling of biotechnology

5.6.1 To consider the need for and modalities of a protocol for safe handling and transfer of living modified organisms.

5.7 Report on the financial mechanism

5.7.1 Consideration of the study prepared by the Secretariat on the availabil-

3 The order given does not reflect any prioritization of items, but merely reflects the general structure of the Convention.

ity of financial resources additional to those provided through the restructured Global Environment Facility (GEF), and on the ways and means for mobilizing and channelling these resources in support of the objectives of the Convention taking into account the views expressed by participants on the subject at the Conference of the Parties at its first meeting.

5.8 Reports by Parties

5.8.1 To provide the form for reporting;

5.8.2 To decide on intervals for reporting.

5.9 Relationship with the FAO Global System for Plant Genetic Resources for Food and Agriculture

5.9.1 To be informed and to be able to consider progress made revising the International Undertaking on Plant Genetic Resources for Food and Agriculture in order to consider its consistency with the objectives and provisions of the Convention and implementation of Resolution 3 of the Nairobi Final Act;

5.9.2 To be informed about and to be able to consider the preparation for the forthcoming International Technical Conference on the Conservation and Utilization of Plant Genetic Resources for Food and Agriculture in 1996;

5.9.3 To be informed about developments with regard to *ex situ* collections of plant genetic resources.

6. In 1996, the third meeting of the Conference of the Parties may consider, *inter alia*, the following items:

6.1 General measures for conservation and sustainable use;

6.2 Identification, monitoring and assessment

6.2.1 To consider options for implementing Article 7;

6.2.2 Appraisal of SBSTTA's review of assessment of biological diversity for the implementation of Article 25 (2) (a) and advice on methodologies for future assessments;

6.3 Conservation and sustainable use of agricultural biological diversity

6.3.1 To consider agricultural biological diversity within the context of the Convention's three objectives and its provisions;

6.4 Consideration of the future programme of work for terrestrial biological diversity in the light of the outcome of deliberations of the third session of the Commission on Sustainable Development in 1995;

6.5 Knowledge, innovations and practices of indigenous and local communities;

6.5.1 Implementation of Article 8 (j);

6.6 Access to genetic resources

6.6.1 To compile the views of Parties on possible options for developing national legislative, administrative or policy measures, as appropriate, to implement Article 15.

6.7 Issues related to technology

6.7.1 To consider ways to promote and facilitate access to and transfer and development of technology, as envisaged by Articles 16 and 18 of the Convention.

6.8 Incentive measures

6.8.1 To consider options for implementing Article 11.

6.9 Special session of the General Assembly to review implementation of Agenda 21

6.9.1 To consider possible inputs from the perspective of the Convention's three objectives.

7. In 1997, the fourth meeting of the Conference of the Parties may consider, *inter alia*, the following items:

7.1 Review of medium-term programme of work (1995–1997)

7.1.1 To undertake an overall review and consider a longer-term work programme;

7.2 Models and mechanisms for linkages between *in situ* and *ex situ* conservation;

7.3 Measures for implementing the Convention

7.3.1 To provide information and share experiences on the implementation of Article 13;

7.3.2 To provide information and share experiences on the implementation of Article 14;

7.4 Consideration of matters related to benefit sharing

7.4.1 To consider measures to promote and advance the distribution of benefits from biotechnology in accordance with Article 19;

7.5 Technical and scientific cooperation.

Decision I/10: Location of the Secretariat

The Conference of the Parties,

1. *Decides* to consider and take a decision on the location of the Secretariat at its second meeting;

2. *Decides* to invite Parties interested in hosting the Secretariat to submit their offers to the Secretariat by 31 March 1995;

3. *Decides* to invite those Parties to include in their offers, to the extent possible, details relating to *inter alia*:

(a) Facilities to be made available, including offices, meeting rooms and conference facilities;

(b) Availability of institutional support, including programmes of relevance to the Convention, academic programmes and representation of Parties through diplomatic offices;

(c) Direct support, including financial and technical support;

(d) Privileges and immunities to be extended to the Secretariat and its staff, including the nature of the headquarters agreement or other arrangement to be established with the Secretariat and diplomatic privileges for Secretariat staff and families;

(e) State of civic amenities, including health and education facilities.

4. *Decides* to request the Secretariat to transmit all offers to the Parties, as an official document of the second meeting of the Conference of the Parties, by 31 May 1995;

5. *Decides* that the second meeting of the Conference of the Parties will not be held in a country making an offer to host the Secretariat;

6. *Decides* that, at its second meeting, it will make every effort to reach a decision on the location of the Secretariat by consensus. Recognizing the requirement of paragraph 1 of this decision, and, in the event consensus is not possible and, at the time of voting, rule 40, paragraph 1 of the rules of procedure has not been adopted, will for this item:

(a) Take a decision by a two-thirds majority of the Parties present and voting; and

(b) If a two-thirds majority does not emerge for any one offer after the first round of voting, successive rounds will be taken, the offer receiving the least votes being eliminated after each round, until only two offers remain and one receives a two-thirds majority vote of the Parties present and voting.

Decision I/11: Preparation for the second meeting of the Conference of the Parties

The Conference of the Parties,

1. *Requests* the Secretariat to assist in the organization of regional and sub-regional meetings for the preparation of the second meeting of the Conference of the Parties;

2. *Invites* the developed countries and the international organizations to make voluntary contributions to fund such regional and sub-regional meetings and to facilitate the participation of the developing countries, and in particular the least developed amongst them, in such meetings as well as in the meetings convened under the Convention.

Decision I/12: International Day for Biological Diversity

The Conference of the Parties,

Decides to recommend to the United Nations General Assembly at its forty-ninth session to consider 29 December, the date of entry into force of the Convention on Biological Diversity, International Day for Biological Diversity.

Decision I/13: Tribute to the Government of the Commonwealth of the Bahamas

The Conference of the Parties,

Having met in Nassau from 28 November to 9 December 1994, at the gracious invitation of the Government of the Commonwealth of the Bahamas,

Deeply appreciative of the special courtesy and the warm hospitality extended by the Government and people of the Bahamas to the Ministers, members of the delegations, observers and members of the Secretariat attending the Conference,

Expresses its sincere gratitude to the Government of the Commonwealth of the Bahamas and to its people for the cordial welcome which they accorded to the Conference and to those associated with its work and for their contribution to the success of the Conference.

Decisions adopted by the second meeting of the Conference of the Parties

Jakarta, Indonesia, 6–17 November 1995

Decision II/1: Report of the first meeting of the Subsidiary Body on Scientific, Technical and Technological Advice

The Conference of the Parties,

1. *Takes note* of the report of the first meeting of the Subsidiary Body on Scientific, Technical and Technological Advice, held at the headquarters of the United Nations Educational, Scientific and Cultural Organization in Paris from 4 to 8 September 1995, contained in document UNEP/CBD/COP/2/5;

2. *Endorses* recommendation I/1 on the *modus operandi* of the Subsidiary Body on Scientific, Technical and Technological Advice;

3. *Requests* the Subsidiary Body on Scientific, Technical and Technological Advice to keep under review its *modus operandi* with a view to improving its functioning on the basis of experience gained;

4. *Endorses also* recommendation I/6 on the global biodiversity outlook and decides that the outlook should be financed through voluntary contributions;

5. *Calls upon* the international community to make contributions for the preparation and publication of the first global biodiversity outlook, to be issued in 1997;

6. *Further requests* the second meeting of the Subsidiary Body on Scientific, Technical and Technological Advice, in considering its programme of work for 1996, to ensure that the programme is based on the priorities set in the programme of work of the Conference of the Parties for 1996 and 1997, as contained in decision II/18, and specific requests to the Subsidiary Body on Scientific, Technical and Technological Advice, contained in other decisions of the second meeting of the Conference of the Parties.

Recommendation I/6: Global Biodiversity Outlook

In view of the need for a large dissemination of scientific and technical information relevant to the conservation and the sustainable use of biological diversity;

In view also of the importance of scientific and technical research in achieving the goals and objectives of the Convention on Biological Diversity;

The first meeting of the Subsidiary Body on Scientific, Technical and Technological Advice (SBSTTA), held in Paris from 4 to 8 September, recommends that the second meeting of the Conference of the Parties to the Convention on Biological Diversity, to be held in Jakarta, Indonesia, from 6 to 17 November 1995, consider:

1. Requesting the Secretariat to prepare, under the guidance of the Bureau of the Conference of the Parties and the SBSTTA, a periodic report on biological diversity. Such a report, which may also reflect the views of the scientific community, may include, *inter alia*:

(a) A brief summary of the status and trends of biological diversity at global and regional level;

(b) An analysis of the global and regional trends in the implementation of the objectives of the Convention on Biological Diversity on the conservation of biological diversity, the sustainable use of its components, and the fair and equitable sharing of benefits arising out of the utilization of genetic resources;

(c) A summary of the implementation of the Convention on Biological Diversity at the national level on the basis of the information contained in national reports to be submitted by Parties in accordance with Article 26 of the Convention;

(d) An overview of the cooperation with other biological-diversity-related conventions and intergovernmental processes; and

(e) A presentation on the implementation of the decisions of the Conference of the Parties and the recommendations adopted by the SBSTTA.

2. The implications of this proposal in terms of financial and human resources in relation to other tasks to be fulfilled by the Secretariat.

Decision II/2: Publication and distribution of scientific and technical information

The Conference of the Parties,

Noting the importance of scientific and technical work being undertaken by other international and intergovernmental organizations to the medium-term programme of work;

Aware that such inputs have already contributed to advancing the work of the Subsidiary Body on Scientific, Technical and Technological Advice;

Requests the Executive Secretary, in consultation with the Bureau of the Subsidiary Body, to identify and mobilize, for publication and distribution, scientific and technical information of relevance to the medium-term programme of work, recognizing the limitations of the budget.

Decision II/3: Clearing-house mechanism

The Conference of the Parties,

1. *Takes note* of the document prepared by the Secretariat on the establishment of the clearing-house mechanism to promote and facilitate technical and scientific cooperation (document UNEP/CBD/COP/2/6);

2. *Notes* that many information systems and activities relevant to the objectives of the Convention have been and are being established at international, subregional, regional and national levels;

3. *Notes* that the enhanced cooperation between these information systems and activities will contribute to capacity-building, and notes that, in this context, the role of the Secretariat is to promote and facilitate access to this clearing-house mechanism;

4. *Decides*, as a contribution to the implementation of the objectives of the Convention, that the clearing-house mechanism, established by decision I/3 adopted at its first meeting in accordance with Article 18, paragraph 3 of the Convention, should be developed:

(a) Starting with a pilot phase for 1996–1997;

(b) Through specific and focused areas of activities related to the promotion of international technical and scientific cooperation;

(c) By gradually building up its functions in response to clear and identified demand based on experience gained and resources available;

(d) In a neutral, transparent, cost-effective, efficient and accessible manner;

(e) As a decentralized mechanism using such resources as print and electronic media, including the Internet;

(f) By making full use of existing facilities, which will avoid any duplication or overlap of activities and allow for the early implementation of the mechanism;

(g) In close cooperation with relevant international organizations and entities as active partners in the clearing-house mechanism to maximize the existing experience and expertise;

(h) By enhancing networking between existing national, regional, subregional and international centres of relevant expertise, as well as governmental and non-governmental institutions and the private sector;

5. *Decides also* that, during the pilot phase for 1996–1997, the Secretariat should act as a focal point and should:

(a) Encourage the development of a network of active partners, such as those specified in 4 (h). These partners should focus initially on:

(i) developing national capabilities through exchanging and disseminating information on the experiences and lessons learned by Parties on the implementation of the Convention. This can be done through guidelines, training programmes, seminars, workshops, where appropriate, and upon request, and by using the clearing-house mechanism;

(ii) facilitating access to and dissemination of research relevant to the objectives of the Convention;

(iii) facilitating the transfer of technology through exchanging and disseminating information on experiences and technologies relevant to the conservation and sustainable use of biological diversity;

(b) Provide information on and facilitate access to these operating active partners;

(c) Support the active partners to develop specific training for the effective participation of users in the clearing-house network;

6. (a) *Decides also* to provide funding for the pilot phase through the budget of the Convention;

(b) *Calls also* upon the international community to make additional voluntary contributions for the implementation of the pilot phase;

7. *Takes note* of the designation by Parties of their national focal point for the clearing-house mechanism (document UNEP/CBD/COP/2/Inf.5) and calls upon those who have not designated their focal point to do so, where appropriate, as soon as possible, and no later than February 1996;

8. *Invites* all relevant international, regional, subregional and national organizations and entities willing to offer their cooperation as active partners in the operation of the clearing-house mechanism to communicate the details of their offer and requests the Executive Secretary of the Secretariat to enter into collaborative arrangements and to report to its third meeting on the results of such arrangements;

9. *Requests* the Global Environment Facility to explore the modalities of providing support through the financial mechanism to developing country Parties for capacity-building in relation to the operation of the clearing-house mechanism and report to the Conference of the Parties at its third meeting;

10. *Decides* to review the implementation of the pilot phase of the clearing-house mechanism at its third meeting and requests the Executive Secretary to submit a progress report;

11. *Decides also* to review the implementation of the pilot phase at its fourth meeting and requests the Subsidiary Body on Scientific, Technical and Technological Advice to provide scientific and technical advice.

Decision II/4: Ways and means to promote and facilitate access to, and transfer and development of technology

The Conference of the Parties,

1. *Takes note* of recommendation I/4 on ways and means to promote and facilitate access to, and transfer and development of technology as envisaged in Articles 16

and 18 of the Convention, adopted by the first meeting of the Subsidiary Body on Scientific, Technical and Technological Advice, held in Paris, at the headquarters of the United Nations Educational, Scientific and Cultural Organization, from 4 to 8 September 1995;

2. *Endorses* paragraph 1 (d) of recommendation I/4, requesting the Executive Secretary to prepare, for consideration by the Subsidiary Body on Scientific, Technical and Technological Advice at its second meeting, a substantive and well-focused background document, taking into account the views expressed by States Parties and observers during the first meeting of the Subsidiary Body on Scientific, Technical and Technological Advice, the first and second meetings of the Conference of the Parties, including those decisions related to the clearing-house mechanism, and the deliberations of the first and second sessions of the Intergovernmental Committee on the Convention on Biological Diversity, and of the open-ended Intergovernmental Meeting of Scientific Experts on Biological Diversity, held in Mexico in April 1994, including its annexed UNEP Expert Panel Reports I to IV. Such a background document should consider the importance of biotechnology to the conservation and sustainable use of biological diversity, especially to developing countries, as well as the enabling roles of capacity-building and the provision of adequate financial resources;

3. *Endorses also* paragraph 1 (e) of recommendation I/4, requesting the Executive Secretary to invite relevant submissions by States Parties, observers and relevant international and non-governmental organizations, including, in particular, the Commission on Sustainable Development and the private sector and to take these into account in the preparation of the background document. The document should also take due cognisance of regional and subregional inputs and comments. The background document should identify key priority issues relating to opportunities for and obstacles to the transfer of technology for consideration by the Subsidiary Body on Scientific, Technical and Technological Advice;

4. *Requests* the second meeting of the Subsidiary Body on Scientific, Technical and Technological Advice to submit a detailed report to the third meeting of the Conference of the Parties.

Decision II/5: Consideration of the need for and modalities of a protocol for the safe transfer, handling and use of living modified organisms

The Conference of the Parties,

Recalling Article 19, paragraph 3, of the Convention on Biological Diversity,

Recognizing the link between paragraphs 3 and 4 of Article 19,

Recognizing also the link between Articles 8 (g) and 19, paragraph 3,

Recalling its decision I/9 made at its first meeting, held in Nassau, Bahamas, from 28 November to 9 December 1994,

Having considered the report and recommendations prepared for its second meeting by the Open-ended Ad Hoc Group of Experts on Biosafety, which met in Madrid from 24 to 28 July 1995,

Recognizing that modern biotechnology has great potential for human well-being if developed and used with adequate safety measures for the environment and human health,

Recognizing also that, although considerable knowledge has accumulated, significant gaps in knowledge have been identified, specifically in the field of interaction between living modified organisms (LMOs) resulting from modern biotechnology and the environment, taking into account the relatively short period of experience with releases of such organisms, the relatively small number of species and traits used, and the lack of experience in the range of environments, specifically those in centres of origin and genetic diversity,

Noting that there is a need for further analysis of existing national, regional and international regulations and legally binding instruments of relevance to the impact of LMOs on the conservation and sustainable use of biological diversity,

Affirming that international action on biosafety should offer an efficient and effective framework for the development of international cooperation aimed at ensuring safety in biotechnology through effective risk assessment and risk management for the transfer, handling and use of any LMO resulting from modern biotechnology that may have adverse environmental impacts that could affect the conservation and sustainable use of biological diversity, taking into account the risks to human health, and taking also into account Articles 8 (g) and 19, paragraph 4, of the Convention,

Considering that, although there are existing international agreements of relevance to the impact of LMOs resulting from modern biotechnology that may have adverse effect on the conservation and sustainable use of biological diversity, none of these specifically address the transboundary movements of such LMOs, and therefore there is an urgent need to give attention to this issue,

Taking into account that the large majority of delegations present at the meeting of the Open-ended Ad Hoc Group of Experts on Biosafety favoured the development, within the context of an international framework for safety in biotechnology, of a protocol on biosafety under the Convention on Biological Diversity,

Stressing the importance of the urgent finalization of the United Nations Environment Programme International Technical Guidelines on Safety in Biotechnology and that this could contribute to the development and implementation of a protocol on biosafety, but noting that this does not prejudice the development and conclusion of such a protocol,

Noting that guidelines on biosafety, including the proposed United Nations Environment Programme International Technical Guidelines on Safety in Biotechnology, may be used as an interim mechanism during the development of the protocol and to complement it after its completion, for the purposes of facilitating the development of national capacities to assess and manage risks, establish adequate information systems and develop expert human resources in biotechnology,

1. *Decides* to seek solution to the above-mentioned concerns through a negotiation process to develop, in the field of the safe transfer, handling and use of living modified organisms, a protocol on biosafety, specifically focusing on transboundary movement, of any living modified organism resulting from modern biotechnology that may have adverse effect on the conservation and sustainable use of biological diversity, setting out for consideration, in particular, appropriate procedure for advance informed agreement;

2. *Decides* to establish an Open-ended Ad Hoc Working Group under the Conference of the Parties which shall operate in accordance with the terms of reference in the annex to this decision;

3. *Requests* the Executive Secretary of the Convention to make the necessary arrangements for the Open-ended Ad Hoc Working Group to meet as soon as possible, at least once before the next meeting of the Conference of the Parties.

Annex:
Terms of reference for the Open-ended Ad Hoc Working Group

1. The Open-ended Ad Hoc Working Group should be composed of representatives, including experts, nominated by Governments and regional economic integration organizations.

2. The Open-ended Ad Hoc Working Group shall, in accordance with operative paragraph 1 of the present decision:

(a) elaborate, as a priority, the modalities and elements of a protocol based on appropriate elements from Sections I, II and III, paragraph 18 (a), of Annex I of the report of the Open-ended Ad Hoc Group of Experts on Biosafety;

(b) consider the inclusion of the elements from Section III, paragraph 18 (b), and other elements, as appropriate;

3. The development of the draft protocol shall, as a priority:

(a) elaborate the key concepts and terms that are to be addressed in the process;

(b) include consideration of the form and scope of advance informed agreement procedures;

(c) identify relevant categories of LMOs resulting from modern biotechnology.

4. The protocol will have to reflect that its effective functioning requires that Parties establish or maintain national measures, but the absence of such national measures should not prejudice the development, implementation and scope of the protocol.

5. The protocol will take into account the principles enshrined in the Rio Declaration on Environment and Development and, in particular, the precautionary approach contained in Principle 15 and will:

(a) not exceed the scope of the Convention;

(b) not override or duplicate any other international legal instrument in this area;

(c) provide for a review mechanism;

(d) be efficient and effective and seek to minimize unnecessary negative impacts on biotechnology research and development and not to hinder unduly access to and transfer of technology.

6. The provisions of the Convention will apply to the protocol.

7. The process will take into full account the gaps in the existing legal framework identified through analysis of existing national and international legislation.

8. The process shall be guided by the need for all Parties to cooperate in good faith and to participate fully, with a view to the largest possible number of Parties to the Convention ratifying the protocol.

9. The process will be carried out on the basis of the best available scientific knowledge and experience, as well as other relevant information.

10. The process of developing a protocol should be conducted as a matter of urgency by an open-ended ad hoc group, which will report on progress to each subsequent meeting of the Conference of the Parties. The Open-ended Ad Hoc Working Group should endeavour to complete its work in 1998.

Decision II/6: Financial resources and mechanism

The Conference of the Parties,

Taking note of the information provided by the reports contained in documents UNEP/CBD/COP/2/9 and UNEP/CBD/COP/2/8 and the collaboration between the Secretariat of the Convention and the Secretariat of the restructured Global Environment Facility,

1. *Decides* that the restructured Global Environment Facility shall continue to serve as the institutional structure to operate the financial mechanism under the Convention on an interim basis, in accordance with Article 39 of the Convention, until a decision will be taken on which institutional structure is to be designated in accordance with Article 21 of the Convention. The Conference of the Parties shall endeavour to make such a decision at its third meeting;

2. *Decides* to undertake the first review of the effectiveness of the financial mechanism at its fourth meeting in 1997 and a review every three years. The first review will be carried out within the basic approach described in document UNEP/CBD/COP/2/9;

3. *Requests* the Executive Secretary to further develop guidelines of the review for consideration and decision by the Conference of the Parties at its third meeting, taking into account comments made by participants at its second meeting and/or provided by Parties in writing to the Secretariat not later than the end of February 1996;

4. *Takes note* of the draft 'Memorandum of Understanding Between the Conference of the Parties to the Convention on Biological Diversity and the Council of the Global Environment Facility Regarding the Institutional Structure Operating the Financial Mechanism of the Convention', jointly prepared by the Secretariats of the Convention and the restructured Global Environment Facility, and requests the Secretariat of the Convention to continue consultations on the draft Memorandum of Understanding, in order to ensure that comments by Parties are reflected, and to submit a revised draft Memorandum of Understanding for consideration and decision by the Conference of the Parties at its third meeting;

5. *Requests* the interim institutional structure operating the financial mechanism to facilitate urgent implementation of Article 6 of the Convention by availing to developing country Parties financial resources for projects in a flexible and expeditious manner;

6. *Requests* the interim institutional structure to incorporate fully, on an ongoing basis, guidance from the Conference of the Parties into the further develop-

ment of the Operational Strategy and programmes to ensure that the objectives of the Convention are addressed. The Conference of the Parties requests the Global Environment Facility to take the following comments into account when preparing the report to be submitted to the third meeting of the Conference of the Parties:

(a) Detailed information should be provided on the conformity of the approved work programmes with the guidance of the Conference of the Parties;

(b) A list of projects submitted by eligible country Parties and information on their status should be included;

7. *Takes note* of the recently adopted revised project cycle and the Operational Strategy which are anticipated to contribute to more timely approval and implementation of projects, and further requests the Global Environment Facility to take any additional appropriate steps to expedite the project preparation and approval process with a view to implementing fully the guidance of the Conference of the Parties contained in Annex I to decision I/2 on financial resources and mechanism entitled 'Policy, strategy, programme priorities and eligibility criteria for access to and utilization of financial resources' (UNEP/CBD/COP/1/17);

8. *Requests* participation of a representative of the Subsidiary Body on Scientific, Technical and Technological Advice of the Convention and of the Scientific and Technical Advisory Panel of the Global Environment Facility in respective meetings of the Subsidiary Body on Scientific, Technical and Technological Advice and the Scientific and Technical Advisory Panel on a reciprocal basis, as provided for in the *modus operandi* of the Subsidiary Body on Scientific, Technical and Technological Advice and in the terms of reference of the Scientific and Technical Advisory Panel;

9. *Requests* the Executive Secretary to:

(a) Further explore possibilities to identify additional financial resources to support the objectives of the Convention;

(b) Continue to monitor the availability of additional financial resources and further identify where and how country Parties might gain access to these resources;

(c) Study characteristics specific to biodiversity activities to allow the Conference of the Parties to make suggestions to funding institutions on how to make their activities in the area of biodiversity more supportive of the Convention;

10. *Recommends*, for more effective implementation of its policies, strategies and programme priorities, that the Global Environment Facility explore the possibility of promoting diverse forms of public involvement and more effective collaboration between all tiers of government and civil society, including the feasibility of a programme of grants for medium-sized projects. Such exploration should take into account the eligibility criteria set out by the Conference of the Parties in Annex I to decision I/2 on financial resources and mechanism, contained in document UNEP/CBD/COP/1/17;

11. *Requests* the interim institutional structure to implement the relevant provisions of the following decisions: II/3 on clearing-house mechanism, II/7 on consideration of Articles 6 and 8 of the Convention, II/8 on preliminary consideration of components of biological diversity particularly under threat and action which could be taken under the Convention, and II/17 on form and intervals of national reports by Parties;

12. *Requests* the Executive Secretary to present a report to the Conference of the Parties at its third meeting on the implementation of the present decision.

Decision II/7: Consideration of Articles 6 and 8 of the Convention

The Conference of the Parties,

Mindful of the crucial importance of the provisions of Articles 6 and 8 in the fulfillment of the objectives of the Convention,

1. *Urges* all Parties and Governments and other interested stakeholders to exchange relevant information and share experience on measures taken for the implementation of Articles 6 and 8;

2. *Stresses* the importance of regional and international cooperation for the implementation of Articles 6 and 8 of the Convention;

3. *Requests* the Executive Secretary to make available through the clearing-house mechanism such information and lessons drawn from national experience and also to make available relevant information on the implementation of Articles 6 and 8 contained in national reports submitted by Parties in accordance with Article 26 of the Convention as well as decision II/17 adopted at its second meeting;

4. *Further requests* the Executive Secretary:

(a) To compile and disseminate that information as widely as possible, including experience of relevant conventions, United Nations bodies and intergovernmental and nongovernmental organizations in dealing with the provisions of Articles 6 and 8;

(b) To prepare, on the basis of available information, suggestions on how the collection and sharing of relevant information and experience might be enhanced;

5. *Encourages* Parties, in preparing and implementing their national strategies and action plans, to collaborate with relevant organizations and, if so desired, to take into consideration existing guidelines such as 'National Biodiversity Planning' published by the United Nations Environment Programme, the World Resources Institute and the World Conservation Union (IUCN);

6. *Emphasizes* the importance of capacity-building as well as the availability of adequate financial resources to assist Parties in the implementation of Articles 6 and 8 of the Convention, and in this context requests the interim financial mechanism under the Convention to facilitate urgent implementation of Articles 6 and 8 of the Convention by availing to developing country Parties financial resources for projects in a flexible and expeditious manner;

7. *Also requests* the Executive Secretary to present to it a report on the implementation of this decision for consideration at its third meeting.

Decision II/8: Preliminary consideration of components of biological diversity particularly under threat and action which could be taken under the Convention

The Conference of the Parties,

1. *Reaffirms* that the conservation and sustainable use of biological diversity and its components should be addressed in a holistic manner, taking into account the three levels of biological diversity and fully considering socio-economic and cultural factors. However, the ecosystem approach should be the primary framework of action to be taken under the Convention;

2. *Endorses* paragraphs 2, 4 and 5 of recommendation I/3 on preliminary consideration of components of biological diversity that are particularly under threat and the action that could be taken under the Convention, adopted by the first meeting of the Subsidiary Body on Scientific, Technical and Technological Advice, held in Paris, at the headquarters of the United Nations Educational, Scientific and Cultural Organization, from 4 to 8 September 1995;

3. *Stresses* that, as reflected in paragraph 3 of recommendation I/3, it is essential to identify the driving forces determining the status and trends of components of biological diversity, so that appropriate action can be taken to control them;

4. *Stresses also* the importance of making full use of existing knowledge and available expertise;

5. *Emphasizes* the need for capacity-building as well as adequate financial resources for the implementation of the tasks identified in this decision;

6.(i) *Encourages* Parties, as part of their first national report which will focus particularly on Article 6, to identify priority issues specifically related to those components of biological diversity under threat, based upon paragraphs 1, 2, 4 and 5 of recommendation I/3 of the report of the first meeting of the Subsidiary Body on Scientific, Technical and Technological Advice to the second meeting of the Conference of the Parties;

(ii) *Requests* the Executive Secretary to prepare a paper which identifies issues of common concern in the context of examining the national reports;

(iii) *Directs* the Subsidiary Body on Scientific, Technical and Technological Advice to consider the findings of the Executive Secretary's paper and to identify possible options for actions to be considered by the Conference of the Parties;

7. *Further requests* the Subsidiary Body at its second meeting to address the issue of the lack of taxonomists, who would be needed for the national implementation of the Convention, and to advise the Conference of the Parties at its third meeting on ways and means to overcome this problem, taking into account existing studies and ongoing initiatives while adopting a more practical direction of taxonomy linked to bioprospecting and ecological research on conservation and sustainable use of biological diversity and its components.

Recommendation I/3: Alternative ways and means in which the Conference of the Parties could start the process of considering the components of biological diversity particularly those under threat and the identification of action which could be taken under the Convention

2. Assessment of the status and trends of components of biological diversity and causes of biodiversity losses provides baseline data which can assist countries to formulate their biodiversity strategies, plans and programmes to implement the provisions of the Convention. This activity leads to the identification of both components under threat and those components that might become threatened, and for which urgent action might be needed to stop or prevent their loss. There is, however, a need to identify, evaluate, develop and share methods needed for the assessment and conservation and sustainable use of biological diversity. Specifically there is a need to:

(i) Further describe the categories of components of biological diversity set down in Annex I of the Convention;

(ii) Evaluate methodologies for identification, characterization and classification of biological diversity and their components so as to identify methods suitable for different conditions of data availability and how their effectiveness can be enhanced;

(iii) Identify methodologies for detecting national and international negative trends in biological diversity;

(iv) Promote exchange of information on existing methodologies through various information systems including electronic mail;

(v) Identify and develop methods for integration of biodiversity concerns into all relevant sectoral policies, plans and actions; integrate biodiversity considerations into area planning mechanisms and processes; and to develop methods for an integrated management approach;

(vi) Develop methods for identifying the links between socio-economic and cultural factors and biological diversity change or loss, and also identify how these factors should be included when deciding upon effective action to correct for unsustainable use/influence, including environmental impact assessment;

(vii) Develop methods for management of biological diversity based on limited knowledge;

(viii) Develop or refine models of processes responsible for biological diversity maintenance and those relating to ecological services provided by biological diversity for different ecosystems through multidisciplinary groups consisting, *inter alia*, of ecologists, natural history experts, oceanographers, economists and sociologists. Identification and targeting of ecological processes and functions should be the basis for conservation and sustainable use of biological diversity and its components;

(ix) Encourage Governments to carry out case studies to learn about ecosystem management efforts, identifying barriers to implementing the ecosystem approach as well as ways and means of overcoming such barriers. Major issue areas influencing the effectiveness of the ecosystem approach may be examined in such studies, including, *inter alia*, budget issues, institutional issues, public participation, science and information as well as legal authorities. The results of such studies should be reported to the Secretariat of the Convention on Biological Diversity for dissemination and further methodological work.

4. There is a need for each Party to start assessing the effectiveness of measures taken under the Convention. However, methods for assessing the effectiveness of measures to conserve or sustainably use biological diversity should be reviewed. The use of indicators of biological diversity and the status of its components is particularly time- and cost-effective. Several indicators are currently being used and developed. They should be reviewed and their use promoted.

5. The Conference of the Parties should organize international cooperation:

(i) To respond to the needs formulated under paragraphs 1 to 4 above and, more specifically, to compile and assess the above-mentioned methodologies, taking into account existing data, processes and reference materials;

(ii) To identify possible concrete actions for the conservation of biological diversity and to use its components sustainably;

(iii) To make these studies available through the clearing-house mechanism established by the Convention to promote technical and scientifical cooperation, and to promote a regional approach to further enhance the collection and analysis of relevant information.

Decision II/9: Forests and biological diversity

The Conference of the Parties,

1. *Decides* to invite its President to transmit the Statement contained in the annex to this decision to the Intergovernmental Panel on Forests at its second meeting;

2. *Requests* the Executive Secretary:

(a) To provide advice and information pertaining to the relationship between indigenous and local communities and forests, as invited by the Inter-Agency Task Force of the Intergovernmental Panel on Forests;

(b) To commission and carry out work on forests and biological diversity, with a view to producing a background document on the links between forests and biological diversity in order to consider, at its third meeting, whether further input to the Intergovernmental Panel on Forests is required, and to transmit this document to the Intergovernmental Panel on Forests for information;

(c) To invite all Parties, relevant intergovernmental agencies and bodies to contribute to the preparation of the documents on forests and biological diversity to be prepared by the Executive Secretary, and to welcome the input of other Governments, non-governmental organizations and indigenous and local communities;

3. *Invites* all Parties to include expertise on forest biological diversity in their delegations to the Intergovernmental Panel on Forests;

4. *Invites* the Secretariat of the Intergovernmental Panel on Forests to communicate progress on issues relevant to forests and biological diversity to the third meeting of the Conference of the Parties.

Annex:
Statement on biological diversity and forests from the Convention on Biological Diversity to the Intergovernmental Panel on Forests

1. The Conference of the Parties to the Convention on Biological Diversity welcomes the decision by the Commission on Sustainable Development to establish an open-ended Intergovernmental Panel on Forests (IPF) to pursue consensus and coordinated proposals for action to support the management, conservation and sustainable development of forests.

2. Wishing to avoid duplication of efforts and coordinate with other relevant organizations on issues of biological diversity, the Conference of the Parties stands ready to contribute to the fulfilment of the mandate of the IPF.

3. Keeping in mind the crucial role of forests in maintaining global biological diversity, the Conference of the Parties wishes to establish a dialogue with the IPF on issues related to forests and biological diversity.

4. Together, tropical, temperate and boreal forests provide the most diverse sets of habitats for plants, animals and micro-organisms, holding the vast majority of the world's terrestrial species. This diversity is the fruit of evolution, but also reflects the combined influence of the physical environment and people.

5. The maintenance of forest ecosystems is crucial to the conservation of biological diversity well beyond their boundaries, and for the key role they play in global climate dynamics and bio-geochemical cycles. Forests provide ecological services and, at the same time, livelihoods or jobs for hundreds of millions of people worldwide.

6. Forest biological diversity results from evolutionary processes over thousands and even millions of years which, in themselves, are driven by ecological forces such as climate, fire, competition and disturbance. Furthermore, the diversity of forest ecosystems (in both physical and biological features) results in high levels of adaptation, a feature of forest ecosystems which is an integral component of their biological diversity. Within specific forest ecosystems, the maintenance of ecological processes is dependent upon the maintenance of their biological diversity. Loss of biological diversity within individual ecosystems can result in lower resilience.

7. Forests are becoming degraded and their biological diversity is being lost. The loss of forest biological diversity is linked to the substantial deforestation, fragmentation and degradation of all types of forests. The reasons for the loss of forest biological diversity are many, both direct and indirect, and the Conference of the Parties takes note of the Terms of Reference of the IPF in this regard. (IPF Agenda item I.2.)

8. Forests and forest biological diversity play important economic, social and cultural roles in the lives of many indigenous and local communities. The Convention on Biological Diversity addresses specifically the need to respect, preserve and maintain knowledge, innovations and practices of indigenous and local communities relevant for the conservation and sustainable use of biological diversity, as well as the need to protect and encourage customary use of biological resources in accordance with traditional cultural

practices. It also encourages countries to cooperate in the development and use of indigenous and traditional technologies, and encourages the equitable sharing of the benefits arising from the utilization of such knowledge, innovations and practices, in pursuance of the objectives of the Convention. Articles 8 (j), 10 (c) and 18.4 of the Convention provide the general framework for this.

9. In addition, the Convention on Biological Diversity recognizes in Article 15 the sovereign rights of States over their genetic resources and also recognizes that the authority to determine access to these resources rests with the national Governments and is subject to national legislation. It also states that each Contracting Party shall endeavour to create conditions to facilitate access to genetic resources for environmentally sound uses by other Contracting Parties and not to impose restrictions that run counter to the objectives of the Convention. Such access, including forest-based genetic resources, shall be subject to prior informed consent by the Party providing such resources and shall be on mutually agreed terms. Measures shall be taken with the aim of sharing in a fair and equitable way the results of research and development and the benefits arising from the commercial and other utilization of genetic resources with the party providing such resources. Such sharing shall be on mutually agreed terms.

10. The Conference of the Parties emphasizes and requests the IPF to acknowledge the need to integrate the conservation and sustainable use of biological diversity into relevant sectoral and cross-sectoral plans, programmes and policies (Convention on Biological Diversity Article 6 (b)). The Conference of the Parties requests the IPF to note that it intends to explore how the conservation and sustainable use of forest biological diversity could be assisted by the establishment of specific environmental goals in the forest and other sectors. The Conference of the Parties also requests the IPF to consider appropriate Environmental Impact Assessment of sectoral activities, plans, programmes and policies with expected negative impact on forest ecosystems (Convention on Biological Diversity Article 14). (IPF Agenda item I.2)

11. The Conference of the Parties notes the mandate of the IPF concerning methods for the proper valuing of the multiple benefits derived from forests. In this context, it requests the IPF to consider the economic (monetized and non-monetized) benefits, the environmental services and non-consumptive values provided by forest biological diversity, including the important cultural, religious and recreational values of forests. (IPF Agenda items III.1 and IV.1.)

12. The Conference of the Parties recognizes the need to develop and implement methods for sustainable forest management which combine production goals, socio-economic goals of forest-dependent local communities, and environmental goals, particularly those related to biological diversity. Sustainable forest management should ensure that components of biological diversity are used in a way and at a rate that does not lead to the long-term decline of biological diversity, thereby maintaining its potential to meet the needs of present and future generations (Convention on Biological Diversity Article 2). Sustainable forest management should take an ecosystem approach and aim at securing forest quality as related to the Convention on Biological Diversity, comprising such elements as forest composition, natural regeneration, patterns of ecosystem variation, ecosystem functions and ecosystem processes over time. Special attention should be paid to components of biological diversity under threat. (IPF Agenda items III.2 and I.5.)

13. *In situ* forest conservation activities in accordance with Article 8 of the Convention on Biological Diversity, including the establishment and management of protected areas, have an important role to play in the achievement of biological diversity goals for sustain-

able forest management, and should be integrated in national forest and land-use plans. In this context, the conservation of primary/old-growth and ecologically mature secondary forest ecosystems is of particular importance. All stakeholders, in particular managers, should engage in an open, transparent and participatory decision-making process that can explicitly incorporate the multiple functions of forests and involve all interested parties, including indigenous and local communities. (IPF Agenda item I.1.)

14. The issue of public education and awareness has not been explicitly addressed in the Terms of Reference of the IPF. The importance of education and awareness-raising at all levels of society, including local communities, local and national policy makers, forest managers, and users of forests and forest products, related to the importance of biological diversity, especially those components under threat, should have a high priority in both national and international efforts. (Convention on Biological Diversity Article 13.)

15. More effort on biological diversity is needed in research, training and other capacity-building activities (Convention on Biological Diversity Article 12). Important topics include development of policies, criteria and indicators, methodologies and technologies for sustainable forest management, and the impact of utilization of components of biological diversity, particularly those under threat, on ecological processes. (IPF Agenda items III.1 and III.2.)

16. In response to the invitation of the IPF, the Conference of the Parties has requested its Executive Secretary to provide advice and information pertaining to the relationship between indigenous and local communities and forests. The Conference of the Parties has further requested the Executive Secretary to provide advice and information concerning the contents, work and medium-term programme of work of the Convention relevant to the Terms of Reference of the IPF. Such advice and information will be provided in time for the Panel's third session.

17. The IPF may also receive substantive inputs from the Convention following the third meeting of the Conference of the Parties on, *inter alia*, the underlying causes of biological diversity loss in forest ecosystems, components and dynamics of biological diversity, and ways and means for the effective protection and use of traditional forest-related knowledge, innovations and practices of forest dwellers, indigenous and local communities, as well as fair and equitable sharing of benefits arising from such knowledge, innovations and practices.

Decision II/10: Conservation and sustainable use of marine and coastal biological diversity

The Conference of the Parties,

Recalling that the Conference of the Parties decided to address, at its second meeting, advice from the Subsidiary Body on Scientific, Technical and Technological Advice on the scientific, technical and technological aspects of the conservation and sustainable use of marine and coastal biological diversity,

Being deeply concerned at the serious threats to marine and coastal biological diversity caused by factors including physical alteration, destruction and degradation of habitats, pollution, invasion of alien species, and over-exploitation of living marine and coastal resources,

1. *Takes note* of recommendation I/8 on scientific, technical and technological aspects of the conservation and sustainable use of marine and coastal biological diversity, adopted by the first meeting of the Subsidiary Body on Scientific, Technical and Technological Advice, held in Paris at the headquarters of the United Nations Educational, Scientific and Cultural Organization, from 4 to 8 September 1995, and;

(a) *Affirms* that it represents a solid basis for future elaboration of the issues presented;

(b) *Supports* the recommendations in paragraphs 10–19 of recommendation I/8, subject to Annex I of the present decision and its further elaboration by the Subsidiary Body on Scientific, Technical and Technological Advice and the Conference of the Parties;

(c) *Reaffirms* the importance of future work by the Subsidiary Body on Scientific, Technical and Technological Advice to provide a balanced perspective on the remaining issues presented by the recommendations in I/8 and Annex I of the present decision relevant to the conservation and sustainable use of marine and coastal biodiversity;

2. *Encourages the use* of integrated marine and coastal area management as the most suitable framework for addressing human impacts on marine and coastal biological diversity and for promoting conservation and sustainable use of this biodiversity;

3. *Encourages* Parties to establish and/or strengthen, where appropriate, institutional, administrative, and legislative arrangements for the development of integrated management of marine and coastal ecosystems, plans and strategies for marine and coastal areas, and their integration within national development plans;

4. *Takes note* of the recently finalized Food and Agriculture Organization of the United Nations Code of Conduct for Responsible Fisheries, the Agreement for the Implementation of the Provisions of the United Nations Convention on the Law of the Sea of 10 December 1982 Relating to the Conservation and Management of Straddling Fish Stocks and Highly Migratory Fish Stocks, and the Washington Declaration and Global Programme of Action for the Protection of the Marine Environment from Land-based Activities, and supports their implementation, including that by Parties, in ways that are consistent with, and conform to, the objectives of the Convention on Biological Diversity;

5. *Welcomes* the International Coral Reef Initiative as a means to address threats to coral reefs and related ecosystems and encourages participation in International Coral Reef Initiative activities to implement its Framework for Action;

6. *Reaffirms* that under Article 25 the Subsidiary Body on Scientific, Technical and Technological Advice is the only scientific, technical and technological authority under the Convention to provide advice to the Conference of the Parties;

7. *Instructs* the Executive Secretary to provide, in accordance with Annex II, the Subsidiary Body on Scientific, Technical and Technological Advice with scientific, technical, and technological advice and options for recommendations to the Conference of the Parties in further elaborating the recommendations contained in recommendation I/8, with the exception of paragraphs 3 and 4;

8. *Offers* the Executive Secretary the following guidance for conducting the work described in paragraph 6:

(a) Solicit input from all Parties and, as appropriate, from other countries and relevant bodies;

(b) Establish, on the basis of country input, a roster of experts with specialization appropriate to the work described in paragraph 6;

(c) The roster will draw upon expertise from scientific, technical, technological, social, management, economic, policy, legal, and indigenous and traditional knowledge;

(d) Convene, as appropriate, meetings of experts, drawn from the roster to support the Secretariat in advancing the work described in paragraph 6. Each meeting shall be for a duration of no longer than five days, and shall be comprised of no more than 15 experts with due regard to geographical representation and to the special conditions of least-developed countries and small island developing States;

9. *Welcomes* the offer from Indonesia to be host country for the first such meeting of Experts on Marine and Coastal Biological Diversity;

10. *Decides* to forward this decision and its annexes to the next session of the Commission on Sustainable Development for its information when considering its review of Agenda 21, chapter 17, on oceans;

11. *Decides* to forward this decision and annexes to the Global Environment Facility, other funding agencies and other relevant international bodies, to be taken into account in considering activities related to the conservation and sustainable use of marine and coastal biological diversity;

12. *Requests* the Executive Secretary, in consultation with the United Nations Office for Ocean Affairs and the Law of the Sea, to undertake a study of the relationship between the Convention on Biological Diversity and the United Nations Convention on the Law of the Sea with regard to the conservation and sustainable use of genetic resources on the deep seabed, with a view to enabling the Subsidiary Body on Scientific, Technical and Technological Advice to address at future meetings, as appropriate, the scientific, technical, and technological issues relating to bio-prospecting of genetic resources on the deep seabed;

13. *Invites* international and regional bodies responsible for legal instruments, agreements and programmes which address activities relevant to the conservation and sustainable use of marine and coastal biodiversity, including the United Nations General Assembly, the Food and Agriculture Organization of the United Nations, the United Nations Environment Programme, the International Maritime Organization, the United Nations Office for Ocean Affairs and the Law of the Sea, the United Nations Educational, Scientific and Cultural Organization including its Intergovernmental Oceanographic Commission, the World Conservation Union (IUCN), the Commission on Sustainable Development, the International Coral Reef Initiative, regional fisheries bodies, migratory species agreements, secretariats of regional agreements for the conservation of the marine environment and other relevant international and regional organizations and institutions, to review their programmes with a view to improving existing measures and developing new actions which promote conservation and sustainable use of marine biological diversity, taking into account the recommendations for action by the Parties to the Convention on Biological Diversity adopted by the Conference of the Parties at its second meeting, and provide information on their actions on a regular basis to the Conference of the Parties and, in a first instance, as soon as possible through the Executive Secretary. Furthermore, these various institutions are invited to

cooperate with the Conference of the Parties through the Subsidiary Body on Scientific, Technical and Technological Advice in planning and implementation of programmes affecting marine and coastal biological diversity, so as to reduce any unnecessary duplication or gaps in coverage;

14. *Decides* to request the Subsidiary Body on Scientific, Technical and Technological Advice to carry out a summary review at its next meeting of the first report from the Executive Secretary and to submit in its report to the Conference of the Parties its recommendation on the work of the Executive Secretary.

Annex I: Additional conclusions on recommendation I/8 adopted by the Subsidiary Body on Scientific, Technical and Technological Advice at its first meeting (UNEP/CBD/COP/2/5)

(i) Some delegations indicated their concern that paragraphs 10–19 were unbalanced in that they over-emphasized fishery issues, rather than some other issues such as pollution. Other delegations had an interest in highlighting the impacts of unsustainable fishing activities on marine and coastal biodiversity.

(ii) In relation to paragraph 10, crucial components of integrated marine and coastal area management are relevant sectoral activities, such as construction and mining in coastal areas, mariculture, mangrove management, tourism, recreation, fishing practices and land-based activities, including watershed management. Parties should, where appropriate and practical, prevent physical alteration, destruction and degradation of vital habitats and pursue restoration of degraded habitats, including spawning areas, nurseries of stocks of living marine resources, bearing in mind the objectives of the Convention on Biological Diversity and the need to provide a balanced approach to the use and conservation of marine and coastal biological diversity.

(iii) Parties are encouraged to undertake and exchange information on demonstration projects as practical examples of integrated marine and coastal area management.

(iv) In relation to paragraph 11, critical habitats for living marine resources should be an important criterion for the selection of marine and coastal protected areas, within the framework of integrated marine and coastal area management, taking into consideration the objectives of the Convention on Biological Diversity. Conservation measures should emphasize the protection of ecosystem functioning, in addition to protecting specific stocks.

(v) In reference to paragraph 12, the present mono-species approach to modelling and assessment should be augmented by an ecosystem process-oriented approach, based on research of ecosystem processes and functions, with an emphasis on identifying ecologically critical processes that consider the spatial dimension of these processes. Models of ecosystem processes should be developed through trans-disciplinary scientific groups (ecologists, oceanographers, economists, and fisheries experts) and be applied in the development of sustainable land and coastal resource use practices.

(vi) Paragraph 13 refers to the draft Food and Agriculture Organization of the United Nations Code of Conduct for Responsible Fisheries. The Code was adopted by the 28th session of the Conference of the Food and Agriculture Organization of the United Nations, in October 1995. The Food and Agriculture Organization of the United Nations is now undertaking the development of technical guidelines for the implementation of the Code. The Conference of the Parties can offer the technical expertise of the Subsidiary Body on Scientific, Technical and Technological Advice in the elaboration and implementation of these guidelines, in line with the objectives and provisions of the Convention on Biological Diversity.

(vii) In relation to paragraph 14 (a), the inclusion of subsidies was contentious. Some delegates stressed that the issue of subsidies was politically sensitive, with potential trade implications. It was noted that these issues address one of the underlying causes of biological diversity loss, viz, the result of over-fishing, and this consideration remained an important recommendation from the report of the Subsidiary Body on Scientific, Technical and Technological Advice. It was also noted that there were a variety of other subsidies which had impacts on the conservation and sustainable use of marine and coastal biological diversity. The Executive Secretary is entitled to evaluate these aspects using a meeting of experts. Some delegations argued that the phrase 'subsidies for fisheries' appeared ambiguous. Government subsidies related to fishing activities have a great variety in their modalities. In addition, subsidies should not be evaluated alone. Evaluation of subsidies for fisheries should be conducted in relation to, or in conjunction with, considerations of fisheries management. It would be most appropriate to examine the various existing subsidies in the light of Article 11, which refers to economically and socially sound incentive measures.

(viii) Also, in relation to paragraph 14, cooperation between regional fisheries bodies and regional organizations for protection and conservation of the marine environment should be promoted.

(ix) In relation to paragraph 15, the Parties should enhance and improve the knowledge regarding the genetic structure of the local populations of marine species subjected to stock enhancement and sea-ranching activities. Considering that the captive-bred populations are likely to interact genetically and ecologically with wild populations, this knowledge should be used in the management of breeding stocks according to sound genetic principles that take into account the use of local populations for stock selection, minimum breeding numbers and the renewal frequency of the breeding stock from the wild population.

(x) Mariculture (paragraph 15) is assumed to include culture-based fisheries and is defined here to be aquaculture in marine or brackish water. According to the Food and Agriculture Organization of the United Nations, 'aquaculture is the farming of aquatic organisms including fish, molluscs, crustaceans and aquatic plants. Farming implies some form of intervention in the rearing process to enhance production, such as regular stocking, feeding, protection from predators, etc. Farming also implies individual or corporate ownership of the stock being cultivated'. Although the Food and Agriculture Organization of the United Nations requires 'ownership of the stock being cultivated' in its definition, no such restriction is adopted here for the purpose of this document.

(xi) Some Parties thought paragraph 15 (I) (e) would be better expressed as 'because of the difficulties of complete containment, introduction of alien species, products of selective breeding, and living modified organisms resulting from modern biotechnology that may have adverse effects on the conservation and sustainable use of marine and coastal biodiversity should be responsibly conducted using the precautionary approach. Therefore, adherence to international codes of practice such as the Food and Agriculture Organization of the United Nations Code of Conduct for Responsible Fisheries, the International Commission for the Exploration of the Sea, and the Organisation

Internationale Epizootique should be a minimum requirement. Assessments and an appropriate monitoring programme should be put in place if introduction goes ahead. Preference should be given to the use of local species. Furthermore, development of technology to ensure a more complete containment should be encouraged.'

Annex II: Draft programme for further work on marine and coastal biological diversity

1. The Executive Secretary will use as the basis of work recommendation I/8 of the Subsidiary Body on Scientific, Technical and Technological Advice (contained in document UNEP/CBD/COP/2/5), this decision and further inputs, if any, from the Conference of the Parties.

2. The Executive Secretary should use the roster of experts on Marine and Coastal Biodiversity to address the following topics:

(a) Identify options for a pragmatic but comprehensive approach in addressing marine and coastal biological diversity on the basis of an ecosystems approach, including its components at the levels of species and genetic resources, distinguishing regions at relevant scales. Use the results from this activity in identifying the gaps in knowledge of the distribution and abundance of marine and coastal biodiversity;

(b) Identify the particular needs for conservation and sustainable use of marine and coastal biological diversity in the context of activities which will impact on marine resources;

(c) Review the mandates and activities under international agreements that affect marine and coastal biological diversity, and develop analyses that can be offered by the Conference of the Parties to the relevant institutions as to the implications of the Convention on Biological Diversity for these activities.

3. In addressing these issues, the following approaches should be applied:

(a) The work should not be impeded by the lack of full scientific information and will incorporate explicitly the precautionary approach in addressing conservation and sustainable use issues;

(b) The Executive Secretary may interact with a wide range of agencies and organizations competent in the aspects of marine and coastal biodiversity under deliberation to avoid unnecessary duplication and ensure effectiveness and cost-effectiveness;

(c) Recommendations should be made for scientific, technical and technological needs for capacity-building and technology transfer for the conservation and sustainable use of marine and coastal resources at the national, regional, and international levels in the context of the issue being addressed;

(d) The scientific, technical, and technological knowledge of local and indigenous communities should be incorporated, as appropriate, as well as community and user-based approaches, in the conservation and sustainable use of marine and coastal biodiversity;

(e) Use should be made, as appropriate, of the clearing-house mechanism and national reports of Parties.

4. The Executive Secretary shall produce, among other relevant documents, the following outputs:

(a) Options for the conservation and sustainable use of biological diversity and its components in the implementation of marine and coastal management and planning practices, including options for the development of integrated marine and coastal area management at regional and national levels;

(b) Annual reports to the Subsidiary Body on Scientific, Technical and Technological Advice, submitted 90 days prior to each meeting of that body. The first annual report will include a three-year work plan.

Decision II/11: Access to genetic resources

The Conference of the Parties,

Recalling that the charge from its second meeting is to prepare for agenda item 6.6.1 of the programme of work for its third meeting where the Secretariat is asked to compile the views of Parties on possible options for developing national legislative, administrative or policy measures, as appropriate to implement Article 15;

Noting that regional efforts, based in part on the similarity of the genetic resources found in the region, are important to common strategies and therefore should be encouraged;

1. *Requests* the Executive Secretary to:

(a) Further elaborate the survey of measures taken by Governments to implement Article 15, including any national interpretations of key terms used in that article, with a view to completing the survey in time for circulation at the third meeting of the Conference of the Parties;

(b) Compile an annotated list of studies and other relevant information on the social and economic valuation of genetic resources, including the demand by industry for genetic resources;

2. *Reaffirms* that human genetic resources are not included within the framework of the Convention;

3. *Urges* Governments to send information on national measures to the Secretariat at their earliest convenience;

4. *Recommends* that the Secretariat not duplicate work underway in other forums.

Decision II/12: Intellectual property rights

The Conference of the Parties,

Requests the Executive Secretary to:

(a) Liaise with the Secretariat of the World Trade Organization to inform it of the goals and the ongoing work of the Convention on Biological Diversity and to invite the Secretariat of the World Trade Organization to assist in the preparation of a paper for the Conference of the Parties that identifies the synergies and relationship between the objectives of the Convention on Biological Diversity and the TRIPs Agreement. This paper could be the basis for consideration by the third meeting of the Conference of the Parties in preparing a possible input for negotiations that are taking place in the Committee on Trade and Environment of the World Trade Organization;

(b) Consult with all stakeholders, in particular the private sector and indigenous and local communities, in order to gain understanding of the needs and concerns of those groups whose participation will be required for cooperative arrangements to be meaningful and effective in achieving the Convention's objectives. These consultations may take place in the form of roundtable discussions;

(c) Undertake a preliminary study which analyses the impact of intellectual property rights systems on the conservation and sustainable use of biological diversity and the equitable sharing of benefits derived from its use in order to gain a better understanding of the implications of Article 16 (5). The study may focus on: (i) exploring the relationship between intellectual property rights and the preservation and maintenance of traditional knowledge and practices of indigenous and local communities and the possible role of intellectual property rights in encouraging the equitable sharing of benefits arising from the use of such knowledge and practices; and (ii) inviting Governments and other relevant stakeholders to submit case studies that address the role of intellectual property rights in the technology transfer process, in particular the role of intellectual property rights in the transfer of biotechnology.

Decision II/13: Cooperation with other biodiversity-related conventions

The Conference of the Parties,

1. *Takes note* of the information note UNEP/CBD/COP/2/Inf.2 prepared by the Secretariat on cooperation with other biodiversity-related conventions;

2. *Stresses* the need to make mutually supportive the implementation of activities undertaken by the Convention on Biological Diversity and by other international and regional conventions and agreements related to biological diversity and its components, building particularly on the consultations which have already taken place with certain key conventions, as outlined in UNEP/CBD/COP/2/Inf.2;

3. *Stresses also* the need to avoid unnecessary duplication of activities and costs on the part of Parties and of the organs of the Convention;

4. *Requests* the Executive Secretary to coordinate with the Secretariats of relevant biodiversity-related conventions with a view to:

(a) Facilitating exchange of information and experience;

(b) Exploring the possibility of recommending procedures for harmonizing, to the extent desirable and practicable, the reporting requirements of Parties under those instruments and conventions;

(c) Exploring the possibility of coordinating their respective programmes of work;

(d) Consulting on how such conventions and other international legal instruments can contribute to the implementation of the provisions of the Convention on Biological Diversity;

5. *Invites also* the governing bodies of such conventions and other international legal instruments related to biological diversity to consider at their next meetings their possible contribution to the implementation of the goals and objectives of the Convention;

6. *Further requests* the Executive Secretary to prepare, for its third meeting, a report on the implementation of this decision, containing concrete recommendations aimed at promoting and strengthening institutional cooperation with other global and regional biodiversity-related conventions;

7. *Requests* the Executive Secretary also to report to the Conference of the Parties at its third meeting on modalities for enhanced cooperation with relevant international biodiversity-related bodies such as the Food and Agriculture Organization of the United Nations, the United Nations Educational, Scientific and Cultural Organization and the Commission on Sustainable Development, taking into account the medium-term programme of work on this issue.

Decision II/14: Convening of an open-ended intergovernmental workshop on cooperation between the Convention on Biological Diversity and other international conventions on related issues

The Conference of the Parties,

Having examined Point 8.2 of UNEP/CBD/COP/2/1, related to the cooperation between the Convention on Biological Diversity and other related international conventions on related issues,

Noting that an identification and harmonization of the points in common within these conventions on biological diversity issues would help the Parties, especially the developing countries, to come up with an appropriate and integrated national legislation on biodiversity matters,

Noting also that cooperation among international conventions would help the Parties to exchange information through the clearing-house mechanism in the context of sharing of scientific and technical information,

1. *Invites*, subject to the availability of funds, the United Nations Environment Programme (UNEP), in accordance with its mandate established by chapter 38 of Agenda 21, to liaise with the Commission on Sustainable Development to organize an open-ended intergovernmental workshop on the study of the relationships between the Convention on Biological Diversity and other related international conventions on related issues, taking into consideration existing studies and the expertise available in nongovernmental organizations and relevant institutions;

2. *Invites* all international organizations or donor countries to contribute financially to the organization of the workshop.

Decision II/15: FAO Global System for the Conservation and Utilization of Plant Genetic Resources for Food and Agriculture

The Conference of the Parties,

Recognizing the special nature of agricultural biodiversity, its distinctive features and problems needing distinctive solutions,

Taking note of the Global System for the Conservation and Utilization of Plant Genetic Resources for Food and Agriculture developed by member countries of the Food and Agriculture Organization of the United Nations (FAO) through the FAO Commission on Plant Genetic Resources, and the recommendation for strengthening it expressed in chapter 14 of Agenda 21;

Recalling that Resolution 3 of the Nairobi Final Act of the Conference for the Adoption of the Agreed Text of the Convention on Biological Diversity recognized 'the need to seek solutions to outstanding matters concerning plant genetic resources within the Global System for the Conservation and Use of Plant Genetic Resources for Food and Sustainable Agriculture, in particular (a) access to *ex-situ* collections not acquired in accordance with this Convention; and (b) the question of farmers' rights',

1. *Considers* that the outstanding matters should be resolved as soon as possible;

2. *Declares* its support for the process engaged in the FAO Commission on Plant Genetic Resources to comply with these recommendations, especially through:

   (1) The implementation of FAO Conference Resolution 7/93 for the adaptation of the International Undertaking on Plant Genetic Resources, in harmony with the Convention of Biological Diversity;

   (2) Convening the Fourth International Technical Conference on Plant Genetic Resources for Food and Agriculture through which two important elements of the Global System, the first State of the World report on Plant Genetic Resources for Food and Agriculture and the first Global Plan of Action for Plant Genetic Resources for Food and Agriculture, are being developed through a country-driven process.

Decision II/16: Statement to the International Technical Conference on the Conservation and Utilization of Plant Genetic Resources for Food and Agriculture

The Conference of the Parties,

1. *Requests* the Food and Agriculture Organization of the United Nations to present the outcome of the International Technical Conference on the Conservation and Utilization of Plant Genetic Resources for Food and Agriculture to the third meeting of the Conference of the Parties and to make the Global Plan of Action and State of the World reports available to that meeting;

2. *Welcomes* the offer of the Food and Agriculture Organization of the United Nations to link its information mechanisms to the clearing-house mechanism under the Convention;

3. *Decides* to invite its President to transmit the statement contained in the annex to this decision to the International Technical Conference on the Conservation and Utilization of Plant Genetic Resources for Food and Agriculture.

Annex: Statement from the Conference of the Parties to the Convention on Biological Diversity to the International Technical Conference on the Conservation and Utilization of Plant Genetic Resources for Food and Agriculture

1. The planet's essential goods and services depend on the variety and variability of genes, species, populations and ecosystems. If humanity is to have a future on this Earth, biological diversity must be conserved so that these functions and services are maintained. The current decline in biodiversity is largely the result of human activity and represents a serious threat to human development. Despite efforts to conserve the world's biological diversity, its depletion has continued. The entry into force of the Convention provides an international framework through which to address this depletion which causes threats to ecosystems that are vital for the sustenance of human societies in all countries. By becoming Parties to the Convention, Governments have committed themselves to the conservation of biological diversity, the sustainable use of its components, and the fair and equitable sharing of the benefits arising out of the utilization of genetic resources.

2. The Convention on Biological Diversity advances the conservation of biological diversity and the sustainable use of its components and the fair and equitable sharing of the benefits arising out of the use of genetic resources, while recognizing the important role of other conventions to the objectives of the Convention.

3. The Conference of the Parties guides the implementation of the provisions of the Convention on Biological Diversity, reviews the further development of matters relating to the conservation of biological diversity, the sustainable use of its components, and the fair and equitable sharing of the benefits arising from the use of genetic resources and, where appropriate, brings these within the purview of the Convention.

4. Within the overarching framework established by the Convention on Biological Diversity, it is the case that there are many international forums through which the objectives of the Convention can be progressed. The Conference of the Parties urges all such forums to work together to achieve these objectives.

5. In this regard, the Conference of the Parties recognizes the substantial contribution that the Food and Agriculture Organization of the United Nations can make, applying its experience and skills to tackle the very important issues associated with genetic resources for food and agriculture.

6. It is important for us to recognize that there are very many Parties to the Convention that are also members of the Food and Agriculture Organization of the United Nations. This forms a strong basis of common ground from which the Convention and the Food

and Agriculture Organization of the United Nations could build complementary programmes in the area of genetic resources for food and agriculture.

7. At its second meeting, held in Jakarta from 6 to 17 November 1995, the Conference of the Parties considered advice provided by its Subsidiary Body on Scientific, Technical and Technological Advice on the contribution of the Convention to the preparation for the forthcoming International Technical Conference on the Conservation and Utilization of Plant Genetic Resources for Food and Agriculture.

8. As a result of these considerations, the Conference of the Parties to the Convention on Biological Diversity wishes to draw to the attention of the fourth International Technical Conference on the Conservation and Utilization of Plant Genetic Resources for Food and Agriculture the following considerations:

(a) The comprehensive nature and the multidisciplinary character of the Convention on Biological Diversity, aimed at addressing all facets of biological diversity within its threefold objectives: the conservation of biological diversity, the sustainable use of its components and the fair and equitable sharing of its benefits;

(b) The importance attached by the Conference of the Parties to the conservation of plant genetic resources for food and agriculture and their use in a sustainable manner;

(c) The recognition that plant genetic resources for food and agriculture are critical components of biological diversity;

(d) In recognition of the need to assess the current situation of plant genetic resources for food and agriculture and identify gaps and needs for priority action, the Conference of the Parties welcomes the preparation of the Global Plan of Action and the State of the World's Genetic Resources for Food and Agriculture;

(e) The need to strengthen capacity-building, in particular in developing countries;

(f) The relevance of the issues to be considered by the fourth International Technical Conference on the Conservation and Utilization of Plant Genetic Resources for Food and Agriculture to the provisions of the Convention on Biological Diversity;

(g) The Conference of the Parties' support for the recognition by the Food and Agriculture Organization of the United Nations of the need to make the processes of the fourth International Technical Conference on the Conservation and Utilization of Plant Genetic Resources for Food and Agriculture and the Convention on Biological Diversity mutually supportive and complementary, in harmony with the provisions of the Convention.

(h) The sovereign rights of States over their natural resources.

9. Recalling the recommendations of Agenda 21, chapter 14 (g) and of Resolution 3 of the Nairobi Final Act, the Conference of the Parties urges the International Technical Conference to make every effort to promote complementarity and consistency between the outcome of the Conference and the provisions of the Convention, making them mutually supportive and enhancing the success of both.

10. The Conference of the Parties compliments the Secretariat of the Food and Agriculture Organization of the United Nations responsible for the programme and processes for the fourth International Technical Conference on the Conservation and Sustainable Utilization of Plant Genetic Resources for Food and Agriculture on its exemplary preparatory process based upon national reports, regional and subregional

meetings leading to a global assessment of biological diversity of unique ecosystems. The process provides an innovative model.

11. The Conference of the Parties to the Convention on Biological Diversity hopes that this statement will be helpful to the International Technical Conference on the Conservation and Utilization of Plant Genetic Resources for Food and Agriculture and plans to consider, at its third meeting, the outcome of the Conference.

Decision II/17: Form and intervals of national reports by Parties

The Conference of the Parties,

1. *Takes note* of the note prepared by the Secretariat on form and intervals of national reports by Parties, document UNEP/CBD/COP/2/14;

2. *Endorses* recommendation I/5 on 'Scientific and Technical Information to be contained in the national reports', adopted by the first meeting of the Subsidiary Body on Scientific, Technical and Technological Advice;

3. *Decides* that the first national reports by Parties will focus in so far as possible on the measures taken for the implementation of Article 6 of the Convention, 'General Measures for Conservation and Sustainable Use', as well as the information available in national country studies on biological diversity, using as a guide the annex to this decision;

4. *Decides* that the first national reports will be due at the fourth meeting of the Conference of the Parties in 1997;

5. *Decides* that, at its fourth meeting in 1997, the Conference of the Parties will determine the intervals and form of subsequent national reports. This determination will be based on the experience of Parties in preparing their first national reports and taking into account the state of implementation of the Convention;

6. *Decides* that Parties shall submit their national reports in one of the working languages of the Conference of the Parties and, for the benefit of others, encourages Parties to also make available their reports electronically and, where possible, on the Internet;

7. *Decides* that national reports submitted by Parties will not be distributed as official documents of the Conference of the Parties, but will be made available to Parties, upon request, and in the language of submission;

8. *Requests* that the Subsidiary Body on Scientific, Technical and Technological Advice instruct any technical panels that it may establish on topical issues to comment on the feasibility and practicalities of developing technical guidelines for national reporting on the subject matter being considered by the panels, and report to the meeting of the Conference of the Parties in 1997;

9. *Requests* the Executive Secretary to prepare a report based on the synthesis of information contained in national reports and other relevant information and containing also suggested next steps, for consideration by the Conference of the Parties;

10. *Requests also* the Executive Secretary to make available to Parties, through the clearing-house mechanism for technical and scientific cooperation, relevant information contained in national reports submitted by Parties in accordance with Article 26 of the Convention;

11. *Urges* all Parties to submit their first national reports to the Secretariat no later than 30 June 1997 to allow consideration of this item by the Conference of the Parties at its fourth meeting;

12. *Urges* the financial mechanism under the Convention to make available financial resources to developing country Parties to assist in the preparation of their national reports;

13. *Commends* the guidance provided in the document 'Guidelines for Preparation of Biodiversity Country Studies', prepared by the United Nations Environment Programme, and the document 'National Biodiversity Planning: Guidelines Based on Early Country Experiences', prepared by the World Resources Institute, the United Nations Environment Programme and the World Conservation Union (IUCN), and its relevance in assisting Parties to implement Article 6 of the Convention and in the preparation of national reports.

Annex:
Suggested guidelines for national reporting on the implementation of Article 6

(a) **Executive summary:** a brief summary of the action plan report, stating succinctly the importance of biodiversity, the commitment to the Convention, the mandate, the participants list, the biotic wealth and national capacity, the goals and gaps, strategic recommendations and characteristics of the action (who will do what, when, where, with what means and funding).

(b) **Introduction:** describe why biodiversity is important to the country and its local communities. Explain the Convention and the nation's commitment to its provisions. Present the aim of the national biodiversity action plan and specify to whom it is directed.

(c) **Background:** describe the legal and policy framework that provides the mandate and instructions for preparing the action plan report. Provide a short summary of the nation's biotic assets, capacity (human resources, institutions, facilities, and funding) and ongoing programmes. Explain the institutional arrangements and responsibilities, with a view to informing people of the manner in which the strategic recommendations will be implemented.

(d) **Goals and objectives:** state the vision for biodiversity and its place in the society, focusing on its protection, scientific understanding, sustainable use, and on the equitable sharing of its benefits and costs. The specific targets to meet the local, national, and international goals in terms of protecting, assessing, utilizing, and benefiting from biodiversity and its components need to be determined.

(e) **Strategy:** summarize the gaps between the current situation in the country and the stated vision, goals and objectives. Summarize the strategic recommendations, including the activities, policies, and tasks that have been selected for implementation to cover the gaps. Assign relative priorities to each.

(f) **Partners:** describe the public and private entities, communities and industries that have participated in the process and have agreed to be responsible for particular activities and investments.

(g) **Action:** present the detailed activities, tasks and policies to be implemented. Explain which partner (Ministry, industry, indigenous group, NGO, or university) will implement each item, where, and what measures the partners will employ.

(h) **Schedule:** present a timetable for the implementation of the various tasks, reflecting the priorities that have been assigned. Note signposts to help signal progress or delay.

(i) **Budget:** provide the budget for the plan of action, showing funding requirements for operating expenses, capital purchases, transport, field costs, etc. List the personnel needed by category of skill or background, the facilities and services required, and possible international technical and financial cooperation.

(j) **Monitoring and evaluation:** explain the measures to be used for tracking the results of the action plan and for monitoring changes in the economy, environment and society. Give the indicators that will be used. Present the individuals and organizations who will carry these responsibilities and how they were selected. Note the audience for the reports, along with the document's content and timing of implementation.

(k) **Sharing of national experience:** present information and case studies which reflect the range of experiences of countries encountered in the implementation of Article 6, taking into account local and external factors.

Recommendation I/5: Scientific and technical information to be contained in the national reports

Recalling Article 26 of the Convention on Biological Diversity, as well as Article 20, paragraph 4;

Recalling also decision 1/7 of the first meeting of the Conference of the Parties which requested the first meeting of the Subsidiary Body on Scientific, Technical and Technological Advice (SBSTTA) to consider as a matter of priority what kind of scientific and technical information should be contained in national reports on measures taken for the implementation of the provisions of the Convention and their effectiveness in meeting the objectives of the Convention;

The first meeting of the SBSTTA recommends to the second meeting of the Conference of the Parties to consider the following elements in deciding on the form and intervals of national reports:

1. The scientific and technical information to be contained in national reports will depend on the expected decisions of the Conference of the Parties on the form and intervals of national reports;

2. Such decisions on the form of national reports should take into account:

   (a) the three-fold objectives of the Convention;

(b) the different socio-economic conditions of Parties, as well as the various stages of the implementation of the Convention at the national level;

(c) the evolving tasks required under the Convention, as well as the evolutionary character of the reporting requirement contained in Article 26 of the Convention;

(d) the comprehensive scope of the Convention, as well as its multisectoral and multidisciplinary approach;

(e) the need for an agreed standard and methodologies for reporting, with particular regard to biological diversity data gathering;

(f) the purposes of reporting, as well as the need to share national experiences and relevant information between Parties;

(g) the need for a flexible form of reporting so that it may be adjusted in the light of progress achieved and experience gained in the implementation of the Convention at the national level;

3. Such decisions on intervals of reporting should take into account the following elements:

(a) the human, technical and financial implications related to the interval of reporting agreed upon;

(b) the time required for the preparation by the Parties and, in particular, the developing countries and countries with economies in transition Parties, of their national reports;

(c) the need to avoid placing a heavy burden on Parties with regard to reporting requirements;

(d) the need also to streamline information contained in national reports of Parties addressed to various fora related to biological diversity, including the Commission on Sustainable Development, so as to avoid duplication of efforts and overlap of reporting activities;

(e) the need to proceed in a step-wise approach.

4. In the light of paragraphs 2 and 3 above, the Conference of the Parties may wish to recommend that the first report of Parties may focus on the measures taken for the implementation of Article 6 of the Convention, as well as the information available in the national country studies on biological diversity. In this regard, the Conference of the Parties may wish to recommend the format contained in the annex of this recommendation. The content of such subject-oriented reports will be based on the outcome of the deliberations of the second meeting of the Conference of the Parties on approaches and experiences related to the implementation of Article 6.

5. The subsequent national reports may focus on selected subjects contained in the medium-term programme of work of the Conference of the Parties and the programme of work of the SBSTTA.

6. Such subject-oriented reports may lead, at a later stage, to a comprehensive report to be submitted by Parties on the implementation of the Convention.

7. In deciding on the form and intervals of national reports, due regard should also be paid to the need to strengthen capacity-building of developing countries and countries with economies in transition Parties, as well as to reflect the financial impli-

cations of such decisions in the budget of the Convention on Biological Diversity, so as to establish adequate administrative and human capacities.

Annex: Possible format of national report on the implementation of Article 6

(a) **Executive summary:** a brief summary of the action plan report, stating succinctly the importance of biodiversity, the commitment to the Convention, the mandate, the participants list, the biotic wealth and national capacity, the goals and gaps, strategic recommendations and characteristics of the action (who will do what, when, where, with what means and funding).

(b) **Introduction:** describe why biodiversity is important to the country and its local communities. Explain the Convention and the nation's commitment to its provisions. Present the aim of the national biodiversity action plan and specify to whom it is directed.

(c) **Background:** describe the legal and policy framework that provides the mandate and instructions for preparing the action plan report. Provide a short summary of the nation's biotic assets, capacity (human resources, institutions, facilities, and funding) and ongoing programmes. Explain the institutional arrangements and responsibilities, with a view to informing people of the manner in which the strategic recommendations will be implemented.

(d) **Goals and objectives:** state the vision for biodiversity and its place in the society, focusing on its protection, scientific understanding, sustainable use, and on the equitable sharing of its benefits and costs. The specific targets to meet the local, national, and international goals in terms of protecting, assessing, utilizing, and benefiting from biodiversity and its components need to be determined.

(e) **Strategy:** summarize the gaps between the current situation in the country and the stated vision, goals and objectives. Summarize the strategic recommendations, including the activities, policies, and tasks that have been selected for implementation to cover the gaps. Assign relative priorities to each.

(f) **Partners:** describe the public and private entities, communities and industries that have participated in the process and have agreed to be responsible for particular activities and investments.

(g) **Action:** present the detailed activities, tasks and policies to be implemented. Explain which partner (ministry, industry, indigenous group, NGO, or university) will implement each item, where, and what measures the partners will employ.

(h) **Schedule:** present a timetable for the implementation of the various tasks, reflecting the priorities that have been assigned. Note signposts to help signal progress or delay.

(i) **Budget:** provide the budget for the plan of action, showing funding requirements for operating expenses, capital purchases, transport, field costs, etc. List the personnel needed by category of skill or background, the facilities and services required, and possible international technical and financial cooperation.

(j) **Monitoring and evaluation:** explain the measures to be used for tracking the results of the action plan and for monitoring changes in the economy, environment and society. Give the indicators that will be used. Present the individuals and organizations who will carry these responsibilities and how they were selected. Note the audience for the reports, along with the document's content and timing of implementation.

(k) **Sharing of national experience:** present success stories on the implementation of Article 6 which might be useful for other Parties.

Decision II/18: Medium-term programme of work of the Conference of the Parties for 1996–1997

The Conference of the Parties,

1. *Decides* to adopt the medium-term programme of work for the period 1996 to 1997 contained in the annex to the present decision;

2. *Also decides* to review at its next meeting the medium-term programme of work in light of the progress achieved in the implementation of the Convention;

3. *Requests* the Executive Secretary to prepare the draft provisional agenda of the third meeting of the Conference of the Parties, pursuant to rules 8 and 9 of the rules of procedure, and include therein all issues arising from its previous meetings and for which actions are required by the Conference of the Parties.

Annex: Medium-term programme of work of the Conference of the Parties 1996–1997

1. The medium-term programme of work will be constructed on the basis of standing and rolling issues.

2. Standing items will include, *inter alia*:

2.1 Matters relating to the financial mechanism, including a report from the interim institutional structure entrusted with its operation;

2.2 Report from the Secretariat on the administration of the Convention and budget for the Secretariat;

2.3 Report from, instructions to and consideration of recommendations from the Subsidiary Body on Scientific, Technical and Technological Advice (SBSTTA);

2.4 Reports by Parties on implementation of the Convention;

2.5 Report on assessment and review of the operation of the clearing-house mechanism;

2.6 Relationship of the Convention on Biological Diversity with the Commission on Sustainable Development and biodiversity-related conventions, other international agreements, institutions and processes of relevance.

3. The other issues and derived activities necessary to implement the Convention should be dealt with on a year-by-year agenda, on the understanding that these relevant rotating issues will be developed and continually dealt with in accordance with the

decisions of the Conference of the Parties by the Subsidiary Body on Scientific, Technical and Technological Advice and any eventual working groups appointed by the Conference of the Parties. The year-by-year agenda has to be flexible.

4. Treatment of the items on the programme of work should also reflect the importance of capacity-building as one of the elements of successful Convention implementation. The programme of work should always reflect a balance among the Convention's objectives, as set forth in Article 1.

5. In 1996, the third meeting of the Conference of the Parties may continue to consider pending issues of the 1995 programme of work.

6. The third meeting of the Conference of the Parties may consider, *inter alia*, the following items in 1996:

6.1 General measures for conservation and sustainable use

6.1.1 Implementation of Articles 6 and 8.

6.2 Identification, monitoring and assessment

6.2.1 To consider options for implementing Article 7;

6.2.2 Appraisal of the SBSTTA review of assessment of biological diversity for the implementation of Article 25 (2) (a) and advice on methodologies for future assessments.

6.3 Conservation and sustainable use of agricultural biological diversity

6.3.1 To consider agricultural biological diversity within the context of the Convention's three objectives and its provisions;

6.3.2 To consider a report on progress under the FAO Global System for the Conservation and Utilization of Plant Genetic Resources for Food and Agriculture.

6.4 Consideration of the future programme of work for terrestrial biological diversity in the light of the outcome of deliberations of the third session of the Commission on Sustainable Development in 1995

6.5 Knowledge, innovations and practices of indigenous and local communities

6.5.1 Implementation of Article 8 (j).

6.6 Access to genetic resources

6.6.1 To consider the compilation of views of Parties on possible options for developing national legislative, administrative or policy measures, as appropriate, to implement Article 15.

6.7 Issues related to technology

6.7.1 To consider ways to promote and facilitate access to and transfer and development of technology, as envisaged by Articles 16 and 18 of the Convention.

6.8 Incentive measures

6.8.1 To consider the compilation of information and experiences shared on the implementation of Article 11.

6.9 Special session of the General Assembly to review implementation of Agenda 21

6.9.1 To provide a report from the perspective of the Convention's three objectives.

6.10 Issues related to biosafety

6.10.1 To consider the first report of the ad hoc working group on biosafety.

7. In 1997, the fourth meeting of the Conference of the Parties may consider, *inter alia*, the following items:

7.1 Review of medium-term programme of work (1995–1997)

7.1.1 To review the operations of the Conference of the Parties and subsidiary organs;

7.1.2 To undertake an overall review and consider a longer-term programme of work.

7.2 Models and mechanisms for linkages between *in situ* and *ex-situ* conservation

7.2.1 To generate options of models and linkage.

7.3 Measures for implementing the Convention

7.3.1 To provide information and share experiences on the implementation of Article 13;

7.3.2 To provide information and share experiences on the implementation of Article 14;

7.3.3 Consideration of biodiversity under threat.

7.4 Consideration of matters related to benefit-sharing

7.4.1 To consider measures to promote and advance the distribution of benefits from biotechnology in accordance with Article 19;

7.4.2 To be considered in the light of the outcome of item 6.7.1 above.

7.5 Technical and Scientific Cooperation

7.6 Terrestrial biological diversity

To assess the status and trends of the biodiversity of inland water ecosystems and identify options for conservation and sustainable use.

Decision II/19: Location of the Secretariat

The Conference of the Parties,

1. *Expresses* its sincere gratitude to the Governments of Canada, Kenya, Spain and Switzerland for their generous offers to host the permanent Secretariat of the Convention;

2. *Decides* to accept the offer of the Government of Canada, contained in document UNEP/CBD/COP/2/Rev.1, to host in Montreal the Secretariat of the Convention on Biological Diversity, established under Article 24 of the Convention;

3. *Requests* the Executive Secretary without delay to discuss and agree with the Government of Canada the practical arrangements for the transfer and hosting of the Secretariat of the Convention in Montreal;

4. *Stresses* that such a transfer should, to the maximum extent possible, minimize the negative impact on the substantive preparation by the Secretariat of the meetings to be convened in 1996 under the auspices of the Convention, and other related activities;

5. *Requests* the Executive Director of the United Nations Environment Programme to negotiate and finalize the headquarters agreement with the Government of Canada;

6. *Further requests* the Executive Secretary to report to its third meeting on the implementation of this decision.

Decision II/20: Financing of and budget for the Convention

The Conference of the Parties,

1. *Decides* that the Trust Fund shall be extended for a period of one year, beginning 1 January 1997 and ending on 31 December 1997;

2. *Adopts* the budget for 1996, which is attached as annex I to this decision;

3. *Urges* all the Parties to pay promptly their contributions to the Trust Fund, based on the scale set forth in Appendix II to the budget (annex I);

4. *Requests* the Parties and States not Parties to the Convention, as well as governmental, intergovernmental and non-governmental organizations and other sources, to contribute to the Trust Fund;

5. *Directs* the Executive Secretary to prepare a report for the Conference of the Parties on the amount of contributions received under the voluntary budget and on ways in which that income has been spent;

6. *Takes note* that the indicative budget for 1997, also attached as annex I to the present decision, is based on Geneva costings;

7. *Requests* the Executive Secretary in presenting a draft 1997 budget for consideration by the third meeting of the Conference of the Parties, to also provide the indicative budget for 1997, attached as annex I to this decision, revised so as to be based on Montreal costings;

8. *Directs* the Executive Secretary to prepare an indicative budget for 1998;

9. *Directs* the Executive Secretary to consider carefully all offers of support from other organizations and to cooperate with them with a view to making the most effective use of the competencies and resources;

10. *Adopts* for 1996 the scale of contributions contained in Appendix II to the budget (annex I), based on the United Nations scale of assessments for the apportionment of the expenses of the United Nations, adjusted to provide that no one contribution shall exceed 25 per cent of the total and that no contribution from a least developed country Party shall exceed 0.01 per cent of the total;

11. *Decides* to transfer to the third meeting of the Conference of the Parties, for further consideration, paragraph 4 of the Financial Rules contained in annex II of the present decision;

12. *Also decides* to transmit paragraph 16 of the Financial Rules to the third meeting of the Conference of the Parties for further consideration.

Annex I:
Proposed budget of the Trust Fund for the Convention on Biological Diversity in 1996–1997

	Inputs	*1996 (US$ thousands)*	*1997***** *(US$ thousands)*
1	**Executive direction and management**		
	Executive Direction		
	Executive Secretary D-2	190	200
	Special Assistant to the Executive Secretary P-3	119	125
	Senior Secretary G-5	84	88
	Support Activities and Technical Reviews	75	79
	Fund Management and Administration		
	Fund Management/Administration Officer P-4 (UNEP/Host country)***	0	–
	Administrative Assistant G-6	105	110
	Clerk G-3	75	79
	subtotal 1	**648**	**680**
2	**Intergovernmental processes and cooperative affairs**		
	Intergovernmental processes		
	Principal Officer D-1	176	185
	Associate Administrative Officer P-2	96	101
	Research Assistant G-5	84	88
	Secretary G-4	80	84
	Support Activities and Technical Reviews	40	42
	Financial Resources and Instruments		
	Programme Officer P-4	142	149
	Support Activities and Technical Reviews	30	32
	Legal Advice and Support		
	Programme Officer P-4	142	149
	Support Activities and Technical Reviews	30	32
	Servicing the Conference of the Parties		
	Servicing COP	930	977
	subtotal 2	**1,750**	**1,838**

3	**Scientific, technical and technological matters**		
	Office of the Principal Officer		
	Principal Officer D-1	176	185
	Programme Officer – Economist P-4	142	149
	Research Assistant G-5	84	88
	Research Assistant G-5	84	88
	Secretary G-4	80	84
	Support Activities and Technical Reviews	60	63
	Conservation Ecology		
	Programme Officer P-4	142	149
	Genetic Resources/Agrobiodiversity		
	Programme Officer P-4 (FAO)+	0	0
	Biotechnology		
	Programme Officer P-5	160	168
	Marine Ecology		
	Programme Officer P-4 (UNESCO)+	0	0
	*Indigenous Knowledge**		
	Programme Officer P-3	0	125
	Servicing of SBSTTA Meetings		
	Servicing of SBSTTA meeting	350	368
	Servicing SBSTTA Panel	23	24
	Servicing and communication of SBSTTA liaison group	20	21
	Servicing of Open-ended working group on Biosafety	492	517
	Servicing Panel meeting on marine and coastal areas	20	21
	subtotal 3	**1,833**	**2,050**
4	**Implementation and communication**		
	Office of the Senior Programme Officer		
	Senior Programme Officer P-5	160	168
	Research Assistant G-5	84	88
	Secretary G-4	80	84
	Support Activities and Technical Reviews	40	42
	Clearing-House Mechanism		
	Programme Officer P-4	142	149
	Data Base Operator P-2	96	101
	Equipment, supplies and material	60	63
	Training Workshops	0	0
	Reports		
	Programme Officer P-3**	50	125
	Library and Documentation Services		
	Librarian/Documentalist P-3	119	125
	Clerk G-3	75	79
	Library acquisitions	50	53

	Communication		
	Programme Officer-Communication P-2 (UNEP)	0	0
	Promotion, awareness raising and publication	138	145
	GBO Publication	0	0
	subtotal 4	**1,094**	**1,221**
5	**Common costs**		
	Travel of staff		
	Travel on official missions	140	147
	Travel to service meetings	70	74
	subtotal 5	**210**	**221**
6	**Equipment**		
	Equipment, (office furniture, pcs, photocopy/printer)	0	0
	Supplies and material	50	53
	subtotal 6	**50**	**53**
7	**Premises*****		
	Rent	–	–
	Security services	–	–
	Building maintenance	–	–
	Utilities (gas, electricity, cleaning, etc.)	70	–
	Insurance	5	–
	subtotal 7	**75**	**0**
8	**Miscellaneous**		
	Temporary assistance and overtime	98	103
	Communications (phone, fax, email, etc)	170	179
	Recruitment costs/travel on interviews	30	30
	Relocation of staff and removal expenses***	–	–
	Hospitality	20	21
	Other	5	5
	subtotal 8	**323**	**338**
	subtotal 1 to 8	**5,983**	**6,399**
9	**Contingencies (2% – subtotal 1 to 8)**	**120**	**128**
	subtotal 1 to 9	**6,103**	**6,527**
10	**Administrative support charge (13%)**	**793**	**849**
11	**Less – contributions from host country*****	–	–
12	**Total Secretariat budget (1 to 11)**	**6,896**	**7,376**

Notes: * The Government of Australia has offered to cover the 1996 salary of Programme Officer on Indigenous Knowledge

** The post of Programme Officer – Reports may be filled towards the end of 1996

*** Amounts to be provided upon completion of host government agreement

**** Geneva costings to be revised to reflect Montreal costings as provided by paragraph 7 of the decision

+ These positions are to be filled by secondees from FAO and UNESCO respectively as of 1 January 1996 on terms and conditions agreed to by the Executive Secretary

Proposed budget for the Convention on Biological Diversity in 1996–1997 covered by additional voluntary contributions

	Inputs	*1996 (US$ thousands)*	*1997**** (US$ thousands)*
1	**Intergovernmental processes and cooperative affairs**		
	Travel of LDCs to COP meeting	270	284
	Travel of COP Bureau	42	44
	Travel of LDCs for COP preparatory meetings	50	53
	subtotal 1	**362**	**380**
2	**Scientific, technical and technological matters**		
	Travel of LDCs to SBSTTA	200	210
	Travel of SBSTTA Bureau	30	32
	Travel of SBSTTA Panel	75	79
	Travel of LDCs to Biosafety meeting	200	210
	Trave of Panel on Marine and Coastal Areas	70	74
	Research Assistant++	84	88
	Support Activities	80	84
	subtotal 2	**739**	**776**
3	**Implementation and communication**		
	Support Activities and Technical Reviews	70	74
	Clearing-House Mechanism (5 workshops a year)	150	158
	subtotal 3	**220**	**231**
	Total (1 TO 3)	**1,321**	**1,387**
4	**Administrative support charge (13%)**	**172**	**180**
5	**Total budget (1 to 4)**	**1,493**	**1,567**

Note: ++ To work under Principal Officer – Scientific, Technical and Technological matters with most of the incumbent's time spent on research on indigenous knowledge

Appendix I to annex I: Convention on Biological Diversity organization chart, 1996–1997

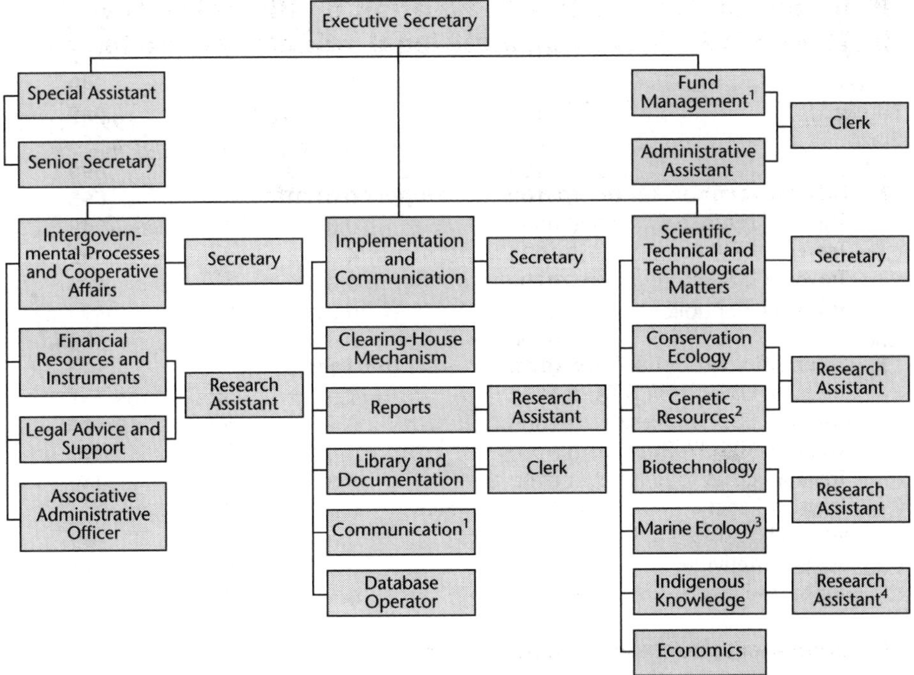

Notes:
1 Seconded by UNEP. 2 Seconded by FAO. 3 Seconded by UNESCO. 4 To be funded through voluntary contributions.

Appendix II to annex I: Scale of 1996 contributions to the Trust Fund for the Convention on Biological Diversity

	United Nations scale of assessments 1996[1] *(%)*	*Scale for the Trust Fund with 25% ceiling and no least developed country Party paying more than 0.01% (%)*	*Contributions as per 1 January 1996 (US$ thousands)*
Albania	0.0100	0.0138	949
Algeria	0.1600	0.2201	15,180
Antigua & Barbuda	0.0100	0.0138	949
Argentina	0.4800	0.6604	45,539
Armenia	0.0550	0.0757	5,218
Australia	1.4800	2.0361	140,411
Austria	0.8650	1.1900	82,065
Bahamas	0.0200	0.0275	1,897

Bangladesh	0.0100	0.0100	690
Barbados	0.0100	0.0138	949
Belarus	0.2925	0.4024	27,750
Belize	0.0100	0.0138	949
Benin	0.0100	0.0100	690
Bhutan	0.0100	0.0100	690
Bolivia	0.0100	0.0138	949
Botswana	0.0100	0.0138	949
Brazil	1.6200	2.2287	153,693
Burkina Faso	0.0100	0.0100	690
Cambodia	0.0100	0.0100	690
Cameroon	0.0100	0.0138	949
Canada	3.1025	4.2683	294,342
Cape Verde	0.0100	0.0100	690
Central African Republic	0.0100	0.0100	690
Chad	0.0100	0.0100	690
Chile	0.0800	0.1101	7,590
China	0.7350	1.0112	69,731
Colombia	0.1000	0.1376	9,487
Comoros	0.0100	0.0100	690
Cook Islands	0.0100	0.0138	949
Costa Rica	0.0100	0.0138	949
Cote d'Ivoire	0.0100	0.0138	949
Cuba	0.0525	0.0722	4,981
Czech Republic	0.2600	0.3577	24,667
Democratic People's Republic of Korea	0.0500	0.0688	4,744
Denmark	0.7175	0.9871	68,071
Djibouti	0.0100	0.0100	690
Dominica	0.0100	0.0138	949
Ecuador	0.0200	0.0275	1,897
Egypt	0.0700	0.0963	6,641
El Salvador	0.0100	0.0138	949
Equatorial Guinea	0.0100	0.0100	690
Estonia	0.0425	0.0585	4,032
Ethiopia	0.0100	0.0100	690
European Community		2.5000	172,400
Fiji	0.0100	0.0138	949
Finland	0.6175	0.8495	58,584
France	6.4075	8.8152	607,895
Gambia	0.0100	0.0100	690
Georgia	0.1175	0.1617	11,148
Germany	9.0425	12.4403	857,884
Ghana	0.0100	0.0138	949
Greece	0.3800	0.5228	36,052
Grenada	0.0100	0.0138	949
Guatemala	0.0200	0.0275	1,897
Guinea	0.0100	0.0100	690
Guinea-Bissau	0.0100	0.0100	690
Guyana	0.0100	0.0138	949
Honduras	0.0100	0.0138	949

Hungary	0.1400	0.1926	13,282
Iceland	0.0300	0.0413	2,846
India	0.3100	0.4265	29,410
Indonesia	0.1400	0.1926	13,282
Israel	0.2675	0.3680	25,378
Italy	5.1975	7.1505	493,100
Jamaica	0.0100	0.0138	949
Japan	15.4350	21.2349	1,464,357
Jordan	0.0100	0.0138	949
Kazakhstan	0.2000	0.2752	18,974
Kenya	0.0100	0.0138	949
Kiribati	0.0100	0.0100	690
Lebanon	0.0100	0.0138	949
Lesotho	0.0100	0.0100	690
Luxembourg	0.0700	0.0963	6,641
Malawi	0.0100	0.0100	690
Malaysia	0.1400	0.1926	13,282
Maldives	0.0100	0.0100	690
Mali	0.0100	0.0100	690
Marshall Islands	0.0100	0.0138	949
Mauritius	0.0100	0.0138	949
Mexico	0.7875	1.0834	74,712
Micronesia (Federated States of)	0.0100	0.0138	949
Monaco	0.0100	0.0138	949
Mongolia	0.0100	0.0138	949
Morocco	0.0300	0.0413	2,846
Mozambique	0.0100	0.0100	690
Myanmar	0.0100	0.0100	690
Nauru	0.0100	0.0138	949
Nepal	0.0100	0.0100	690
Netherlands	1.5875	2.1840	150,610
New Zealand	0.2400	0.3302	22,769
Niger	0.0100	0.0100	690
Nigeria	0.1150	0.1582	10,910
Norway	0.5600	0.7704	53,129
Oman	0.0400	0.0550	3,795
Pakistan	0.0600	0.0825	5,692
Panama	0.0100	0.0138	949
Papua New Guinea	0.0100	0.0138	949
Paraguay	0.0100	0.0138	949
Peru	0.0600	0.0825	5,692
Philippines	0.0600	0.0825	5,692
Portugal	0.2750	0.3783	26,090
Republic of Korea	0.8175	1.1247	77,558
Republic of Moldova	0.0850	0.1169	8,064
Romania	0.1500	0.2064	14,231
Russian Federation	4.4500	6.1221	422,183
Saint Kitts and Nevis	0.0100	0.0138	949
Saint Lucia	0.0100	0.0138	949
Samoa	0.0100	0.0100	690

San Marino	0.0100	0.0138	949
Senegal	0.0100	0.0138	949
Seychelles	0.0100	0.0138	949
Sierra Leone	0.0100	0.0100	690
Slovakia	0.0825	0.1135	7,827
Solomon Islands	0.0100	0.0100	690
South Africa	0.3225	0.4437	30,596
Spain	2.3625	3.2502	224,136
Sri Lanka	0.0100	0.0138	949
Sudan	0.0100	0.0100	690
Swaziland	0.0100	0.0138	949
Sweden	1.2275	1.6887	116,456
Switzerland	1.2100	1.6647	114,796
Togo	0.0100	0.0100	690
Tunisia	0.0300	0.0413	2,846
Uganda	0.0100	0.0100	690
Ukraine	1.1400	1.5684	108,155
United Kingdom of Great Britain and Northern Ireland	5.3150	7.3122	504,247
Uruguay	0.0400	0.0550	3,795
Uzbekistan	0.1375	0.1892	13,045
Vanuatu	0.0100	0.0100	690
Venezuela	0.3375	0.4643	32,019
Viet Nam	0.0100	0.0138	949
Zaire	0.0100	0.0100	690
Zambia	0.0100	0.0100	690
Zimbabwe	0.0100	0.0138	949
	70.9600	**100.0000**	**6,896,000**

Note: 1 United Nations Report of the Committee on Contributions, Supplement No. 11 (A/49/11).

Annex II:
Financial rules for the administration of the Trust Fund for the Convention on Biological Diversity

1. The Conference of the Parties to the Convention shall designate an organization (hereinafter referred to as the Trustee) which shall establish and manage the Trust Fund for the Convention on Biological Diversity (hereinafter referred to as the Trust Fund) in accordance with these rules.

2. The Trust Fund shall be used for funding the administration of the Convention including the functions of the Secretariat.

3. The Trust Fund shall be financed from:

(a) Contributions made by Parties to the Convention based on the scale set forth in the Appendix to the budget;

(b) Additional contributions made by such Parties;

(c) Contributions from States not Parties to the Convention, as well as governmental, intergovernmental and non-governmental organizations, and other sources.

4. It is for the Conference of the Parties to determine the scale referred to in paragraph 3 (a) above. The scale is to be based on the United Nations scale of assessments for the apportionment of the expenses of the United Nations [adjusted to provide that no one contribution shall exceed 25 per cent of the total, [and] no contributions shall be required when the United Nations scale provides for a contribution of less than 0.1 per cent], [and no developing country Party shall be required to pay more than any developed country Party]. [The Conference of the Parties will develop possible methodologies for the principle of common but differentiated responsibility of developed and developing countries to be reflected in the scale of assessment.] [This scale of assessment shall apply unless amended by the Conference of the Parties.] The contributions referred to in paragraph 3 (a) shall be due on 1 January of each calendar year.

5. All contributions shall be paid in United States dollars or its equivalent in a convertible currency and into a bank account to be specified by the Trustee. In conversion of currencies into United States dollars, the United Nations operational rate of exchange shall be used.

6. Accounting records shall be kept in such currency or currencies as the Trustee deems necessary.

7. (a) Budget proposals expressed in United States dollars covering the expenditure and income from contributions referred to in paragraph 3 (a) above shall be prepared by the head of the Secretariat (hereinafter referred to as the Executive Secretary) for periods of two calendar years at the minimum. At least 90 days before the date fixed for the opening of each ordinary meeting of the Conference of the Parties, these budget proposals shall be dispatched by the Executive Secretary to all Parties to the Convention.

(b) The budget shall, in accordance with Rule 16, be approved by the Conference of the Parties and, if necessary, be revised at an ordinary or extraordinary meeting of the Parties.

8. Contributions referred to in paragraphs 3 (b) and (c) shall be used in accordance with any terms and conditions agreed between the Executive Secretary and the respective contributor. At each ordinary meeting of the Conference of the Parties, the Executive Secretary shall present a report on contributions received and expected as well as their sources, amounts, purposes and conditions.

9. The Executive Secretary may commit resources against the Trust Fund only if such commitments are covered by contributions already received. In the event that the Trustee anticipates that there might be a shortfall in resources over the financial period as a whole, it shall notify the Executive Secretary, who shall adjust the budget so that expenditures are at all times fully covered by contributions received.

10. The Trustee, on the advice of the Executive Secretary, may make transfers from one budget line to another within the budget in accordance with the Financial Regulations and Rules of the United Nations.

11. Contributions referred to in paragraph 3 (a) above from States and regional economic integration organizations that become Parties to the Convention after the beginning of a financial period shall be made *pro rata temporis* for the balance of that financial period. Consequent adjustments shall be made at the end of each financial period for other Parties.

12. Contributions not immediately required for the purposes of the Trust Fund shall be invested, and any interest so earned shall be credited to the Trust Fund.

13. It is for the Conference of the Parties and the Trustee to agree on an administrative support charge to be paid to the Trustee.

14. At the end of each calendar year, the Trustee shall transfer any balance to the following calendar year and submit to the Conference of the Parties, through the Executive Secretary, the certified and audited accounts for that year as soon as practicable. The Trust Fund shall be subjected to the internal and external auditing procedure of the United Nations as laid down in its Financial Regulations and Rules of the United Nations.

15. In the event that the Conference of the Parties decides to terminate the Trust Fund, a notification to that effect shall be presented to the Trustee at least six months before the date of termination selected by the Conference of the Parties. The Conference of the Parties shall decide, in consultation with the Trustee, on the distribution on any unspent balance after all liquidation expenses have been met.

[16A. The Parties shall reach agreement by consensus on:

(a) The scale and any subsequent revision to it;

(b) The budget.]

[16B. The Parties shall make every effort to reach agreement on the budget by consensus. If all efforts to reach consensus on the budget have been exhausted and no agreement has been reached, the budget shall, as a last resort, be adopted by a [two-thirds] [four-fifths] majority vote of the Parties present and voting representing a [two-thirds] [four-fifths] majority vote of the developing country Parties present and voting and a [two-thirds] [four-fifths] majority vote of the other Parties present and voting.]

17. Any amendments to these rules shall be adopted by the Conference of the Parties by consensus.

Decision II/21: Venue and date of the third meeting of the Conference of the Parties

The Conference of the Parties,

1. *Welcomes* the kind offer of the Government of Argentina to host the third meeting of the Conference of the Parties ;

2. *Decides* that the third meeting of the Conference of the Parties will take place in Buenos Aires, Argentina, from 4 to 15 November 1996, including the Ministerial-level segment on 13 and 14 November 1996 ;

3. *Decides also* that Argentina will be an ex officio member of the Bureau of the second meeting of the Conference of the Parties.

Decision II/22: Convening of regional and subregional meetings for Parties to the Convention

The Conference of the Parties,

Appreciating the assistance of the Secretariat of the Convention on Biological Diversity in convening regional and subregional meetings for the Parties to the Convention, especially developing country Parties, in preparation for the second meeting of the Conference of the Parties,

Having benefited from such regional meetings by adopting decisions on the second meeting of the Conference of the Parties' agenda items,

1. *Requests* the Secretariat of the Convention on Biological Diversity to convene regional and subregional meetings, especially for developing country Parties, to prepare for the third meeting of the Conference of the Parties;

2. *Urges* the Secretariat of the Convention to seek voluntary contributions for such meetings and to facilitate the participation of developing country Parties and, in particular, the least developed countries.

Decision II/23: Tribute to the Government and people of the Republic of Indonesia

The Conference of the Parties,

Having met in Jakarta from 6 to 17 November 1995, at the gracious invitation of the Government of the Republic of Indonesia,

Deeply appreciative of the special courtesy and the warm hospitality extended by the Government and people of Indonesia to the Ministers, members of the delegations, observers and members of the Secretariat attending the meeting;

Expresses its sincere gratitude to the Government of the Republic of Indonesia and to its people for the cordial welcome which they accorded to the Conference of the Parties and to those associated with its work and for their contribution to the success of the second meeting of the Conference of the Parties to the Convention on Biological Diversity.

Decisions adopted by the third meeting of the Conference of the Parties

Buenos Aires, Argentina, 4–15 November 1996

Decision III/1: Pending issues arising from the work of the second meeting of the Conference of the Parties

The Conference of the Parties,

Having considered paragraphs 4 and 16 of the financial rules for the administration of the Trust Fund for the Convention on Biological Diversity and paragraph 1 of rule 40 of the rules of procedure for meetings of the Conference of the Parties,

1. *Decides* to transmit to the fourth meeting of the Conference of the Parties, for further consideration, paragraph 4 of the financial rules as contained in the annex to the present decision;

2. *Also decides* to transmit to the fourth meeting of the Conference of the Parties, for further consideration, paragraph 16 of the financial rules as contained in annex II of decision II/20, entitled 'Financing of and budget for the Convention', contained in document UNEP/CBD/COP/2/19.

3. *Further decides* to transmit to its fourth meeting for further consideration paragraph 1 of rule 40 of the rules of procedure for meetings of the Conference of the Parties.

Annex

'It is for the Conference of the Parties to determine the scale referred to in paragraph 3 (a) above. The scale is based on the United Nations scale of assessments for the apportionment of the expenses of the United Nations [adjusted to provide that no developing country Party shall be required to pay more than any developed country Party]. This scale of assessments shall apply unless amended by the Conference of the Parties. The contributions referred to in paragraph 3 (a) shall be due on 1 January of each calendar year.'

Appendix to Annex: Financial rules for the administration of the Trust Fund for the Convention on Biological Diversity[4]

Decision III/2: Report and recommendations of the second meeting of the Subsidiary Body on Scientific, Technical and Technological Advice

The Conference of the Parties,

Recalling its decision II/1, which endorsed recommendation I/1 of the Subsidiary Body on Scientific, Technical and Technological Advice on the *modus operandi* of that Body, and which requested it to keep under review its *modus operandi* with a view to improving its functioning on the basis of experience gained,

Noting, in particular, the recommendation of the Subsidiary Body on Scientific, Technical and Technological Advice that it adopt a thematic approach to its work,

1. *Takes note* of the report of the second meeting of the Subsidiary Body on Scientific, Technical and Technological Advice, held at the seat of the Secretariat from 2 to 6 September 1996, contained in document UNEP/CBD/COP/3/3;

2. *Notes* recommendation II/11 of the Subsidiary Body on Scientific, Technical and Technological Advice which contains the proposed revised elements of its *modus operandi*, and decides to consider this recommendation further at its fourth meeting as part of the longer-term review of the programme of work and the operations of the Conference of the Parties and subsidiary organs.

Decision III/3: Use of languages in the meetings of the Subsidiary Body on Scientific, Technical and Technological Advice

The Conference of the Parties,

Recalling the recommendations of the Subsidiary Body on Scientific, Technical and Technological Advice contained in document UNEP/CBD/COP/3/3,

1. *Takes note* of the concern expressed by several delegations that the proceedings of the Subsidiary Body on Scientific, Technical and Technological Advice are conducted only in the working languages of the Conference of the Parties;

2. *Takes note also* of the estimates given by the Secretariat of the cost of holding meetings of the Subsidiary Body on Scientific, Technical and Technological Advice in the six languages of the United Nations;

4 The financial rules for the administration of the Trust Fund for the Convention on Biological Diversity are reproduced in Section V of this Handbook.

3. *Decides* that the meetings of the Subsidiary Body on Scientific, Technical and Technological Advice will be held in the six official languages of the United Nations and that the *modus operandi* of the Subsidiary Body on Scientific, Technical and Technological Advice will be modified accordingly;

4. *Further decides* that the amount of US$500,000 will be allocated in the core budget to cover administrative costs of servicing the Subsidiary Body on Scientific, Technical and Technological Advice meeting in 1997.

Decision III/4: Clearing-house mechanism to promote and facilitate technical and scientific cooperation

The Conference of the Parties,

Recalling decision I/3 of the Conference of Parties, that a clearing-house mechanism should be established, in accordance with Article 18, paragraph 3, of the Convention, to promote and facilitate technical and scientific cooperation,

Recalling also decision II/3 of the Conference of Parties on the development of the clearing-house mechanism through the establishment of a pilot phase for 1996–1997 and related activities to promote technical and scientific cooperation,

Having examined the note by the Executive Secretary, contained in document UNEP/CBD/COP/3/4, which emphasizes the main features of the operational framework of the pilot phase of the clearing-house mechanism, namely, information linking and organization, visualization and the decision support function,

Noting that progress made to date in the implementation of the pilot phase has produced valuable insights as to the future development of the clearing-house mechanism and *concerned* that it is now time for these initial experiences to be brought together and advanced in a systematic manner so as to ensure that the clearing-house mechanism is expeditiously implemented in accordance with the expectations of the Parties,

Noting also:

(a) The crucial part played by technical and scientific cooperation on all aspects of biological diversity, including taxonomy and transfer of technology, in ensuring the capacity of the clearing-house mechanism to play an important role in the implementation of the Convention;

(b) The need for the clearing-house mechanism to be clearly focused on the implementation of the Convention;

(c) The need for the clearing-house mechanism activities to include information exchange modalities additional to the Internet to ensure the participation of Parties without Internet access;

(d) The need for capacity-building for the purposes of the clearing-house mechanism in developing countries, including training on information systems technologies that will allow developing countries to take advantage of the recent developments in electronic communication, including the Internet;

(e) The advantages of country-driven pilot projects focused on priority areas identified by the Conference of Parties which would enable developing countries to begin to implement the main features of the pilot phase of the clearing-house mechanism,

1. *Decides* that the pilot phase approved in its decision II/3 shall be extended for a further year, until December 1998;

2. *Requests* the Global Environment Facility to support the activities referred to in paragraphs (d) and (e) above as critical components in the implementation of the clearing-house mechanism at the national, subregional and regional levels, including in the pilot phase;

3. *Further requests* the interim financial mechanism to implement its revised operational criteria for enabling activities in relation to the clearing-house mechanism to give effect, as quickly as possible, to the recommendations contained in paragraph 2 above;

4. *Also requests* Governments and other bilateral and multilateral funding institutions, as far as possible and as appropriate, to provide funding for capacity-building related to the implementation of the clearing-house mechanism;

5. *Requests* Governments and relevant financial, scientific and technical institutions to facilitate, including through the provision of voluntary contributions, regional workshops with a view to attaining a clear definition of country and regional-level scientific and technical information needs and priorities identified and modalities to deliver information and evaluate national capacities for the implementation of the Convention. Such workshops should also review experience in scientific and technical cooperation in support of the objectives of the Convention, in order to identify ways by which the clearing-house mechanism can best facilitate such cooperation;

6. *Emphasizes* that the key characteristics of the clearing-house mechanism are, *inter alia*, that it should be compatible with national capacities, needs-driven and decentralized in nature, should provide access to meta-data, should provide support to the decision-making process, and should to the extent possible involve the private sector;

7. *Recommends* that the clearing-house mechanism should disseminate, in addition to scientific and technical information, information on policy and management issues relevant to the implementation of the Convention;

8. *Endorses* the proposal of the Secretariat for the publication of a clearing-house mechanism newsletter;

9. *Recognizes* that ownership of all information made available through the clearing-house mechanism shall remain with the provider of the information;

10. *Agrees* that the clearing-house mechanism shall be assisted in its functioning by an informal advisory committee, constituted and coordinated by the Executive Secretary in a transparent manner, which will guide and integrate the development of the pilot phase activities and endeavour to ensure that all Parties can participate in the pilot phase of the clearing-house mechanism;

11. *Recommends* that one important role of the clearing-house mechanism at the national level should be to provide relevant information linkages to the national focal points and relevant thematic focal points, in order to facilitate the fair and

equitable sharing of the benefits arising out of the utilization of genetic resources. Linkages to patent offices in each country for up-to-date information on new patent registrations and patents in the public domain provide an example of one mechanism;

12. *Recommends* that the work of the clearing-house mechanism at the international level focus on providing thematic focal points for linking to the activities at the national and regional level;

13. *Recognizes* that close cooperation is needed with other conventions and agreements, and requests the Secretariat to identify those activities and organizations which could support the clearing-house mechanism, and to provide appropriate advice to the Subsidiary Body on Scientific, Technical and Technological Advice at its next meeting;

14. *Recognizes* the role of the Secretariat in the coordination of the successful implementation of the clearing-house mechanism, and recommends that the clearing-house mechanism posts within the Secretariat should be filled as soon as possible;

15. *Requests* all Parties to designate their clearing-house mechanism national focal points and make them operational as soon as possible;

16. *Requests* those Parties with access to the Internet to connect their national clearing-house mechanism homepage to the Secretariat's clearing-house mechanism homepage on the Internet, where possible, and further requests the Executive Secretary and partners to collaborate on the provision of advice to Parties and others on, *inter alia*, the necessary layout and system specifications.

Decision III/5: Additional guidance to the financial mechanism

The Conference of the Parties,

Bearing in mind Articles 20 and 21 of the convention,

Underlining the importance of paragraphs 1 and 4 of Article 20 of the Convention,

Taking into account, in particular, paragraph 6 of decision II/6,

Recalling paragraph 6 of decision II/7, which emphasizes the importance of capacity/building and requests the interim financial mechanism under the convention to facilitate the urgent implementation of Articles 6 and 8 of the Convention by making available to developing country Parties financial resources for projects in a flexible and expeditious manner,

Recognizing that the Global Environment Facility, as stated in its Operational Principles for Development and Implementation of its Work Programme will maintain sufficient flexibility to respond to changing circumstances, including evolving guidance of the Conference of the Parties and experience gained from monitoring and evaluation activities,

Recognizing further that the Global Environment Facility, in its operational criteria for enabling activities for biodiversity, anticipates that these criteria will need to be reviewed and revised on the basis of early implementation experience, as necessary,

Recognizing progress made by the Global Environment Facility, in particular, concerning the Global Environment Facility decisions on medium-sized projects and enabling activities,

Recognizing also difficulties encountered with the application of the Operational Strategy of the Global Environment Facility, the project appraisal process, the application of the criteria for determining incremental costs and the procedures applied by the Implementing Agencies,

Recognizing further the need for a balanced implementation of the provisions of the Convention,

Taking note of the report of the Global Environment Facility to the third meeting of the Conference of the Parties, in which information was provided on the efforts to ensure that funding of its activities is in conformity with the policy, strategy, eligibility criteria and programme priorities of the Conference of the Parties, and in particular, the expedited procedures adopted for enabling activities in the biodiversity focal area,

1. *Urges* the Implementing Agencies of the Global Environment Facility to enhance cooperation to increase efforts to improve the processing and delivery systems of the Global Environment Facility;

2. *Decides* to provide the following additional guidance to the Global Environment Facility in the provision of financial resources in conformity with decisions I/2 and II/6 of the first and second meetings of the Conference of the Parties. In this regard, the Global Environment Facility shall provide financial resources to developing countries for country-driven activities and programmes, consistent with national priorities and objectives, recognizing that economic and social development and poverty eradication are the first and overriding priorities of developing countries:

(a) For capacity-building in biosafety, including for the implementation by developing countries of the UNEP International Technical Guidelines on Safety in Biotechnology;

(b) For capacity-building, including taxonomy, to enable developing countries to develop and carry out an initial assessment for designing, implementing and monitoring programmes in accordance with Article 7, taking into account the special need of small island States (*Note:* The Conference of the Parties endorsed recommendation II/2 of the Subsidiary Body on Scientific, Technical and Technological Advice, concerning capacity-building for taxonomy);

(c) For supporting, as a priority, efforts for the conservation and sustainable use of biological diversity important to agriculture, in accordance with decision 3/11;

(d) For supporting the following activities as critical components in the implementation of the clearing-house mechanism at the national, subregional and regional levels, including in the pilot phase, to which critical components the Global Environment Facility shall give effect by implementing its revised operational criteria for enabling activities in relation to the clearing-house mechanism as quickly as possible:

(i) capacity-building for the purpose of the clearing-house mechanism, including training in information systems technologies that will allow developing countries to take advantage of the recent developments in electronic communication, including the Internet;

(ii) country-driven pilot projects, focused on priority areas identified by the Conference of the Parties which would enable developing countries to begin to implement the main features of the pilot-phase of the clearing-house mechanism;

3. *Reconfirms* the importance of the Global Environment Facility's support for incentive measures, guidance for which was contained in Annex I to decision I/2, paragraph 4 (i), taking note of decision III/18;

4. *Urges* the Global Environment Facility, along with Governments, regional economic integration organizations, and competent international, regional and national organizations, to support human and institutional capacity-building programmes for Governments, non-governmental organizations and local and indigenous communities, as appropriate, to promote the successful development and implementation of legislative, administrative and policy measures and guidances on access to genetic resources, including scientific, technical, business, legal and management skills and capacities;

5. *Requests* the Global Environment Facility to examine the support of capacity-building projects for indigenous and local communities embodying traditional lifestyles related to the preservation and maintenance of their knowledge, innovations and practices relevant for the conservation and sustainable use of biological diversity with their prior informed consent and their participation;

6. *Requests* the Global Environment Facility, in preparing projects in conformity with the Conference of the Parties guidance on policy, strategy, programme priorities and eligibility criteria, to include in such projects, when relevant to the project's objectives and consistent with national priorities, project components addressing:

(a) Targeted research which contributes to conservation of biological diversity and the sustainable use of its components including research for reversing current trends of biodiversity loss and species extinction;

(b) Promotion of the understanding of the importance of, and measures required for, the conservation and sustainable use of biological diversity;

7. *Requests* the Secretariat of the Convention and the Global Environment Facility to collaborate in preparing, for consideration by the Conference of the Parties at its fourth meeting, a proposal on the means to address the fair and equitable sharing of the benefits arising out of genetic resources including assistance to developing country Parties.

Decision III/6: Additional financial resources

The Conference of the Parties,

Recalling Article 21, paragraph 4, of the Convention, which states that 'the Contracting Parties shall consider strengthening existing financial institutions to provide financial resources for the conservation and sustainable use of biological diversity', as well as Article 20, paragraph 2,

Recalling also decision II/6, by which it requested the Executive Secretary to explore possibilities to identify additional financial resources, to continue to monitor the availability of additional financial resources, and to study characteristics specific to biological diversity activities to allow the Conference of the Parties to make suggestions to funding institutions on how to make their activities in the area of biological diversity more supportive of the Convention,

Recognizing the importance of identifying alternative sources of funding in support of the Convention,

Taking note of elements contained in documents UNEP/CBD/COP/3/7 and UNEP/CBD/COP/3/37,

1. *Urges* all funding institutions, including bilateral and multilateral donors as well as regional funding institutions and non-governmental organizations, to strive to make their activities more supportive of the Convention, taking into account, *inter alia*, relevant elements contained in document UNEP/CBD/COP/3/7;

2. *Requests* the Executive Secretary:

(a) To explore as soon as possible ways of collaborating with funding institutions to facilitate these efforts to achieve greater support for the Convention;

(b) To invite all funding institutions to provide information to the Secretariat on ways in which their activities support the Convention, and further requests the Secretariat to submit a report to the next Conference of the Parties on the basis of this information;

3. *Requests* the Executive Secretary to explore further possibilities for encouraging the involvement of the private sector in supporting the Convention's objectives;

4. *Urges* developed country Parties to cooperate in the development, where possible, of standardized information on their financial support for the objectives of the Convention on Biological Diversity. Where possible, these Parties should submit this information to the Secretariat of the Convention on Biological Diversity in their national reports;

5. *Invites* other funding institutions, including bilateral and multilateral donors as well as regional funding institutions and non-governmental organizations, to compile information on their financial support for the Convention and to provide the Secretariat with such information;

6. *Requests* the Executive Secretary to make the information referred to above available to the Conference of the Parties.

Decision III/7: Guidelines for the review of the effectiveness of the financial mechanism

The Conference of the Parties,

Recalling paragraph 3 of Article 21 of the Convention on Biological Diversity, which provides for the Conference of Parties to review the effectiveness of the financial mechanism,

Recalling further decision II/6, paragraph 3, on the further development of the guidelines for the review of the effectiveness of the financial mechanism for consideration and decision by the Conference of the Parties at its third meeting,

1. *Decides* to adopt the attached Annex, containing the objectives and criteria for the first review of the effectiveness of the financial mechanism to be conducted in time for the fourth meeting of the Conference of the Parties;

2. *Decides also* that the review referred to in paragraph 3 of Article 21 of the Convention should be conducted under the authority of the Conference of the Parties;

3. *Decides further* that, based on the results of the review, the Conference of the Parties shall take appropriate action to improve the effectiveness of the mechanism if necessary.

Annex:
Objectives and criteria for the first review of the effectiveness of the financial mechanism

A Objectives

1. In accordance with Article 21, paragraph 3, of the Convention, the objectives shall be to review and take appropriate action, if necessary, to improve:

(a) The effectiveness of the financial mechanism in providing financial resources;

(b) The conformity of the activities of the restructured Global Environment Facility (GEF), as the institutional structure operating the financial mechanism on an interim basis, with the guidance of the Conference of the Parties; and

(c) The effectiveness of GEF-funded activities on the implementation of the Convention.

B Methodology

2. The review shall draw upon, *inter alia*, the following sources of information:

(a) Information provided by the Parties on their experiences gained through activities funded by the financial mechanism;

(b) Annual reviews by the Conference of the Parties on the conformity of the activities of the financial mechanism with the guidance of the Conference of the Parties;

(c) The GEF annual report to the Conference of the Parties on its activities as the institutional structure to operate the financial mechanism, the annual reports of GEF and other relevant GEF policy and information documents;

(d) Reports from the GEF monitoring and evaluation programme;

(e) Information available from the United Nations Commission on Sustainable Development and the Organisation for Economic Cooperation and Development, and relevant bilateral and multilateral funding institutions; and

(f) Information provided by inter-governmental organizations and non-governmental organizations.

C Criteria

3. The effectiveness of the financial mechanism shall be assessed against, *inter alia*, the following criteria:

(a) The effectiveness of the financial mechanism in providing financial resources for the implementation of the Convention's objectives in respect of, *inter alia*:

- (i) the adequacy, predictability and timely disbursement of funds for projects;
- (ii) the responsiveness and efficiency of the GEF project cycle and operational strategy as it relates to biological diversity;
- (iii) the ability of GEF to leverage additional finance; and
- (iv) the sustainability of funded projects;[5] and

(b) Application of the criteria of agreed full incremental costs to enable developing country Parties to implement the Convention, keeping in mind the provision of new and additional financial resources, in accordance with Article 20.2;

(c) The conformity of the activities of the financial mechanism with the guidance of the Conference of the Parties, as contained in decisions I/2, II/3, II/6, II/7, II/17 and III/5, which include:

- (i) the eligibility criteria;
- (ii) programme priorities;
- (iii) the provision of financial resources for projects in a flexible and expeditious manner to facilitate the Parties' urgent implementation of Articles 6 and 8 of the Convention;
- (iv) the programme of grants for medium-sized projects; and
- (v) decision II/17 on national reporting by the Parties; and

(d) The effectiveness of GEF-funded activities on the implementation of the Convention.[6]

D Procedures

4. Under the authority and with the support of the Conference of the Parties, the Secretariat shall prepare background documentation for review by the Conference of the Parties and submit this documentation to the Parties at least three months before the fourth meeting of the Conference of the Parties, according to the above criteria, and shall, if necessary, appoint a consultant for this purpose.

5. In compiling the information for the review the Secretariat shall develop a questionnaire using the criteria adopted in this decision to be sent to the Parties for the provision of required information.

---

5 The Conference of the Parties recognizes that sustainability is a shared responsibility of the financial mechanism and the Parties.

6 The impact that the activities funded have on the realization of the Convention's objectives is of a long-term nature and thus information on impacts may not be available until further project experience has been gained.

6. The Secretariat shall also ensure that field visits are effected in a selected number of country Parties in all geographical regions, in order to assess the process and to identify impediments, if any.

7. The Secretariat shall take the opportunity of relevant meetings to meet and interview stakeholders, including GEF and its Implementing Agencies.

8. On the basis of all information received, the Secretariat will prepare a synthesis to assess the progress in meeting the requirements of this annex. This synthesis will be sent for appraisal by five representatives of Parties nominated on a regional basis to ensure that the requirements of this annex will be met in a timely and comprehensive manner. Taking account of comments received, the Secretariat will distribute copies of the synthesis to all Parties and relevant bodies for their comments and any further contributions. On the basis of these, the Secretariat will prepare a draft report, which will be presented to the above regional representatives to ensure its compliance with the terms of this annex. The draft report will also be made available to GEF and the Implementing Agencies. The Secretariat will submit the synthesis report, with supporting documents as necessary, to Parties not later than three months prior to the fourth meeting of the Conference of the Parties. The supporting documents will include any comments and other information identified by source.

9. The Conference of the Parties shall, if necessary, take appropriate actions to improve the effectiveness of the financial mechanism and/or the effectiveness of this review procedure.

Decision III/8: Memorandum of understanding between the Conference of the Parties to the Convention on Biological Diversity and the Council of the Global Environment Facility

The Conference of the Parties,

Recalling Articles 20 and 21 of the Convention on Biological Diversity,

Recalling further decision 11/6 on financial resources and mechanism,

1. *Adopts* the Memorandum of Understanding contained in the annex to the present decision;

2. *Requests* the Executive Secretary to transmit this decision to the Council of the Global Environment Facility.

Annex:
Memorandum of Understanding between the Conference of the Parties to the Convention on Biological Diversity and the Council of the Global Environment Facility

Preamble

The Conference of the Parties to the Convention on Biological Diversity (hereinafter the Conference of the Parties) and the Council of the Global Environment Facility (hereinafter the Council),

Recognizing the characteristics of the financial mechanism for the provision of financial resources for the purposes of the Convention on Biological Diversity (hereinafter the Convention) outlined in Article 21, paragraph 1, of the Convention, and the provisions of Article 21, paragraph 2, of the Convention, which call upon the Conference of the Parties to decide on the arrangements to give effect to Article 21, paragraph 1, after consultation with the institutional structure entrusted with the operation of the financial mechanism,

Recognizing further the willingness of the Global Environment Facility (hereinafter GEF) to serve for the purposes of the financial mechanism for the implementation of the Convention,

Recognizing that the financial mechanism shall function under the authority and guidance of and be accountable to the Conference of the Parties for the purposes of the Convention and that GEF as decided by the Conference of the Parties will operate the financial mechanism of the Convention on an interim basis in accordance with Article 39 of the Convention,

Having consulted with each other and taking into account the relevant aspects of their governance structures as reflected in their constituent instruments,

Have reached the following understanding:

1. *Purpose*

1.1 The purpose of the present Memorandum of Understanding is to make provision for the relationship between the Conference of the Parties and the Council in order to give effect to the provisions of Article 21, paragraph 1, of the Convention and paragraph 26 of the GEF Instrument and, on an interim basis, in accordance with Article 39 of the Convention.

2. *Guidance from the Conference of the Parties*

2.1 In accordance with Article 21 of the Convention the Conference of the Parties will determine the policy, strategy, programme priorities and eligibility criteria for access to and utilization of financial resources available through the financial mechanism, including monitoring and evaluation on a regular basis of such utilization. GEF, in operating the financial mechanism under the Convention, will finance activities that are in full conformity with the guidance provided to it by the Conference of the Parties. For this purpose, the Conference of the Parties will communicate its guidance, and any revisions to such guidance as it may adopt, on the following matters:

(a) Policy and strategy;

(b) Programme priorities;

(c) Eligibility criteria;

(d) An indicative list of incremental costs;

(e) A list of developed country Parties and other Parties which voluntarily assume the obligations of developed country Parties;

(f) Any other matter relating to Article 21, including periodic determination of the amount of resources needed as detailed in paragraph 5 of this Memorandum.

2.2 The Council will communicate to the Conference of the Parties all relevant information, including information on the projects in the area of biological diversity funded by GEF outside the framework of the financial mechanism of the Convention.

3. *Reporting*

3.1 The Council will prepare and submit a report for each ordinary meeting of the Conference of the Parties.

3.2 The reports will include specific information on how the GEF Council, its Secretariat and its Implementing and Executing Agencies have applied the guidance and implemented the policy, strategies, programme priorities and eligibility criteria determined by the Conference of the Parties, as well as any other decision of the Conference of the Parties communicated to GEF, under Article 21 of the Convention. The Council should also report on its monitoring and evaluation activities concerning projects in the biodiversity focal area.

3.3. In particular, the reports will provide detailed information on the GEF biodiversity focal area, including:

(a) Information on how GEF has responded to the guidance provided by the Conference of the Parties as described by paragraph 2, including, where appropriate, through its incorporation in the GEF operational strategy and operational programmes;

(b) The conformity of the approved work programmes with guidance of the Conference of the Parties;

(c) A synthesis of the different projects under implementation and a listing of the projects approved by the Council in the biodiversity focal area, as well as a financial report with an indication of the financial resources allocated to these projects;

(d) A list of project proposals submitted for approval to the Council, through the GEF Implementing Agencies, by eligible Parties, including reporting on their approval status and, in cases of projects not approved, the reasons therefore;

(e) A review of the project activities approved by GEF and their outcomes, including information on funding and progress in implementation; and

(f) Additional financial resources leveraged by GEF for the implementation of the Convention.

3.4 In order to meet the requirements of accountability to the Conference of the Parties, reports submitted by the Council will cover all GEF-financed activities carried out for the purpose of the Convention, whether decisions on such activities are made by the Council or by the GEF Implementing and/or Executing Agencies. To this end, the Council will make arrangements as might be necessary with the Implementing Agencies regarding disclosure of information.

3.5 The Council will also provide information on other matters concerning the discharge of its functions under Article 21, paragraph 1, as may be requested by the Conference of the Parties. If the Council has difficulties in responding to any such request, it will explain its concerns to the Conference of the Parties and the Conference of the Parties and the Council will find a mutually agreed solution.

4. *Monitoring and evaluation*

4.1 The Conference of the Parties may raise with the Council any matter arising from the reports received.

4.2 The funding decisions for specific projects should be agreed between the developing country Party concerned and GEF in accordance with policy, strategy, programme priorities and eligibility criteria established by the Conference of the Parties. The GEF Council is responsible for approving the GEF work programmes. If a Party considers that a decision of the Council regarding a specific project was not made in compliance with the policies, programme priorities and eligibility criteria established by the Conference of the Parties in the context of the Convention, the Conference of the Parties should analyse the observations presented to it by the Party and take decisions on the basis of compliance with such policy, strategy, programme priorities and eligibility criteria. In the event that the Conference of the Parties considers that this specific project decision does not comply with the policy, strategy, programme priorities and eligibility criteria established by the Conference of the Parties, it may ask the GEF Council for further clarification on the specific project decision.

4.3 As provided for in Article 21, paragraph 3, of the Convention, the Conference of the Parties will periodically review the effectiveness of the financial mechanism in implementing the Convention and communicate to the Council relevant decisions taken by the Conference of the Parties as the result of such review, to improve the effectiveness of the financial mechanism in assisting developing country Parties to implement the Convention.

5. *Determination of funding requirements*

5.1 In anticipation of the replenishment of GEF, the Conference of the Parties will make an assessment of the amount of funds that are necessary to assist developing countries, in accordance with the guidance provided by the Conference of the Parties, in fulfilling their commitments under the Convention over the next GEF replenishment cycle, taking into account:

(a) Article 20, paragraph 2, and Article 21, paragraph 1, of the Convention;

(b) Guidance to the financial mechanism from the Conference of the Parties which calls for future financial resources;

(c) The information communicated to the Conference of the Parties in the national reports submitted in accordance with Article 26 of the Convention;

(d) National strategies, plans or programmes developed in accordance with Article 6 of the Convention;

(e) Information communicated to the Conference of the Parties from GEF on the number of eligible programmes and projects that were submitted to GEF, the number that were approved for funding, and the number that were turned down owing to lack of resources;

(f) Experience gained by those concerned in the implementation of projects.

5.2 On the occasion of each replenishment, GEF will, in its regular report to the Conference of the Parties as provided for in paragraph 3 of this Memorandum of Understanding, indicate how it has responded during the replenishment cycle to the previous assessment by the Conference of the Parties prepared in accordance with paragraph 5.1 and inform the Conference of the Parties of the conclusion of replenishment negotiations.

5.3 On the basis of the report referred to in paragraph 5.2 of this Memorandum of Understanding the Conference of the Parties will review the amount of funding necessary for the implementation of the Convention, on the occasion of each replenishment of the financial mechanism.

6. *Reciprocal representation*

On a reciprocal basis, representatives of GEF will be invited to attend meetings of the Conference of the Parties and representatives of the Convention will be invited to attend meetings of GEF.

7. *Inter-secretariat cooperation*

The Secretariat of the Convention and the Secretariat of GEF will communicate and cooperate with each other and consult on a regular basis to facilitate the effectiveness of the financial mechanism in assisting developing country Parties to implement the Convention. In particular, the two secretariats will consult on the project proposals under consideration for inclusion in a proposed work programme, especially with regard to the consistency of the project proposals with the guidance of the Conference of the Parties. Official documentation of GEF will be made available to the Secretariat of the Convention on Biological Diversity.

8. *Amendments*

Any amendments to the present Memorandum of Understanding will be decided upon by the Conference of the Parties and the Council in writing.

9. *Interpretation*

If differences arise in the interpretation of the present Memorandum of Understanding, the Conference of the Parties and the Council will reach a mutually acceptable solution.

10. *Entry into effect*

10.1 The present Memorandum of Understanding will come into effect upon approval by the Conference of the Parties and by the Council. Either participant may withdraw this Memorandum of Understanding at any time by written notification addressed to the other. The withdrawal will take effect six months after its notification.

10.2 The withdrawal of this Memorandum of Understanding by either Party to this Memorandum of Understanding shall not affect any projects considered and/or approved in accordance with the Memorandum of Understanding prior to the withdrawal.

Decision III/9: Implementation of Articles 6 and 8 of the Convention

The Conference of the Parties,

Reaffirming the great importance of the development and implementation by all Parties of national strategies, plans and programmes in accordance with Article 6 of the Convention,

Welcoming the work already undertaken by the Parties in implementing Article 6,

Recalling paragraph 5 of decision II/6, in which the Conference of the Parties requested the interim institutional structure operating the financial mechanism to facilitate urgent implementation of Article 6 of the Convention by making available to developing country Parties financial resources for projects in a flexible and expeditious manner,

Recalling also that in decision II/17 the Conference of the Parties decided that the first national reports by Parties would focus in so far as possible on measures taken for the implementation of Article 6,

Reaffirming that Article 8 of the Convention sets out a clear framework of the necessary elements for *in-situ* conservation, which should be addressed in a coherent manner,

Noting that the reduction in the number of species and the fragmentation and degradation of ecosystems and habitats call not only for conservation but also for *inter alia* sustainable use and restoration of habitats, including their biological diversity components, together with other measures provided for by Article 8 of the Convention,

Noting the conclusions and recommendations of the United Nations-Norway Conference on Alien Species, Trondheim, Norway, 1–5 July 1996, and suggesting that Parties may wish to use these results in their implementation of Article 8 (h) of the Convention,

Believing that a central role of the clearing-house mechanism should be the sharing of experiences and dissemination of information relevant to Articles 6 and 8,

Emphasizing that the compilation and dissemination under the Convention of information relevant to the implementation of Articles 6 and 8 should complement and enhance existing efforts, rather than duplicate them,

1. *Stresses* the need for Parties to ensure the cross-border coordination of their respective strategies, on a bilateral as well as on a regional basis;

2. *Urges* Parties to include in their national plans or strategies and legislation measures for:

(a) The conservation of biological diversity both *in situ* and *ex situ*;

(b) The integration of biological diversity objectives in relevant sectoral policies in order to achieve conservation and sustainable use of biological diversity;

(c) The equitable sharing of benefits arising out of the use of genetic resources;

3. *Further urges* Parties to submit their first national reports on time;

4. *Requests* the interim financial mechanism under the Convention to make available to developing country Parties resources to enable them to facilitate urgent implementation of paragraphs 2 and 3 above;

5. *Encourages* all Parties to set measurable targets in order to achieve biological diversity conservation and sustainable use objectives;

6. *Requests* Parties to take action to achieve the restoration of habitats, including their biological diversity components;

7. *Requests* the Executive Secretary to explore ways of enhancing the collection and dissemination to Parties of information on the implementation of Articles 6

and 8 by involving in a more regular and systematic fashion organizations already concerned with the collection and dissemination of such information;

8. *Requests* the Executive Secretary to prepare a paper for consideration by the next meeting of the Subsidiary Body on Scientific, Technical and Technological Advice, identifying existing conventions and other international agreements relevant to the implementation of the various paragraphs of Article 8;

9. *Recommends* the development of a thematic approach in the further compilation and dissemination of information on the implementation of Articles 6 and 8 and commends the inclusion of the following work areas within this approach:

(a) Methodologies to evaluate and mitigate threats to biological diversity;

(b) Ways to suppress or mitigate perverse or negative incentives having a deleterious effect on biological diversity;

(c) Alien species; and

(d) Protected areas;

10. *Encourages* the Scientific Committee on Problems of the Environment and the Invasive Species Specialist Group of the World Conservation Union to continue their efforts to develop a global strategy and action plan to deal with the problem of alien invasive species;

11. *Decides* that the first national reports referred to in decision II/17 should be submitted no later than 1 January 1998, taking into account decision III/25 of the third meeting of the Conference of the Parties on the date and venue of its next meeting.

Decision III/10: Identification, monitoring and assessment

The Conference of the Parties,

Reaffirming the central importance of the implementation of Article 7 in ensuring that the objectives of the Convention are met,

Stressing the fundamental role of taxonomy in identifying the components of biological diversity,

Recognizing the lack of taxonomic capacity in many countries,

Recognizing also the necessity of capacity-building to enable Parties to carry out identification, monitoring and assessment within the remit of the Convention,

Noting the review of methodologies for assessment of biological diversity contained in Annex I of document UNEP/CBD/COP/3/13 and the discussion of indicators contained in Annex II of that document,

1. *Urges* Parties to identify indicators of biological diversity and to develop innovative methods of implementing Article 7 as a high priority, in particular commending the value of rapid biological diversity assessment approaches as an efficient and cost-effective way of assessing biological diversity and identifying priorities for action, and recognizing also the role of remote sensing as a useful tool for monitoring;

2. *Endorses* the recommendation II/1 of the Subsidiary Body on Scientific, Technical and Technological Advice concerning indicators, monitoring and assessment of biological diversity;

3. *Endorses* the recommendation II/2 of the Subsidiary Body on Scientific, Technical and Technological Advice concerning capacity-building for taxonomy;

4. *Recommends* that Parties consider a step-by-step approach to the implementation of Article 7, paying attention to the indicative list of categories of important components of biological diversity set out in Annex I of the Convention, beginning with the rapid implementation of Article 7 (a) and the first part of Article 7 (c), concerning identification of important components of biological diversity and the processes and categories of activities which have or are likely to have significant adverse impacts on biological diversity;

5. *Stresses*, however, that such an approach should not preclude the timely implementation of other Articles of the Convention, particularly Articles 6 and 8, with respect to those components of biological diversity that have been identified;

6. *Calls on* Parties to cooperate on a voluntary pilot project to demonstrate the use of successful assessment and indicator methodologies;

7. *Also calls on* Parties to prepare, where appropriate, reports on experiences on the application of assessment methodologies and results from assessments and to disseminate these reports by appropriate mechanisms such as the clearing-house mechanism;

8. *Recommends* to Parties that they explore ways to make taxonomic information housed in collections world-wide readily available, in particular to countries of origin;

9. *Instructs* the Subsidiary Body on Scientific, Technical and Technological Advice:

(a) To provide scientific advice and further guidance, through its thematic work on ecosystems, to the fourth meeting of the Conference of the Parties, to assist in the national elaboration of Annex I of the Convention, using as guidance the elaboration of the terms as set out in paragraphs 12–29 of document UNEP/CBD/COP/3/12;

(b) Further to review methodologies for assessment of biological diversity and make recommendations for their application to the fourth meeting of the Conference of the Parties;

10. *Requests* the institutional structure of the interim financial mechanism of the Convention to provide financial resources to developing countries in order to address the need for capacity-building, including taxonomy, to enable them to develop and carry out an initial assessment for designing, implementing and monitoring programmes in accordance with Article 7, taking into account the special need of small island States.

Recommendation II/1: Agenda item 3.1: Assessment of biological diversity and methodologies for future assessments Agenda item 3.2: Identification, monitoring and assessment of components of biological diversity and of processes that have adverse impacts Agenda item 3.3: Review and promotion of indicators of biological diversity

1 General advice

1. There was broad agreement that agenda items 3.1, 3.2 and 3.3 were inextricably interlinked and should therefore be considered together. It was acknowledged that the subject matter dealt with was highly complex and central to the Convention, particularly with respect to Article 7 but also to other Articles such as 6, 8, 16, 25 and 26. The background documents prepared by the Secretariat (documents UNEP/CBD/SBSTTA/2/2, UNEP/CBD/SBSTTA/2/3, UNEP/CBD/SBSTTA/2/4) were generally considered to contain useful approaches to dealing with these issues.

2. The importance of capacity-building, development and enhancement of institutions (and concomitant financial support) in assisting developing countries in all aspects of their assessments was repeatedly emphasized.

3. The role the clearing-house mechanism should have in improving the flow of information was stressed. The possible need to develop interim measures within the clearing-house mechanism was raised.

4. It was noted that improvement of taxonomic knowledge was fundamental to the development of indicators and assessments.

5. It was emphasized that the assessment of biological diversity was ultimately the responsibility of each Party, so that national reporting should be the focus of assessment efforts. When necessary, regional bodies should be called upon to provide information to facilitate the assessment of biological diversity beyond national jurisdictions. The question of how the Secretariat and the SBSTTA would deal with national reports when they began to arrive was raised.

6. There was wide agreement that assessments should be: transparent; based on scientific principles; based initially on existing knowledge; focused; pragmatic; cost-effective; within a socio-economic context; management- or policy-oriented. Indicators were recognized as being a vital aspect of such assessments with the pressure-state-response framework being particularly useful. A distinction was made between assessments of biological diversity itself and the assessment of the state of knowledge of biological diversity. The former was relevant principally at national level, the latter principally at regional and global levels.

7. Calls were made for development and refinement of guidelines for national reporting. The UNEP country studies guidelines were mentioned in this context. The desirability of harmonization was emphasized as this would allow comparisons with similar ecosystems in different countries to be made, and also facilitate the development of overviews such as the Global Biodiversity Outlook. The need to develop a core set of indicators for

national reporting which should be easily and widely measurable and policy-relevant was raised. Initially, emphasis should be laid on indicators already known to be successful. Traditional knowledge could play a valuable role in the development of indicators, as well as in monitoring and assessment.

8. However, the need for flexibility in approach to assessment, national reporting and indicator development in response to widely varying ecological conditions and national capacities was repeatedly raised. Regional or ecosystem approaches to the development of guidelines and indicators were widely advocated and it was noted that there was unlikely ever to be any one optimum method for assessment. The annex to the document prepared by the Secretariat (UNEP/CBD/SBSTTA/2/2) may be useful in this regard as it sets out a series of methodologies, allowing choice of the most appropriate for a given set of circumstances.

9. A two-track approach to assessment and indicator development was suggested. In the short term actual assessments should be carried out of sectors and components of biological diversity which were already reasonably well known and understood; longer-term programmes involving research and capacity-building should be developed in areas needing advances in knowledge.

10. The distinction was made between inventorying and assessment or monitoring of biological diversity. The latter must be related to human impacts. It was also noted that, although in themselves costly and difficult processes, inventories of biological diversity were more straightforward than assessment of impacts on and changes to biological diversity. The latter required both improved knowledge and long-term monitoring. Biosphere reserves were noted as being potentially extremely valuable in the latter regard.

11. Coordination with related international conventions and processes was considered of great importance. This should serve to minimize duplication of effort. In addition, experience gained in reporting to these could be used to develop guidelines for reporting and indicator development within the remit of the Convention on Biological Diversity.

12. The desirability of preparing thematic assessments in line with the major themes and specific needs of the Convention was underlined. In particular, freshwater ecosystems were widely recognized as being in urgent need of global assessment. Calls for assessment of coastal and marine, grassland and wetland ecosystems, in addition to those others mentioned in the Secretariat document (UNEP/CBD/SBSTTA/2/2), were also made.

13. The importance of assessing biological diversity in agricultural systems was widely acknowledged. It was stressed that such an assessment should take into account the work of the FAO. It was noted that there exists an interdependence between sustaining biological diversity and sustaining agriculture. It was also recognized that agricultural practices may affect biological diversity in agricultural ecosystems in both negative and positive ways and that when individual activities of many producers are considered in aggregate, the potential for significant offsite impacts on biological diversity exists. Because agriculture takes place across landscapes that often include other types of land-use, an improved understanding of the role of agriculture in the overall context of a region is needed.

14. It was also stressed that assessments of the status of biological diversity should, as a matter of priority, be incorporated into regional and global resource assessments as the basis for management decisions in sectors which had serious impacts on the status of biological diversity, particularly those concerning marine, agricultural and forest ecosystems. This would entail cooperation with agencies and organizations responsible for regional and global resource assessments, such as the FAO, and should operate with relevant conventions such as that covering straddling and highly migratory fish stocks.

15. It was noted that coordinated thematic assessments by countries would allow development of thematic overviews within the Global Biodiversity Outlook.

16. The proposed framework of processes and categories of activities that are or are likely to have significant adverse impacts on biological diversity (paragraphs 39–41 of document UNEP/CBD/SBSTTA/2/3) received general support. A number of specific recommendations for amendment or modification were made. Radioactive contaminants were identified as an additional proximate threat, improper land management was identified as an activity having adverse effects on biological diversity, and national policy failure was considered an additional ultimate cause of threats. In addition, it was noted that consumptive use of wild species could be a contribution to conservation. It was suggested that assessments should be carried out using this framework to set priorities, it being acknowledged that these priorities would differ in different countries.

17. Some form of intersessional activity (for example a liaison group or informal working group) was considered appropriate to examine issues such as development of guidelines for national reporting and a review of indicator initiatives. It was also suggested that indicators and monitoring should be considered together as a standing item on the agenda of the SBSTTA.

2 Conclusions and recommendations

18. The SBSTTA recognizes the vital importance of monitoring and assessment of biological diversity, particularly with regard to Article 7 of the Convention, and further recognizes that the primary responsibility for undertaking monitoring and assessment of biological diversity lies with individual Parties.

19. The SBSTTA advocates a two-track approach to assessment and indicator development. In the short term, actual assessment should be carried out of sectors and components of biological diversity which were already reasonably well-known and understood. Use should, in particular, be made of indicators known to be operational. Longer-term programmes involving research and capacity-building should be developed in areas needing advances in knowledge.

2.1 Priority tasks

20. The SBSTTA considered that the following tasks should be accorded a high priority:

(i) Enhancing capacity-building, strengthening of institutions and funding in developing countries to carry out identification, monitoring and assessment within the remit of the Convention;

(ii) Development of the clearing-house mechanism to improve the flow of information both from national reporting and from the international scientific community;

(iii) Development and refinement of national guidelines to include: assessment and monitoring methodologies; indicators; thematic approaches; definition and clarification of terms; recommendations for harmonization;

(iv) Provision of a critical review of methodologies for inventory and assessment along the lines of that provided in Annex 1 of document UNEP/CBD/SBSTTA/2/2;

(v) Development of a core set of indicators for national reports. Such indicators should in the first instance be based on those which are known to be operational;

(vi) Development of indicators in thematic areas important to the Convention, particularly coastal and marine ecosystems (including mangroves), agricultural biological diversity, forests and freshwater ecosystems;

(vii) Development of an indicative framework of processes and categories of activities that are or are likely to have significant adverse impacts on biological diversity;

(viii) Development of methods to strengthen links between natural resource assessments and assessments of biological diversity by introducing biological diversity dimensions into resource assessments, including assessments of forests, land resources, soils and marine living resources.

21. The SBSTTA noted that development of a core set of indicators would entail a review of current approaches to indicator development and development of indicators in thematic areas important to the Convention.

22. The SBSTTA considered that the following tasks were also important:

(i) Development of regional- or ecosystem-based guidelines for assessments;

(ii) Preparation of thematic assessments of knowledge and status of biological diversity on one or more of the following ecosystems: freshwater; coastal and marine; forests and woodlands; montane systems; rangelands, arid and semi-arid lands; grasslands; wetlands; agricultural systems;

(iii) Establishment of the costs and benefits of the conservation of biological diversity and its sustainable use;

(iv) Assistance in preparation of the Global Biodiversity Outlook;

(v) Elaboration and further interpretation of the terms in Annex I of the Convention, as discussed in detail in document UNEP/CBD/SBSTTA/2/3;

(vi) Development of a review of methods for monitoring activities which have or may have adverse impacts on biological diversity, particularly with regard to pressure indicators and to the socio-economic context of the use of biological diversity as well as the impact from technology including biotechnology. Such a review should include options for mitigating the effects of these activities.

2.2 Proposed specific recommendations

23. In response to these priorities, the SBSTTA recommends to the Conference of the Parties that the Executive Secretary be requested to produce in consultation with a liaison or expert group, and for consideration by the next SBSTTA:

(i) A guideline report to assist Parties in addressing these issues. Such a report should contain an elaboration of assessment methodologies for meeting the requirements of the Convention, taking into account the contents of those national reports already prepared and reports to other conventions and international processes. Such a report should also contain: information on indicators and monitoring techniques; definitions and clarification of terms and recommendations for harmonization. Preparation of the guidelines should not delay production of national reports already in progress;

(ii) A list of options for consideration by the SBSTTA for capacity-building in developing countries in the application of guidelines and indicators for subsequent national reports;

(iii) A listing of current approaches to indicator development to be tabled at the next meeting of the SBSTTA and recommendations for a preliminary core set of indicators of biological diversity, particularly those related to threats.

24. The SBSTTA recommends that the Conference of the Parties request that any guidelines or other products so produced be peer-reviewed by a roster of experts and competent institutions.

25. The SBSTTA also recommends to the Conference of the Parties that the Executive Secretary be requested to initiate consultation with other regional and global organizations, particularly the FAO, involved in assessments of biological resources within relevant economic sectors, to attempt to ensure that biological diversity is included in resource assessments undertaken by these regional and global organizations with the aim of influencing management decisions.

26. In view of the complexity of these issues and their central importance in the implementation of the Convention, the SBSTTA recommends that indicators, assessment and monitoring should be considered together as a standing item on the agenda of the SBSTTA.

Recommendation II/2: Agenda item 3.4: Practical approaches for capacity-building for taxonomy

The SBSTTA,

Recalling paragraph 7 of decision II/8, which requested the second meeting of the SBSTTA to address the issue of the lack of taxonomists that are required for Parties to implement the Convention and to advise the Conference of the Parties at its third meeting on ways and means to overcome this problem, taking into account existing studies and ongoing initiatives while adopting more practical direction of taxonomy linked to bio-prospecting and ecological research on conservation and sustainable use of biological diversity and its components;

Recognizing that biological collections are the basis of taxonomy and are also sources of genetic resources;

Having examined the note by the Secretariat (UNEP/CBD/SBSTTA/2/5) and finding an extraordinary level of agreement that enhanced taxonomic capacity is a *sine qua non* for the implementation of the Convention;

Recommends that the Conference of the Parties consider the following:

1. There is a scarcity of taxonomists, taxonomic collections, and institutional facilities, and there is a need to take measures to alleviate this situation worldwide, to facilitate and assist countries in implementing the Convention on Biological Diversity. In particular, national institutions and regional and subregional networks should be established or strengthened and linkages enhanced with taxonomic institutions in developing and developed countries. In strengthening the taxonomic base, considera-

tion must be given to the information needs for bio-prospecting, habitat conservation, sustainable agriculture and the sustainable utilization of biological resources.

2. Capacity-building for taxonomy should be linked to the effective implementation of the Convention on Biological Diversity, particularly the national identification of areas of high diversity; improving the understanding of ecosystem functioning; giving priority to threatened taxa, taxa that are or may be of value to humanity, and those with potential use as biological indicators for conservation and sustainable use of biological diversity.

3. Development of guidelines and programme priorities for funding, including for the financial mechanism under the Convention, should take account of the specific needs for capacity-building in taxonomy to serve areas such as bio-prospecting, habitat conservation and the sustainable use of biological diversity. Such support should recognize the need for adequate, long-term housing of collections and records and long-term research.

4. For new taxonomists to be recruited, there is a need to provide employment opportunities. It is urgent that Parties take this need into consideration and integrate it into the programme of capacity-building.

5. Where appropriate, national taxonomic needs assessment and action plans should be developed by setting national priorities, mobilizing available institutional resources, and identifying available funds. Countries could benefit from regional and subregional collaboration.

6. The importance of establishing regional and subregional training programmes was recognized. Attention should also be given to the training of specialists, parataxonomists, and technicians in this field. The field of taxonomy must be integrated with training activities such as biological monitoring and assessments. Maximum use should be made of existing institutions and those organizations active in these fields.

7. There is an urgent need to make the information on existing taxonomic knowledge, including information about the taxa in worldwide collections, available to countries of origin.

8. Taxonomic information to assist capacity-building in taxonomy should be included within the clearing-house mechanism. The taxonomic work embodied in existing archives and inventories, field guides and publications needs to be updated and readily accessible through worldwide services and the duplication of work already conducted should be avoided. The dissemination of information should further the objectives of the Convention and be linked to user needs. This sharing of information will require greater international collaboration. It should also be recognized that traditional taxonomic systems offer a valuable perspective on biological diversity and should be considered part of the total taxonomic knowledge base at national, regional and subregional levels.

9. Since taxonomy generally involves the use of biological collections, those concerned should consider the adoption of mutually agreed upon material transfer agreements or equivalent instruments in accordance with the provisions of the Convention on Biological Diversity for exchange of biological specimens and information relating to them.

10. The Conference of the Parties should consider instructing the Global

Environment Facility to support a Global Taxonomy Initiative, providing the necessary funds for the following actions related to capacity-building in taxonomy:

(a) developing national, regional and subregional training programmes;

(b) strengthening reference collections in countries of origin including, where appropriate, the exchange of paratypes on mutually agreed upon terms;

(c) making information housed in collections worldwide and the taxonomy based on them available to the countries of origin;

(d) producing and distributing regional taxonomic guides;

(e) strengthening infrastructure for biological collections in countries of origin, and the transfer of modern technologies for taxonomic research and capacity-building; and

(f) disseminating taxonomic information worldwide, *inter alia*, by the clearing-house mechanism.

Decision III/11: Conservation and sustainable use of agricultural biological diversity

The Conference of the Parties,

Recalling resolution 3 of the Nairobi Final Act,

Also recalling decisions II/15 and II/16 of the second meeting of the Conference of the Parties,

Further recalling recommendation II/7 of the second meeting of the Subsidiary Body on Scientific, Technical and Technological Advice related to agricultural biological diversity,

Welcoming the outcome of the fourth International Technical Conference on the Conservation and Sustainable Utilization of Plant Genetic Resources for Food and Agriculture, held in June 1996 in Leipzig, and taking note of the follow-up process agreed in Leipzig and of the periodic updating of the report on the State of the World's Plant Genetic Resources for Food and Agriculture and the Global Plan of Action for the Conservation and Sustainable Utilization of Plant Genetic Resources for Food and Agriculture by the Food and Agriculture Organization of the United Nations, as well as the implementation of the Global Plan of Action,

Considering the importance of biological diversity for agriculture and taking note of the interrelationship of agriculture with biological diversity as detailed in the basis for action attached hereto as Annex 1,

Believing that the field of agriculture offers a unique opportunity for the Convention on Biological Diversity to link concerns regarding biological diversity conservation and sharing of benefits arising from the use of genetic resources with the mainstream economy, taking into account the need for a balanced development of the three objectives of the Convention,

Recognizing the close relationship between agriculture and biological and cultural diversity and that the Conference of the Parties has a clear role and mandate to address issues relating to agricultural biological diversity within the framework of the Convention on Biological Diversity,

Further recognizing agricultural biological diversity as a focal area in view of its social and economic relevance and the prospects offered by sustainable agriculture for reducing the negative impacts on biological diversity, enhancing the value of biological diversity and linking conservation efforts with social and economic benefits,

Urging the expeditious provision of funds from appropriate sources necessary for the implementation of this decision,

Recognizing that traditional farming communities and their agricultural practices have made a significant contribution to the conservation and enhancement of biodiversity and that these can make an important contribution to the development of environmentally sound agricultural production systems,

Recognizing also that the inappropriate use of and excessive dependence on agrochemicals has produced substantial negative effects on terrestrial systems, including soil, coastal and aquatic organisms, thus affecting biological diversity in different ecosystems,

Reaffirming the sovereign rights of States over their own genetic resources, including their genetic resources for food and agriculture,

Urging Parties to establish or maintain means to regulate, manage or control the risks associated with the use and release of living modified organisms resulting from biotechnology which are likely to have adverse environmental impacts that could affect the conservation and sustainable use of biological diversity, taking also into account the risks to human health,

Considering that its activities in this field relating to the implementation of Article 6 (b) of the Convention should focus on the interface between agricultural sustainability and environmental issues and should promote the integration of social, economic and environmental objectives and facilitate the development of solutions to problems relating to agricultural biological diversity in the context of the Convention's provisions,

Further considering that the contributions of conservation and sustainable use of agricultural biological diversity to sustainable agriculture should be a key focal area within the context of terrestrial, freshwater and marine biological diversity, to be pursued in collaboration with, and with the cooperation and initiative of, relevant international organizations thus avoiding duplication,

1. *Decides* to establish a multi-year programme of activities on agricultural biological diversity aiming, first, to promote the positive effects and mitigate the negative impacts of agricultural practices on biological diversity in agro-ecosystems and their interface with other ecosystems; second, to promote the conservation and sustainable use of genetic resources of actual or potential value for food and agriculture; and third, to promote the fair and equitable sharing of benefits arising out of the utilization of genetic resources; and which, in support of the implementation of ongoing or the initiation of new policies, programmes and plans in the field of agrobiodiversity, will have the following components:

(a) The identification and assessment of relevant ongoing activities and existing instruments at the international level;

(b) The identification and assessment of relevant ongoing activities and existing instruments at the national level;

(c) The identification of issues that need to be addressed and relevant knowledge;

(d) The identification of priority issues for further development of the programme;

(e) The identification and implementation of case studies on issues identified;

(f) The sharing of experiences and the transfer of knowledge and technologies;

2. *Requests* the Executive Secretary to invite the Food and Agriculture Organization of the United Nations, in close collaboration with other relevant United Nations bodies and regional and international organizations, to identify and assess relevant ongoing activities and existing instruments at the international level, choosing among the thematic areas in the indicative list in Annex 2. The results should be reported back on a phased basis to the Conference of the Parties through the Subsidiary Body on Scientific, Technical and Technological Advice;

3. *Welcomes* the offer by the Food and Agriculture Organization of the United Nations to continue serving countries in implementing the Convention on Biological Diversity in the area of agricultural biological diversity, and, referring to its earlier decisions, underlines the necessity of avoiding any duplication of work with respect to the activities being undertaken by the Food and Agriculture Organization of the United Nations in this programme of work;

4. *Requests* Parties, as far as possible and as appropriate, to identify and assess relevant ongoing activities and existing instruments at the national level and to report back to the Conference of the Parties;

5. *Requests* Parties, as far as possible and as appropriate, to identify issues and priorities that need to be addressed at the national level and to report back to the Conference of the Parties;

6. *Suggests* that, in carrying out the initiatives described in paragraphs 3 and 4 above, Parties consider the thematic areas in the indicative list in Annex 2, as appropriate;

7. *Requests* the Executive Secretary, in close collaboration with the Food and Agriculture Organization of the United Nations, as appropriate, to report the results, together with advice from the Subsidiary Body on Scientific, Technical and Technological Advice, of the above initiatives as a basis for setting priorities by the Conference of the Parties for further work within this programme of work using as criteria, *inter alia*:

(a) The relevance of the issue to the objectives of the Convention;

(b) The extent to which work on the issue is not already being undertaken;

8. *Requests* that the clearing-house mechanism be used to promote and facilitate the development and transfer of technology relevant to the conservation and sustainable use of agricultural biological diversity by facilitating contacts among:

(a) Groups needing solutions to specific problems;

(b) Holders of technologies developed and maintained by many sources;

(c) Technology-transfer brokers;

(d) Enabling agencies which fund technology transfer;

9. *Encourages the Parties*, in accordance with decision I/2 of the Conference of the Parties, to use and/or study and develop methods and indicators to monitor the impacts of agricultural development projects, including the intensification and extensification of production systems, on biological diversity and to promote their application;

10. *Invites* countries to share case-study experiences addressing the conservation and sustainable use of agricultural biological diversity, which, among other ways of sharing information, should be posted through the clearing-house mechanism of the Convention;

11. *Encourages* interested Parties and international agencies to conduct case studies on the two initial issues identified by the Subsidiary Body on Scientific, Technical and Technological Advice in recommendation II/7, described in Annex 3;

12. *Instructs* the Subsidiary Body on Scientific, Technical and Technological Advice to coordinate and assess the lessons learned from work on the topics described in Annex 3 and to report back thereon to the Conference of the Parties, as appropriate;

13. *Recognizes* that the successful implementation of policies aiming at the sustainable use of agrobiodiversity components largely depends on the degree of public awareness and understanding of its basic importance for society, and recommends Parties to establish or enhance mechanisms for information and education, including the use of the clearing-house mechanism, specific to groups of concern at national, regional and international levels;

14. *Endorses* the conclusions of the relevant sections of the 1995 Commission on Sustainable Development sectoral review of Agenda 21, which, *inter alia*, recognized the need for an integrated and multidisciplinary approach to the planning, development and management of land resources, and that the achievement of the multiple objectives related to sustainable agriculture and rural development requires a whole system approach that recognizes that it is not possible to focus on agricultural activities alone;

15. *Encourages* Parties to develop national strategies, programmes and plans which, *inter alia*:

(a) Identify key components of biological diversity in agricultural production systems responsible for maintaining natural processes and cycles, monitoring and evaluating the effects of different agricultural practices and technologies on those components and encouraging the adoption of repairing practices to attain appropriate levels of biological diversity;

(b) Redirect support measures which run counter to the objectives of the Convention regarding agricultural biodiversity;

(c) Internalize environmental costs;

(d) Implement targeted incentive measures which have positive impacts on agrobiodiversity, in order to enhance sustainable agriculture, in accordance with Article 11 and consistent with Article 22, as well as to undertake impact assessments in order to minimize adverse impacts on agrobiodiversity, in accordance with Article 14;

(e) Encourage the development of technologies and farming practices that not only increase productivity, but also arrest degradation as well as reclaim, rehabilitate, restore and enhance biological diversity and monitor adverse effects on sustainable agricultural biodiversity. These could include, *inter alia*, organic farming, integrated pest management, biological control, no-till agriculture, multi-cropping, inter-cropping, crop rotation and agricultural forestry;

(f) Empower their indigenous and local communities and build their capacity for *in situ* conservation and sustainable use and management of agricultural biological diversity, building on the indigenous knowledge systems;

(g) Encourage *ex ante* and/or *ex post* evaluation of impacts on biological diversity from agricultural development projects, to assure the use of best practices to promote the conservation and sustainable use of biological diversity;

(h) Integrate with other plans, programmes and projects relating to the conservation and sustainable use of other terrestrial, freshwater, coastal and marine ecosystems, in accordance with Article 6 (b) of the Convention on Biological Diversity;

(i) Promote partnerships with researchers, extension workers and farmers in research and development programmes for biological diversity conservation and sustainable use of biological diversity in agriculture. To achieve this, countries should be encouraged to set up and maintain local level forums for farmers, researchers, extension workers and other stakeholders to evolve genuine partnerships;

(j) Promote at national and regional levels adequate and appropriate services to farmers and responsiveness of public research and extension services and development of genuine partnerships;

(k) Promote research into, and development and implementation of, integrated pest management strategies, in particular, methods and practices alternative to the use of agro-chemicals, that maintain biodiversity, enhance agro-ecosystem resilience, maintain soil and water quality and do not affect human health;

(l) Encourage the consideration of introducing necessary measures and/or legislation, as appropriate, to encourage appropriate use of and discourage excessive dependence on agro-chemicals with a view to reducing negative impacts on biological diversity;

(m) Study, use and/or develop, in accordance with decision I/2, methods and indicators to monitor the impacts of agricultural development projects on biological diversity, including intensification and extensification, of production systems on biological diversity, and to promote their application;

(n) Study the positive and negative impacts on ecosystems and biomes of agricultural transformation resulting from intensification or extensification of production systems in their countries;

16. *Encourages* Parties to develop national strategies, programmes and plans, which should focus on, *inter alia*:

(a) The key elements of the Global Plan of Action, such as broadening the genetic base of major crops; increasing the range of genetic diversity available to farmers; strengthening the capacity to develop new crops and varieties that are specifically adapted to local environments; exploring and promoting the use of underutilized crops; and deploying genetic diversity to reduce crop vulnerability;

(b) The development of inventories which consider the status of farm animal genetic resources and measures for their conservation and sustainable utilization;

(c) Micro-organisms of interest for agriculture;

17. *Encourages* Parties at the appropriate level, with the support of the relevant international and regional organizations, to promote:

(a) The transformation of unsustainable agricultural practices into sustainable production practices adapted to local biotic and abiotic conditions, in conformity with the ecosystem or integrated land use approach;

(b) The use of farming practices that not only increase productivity, but also arrest degradation as well as reclaim, rehabilitate, restore and enhance biological diversity;

(c) Mobilization of farming communities including indigenous and local communities for the development, maintenance and use of their knowledge and practices in the conservation and sustainable use of biological diversity in the agricultural sector with specific reference to gender roles;

18. *Notes* that the various options for the legal status of a revised International Undertaking on Plant Genetic Resources, which include a voluntary agreement, binding instrument, or protocol to the Convention on Biological Diversity, have not been decided upon by the Food and Agriculture Organization of the United Nations, requests the Food and Agriculture Organization of the United Nations to inform the Conference of the Parties of its deliberations, affirms its willingness to consider a decision by the Conference of the Food and Agriculture Organization of the United Nations that the International Undertaking should take the form of a protocol to this Convention once revised in harmony with this Convention and further requests the Executive Secretary to inform the Commission on Genetic Resources for Food and Agriculture accordingly;

19. *Welcomes* the contribution that the Global Plan of Action for the Conservation and Sustainable Utilization of Plant Genetic Resources, as adopted by the fourth International Technical Conference on Plant Genetic Resources, provides to the implementation of the Convention on Biological Diversity in the field of plant genetic resources for food and agriculture and encourages Parties actively to implement the Global Plan of Action, in accordance with their national capacities, and endorses its priorities and policy recommendations; recognizes that several issues require further work in the context of the FAO Global System for the Conservation and Utilization of Plant Genetic Resources for Food and Agriculture, in particular: financing; the realization of Farmers' Rights as discussed in the Global Plan of Action; as well as terms of technology transfer to developing countries and access and benefit-sharing arrangements, in accordance with relevant provisions of the Convention. In this regard, calls for effective and speedy completion of the revision of the International Undertaking and strengthening of the FAO Global System;

20. *Appreciates* the importance of the country-based Global Strategy for the Management of Farm Animal Genetic Resources under the Food and Agriculture Organization of the United Nations and strongly supports its further development;

21. *Draws the attention* of Parties to Article 20.1 of the Convention, in the context of providing, in accordance with their capabilities, financial support and incentives for the conservation and sustainable use of biological diversity important to agriculture in accordance with national plans, priorities and programmes;

22. *Draws the attention* of international funding agencies to the urgent need to support the conservation and sustainable use of biological diversity important to

agriculture and invites these agencies to provide information and feedback in this respect to the Conference of the Parties and in this context, requests the interim financial mechanism to give priority to supporting efforts for the conservation and sustainable use of biological diversity important to agriculture in accordance with this decision;

23. *Encourages* the United Nations Environment Programme/Food and Agriculture Organization of the United Nations process developed by the Intergovernmental Committee negotiating an international binding instrument for the application of the prior informed consent procedure on hazardous chemical substances, including pesticides;

24. *Recalls* paragraph 39 (g) from the World Food Summit Plan of Action and encourages the World Trade Organization through its Committee on Trade and Environment, in collaboration with other relevant organizations, to consider developing a better appreciation of the relationship between trade and agricultural biodiversity and, in this consideration, recommends the collaboration with the Convention on Biological Diversity and requests the Executive Secretary to convey this request to the World Trade Organization.

Annex 1:
Basis for action

A Impact of biological diversity on agriculture

1. Biological diversity has enabled farming systems to evolve since agriculture was first developed some 12,000 years ago, and an understanding of the dynamic evolutionary and environmental processes which shape and influence agricultural biodiversity is fundamental to improving the sustainable management and conservation of agricultural ecosystems today. In recent years, as the world's population continues to grow and agricultural production must meet the rising demand for food, agricultural expansion into forests and marginal lands, combined with overgrazing and urban and industrial growth, has substantially reduced levels of biological diversity over significant areas. Current patterns of agricultural land use based on limited numbers of species and varieties have also diminished the biological diversity within agricultural ecosystems and are undermining the long-term sustainability of agricultural production itself.

2. Agricultural intensification has the potential to balance the world's need for increasing food supplies while reducing pressures to expand agricultural areas still further, but it is also harmful when accompanied by excessive dependence on agrochemicals and external energy and water inputs. Agro-ecological forms of intensification can, however, blend improved knowledge about agricultural ecosystems, intercropping, uses of diverse species, integrated pest management and the efficient use of resources. Beneficial mixes of land use also raise the overall level of biodiversity in agricultural landscapes. These approaches currently represent a small but growing portion of intensification efforts. Meeting the imperative of increasing agricultural production in such sustainable ways while conserving and prudently using biological diversity is the major challenge which we must urgently address.

3. The importance of agrobiodiversity is of widespread and complex significance to society, encompassing socio-cultural, economic and environmental elements. It is essential to food security and poverty alleviation and much of the knowledge about

agrobiodiversity is maintained by farmers themselves, many of whom are women. All domesticated crops and animals result from human management of biological diversity, which is constantly responding to new challenges to maintain and increase productivity. Biological diversity itself presents opportunities for naturally controlling pests and reducing the use of pesticides, while maintaining high yields, and a large proportion of crops depend on insect pollinators for good yields. Landraces and wild species of animals and plants are the essential source of genetic variability for responding to biotic and abiotic stress through genetic adaptation.

4. The biological diversity of the soil is responsible for nutrient circulation and fertility within agricultural ecosystems. Diversified agricultural production provides protection against uncertainties in the market, especially for less capitalized producers, and increases the opportunities to add value and exploit new markets. Farmers all over the world have also managed a variety of wild species and habitats which benefit the sustainability of both agricultural and natural ecosystems.

5. At the more fundamental level, the living organisms which constitute agricultural biodiversity play an important role in the resilience of all natural, life-support processes. They are essential agents for, *inter alia*, nitrogen, carbon, energy and water cycles. Moreover, the species composition and their relationships will affect the functioning and yields of agricultural ecosystems themselves. A diverse environment also offers a shield for agricultural ecosystems against perturbations, natural or man-made, contributing to their resilience and that of their surrounding ecosystems.

6. Agricultural production utilizes natural resources of diverse ecosystems worldwide and is the economic activity most representative as far as extensive land-use is concerned – nearly one third of the world's land area is used for food production. Serious adverse effects may occur on biological diversity at on and off-farm levels. Most of the world's biological diversity on land is harboured by areas under exploitation by humans; consequently, conserving biological diversity implies improving the ways in which agricultural ecosystems are managed.

B Impacts of agriculture on biodiversity

7. Different agricultural practices lead to diverse impacts upon biological diversity. These impacts occur at the ecosystem, species and genetic levels.

(a) Unsustainable agricultural practices have caused negative impacts on biological diversity, world-wide, at all levels – ecosystem, species and genetic – on both natural and domestic diversity. They have resulted in the large-scale degradation of agrobiodiversity and habitats through the destruction of biotic and abiotic resources, as well as by threatening the natural resource base to agriculture and through socio-economic problems created by destruction of the local resource base. Inappropriate reliance on monoculture, over-mechanization, and misuse of agricultural chemicals diminish the diversity of fauna, flora and micro-organisms, including beneficial organisms. These practices normally lead to a simplification of the components of the environment and to unstable production systems. Expansion of agriculture to frontier areas, including forests, savannahs, wetlands, mountains, and arid lands, combined with overgrazing, and inadequate crop management and pest control strategies contribute to degradation of biological diversity, as well as to the loss of the cultural diversity of traditional communities.

(b) Agricultural practices have, however, also facilitated enhanced biodiversity as a result of both traditional and modern sustainable farming practices. Agricultural ecosystems can provide habitats for plants, birds and other animals. Many agriculturalists have made strong efforts to preserve biological diversity important to agriculture, both *in situ* and *ex situ*. Currently, progress is being made in many regions of the world in implementing biological diversity-friendly agricultural practices in soil conservation, withdrawing production from marginal areas, mastering chemical and nutrient runoff, and breeding crop varieties which are genetically resistant to diseases, pests and abiotic stresses.

Annex 2
Indicative list of thematic areas

1 Land resources

(i) soil erosion control;

(ii) sustainable tillage;

(iii) sustainable farming or cropping;

(iv) marginal land use;

(v) stock of agricultural land including pressures of urbanization;

(vi) integrated land and resource management;

(vii) restoration of degraded landscapes.

2 Water resources

(i) precipitation;

(ii) irrigation management;

(iii) sustainable use;

(iv) water quality;

(v) farm waste.

3 Plant, animal and microbial genetic resources

(i) *in situ*;

(ii) *ex situ*;

(iii) role of botanical gardens and zoos vis-à-vis agricultural biological diversity;

(iv) sustainable use.

4 Wildlife

(i) habitats;

(ii) populations (eg, pollinators, nematodes, soil micro-organisms);

(iii) biocontrol organisms;

(iv) border habitats for natural organisms beneficial to agriculture.

5 Air and climate

(i) greenhouse gas emissions;

(ii) temperature and precipitation variability.

6 Farm inputs

(i) sustainable/water use efficiency;

(ii) energy use efficiency;

(iii) input costs;

(iv) pesticide use involving integrated pest management;

(v) nutrient balance including symbiotic soil micro-organisms.

7 Wild sources of food

(i) wild relatives of domesticated species;

(ii) other wild species.

8 Traditional knowledge

9 Marketing conditions for agricultural products

The relationship between biological diversity-friendly agricultural practices and market forces.

10 Land-use pressures

Examining land-use pressures which make it more difficult to maintain biodiversity-friendly practices, such as lack of services for rural people, and the artificial maintenance of some land far below productive capacity;

11 Agroforestry

Annex 3
Initial issues for conducting case studies

1. Pollinators, including consideration of the monitoring of the loss of pollinators worldwide; the identification of the specific causes of pollinator decline; the estimation of the economic cost associated with reduced pollination of crops; the identification and promotion of best practices and technologies for more sustainable agriculture; and the identification and encouragement of the adoption of conservation practices to maintain pollinators or to promote their re-establishment.

2. Soil micro-organisms in agriculture, including consideration of: the measurement and monitoring of the worldwide loss of symbiotic soil micro-organisms, in particular nitrogen-fixing bacteria and mycorrhizal fungi; the identification and promotion of the transfer of technologies for the detection of symbiotic soil micro-organisms and their use to enhance nitrogen fixation and phosphorous absorption; the estimation of the potential and actual economic gain associated with reduced use of nitrogen and phosphorus chemical fertilization of crops with the enhanced use and conservation of symbiotic soil micro-organisms; the identification and promotion of best practices for more sustainable agriculture; and the identification and promotion of conservation measures to conserve symbiotic soil micro-organisms or to promote their re-establishment.

Decision III/12: Programme of work for terrestrial biological diversity: Forest biological diversity

The Conference of the Parties,

Affirming that some forests can play a crucial role in conserving biological diversity, and recognizing that some forests are becoming degraded and their biological diversity lost,

Recognizing that issues related to forests must be dealt with in a comprehensive and holistic manner, including environmental, economic and social values and issues,

Affirming also that the Convention has a clear role and mandate in issues of forest biological diversity,

Noting that the conservation and sustainable use of forests cannot be isolated from the conservation and sustainable use of biological diversity in general,

Noting also that the conservation and sustainable use of biological diversity must be an integral part of sustainable forest management practices,

Noting further that the implementation of forest conservation and sustainable use policies depends, *inter alia*, on the level of public awareness and policies outside the forest sector,

Recognizing the vital role played by forest ecosystems for many indigenous and local communities,

Reaffirming the statement on biological diversity and forests contained in the annex to decision II/9 transmitted from the Convention on Biological Diversity to the Intergovernmental Panel on Forests,

1. *Welcomes* the comprehensive work taking place under the Intergovernmental Panel on Forests and acknowledges the cooperation between the Intergovernmental Panel on Forests and the Convention on Biological Diversity;

2. *Endorses* recommendation II/8 of the Subsidiary Body on Scientific, Technical and Technological Advice as contained in the annex to this decision;

3. *Affirms* that the Convention on Biological Diversity will be working in a complementary way with the Intergovernmental Panel on Forests and other forest-related forums on forests and biological diversity, with a view to avoiding duplication of effort;

4. *Decides* to invite its President to transmit this decision on forests and its annex to the Intergovernmental Panel on Forests at its fourth meeting;

5. *Requests* the Executive Secretary to explore ways and means to cooperate with the Intergovernmental Panel on Forests or any successor process on matters relating to biological diversity and forests including inter-sessional work, with a view to developing common priorities for further consideration. In this process the Executive Secretary should take account of the research and technical priorities listed in recommendation II/8 of the Subsidiary Body on Scientific, Technical and Technological Advice;

6. *Further requests* the Executive Secretary to develop a focused work programme for forest biological diversity. Optional elements for such a work programme should initially focus on research, cooperation and the development of technologies necessary for the conservation and sustainable use of forest biological diversity. In addition the programme should:

(a) Take account of the outcome of the Intergovernmental Panel on Forests and other forest-related forums;

(b) Facilitate the application and integration of the objectives of the Convention on Biological Diversity in the sustainable management of forests at the national, regional and global levels, in accordance with the ecosystem approach;

(c) Complement and not duplicate the work of relevant international forums, notably the Intergovernmental Panel on Forests;

(d) Complement existing national, regional or international criteria and indicator frameworks for sustainable forest management;

(e) Incorporate traditional systems of forest biological diversity conservation;

7. *Requests* the Executive Secretary in developing this draft work programme, to work closely with the Intergovernmental Panel on Forests and relevant institutions, and also to take full account of the decisions of the United Nations Commission on Sustainable Development, noting in particular the report on institutional aspects contained in the programme element V.1 of the Intergovernmental Panel on Forests mandate resulting from the Swiss/Peruvian initiative on forests held in support of the Intergovernmental Panel on Forests, and encourages all Parties actively to assist the Executive Secretary in carrying out this work;

8. *Requests* the Executive Secretary to report on progress in the draft programme of work to the next meeting of the Conference of the Parties for its discussion and consideration;

9. *Requests* the Subsidiary Body on Scientific, Technical and Technological Advice to contribute advice on this draft programme of work and report back to the fourth meeting of the Conference of the Parties, and also requests the Subsidiary Body on Scientific, Technical and Technological Advice, in providing its advice, to bear in mind for possible future action, *inter alia*, the remaining forest research priority items listed in its recommendation II/8;

10. *Directs* the Subsidiary Body on Scientific, Technical and Technological Advice, in the light of the proposed work programme and taking account of the research and technical priorities already identified in its recommendation II/8, to advance its scientific, technical, and technological consideration of forest biological diversity by initially focusing on the synthesis and development of scientific information in the following research areas:

(a) Methodologies necessary to advance the elaboration and implementation of criteria and indicators for the conservation of biological diversity as part of sustainable forest management;

(b) Scientific analysis of the ways in which human activities, in particular forest management practices, influence biological diversity and assessment of ways to minimize or mitigate negative influences.

Annex
Input to the Intergovernmental Panel on Forests

The Conference of the Parties of the Convention on Biological Diversity wishes to transmit to the fourth session of the Intergovernmental Panel on Forests (IPF), for its consideration, the decision of the third meeting of the Conference of the Parties on biological diversity and forests, as well as the related recommendation II/8 of Subsidiary Body on Scientific, Technical and Technological Advice (SBSTTA). The decision by the third meeting of the Conference of the Parties requested the Executive Secretary to develop a draft work programme for forest biological diversity and gives guidance to SBSTTA on research priorities. These documents are presented as contributions to the IPF deliberations and in the spirit of continuing our positive dialogue and cooperation.

Related recommendations

(a) Biodiversity considerations should be integrated fully into the IPF recommendations and proposals for action. IPF should also consider ways to deal with identified gaps in forest biodiversity knowledge.

(b) In relation to the programme element I.1 of IPF on national forest and land use plans, strategies for sustainable forest management should be based on an ecosystem approach, which will integrate conservation measures (eg, protected areas) and sustainable use of biological diversity. Methodologies need to be developed to assist countries in identifying sites of high interest for biodiversity. These recommendations should take into account national financial circumstances, laws and regulations.

(c) In relation to the programme element 3.2 of IPF dealing with criteria and indicators, conservation of biological diversity and the sustainable use of its components, as well as the maintenance of forest quality, as part of sustainable forest management, should be substantively included in the deliberations of IPF.

The following research and technological priorities were also identified:

(a) Building the scientific foundation and methodologies necessary to advance the elaboration and implementation of criteria and indicators for forest quality and biodiversity conservation as part of sustainable forest management;

(b) Analysing the role of biodiversity in forest ecosystem functioning;

(c) Analysing measures for mitigating the underlying causes of biodiversity loss;

(d) Advancing scientific and technical approaches to (i) rehabilitating degraded and deforested ecosystems and (ii) enriching biodiversity in forest plantations;

(e) Identifying gaps in knowledge in the areas of fragmentation and population viability, to include mitigation options such as corridors and buffer zones;

(f) Assessing ecological landscape models, the integration of protected areas in the ecosystem approach to sustainable forest management and the representativeness and adequacy of protected areas networks;

(g) Analysing scientifically the ways in which human activities, in particular forest management practices, influence biodiversity and assessing ways to minimize or mitigate negative influences; and

(h) Developing assessment and evaluation methodologies for the multiple benefits derived from forest biodiversity.

Decision III/13: Future programme of work for terrestrial biological diversity: Dryland, mountain and inland water ecosystems

The Conference of the Parties,

Taking note of the relevant parts of the report of the third session of the Commission on Sustainable Development, on the review of sectoral cluster: Land, desertification, forests and biodiversity (chapters 10–15 of Agenda 21), as contained in document UNEP/CBD/COP/3/Inf.45,

Recognizing the need for an integrated approach to the planning and management of land resources,

Reaffirming the central importance of biological diversity to sustainable development in drylands and montane areas as well as in other terrestrial ecosystems,

Recalling decision II/18 of the Conference of the Parties, in which it decided that it may consider at its fourth meeting in 1997, *inter alia*, an assessment of the status and trends of the biological diversity of inland water ecosystems and the identification of options for conservation and sustainable use,

Concerned that activities carried out under the Convention should not duplicate existing efforts, but rather should complement them,

1. *Endorses* paragraph 5 of recommendation II/8 of the Subsidiary Body on Scientific, Technical and Technological Advice and thereby requests the Executive Secretary:

(a) To explore ways and means to cooperate with the United Nations Convention to Combat Desertification in those Countries Experiencing Serious Drought and/or Desertification particularly in Africa on matters relating to biological diversity and drylands, with a view to identifying common priorities;

(b) To contact those agencies and networks working on sustainable mountain development with a view to examining forms of cooperation on matters relating to biological diversity and mountains;

(c) To make the results of these activities available to the third meeting of the Subsidiary Body on Scientific, Technical and Technological Advice;

2. *Requests* the Subsidiary Body on Scientific, Technical and Technological Advice to provide the fourth meeting of the Conference of the Parties with scientific, technical and technological advice on the status and trends of biological diversity in inland water ecosystems and the identification of options for conservation and sustainable use.

Decision III/14: Implementation of Article 8 (j)

The Conference of the Parties,

Reaffirming the spirit and the intent of the Convention as expressed in Article 8 (j),

Recognizing that Article 8 (j) is closely linked with other articles of the Convention, in particular Articles 10 (c), 17.2 and 18.4,

Taking note of relevant activities within the United Nations system, in particular under the Commission on Human Rights, and of relevant international instruments, such as Convention 169 of the International Labour Organization,

Stressing the need for Contracting Parties to implement Article 8 (j) and related articles and to initiate a process toward this end,

Realizing the importance of biological diversity for indigenous and local communities embodying traditional lifestyles relevant for the conservation and sustainable use of biological diversity,

Emphasizing the need for dialogue with representatives of indigenous and local communities embodying traditional lifestyles relevant for the conservation and sustainable use of biological diversity within the framework of the Convention,

Recognizing rights under national legislation of indigenous and local communities to control access to their knowledge, innovations and practices relevant for the conservation and sustainable use of biological diversity,

Reaffirming the dynamic nature of traditional knowledge, innovations and practices,

Recognizing that traditional knowledge should be given the same respect as any other form of knowledge in the implementation of the Convention,

Emphasizing the need for Parties to initiate projects on capacity-building with indigenous and local communities to address concerns in the conservation and sustainable use of biological diversity and of equitable sharing of the benefits arising from the utilization of their knowledge, innovations and practices,

Recognizing that issues related to traditional knowledge, innovations and practices go beyond the scope of the Convention,

Expressing its sincere appreciation for the valuable contribution made by the participating representatives of the indigenous and local communities at the third meeting of the Conference of the Parties,

1. *Requests* those Parties that have not yet done so to develop national legislation and corresponding strategies for the implementation of Article 8 (j) in consultation particularly with representatives of their indigenous and local communities;

2. *Urges* Parties to supply information about the implementation of Article 8 (j) and related articles, for example, national legislation and administrative and incentive measures, and to include such information in national reports;

3. *Invites* Governments, international agencies, research institutions, representatives of indigenous and local communities and non-governmental organizations to submit case studies to the Executive Secretary in time for consideration by the workshop referred to in paragraph 9 below on measures taken to develop and implement the Convention's provisions relating to indigenous and local communities. These studies could highlight key areas of discussion and help in considering the implementation of Article 8 (j) and related articles, including, *inter alia*, interactions between traditional and other forms of knowledge relating to conservation and sustainable use of biological diversity; the influence of current laws and policies on knowledge, innovations and practices of indigenous and local communities embodying traditional lifestyles relevant for the conservation and sustainable use of biological diversity; and incentive measures;

4. *Requests* the Executive Secretary to remain informed as to relevant international processes and bodies, including, *inter alia*, those under the auspices of the Commission on Human Rights and the Commission on Sustainable Development, Convention 169 of the International Labour Organization, the World Intellectual Property Organization, the World Bank, the Food and Agriculture Organization of the United Nations, the United Nations Educational, Social and Cultural Organization, and the World Trade Organization, and to provide periodic reports related to Article 8 (j) and related articles to the Conference of Parties;

5. *Requests* the interim financial mechanism to examine the support of capacity-building projects for indigenous and local communities embodying traditional lifestyles related to the preservation and maintenance of their knowledge, innovations and practices relevant for the conservation and sustainable use of biological diversity with their prior informed consent and their participation;

6. *Recommends* that the indigenous knowledge post in the Secretariat should be filled as soon as possible;

7. *Decides* that an intersessional process should be established to advance further work on the implementation of Article 8 (j) and related provisions with a view to producing a report for consideration at the fourth meeting of the Conference of the Parties;

8. *Decides* that activities as part of the intersessional process referred to in paragraph 7 should include representation by Governments, indigenous and local communities embodying traditional lifestyles relevant for the conservation and sustainable use of biodiversity, and other relevant bodies;

9. *Requests* the Executive Secretary to arrange, as part of the intersessional process referred to in paragraph 7, a five-day workshop before the fourth meeting of the Conference of the Parties according to the terms of reference in the Annex;

10. *Further requests* the Executive Secretary to produce, in support of the intersessional process referred to in paragraph 7, a background document containing the following:

(a) The consideration of the linkages between Article 8 (j) and related issues including, *inter alia*, technology transfer, access to genetic resources, ownership, intellectual property rights, alternative systems of protection of knowledge, innovations and practices, incentives and Articles 6 and 7 and the remainder of Article 8;

(b) The elaboration of concepts of key terms of Article 8 (j) and related provisions such as Articles 10 (c), 17.2 and 18.4;

(c) A survey of the activities undertaken by relevant organizations and their possible contribution to Article 8 (j) and related articles;

11. *Further requests* the Executive Secretary to invite representatives of indigenous and local communities embodying traditional lifestyles relevant for the conservation and sustainable use of biodiversity to provide input to the meeting;

12. *Calls* upon Parties to make additional voluntary contributions to help fund the workshop.

Annex

1. The workshop would seek:

(a) To identify the extent to which the various organizations, individually or collectively, could address interests in Article 8 (j), such as guidance to Governments on implementation;

(b) To identify any gaps which would help set future priorities of the Conference of the Parties;

(c) To consider the background document prepared by the Executive Secretary according to operative paragraph 9 to the present decision;

(d) To consider the input provided by the indigenous and local communities embodying traditional lifestyles according to paragraph 10 to the present decision;

(e) To consider the information provided by the Parties on national implementation under Article 8 (j) and related articles and seek to draw conclusions which will be of assistance in an assessment of priorities for future work by Parties and by the Conference of the Parties relevant to Article 8 (j) and related articles;

(f) To provide advice to the Conference of the Parties on the possibility of developing a workplan on Article 8 (j) and related articles including the modalities for such a workplan;

(g) To examine the need to establish an open-ended intersessional working group or a subsidiary body to address the role of traditional knowledge, innovations and practices of indigenous and local communities embodying traditional lifestyles relevant to the conservation and sustainable use of biological diversity.

2. In organizing the workshop,

(a) The Executive Secretary will consult with the Centre for Human Rights and other relevant bodies on organizational considerations in sessions of the United Nations Working Group on Indigenous Populations in order to inform the process of organizing this workshop;

(b) The Parties shall, as far as possible and as appropriate, promote consultations among indigenous and local communities embodying traditional lifestyles relevant for the conservation and sustainable use of biodiversity in order for them to choose their representatives to the workshop;

(c) A set number of funded participants will be determined according to the amount of voluntary contributions received and will be allocated taking into account regional and gender representations;

(d) A core figure of US$350,000 will be allocated in the budget of the Convention on Biological Diversity to cover the administrative costs of the workshop;

(e) Consideration could be given to holding it back-to-back with the third meeting of the Subsidiary Body on Scientific, Technical and Technological Advice or at a venue offered by a voluntary host.

Decision III/15: Access to genetic resources

The Conference of the Parties,

Recognizing the importance of the implementation of Article 15 with all of its provisions,

Noting that the implementation of Article 15 is closely linked to that of other Articles, such as 8 (j), 11, 16.2, 16.5, 17.2, 19.1 and 19.2;

Taking note of the importance of national and regional efforts, as set out in its decision II/11,

Recalling the support expressed in decision II/15 for the harmonization of the International Undertaking on Plant Genetic Resources for Food and Agriculture with the Convention on Biological Diversity, and noting the linkages of Article 15 with the further development and implementation of the work by the Food and Agriculture Organization of the United Nations on the Global System,

Recognizing that there is a variety of approaches to managing access to genetic resources based on their diversity and other considerations,

Recalling decision II/18, that placed the distribution of the benefits from technology, including biotechnology, on the agenda of the fourth meeting of the Conference of the Parties,

1. *Urges* Governments, regional economic integration organizations and other international, regional and national competent organizations to send to the Secretariat, five months before the fourth meeting of the Conference of the Parties, information on:

(a) National, regional, and sectoral legislative, administrative and policy measures and guidelines for activities covered by Article 15, and in particular, on access and benefit-sharing, both adopted and under development, including information on their implementation;

(b) National participatory processes for the activities covered by Article 15, and in particular, ways by which access and benefit-sharing measures and guidelines, including related institutional arrangements, are developed and implemented;

(c) As appropriate, research programmes on genetic resources;

2. *Requests* the Executive Secretary, in time for the fourth meeting of the Conference of the Parties:

(a) To prepare a note based on information provided in response to paragraph 1, further summarizing legislative, administrative and policy measures, including guidelines and regional and sectoral measures for the activities covered by Article 15, and in particular on access and benefit-sharing, both under development and adopted. The note should include a summary of the scope of the genetic resources included and being considered; any national and regional interpretations of key terms; the elements included in access measures and consideration of the process by which such measures are prepared and implemented, including interim measures; and relevant national experiences in the development and implementation of such measures, including, as available, case studies;

(b) To disseminate this information, including through the clearing-house mechanism;

3. *Urges* Governments, regional economic integration organizations, the interim financial mechanism, and competent international, regional and national organizations to support and implement human and institutional capacity-building programmes for Governments, non-governmental organizations and local and indigenous communities, as appropriate, to promote the successful development and implementation of legislative, administrative and policy measures and guidelines on access, including scientific, technical, business, legal and management skills and capacities;

4. *Invites* Governments, regional economic integration organizations and competent international, regional and national organizations to conduct analyses of ongoing experiences of legislative, administrative and policy measures and guidelines on access, including regional efforts and initiatives, and to disseminate these widely to assist Parties and stakeholders involved in developing and implementing measures and guidelines on access;

5. *Encourages* Governments and regional economic integration organizations to explore and develop, in collaboration with relevant stakeholders, guidelines and practices to ensure mutual benefits to providers and users of access measures and to implement them effectively at the national, regional or international level, as appropriate;

6. *Encourages* Governments and regional economic integration organizations to identify and communicate to the Secretariat competent national authorities responsible for granting access to genetic resources and/or competent national authorities to provide information on the granting of access to genetic resources;

7. *Urges* Governments and regional economic integration organizations to bring to a rapid conclusion the negotiation for the adaptation of the International Undertaking on Plant Genetic Resources for Food and Agriculture, in harmony with the Convention on Biological Diversity, in particular, providing solutions to access to *ex situ* collections not acquired in accordance with the Convention;

8. *Requests* the Executive Secretary to cooperate closely with the World Trade Organization through the Committee on Trade and Environment to explore the extent to which there may be linkages between Article 15 and relevant articles of the Agreement on Trade-related Aspects of Intellectual Property Rights;

9. *Urges* the Executive Secretary to coordinate closely with the Food and Agriculture Organization of the United Nations, United Nations Conference on Trade

and Development and other relevant organizations working on access to genetic resources to ensure complementary efforts.

Decision III/16: Ways to promote and facilitate access to and transfer and development of technology, as envisaged in Articles 16 and 8 of the Convention

The Conference of the Parties,

Recalling the provisions of the Convention as contained in paragraphs 16.1 and 16.2,

Taking note of document UNEP/CBD/COP/3/21 on promoting and facilitating access to and transfer and development of technology,

1. *Takes note* of decision II/4 of the second meeting of the Conference of the Parties, and recommendation II/3 of the second meeting of the Subsidiary Body on Scientific, Technical and Technological Advice;

2. *Notes also* that the issue of technology will be dealt with at its fourth meeting *inter alia* in the context of agenda item 7.4 on consideration of matters related to benefit-sharing, and specifically agenda item 7.4.1: Consideration of measures to promote and advance the distribution of benefits from biotechnology in accordance with Article 19 and agenda item 7.4.2: Consideration of benefit-sharing in the light of the present decision;

3. *Endorses* the recommendation II/3 of the second meeting of the Subsidiary Body on Scientific, Technical and Technological Advice, and requests the third meeting of the Subsidiary Body on Scientific, Technical and Technological Advice to conduct its work on technology transfer within sectoral themes related to the priority issues under its programme of work, as set out in recommendation II/12;

4. *Emphasizes* the importance of technology transfer in the achievement of each of the three objectives of the Convention.

Recommendation II/3: Agenda item 3.5: Ways and means to promote and facilitate access to, and transfer and development of technology, including biotechnology

The SBSTTA,

Recalling the relevant provisions of the Convention and, in particular, Article 25, paragraph 2 (c) and Article 20, paragraph 4;

Having examined the note produced by the Secretariat (UNEP/CBD/SBSTTA/2/6) and concluded that it met the terms of decision II/4 of the Conference of the Parties;

Recommends to the Conference of the Parties that:

(a) The work of the SBSTTA on access to and transfer of technology should now adopt an integrated approach. It should be conducted within sectoral themes related to the priority issues under the programme of work of the SBSTTA, for example technologies relevant to the conservation and sustainable use of, or making use of, marine biological diversity or agricultural biological diversity; Recommendation II/5 Capacity-Building for Biosafety;

(b) The future work of the SBSTTA on access to and transfer of technologies should examine technologies that do not cause significant damage to the environment and are: (i) relevant to the conservation and sustainable use of biological diversity and that (ii) make use of genetic resources, pursuant to Article 16 (1) of the Convention. In this respect, the role of the financial mechanism to facilitate the transfer of technology to developing countries should be explored;

(c) The work of the SBSTTA on technologies should examine these categories of technology in the context of the three objectives of the Convention, and should emphasize the importance of the third objective, namely the fair and equitable sharing of the benefits arising from the utilization of genetic resources;

(d) The identification of appropriate technologies relevant to the conservation and sustainable utilization of biological diversity should be based on an assessment, at the national level, of technological needs in the Parties, and should focus, *inter alia*, on means of gaining economic and commercial value from genetic resources;

(e) The SBSTTA should consider ways and means to encourage the greater involvement of the private sector in its work on access to and transfer of technologies by all Parties, particularly by examining options for incentive mechanisms. The Conference of the Parties should encourage all Parties to facilitate the transfer of technologies from the private sector;

(f) The clearing-house mechanism should facilitate the sharing of information and experiences about technological innovation available for Governments to fulfil their obligations under the Convention;

Decision III/17: Intellectual property rights

The Conference of the Parties,

Recognizing that intellectual property rights are relevant to and may have implications for the implementation of the Convention and the achievement of its objectives,

Noting that intellectual property rights are the focus of other international agreements and organizations,

Recalling Article 16, paragraph 5, of the Convention,

Recognizing the importance of implementing intellectual property rights-related provisions of the Convention on Biological Diversity and of international agreements relating to intellectual property rights in a mutually supportive way,

Recalling decision II/12 of the second meeting of the Conference of the Parties,

1. *Encourages* Governments, and relevant international and regional organizations, to conduct and communicate to the Executive Secretary, for dissemination through means such as the clearing-house mechanism, case studies of the impacts of intellectual property rights on the achievement of the Convention's objectives, including relationships between intellectual property rights and the knowledge, practices and innovations of indigenous and local communities embodying traditional lifestyles relevant for the conservation and sustainable use of biological diversity. Such studies could:

(a) Take into account the information and options for future work contained in the preliminary study prepared by the Executive Secretary, contained in document UNEP/CBD/COP/3/22;

(b) Take into consideration existing and potential interrelationships between intellectual property rights and other aspects of the Convention's implementation, including, for example, implementation of Articles 8 (j), 15 and 16;

(c) Involve, through consultation or cooperation, relevant international organizations, as well as relevant regional and national bodies, stakeholders, and others with relevant expertise, as appropriate;

(d) Consider the role and the potential of existing intellectual property rights systems in achieving the objectives of the Convention, including, *inter alia*, in facilitating technology transfer and in arrangements by which interested parties including indigenous and local communities embodying traditional lifestyles relevant for the conservation and sustainable use of biological diversity and countries may determine access to and share equitably the benefits of genetic resources or knowledge, innovations and practices;

(e) Consider the development of intellectual property rights, such as *sui generis* systems/approaches, or alternative forms of protection that could promote achievement of the Convention's objectives, consistent with the Parties' international obligations;

(f) Reflect the importance of coordinating efficiently with work undertaken pursuant to other elements of the work programme of the Conference of the Parties and work programmes of other relevant organizations;

2. *Notes* that the possible establishment of a new international intellectual property rights regime for databases could have implications for scientific and technical cooperation related to conservation and sustainable use of biological diversity, and calls for an open and transparent evaluation of these implications;

3. *Requests* the Executive Secretary to contact relevant international organizations, particularly the World Intellectual Property Organization, to invite them to take into account in their development cooperation programmes, where appropriate, the need to build capacity to achieve the objectives of the Convention on Biological Diversity as related to intellectual property rights;

4. *Requests* the Executive Secretary to transmit to the Secretariat of the World Trade Organization, for use by appropriate World Trade Organization bodies, decisions of the third meeting of the Conference of the Parties, as well as the documents placed before the third meeting of the Conference of the Parties, and to endeavour to undertake further cooperation and consultation with the World Trade Organization Secretariat, as appropriate. The documents shall be accompanied by the note from the Conference of the Parties included as the annex to this decision;

5. *Welcomes* the decision of the Committee on Trade and Environment of the World Trade Organization to de-restrict and transmit documents to the Executive Secretary relating to its work, and invites the Committee on Trade and Environment to transmit future relevant documents to the Executive Secretary as they are produced;

6. *Requests* the Executive Secretary to apply for observer status in the Committee on Trade and Environment of the World Trade Organization, for the purpose of representing the Convention on Biological Diversity in meetings whose agendas have a relationship with the Convention;

7. *Notes* the potential mutual benefits of exchanging information related to Article 16 of the Convention on Biological Diversity and the laws and regulations received by the Council on Trade-related Aspects of Intellectual Property Rights pursuant to the notification requirement of Article 63 of the Agreement on Trade-Related Aspects of Intellectual Property Rights;

8. *Recognizes* that further work is required to help develop a common appreciation of the relationship between intellectual property rights and the relevant provisions of the Agreement on Trade-related Aspects of Intellectual Property Rights and the Convention on Biological Diversity, in particular on issues relating to technology transfer and conservation and sustainable use of biological diversity and the fair and equitable sharing of benefits arising out of the use of genetic resources, including the protection of knowledge, innovations and practices of indigenous and local communities embodying traditional lifestyles relevant for the conservation and sustainable use of biological diversity.

Annex:
The Convention on Biological Diversity and the Agreement on Trade-related Aspects of Intellectual Property Rights

The Conference of the Parties hereby transmits to the Secretariat of the World Trade Organization, for use by appropriate bodies of the World Trade Organization, the decisions of the third meeting of the Conference of the Parties, as well as the documents placed before the third meeting of the Conference of the Parties. In particular, attention is drawn to document UNEP/CBD/COP/3/22, entitled 'The impact of intellectual property rights systems on the conservation and sustainable use of biological diversity and on the equitable sharing of benefits from its use', and document UNEP/CBD/COP/3/23, entitled 'The Convention on Biological Diversity and the Agreement on Trade-related Aspects of Intellectual Property Rights (TRIPs): Relationships and synergies'. These documents were prepared for the consideration of the Conference of the Parties and their inclusion does not imply full endorsement by the Conference of the Parties. They are offered as contributions to what is hoped will be a continuing process of consultation and cooperation, aimed at promoting the harmonious implementation of the two agreements.

Decision III/18: Incentive measures

The Conference of the Parties,

Affirming that the implementation of incentive measures, in a broad social, cultural and economic context, is of central importance to the realization of the three objectives of the Convention,

Recalling that economic and social development and poverty eradication are the first and overriding priorities of developing countries,

Recognizing that incentive measures are country-specific and need to take into account varying legal, political, economic and social conditions,

Noting that local and indigenous communities and the private sector have an important role in the design and implementation of incentive measures,

Taking note of document UNEP/CBD/COP/3/24,

1. *Endorses* recommendation II/9 of the Subsidiary Body on Scientific, Technical and Technological Advice;

2. *Resolves* that incentive measures shall be included as appropriate on the agenda of the Conference of the Parties and be integrated into the sectoral and thematic items under the medium-term programme of work of the Conference of the Parties;

3. *Encourages* Parties to review their existing legislation and economic policies, to identify and promote incentive for the conservation and sustainable use of components of biological diversity, stressing the importance of taking appropriate action on incentives that threaten biological diversity;

4. *Encourages* Parties to ensure adequate incorporation of the market and non-market values of biological diversity into plans, policies and programmes and other relevant areas, *inter alia*, national accounting systems and investment strategies;

5. *Encourages* Parties to develop training and capacity-building programmes to implement incentive measures and promote private-sector initiatives in this regard;

6. *Encourages* Parties to incorporate biological diversity considerations into impact assessments, consistent with Article 14 of the Convention, as a step in the design and implementation of incentive measures;

7. *Invites* Parties to share experiences on incentive measures and make relevant case studies available to the Secretariat, and requests the Executive Secretary to facilitate the exchange of information on incentive measures, including case studies, amongst Parties, through appropriate means such as the clearing-house mechanism and regional workshops;

8. *Requests* the Executive Secretary to provide an initial background document for consideration by the Conference of the Parties at its fourth meeting, providing guidance to the Parties on the design and implementation of incentive measures;

9. *Requests* the Executive Secretary to take into consideration relevant work under way in other forums, such as United Nations Conference on Trade and Development and the Organisation for Economic Cooperation and Development;

10. *Requests* the Subsidiary Body on Scientific, Technical and Technological Advice, as appropriate, to provide in its recommendations to the Conference of the Parties scientific, technical and technological advice on the implementation of Article 11 in relevant thematic areas.

Recommendation II/9: Agenda item 3.11: Economic valuation of biological diversity

The SBSTTA,

Recalling that recommendation I/9 decided that the SBSTTA would consider at its second meeting advice to the Conference of the Parties on the economic valuation of biological diversity and its components, in particular in relation to access to genetic resources,

Recalling also that decision II/11 of the Conference of the Parties requested the Executive Secretary to compile an annotated list of studies and other relevant information on the social and economic valuation of genetic resources, including the demand by industry for genetic resources,

Having examined the Note prepared by the Secretariat (UNEP/CBD/SBSTTA/2/13),

Recognizing that a better understanding of the full value of biological diversity at the genetic, species, and ecosystem level will greatly assist Parties in their efforts to implement effective policy and management measures to meet the threefold objectives of the Convention,

Recognizing that information on the economic value of biological diversity and its components is severely deficient, and that methods for providing this information need further development,

Recognizing also that biological diversity and its components provide a wide range of benefits, representing significant use and non-use values. Some of these values are difficult to define fully in terms of economic value. These include intangible, yet critical, socio-cultural values and existence values,

Further recognizing that, while more information on economic values is needed, the lack of this information need not delay the implementation of economically and socially sound incentive measures to sustainably manage biological diversity. In this regard, consideration of incentives having a perverse impact on biological diversity and its components should be regarded as a priority area,

Recommends:

1. That future work should include regular review and syntheses of current information, case studies of economic value, research into appropriate and cost-effective methodologies for determining these values, and means of facilitating access to this information.

2. That economic valuation should be integrated into the sectoral and thematic items under the Medium-Term Programme of Work of the Conference of the Parties, and should be reflected as appropriate in relevant agenda items including, in particular, incentive measures, and also agricultural biodiversity, genetic resources, environmental impact assessments, inland water ecosystems, and marine and coastal biodiversity, taking the ecosystem approach as the primary framework of action to be taken under the Convention.

3. That the Conference of the Parties encourage Parties to draw upon research into the economic valuation of biological diversity produced by, *inter alia*, regional and

economic groupings in order to assist the appropriate development of policy and management measures for conservation and sustainable use;

4. That the Conference of the Parties, in its consideration of Incentive Measures at its third meeting, emphasize the importance of developing well-targeted local level incentives, participatory approaches to the design of new measures, and capacity-building.

Decision III/19: Special Session of the General Assembly to review implementation of Agenda 21

The Conference of the Parties,

Recalling the provisions of the Convention on Biological Diversity and the relevant chapters of Agenda 21,

Recalling General Assembly resolution 50/113, which invited the Conference of the Parties to the Convention on Biological Diversity to provide inputs to the special session of the General Assembly to review progress in implementing Agenda 21,

Recognizing the importance of the special session of the General Assembly in 1997 to review progress made to date in the implementation of Agenda 21,

Mindful of the role of the Convention on Biological Diversity in promoting sustainable development, and reaffirming its commitment to the three objectives of the Convention,

1. *Requests* the President of the Conference of the Parties to transmit the annexed statement from the Conference of the Parties to the special session of the General Assembly in 1997;

2. *Also requests* the Executive Secretary to provide to the special session of the General Assembly and to the preparatory process such information related to activities and developments under the Convention as may be required, including the reports of the meetings of the Conference of the Parties.

Annex:
Statement from the Conference of the Parties to the Convention on Biological Diversity to the Special Session of the United Nations General Assembly

1. The Conference of the Parties to the Convention on Biological Diversity takes this opportunity to reaffirm its commitment to the three objectives of the Convention, namely the conservation of biological diversity, the sustainable use of its components and the fair and equitable sharing of benefits arising out of the utilization of genetic resources.

A The Convention on Biological Diversity and Agenda 21

2. The Conference of the Parties emphasizes the significance of the Convention, and activities carried out in implementation of the Convention, to the achievement of

goals set out in many of the chapters of Agenda 21. Sustainable development cannot be achieved without the sustainable use of the world's biological diversity. The Convention provides a set of legally binding commitments and is an important tool for translating the principles of the Rio Declaration on Environment and Development and Agenda 21 into concrete actions.

3. The Convention on Biological Diversity entered into force on 29 December 1993. The Conference of the Parties, at its first three meetings, adopted a number of decisions aimed at elaborating and implementing the provisions of the Convention. The Convention adopts an ecosystem approach, both in its provisions and in its programme of work. The integration of biological diversity considerations into relevant sectoral or cross-sectoral plans, programmes and policies is central to the Convention. In addition, the Conference of the Parties attaches particular importance to cooperation with other biological diversity-related conventions, institutions and processes.

4. The Conference of the Parties recognizes that biological diversity is a cross-cutting issue. The provisions of the Convention are of the utmost relevance to a number of the issues reviewed by the Commission on Sustainable Development to date, including: the planning and management of land resources; combating deforestation; managing fragile ecosystems; promoting sustainable agriculture and rural development; and consideration of marine and coastal biological diversity.

5. The provisions of the Convention are also relevant to the cross-sectoral issues reviewed by the Commission on Sustainable Development. In its statement to the third session of the Commission on Sustainable Development, the Conference of the Parties noted in particular the relevance of the following cross-sectoral issues on the agenda of the third session of the Commission on Sustainable Development: combating poverty; demographic dynamics and sustainability; integrating environment and development in decision-making; environmentally sound management of biotechnology; roles of major groups; financial resources and mechanisms; transfer of technology; science for sustainable development; and information for decision-making.

B The Convention and chapter 15 of Agenda 21

6. The Convention is the principal global instrument relevant to achieving the goals set out in chapter 15 of Agenda 21, Conservation of Biological Diversity. At its third session, the Commission on Sustainable Development urged States to sign, ratify, accede to and implement the Convention on Biological Diversity. At the time of the third meeting of the Conference of the Parties, 161 States and one regional economic integration organization had done so, making this Convention the principal instrument for advancing global cooperation and practical action in its field.

7. The first meeting of the Conference of the Parties, held in Nassau, the Bahamas, in December 1994, set in place the mechanisms provided for by the Convention. The second meeting, held in Jakarta, Indonesia, in November 1995, adopted substantive decisions aimed at facilitating the implementation of the Convention.

C The relevance of the Convention to other chapters of Agenda 21

8. Significant work has already been undertaken or initiated under the Convention in relation to a number of key areas. For example:

(a) National planning processes

9. The Convention requires Parties, in accordance with their particular conditions and capabilities, to develop national strategies, plans and programmes for the conservation and sustainable use of biological diversity. The second meeting of the Conference of the Parties decided that the first national reports of the Parties, due at its fourth meeting, will focus on measures taken for the implementation of Article 6 of the Convention (General measures for conservation and sustainable use).

(b) Marine and coastal biological diversity

10. The second meeting of the Conference of the Parties adopted decision II/10 on marine and coastal biological diversity, the Jakarta Mandate. This decision proposes a framework for global action. The salient features of the mandate are:

(i) support for and cooperation with other international efforts;

(ii) development of a programme of work for the Convention process, on the basis of five thematic areas, namely: integrated marine and coastal area management; marine and coastal protected areas; sustainable use of coastal and marine living resources; mariculture; and alien species; and

(iii) the establishment of a roster of experts on the basis of country input, which will draw upon expertise from scientific, technical, technological, social, management, economic, policy, legal and indigenous and traditional knowledge.

11. The first meeting of experts drawn from the roster is to be held in Jakarta early in 1997. The Conference of the Parties also forwarded its decision on marine and coastal biological diversity to the fourth session of the Commission on Sustainable Development in 1996. Integral to the implementation of the Jakarta Mandate will be cooperation with other relevant institutions, processes and international agreements.

(c) Terrestrial biological diversity

12. The second meeting of the Conference of the Parties submitted a statement to the Intergovernmental Panel on Forests, and the Conference of the Parties has considered further inputs. The Conference of the Parties has also begun to consider further work in the area of terrestrial biological diversity, including in relation to drylands and to the biological diversity of mountain regions. At its third meeting, major consideration was given to agricultural biological diversity.

(d) Environmentally sound management of biotechnology

13. Chapter 16 of Agenda 21 addresses the environmentally sound management of biotechnology. The second meeting of the Conference of the Parties established an Open-ended Ad Hoc Working Group on Biosafety to develop, in the field of the safe transfer, handling and use of living modified organisms, a protocol on biosafety, specifically focusing on transboundary movement, of any living modified organism resulting from modern biotechnology that may have adverse effects on the conservation and sustainable use of biological diversity, setting out for consideration, in particular, appropriate procedure for advance informed agreement. The Working Group held its first meeting in July 1996 and reported to the third meeting of the Conference of the Parties. The Working Group aims to complete its work by 1998.

(e) Technical and scientific cooperation, and capacity-building

14. A number of articles of the Convention address the issues of technical and scientific cooperation and capacity-building, in which the clearing-house mechanism will play a significant role. The second meeting of the Conference of the Parties reaffirmed the importance of the clearing-house mechanism, accessible to all countries, to support implementation of the Convention at the national level. The Conference of the Parties noted that enhanced cooperation with other information systems and activities would contribute to the development of the clearing-house mechanism. A pilot phase of the clearing-house mechanism was established.

(f) Financial resources

15. The Convention recognizes the need for new and additional financial resources to enable developing country Parties to meet their commitments under the Convention and to benefit from its provisions. The Conference of the Parties has encouraged exploration of availability of additional financial resources, and ways in which the activities of funding institutions might be more supportive of the objectives of the Convention. In this regard, the Conference of the Parties encourages bilateral and multilateral funding agencies to incorporate more fully biological diversity considerations into their activities.

(g) Financial mechanism

16. The Convention foresees that there shall be a mechanism for the provision of financial resources to developing country Parties for the purposes of the Convention. The Conference of the Parties decided at its second meeting that the restructured Global Environment Facility should continue to serve on an interim basis as the institutional structure to operate the financial mechanism under the Convention. It also decided to undertake the first review of the effectiveness of the financial mechanism at its fourth meeting and to undertake a review every three years thereafter.

17. The Conference of the Parties specifically requested the Global Environment Facility as the interim institutional structure to implement the relevant provisions of the following decisions: II/3 and III/4 on the clearing-house mechanism; II/7 and III/9 on consideration of Articles 6 and 8 of the Convention; II/8 on preliminary consideration of components of biological diversity particularly under threat and action which could be taken under the Convention; II/17 on the form and intervals of national reports by Parties; III/10 on identification, monitoring and assessment; III/11 on conservation and sustainable use of agricultural biological diversity; III/14 on implementation of Article 8 (j); III/15 on access to genetic resources; III/18 on incentive measures; and III/20 on issues related to biosafety. The additional guidance to the financial mechanism given by the Conference of the Parties at its third meeting is contained in consolidated form in decision III/5.

(h) Major groups

18. The major groups, identified in Section 3 of Agenda 21, participate in the processes of the Convention, allowing them an opportunity to engage with Governments over the implementation of the commitments made under the Convention. In particular, certain provisions of the Convention specifically address the interests of indigenous people and their communities, as well as of other local communities.

D Recent developments

19. The Conference of the Parties also draws to the attention of the special session of the General Assembly the report of its third meeting, held in Buenos Aires, Argentina (document UNEP/CBD/COP/3/38). The third meeting considered, *inter alia*:

(a) The financial mechanism and financial resources for the effective implementation of the Convention;

(b) Implementation of Articles 6 and 8 of the Convention;

(c) The conservation and sustainable use of agricultural biological diversity;

(d) Terrestrial biological diversity;

(e) The implementation of Article 8 (j);

(f) Access to genetic resources;

(g) Technology transfer;

(h) The impacts of intellectual property rights on the conservation and sustainable use of biological diversity;

(i) Incentive measures; and

(j) Cooperation with other conventions, institutions and processes.

E Future work under the Convention

20. The Conference of the Parties draws to the attention of the special session the further work envisaged under the Convention's medium-term programme of work, including such areas as:

(a) Consideration of inland water ecosystems;

(b) Linkages between *in situ* and *ex situ* conservation;

(c) Public awareness and education;

(d) Impact assessment and minimizing adverse impacts;

(e) Matters related to benefit sharing;

(f) Technical and scientific cooperation;

(g) Conservation and sustainable use of agricultural biological diversity;

(h) Forest biological diversity;

(i) Implementation of Article 8 (j); and

(j) Indicators and methodologies for assessments.

21. At its fourth meeting, the Conference of the Parties will undertake a longer-term review of the work programme of the Convention and the operation of the Conference of the Parties and subsidiary organs, in the light of progress and experience to date.

F Cooperation with other conventions, institutions and processes

22. The Conference of the Parties affirms the importance it attaches to cooperation and

coordination between the Convention on Biological Diversity and other conventions, institutions and processes of relevance. A number of measures have already been taken to enhance such cooperation, including the agreement of memoranda of cooperation between the Convention Secretariat and the secretariats of certain other biological diversity-related conventions. The Conference of the Parties emphasizes its commitment to continue to explore effective mechanisms to cooperate with other conventions, institutions and processes of relevance, and in particular the Commission on Sustainable Development, to avoid duplication and promote efficient use of resources in implementing its objectives and objectives contained in Agenda 21 in an expeditious manner.

G Future challenges

23. In spite of the progress made to date in implementing the objectives of the Convention, Parties remain aware that biological diversity is being destroyed by human activities at unprecedented rates. The Conference of the Parties notes that a significant amount of work remains to be undertaken, in collaboration with relevant conventions, institutions and processes, in order fully to implement the Convention. It therefore calls upon the special session to recognize the urgency of this work and to support it.

24. In particular, the Conference of the Parties recognizes that attention needs to be paid, *inter alia*, to:

(a) The further raising of public awareness and the understanding of the importance of biological diversity through educational programmes and information;

(b) The rapid development and implementation of national strategies, plans or programmes for the conservation and sustainable use of biological diversity;

(c) The consideration of appropriate arrangements for access to genetic resources, and for the fair and equitable sharing of benefits arising out of the utilization of such resources;

(d) The development of effective means to respect, preserve and maintain the knowledge, innovations and practices of indigenous and local communities and the equitable sharing of the benefits arising out of the utilization thereof;

(e) The transfer of and access to technologies relevant to the Convention; and

(f) The provision of new and additional financial resources for the implementation of the Convention.

Decision III/20: Issues related to biosafety

The Conference of the Parties,

Recalling decision II/5 adopted at its second meeting,

Having considered the report and recommendations of the first meeting of the Open-ended Ad Hoc Working Group on Biosafety, which met in Aarhus, Denmark, from 22 to 26 July 1996,

Recalling paragraph 10 of the terms of reference for the Open-ended Ad Hoc Working Group, contained in the annex to decision II/5, which states that the process of developing a protocol shall be conducted as a matter of urgency and that the Open-ended Ad Hoc Working Group shall endeavour to complete its work in 1998,

Welcoming the adoption of the UNEP International Technical Guidelines for Safety in Biotechnology at the Global Consultation of Government-designated Experts, held in Cairo, Egypt, from 11 to 14 December 1995,

Affirming its support for a two-track approach through which the promotion of the application of the UNEP International Technical Guidelines for Safety in Biotechnology can contribute to the development and implementation of a protocol on biosafety, without prejudicing the development and conclusion of such a protocol,

1. *Decides:*

(a) That each of the five groups of States referred to in section 1, paragraph 1, of General Assembly resolution 2997 (XXVII), of 15 December 1972, shall send to the Secretariat nominations for two representatives to the Bureau as soon as possible, and in any event before the commencement of the second meeting of the Open-ended Ad Hoc Working Group established by the second meeting of the Conference of the Parties in decision II/5;

(b) That the Bureau shall remain in office, under the chairmanship of Mr. Veit Koester, (Denmark), until the fourth meeting of the Conference of the Parties;

(c) That two meetings of the Open-ended Ad Hoc Working Group will be held in 1997, and that a sufficient number of meetings will be held in 1998 to allow the Working Group to complete its work in 1998;

2. *Endorses* recommendation II/5 of the Subsidiary Body on Scientific, Technical and Technological Advice and, in particular:

(a) The realization of activities to promote the application of the UNEP International Technical Guidelines for Safety in Biotechnology, in accordance with paragraph 2 of recommendation II/5;

(b) The importance of funding for capacity-building in biosafety;

(c) The request to the interim institutional structure operating the financial mechanism to provide financial resources to developing country Parties for capacity-building in biosafety, in accordance with paragraph 3 of recommendation II/5, as set out in paragraph 2 (a) of decision III/5.

Recommendation II/5: Agenda item 3.7: Capacity-building for biosafety

The SBSTTA,

Recalling decision II/5 of the Conference of Parties that capacity-building related to biosafety was recognized as an area of priority requiring global attention as an element that will facilitate the effective implementation of any biosafety regulations, guidelines or future agreements on biosafety;

Recalling also decision II/5 of the Conference of Parties that established an Open-ended Ad Hoc Working Group on a Protocol for Biosafety, which held its first meeting from 22 to 26 July 1996 in Aarhus, Denmark, and its report contained in document UNEP/CBD/COP/3/24;

Having examined the Note by the Secretariat (UNEP/CBD/SBSTTA/2/8) and the report of the first meeting of the Open-ended Ad Hoc Working Group;

Recommends the following for the consideration of the Conference of Parties:

1. It is necessary to avoid duplication between the work of the SBSTTA and the work of the Ad Hoc Working Group. The SBSTTA offers full support and will only provide input into the work of the Ad Hoc Working Group upon request;

2. The UNEP International Technical Guidelines for Biosafety in Biotechnology represent a useful tool with respect to capacity-building and should not preempt the work of the protocol on biosafety. The guidelines can be used as an interim measure in view of the development of a biosafety protocol and to complement it after its completion and in the course of its implementation for the purpose of facilitating national capacities for risk assessment and risk management, adequate information systems, and to develop, through training, expert resources in the area of biotechnology.

3. Recognizing the importance of funding for capacity-building in biosafety (including scientific capacity and impact assessment) and considering its cross-sectoral nature, the Conference of Parties should consider the development of guidance to the Global Environment Facility for the provision of financial resources to developing countries in biosafety, including the implementation by them of the UNEP Guidelines. Furthermore, the Conference of Parties should encourage funding within programmes from organizations such as UNEP, the United Nations Development Programme, the United Nations Industrial Development Programme, World Health Organization, the Food and Agriculture Organization of the United Nations and other multilateral and bilateral sources, in the priority areas identified by the Conference of Parties;

4. Capacity-building for biosafety should also be discussed in conjunction with the issues of technology transfer, risk assessment and risk management in order to ensure the safe use of the products of biotechnology; and

5. Specific information related to biosafety capacity-building should be included within the clearing-house mechanism as described in decision II/3.

Decision III/21: Relationship of the Convention with the Commission on Sustainable Development and biodiversity-related conventions, other international agreements, institutions and processes of relevance

The Conference of the Parties,

Recalling decisions II/13 and II/14 adopted at its second meeting,

Reaffirming the need to make mutually supportive activities under the Convention on Biological Diversity and activities under other conventions, processes and institutions relevant to the achievement of the objectives of the Convention, while avoiding unnecessary duplication of activities and costs on the part of Parties and of the organs of the Convention,

Welcoming the progress made to date in the development of cooperative arrangements with relevant conventions, institutions and processes, as described in document UNEP/CBD/COP/3/29,

1. *Expresses* its appreciation to those conventions and institutions which have provided documentation and information to assist the deliberations of the Conference of the Parties at its third meeting;

2. *Endorses* the memoranda of cooperation entered into by the Executive Secretary with the secretariats of the Convention on Wetlands of International Importance, especially as Waterfowl Habitat, the Convention on International Trade in Endangered Species of Wild Fauna and Flora and the Convention on the Conservation of Migratory Species of Wild Animals, and encourages the development of further such arrangements with relevant international biological diversity-related bodies, including regional conventions;

3. *Requests* the Executive Secretary to continue to coordinate with the secretariats of relevant biological diversity-related conventions, institutions, and processes, with a view to: facilitating the exchange of information and experience; exploring the possibility of recommending procedures for harmonizing, to the extent desirable and practicable, the reporting requirements of Parties under those instruments and conventions; exploring the possibility of coordinating their respective programmes of work; and consulting on how such conventions and other international legal instruments can contribute to the implementation of the provisions of the Convention on Biological Diversity;

4. *Also requests* the Executive Secretary to develop closer relationships with, in particular, the United Nations Framework Convention on Climate Change and the United Nations Convention to Combat Desertification in those Countries Experiencing Serious Drought and/or Desertification, particularly in Africa, with a view to making implementation activities and institutional arrangements mutually supportive;

5. *Encourages* the further development of cooperative arrangements at the scientific and technical level with appropriate biological diversity-related conventions and institutions, such as the Scientific Council of the Convention on Conservation of Migratory Species and the Scientific and Technical Review Panel of the Convention on Wetlands of International Importance, through the Subsidiary Body on Scientific, Technical and Technological Advice;

6. *Takes note* of document UNEP/CBD/COP/3/35 and the comments made by participants at its third meeting, and invites the Executive Secretary to continue to investigate, in collaboration with relevant global and regional conventions, institutions and processes, modalities for cooperation, and to report back to the Conference of the Parties at its fourth meeting in the light of the longer-term review of work;

7. *Decides:*

(a) In relation to cooperation with the Convention on Wetlands of International Importance:

(i) to note the Strategic Plan for 1997–2002 adopted by the Conference of Contracting Parties to the Convention on Wetlands of International Importance, in March 1996, which includes actions aimed at creating synergy between that Convention and the Convention on Biological Diversity;

(ii) to invite the Convention on Wetlands of International Importance to cooperate as a lead partner in the implementation of activities under the

Convention related to wetlands, and, in particular, requests the Executive Secretary to seek inputs from the Convention on Wetlands of International Importance, in the preparation of documentation concerning the status and trends of inland water ecosystems for the consideration of the Conference of the Parties at its fourth meeting;

(b) In relation to cooperation with the Convention on the Conservation of Migratory Species, to request the Executive Secretary, in consultation with the Secretariat of that Convention, to evaluate how the implementation of that Convention can complement the implementation of the Convention on Biological Diversity through its transboundary coordinated and concerted action on a regional, continental and global scale;

8. *Urges* the Parties to ensure that the conservation and sustainable use of wetlands, and of migratory species and their habitats, are fully incorporated into national strategies, plan and programmes to preserve biological diversity;

9. *Invites* the governing bodies of biological diversity-related conventions to consider the possible contributions of those conventions to the implementation of the objectives of the Convention on Biological Diversity, and to share experience with the Conference of the Parties on, *inter alia*, successful management and conservation practices;

10. *Calls on* the national focal points of the Convention on Biological Diversity, and the competent authorities of the Convention on Wetlands of International Importance, the Convention on the Conservation of Migratory Species and the Convention on International Trade in Endangered Species of Wild Fauna and Flora to cooperate on the implementation of these conventions at the national level to avoid duplication of effort;

11. *Urges* the United Nations Environment Programme to undertake early implementation of decision II/14 of the Conference of the Parties;

12. *Invites* contracting parties to relevant biological diversity-related conventions to explore opportunities for accessing funding through the Global Environment Facility for relevant projects, including projects involving a number of countries, which fulfil the eligibility criteria and guidance provided by the Conference of the Parties to the Convention on Biological Diversity to the Global Environment Facility.

Decision III/22: Medium-term programme of work for 1996–1997

The Conference of the Parties,

Recalling decision II/18 of the Conference of the Parties in which the Conference of the Parties adopted its medium-term work programme for the biennium 1996–1997,

Recalling also that decision II/18 provides for the review of the medium-term programme of work for the biennium 1996–1997, particularly the review of the operations of the Conference of the Parties and its subsidiary organs as well as the overall review and consideration of a long-term programme of work,

1. *Recognizes* that it may be necessary for the Executive Secretary, with the guidance of the Bureau of the Conference of the Parties, to adjust further the servicing of the programme of work in the light of the resources available to the Secretariat;

2. *Invites* Parties, participants and other relevant institutions to submit by 31 March 1997 their views to the Executive Secretary on:

(a) The operations of the Conference of the Parties;

(b) The overall review of the medium-term programme of work for 1995–1997;

(c) A longer-term programme of work;

3. *Requests* the Executive Secretary to submit a synthesis of these views to the Conference of the Parties for consideration at its fourth meeting;

4. *Welcomes* offers to contribute to efforts to facilitate the review process;

5. *Takes note* of the provisional agenda for the fourth meeting of the Conference of the Parties, contained in Annex I of document UNEP/CBD/COP/3/31;

6. *Takes note* of the draft provisional agenda of the third meeting of the Subsidiary Body on Scientific, Technical and Technological Advice, contained in recommendation II/12 of the second meeting of the Subsidiary Body on Scientific, Technical and Technological Advice, in document UNEP/CBD/COP/3/3;

7. *Requests* the bureau of the Subsidiary Body on Scientific, Technical and Technological Advice to focus the agenda of the third meeting of the Subsidiary Body on Scientific, Technical and Technological Advice, in line with the comments given at the third meeting of the Conference of the Parties on the work of the Subsidiary Body on Scientific, Technical and Technological Advice, and to submit it to the Parties sufficiently in advance of the third meeting of the Subsidiary Body on Scientific, Technical and Technological Advice.

Appendix:[7] Medium-term programme of work of the Conference of the Parties 1996–1997

1. The medium-term programme of work will be constructed on the basis of standing and rolling issues.
2. Standing items will include, *inter alia*:
   - 2.1 Matters relating to the financial mechanism, including a report from the interim institutional structure entrusted with its operation;
   - 2.2 Report from the Secretariat on the administration of the Convention and budget for the Secretariat;
   - 2.3 Report from, instructions to and consideration of recommendations from the Subsidiary Body on Scientific, Technical and Technological Advice;
   - 2.4 Reports by Parties on the implementation of the Convention;

7 As contained in the annex to decision II/18 (UNEP/CBD/COP/2/19).

2.5 Report on the assessment and review of the operation of the clearing-house mechanism;

2.6 Relationship of the Convention on Biological Diversity with the Commission on Sustainable Development and biodiversity-related conventions, other international agreements, institutions and processes of relevance.

3. The other issues and derived activities necessary to implement the Convention should be dealt with on a year-by-year agenda, on the understanding that these relevant rotating issues will be developed and continually dealt with in accordance with the decisions of the Conference of the Parties by the Subsidiary Body on Scientific, Technical and Technological Advice and any eventual working groups appointed by the Conference of the Parties. The year-by-year agenda has to be flexible.

4. Treatment of the items on the programme of work should also reflect the importance of capacity-building as one of the elements of successful Convention implementation. The programme of work should always reflect a balance among the Convention's objectives, as set forth in Article 1.

5. In 1996, the third meeting of the Conference of the Parties may continue to consider pending issues of the 1995 programme of work.

6. The third meeting of the Conference of the Parties may consider, *inter alia*, the following items in 1996:

6.1 General measures for conservation and sustainable use:

6.1.1 Implementation of Articles 6 and 8.

6.2 Identification, monitoring and assessment:

6.2.1 To consider options for implementing Article 7;

6.2.2 Appraisal of the SBSTTA review of assessment of biological diversity for the implementation of Article 25 (2) (a) and advice on methodologies for future assessments.

6.3 Conservation and sustainable use of agricultural biological diversity:

6.3.1 To consider agricultural biological diversity within the context of the Convention's three objectives and its provisions;

6.3.2 To consider a report on progress under the FAO Global System for the Conservation and Utilization of Plant Genetic Resources for Food and Agriculture.

6.4 Consideration of the future programme of work for terrestrial biological diversity in the light of the outcome of deliberations of the third session of the Commission on Sustainable Development in 1995.

6.5 Knowledge, innovations and practices of indigenous and local communities:

6.5.1 Implementation of Article 8 (j).

6.6 Access to genetic resources:

6.6.1 To consider the compilation of views of Parties on possible options for developing national legislative, administrative or policy measures, as appropriate, to implement Article 15.

6.7 Issues related to technology:

6.7.1 To consider ways to promote and facilitate access to and transfer and development of technology, as envisaged by Articles 16 and 18 of the Convention.

6.8 Incentive measures:

6.8.1 To consider the compilation of information and experiences shared on the implementation of Article 11.

6.9 Special session of the General Assembly to review implementation of Agenda 21:

6.9.1 To provide a report from the perspective of the Convention's three objectives.

6.10 Issues related to biosafety:

6.10.1 To consider the first report of the ad hoc working group on biosafety.

7. In 1997, the fourth meeting of the Conference of the Parties may consider, *inter alia*, the following items:

7.1 Review of the medium-term programme of work (1995–1997):

7.1.1 To review the operations of the Conference of the Parties and subsidiary organs;

7.1.2 To undertake an overall review and consider a longer-term programme of work.

7.2 Models and mechanisms for linkages between *in situ* and *ex situ* conservation:

7.2.1 To generate options of models and linkage.

7.3 Measures for implementing the Convention:

7.3.1 To provide information and share experiences on the implementation of Article 13;

7.3.2 To provide information and share experiences on the implementation of Article 14;

7.3.3 Consideration of biodiversity under threat.

7.4 Consideration of matters related to benefit-sharing:

7.4.1 To consider measures to promote and advance the distribution of benefits from biotechnology in accordance with Article 19;

7.4.2 To be considered in the light of the outcome of item 6.7.1 above.

7.5 Technical and scientific cooperation.

7.6 Terrestrial biological diversity:

7.6.1 To assess the status and trends of the biodiversity of inland water ecosystems and identify options for conservation and sustainable use.

Decision III/23: Administrative matters

The Conference of the Parties,

Recalling decision I/4 of the first meeting of the Conference of the Parties,

Reiterating its gratitude to the Government of Canada for the generous offer to host the Permanent Secretariat of the Convention on Biological Diversity,

Welcoming the speed with which the relocation of the Permanent Secretariat from Geneva to Montreal took place,

Expressing appreciation to the Executive Director of the United Nations Environment Programme for finalizing negotiations for the headquarters agreement between the Permanent Secretariat of the Convention and the Government of Canada,

Noting with concern the difficulties encountered by the Permanent Secretariat in making the transition, in particular the difficulties associated with the establishment of efficient and timely services and with recruitment of staff,

Taking note with appreciation of the efforts of the Executive Secretary to continue the functions of the Permanent Secretariat in these circumstances and urging him to continue his efforts to meet the needs of the Convention,

1. *Invites* the Executive Director of the United Nations Environment Programme and the Executive Secretary of the Convention on Biological Diversity to develop procedures, making an effort to conclude by 27 January 1997, with respect to the functioning of the Permanent Secretariat of the Convention on Biological Diversity, to clarify and make more effective their respective roles and responsibilities;

2. *Stresses* that these procedures must provide for the managerial autonomy and efficiency of the Permanent Secretariat and its responsiveness to the needs of the Convention, and must ensure the administrative accountability of the Executive Secretary to the Conference of the Parties;

3. *Stresses also* that the procedures must be in accordance with the United Nations financial and staff rules and regulations and with decision I/4 of the Conference of the Parties and should as far as possible, and where appropriate, follow the Personnel, Financial and Common Services arrangements agreed to between the United Nations and the Framework Convention on Climate Change;

4. *Requests* the Executive Secretary to make available to the Parties copies of the agreed procedures on a timely basis and to report to the Conference of the Parties through its Bureau at its fourth meeting on the implementation of these arrangements.

Decision III/24: Budget of the Trust Fund for the Convention on Biological Diversity

The Conference of the Parties,

1. *Approves* the Convention budget for the biennium 1997–1998 as set forth in the annex to the present decision;

2. *Decides* that the Trust Fund shall be extended for a period of two years, beginning 1 January 1998 and ending 31 December 1999;

3. *Urges* all the Parties to pay promptly their contributions to the Trust Fund, based on the indicative scale set forth in the appendix to the budget (annex, part A) and in accordance with the terms of paragraph 10 of its decision II/20;

4. *Requests* the Parties and States not Parties to the Convention, as well as governmental, intergovernmental and non-governmental organizations and other sources, to contribute to the Trust Fund;

5. *Decides:*

(a) That two special trust funds shall be established: (i) a special voluntary trust fund for additional voluntary contributions to the core budget for approved activities under the Convention on Biological Diversity (annex, part B), and (ii) a special voluntary trust fund for facilitating participation of Parties in the Convention process (annex, part C);[8]

(b) That the Executive Director of the United Nations Environment Programme should be requested to establish the special trust funds referred to in paragraph 5 (a) above, for which the Financial Rules for the Administration of the Trust Fund for the Convention on Biological Diversity and other arrangements for that Fund shall apply *mutatis mutandis*, with the exception of the modification in sub-paragraph 5 (f) below;

(c) That all the Parties and States not Parties to the Convention, as well as governmental, intergovernmental and non-governmental organizations and other sources should be invited to contribute to the special trust funds;

(d) That the Trustee shall promptly advise the Executive Secretary of the receipt of all the contributions and acknowledge receipt of such contributions;

(e) That on a monthly basis the Trustee shall provide the Executive Secretary with information on the status of allotments, expenditures, trial balances and unliquidated obligations;

(f) That the Executive Secretary may make transfers from one budget line to another in accordance with the Financial Rules and Regulations of the United Nations;

6. *Requests* the Executive Secretary to explore in conjunction with the Executive Secretaries of the United Nations Framework Convention on Climate Change and the United Nations Convention to Combat Desertification in those Countries Experiencing Serious Drought and/or Desertification, particularly in Africa, the availability, cost and funding of suitable liaison arrangements in Geneva and/or New York and to report thereon to the Conference of the Parties at its next meeting;

7. *Urges* all those making financial contributions to a trust fund of the Convention to provide details promptly to the Executive Secretary regarding the amounts, date of payment, conditions and any other relevant information;

8. *Requests* the Executive Secretary to ensure that duplicates of all the information on financial matters and the relevant documents are kept in custody at the seat of the Permanent Secretariat according to the Financial Rules and Regulations of the United Nations;

9. *Directs* the Executive Secretary to consider carefully all offers of support from other organizations and to cooperate with them with a view to making the most effective use of the available competencies, resources and services and to enter into such administrative and contractual arrangements as may be necessary for the effective discharge of the functions of the Permanent Secretariat;

8 Developing country Parties, in particular the least developed among them, and small island developing States.

10. *Requests* the Executive Secretary to prepare and submit to Parties a quarterly report on the administration of the Convention including such matters as staff lists, status of contributions, progress on the implementation of the medium-term work programme and financial expenditures;

11. *Requests* the Executive Secretary to include in the documents circulated for consideration at future meetings of the Conference of the Parties estimates of the likely costs of the recommendations contained therein, where such recommendations would have significant implications for the budget of the Convention.

Annex
A Budget of the Trust Fund for the Convention on Biological Diversity for the biennium 1997–1998

		1997 (US$)	*1998 (US$)*
1	**EXECUTIVE DIRECTION AND MANAGEMENT**		
	Executive direction		
	Executive Secretary (D-2)	95,432	100,203
	Principal Officer (D-1)	91,948	96,546
	Programme Officer – Legal affairs (P-4/L-4)	78,943	82,891
	Special Assistant to the Executive Secretary (P-3/L-3)	68,124	71,531
	Research Assistant (G-7)	25,453	26,726
	Senior Secretary (G-7)	25,453	26,726
	Fund management and administration		
	Fund Management/Administration Officer (P-4) (UNEP)	0	0
	Finance and Administration Officer (Quebec) b/	0	0
	Associate Administrative Officer (P-2/L-2)	54,296	57,011
	Associate Administrative Officer – Correspondence (P-2/L-2)	54,296	57,011
	Financial Assistant (G-7)	25,453	26,726
	Administrative Assistant (G-6)	23,302	24,467
	Travel Clerk (G-6)	23,302	24,467
	Receptionist (G-4)	19,535	20,512
	Messenger (G-4)	19,535	20,512
	Subtotal	**605,072**	**635,327**
	Servicing the Conference of the Parties		
	Review of *modus operandi* of the Convention	60,000	0
	Servicing the Conference of the Parties *a/, e/*	0	1,000,000
	Subtotal 1	**665,072**	**1,635,327**

a/ Additional costs for all meetings under the conventions held outside the seat of the Secretariat shall be borne by the host.

b/ Positions to be filled by secondees should be filled by 1 January 1997 on terms and conditions agreed to by the Executive Secretary. Parties should be informed in a timely manner if this deadline is not met and the reasons why.

e/ See item 14.

2 SCIENTIFIC, TECHNICAL AND TECHNOLOGICAL MATTERS		
Office of the Principal Officer		
Principal Officer (D-1)	91,948	96,546
Secretary (G-5)	21,340	22,407
Scientific, technical and technological analysis		
Programme Officer – Conservation ecology (P-4/L-4)	78,943	82,891
Programme Officer – Economics (P-4/L-4)	78,943	82,891
Programme Officer – Genetic resources/ agrobiodiversity (FAO) (P-4) b/	0	0
Programme Officer – Indigenous knowledge (P-4/L-4) b/, c/	0	82,890
Research Assistant – Indigenous knowledge (G-7) b/, c/	0	26,726
Research Assistant (G-7)	25,453	26,726
Research Assistant (G-7)	25,453	26,726
SBSTTA activities		
Preparation of Global Biodiversity Outlook	80,000	250,000
Servicing of SBSTTA activities	120,000	120,000
Servicing of workshop on Article 8 (j) d/	350,000	0
Servicing of SBSTTA meetings	500,000	0
Subtotal 2	**1,372,081**	**817,801**
3. BIOSAFETY PROTOCOL		
Senior Programme Officer (P-5)	85,000	93,500
Associate Programme Officer (P-2/L-2)	54,296	57,011
Research Assistant (G-7)	25,453	26,726
Secretary (G-5)	21,340	22,407
Biosafety Protocol meetings		
Servicing meetings of Open-ended Ad Hoc Working Group on Biosafety	700,000	700,000
Subtotal 3	**886,089**	**899,643**

b/ Positions to be filled by secondees should be filled by 1 January 1997 on terms and conditions agreed to by the Executive Secretary. Parties should be informed in a timely manner if this deadline is not met and the reasons why.

c/ See part B: Special Trust Fund for additional voluntary contributions to the core budget for approved activities.

d/ Servicing of the workshop in six languages.

4. IMPLEMENTATION AND COMMUNICATION		
Office of the Principal Officer		
Principal Officer (D-1)	91,948	96,546
Junior Programme Officer (Finland) (L-2)	0	0
Secretary (G-5)	21,340	22,407

Clearing-house mechanism		
Programme Officer – Clearing-house mechanism (P-4)	78,943	82,891
Librarian/documentalist (P-3/L-3)	68,124	71,531
Programme Officer – Information (P-3)	68,124	71,531
Programme Officer – Communications (UNEP) (P-2)	0	0
Associate Programme Officer – Database management (P-2/L-2)	54,296	57,011
Associate Programme Officer – Documentation control (P-2/L-2)	54,296	57,011
Database Clerk (G-5)	21,340	22,407
Clerk – Publications (G-4)	19,535	20,512
Servicing of workshops on clearing-house mechanism e/	150,000	0
Library development and acquisitions	80,000	80,000
Promotion, awareness-raising and publications	150,000	150,000
Jakarta Mandate on Marine and Coastal Biological Diversity		
Programme Officer, Marine Ecology (UNESCO) (P-4) b/	0	0
Programme Officer (P-3/L-3)	68,124	71,531
Junior Programme Officer (Italy) (L-2) b/, c/	0	0
Meeting of Marine and Coastal Experts	80,000	0
Financial resources and instruments		
Programme Officer – Financial resources and instruments (P-4)	78,943	82,891
Programme Officer – Financial mechanism (P-3/L-3)	68,124	71,531
Research Assistant (G-7)	25,453	26,726
Review of the effectiveness of the financial mechanism e/	150,000	0
National reports and reviews		
Programme Officer (P-4/L-4)	78,943	82,891
Programme Officer (P-3/L-3) (Quebec) b/	0	0
Research Assistant (G-7)	25,453	26,726
Subtotal 4	**1,432,989**	**1,094,138**

b/ Positions to be filled by secondees should be filled by 1 January 1997 on terms and conditions agreed to by the Executive Secretary. Parties should be informed in a timely manner if this deadline is not met and the reasons why.
c/ See Part B: Special Trust Fund for additional voluntary contributions to the core budget for approved activities.
e/ See item 14.

5	**CONSULTANCIES**	**300,000**	**400,000**
6	**TRAVEL OF STAFF**		
	Travel on official missions	400,000	400,000
	Travel to service meetings	70,000	70,000
	Subtotal 6	**470,000**	**470,000**

7	**EQUIPMENT**		
	Expendable equipment (supplies and material)	70,000	70,000
	Non-expendable equipment (furniture, computers, photocopiers, etc)	50,000	50,000
	Subtotal 7	**120,000**	**120,000**
8	**PREMISES**		
	Rent	0	0
	Utilities (gas, electricity, cleaning, etc.)	60,000	60,000
	Insurance	20,000	20,000
	Subtotal 8	**80,000**	**80,000**
9	**MISCELLANEOUS**		
	Temporary assistance and overtime	100,000	100,000
	Communications (telephone, fax, mail, email, etc.)	300,000	300,000
	Recruitment costs/costs on interviews	30,000	20,000
	Hospitality	50,000	50,000
	Subtotal 9	**480,000**	**470,000**
	Subtotal 1 to 9	5,806,231	5,986,910
10	**ADMINISTRATIVE SUPPORT CHARGE (13%)**	**754,810**	**778,298**
	Subtotal 1 to 10	6,561,041	6,765,208
11	**CONTINGENCIES (0% – subtotal 1 to 9)**	**0**	**0**
12	**TOTAL**	**6,561,041**	**6,765,208**
13	**LESS – CONTRIBUTIONS FROM HOST COUNTRY**	**1,000,000**	**1,000,000**
14	**LESS ITEMS FUNDED FROM SAVINGS FROM PREVIOUS YEARS**		
	(a) Servicing of workshops on clearing-house mechanism	150,000	
	(b) Review of the effectiveness of the Financial Mechanism	150,000	
	(c) Servicing of the fourth meeting of the Conference of the Parties		1,000,000
15	**BUDGET TO BE SHARED BY PARTIES**	**5,261,041**	**4,765,208**

Appendix to part A: Assessments

	Party	United Nations scale of assessments 1997* (%)	Scale for the Trust Fund with 25% ceiling and no least developed country Party paying more than 0.01% (%)	Contributions as per 1 January 1997 (US$)	Contributions as per 1 January 1998 (US$)
1	Albania	0.01	0.01	705	638
2	Algeria	0.16	0.21	11,274	10,211
3	Antigua & Barbuda	0.01	0.01	705	638
4	Argentina	0.48	0.64	33,822	30,634
5	Armenia	0.05	0.07	3,523	3,191
6	Australia	1.48	1.98	104,283	94,455
7	Austria	0.87	1.17	61,302	55,524
8	Bahamas	0.02	0.03	1,409	1,276
9	Bangladesh	0.01	0.01	526	477
10	Barbados	0.01	0.01	705	638
11	Belarus	0.28	0.38	19,729	17,870
12	Belize	0.01	0.01	705	638
13	Benin	0.01	0.01	526	477
14	Bhutan	0.01	0.01	526	477
15	Bolivia	0.01	0.01	705	638
16	Botswana	0.01	0.01	705	638
17	Brazil	1.62	2.17	114,148	103,390
18	Bulgaria	0.08	0.11	5,637	5,106
19	Burkina Faso	0.01	0.01	526	477
20	Cambodia	0.01	0.01	526	477
21	Cameroon	0.01	0.01	705	638
22	Canada	3.11	4.17	219,136	198,483
23	Cape Verde	0.01	0.01	526	477
24	Central African Republic	0.01	0.01	526	477
25	Chad	0.01	0.01	526	477
26	Chile	0.08	0.11	5,637	5,106
27	China	0.74	0.99	52,142	47,227
28	Colombia	0.10	0.13	7,046	6,382
29	Comoros	0.01	0.01	526	477
30	Congo	0.01	0.01	705	638
31	Cook Islands	0.01	0.01	705	638
32	Costa Rica	0.01	0.01	705	638
33	Cote d'Ivoire	0.01	0.01	705	638
34	Croatia	0.09	0.12	6,342	5,744
35	Cuba	0.05	0.07	3,523	3,191
36	Cyprus	0.03	0.04	2,114	1,915
37	Czech Republic	0.25	0.33	17,615	15,955
38	DPR of Korea	0.05	0.07	3,523	3,191

39	Denmark	0.72	0.96	50,732	45,951
40	Djibouti	0.01	0.01	526	477
41	Dominica	0.01	0.01	705	638
42	Ecuador	0.02	0.03	1,409	1,276
43	Egypt	0.08	0.11	5,637	5,106
44	El Salvador	0.01	0.01	705	638
45	Equatorial Guinea	0.01	0.01	526	477
46	Eritrea	0.01	0.01	526	477
47	Estonia	0.04	0.05	2,818	2,553
48	Ethiopia	0.01	0.01	526	477
49	Fiji	0.01	0.01	705	638
50	Finland	0.62	0.83	43,686	39,569
51	France	6.42	8.60	452,364	409,730
52	Gambia	0.01	0.01	526	477
53	Georgia	0.11	0.15	7,751	7,020
54	Germany	9.06	12.13	638,383	578,218
55	Ghana	0.01	0.01	705	638
56	Greece	0.38	0.51	26,775	24,252
57	Grenada	0.01	0.01	705	638
58	Guatemala	0.02	0.03	1,409	1,276
59	Guinea	0.01	0.01	526	477
60	Guinea-Bissau	0.01	0.01	526	477
61	Guyana	0.01	0.01	705	638
62	Haiti	0.01	0.01	526	477
63	Honduras	0.01	0.01	705	638
64	Hungary	0.14	0.19	9,865	8,935
65	Iceland	0.03	0.04	2,114	1,915
66	India	0.31	0.42	21,843	19,784
67	Indonesia	0.14	0.19	9,865	8,935
68	Iran (Islamic Republic of)	0.45	0.60	31,708	28,719
69	Ireland	0.21	0.28	14,797	13,402
70	Israel	0.27	0.36	19,025	17,232
71	Italy	5.25	7.03	369,924	335,060
72	Jamaica	0.01	0.01	705	638
73	Japan	15.65	20.96	1,102,725	998,797
74	Jordan	0.01	0.01	705	638
75	Kazakstan	0.19	0.25	13,388	12,126
76	Kenya	0.01	0.01	705	638
77	Kiribati	0.01	0.01	526	477
78	Kyrgyztan	0.03	0.04	2,114	1,915
79	Lao PDR	0.01	0.01	526	477
80	Latvia	0.08	0.11	5,637	5,106
81	Lebanon	0.01	0.01	705	638
82	Lesotho	0.01	0.01	526	477
83	Lithuania	0.08	0.11	5,637	5,106
84	Luxembourg	0.07	0.09	4,932	4,467
85	Madagascar	0.01	0.01	526	477
86	Malawi	0.01	0.01	526	477
87	Malaysia	0.14	0.19	9,865	8,935
88	Maldives	0.01	0.01	526	477
89	Mali	0.01	0.01	526	477

90	Marshall Islands	0.01	0.01	705	638
91	Mauritania	0.01	0.01	526	477
92	Mauritius	0.01	0.01	705	638
93	Mexico	0.79	1.06	55,665	50,419
94	Micronesia (Federated States of)	0.01	0.01	705	638
95	Monaco	0.01	0.01	705	638
96	Mongolia	0.01	0.01	705	638
97	Morocco	0.03	0.04	2,114	1,915
98	Mozambique	0.01	0.01	526	477
99	Myanmar	0.01	0.01	526	477
100	Nauru	0.01	0.01	705	638
101	Nepal	0.01	0.01	526	477
102	Netherlands	1.59	2.13	112,034	101,475
103	New Zealand	0.24	0.32	16,911	15,317
104	Nicaragua	0.01	0.01	705	638
105	Niger	0.01	0.01	526	477
106	Nigeria	0.11	0.15	7,751	7,020
107	Niue	0.01	0.01	705	638
108	Norway	0.56	0.75	39,459	35,740
109	Oman	0.04	0.05	2,818	2,553
110	Pakistan	0.06	0.08	4,228	3,829
111	Panama	0.01	0.01	705	638
112	Papua New Guinea	0.01	0.01	705	638
113	Paraguay	0.01	0.01	705	638
114	Peru	0.06	0.08	4,228	3,829
115	Philippines	0.06	0.08	4,228	3,829
116	Poland	0.33	0.44	23,252	21,061
117	Portugal	0.28	0.38	19,729	17,870
118	Qatar	0.04	0.05	2,818	2,553
119	Republic of Korea	0.82	1.10	57,779	52,333
120	Republic of Moldova	0.08	0.11	5,637	5,106
121	Romania	0.15	0.20	10,569	9,573
122	Russian Federation	4.27	5.72	300,871	272,515
123	Rwanda	0.01	0.01	526	477
124	Saint Kitts and Nevis	0.01	0.01	705	638
125	Saint Lucia	0.01	0.01	705	638
126	Saint Vincent and the Grenadines	0.01	0.01	705	638
127	Samoa	0.01	0.01	526	477
128	San Marino	0.01	0.01	705	638
129	Senegal	0.01	0.01	705	638
130	Seychelles	0.01	0.01	705	638
131	Sierra Leone	0.01	0.01	526	477
132	Singapore	0.14	0.19	9,865	8,935
133	Slovakia	0.08	0.11	5,637	5,106
134	Slovenia	0.07	0.09	4,932	4,467
135	Solomon Islands	0.01	0.01	526	477
136	South Africa	0.32	0.43	22,548	20,423
137	Spain	2.38	3.19	167,699	151,894
138	Sri Lanka	0.01	0.01	705	638

139 Sudan	0.01	0.01	526	477
140 Suriname	0.01	0.01	705	638
141 Swaziland	0.01	0.01	705	638
142 Sweden	1.23	1.65	86,668	78,500
143 Switzerland	1.21	1.62	85,259	77,223
144 Syrian Arab Republic	0.05	0.07	3,523	3,191
145 Togo	0.01	0.01	526	477
146 Trinidad and Tobago	0.03	0.04	2,114	1,915
147 Tunisia	0.03	0.04	2,114	1,915
148 Turkmenistan	0.04	0.05	2,818	2,553
149 Uganda	0.01	0.01	526	477
150 Ukraine	1.09	1.46	76,803	69,565
151 United Kingdom	5.32	7.13	374,856	339,527
152 United Republic of Tanzania	0.01	0.01	526	477
153 Uruguay	0.04	0.05	2,818	2,553
154 Uzbekistan	0.13	0.17	9,160	8,297
155 Vanuatu	0.01	0.01	526	477
156 Venezuela	0.33	0.44	23,252	21,061
157 Viet Nam	0.01	0.01	705	638
158 Yemen	0.01	0.01	705	638
159 Zaire	0.01	0.01	526	477
160 Zambia	0.01	0.01	526	477
161 Zimbabwe	0.01	0.01	705	638
162 European Community	0.00	2.50	131,526	119,130
	72.9000	**100.0**	**5,261,041**	**4,765,208**

* General Assembly resolution 49/19. Scale of assessments for the apportionment of the expenses of the United Nations.

B Special Trust Fund for additional voluntary contributions to the core budget for approved activities

		1997 (US$)	1998 (US$)
1	**EXECUTIVE DIRECTION AND MANAGEMENT**		
	Conference of the Parties		
	Meetings of Bureau of the Conference of the Parties	75,000	50,000
	Liaison functions	150,000	200,000
	Subtotal 1	**225,000**	**250,000**
2	**SCIENTIFIC, TECHNICAL AND TECHNOLOGICAL MATTERS**		
	Scientific, technical and technological analysis		
	Programme Officer – Indigenous knowledge (P-4/L-4) a/, b/, c/	78,943	0
	Research Assistant – Indigenous knowledge (G-7) a/, b/, c/	25,453	0
	Miscellaneous a/, c/	20,604	0

	SBSTTA meetings		
	Meetings of SBSTTA Bureau	75,000	50,000
	Subtotal 2	**200,000**	**50,000**
3	**BIOSAFETY PROTOCOL**		
	Meetings of Biosafety Protocol Bureau	75,000	50,000
	Subtotal 3	**75,000**	**50,000**
4	**IMPLEMENTATION AND COMMUNICATION**		
	Office of the Principal Officer		
	Junior Programme Officer (L-2) a/, b/	54,296	57,011
	Clearing-house mechanism		
	Clearing-house mechanism activities	50,000	50,000
	Servicing of workshops on clearing-house mechanism	0	158,000
	Jakarta Mandate on Marine and Coastal Biological Diversity		
	Junior Programme Officer (L-2) b/	54,296	57,011
	Subtotal 4	**158,592**	**322,022**
	Subtotal 1 to 4	**658,592**	**672,022**
5	**ADMINISTRATIVE SUPPORT CHARGE (13%)**	**85,617**	**87,363**
6	**TOTAL**	**744,209**	**759,384**

a/ Carried over from 1996.

b/ Positions to be filled by secondees by 1 January 1997 on terms and conditions agreed to by the Executive Secretary. Parties should be informed in a timely manner if this deadline is not met and the reasons why.

c/ Contribution of the Government of Australia.

C Special voluntary trust fund for facilitating participation of Parties in the Convention process

		1997 (US$)	*1998 (US$)*
1	**EXECUTIVE DIRECTION AND MANAGEMENT**		
	Conference of the Parties		
	Travel of participants to meeting of the Conference of the Parties a/	0	400,000
	Travel of participants to regional preparatory meetings of the Conference of the Parties a/	0	250,000
	Subtotal 1	**0**	**650,000**

2	**SCIENTIFIC, TECHNICAL AND TECHNOLOGICAL MATTERS**		
	SBSTTA meetings		
	Travel of participants to SBSTTA meeting a/	338,372	0
	Travel of participants to workshop on Article 8 (j) a/	338,372	0
	Subtotal 2	**676,744**	**0**
3	**BIOSAFETY PROTOCOL**		
	Biosafety Protocol meetings		
	Travel of participants to Ad Hoc Working Group on Biosafety a/	676,744	676,744
	Subtotal 3	**676,744**	**676,744**
4	**IMPLEMENTATION AND COMMUNICATION**		
	Clearing-house mechanism		
	Travel of participants to workshops on clearing-house mechanism a/	200,000	200,000
	Subtotal 4	**200,000**	**200,000**
	Subtotal 1 to 4	**1,553,488**	**1,526,744**
5	**ADMINISTRATIVE SUPPORT CHARGE (13%)**	**201,953**	**198,477**
6	**TOTAL**	**1,755,441**	**1,725,221**

a/ Participants from developing countries, in particular least developed countries and small-island developing States.

Decision III/25: Date and venue of the fourth meeting of the Conference of the Parties

The Conference of the Parties,

1. *Welcomes* the kind offer of the Government of the Republic of Slovakia to host the fourth meeting of the Conference of the Parties;

2. *Decides* that the fourth meeting of the Conference of the Parties will take place in Bratislava, Slovakia, from 4 to 15 May 1998.

Decision III/26: Convening of regional and subregional meetings for Parties to the Convention

The Conference of the Parties,

Recalling its decision II/22,

Having benefited from such meetings by adopting decisions on agenda items of the third meeting of the Conference of the Parties,

1. *Requests* the Executive Secretary to seek voluntary contributions to meet the administrative costs of the regional/subregional meetings;

2. *Urges* the Secretariat of the Convention to seek additional voluntary contributions for such meetings to facilitate the participation of developing country Parties, in particular the least developed countries and small island developing States.

Decision III/27: Tribute to the Government and people of the Argentine Republic

The Conference of the Parties,

Having met in Buenos Aires, from 4 to 15 November 1996, at the gracious invitation of the Government of Argentina,

Deeply appreciative of the special courtesy and warm hospitality extended by the Government and people of Argentina, to the Ministers, members of delegations, observers and members of the Secretariat attending the meeting,

Expresses its sincere gratitude to the Government of the Argentine Republic and its people for the cordial welcome which they accorded to the Conference of the Parties and to those associated with its work and for their contribution to the success of the third meeting of the Conference of the Parties to the Convention on Biological Diversity.

Decisions adopted by the fourth meeting of the Conference of the Parties

Bratislava, Slovak Republic, 4–15 May 1998

Decision IV/1: Report and recommendations of the third meeting of the Subsidiary Body on Scientific, Technical and Technological Advice, and instructions by the Conference of the Parties to the Subsidiary Body on Scientific, Technical and Technological Advice

A Report and recommendations of the third meeting of the Subsidiary Body on Scientific, Technical and Technological Advice

The Conference of the Parties,

Recalling its decision III/2, which, *inter alia,* noted recommendation II/11 of the Subsidiary Body on Scientific, Technical and Technological Advice and decided to consider the recommendation further at its fourth meeting as part of the longer-term review of the programme of work and the operations of the Conference of the Parties and subsidiary organs,

Also recalling its decision III/10 on identification, monitoring and assessment,

Further recalling past practice of noting the reports of the Subsidiary Body on Scientific, Technical and Technological Advice,

1. *Takes note* of the report of the third meeting of the Subsidiary Body on Scientific, Technical and Technological Advice, held in Montreal from 1 to 5 September 1997, contained in document UNEP/CBD/COP/4/2, bearing in mind that five of the seven recommendations — III/1 (Inland water ecosystems); III/2 (Marine and coastal biological diversity); III/3 (Forest biological diversity); III/4 (Agricultural biological diversity); and III/6 (Clearing-house mechanism) — contain advice on matters that have been considered under other items on the agenda of the present meeting;

2. *Takes note* that the recommendations made at the third meeting of the Subsidiary Body on Scientific, Technical and Technological Advice constitute major inputs into the thematic work under the Convention;

Indicators

3. *Endorses* recommendation III/5 of the Subsidiary Body on Scientific, Technical and Technological Advice, and requests the Executive Secretary to undertake the work outlined in its annex, in accordance with the guidance contained in the same recommendation, for consideration by the Subsidiary Body on Scientific, Technical and Technological Advice at its fourth meeting;

4. *Proposes* that further work on indicators by the Parties and by the Subsidiary Body on Scientific, Technical and Technological Advice should take account of, *inter alia*, further work by the Subsidiary Body on Scientific, Technical and Technological Advice on the development of the ecosystem approach;

Identification monitoring and assessment

5. *Welcomes* the contributions provided by the DIVERSITAS working group of experts to the Executive Secretary, in its recommendations on scientific research that should be undertaken for the effective implementation of Articles 7, 8, 9, 10 and 14 of the Convention on Biological Diversity, as contained in document UNEP/CBD/COP/4/Inf.18;

6. *Decides* to transmit those recommendations to the Subsidiary Body on Scientific, Technical and Technological Advice for further consideration and use and encourages the Subsidiary Body on Scientific, Technical and Technological Advice to further cooperate with DIVERSITAS and with other relevant international, regional and national organizations and institutions on such issues.

B Ecosystem approach

The Conference of the Parties,

Recognizing that in several decisions adopted at the third meeting of the Conference of the Parties the ecosystem approach has been addressed as a guiding principle, although the terminology used has varied, including: 'ecosystem approach', 'ecosystem process-oriented approach', 'ecosystem management approach' and 'ecosystem-based approach',

Acknowledging that, by paragraph 1 of its decision II/8, the ecosystem approach has been adopted as a framework for the analysis and implementation of the objectives of the Convention on Biological Diversity, and in the elaboration and implementation of the various thematic and cross-cutting work programmes under the Convention, as appropriate,

Acknowledging the need for a workable description and further elaboration of the ecosystem approach,

1. *Takes note* of the report of the workshop on the ecosystem approach, held in Lilongwe, Malawi, from 26 to 28 January 1998, as contained in document UNEP/CBD/COP/4/Inf.9;

2. *Requests* the Subsidiary Body on Scientific, Technical and Technological Advice to develop principles and other guidance on the ecosystem approach, taking into consideration, *inter alia*, the results of the Malawi workshop, and to report thereon to the Conference of the Parties at its fifth meeting.

C Alien species that threaten ecosystems, habitats or species

The Conference of the Parties,

Noting the significant adverse ecological and economic effects of certain alien species on biological diversity and human health,

Recalling that the Subsidiary Body on Scientific, Technical and Technological Advice, at its second meeting, considered the development of an indicative framework of processes and categories of activities that are likely to have significant adverse impacts on biological diversity to be a priority,

Recalling paragraphs 9 and 10 of its decision III/9, on the implementation of Articles 6 and 8 of the Convention, which address alien species that threaten ecosystems, habitats or species,

Recalling recommendations III/1, III/2 and III/3 of the Subsidiary Body on Scientific, Technical and Technological Advice, related to alien species as they affect inland water, marine and coastal, forest and agricultural biological diversity respectively in accordance with decisions II/10, III/11, III/12 and III/13 of the Conference of the Parties,

Recognizing the particular endemic biological diversity of geographically and/or evolutionarily isolated ecosystems, such as small islands, and the particularly damaging impacts, in terms of biological-diversity loss, that species introduction can have on such ecosystems,

Noting the importance of taking a precautionary and ecosystem approach when dealing with issues related to alien species,

Noting the need to address the issue of alien species as an integrated component of the various sectoral and thematic items under the programme of work of the Conference of the Parties,

Recognizing that there is also a need for complementary and consolidated action on alien species,

1. *Decides* that alien species is a cross-cutting issue for implementation of many of the themes of the Convention;

2. *Requests* the Subsidiary Body on Scientific, Technical and Technological Advice to develop guiding principles for the prevention, introduction and mitigation of impacts of alien species and to report on those principles and any related work programme to the Conference of the Parties at its fifth meeting;

3. *Invites* Parties to develop country-driven projects at national, regional, subregional and international levels to address the issue of alien species and requests the financial mechanism to provide adequate and timely support for those projects;

4. *Invites* the Parties to address the issue of alien species for the conservation and sustainable use of biological diversity and to incorporate such activities into their national strategies, programmes and action plans;

5. *Requests* the Subsidiary Body on Scientific, Technical and Technological Advice to identify the priority work pertinent to the issue of alien species in geographically and evolutionarily isolated ecosystems and to report thereon to the Conference of the Parties at its fifth meeting;

6. *Requests* the Subsidiary Body on Scientific, Technical and Technological Advice, at its next meeting, to examine the Global Invasive Species Programme (GISP), with a view to considering concerted action and developing proposals for further action under the Convention on this issue.

D Global Taxonomy Initiative

The Conference of the Parties,

Noting decision III/10, supporting a Global Taxonomy Initiative, and the activities being supported by the financial mechanism on taxonomy,

Recognizing the need for taxonomic input in many activities aimed at the conservation and sustainable use of biological diversity and the lack of taxonomic capacity in a majority of countries,

Recalling that paragraph 3 of decision III/10, in which the Conference of the Parties endorsed the recommendation II/2 of the Subsidiary Body on Scientific, Technical and Technological Advice concerning capacity-building for taxonomy through a Global Taxonomy Initiative,

Taking into account the urgency for the availability of taxonomic information to countries of origin, and the need of developing countries to develop national collections and human and institutional capacities in taxonomy,

1. *Acknowledges* the work already under way by the financial mechanism in response to decision III/10 of the Conference of the Parties, and *requests* the Global Environment Facility to report on these experiences at the fifth meeting of the Conference of the Parties;

2. *Stresses* the urgent need for the further implementation of recommendation II/2 of the Subsidiary Body on Scientific, Technical and Technological Advice concerning capacity-building in all fields of taxonomy to assist in the implementation of the Convention, through the incorporation of targeted actions in its workplan, including promoting regional activities to set regional agendas;

3. *Endorses*, as initial advice, the Suggestions for Action in the annex to the present decision to develop and implement a Global Taxonomy Initiative, and *requests* the Subsidiary Body on Scientific, Technical and Technological Advice to examine and provide advice on the further advancement of a Global Taxonomy Initiative;

4. *Recognizes* that the implementation of a Global Taxonomy Initiative should occur on the basis of country-driven projects at the national, regional and subregional levels;

5. *Invites* the United Nations Environment Programme to assist in the global implementation of a Global Taxonomy Initiative, as offered by the Executive Director in his address to the Conference of the Parties at its fourth meeting;

6. *Encourages* Governments to make available appropriate resources to enhance the availability of taxonomic information;

7. *Encourages* Governments to develop bilateral and multilateral training and employment opportunities for taxonomists, particularly for those dealing with poorly known organisms;

8. *Stresses* the need to consider indigenous and traditional knowledge as an important existing information source that should be taken into account, and made available through appropriate mechanisms;

9. *Stresses* the urgent need for adequate financial resources to implement a Global Taxonomy Initiative and *requests* the institutional structure of the financial mechanism of the Convention to provide financial resources, particularly to assist in implementing, through country-driven activities within the context of the operational programmes of the Global Environment Facility, the Suggestions for Action annexed to the present decision.

Annex: Suggestions for action

1. The Executive Secretary should, as a matter of urgency, seek means outside of core funding of the Convention, to appoint a Programme Officer with appropriate operational resources to have responsibility for the further development of a Global Taxonomy Initiative, through the network of existing global, regional and national relevant institutions and organizations. The officer should especially coordinate actions to meet the need, recognized by the meeting, for each country to conduct a national taxonomic needs assessment, and to link to national reporting under the Convention on Biological Diversity and immediately coordinate a global directory of taxonomic expertise and biological collections. This information resource should be made available in both electronic and paper form.

2. Parties and authorities responsible for museums and herbaria should invest, on a long-term basis, in the development of appropriate infrastructure for their national collections. As part of that investment, donors, both bilateral and multilateral, in their commitment to the conservation and sustainable use of biological diversity in countries where they provide investment support, should support infrastructural needs of collection-holding institutions.

3. Parties and international donors should encourage partnerships between institutions in developed and developing countries so as to promote scientific collaboration and infrastructure rationalization. Such collaboration should include the development of national, subregional, regional and global training initiatives. Taxonomic institutions in each nation, both individually and regionally, should develop national priorities in taxonomic training, infrastructure, new technology, capacity-building and market needs.

4. Parties and authorities should adopt internationally agreed levels of collection housing (climate control, fire protection systems, pest control, acceptable levels of workplace health and safety) that ensure protection of collections and the well-being of all people working on and accessing collections.

5. Parties and international donors should provide training programmes at different educational levels, relevant to the needs of individual countries, including vocational, technical and academic training. Parties should also recognize that ongoing employment for trainees is part of an effective training scheme.

6. Parties and authorities should utilize information systems to maximum effect in taxonomic institutions. In developing priority-setting criteria for information

products, taxonomic institutions should consider the needs of the wide range of users of that information, including biological diversity managers. In particular, taxonomic information, literature and checklists should be put into electronic form.

7. Parties to the Convention on Biological Diversity should report on measures adopted to strengthen national capacity in taxonomy, to designate national reference centres, and to make information housed in collections available to countries of origin.

8. Institutions, supported by Parties and international donors, should coordinate their efforts to establish and maintain effective mechanisms for the stable naming of biological taxa.

9. Governments members of the Organization for Economic Cooperation and Development (OECD) should endorse and support the recommendations from the OECD Megascience Forum's Biodiversity Informatics Subgroup, regarding the development of a Global Biodiversity Informatics Facility (GBIF) to allow people in all countries to share biological diversity information and to provide access to critical authority files.

Implementing the actions

10. The Executive Secretary should ensure that the clearing-house mechanism (in collaboration with the OECD Megascience Forum's Biodiversity Informatics Subgroup Initiative) develop protocols and strategies for coordinating access to and distribution of taxonomic information contained in collections. In addition, the clearing-house mechanism, through its national focal points, should establish and update directories of taxonomists and their research and identification expertise.

11. *In addition, Parties should:*

(a) Ensure that institutions responsible for biological diversity inventories and taxonomic activities are financially and administratively stable, so as to have potential for continued and growing training and employment opportunities;

(b) Assist institutions to establish consortia to conduct regional projects;

(c) Select or use centres of expertise at different geographical levels, capable of offering training programmes individually or in combination, where such centres include universities, museums, herbaria, botanical and zoological gardens, research institutes and international or regional organizations;

(d) Give special attention to international funding of fellowships for specialist training abroad or for attracting international experts to national or regional courses. Appropriate areas for funding should include conventional academic courses, expeditions, collaborative research projects, secondments, institutional partnerships, regional flora and fauna, internships and tutorial guidance;

(e) Provide programmes for re-training of qualified professionals moving into taxonomy-related fields;

(f) Adapt training methods to the particular technical or academic backgrounds and experience of candidates. Content of courses should respond to external user demands and modern needs, taking into account cost-effectiveness in their delivery;

(g) Ensure training programmes address gaps in knowledge and the need for specialists in given taxonomic groups, and offer a comprehensive view of biological-diversity issues, including new scientific/technological approaches to taxonomy (eg molecular biology/informatics);

(h) Provide business management training, of the nature commonly offered to private-sector executives, for managers of biological-diversity institutions, as part of other efforts to strengthen those organizations;

(i) Develop and maintain a register of practising taxonomists, areas of expertise and description of collections through electronic and other means, which should be available on the Internet;

(j) Hold workshops to determine national taxonomic priorities, in the context of national biological-diversity studies and action plans. Once national priorities have been identified, support development of regional taxonomic priorities, including plans to database collections using mutually agreed software, quality control and core-data requirements.

Recommendation III/5: Agenda item 7.3: Current approaches to indicator development and recommendations for a preliminary core set of indicators of biological diversity, particularly those related to threats, and options for capacity-building in developing countries in the application of guidelines and indicators for subsequent national reports

The SBSTTA,

Reaffirming the vital importance of indicators of all levels of biological diversity in the implementation of the Convention, particularly with respect to Article 7, and recognizing the need to provide urgent, practical advice to Parties in the implementation of identification and monitoring,

Having examined the documents prepared by the Executive Secretary in consultation with a liaison group concerning recommendations for a core set of indicators of biological diversity (UNEP/CBD/SBSTTA/3/9 and UNEP/CBD/SBSTTA/3/Inf.13),

1. *Considers* that these provide a good basis for the development of further work on indicators and generally supports the proposed work programme on indicators as set out in UNEP/CBD/SBSTTA/3/9;

2. *Stresses* that the primary role of indicators in this context should be as a tool for management of biological diversity at local and national levels and assessing the implementation of the Convention, but recognizes also that they may have a wider role, for example in increasing public awareness;

3. *Stresses* that, in the future, the development of regional and global indicators will be necessary to assess specific aspects of the world's biological diversity;

4. *Stresses also* that all work undertaken by the secretariat and any liaison group on indicators should be integrated with any work on indicator development

undertaken within thematic areas under the Convention, for example concerning forests, inland water ecosystems and agricultural biological diversity;

5. *Recognizes* that the development and application of indicators requires the collection and analysis of data on a continuing basis, and that this is likely to be a costly activity;

6. *Recognizes also* that every attempt should be made to avoid duplication of effort in the development and application of indicators;

7. *Recommends* to the Conference of the Parties:

(a) That any liaison group on indicators of biological diversity have as wide as possible a range of expertise, both geographical and sectoral, represented on it;

(b) That the secretariat and any such liaison group be requested to ensure that all their work on indicators take as full as possible account of other relevant indicator initiatives undertaken by different international processes and organizations, particularly those relating to sustainable development and biological diversity;

(c) That the secretariat and any such liaison group be requested to develop a key set of standard questions, using as a basis the material on pages 12 and 13 of document UNEP/CBD/SBSTTA/3/Inf.14;

(d) That the secretariat and any such liaison group be requested to compile a set of principles for designing national-level monitoring programmes and indicators. These should address matters such as:

(i) the way indicators relate to management questions;

(ii) the ability to show trends;

(iii) the ability to distinguish between natural and human-induced change;

(iv) the ability to provide reliable results (ie through the establishment of standard methodologies);

(v) the degree to which indicators are amenable to straightforward interpretation;

(vi) the question of baselines for measurement, in light of the fact that application of a pre-industrial baseline may often prove problematic;

(e) That the Executive Secretary be requested to invite countries and relevant organizations to forward case studies to the secretariat. The secretariat and any liaison group should use these to provide a menu of possible approaches and a synthesis of best practice and lessons, to provide further advice to Parties on identification and monitoring;

(f) That consideration be given to providing means for regional coordination of indicator development;

(g) That Parties be urged to share relevant experience concerning the development and application of indicators through the clearing-house mechanism and other means; and also be urged to include in their future National Reports specific reference to indicator development activities and their capacity to implement indicators;

(h) That the need for capacity-building in indicator development and application be stressed;

(i) That the work programme on indicators as set out in Table 5 of UNEP/CBD/SBSTTA/3/9 be adopted, as amended, in the annex to the present recommendation.

Annex:
Preliminary outline of work under the two-track approach

Activity	*Details*	*Ways and means*	*Time scale*
FIRST TRACK			
Roster of experts	Establish a roster based upon submissions of names by Contracting Parties, countries and relevant organizations	Secretariat	Immediately
Contributions	Contact relevant institutions and processes to seek information and expertise, and to explore collaboration	Secretariat	Immediately
Further development of indicator framework, including standard questions and principles.	Incorporate recommendations from SBSTTA 3 and other reports	Liaison group, incorporating further expertise	Further meeting in 1997 if funds available
Support from financial mechanism	Liaison with GEF secretariat on methodologies and priorities for supporting national development of indicators	Secretariat	Ongoing
Development of menu of indicators in thematic areas	Case studies (compilation and synthesis) of indicators for coastal and marine, agro-biological diversity, forest and freshwater systems	Liaison group	For SBSTTA 4
Capacity assessment	Questionnaire distributed to countries following agreement on indicator framework and analysis of first national reports	Developed by secretariat with assistance of liaison group	Question-naire ready by COP 4
Training	Development of methodology sheets, guidelines and public information	Liaison group	Guidelines by SBSTTA 4
Training	Development of training systems to meet identified needs	Liaison group	After COP 4
Agreed indicator framework	Recommendations made available to Parties for inclusion in the second national report	Secretariat	As soon as available, and one year prior to deadline for report

Global Biodiversity Outlook	Data from initial national report and other sources for inclusion in GBO-2	Secretariat	Publication likely by COP 5
SECOND TRACK			
Research and development	Develop research proposal		Submission to agencies by mid-1999
Pilot programme	Set up pilot programmes to develop and test indicators		Completed by May 1999
Second set of indicators	Further development of indicators		Available for preparation of third national reports

Decision IV/2: Review of the operations of the clearing-house mechanism

The Conference of the Parties,

Noting that decisions I/3, II/3, II/4, II/7, II/8, II/10, II/11, II/14, II/16, II/17, III/4, III/5, III/9, III/10, III/11, III/15, III/17, III/18 and III/19 of the Conference of the Parties have clearly stressed and broadened the roles of the clearing-house mechanism as a key instrument to promote and facilitate the implementation of the objectives of the Convention,

Recalling that four clearing-house regional workshops were held prior to the fourth meeting of the Conference of the Parties and drawing upon those experiences,

Recognizing the urgent need for the private sector to be involved in clearing-house mechanism activities to ensure that the facilitation and promotion of the transfer of technology meet the needs of Contracting Parties,

Acknowledging the need to establish a reliable network of existing and evolving biodiversity institutions and initiatives which can serve the needs and demands of Parties, not only during the pilot phase but also in the long term,

1. *Requests* all Governments and bilateral and multilateral funding institutions to provide funding for the development and implementation of the clearing-house mechanism, including support for national as well as regional and subregional clearing-house mechanism activities;

2. *Recommends* that Parties include in their national reports the lessons learned through activities undertaken to implement their national clearing-house mechanisms, as appropriate;

3. *Recommends* that each Party organize an appropriate national clearing-house mechanism steering committee or working group composed of multisectoral and interdisciplinary representatives, to achieve broad participation of different stakeholders in the implementation process of the clearing-house mechanism;

4. *Invites* the Parties and other partners to use the clearing-house mechanism logo as a unifying element creating a clearing-house mechanism identity;

5. *Recommends* that, in building up the content of information in the clearing-house mechanism either at the secretariat or other level, the following major content elements, among others, be used:

(a) *National, subregional and regional levels*: country profiles, biodiversity strategy and action plans, appropriate legislation, scientific and technological information, financial sources;

(b) *Secretariat level*: Convention on Biological Diversity and its implementation, national focal points, international themes, financial sources;

6. *Requests* those Parties with access to the Internet to link their national clearing-house mechanism home page to the Secretariat's clearing-house mechanism home page, where possible;

7. *Recommends* that the development of a common format be investigated, under which the orderly sequence of the articles of the Convention should be followed; alternatively, the sequence of the three objectives of the Convention could be considered as the organizing format for information in the clearing-house mechanism;

8. *Agrees* that the clearing-house mechanism should act as the clearing-house mechanism for future programmes and activities under the Convention on Biological Diversity, subject to budgetary considerations;

9. *Requests* the Global Environmental Facility:

(a) To be a catalyst in the development and implementation of the clearing-house mechanism, so as to assist it to fulfil its role in promoting and facilitating the implementation of the Convention, in a participatory manner and fully incorporating available modern information and communication tools;

(b) To support capacity-building activities and country-driven pilot projects focused on priority areas, as critical components in the implementation of the clearing-house mechanism at the national, subregional, biogeographic, and regional levels, both during and after the pilot phase;

(c) To provide by all possible means, as appropriate, increased support for country-driven projects to establish and strengthen biodiversity information systems such as, *inter alia*, training, technology and processes related to the collection, organization, maintenance and updating of data and information and its communication to users through the clearing-house mechanism;

(d) To evaluate at the end of the clearing-house mechanism pilot phase the experience of the Global Environment Facility's support for developing countries' activities, to consider additional efforts to meet the increasing interest in taking part in and having access to the clearing-house mechanism, including in regional networking, and to report to the Executive Secretary prior to the next meeting of the Subsidiary Body on Scientific, Technical and Technological Advice;

10. *Instructs* the Executive Secretary:

(a) To put in place a list server with all officially designated clearing-house mechanism national focal points and other partners for the purpose of disseminating information on new and recent developments regarding the clearing-house mechanism, at either the national, regional or international level;

(b) To act as a focal point, during and after the pilot phase, to encourage the development of a network of partners, including indigenous and local communities, and to facilitate these in developing specific training for the effective participation of users in the clearing-house network;

(c) To ensure that the clearing-house mechanism should be continuously assisted in its functioning by the Informal Advisory Committee which is to provide guidance to the Executive Secretary during and after the pilot phase, and to play a full role in the further development of the clearing-house mechanism;

(d) To provide encouragement for and facilitate the coordination of biodiversity-related networks, activities and focal points that may constitute the clearing-house mechanism, to encourage their linkages within the clearing-house mechanism network and to make available information arising from the Secretariat's own functions as outlined in Article 24 of the Convention;

(e) To assist in ensuring that the implementation of Articles 16 (Transfer of and access to technology), 17 (Information exchange) and 18 (Scientific and technical cooperation) of the Convention on Biological Diversity is facilitated by the clearing-house mechanism;

(f) To produce an informative and widely disseminated clearing-house mechanism brochure and newsletter to increase awareness of the activities of the clearing-house mechanism;

(g) To improve synergy in regard to information exchange with other biodiversity-related conventions and ongoing international or supranational information initiatives, and to contribute to the harmonization of the information management of other biodiversity-related treaties and to continue to discuss the possibilities of joint and harmonized approaches with the United Nations Framework Convention on Climate Change and the United Nations Convention to Combat Desertification;

(h) To facilitate support to those Parties without adequate Internet access, preparing and disseminating to them updated information arising from the Secretariat's own functions as outlined in Article 24 of the Convention on, *inter alia*, CD-ROM or diskettes, either periodically or as required, and facilitating the dissemination of appropriate information to those Parties;

(i) To collaborate, with partners, on the provision of advice to Parties and others on, *inter alia*, the necessary layout and system specifications of the clearing-house mechanism;

(j) To produce a tool-kit prototype containing necessary information for national focal points to build their national clearing-house mechanisms, drawing upon the recommendations of the regional workshops and following an informal assessment of national practices in collaboration with the Informal Advisory Committee on the clearing-house mechanism;

(k) To undertake an independent review of the pilot phase of the clearing-house mechanism, starting at the end of 1998, to be presented to the Subsidiary Body on Scientific, Technical and Technological Advice for its consideration together with a longer-term programme of work for the clearing-house mechanism. The following elements for evaluation of the pilot phase, among others, are recommended to be used:

(i) Number of national focal points fully and effectively connected;

(ii) Number and relevance of thematic networks and activities connected;

(iii) Amount of information transferred from participating nodes;

(iv) Number and effectiveness of training events;

(v) Effectiveness of guidelines in achieving their aims;

(vi) Whether the clearing-house mechanism is being effectively used by Parties to further the aims of the Convention;

(vii) Number of nodes supplying relevant information such as national reports, legislation and policies;

(viii) Use made of list servers;

(ix) Financial support, other resources, and time allocated for the implementation of the clearing-house mechanism, in particular by the Secretariat and the clearing-house mechanism national focal points.

Decision IV/3: Issues related to biosafety

The Conference of the Parties,

Recalling its decisions II/5 and III/20 on issues related to biosafety,

Recalling also part A of the annex to its decision III/24, and table 1 of its decision IV/17, which contain the budgets of the Trust Fund for the Convention on Biological Diversity for the bienniums 1997–1998 and 1999–2000, respectively,

Having considered the report of the fourth meeting of the Open-ended Ad Hoc Working Group on Biosafety, which met in Montreal, from 5 to 13 February 1998,

Recalling the recommendations of the fourth meeting of the Open-ended Ad Hoc Working Group on Biosafety that:

(a) In order to complete its work, the Open-ended Working Group on Biosafety should hold two further meetings, with a duration of two weeks and one week, respectively;

(b) The first of those two meetings should be held in Montreal, from 17 to 28 August 1998; and

(c) In the event of it not being possible to hold in 1998 the final meeting of the Open-ended Ad Hoc Working Group on Biosafety, followed by a meeting of the Conference of the Parties to adopt the Protocol, these meetings should be convened early in 1999 but, in any event, no later than February 1999,

1. *Accepts* the recommendations of the Open-ended Ad Hoc Working Group on Biosafety;

2. *Decides*:

(a) That the bureau of the Open-ended Ad Hoc Working Group on Biosafety shall be composed of representatives of Argentina, Bahamas, Denmark, Ethiopia, Hungary, India, Mauritania, New Zealand, Russian Federation and Sri Lanka;

(b) That the members of the bureau shall remain in office, under the chairmanship of Mr. Veit Koester (Denmark) until the adoption of the Protocol on Biosafety;

3. *Decides* that the final meeting of the Open-ended Ad Hoc Working Group on Biosafety and an extraordinary meeting of the Conference of the Parties will be held in February 1999. These meetings shall be held at the seat of the Secretariat of the Convention on Biological Diversity in Montreal, Canada, unless an offer to host these meetings is received by the Executive Secretary no later than 1 August 1998;

4. *Decides*, in accordance with rule 13 of the rules of procedure, that the agenda of the extraordinary meeting will address all matters relating to:

(a) Adoption of the Protocol on Biosafety; and

(b) Preparations for the first Meeting of the Parties to the Protocol with regard to, *inter alia*, interim arrangements, taking into account the budgetary provision made for this purpose in accordance with decision IV/17 on the budget of the Trust Fund for the Convention;

5. *Decides* that written submissions by Governments of provisions to be included in the Protocol must be received by the Executive Secretary by 1 July 1998, in accordance with the six-month rule for consideration of the draft Protocol under Article 28, paragraph 3, of the Convention, thereby enabling the Open-ended Ad Hoc Working Group on Biosafety to consider those proposals during its meeting in August 1998;

6. *Decides* that the Protocol shall be opened for signature at the Headquarters of the United Nations in New York no later than three months from the date of its adoption by the Conference of the Parties;

7. *Calls on* Parties to consider providing voluntary contributions to facilitate participation in the above meetings by developing country Parties, in particular least developed States and small island developing countries, and Parties with economies in transition.

Decision IV/4: Status and trends of the biological diversity of inland water ecosystems and options for conservation and sustainable use

The Conference of the Parties,

1. *Adopts*, on the basis of modified recommendation III/1 of the Subsidiary Body on Scientific, Technical and Technological Advice as contained in document UNEP/CBD/COP/4/2, annex I to the present decision as a work programme under the Convention on Biological Diversity, on the biological diversity of inland water ecosystems and the associated matters of identification and monitoring, assessment methodology and taxonomy;

2. *Welcomes* the recommendations on strategic approaches to freshwater management of the Commission on Sustainable Development at its sixth session and *urges* Parties and Governments to:

(a) Include information on the biological diversity of inland waters when providing voluntary national communications and reports on actions further to the recommendations of the Commission on Sustainable Development; and

(b) Consider inland water biological diversity in the agenda of subsequent meetings held to further the recommendations of the Commission on Sustainable Development.

3. *Urges* Parties and Governments to include inland water biological diversity considerations in their participation and collaboration with organisations, institutions and conventions affecting or working with inland water resources, consistent with the guidance provided to the Conference of the Parties and the Executive Secretary in part A 'General', paragraphs 1–3 of annex I to the present decision;

4. *Encourages* the implementation of the Joint Work Plan with the Convention on Wetlands in document UNEP/CBD/COP/4/Inf.8, as recommended by the Conference of the Parties in its decision III/21 and by the Subsidiary Body on Scientific, Technical and Technological Advice in recommendation III/1, part A, section I, paragraph (b) and endorsed by the Conference of the Parties at its fourth meeting as a framework for enhanced cooperation between the Conventions through decision IV/15;

5. *Urges* Parties and Governments to integrate those elements highlighted by the Subsidiary Body on Scientific, Technical and Technological Advice as important for Parties, contained in annex I, sections A, B, C and D, to the present decision (respectively concerning inland water ecosystems, identification and monitoring, methodologies for assessment and taxonomy), as appropriate, into their national and sectoral plans and to implement these as soon as possible;

6. *Recognizing* that Global Environment Facility projects are country-driven, *requests* the Financial Mechanism, within the context of implementing national biological diversity strategies and action plans, to provide adequate and timely support to eligible projects which help Parties to develop and implement national, sectoral and cross-sectoral plans for the conservation and sustainable use of biological diversity of inland water ecosystems.

7. *Urges* Parties when requesting support, for projects related to inland water ecosystems, from the Financial Mechanism that priority be given to:

(a) Identifying inland water ecosystems in accordance with Article 7 and Annex I to the Convention, taking into account the criteria for Wetlands of International Importance as adopted under the Convention on Wetlands;

(b) Preparing and implementing integrated watershed, catchment and river basin management plans based on an ecosystem approach including transboundary watersheds, catchments and river basins, and those which include ecosystems identified under subparagraph (a) above;

(c) Investigating where appropriate, the processes contributing to the loss of biological diversity of inland water ecosystems, through targeted research, such as: investigations into the impacts of harmful substances, alien invasive species and saltwater intrusions; and the identification of measures needed to address these issues where they constitute threats to inland water ecosystem biological diversity;

8. *Requests* the Subsidiary Body on Scientific, Technical and Technological Advice to:

(a) Implement the programme of work respecting the relevant tasks described in annexes I and II to the present decision, taking into account the decisions adopted at the fourth meeting of the Conference of the Parties and the schedule as contained in annex II to the present decision, subject to amending the time schedule so as to immediately commence development of regional guidelines for rapid assessment for small island States, and to report on progress to the Conference of the Parties at its fifth meeting;

(b) Incorporate, as appropriate, the outcome of the sixth session of the Commission on Sustainable Development on strategic approaches to freshwater management into its work plan and report back thereon to the Conference of the Parties at its fifth meeting;

(c) Continue to take note of the approved work programme and results, and pursue opportunities for cooperation with, the Scientific and Technical Review Panel of the Convention on Wetlands.

9. *Invites* all relevant organizations to support efforts by Parties and Governments to implement their national and sectoral plans for the conservation and sustainable use of the biological diversity of inland water ecosystems;

10. *Requests* the Executive Secretary to facilitate the programme of work outlined in the present decision, including in its annexes I and II; including implementation of the tasks outlined for the Executive Secretary in paragraphs 1, 2 and 4 of annex I to the present decision, and additionally, in particular, to begin compiling information and case studies for use by the Subsidiary Body on Scientific, Technical and Technological Advice in addressing paragraphs 8 (a) and (c) of annex I to the present decision;

11. *Notes* that, while the implementation of the programme of work is subject to the availability of financial resources, particular attention should be given to early progress in the development of rapid assessment methodologies especially related to small island States.

Annex I:
Biological diversity of inland water ecosystems

The Conference of the Parties,

Recalling that decision III/13 of the Conference of the Parties requested the Subsidiary Body on Scientific, Technical and Technological Advice to provide the fourth meeting of the Conference of the Parties with scientific, technical and technological advice on the status and trends of biological diversity in inland water ecosystems and the identification of options for conservation and sustainable use,

Having examined the Notes prepared by the Executive Secretary (UNEP/CBD/COP/4/2, UNEP/CBD/COP/4/4 and UNEP/CBD/COP/4/Inf.8); and the other information provided to the fourth meeting of the Conference of the Parties,

Recognizing the importance of inland water ecosystems for global biological diversity and human welfare, and also their vulnerability to human actions,

Recognizing the importance of adopting an ecosystem approach that integrates the conservation and sustainable use of biological diversity and the fair and equitable sharing of benefits of inland waters,

Recognizing the link between human communities, inland waters and biological diversity of inland waters and the importance of local community participation and awareness in achieving conservation and sustainable use of inland water biological diversity, and

Recognizing the crucial part played by technical and scientific cooperation in all aspects of biological diversity, including the transfer of technology, and recognizing also the necessity of capacity-building to enable Parties to carry out identification, monitoring and assessment of biological diversity as required by Article 7 of the Convention,

Adopts the following programme of work:

A Assessment of the status and trends of the biological diversity of inland water ecosystems and identification of options for conservation and sustainable use

1 General

1. The Executive Secretary should continue and further develop the collaboration with organizations, institutions, and conventions working with research, management and conservation of inland water biological diversity. These include (but are not limited to) the Convention on Wetlands, FAO, the International Center for Living Aquatic Resources Management (ICLARM), Global Water Partnership, World Water Council, UNDP, UNEP, DIVERSITAS, Wetlands International, IUCN, World Bank, Bonn Convention, *et al.*

2. The Executive Secretary of this Convention and the Secretary-General of the Convention on Wetlands are encouraged to elaborate a work plan that ensures cooperation, and avoids overlap between the two conventions, noting the Memorandum of Cooperation with the Convention on Wetlands, and decision III/21 of the Conference of the Parties, whereby the Convention on Wetlands would be a lead partner in inland water ecosystems.

3. The Conference of the Parties wishes to continue the close cooperation with the Commission on Sustainable Development in its development of the Strategic Approach to Freshwater Management to ensure that biological diversity issues are considered in this process.

4. The Conference of the Parties requests the Executive Secretary to develop a roster of experts on the conservation and sustainable use of the biological diversity of inland waters, and urge Governments to nominate experts to the roster, noting also that the Ramsar Bureau is establishing a similar list of experts.

5. The clearing-house mechanism should be used to promote and facilitate the exchange of information and the transfer of technology relevant to the conservation and sustainable use of inland water biological diversity.

6. Recognizing the immediate threats to the inland water ecosystems and associated biological diversity of small island States, the Conference of the Parties requests the Executive Secretary and the Subsidiary Body on Scientific, Technical and Technological Advice to pay special attention to early cooperation with the small island States in the development of rapid-assessment methodologies.

7. Recognizing that in the territories of certain States there are inland water ecosystems suffering from ecological disaster, the Conference of the Parties requests the Executive Secretary and the Subsidiary Body on Scientific, Technical and Technological Advice to pay special attention to early cooperation in assessing such disasters and mitigating activities and in developing rapid assessment methodologies within these States.

2 Work plan of the Subsidiary Body on Scientific, Technical and Technological Advice

8. A work plan for the Subsidiary Body on Scientific, Technical and Technological Advice should be developed in cooperation with relevant organizations, Governments and Parties that should build upon the ongoing efforts in inland water ecosystem conservation. The work plan should include:

Status and trends:

(a) Using existing information and drawing upon relevant organizations and experts, develop an improved picture of inland water biological diversity, its uses and its threats, around the world. The output should identify areas where the lack of information severely limits the quality of assessments. This will help to focus attention on these areas;

(b) Developing and disseminating regional guidelines for rapid assessment of inland water biological diversity for different types of inland water ecosystems;

Conservation and sustainable use:

(c) Compiling case studies of watershed, catchment and river basin management experiences and best practices, to synthesize the lessons that emerge from these studies, and to disseminate information through the clearing-house and other appropriate mechanisms. Areas where the Subsidiary Body on Scientific, Technical and Technological Advice should concentrate its efforts include:

- (i) Examples of watershed management that incorporate inland water biological diversity with special reference to examples that use the ecosystem-based approach to meet water management goals;
- (ii) Examples of water resource development projects (water supply and sanitation, irrigation, hydropower, flood control, navigation, groundwater extraction) that incorporate biological diversity considerations;
- (iii) Impact assessment and other methodologies that address inland water biological diversity issues in an adaptive management framework;
- (iv) Case studies of successful remedial action, including restoration and rehabilitation of degraded inland water ecosystems;
- (v) Examples of equitable sharing of benefits derived from use of inland water biological diversity;
- (vi) Examples of the impacts of invasive alien species and of programmes used to control their introduction and mitigate negative consequences on inland water ecosystems especially at the watershed, catchment and river basin level;
- (vii) Use of protected areas and their management strategies for conservation and sustainable use of inland water ecosystems;

(d) Developing methods and techniques for the valuation of goods and services of inland water ecosystems, incentives and policy reform, and the understanding of ecosystem function.

3 Recommendations to Parties

9. The Conference of the Parties recommends that Parties:

(a) *Watershed management*:

(i) Encourage the adoption of integrated land and watershed management approaches based on watersheds, catchments and river basins for the protection, use, planning and management of inland water ecosystems;

(ii) Encourage the adoption of integrated watershed, catchment and river basin management strategies to maintain, restore or improve the quality and supply of inland water resources and the economic, social, hydrological, biological diversity and other functions and values of inland water ecosystems;

(b) *Appropriate technologies*:

(i) Encourage the use of low-cost (appropriate) technology, non-structural and innovative approaches to meet watershed management goals, such as using wetlands to improve water quality, using forests and wetlands to recharge groundwater and maintain the hydrological cycle, to protect water supplies and using natural floodplains to prevent flood damage, and to use indigenous species for aquaculture;

(ii) Encourage the development of preventative strategies such as cleaner production, continual environmental improvement, corporate environmental reporting, product stewardship and environmentally sound technologies to avoid degradation and promote restoration of inland water ecosystems;

(c) *Technology transfer*: Emphasize more effective conservation and efficiency in water use, together with non-engineering solutions. Environmentally appropriate technologies should be identified, such as low-cost sewage treatment and recycling of industrial water to assist in the conservation and sustainable use of inland waters;

(d) *Research*: Encourage research on the application of the ecosystem approach;

(e) *Monitoring and assessment*:

(i) Identify the most cost-effective approaches and methods to describe the status, trends and threats of inland waters and indicate their condition in functional as well as species terms;

(ii) Promote the development of criteria and indicators for the evaluation of impact on inland water ecosystems from both physical infrastructure projects and watershed activities, including, *inter alia*, agriculture, forestry, mining and physical alteration, taking into consideration the natural variability of water conditions;

(iii) Initiate studies on ecological functions and services to improve understanding of effects of exploitation on non-target species;

(iv) Undertake assessments in such inland water ecosystems which may be regarded as important in accordance with the terms of Annex 1 of the Convention. Furthermore Parties should undertake assessments of threatened species and conduct inventories and impact assessments of alien species within their inland water ecosystems;

(f) *Sustainable use*:

(i) Encourage valuation of inland water biological diversity;

(ii) Produce and promote guidance on the sustainable use of inland waters to maintain biological diversity;

(iii) Support the conservation and sustainable use of inland water biological diversity through the establishment and implementation of appropriate legal, administrative and incentive measures;

(iv) Consider the use and/or establishment of gene banks for fish and other species;

(g) *Environmental impact assessments*:

(i) Encourage environmental impact assessments (EIAs) of water development projects, aquaculture, and watershed activities including agriculture, forestry, and mining. EIAs need to gather adequate biological data to document effects on biological diversity, provide predictions on the effects of alternative project scenarios on ecosystems and consider the valuation of the goods and services of potentially affected ecosystems, and test predictions with well-designed sampling schemes that can adequately distinguish the effects of anthropogenic activities from natural processes;

(ii) Encourage EIAs which assess the impacts, not only of individual proposed projects, but also the cumulative effects of existing and proposed developments on the watershed, catchment or river basin;

(h) *Alien species, genotypes and genetically modified organisms.* Raise awareness of the possible problems and costs associated with the deliberate or accidental introduction of alien species, genotypes and genetically modified organisms which adversely affect aquatic biological diversity, bearing in mind the activities relating to the development of a Protocol on Biosafety under the Convention. Policies and guidelines should be developed to prevent and control such introductions, and to rehabilitate sites where possible. This work should be coordinated with the cross-cutting work being addressed in the decision regarding the work of the Subsidiary Body on Scientific, Technical and Technological Advice on alien species (decision IV/1 C);

(i) *Education and public awareness.* Strengthen education and awareness programmes, recognizing that responsible environmental stewardship requires an informed public. Participatory-based management approaches are most effective when people are well informed of both the economic and environmental consequences of management. Inland waters provide both a challenge and an opportunity to educate the public and policy makers about the need to take an ecosystem-based approach to management. Environmental education should be built into school curricula and should emphasize integration using inland waters as a model subject to teach problem-solving;

(j) *Collaboration with broader water resource community.* Promote effective collaboration among ecologists, planners, engineers, and economists (both within countries and among countries) in the planning and implementation of development projects to better integrate inland water biological diversity with water resource development when considering projects likely to have an adverse impact on inland water ecosystems;

(k) *Transboundary cooperation*: Develop and maintain effective cooperation for sustainable management of transboundary watersheds, catchments, river basins and migratory species through appropriate mechanisms such as bilateral and multi agreements;

(l) *Involvement of local and indigenous communities*:

(i) Involve, as far as possible and appropriate, local and indigenous communities in the development of management plans and in projects that may affect inland water biological diversity;

(ii) Implement Article 8 (j) as related to inland water biological diversity;

(iii) Encourage the involvement and participation of affected parties including end-users and communities in policy-making, planning and implementation;

(m) *Economic and legal instruments*:

(i) Review the range and effectiveness of national incentives, subsidies, regulations, and other relevant financial mechanisms which have the ability to affect inland water ecosystems, whether adversely or beneficially;

(ii) Redirect financial support measures which run counter to the objectives of the Convention regarding the biological diversity of inland waters;

(iii) Implement targeted incentive and regulatory measures that have positive impacts on the biological diversity of inland waters;

(iv) Develop the policy research capacity needed to inform the decision-making process in a multidisciplinary and sectorally integrated manner;

(v) At appropriate levels (regional, national, subnational and local), encourage the identification of stressed rivers, the allocation and reservation of water for ecosystem maintenance, and the maintenance of environmental flows as an integral component of appropriate legal, administrative and economic mechanisms;

4 Financing

10. Guidance should be provided to the Global Environment Facility regarding the importance of projects concerning inland water biological diversity. The GEF should be encouraged to consider the importance of inland water biological diversity in its other focal areas and should provide necessary funding for inland water biological diversity projects.

11. Ways should be considered for mobilizing financial resources from other sources.

B Provision of scientific advice and further guidance to assist in the national elaboration of annex I of the Convention (as pertaining to inland water ecosystems)

12. The Conference of the Parties advises Parties to prepare indicative lists of inland water ecosystems, using the criteria set out in Annex I of the Convention. The Conference of the Parties requests the Executive Secretary to work closely with the Ramsar Bureau and further direct the Subsidiary Body on Scientific, Technical and Technological Advice to work jointly with the Scientific and Technical Review Panel of the Convention on

Wetlands to achieve desirable convergence between approaches on criteria and classification of inland water ecosystems between the two Conventions.

13. Parties should take note of the work of the IUCN as well as its recommendations in the ongoing review and application of criteria for the assessment of threatened species and populations, including the further development of such criteria for application at the regional and national levels.

C Review of methodologies for assessment of biological diversity (as pertaining to inland water ecosystems)

14. Parties are urged to adopt an integrated approach in their assessment, management and where possible remedial action of inland water ecosystems, including associated terrestrial and inshore marine ecosystems. Assessments should involve all stakeholders, should be cross-sectoral and should make full use of indigenous knowledge.

15. Suitable organisms should be identified as being particularly important in the assessment of inland water ecosystems. Ideally, such groups should meet the following criteria:

(a) The group should contain a reasonable number of species with varied ecological requirements;

(b) The taxonomy of the group should be reasonably well understood;

(c) The species should be easy to identify;

(d) The group should be easy to sample or observe so that density – absolute or as indices – can be assessed, used objectively and treated statistically;

(e) The group should serve as indicators of overall ecosystem health or indicators of development of a key threat to ecosystem health;

16. In view of the great economic importance of some groups (eg inland water fish species), and of the large gaps in taxonomic knowledge for many species, the Conference of the Parties considers this as a specific focus of the capacity-building in taxonomy recommended by the Subsidiary Body on Scientific, Technical and Technological Advice in its recommendation II/2 and endorsed by the Conference of the Parties in decision III/10.

17. The Conference of the Parties advises Parties and relevant international organizations that issues of biological diversity and subsistence use of fisheries should be more fully addressed in fisheries reporting as regards biological diversity and in fisheries management. In particular, species composition of total catch should be reported and the contribution that indigenous species make to capture fisheries should be reported separately.

18. The transboundary nature of many inland water ecosystems should be fully taken into account in assessments, and it may be appropriate for relevant regional and international bodies to contribute to such assessments.

19. In accordance with recommendation II/1 of the Subsidiary Body on Scientific, Technical and Technological Advice, endorsed by the Conference of the Parties in decision III/10, assessments should be simple, inexpensive, rapid and easy to use. Such rapid assessment programmes will never replace thorough inventories. The Conference of the Parties takes note of the need to evaluate specific rapid assessment programmes for inland water ecosystems currently under development.

20. Assessments should be carried out with a view to implementing other articles of the Convention and, in particular, to addressing the threats to inland water ecosystems within an appropriate framework such as that included in paragraphs 39–41 of document UNEP/CBD/COP/3/12. Of particular importance is the undertaking of environmental impact assessments on biological diversity of development projects involving inland water ecosystems.

D The urgency of needed action on taxonomy

21. The Executive Secretary is requested to take decisive action to advance the Global Taxonomy Initiative as detailed in decisions III/10 and IV/1 D, which should be implemented as soon as possible.

Annex II:
Possible time-frame of a work programme pertaining to the activities of the Subsidiary Body on Scientific, Technical and Technological Advice

Activities	*Year*	*COP**	*SBSTTA***	*Secretariat*	*Other*
Implication of the outcome of the sixth session of the Commission on Sustainable Development (CSD)					
Integration of the outcome of the sixth session of the Commission on Sustainable Development	1998	Consideration of the outcome of the CSD-6	Consideration of the follow-up of the CSD-6 and make recommendation to the COP		
(CSD-6)	1999	Consideration of the recommendation of the Subsidiary Body on Scientific, Technical and Technological Advice	Possible follow-up activities	Possible follow-up activities	
Status and trends					
Using existing information and drawing upon relevant organizations and experts, develop an	1998		Consideration of ways and means for the activity	Preparation of proposal for the ways and means of the assessment	
improved picture of inland water biological	1998–2002		Carrying out the activity	Assist the SBSTTA in carrying out the activity	Establishing network of experts

diversity, its uses and the threats to it, around the world. Identification of gap	2002		Consideration of the outcome and make recommendation to the COP		Possible regional workshops
	2003	Consideration of the recommendation of the SBSTTA			
Develop regional guidelines for rapid assessment	2002		Consideration of ways and means for the activity	Preparation of proposal for the ways and means for the development of regional guidelines	
	2002–2004		Development of regional guidelines	Assist the SBSTTA in the development of regional guidelines	Possible regional workshops
	2004		Consideration of the regional guidelines and recommendation to the COP		
	2005	Consideration of the SBSTTA recommendation			
Conservation and sustainable use					
Compilation of case studies on conservation and sustainable use	1998–2002			Compilation of case studies and make synthesis	Disseminate through the clearing-house mechanism
	2002		Consideration of case studies and make recommendation		
	2003	Consideration of the SBSTTA recommendation			
	2003–		Activities may be continued		

DECISION IV/4

Development of methods and techniques for the valuation of goods and services of inland water ecosystems, incentives and policy reforms and understanding of ecosystem function	2002		Consideration of ways and means for the activity	Preparation of proposal for the development of methods and techniques for the proposed topics	
	2002–2005		Development of methods and techniques for the proposed topics	Assist the SBSTTA in the activity	Expert meetings/ Liaison group meetings
	2005		Consideration of the methods and techniques for the proposed topics and make recommendation to the COP		
	2006	Consideration of the SBSTTA recommendation			
The national elaboration of Annex I of the Convention on Biological Diversity					
Work closely with the Convention on Wetlands to achieve desirable convergence between approaches on criteria and classification of inland water ecosystems between the two Conventions	1998–2001		Work closely with the Scientific and Technical Review Panel of the Convention on Wetlands	Work closely with the Bureau of the Convention on Wetlands	
	2001		Consideration of the outcome and make report to the Conference of the Parties		
	2002	Consideration of the report of the Subsidiary Body on Scientific, Technical and Technological Advice			

Urgency of needed action on taxonomy

Global Taxonomy Initiative	1998–2001	Regional workshops

* Conference of the Parties
** Subsidiary Body on Scientific, Technical and Technological Advice
Budget implication:

Studies for assessments:	US$300,000–500,000 per study
Scientific/technical meetings:	US$100,000–300,000 per meeting

The Secretariat will require a Programme Officer at P-4 level, specialized in the biological diversity of inland waters. The Secretariat will benefit from the services of a Junior Professional Officer (P-2) for this programme of work. However, as Junior Professional Officers are seconded by Governments, there will be no budget implications in this regard.

Decision IV/5: Conservation and sustainable use of marine and coastal biological diversity, including a programme of work

The Conference of the Parties,

I Programme of work arising from decision II/10 (Jakarta Mandate on Marine and Coastal Biological Diversity)

Reaffirming its decision II/10 on the conservation and sustainable use of marine and coastal biological diversity,

Having considered recommendation III/2 of its Subsidiary Body on Scientific, Technical and Technological Advice,

1. *Adopts* the programme of work on marine and coastal biological diversity, as contained in the annex to the present decision;

2. *Urges* Parties, countries, relevant organizations and donor agencies to contribute to the implementation of specific elements of the programme of work;

3. *Urges* Parties, when requesting for assistance through the financial mechanism of the Convention, to propose projects which, while being fully consistent with previous guidance of the Conferences of the Parties, promote the implementation of the programme of work;

4. *Urges* the Executive Secretary to cooperate with the Convention on Wetlands of International Importance, especially as Waterfowl Habitat, where appropriate, in relation to the implementation of the joint work plan having regard to linkages with the programme of work on inland water biological diversity adopted by decision IV/4;

II Coral reefs

Being deeply concerned at the recent extensive and severe coral bleaching, such as that reported by the African countries, caused by abnormally high water temperatures experienced since January 1998,

Recognizing the potentially severe loss of biological diversity and consequent socio-economic impacts, and

Noting this occurrence as a possible consequence of global warming and in light of the precautionary approach,

1. *Requests* the Subsidiary Body on Scientific, Technical and Technological Advice to make an analysis of this phenomenon and provide relevant information to the fifth meeting of the Conference of the Parties for its consideration;

2. *Instructs* the Executive Secretary to express its concern to the Executive Secretary of the United Nations Framework Convention on Climate Change and the Secretary-General of the Convention on Wetlands and convey it to the conferences of the Parties to the United Nations Framework Convention on Climate Change and the Convention on Wetlands at their next meetings;

3. *Invites* the United Nations Framework Convention on Climate Change to urgently address this issue in its deliberations; and

4. *Urges* Parties, with reference to programme element 1.3 (c) of the programme of work, to take appropriate actions to mitigate impacts upon marine and coastal biological diversity and consequent socio-economic effects;

III Small island developing States

Recognizing the uniqueness and extreme fragility of marine and coastal biological diversity of small island developing States (SIDS), the disproportionate responsibility facing small island developing States in the conservation of these biological resources, and the limited capacity of small island developing States to implement the Jakarta Mandate on Marine and Coastal Biological Diversity,

Strongly recommends to Parties, countries, relevant organizations and donor agencies that the special needs and considerations of small island developing States be a focus for implementing each of the elements of the programme of work, as appropriate.

Annex: Programme of work on marine and coastal biological diversity

A Introduction

1. The aim of this programme of work is to assist the implementation of the Jakarta Mandate on Marine and Coastal Biological Diversity at the national, regional and global levels. It identifies key operational objectives and priority activities within the five key programme elements: integrated marine and coastal area management, marine and coastal living resources, marine and coastal protected areas, mariculture and alien species and genotypes. It also provides a general programme element to encompass the coordination role of the Secretariat, the collaborative linkages required and the effective use of experts.

B Basic principles

1 Ecosystem approach

2. The ecosystem approach should be promoted at global, regional, national and local levels taking into account the report of the Malawi workshop (document UNEP/CBD/COP/4/Inf.9) and in accordance with decision IV/1 B.

3. Protected areas should be integrated into wider strategies for preventing adverse effects to marine and coastal ecosystems from external activities and take into consideration, *inter alia*, the provisions of Article 8 of the Convention.

2 Precautionary approach

4. The precautionary approach, as set out in decision II/10, annex II, paragraph 3 (a), should be used as a guidance for all activities affecting marine and coastal biological diversity, being also relevant to many other international agreements, *inter alia*, the United Nations Agreement on Straddling Fish Stocks and Highly Migratory Fish Stocks and the Code of Conduct for Responsible Fisheries of the Food and Agriculture Organization of the United Nations, the Washington Global Programme of Action for the Protection of the Marine Environment from Land-based Activities and regional agreements such as OSPAR.

3 The importance of science

5. Science should, *inter alia*, provide knowledge on key processes and influences in the marine and coastal ecosystems which are critical for structure, function and productivity of biological diversity. Research should focus on understanding the natural factors outside human influence, including intrinsic factors influencing ecosystems themselves, as well as on human interference with ecosystems.

6. Special efforts should be undertaken to support the Global Taxonomy Initiative in the marine and coastal environment in view of the importance of basic taxonomic work for the implementation of the objectives of the work programme, in accordance with decision IV/1 D.

7. It is important to draw upon regional scientific organizations, such as the International Council for the Exploration of the Sea (ICES). The creation and strengthening of regional scientific centres of excellence on the marine and coastal ecosystems, that provide guidance to regional and national managers, should be given priority.

4 Roster of experts

8. The Executive Secretary should make full use of the roster of experts on marine and coastal biological diversity. The use and administration of the roster by the Executive Secretary should be efficient, effective and transparent. Upon request of the Executive Secretary, Parties or other countries and relevant bodies, the experts on the roster are invited to make available their specific expertise in order to contribute to the further development of the scientific, technical, technological and socio-economic issues. Such requests could entail, *inter alia*, peer reviews, questionnaires, clarifications or examinations of scientific, technical, technological and socio-economic issues, specific contributions to the compilation of documents, participation in the global and regional workshops, and assisting in connecting the Jakarta Mandate and the present programme of work to international, regional, national and local scientific, technical and technological processes.

5 Local and indigenous communities

9. The programme of work will use and draw upon scientific, technical and technological knowledge of local and indigenous communities in keeping with the contents of Article 8 (j) of the Convention as well as community and user-based approaches; in the execution of the programme of work, the involvement of relevant stakeholders including indigenous and local people should be promoted.

6 Levels of implementation

10. *National and local.* The primary basis for this programme of work is action at national and local levels. The Parties should, in accordance with Article 6 of the Convention, develop national strategies, plans and programmes in order to promote the conservation and sustainable use of marine and coastal biological diversity.

11. *Regional.* At the regional level, organizations, arrangements and bodies should be invited to coordinate activities of and/or relevant to the programme of work. These organizations should as appropriate and according to their own rules of procedure report to the Convention on their activities. Where regional organizations have not been established, the Parties and other institutions should examine the need for new regional organizations or other mechanisms for regional integration. Cooperation and information flow between the economic sectors involved should be promoted. Regional scientific and technical centres of excellence should be promoted.

12. *Global.* At the global level, UNEP (including the Global International Water Assessment), FAO, the Intergovernmental Oceanographic Commission of the United Nations Educational, Scientific and Cultural Organization (UNESCO), the International Maritime Organization, the United Nations and other relevant bodies should be encouraged to implement the programme of work. These organizations should be invited to inform the Convention on their efforts to implement the Convention.

13. *Implementation modalities.* This programme of work is the programme of work of the Parties and of the Secretariat. The main function of the Secretariat is to promote the implementation of specific activities and to perform an overall coordination role.

14. Activities associated with the programme of work should be cost-effective and efficient. Duplication of efforts will be avoided, and harmonization of respective programmes of work will be pursued through strong coordination between the Convention and other relevant bodies, with a particular view to the list of partner organizations mentioned in decision II/10, paragraph 13, and the Convention on Wetlands.

C Programme elements

Programme element 1: Implementation of integrated marine and coastal area management (IMCAM)

Operational objective 1.1: To review the existing instruments relevant to IMCAM and their implication for the implementation of the Convention.

Activities:

(a) To identify existing mechanisms and instruments relevant to IMCAM;

(b) To identify focal points for the implementation of IMCAM at different levels (national, regional and global);

(c) Secretariat to gather, compare and analyse information provided by the focal points;

(d) To convene meetings involving representatives of stakeholders at different levels.

Time schedule: 1998–2000 (minimum three-year period)

Ways and means: The activities will be carried out by the Executive Secretary, with the collaboration of an informal inter-agency task force.

Budgetary implications: Costs related to communications and staff travel to inter-agency meetings and to service meetings. Costs related to convening of meeting of stakeholders on the integration of marine and coastal biological diversity into sectoral policies.

Operational objective 1.2: To promote the development and implementation of IMCAM at the local, national and regional level.

Activities:

(a) To promote, within the framework of IMCAM, the integration of biological diversity concerns in all socio-economic sectors adversely impacting the marine and coastal environment;

(b) To promote the identification or establishment of subregional, regional or global processes for developing advice on the application of IMCAM and issues identified under the operational objective;

(c) To promote adequate protection of areas important for reproduction such as spawning and nursery areas and restoration of such areas and other important habitats for marine living resources;

(d) To promote action to reduce and control sea-based sources of pollution;

(e) To assist the development of national and regional capacity-building;

(f) To provide information on relevant legal and institutional issues, having regard to the United Nations Convention on the Law of the Sea (UNCLOS) and other related international and regional agreements;

(g) To assist the development of appropriate education and public awareness programmes at all levels;

(h) To provide guidance on maintenance and wider application of local and traditional knowledge.

Time schedule: 1998–2000 (minimum three-year period)

Ways and means: The activities should be carried out by the Executive Secretary in collaboration with relevant organizations.

Budgetary implications: No significant budgetary implications.

Operational objective 1.3: To develop guidelines for ecosystem evaluation and assessment, paying attention to the need to identify and select indicators, including social and abiotic indicators, that distinguish between natural and human-induced effects.

Activities:

(a) To promote the development of sets of indicators on which to base decision-making; and convene regional workshops to help select key indicators;

(b) To identify existing organizations and initiatives;

(c) To promote the identification of key habitats for marine living resources on a regional basis, with a view to further develop policies for action to prevent physical alteration and destruction of these habitats, and pursue restoration of degraded habitats, including, *inter alia*, coral reef systems;

(d) To promote the establishment or strengthening of mechanisms for research, monitoring and assessment of marine and coastal ecosystems and their living resources;

(e) To promote exchange of information and experience using the clearing-house mechanism and other appropriate mechanisms;

(f) To collaborate with relevant organizations in the preparation of guidelines;

Time schedule: 1998–2000 (minimum three-year programme)

Ways and means: The activities should be carried out by the Executive Secretary and the Subsidiary Body on Scientific, Technical and Technological Advice, as part of the work programme on indicators, monitoring and assessment and in collaboration with relevant organizations.

Budgetary implications: Budgetary implications will be covered under the programmes of work on indicators, monitoring and assessment and public education, training and awareness. Voluntary contributions for regional workshops on indicators and public education, training and awareness activities are needed.

Programme element 2: Marine and coastal living resources

Operational objective 2.1: To promote ecosystem approaches to the sustainable use of marine and coastal living resources, including the identification of key variables or interactions, for the purpose of assessing and monitoring, first, components of biological diversity; second, the sustainable use of such components; and, third, ecosystem effects.

Activities:

(a) To develop collaborative links with relevant organizations and institutions;

(b) To promote the exchange of information and experience using appropriate mechanisms;

(c) To promote the identification and development of ecosystem approaches compatible with the sustainable use of marine and coastal living resources;

(d) To promote the identification both of components of the ecosystems which are critical to the functioning of the ecosystem and of key threats;

(e) To promote capacity-building at local, national and regional levels, including local and traditional knowledge;

(f) To carry out a study on the effects of stock enhancement on marine and coastal biological diversity at the species and genetic levels.

Time schedule: 1998–2000 (minimum three-year period)

Ways and means: The Executive Secretary shall promote the undertaking of the activities by relevant organizations and institutions. The information dissemination aspects should be included in the work plan of the clearing-house mechanism unit. The Executive Secretary shall attempt to establish an informal inter-agency task force for this work.

Budgetary implications: Costs related to communications and travel to inter-agency meetings. Relevant organizations are invited to conduct the study, within the framework of existing cooperative arrangements. Additional contributions from Parties, countries and organizations in the organization of capacity building activities are expected.

Operational objective 2.2: To make available to the Parties information on marine and coastal genetic resources, including bioprospecting.

Activity:

To explore ways to expand the knowledge base on which to make informed and appropriate decisions about how this area might be managed in accordance with the objectives of the Convention.

Time schedule: 1998/ongoing

Ways and means: The activity should be implemented by the Executive Secretary, making full use of the roster of experts.

Budgetary implications: No significant budgetary implications.

Programme element 3: Marine and coastal protected areas

Operational objective 3.1: To facilitate research and monitoring activities related to the value and the effects of marine and coastal protected areas or similarly restricted management areas on sustainable use of marine and coastal living resources.

Activities:

(a) To collaborate with relevant organizations in the preparation of project proposals;

(b) To work with relevant organizations to identify pilot projects;

(c) To conduct a desk study to gather and assimilate information;

(d) To identify the linkages between conservation and sustainable use;

(e) To facilitate Parties, countries or international/regional organizations in conducting research on the effects of marine and coastal protected or closed areas on population size and dynamics, subject to national legislation.

Time schedule: 1998–onwards (three to five-year period)

Ways and means: The Executive Secretary, in collaboration with relevant organizations and agencies, involving also funding agencies or donor countries, will facilitate and assist in the preparation of project documents and identify pilot projects for research and monitoring, as well as conduct the desk study. The projects should be undertaken by Parties and countries or competent organizations. The Executive Secretary, starting from the roster of experts, will select the names of an ad hoc technical expert group and elaborate the terms of reference for it, both to be endorsed by the Subsidiary Body on Scientific, Technical and Technological Advice. The expert group will carry out its activities under the Subsidiary Body on Scientific, Technical and Technological Advice and will work through electronic correspondence and teleconferences.

Budgetary implications: Costs related to communications. Additional voluntary contributions are needed from Parties or donor countries or funding agencies to fund the projects, the amount depending on the number, nature and scale of the projects.

Operational objective 3.2: To develop criteria for the establishment of, and for management aspects of, marine and coastal protected areas.

Activities:

(a) To compile research findings on aspects of marine and coastal protected areas relevant to their selection, design, establishment and management;

(b) To assist in developing criteria for selection of marine and coastal protected areas, where critical habitats for marine living resources should be one important criterion;

(c) Using the clearing-house mechanism, to assist the exchange of information on research, management issues and problems (including incentive measures) between marine protected area managers, to facilitate continuous improvement in management effectiveness across the global network of marine protected areas;

(d) To implement activities as in subparagraphs (e) to (h) under operational objective 1.2.

Time schedule: 1998–2000 (minimum three-year programme)

Ways and means: The basis for undertaking these activities should be collaboration between the Executive Secretary, under the guidance of the Subsidiary Body on Scientific, Technical and Technological Advice, and relevant international, national and non-governmental organizations. The creation of an informal task force may be an appropriate mechanism, conducting its work through regular communication and through periodic meetings as required.

Budgetary implications: Costs related to communications and to staff travel to inter-agency meetings and to service meetings.

Programme element 4: Mariculture

Operational objectives: To assess the consequences of mariculture for marine and coastal biological diversity and promote techniques which minimize adverse impact.

Activities:

(a) To provide guidance on criteria, methods and techniques which avoid the adverse effects of mariculture and also subsequent stock enhancement on marine and coastal biological diversity and enhance the positive effects of mariculture on marine and coastal productivity;

(b) To collect and disseminate information, data, literature and bibliography relevant to the operational objective and best practice of successful sustainable mariculture, including the use of local species where appropriate;

(c) To evaluate the current state of scientific and technological knowledge on the effects of mariculture on marine and coastal biological diversity.

Time schedule: 1999–onwards (minimum three-year period)

Ways and means: Coordination of this programme of activities within the Secretariat creates the need for a professional with specific high-level expertise. This need could probably best be met through the secondment by a Party or specialized institution of an appropriate professional. To be successful and cost-effective, the work would need to draw upon specialist scientific knowledge world-wide. It would thus need to be supported by the establishment of an ad hoc technical expert group under the Subsidiary Body on Scientific, Technical and Technological Advice, taking into consideration the roster of experts. Operational aspects thus suggest that this work be undertaken from 1999 onwards.

Budgetary implications: Voluntary contribution by a Party or institution to cover the costs of the secondee. Costs for communications and travel to service meetings. Costs related to the convening of expert meeting(s).

Programme element 5: Alien species and genotypes

Operational objective 5.1: To achieve better understanding of the causes of the introduction of alien species and genotypes and the impact of such introductions on biological diversity.

Activities:

(a) To analyse and disseminate information, data and case-studies on the subject;

(b) To develop collaboration with relevant organizations;

(c) To ensure exchange of information and experience, using appropriate mechanisms.

Time schedule: 1998–2000 (minimum three-year period)

Ways and means: The Executive Secretary, under the guidance of the Subsidiary Body on Scientific, Technical and Technological Advice, will seek the assistance of relevant organizations through an informal inter-agency task force. In particular, the options will be investigated for collaboration with UNEP, the Scientific Committee on Problems of the Environment (SCOPE), the International Council for the Exploration of the Sea (ICES) and the World Conservation Union (IUCN) Invasive Species Specialist Group and the Global Invasive Species Programme in the development of a global strategy and action plan. In carrying out this work, it is expected that Parties or specialized institutions will second a specialist.

Budgetary implications: Voluntary contribution by a Party or institution to cover the costs of the secondee. Costs for communications.

Operational objective 5.2: To identify gaps in existing or proposed legal instruments, guidelines and procedures to counteract the introduction of and the adverse effects exerted by alien species and genotypes which threaten ecosystems, habitats or species, paying particular attention to transboundary effects; and to collect information on national and international actions to address these problems, with a view to prepare for the development of a scientifically-based global strategy for dealing with the prevention, control and eradication of those alien species which threaten marine and coastal ecosystems, habitats and species.

Activities:

(a) To request views and information from Parties, countries and other bodies;

(b) To analyse the information for the purpose of identifying gaps in legal instruments, guidelines and procedures;

(c) To evaluate the information on the effectiveness of efforts to prevent the introduction of, and to control or eradicate, those alien species which may threaten ecosystems, habitats or species;

(d) To identify means to support capacity-building in developing countries to strengthen their ability to conduct work related to alien species.

Time schedule: 1998–2000 (minimum three-year period)

Ways and means: The activities will be carried out by the Executive Secretary, in collaboration with Parties, countries and other relevant bodies and in cooperation with UNEP, IOC and IMO. It is proposed that a conference with global participation be held and that a Party or specialized institution will be able to host the conference. It is anticipated that the peer review process will be followed for the output of this programme activity.

Budgetary implications: Costs related to communications and staff travel servicing the conference. Voluntary contributions for holding the conference are needed.

Operational objective 5.3: To establish an 'incident list' on introductions of alien species and genotypes through the national reporting process or any other appropriate means.

Activities:

(a) To distil references of incidents from the national reports and other appropriate sources;

(b) To make the information available through the clearing-house mechanism or other appropriate mechanisms.

Time schedule: Such information gathering can begin immediately and be informed by national reports as they are provided.

Ways and means: Secretariat

Budgetary implications: Costs related to additional staff time within the national reports unit and the clearing-house mechanism unit.

Programme element 6: General

Operational objective 6.1: To assemble a database of initiatives on programme elements through a cooperative approach with relevant organizations and bodies, with special emphasis on integrated marine and coastal areas management.

Activities:

(a) To identify sources of relevant information and to make this readily available;

(b) To request inputs from Parties, countries and relevant organizations and bodies;

(c) To carry out desk evaluations with the assistance of the roster of experts of available information and to disseminate the findings through the clearing-house mechanism.

Time schedule: 1998–2000 (minimum three-year programme)

Ways and means: Secretariat.

Budgetary implications: Costs related to additional staff time within the clearing-house mechanism unit associated with the design of appropriate databases and posting information.

Operational objective 6.2: To develop a database of experts from the roster and other sources, to be available for the development and implementation of specific elements of national policies on marine and coastal biological diversity, giving full recognition to the importance of taxonomy and following closely the development of the Global Taxonomy Initiative and in accordance with decision IV/1 D. Special consideration should be given to regional perspectives and the setting up of regional centres of taxonomic expertise, as well as to the taxonomy efforts of other intergovernmental programmes, agencies and relevant institutions.

Activities:

(a) To maintain and update regularly a database of experts on marine and coastal biological diversity;

(b) To make the information available through the clearing-house mechanism;

(c) To promote the strengthening of taxonomic expertise at regional and national levels.

Time schedule: Ongoing

Ways and means: Secretariat, also through relevant organizations, in particular those that deal with taxonomic issues.

Budgetary implications: Costs related to additional staff time within the clearing-house mechanism unit associated with the design of the database and of the Jakarta Mandate on Marine and Coastal Biological Diversity home page.

Decision IV/6: Agricultural biological diversity

The Conference of the Parties,

Recalling its decision III/11, on the conservation and sustainable use of agricultural biological diversity, and reiterating the importance of agricultural biological diversity as containing the most vital elements of biological diversity essential for food and livelihood security,

Emphasizing the need for a worldwide reorientation towards sustainable agriculture which balances production and conservation objectives in such a way as to meet the needs of expanding populations while maintaining an ecological balance,

Welcoming the statement presented by the Food and Agriculture Organization of the United Nations at the fourth meeting of the Conference of the Parties, regarding its offer to provide further technical assistance to Parties in the implementation of the three objectives of the Convention, in particular, in response to decision III/11,

Further welcoming the establishment by the Commission on Genetic Resources for Food and Agriculture, of an intergovernmental Technical Working Group for Animal

Genetic Resources for Food and Agriculture, the first meeting of which is scheduled for September 1998,

1. *Endorses* recommendation III/4 of the Subsidiary Body on Scientific, Technical and Technological Advice and, noting the progress made so far in initiating the development of the multi-year work programme on agricultural biological diversity called for in decision III/11, highlights the importance of speeding up implementation and requests full support of the Convention's instruments in such efforts;

2. *Reiterates its wish*, in accordance with paragraph 2 of decision III/11, that FAO maintain its coordinating role in the assessment of ongoing activities and instruments at regional and international levels and *requests* the Executive Secretary, in collaboration with FAO, to further consult with Parties, Governments and relevant organizations and bodies in the finalization of this review with a view to making available a clear and well structured report, well in advance of the fourth meeting of the Subsidiary Body on Scientific, Technical and Technological Advice, that will facilitate the work of the Subsidiary Body on Scientific, Technical and Technological Advice;

3. *Requests* the Executive Secretary to reiterate the invitation to Parties and Governments for further national submissions, if possible in electronic form, on ongoing activities, existing instruments and lessons learned in the area of agricultural biological diversity, in the light of paragraphs 4, 5 and 6 and annex 2 of decision III/11;

4. *Suggests* that Governments, funding agencies, the private sector and non-governmental organizations should join efforts to identify and promote sustainable agricultural practices, integrated landscape management of mosaics of agriculture and natural areas, as well as appropriate farming systems that will reduce possible negative impacts of agricultural practices on biological diversity and enhance the ecological functions provided by biological diversity to agriculture. In this regard, *invites* Parties, Governments and organizations to begin the process of conducting case-studies based on socio-economic and ecological analyses of different land-use management options and to provide such case-studies to the Executive Secretary.

5. *Decides* to expand the focus placed on soil micro-organisms in annex 3 of decision III/11 to address all soil biota, as outlined in paragraph 8 of recommendation III/4 of the Subsidiary Body on Scientific, Technical and Technological Advice, and invites Parties, Governments and international organizations to conduct case-studies on soil biota in agriculture and to provide them to the Executive Secretary for compilation in the form of a synthesis report for consideration by the Subsidiary Body on Scientific, Technical and Technological Advice;

6. *Requests* Parties, Governments and international organizations, in particular FAO, in the light of paragraphs 9, 15 (a) and 15 (m) of decision III/11 and paragraphs 3 and 4 of decision IV/1 A, to begin to provide inputs on the development and application of methodologies for assessments of agricultural biological diversity and tools for identification and monitoring, including: criteria and indicators for agricultural biological diversity, including those addressing farming systems and agricultural ecosystems; rapid assessment techniques; the identification of underlying causes behind the loss of biological diversity; and the identification of incentives to overcome constraints and enhance the conservation and sustainable use of agricultural biological diversity and the fair and equitable sharing of benefits;

7. *Requests* the Subsidiary Body on Scientific, Technical and Technological Advice at its fourth meeting, in accordance with paragraph 7 of decision III/11 and

decision IV/16, to develop and provide to the Conference of the Parties at its fifth meeting, advice and recommendations for the development of the first phase, and subsequent phases, of the multi-year work programme on agricultural biological diversity;

8. *Welcomes* the close cooperation established between the Executive Secretary and FAO and, with reference to decision II/15 and decision III/11, paragraph 19, of the Conference of the Parties, urges that the momentum in the intergovernmental negotiations of the revision of the International Undertaking on Plant Genetic Resources in harmony with the Convention should be maintained with a view to its timely conclusion before the end of 1999;

9. *Requests* the Executive Secretary, as a complement to decision III/17, paragraph 6, to apply for observer status in the Committee on Agriculture of the World Trade Organization for the purpose of representing the Convention in meetings whose agendas may influence implementation of decision III/11 and related decisions of the Conference of the Parties;

10. *Requests* the Executive Secretary to report to the Conference of the Parties on the impact of trade liberalization on the conservation and sustainable use of agricultural biological diversity in consultation with relevant bodies, such as the World Trade Organization;

11. Reiterating the precautionary approach, *requests* the Subsidiary Body on Scientific, Technical and Technological Advice, to consider and assess, in light of contributions to be provided by Parties, Governments and organizations, whether there are any consequences for the conservation and sustainable use of biological diversity from the development and use of new technology for the control of plant gene expression, such as that described in United States patent 5723765, and to elaborate scientifically based advice to the Conference of the Parties. Moreover, urges Parties, Governments as well as civil society and public and private institutions to consider the precautionary approach in its application;

12. With reference to paragraphs 21 and 22 of decision III/11, *draws the attention* of international funding agencies, including the financial mechanism, of the need to support capacity-building in the development and implementation of this work programme;

13. *Welcomes* the efforts being made by the financial mechanism in the development of its operational policy framework on agricultural biological diversity and urges the early completion of this framework, fully in line with decision III/11, so as to provide effective implementation support to Parties and Governments in all agricultural ecosystems.

Recommendation III/4: Agenda item 6: Review of ongoing activities on agricultural biological diversity

The SBSTTA,

Taking note of the important information contained in document UNEP/CBD/SBSTTA/3/6 and in the supporting documents, both those that had been provided by the Food and Agriculture Organization of the United Nations (FAO) following the seventh session of the Commission on Genetic Resources for Food and Agriculture (CGRFA) (UNEP/CBD/SBSTTA/3/Inf.6, Inf.7 and Inf.8) and those prepared specifically for the third meeting of SBSTTA (UNEP/CBD/SBSTTA/3/Inf.9, Inf.10, Inf.20 and Inf.21),

1. *Congratulates* the secretariat for the significant progress made in initiating the review of the identification and assessment of ongoing activities and instruments at international and national levels, and in particular the proposed process outlined for the development of a multi-year work programme to implement decision III/11 and the focus provided on farming systems and agro-ecosystems approaches, contained in document UNEP/CBD/SBSTTA/3/Inf.10. The SBSTTA notes that the completion of this review, well ahead of its consideration at the next meeting of the SBSTTA, is a top priority;

2. *Thanks* the Government of the Netherlands for its support in facilitating the joint secretariat of the Convention on Biological Diversity–Food and Agriculture Organization of the United Nations technical workshop;

3. *Congratulates* the Food and Agriculture Organization of the United Nations for its work to promote the implementation of decision III/11;

4. *Commends* the establishment of collaboration between the secretariat of the Convention on Biological Diversity and FAO in response to decision III/11 and related decisions and, noting the important progress made, encourages the further development of the joint collaboration between the Convention on Biological Diversity and FAO, so as to reflect the results of the analysis of activities and instruments at international level and the identification of gaps and complementarities resulting from the review;

5. *Notes* the progress made by the CGRFA at its seventh session in May 1997, and recalls the importance, for the implementation of the Convention of Biological Diversity, of a successful conclusion to the negotiation for the adaptation of the International Undertaking in harmony with the objectives of the Convention;

6. *Acknowledges* the complexity of agricultural biological diversity and the breadth and scope of decision III/11; notes the need to address ecosystems, species and genetic levels, to focus on the interface between environment and agriculture and to consider linkages with other ecosystems; and further notes the importance of agricultural biological diversity in ensuring food security and sustainable development and the need for countries to recognize the importance of agricultural biological diversity as an integral component of their overall biodiversity strategies;

7. *Emphasizes* the importance for the conservation and sustainable use of agricultural biological diversity of respecting the knowledge, innovations and practices deriving from traditional farming systems;

8. *Agrees* to expand the focus placed on soil micro-organisms in Annex 2 of decision III/11 to address all soil biota, so as to include other key organisms such as earthworms;

9. *Welcomes* the efforts being made by GEF to incorporate agricultural biological diversity into its operational programmes, revised operational criteria for enabling activities, and short-term response measures;

10. *Notes* the granting, to the secretariat of the Convention of Biological Diversity, of observer status in the Committee on Trade and Environment of the World Trade Organization, and *supports* the proposed collaboration between these bodies,

and with FAO, in order to consider ways to develop a better appreciation of the relationship between trade and agricultural biological diversity and to initiate the identification of issues that will need to be addressed by the Conference of the Parties, while providing an opportunity for Parties and Governments to provide inputs;

11. *Further notes* that relevant information, at national, regional and global levels, should be made available through the clearing-house mechanism and that this mechanism should be used as widely as possible to promote the transfer and development of technology and information exchange;

12. *Agrees* that work undertaken on the development of indicators for agricultural biological diversity be carried out in context of recommendation III/5;

13. *Notes* the contributions received to date in response to paragraphs 1 to 6 of decision III/11, *emphasizes* the importance of the identification and assessment of relevant activities and existing instruments related to agricultural biological diversity to be conducted at national level, and hopes that such information will become more widely available following further contributions and submission of the first national reports;

14. *Recommends* that the Conference of the Parties:

(a) Note the significant progress made so far in initiating the development of the multi-year work programme on agricultural biological diversity called for in decision III/11;

(a) Encourage the Executive Secretary, in collaboration with FAO, to continue ongoing efforts to compile and assess the findings of the review being conducted by Governments and Parties and by international and regional organizations, and to seek closer collaboration with other relevant United Nations bodies, as well as with other regional and international organizations, in particular the Consultative Group on International Agricultural Research (CGIAR) centres, and including non-governmental organizations, with a view to drawing on their experience and expertise;

(b) Reaffirm that the reporting on, and development of, the multi-year work programme is an iterative and phased process;

(c) Provide guidance to GEF and invite other funding institutions to assist countries with the implementation of decision III/11, in particular, through responding to urgent and priority national needs.

Decision IV/7: Forest biological diversity

The Conference of the Parties,

Recalling decision III/12 of the third meeting of the Conference of the Parties, and recommendations II/1, II/8 and III/3 of the Subsidiary Body on Scientific, Technical and Technological Advice,

Having considered the report of the Executive Secretary on the draft programme of work for forest biological diversity (UNEP/CBD/COP/4/7),

Taking note of views expressed by the Parties and countries on the development of the work programme, as contained in document UNEP/CBD/COP/4/Inf.11,

Noting that the development and implementation of national measures that enhance the integration of the conservation and sustainable use of forest biological diversity into national forest and land-use programmes and forest-management systems is an important task for both developed and developing countries,

Looking forward to the outcomes of forthcoming work under the Intergovernmental Forum on Forests (IFF), including the global workshop on underlying causes of deforestation, to be hosted by the Government of Costa Rica in January 1999,

Reaffirming that the proposals for action contained in the final report of the Intergovernmental Panel on Forests (IPF), in particular those related to national forest and land-use programmes, and the objectives of the Intergovernmental Forum on Forests, provide a good basis for the implementation of key provisions of the Convention on Biological Diversity at the national level,

Noting that decision IV/13 gives further guidance to the Global Environment Facility (GEF) with regard to forest biological diversity,

1. *Decides* to endorse the work programme for forest biological diversity as contained in the annex to the present decision;

2. *Urges* Parties, countries, international and regional organizations, major groups and other relevant bodies to collaborate in carrying out the tasks identified in the work programme;

3. *Calls upon* Parties and countries to integrate forest biological diversity considerations in their participation and collaboration with organizations, institutions and conventions affecting or working with forest biological diversity;

4. *Invites* the Food and Agriculture Organization of the United Nations (FAO) to further integrate forest biological diversity into ongoing work with the Global Forest Resources Assessment;

5. *Urges* Parties and countries and international financial institutions, including the Global Environment Facility, to give high priority to the allocation of resources to activities that advance the objectives of the Convention in respect of forest biological diversity;

6. *Calls upon* the Global Environment Facility (GEF) to provide financial support, in accordance with Article 7 of the Convention, for activities and capacity-building for the implementation of the work programme for forest biological diversity and the use of the clearing-house mechanism, particularly for activities to halt and mitigate deforestation effects, basic assessments and monitoring of forest biological diversity, including taxonomic studies and inventories, focusing on forest species, other important components of forest biological diversity and ecosystems under threat;

7. *Invites* Parties, when requesting assistance through the financial mechanism, to propose projects that are being fully consistent with previous guidance of the Conference of the Parties and promote the implementation of the focused work programme on forest biological diversity;

8. *Requests* the financial mechanism of the Convention to consider the operational objectives of the programme of work as a guidance for funding in the field of forest biological diversity and strongly encourages the Global Environment Facility to assist in the implementation of the programme of work at the national, regional and subregional level;

9. *Notes* the potential impact of afforestation, reforestation, forest degradation and deforestation on forest biological diversity and on other ecosystems, and, accordingly, *requests* the Executive Secretary to liaise and cooperate with the Secretariat of the United Nations Framework Convention on Climate Change and the Secretariat of the Convention to Combat Desertification in Those Countries Experiencing Serious Drought and/or Desertification, particularly in Africa to achieve the objectives of the Convention on Biological Diversity;

10. *Requests* the Executive Secretary to compile a synthesized report on the information on forest biological diversity made available to the Conference of the Parties, particularly national reports;

11. *Requests* the Executive Secretary, in implementing the work programme on forest biological diversity to actively continue collaborating and cooperating with the secretariat of the Intergovernmental Forum on Forests and relevant institutions and to inform the Conference of the Parties thereon;

12. *Requests* the Subsidiary Body on Scientific, Technical and Technological Advice, in accordance with its mandate, to provide advice on the status and trends of forest biological diversity and the identification of options for the conservation and sustainable use of forest biological diversity to the Conference of the Parties at its sixth meeting;

13. *Requests* the Executive Secretary to transmit this decision to the Intergovernmental Forum on Forests at its second meeting, to the Conference of the Parties to the United Nations Framework Convention on Climate Change at its fourth meeting and to the Conference of the Parties to the Convention on Desertification at its second meeting.

Annex:
Work programme for forest biological diversity under the Convention on Biological Diversity

I Introduction

1. In accordance with decision III/12 of the Conference of the Parties, this work programme on forest biological diversity focuses on the research, co-operation and development of technologies necessary for the conservation and sustainable use of forest biological diversity of all types of forests in the programme elements and priority areas already identified.

2. The work programme is based on recommendation III/3 of Subsidiary Body on Scientific Technical and Technological Advice and incorporates the views and interests expressed by Parties and countries. The work programme is action-oriented, demand-driven, needs-driven and flexible enough to reflect and respond to changing conditions, including but not limited to, the outcome of and the priorities to be identified by the Intergovernmental Forum on Forests (IFF). The work programme also reflects the varied needs and circumstances of Parties, indicating that inclusion of an activity in the work programme does not necessarily imply full participation in that activity by all Parties. In carrying out work under the identified programme elements, Parties should recall the further research priorities listed in recommendation II/8 of the Subsidiary Body on Scientific, Technical and Technological Advice.

A Objectives

3. The objectives of the programme of work are:

(a) To enhance Parties' abilities to realize the objectives of the Convention through improved implementation, by encouraging and assisting Parties to develop measures for enhancing the integration of conservation and sustainable use of biological diversity into their national forest and land-use programmes and forest-management systems;

(b) To facilitate the implementation of the objectives of the Convention on Biological Diversity based on the ecosystem approach;

(c) To provide an effective and complementary tool to national forest and land-use programmes for the implementation of the Convention on Biological Diversity at the national level;

(d) To identify traditional forest systems of conservation and sustainable use of forest biological diversity and to promote the wider application, use and role of traditional forest-related knowledge in sustainable forest management and the equitable sharing of benefits, in accordance with Article 8 (j) and other related provisions of the Convention;

(e) To identify mechanisms that facilitate the financing of activities for the conservation, incorporation of traditional knowledge and sustainable use of forest biological diversity, taking into account that activities should be complementary to, and should not duplicate, existing efforts;

(f) To contribute to ongoing work in other international and regional organizations and processes, in particular to the implementation of the proposals for action of the Intergovernmental Panel on Forests and to provide input to IFF;

(g) To contribute to the access to and transfer of technology in accordance to Article 16 of the Convention; and

(h) To identify the contribution of networks of protected areas to the conservation and sustainable use of forest biological diversity.

B Time-frame

4. The programme of work reflects a rolling three-year planning horizon in three phases, on the assumption that, in its consideration, the Conference of the Parties will identify a rolling longer-term programme of work.

C Review and planning process

5. Each phase of the work programme should be subject to periodic review and the development of the work programme, including work in its future phases, should take into consideration recommendations made by the Subsidiary Body on Scientific, Technical and Technological Advice. The phases and outputs should take into account the time-frames and work of IFF.

6. Interim reports after each three-year phase to provide the Conference of the Parties with information on progress made in the implementation of the work programme.

D Ways and means

7. In its recommendation III/3, the Subsidiary Body on Scientific, Technical and Technological Advice identified the following ways and means for carrying out the work programme: workshops, regional meetings, the clearing-house mechanism, scientific meetings and case-studies. Other feasible ways and means include:

(a) National mechanisms and pilot projects;

(b) Peer-review mechanisms, including networks of experts or liaison groups and inter-agency task force groups, relying to the extent possible on existing electronic communication systems;

(c) Use of national and international data and meta-databases, especially in the national and regional monitoring of forest biological diversity;

(d) Bearing in mind Articles 16 and 17 of the Convention, use of remote-sensing technologies to assist Parties to assess changes in their forest biological diversity, as well as to enhance their ability to report on certain aspects of criteria and indicators frameworks.

E Collaborative efforts

8. The work programme should support and enhance cooperation on the conservation and sustainable use of forest biological diversity at all levels, ranging from community to inter-organization level, nationally and internationally. At all levels the work programme should be developed and implemented with relevant stakeholders, recognizing that the most important part of work is action at the national level.

9. In the context of this work programme, collaboration should be strengthened in particular with the Convention to Combat Desertification in Those Countries Experiencing Serious Drought and/or Desertification, particularly in Africa and with the United Nations Framework Convention on Climate Change, in order to advance the effective implementation of the Convention on Biological Diversity.

II Work programme

Elements of the proposed work programme

10. The work programme elaborates, as follows, the elements for inclusion therein.

1 Holistic and inter-sectoral ecosystem approaches that integrate the conservation and sustainable use of biological diversity, taking account of social and cultural and economic considerations

11. The IPF proposal for action 17 encourages countries to develop, implement, monitor and evaluate national forest programmes, which include a wide range of approaches for sustainable forest management, including ecosystem approaches that integrate the conservation of biological diversity and the sustainable use of biological diversity.

Research

Approach

12. Synthesize existing knowledge of holistic and inter-sectoral approaches that enhance the integration of forest biological diversity conservation into sustainable forest management, examine how such integration can be better achieved, and assist in identifying priority research areas in relation to these approaches.

Activities

13. Examination of methodologies for enhancing the integration of forest biological diversity conservation and sustainable use into an holistic approach to sustainable forest management.

14. Development of methodologies to advance the integration of traditional forest-related knowledge into sustainable forest management, in accordance with Article 8 (j).

15. Cooperation on the conservation and sustainable use of forest biological resources at all levels, ranging from community to inter-organization level, at the national and international levels in accordance with Articles 5 and 16 on the Convention.

16. Case-studies from countries in which the ecosystem approach has been applied in sustainable forest management practices, including arid and semi-arid areas. This could assist other countries in developing their own national actions and approaches under this work programme.

17. Sharing of relevant technical and scientific information on networks at all levels of protected forest areas and networking modalities, taking into account existing national, regional and international networks and structures, in all types of forest ecosystems.

Ways and means

18. Clearing-house mechanism, national pilot projects, the Convention on Biological Diversity participating in Inter-Agency Task Force on Forests (ITFF) and in the meetings of IFF to actively encourage countries to implement national forest programmes that encompass an ecosystem approach which ensures the maintenance of forest biological diversity values, while also taking into account social, cultural and economic considerations.

19. Consideration of the UNEP guidelines and the FAO document entitled 'Basic principles and operational guidelines for the formulation, execution and revision of national forestry programmes' for the preparation of country studies of biological diversity.

20. The integration of social, cultural and economic considerations into the conservation and sustainable use of forest biological diversity will bring the concept close to sustainable forest management. The issue should also be dealt with thoroughly in other forums, mainly within the work under IFF.

Outcomes

21. A better understanding of the ecosystem approach as it relates to forest biological diversity, and an elaboration of the linkages to other work under the Convention, including the incorporation of Article 8 (j).

22. Guidance of the Convention on Biological Diversity to IFF and other relevant forums and conventions.

23. Cooperation among Parties and with organizations and conventions.

24. A better understanding of the complexity and interdependencies of biological communities and their dependencies on the abiotic site-specific factors.

25. Methodologies to help ensure that forest plans and practices reflect the social, cultural and economic values of forests as well as the views of forest stakeholders.

26. Identification of general guidelines or methodologies to help ensure that forest plans and practices reflect biological diversity conservation considerations, as well as social, cultural and economic factors.

27. Clarification of the links between the ecosystem approach and sustainable forest management.

Development of technologies

Approach

28. Promote activities to support the development of techniques and means for the effective conservation and sustainable use of biological resources, in particular, full support for technology transfer from developed to developing countries, in accordance with Article 16 of the Convention.

2 Comprehensive analysis of the ways in which human activities, in particular forest-management practices, influence biological diversity and assessment of ways to minimize or mitigate negative influences

Research

Approach

29. Promote activities for an enhanced understanding of positive and negative human influences on forest ecosystems by land-use managers, policy makers, scientists and all other relevant stakeholders.

30. Promote activities to assemble management experiences and scientific, indigenous and local information at the national and local levels to provide for the sharing of approaches and tools that lead to improved forest practices with regard to forest biological diversity.

31. Promote activities with the aim of providing options to minimize or mitigate negative and to promote positive human influences on forest biological diversity.

32. Promote activities to minimize the impact of harmful alien species on forest biological diversity, particularly in small island developing States.

Activities

33. Identification of means and mechanisms to improve the identification and prioritization of research activities related to the influences of human activities, in particular forest management practices, on forest biological diversity.

34. Improve dissemination of research results and synthesis of reports of the best available scientific and traditional knowledge on key forest biological diversity issues.

35. Case-studies on assessing impacts of fires and alien species on forest biological diversity and their influences on the management of forest ecosystems and savannahs.

Ways and means

36. Regional workshops and/or liaison meetings that bring together experts in sustainable forest management, sustainable use and science from the forest sector and, if necessary, representatives from other relevant sectors, with experts on biological diversity, bearing in mind the IPF proposal for action contained in paragraph 94 of the report on its fourth session.

37. The sharing of forest and land-use guidelines, for example, through the clearing-house mechanism, to ensure the fuller integration of genetic, species and habitat diversity into sustainable forest management systems.

Outcomes

38. Analysis of human impacts on forest ecosystems, as well as an enhanced ability to prioritise research needs and apply results and an enhanced understanding of the role of traditional knowledge in ecosystem management to minimize or mitigate negative influences, and to promote the positive effects.

39. Expansion of research capacity to develop and assess options incorporating the applications of traditional knowledge to minimize or mitigate negative influences, and to promote the positive effects.

3 Methodologies necessary to advance the elaboration and implementation of criteria and indicators for forest biological diversity

Research

Approach

40. Foster activities to determine and advance the methodology for elaborating and implementing the criteria and indicators of forest biological diversity. These activities could supplement work that has already been developed. In this regard, coordination with IFF, and drawing upon existing and ongoing work at the national, regional and international levels, is recognized as an important approach.

41. Foster activities to determine criteria and indicators for the conservation and sustainable use and the fair and equitable sharing of benefits arising out of utilization of resources of forest biological diversity and to advance methodology for integrating these criteria and indicators into existing criteria and indicators processes.

42. The work related to indicators of forest biological diversity could also imply the need for an inventory to assess current status and trends in forest biological diversity, at the local and national level based on repeated measures of the selected indicators. The work under this programme element could also include, *inter alia*, capacity-building on taxonomy and inventories, taking note of the work under the Global Taxonomy Initiative.

Activities

43. Assessment of experiences gained in the national and regional processes, identifying common elements and gaps in the existing initiatives and improving the indicators for forest biological diversity.

44. Taxonomic studies and inventories at the national level which provide for a basic assessment of forest biological diversity.

Ways and means

45. Collaboration with national institutions and relevant bodies and in coordination with the work on the general development of methods for implementing Article 7 under the Convention. Collaboration with ITFF member agencies; cooperating with and complementing existing criteria and indicators initiatives for sustainable forest management, including regional initiatives to develop appropriate criteria and indicators, such as the Helsinki process for boreal, temperate and Mediterranean-type forests in Europe; the Montreal process for temperate and boreal forests outside Europe; the Tarapoto proposal for the Amazon forest; the UNEP/FAO-initiated processes for dry-zone Africa and the Near East in arid and semi-arid areas; and the 'Lepaterique' process for Central America initi-

ated by FAO and the Central American Commission for Environment and Development (CCAD).[9]

46. Review of specific indicators of forest biological diversity that have been derived by the major ongoing international processes related to sustainable forest management. The prioritization of related activities should consider the development of indicators that are capable of providing the most useful information on national or regional status and trends of forest biological diversity.

Outcomes

47. Methodologies to advance the elaboration and implementation of criteria and indicator frameworks and the improved capacity of countries to implement these frameworks.

48. Contribution to the national and regional initiatives in the development of indicators under the criteria for forest biological diversity.

4 Further research and technological priorities identified in the recommendation II/8 of the Subsidiary Body on Scientific, Technical and Technological Advice as well as issues identified in the review and planning process under the work programme

49. Included under this element is a series of specific research and technological priorities initially identified under recommendation II/8 of the Subsidiary Body on Scientific, Technical and Technological Advice. These represent important issues brought forward into the Convention from the IPF proposals for action. These priorities are among the issues to be discussed by IFF at its scheduled meetings in 1998 and 1999 and within the inter-sessional meetings of the IFF,[10] as part of its attempt to identify and define global and regional research priorities for forests, taking into account national priorities. It is essential that the Convention on Biological Diversity coordinates with IFF in order to enhance synergy on these issues as they intersect with the programme of work for forests under the Convention on Biological Diversity.

50. Following input from IFF on these priorities, the Conference of the Parties may wish to consider incorporating them in phases 2 and 3 of this work programme. When additional scientific and technological priorities are identified, they can similarly be incorporated in the periodic planning activities and reviews of the work programme.

Research

Analysing measures for minimizing or mitigating the underlying causes of forest biological diversity loss

51. Besides unsustainable forest-management practices, there are other causes for the loss of forest biological diversity in forest ecosystems, such as habitat transformation, harmful alien species, pollution, erosion, uncontrolled forest fires and poverty. There is a need for a better understanding of the underlying social, cultural and economic causes of forest biological diversity loss and the improvement of measures for mitigating those causes.

9 See background document for the Intergovernmental Seminar on Criteria and Indicators for Sustainable Forest Management, Helsinki, June 1996.

10 For example, the international seminar on research and information needs in international forest processes, to be held in Vienna in September 1998.

Assessing ecological landscape models, the integration of protected areas in the ecosystem approach to sustainable forest management and the representativeness and adequacy of protected areas networks

52. Conserving the biological diversity of forests should be carried out both by establishing protected areas and by taking into account biological diversity conservation in all types of forests outside the protected areas, taking into account plantation forests. The outcome of this programme element would include the further development of methods to integrate protected areas into sustainable forest management and analysis of the representativeness and adequacy of the protected areas networks.

53. Reducing gaps in knowledge in the areas of fragmentation of habitats and population viability, to include mitigation options such as ecological corridors and buffer zones.

54. The work should also contribute to the preparation of the discussions of the Conference of the Parties on *in situ* conservation.

Advancing scientific and technical approaches

Activities

55. Promoting the development of scientific and technical local approaches to:

(a) Conserve and sustainably manage biological diversity in production forests;

(b) Rehabilitate degraded and deforested ecosystems as appropriate;

(c) Enrich indigenous biological diversity in forest plantations

56. Developing assessment and valuation methodologies for the multiple benefits derived from forest biological diversity.

Decision IV/8: Access and benefit-sharing

The Conference of the Parties,

1. *Requests* the inter-sessional open-ended meeting referred to in decision IV/16, paragraph 2, to explore options for access and benefit-sharing mechanisms and to start work on paragraph 10 of decision IV/15 and to make recommendations for future work;

2. *Requests* the Executive Secretary to invite information from Parties and relevant organizations in time for the inter-sessional meeting in respect of those *ex situ* collections which were acquired prior to the entry into force of the Convention on Biological Diversity and which are not addressed by the Commission on Genetic Resources for Food and Agriculture of the Food and Agriculture Organization, to help the inter-sessional meeting to make recommendations to the fifth meeting of the Conference of the Parties for future work on resolving the issue of such *ex situ* collections, with due regard to the provisions of the Convention;

3. *Decides* to establish a regionally balanced panel of experts appointed by Governments, composed of representatives from the private and the public sectors as well as representatives of indigenous and local communities, operating in accordance with decisions II/15, III/11 and III/15, under the Conference of the Parties and reporting to its next meeting. The mandate of this panel would be to draw upon all relevant sources, including legislative, policy and administrative measures, best practices and

case-studies on access to genetic resources and benefit-sharing arising from the use of those genetic resources, including the whole range of biotechnology, in the development of a common understanding of basic concepts and to explore all options for access and benefit-sharing on mutually agreed terms including guiding principles, guidelines, and codes of best practice for access and benefit-sharing arrangements. These options might address, *inter alia*, the elements set out in the annex to the present decision;

4. *Requests* the financial mechanism to give special emphasis to the following programme priorities to fund initiatives by eligible Parties:

(a) Stock-taking activities, such as, for example, assessments of current legislative, administrative, and policy measures on access to genetic resources and benefit-sharing, evaluation of the strengths and weaknesses of a country's institutional and human capacity, and promotion of consensus-building among its different stakeholders; and, for those developing country Parties that have identified arrangements for benefit-sharing as a national priority;

(b) Formulation of access and benefit-sharing mechanisms at the national, subregional and regional level including monitoring and incentive measures;

(c) Capacity-building for measures on access to genetic resources and sharing of benefits, including capacity-building for economic valuation of genetic resources;

(d) Within biodiversity projects, other specific benefit-sharing initiatives, such as support for entrepreneurial developments by local and indigenous communities, facilitation of financial sustainability of projects promoting the sustainable use of genetic resources, and appropriate targeted research components;

5. *Invites* all relevant organizations and the private sector to support efforts by Parties and Governments to develop and promote legislative or administrative measures, policies and programmes which facilitate the distribution of benefits arising from the use of genetic resources on mutually agreed terms and to update the Executive Secretary on a regular basis regarding their activities and experiences;

6. *Requests* the Executive Secretary:

(a) To explore the possibility of linking the clearing-house mechanism with relevant international and other organizations to access publicly available information on intellectual property rights which are based on biological resources and to report on the progress made on this matter to the Conference of the Parties at its fifth meeting;

(b) To compile information on access and benefit-sharing arrangements and to disseminate such information in a standardized format through the clearing-house mechanism;

(c) To facilitate the exchange of information related to access and benefit-sharing through appropriate means such as the clearing-house mechanism;

(d) To prepare a background document on the review of implementation of measures to promote and advance benefit-sharing arrangements, based on the experiences submitted by Parties, Governments and relevant organizations.

Annex

1. Prior informed consent in provider countries for access to genetic resources and research and development.

2. Clear, established mechanisms to provide such consent, including, *inter alia*, legislative, administrative and policy measures, as appropriate.

3. Reference to the country of origin, where available, in relevant publications and patent applications.

4. Mutually agreed terms including on benefit-sharing and intellectual property rights and technology transfer, where appropriate.

5. Efficient permitting and regulatory procedures that avoid burdensome procedures involving high transaction costs.

6. Incentive measures to encourage the conclusion of contractual partnerships.

Decision IV/9: Implementation of Article 8 (j) and related provisions

The Conference of the Parties,

Recalling its decision III/14,

Realizing the importance for biological diversity of indigenous and local communities embodying traditional lifestyles relevant for the conservation and sustainable use of biological diversity,

Emphasizing the need for dialogue with representatives of indigenous and local communities embodying traditional lifestyles relevant for the conservation and sustainable use of biological diversity within the framework of the Convention,

Welcoming the report of the inter-sessional workshop on Article 8 (j), held in Madrid from 24 to 28 November 1997,

Expressing its sincere appreciation to the Government of Spain for hosting the inter-sessional workshop,

Reaffirming the dynamic nature of traditional knowledge, innovations and practices,

Recognizing that traditional knowledge should be given the same respect as any other form of knowledge in the implementation of the Convention,

Recognizing also that intellectual property rights may have implications for the implementation of the Convention and achievement of its objectives under Article 8 (j),

Further recognizing the importance of making intellectual-property-related provisions of Article 8 (j) and related provisions of the Convention on Biological Diversity and provisions of international agreements relating to intellectual property mutually supportive, and the desirability of undertaking further cooperation and consultation with the World Intellectual Property Organization,

Welcoming the decision of the World Intellectual Property Organization to incorporate biodiversity-related issues under its 1998–1999 main programme item 11 (Global intellectual property issues),

Acknowledging the importance of starting work as soon as possible on priority work programme elements,

Expressing its sincere appreciation for the valuable contribution made by the participating representatives of the indigenous and local communities at the fourth meeting of the Conference of the Parties,

1. *Decides* that an ad hoc open-ended inter-sessional working group be established to address the implementation of Article 8 (j) and related provisions of the Convention. The mandate of this working group shall be:

(a) To provide advice as a priority on the application and development of legal and other appropriate forms of protection for the knowledge, innovations and practices of indigenous and local communities embodying traditional lifestyles relevant for the conservation and sustainable use of biological diversity;

(b) To provide the Conference of the Parties with advice relating to the implementation of Article 8 (j) and related provisions, in particular on the development and implementation of a programme of work at national and international levels;

(c) To develop a programme of work, based on the structure of the elements in the Madrid report (UNEP/CBD/COP/4/10/Add.1) as set out in the annex to the present decision;

(d) To identify those objectives and activities falling within the scope of the Convention; to recommend priorities taking into account the programme of work of the Conference of the Parties, such as the equitable sharing of benefits; to identify for which work-plan objectives and activities advice should be directed to the Conference of the Parties and which should be directed to the Subsidiary Body on Scientific, Technical and Technological Advice; to recommend which of the work-plan objectives and activities should be referred to other international bodies or processes; to identify opportunities for collaboration and coordination with other international bodies or processes with the aim of fostering synergy and avoiding duplication of work;

(e) To provide advice to the Conference of the Parties on measures to strengthen cooperation at the international level among indigenous and local communities embodying traditional lifestyles relevant to the conservation and sustainable use of biological diversity and make proposals for the strengthening of mechanisms that support such cooperation;

2. *Decides* that the working group shall be composed of Parties and observers, including, in particular, representation from indigenous and local communities embodying traditional lifestyles relevant to the conservation and sustainable use of biological diversity with participation to the widest possible extent in its deliberations in accordance with the rules of procedure;

3. *Encourages* Parties to include representatives of indigenous and local communities embodying traditional lifestyles relevant to the conservation and sustainable use of biological diversity in their delegations;

4. *Encourages* Parties to promote consultations among indigenous and local communities embodying traditional lifestyles relevant to the conservation and sustain-

able use of biological diversity concerning the issues to be dealt with in the working group;

5. *Encourages* indigenous and local communities embodying traditional lifestyles relevant to the conservation and sustainable use of biological diversity to participate and to identify the process to select their participants in the working group, taking into account the funds available, the need for geographical balance and the need for the working group to be effective and efficient;

6. *Decides* that the working group should meet in conjunction with Subsidiary Body on Scientific, Technical and Technological Advice, unless a Party offers to host the meeting of the working group;

7. *Decides* that the working group shall report directly to the Conference of the Parties and that the working group may provide advice to the Subsidiary Body on Scientific, Technical and Technological Advice on issues relevant to its agenda;

8. *Decides* that the costs of servicing the meetings of the working group shall be funded in accordance with the relevant provisions of decision IV/17, as related to the budget;

9. *Decides* that there shall be both short- and medium-term activities in the programme of work to facilitate the work of the Parties in the implementation of Article 8 (j) and related provisions.

10. As part of the short-term activities, *invites* Governments, international agencies, research institutions, representatives of indigenous and local communities embodying traditional lifestyles relevant for the conservation and sustainable use of biological diversity and non-governmental organizations to submit case-studies and other relevant information to the Executive Secretary, on the following, as background information for the working group without being a prior condition to or pre-empting the deliberations of the working group in discharging its mandate as set out in paragraph 1 (c) of the present decision:

(a) Interactions between traditional and other forms of knowledge relating to the conservation and sustainable use of biological diversity;

(b) The influence of international instruments, intellectual property rights, current laws and policies on knowledge, innovations and practices of indigenous and local communities embodying traditional lifestyles relevant for the conservation and sustainable use of biological diversity;

(c) The extent to which traditional knowledge of indigenous and local communities has been incorporated into development and resource-management decision-making processes;

(d) Documented examples and related information on ethical guidance for the conduct of research in indigenous and local communities about the knowledge they hold; and

(e) Matters of prior informed consent, fair and equitable sharing of benefits and *in situ* conservation in lands and territories used by indigenous and local communities embodying traditional lifestyles relevant for the conservation and sustainable use of biological diversity;

11. *Requests* the Executive Secretary to prepare a suitable format for the presentation of the information requested in paragraph 10 of the present decision, in order to assist in the preparation of its synthesis in support of the programme of work;

12. *Requests* Parties according to their capabilities to facilitate the representation, and financially and logistically support the active participation in the working group of the indigenous and local communities from their territories;

13. *Encourages* Parties, when making applications to the interim financial mechanism for funding in respect of activities under Article 8 (j) and related provisions, to consider: (a) priorities as set out in paragraph 10 and (b) projects in support of the development of national legislation and corresponding strategies on the implementation of Article 8 (j), as well as (c) projects in support of preparations by indigenous and local communities embodying traditional lifestyles relevant to the conservation and sustainable use of biological diversity for their active participation in and contribution to the working group;

14. *Requests* the Executive Secretary to transmit to the secretariat of the World Intellectual Property Organization, decisions and documents of the fourth meeting of the Conference of the Parties and to apply for observer status in the World Intellectual Property Organization, for the purpose of representing the Convention on Biological Diversity in meetings related to main programme 11.1 and 11.2 of the Organization;

15. *Encourages* Governments, relevant international and regional organizations and representatives of indigenous and local communities embodying traditional lifestyles relevant to the conservation and sustainable use of biological diversity to conduct and communicate to the Executive Secretary, case studies for dissemination through means such as the clearing-house mechanism and *requests* the Executive Secretary to compile case-studies submitted under decisions of the Conference of the Parties at its third and fourth meetings relating to Article 8 (j) and intellectual property rights, including existing *sui generis* systems and/or adapted forms of protection to the knowledge, innovations and practices of indigenous and local communities relevant to the conservation and sustainable use of biological diversity for transmittal to the World Intellectual Property Organization and for use in initiatives on legislating on the implementation of Article 8 (j) and related provisions;

16. *Invites* the World Intellectual Property Organization to take into account the lifestyles and the traditional systems of access and use of the knowledge, technologies and practices of indigenous and local communities embodying traditional lifestyles relevant to the conservation and sustainable use of biological diversity in its work and the relevant recommendations of the Conference of the Parties;

17. *Requests* the Executive Secretary to seek ways, including the possibility of negotiating a memorandum of understanding with the World Intellectual Property Organisation, to enhance cooperation between the Convention on Biological Diversity and the World Intellectual Property Organization on issues arising from Article 8 (j) and related provisions and encourages Parties to forward information to the Executive Secretary to support such cooperation.

Annex:
Structure of work programme options from the Madrid Report (UNEP/CBD/COP/4/10/Add.1)

A Participatory mechanisms for indigenous and local communities

B Status and trends in relation to Article 8 (j) and related provisions

C Traditional cultural practices for conservation and sustainable use

D Equitable sharing of benefits

E Exchange and dissemination of information

F Monitoring elements

G Legal elements

Decision IV/10: Measures for implementing the Convention on Biological Diversity

A Incentive measures: Consideration of measures for the implementation of Article 11

The Conference of the Parties,

Reaffirming the importance for the implementation of the Convention of the design and implementation by Parties and Governments of economically and socially sound measures that act as incentives for the conservation and sustainable use of biological diversity,

Recalling decision III/18 on incentive measures,

Recognizing that incentive measures should be designed using an ecosystem approach and with the targeted resource management audience in mind,

Recognizing that economic valuation of biodiversity and biological resources is an important tool for well-targeted and calibrated economic incentive measures,

(a) *Encourages* Parties, Governments and relevant organizations:

(a) To promote the design and implementation of appropriate incentive measures, taking fully into account the ecosystem approach and the various conditions of the Parties and employing the precautionary approach of Principle 15 of the Rio Declaration on Environment and Development, in order to facilitate achieving the implementation of the objectives of the Convention and to integrate biological diversity concerns in sectoral policies, instruments and projects;

(b) As a first step towards formulating incentive measures, to identify threats to biological diversity and underlying causes of reduction or loss of biological diversity and relevant actors;

(c) To take into account economic, social, cultural and ethical valuation in the development of relevant incentive measures;

(d) To develop supportive legal and policy frameworks for the design and implementation of incentive measures;

(e) To carry out participatory consultative processes at the relevant level to define the clear and target-oriented incentive measures to address the identified underlying causes of biodiversity reduction or loss and unsustainable use;

(f) To identify perverse incentives and consider the removal or mitigation of their negative effects on biological diversity in order to encourage positive, rather than negative, effects on the conservation and sustainable use of biological diversity;

(g) To prepare case-studies on incentive measures in the thematic focus of the fifth meeting of the Conference of the Parties, utilizing the indicative outline prepared by the Executive Secretary as far as possible, and to make them available to the Executive Secretary.

(h) To undertake value addition and enhancement of naturally occurring genetic resources, based on the participatory approach, where appropriate, to work as incentives for their conservation and sustainable use;

2. *Requests* Parties to include information on the design and implementation of incentive measures in their second national reports;

3. *Requests* the financial mechanism to provide to eligible Parties adequate and timely support for the design and approaches relevant to the implementation of incentive measures including, where necessary, assessment of biological diversity of the relevant ecosystems, capacity-building necessary for the design and implementation of incentive measures and the development of appropriate legal and policy frameworks, and projects with components that provide for these incentives;

4. *Invites* all relevant organizations:

(a) To support efforts by Parties to design and implement appropriate incentive measures;

(b) To assist Parties and Governments to identify gaps in national capacity for policy research and analysis relevant to the design of incentive measures and to develop the necessary capacity to conduct such research and analysis;

5. *Requests* the Executive Secretary:

(a) To compile the information received from Parties, Governments and relevant organizations and to facilitate the exchange of information through appropriate means, such as the clearing-house mechanism, taking full advantage of existing and ongoing work of Parties and relevant organizations in this area;

(b) To prepare in collaboration with the Organisation for Economic Development and Cooperation (OECD), the World Conservation Union (IUCN) and other relevant organizations, a background paper containing further analysis of the design and implementation of incentive measures for the conservation and sustainable use of biodiversity, as it is related to the incentive measures in the thematic focus of the fifth meeting of the Conference of the Parties, with the aim of developing guidance to Parties;

(c) To describe, in this document, ways and means to identify perverse incentives and possibilities to remove or mitigate their negative effects on biological diversity.

B Public education and awareness: Consideration of measures for the implementation of Article 13

The Conference of the Parties,

Recalling Article 13 of the Convention, on public education and awareness,

Recognizing the importance of public education and awareness as central instruments to achieve the Convention's goals and to ensure effective implementation of the Convention at the national level, and *also recognizing* the need for capacity-building in this area,

Having taken note of the decision of the Commission on Sustainable Development at its sixth session on transfer of environmentally sound technology, capacity-building, education and public awareness, and science for sustainable development,

Recognizing that the conservation and sustainable use of biological diversity includes social issues which require cultural understanding and sensitivity, and that efforts to promote the goals of Article 13 entail recognition of the diverse needs of people and their differing perceptions, knowledge, attitudes, interests, values and understanding in respect of the goals of the Convention, and that public education and awareness on biological diversity is most effective when it occurs in a social context that is meaningful to a specific audience,

Noting the opportunities for synergy on this particular issue within the Convention, the activities of the Commission on Sustainable Development, the mandate and activities of the United Nations Educational, Scientific and Cultural Organization, the World Conservation Union (IUCN) and relevant activities of other bodies on public education, training and awareness on matters related to biological diversity,

Stressing that modern technologies and expanding access to electronic communication means bring new possibilities for promoting and encouraging understanding of the importance of, and measures required for, the conservation of biological diversity; but also *recognizing* the importance of traditional communication systems among local communities, with emphasis on maintaining their integrity and dynamism,

Further recognizing the role of the public media and non-traditional means of communication in information dissemination and awareness-raising,

Recognizing that non-governmental organizations have an important role in developing and disseminating information on biological diversity, especially in reaching out to marginalized groups who have a significant role to play in the conservation and sustainable use of biological diversity,

1. *Urges* Parties:

(a) To place special emphasis on the requirements of Article 13 of the Convention in the development of their national strategies and action plans;

(b) To promote education on biological diversity through relevant institutions, including non-governmental organizations;

(c) To allocate appropriate resources for the strategic use of education and communication instruments at each phase of policy formulation, planning, implementation and evaluation, including the identification of relevant target groups seeking to provide these with relevant, timely, reliable and understandable information;

(d) To integrate biological diversity concerns into education strategies, recognizing the particular needs of indigenous and local communities; and

(e) To support initiatives by major groups that foster stakeholder participation in biological diversity conservation and sustainable use and that integrate biological diversity conservation matters into their practices and educational programmes;

2. *Also urges* Parties to share experiences on initiatives on public education and awareness and public participation relevant to the Convention, particularly on a sectoral and thematic basis, and to make relevant case studies as well as lessons learned in the preparation of national biological diversity policies, strategies and plans available to the Executive Secretary and for the exchange of information among Parties

through the clearing-house mechanism and to consider how to organize assistance for Parties who may be keen to develop public awareness and education strategies, but lack the ability to do so;

3. *Encourages* Parties to make use of the media, including print and electronic media, to promote public education and awareness about the importance and appropriate methods for the conservation and sustainable use of biological diversity;

4. *Calls upon* Parties, where necessary, to illustrate and translate the provisions of the Convention into the respective local languages to promote public education and awareness-raising of relevant sectors, including local communities;

5. *Decides* that public education and awareness issues shall be integrated into and become an integral component of all sectoral and thematic items under the programme of work of the Conference of the Parties;

6. *Invites* the United Nations Educational, Scientific and Cultural Organization (UNESCO) to consider launching a global initiative on biological diversity education, training and public awareness and *requests* the Executive Secretary to explore the feasibility of such an initiative and to report to the fifth meeting of the Conference of the Parties on the progress of such an initiative;

7. *Invites* the United Nations Environment Programme (UNEP), in cooperation with other United Nations bodies and other relevant international and regional organizations, agreements, processes and institutions, to continue and make use of existing initiatives and to further develop its information dissemination and public-awareness activities in support of the work of the Convention;

8. *Urges* Parties, relevant organizations and donor agencies to support local, national, subregional and regional public education and awareness initiatives;

9. *Urges* Parties, when requesting for assistance through the financial mechanism of the Convention, to propose projects which promote measures for implementing the provisions of the Convention on public education and awareness;

10. *Decides* to review progress in the implementation of the above activities, at the latest at its seventh meeting.

C Impact assessment and minimizing adverse effects: Consideration of measures for the implementation of Article 14

The Conference of the Parties,

Recalling Article 14 of the Convention, on impact assessment and minimizing adverse impacts, including its provision on liability and redress for damage to biological diversity,

Recalling also its decision II/18, on measures to provide information and share experiences on the implementation of Article 14,

Taking note of the note by the Executive Secretary on impact assessment and minimizing adverse impacts; implementation of Article 14 (UNEP/CBD/COP/4/20),

Noting the initiatives in this field, such as the statement submitted to the fourth meeting of the Conference of the Parties on behalf of the International Association for

Impact Assessment, following its 18th annual meeting in Christchurch, New Zealand, in April 1998,

Noting the entry into force of the Economic Commission for Europe Convention on Environmental Impact Assessment in a Transboundary Context (the 'Espoo Convention'), as an example of regional cooperation,

Concerning impact assessment

1. *Invites* Parties, Governments, national and international organizations, and indigenous and local communities embodying traditional lifestyles, to transmit to the Executive Secretary for the purpose of exchanging information and sharing experiences on:

(a) Impact assessments that consider environmental effects and interrelated socio-economic aspects relevant to biological diversity;

(b) Strategic environmental assessments;

(c) Ways and means of fully incorporating biodiversity considerations into environmental impact assessment procedures;

(d) Reports and case studies relating to environmental impact assessment in the thematic areas specifically referred to in its decisions, particularly with respect to biological diversity, including in respect of activities with transboundary implications and for environmental impacts having cumulative effects on biological diversity;

(e) Reports relating to existing legislation, experience with environmental impact assessment procedures and guidelines for environmental impact assessment, particularly with regard to the incorporation of biological diversity considerations into environmental impact assessment;

(f) Reports concerning the implementation of mitigating measures and incentive schemes to enhance compliance with existing national environmental impact assessment systems;

2. *Requests* the Executive Secretary to prepare a synthesis report based on the information contained in such submissions and other relevant information, for the consideration of the Subsidiary Body on Scientific, Technical and Technological Advice;

3. *Instructs* the Subsidiary Body on Scientific, Technical and Technological Advice to identify further actions that would promote implementation of the impact assessment procedures requested by Article 14 of the Convention, including consideration of whether there is a need for additional work to develop guidelines on the incorporation of biological diversity considerations into environmental impact assessment and to report to the Conference of the Parties;

4. *Recommends* that appropriate issues related to environmental impact assessment should be integrated into and become an integral component of relevant sectoral and thematic items under the programme of work of the Conference of the Parties;

5. *Requests* the Executive Secretary to make this information available through the clearing-house mechanism and other appropriate means;

6. *Encourages* the Executive Secretary to initiate collaboration between the Convention and other international organizations and bodies with expertise in this

field and to seek cooperation, in particular with the Convention on Wetlands of International Importance, especially as Waterfowl Habitat and the Bonn Convention on the Conservation of Migratory Species, with the World Conservation Union (IUCN) and the International Association for Impact Assessment, with a view to drawing on their networks of professional expertise and sources of information and advice;

7. *Emphasizes* the need to enable active participation by interested and affected stakeholders in the assessment process, including indigenous and local communities embodying traditional lifestyles and non-governmental organizations;

Concerning liability and redress

8. *Invites* Parties, Governments and relevant international organizations to provide the Executive Secretary with information on national, international and regional measures and agreements on liability and redress applicable to damage to biological diversity, including the nature, scope and coverage of such provisions, and information on experiences in their implementation, as well as information regarding access by foreign citizens to national courts potentially applicable to or in cases involving transboundary environmental harm;

9. *Invites* Parties to include in their national reports information on actions taken with respect to liability and redress for damage to biological diversity;

10. *Requests* the Executive Secretary to prepare a synthesis report based on the information contained in submissions by Parties and other relevant information, for examination by the Conference of the Parties at its fifth meeting;

11. *Notes* that this decision is without prejudice to the consideration of the issue of liability and redress in the negotiation of the protocol on biosafety.

Decision IV/11: Review of the effectiveness of the financial mechanism

The Conference of the Parties,

Recalling its decisions II/6 on financial resources and mechanism and III/7 on the review of the effectiveness of the financial mechanism,

Taking note of the synthesis report on the first review of the effectiveness of the financial mechanism, contained in document UNEP/CBD/COP/4/16,

Taking note also of the Statement of the First Assembly of the Global Environment Facility, held in New Delhi, India, from 1 to 3 April 1998, and the list of measures identified therein for the Global Environment Facility to improve its operational performance, and welcoming the second replenishment of the Global Environment Facility Trust Fund in the amount of US$2.75 billion for its four focal areas,

Taking note of the report on the activities of the Global Environment Facility contained in document UNEP/CBD/COP/4/15,

Recalling the provisions of the Memorandum of Understanding between the Conference of the Parties and the Council of the Global Environment Facility, in particular paragraph 7 therein concerning the significance of inter-secretariat cooperation,

Welcoming the efforts made to date by the Global Environment Facility to address the concerns of Parties on the responsiveness of the financial mechanism to the policy, strategy, programme priorities and eligibility criteria established by the Conference of the Parties,

Taking into account the views and concerns expressed by Parties about the difficulties encountered in carrying out the first review, in particular the inadequacy of the procedures; and the insufficient information provided as compared with that requested in decision III/7,

Recalling decision II/6, paragraph 2, which calls for the effectiveness of the financial mechanism to be reviewed every three years,

Recognizing concerns expressed by several Parties about the need for implementing agencies to improve the processing and delivery systems of the Global Environment Facility, and reaffirming paragraph 1 of decision III/5 in this regard,

Recognizing also that further improvements are needed in the effectiveness of the financial mechanism,

1. *Determines* to further improve the effectiveness of the financial mechanism;

2. *Requests* the Council of the Global Environment Facility to take the action identified in the annex to the present decision with a view to improving the effectiveness of the financial mechanism, and further requests the Global Environment Facility to report thereon to the Conference of the Parties at its fifth meeting;

3. *Decides* that the Conference of the Parties at its fifth meeting will determine terms of reference for the second review of the effectiveness of the financial mechanism;

4. *Requests* the Executive Secretary to advise the Parties on matters relating to recommendations for further guidance to the financial mechanism with respect to:

(a) The relationship of any draft guidance to previous guidance; and

(b) Any possible effects of that draft guidance on the implementation of previous guidance from the Conference of the Parties.

Annex:
Action to improve the effectiveness of the financial mechanism

1. The Council of the Global Environment Facility should improve the effectiveness of the financial mechanism by:

(a) Further streamlining its project cycle with a view to making project preparation simpler, more transparent and more country-driven;

(b) Further simplifying and expediting procedures for approval and implementation, including disbursement, for GEF-funded projects;

(c) Developing policies and procedures that fully comply with the guidance from the Conference of the Parties in a straightforward and timely manner;

(d) Increasing support to priority actions identified in national plans and strategies of developing countries;

(e) Applying in a more flexible, pragmatic and transparent manner the incremental cost principle;

(f) Promoting genuine country ownership through greater involvement of participant countries in GEF-funded activities;

(g) Increasing its flexibility to respond to the thematic longer-term programme of work of the Convention on Biological Diversity, in accordance with the guidance of the Conference of the Parties;

(h) Promoting the catalytic role of the Global Environment Facility in mobilizing funding from other sources for GEF-funded activities;

(i) Including in its monitoring and evaluation activities the assessment of the compliance under its operational programmes with the policy, strategy, programme priorities and eligibility criteria established by the Conference of the Parties;

(j) Promoting efforts to ensure that the implementing agencies fully comply with the policy, strategy, programme priorities and eligibility criteria of the Conference of the Parties in their support for country-driven activities funded by the Global Environment Facility; and

(k) Undertaking efforts to improve the efficiency, effectiveness and transparency of the process of cooperation and coordination between the implementing agencies with a view to improving the processing and delivery systems of the Global Environment Facility, and to avoid duplication and parallel processes.

Decision IV/12: Additional financial resources

The Conference of the Parties,

Recalling Article 20, paragraphs 2 and 3, and Article 21, paragraph 4, of the Convention,

Recalling also decision III/6, by which it requested the Executive Secretary to explore possible ways of collaborating with funding institutions to facilitate efforts to achieve greater support for the Convention, and to explore further possibilities for encouraging the involvement of the private sector in support of the Convention,

Having examined the note by the Executive Secretary contained in document UNEP/CBD/COP/4/17,

Noting concerns expressed by Parties on the downward trend of development assistance in the past few years,

Noting also the lack of comprehensive information about trends in development assistance with respect to biological diversity,

Reaffirming the need to continue the implementation of decision III/6, paragraph 4, with regard to the provision of standardized information on financial support from developed country Parties for the objectives of the Convention on Biological Diversity,

Requests the Executive Secretary to prepare, for consideration by the Parties at the fifth meeting of the Conference of the Parties, a report on additional financial resources to include proposals for:

(a) Monitoring financial support for the implementation of the Convention;

(b) Possible collaboration with international organizations, institutions, conventions and agreements of relevance;

(c) Exploring possibilities for additional financial support to elements in the programme of work outlined in decision IV/16, annex II;

(d) Examining the constraints to, opportunities for and implications of private sector support for the implementation of the Convention.

Decision IV/13: Additional guidance to the financial mechanism

The Conference of the Parties,

Bearing in mind Articles 20 and 21 of the Convention,

Taking into account the guidance provided by the Conference of the Parties at its first, second and third meetings to the Global Environment Facility,

Decides to provide the following additional guidance to the Global Environment Facility in the provision of financial resources, in conformity with decisions I/2, II/6 and III/5 of the Conference of the Parties. In this regard, the Global Environment Facility shall provide financial resources to developing countries for country-driven activities and programmes, consistent with national priorities and objectives, recognizing that economic and social development and poverty eradication are the first and overriding priorities of developing countries:

The Global Environment Facility should:

1. Provide adequate and timely support for country-driven projects at national, regional and subregional levels addressing the issue of alien species in accordance with decision IV/1 C;

2. Provide financial resources for country-driven activities within the context of its operation programmes to participate in the Global Taxonomy Initiative which take into account as appropriate, elements of the Suggestions for Action contained in the annex to decision IV/1 D;

3. Within the context of implementing national biological diversity strategies and action plans, provide adequate and timely support to eligible projects which help Parties to develop and implement national, sectoral and cross-sectoral plans for the conservation and sustainable use of biological diversity of inland water ecosystems in accordance with decision IV/4;

4. In accordance with decision IV/7 and with Article 7 of the Convention and also within the context of implementing national biological diversity strategies and plans, provide adequate and timely financial support to Parties for projects and capacity-building activities for implementing the programme of work of forest biological diversity at the national, regional and subregional levels and the use of the clearing-house mechanism to include activities that contribute to halting and addressing deforestation, basic assessments and monitoring of forest biological diversity, including taxonomic studies and inventories, focusing on forest species, other important components of forest biological diversity and ecosystems under threat;

5. In accordance with decision IV/2:

(a) Support capacity-building activities and country-driven pilot projects focused on priority areas, as critical components in the implementation of the clearing-house mechanism at the national, subregional, biogeographic, and regional levels, both during and after the pilot phase;

(b) Provide, as appropriate, increased support, in the framework of country-driven projects to promote the objectives of the Convention, to establish and strengthen biodiversity information systems such as, *inter alia*, training, technology and processes related to the collection, organization, maintenance and updating of data and information and its communication to users through the clearing-house mechanism;

(c) Evaluate at the end of the clearing-house mechanism pilot phase the experience of the Global Environment Facility's support for developing countries' activities, to consider additional efforts to meet the increasing interest in taking part in and having access to the clearing-house mechanism, including in regional networking, and to report to the Conference of the Parties prior to the next meeting of the Subsidiary Body on Scientific, Technical and Technological Advice;

6. Continue to provide financial assistance for the preparation of national reports, having regard to the constraints and needs identified by Parties in their first national reports, in accordance with decision IV/14;

7. Provide adequate and timely support for the design and approaches relevant to the implementation of incentive measures, including, where necessary, assessment of biological diversity of the relevant ecosystems, capacity-building necessary for the design and implementation of incentive measures and the development of appropriate legal and policy frameworks, and projects with components that provide for these incentives, in accordance with decision IV/10;

8. In accordance with decision IV/8, provide support for:

(a) Stock-taking activities, such as, for example, assessments of current legislative, administrative and policy measures on access to genetic resources and benefit-sharing, evaluation of the strengths and weaknesses of a country's institutional and human capacity, and promotion of consensus-building among its different stakeholders;

(b) Formulation of access and benefit-sharing mechanisms at the national, subregional and regional levels, including monitoring, assessment, and incentive measures;

(c) Capacity-building on measures on access to genetic resources and sharing of benefits, including capacity-building on economic valuation of genetic resources;

(d) Within biodiversity projects, other specific benefit-sharing initiatives such as support for entrepreneurial developments by local and indigenous communities, facilitation of financial sustainability of projects promoting the sustainable use of genetic resources, and appropriate targeted research components.

Decision IV/14: National reports by Parties

The Conference of the Parties,

Recalling Article 26 and Article 23, paragraph 4 (a) of the Convention,

Recalling further decision II/17 on the form and intervals of national reports,

Noting the difficulty experienced by Parties in preparing their national reports and that the first national reports varied in length and scope and that further guidelines are needed to simplify and streamline the national reporting process,

Welcoming the number of first national reports received by the Executive Secretary,

1. *Encourages* those Parties that have submitted interim reports to submit a full report as soon as they are in a position to do so, and urges those that have yet to submit their first national report to do so as soon as they can and, in any event, no later than 31 December 1998;

2. *Requests* the Executive Secretary to prepare, in time for the fourth meeting of the Subsidiary Body on Scientific, Technical and Technological Advice, a revised version of the report referred to in decision II/17 on the basis of the national reports received and other relevant information;

3. *Requests* the Subsidiary Body on Scientific, Technical and Technological Advice, at its fourth meeting, to consider the report of the Executive Secretary and to provide the Conference of the Parties, at its fifth meeting, with advice on the intervals and form of future national reports, taking into account the elements contained in the Annex to the present decision. This advice should cover the nature of the information needed from Parties in order to assess the state of implementation of the Convention; recommendations on improving the reporting process, through guidelines on format, style, length and treatment with a view to ensuring comparability between national reports; and identification of ways and means to further facilitate national implementation of the Convention;

4. *Urges* developed country Parties to include in their national reports information, in a standardized form, on their financial support for the objectives of the Convention;

5. *Requests* the Global Environment Facility, as the operating entity of the financial mechanism, to continue to provide financial assistance for the preparation of national reports, having regard to the constraints and needs identified by Parties in their first national reports.

Annex:
Elements for the recommendation of the Subsidiary Body on Scientific, Technical and Technological Advice on the preparation of national reports

1. A standard format should be developed which would allow comparability, but provide enough flexibility to give appropriate scope to reflect national conditions and capacities.

2. The focus of subsequent national reports should be consistent with the work programme of the Convention, taking into account decisions of the fourth meeting of the Conference of the Parties.

3. Information contained in national reports should include, insofar as possible, a report on the progress of the implementation of the National Biodiversity Strategy and Action Plans, and on lessons learned, including identification of gaps in national capacity for policy research and analysis, along with technical and financial requirements for meeting needs identified in the National Biodiversity Strategies and Action Plans and the possible use of nationally developed indicators.

4. Parties are encouraged to consider the participation of all relevant stakeholders in the preparation and use of national reports.

Decision IV/15: The relationship of the Convention on Biological Diversity with the Commission on Sustainable Development and biodiversity-related conventions, other international agreements, institutions and processes of relevance

The Conference of the Parties,

Recalling its decisions II/13, III/17 and III/21,

Recalling also Article 16, paragraph 5, Article 22, paragraph 1, Article 23, paragraph 4 (h), and Article 24, paragraph 1 (d), of the Convention on Biological Diversity,

Reaffirming the importance of mutually supportive activities under the Convention on Biological Diversity and activities under other conventions, processes and institutions relevant to the achievement of the objectives of the Convention, while avoiding unnecessary duplication of activities and costs on the part of Parties and the organs of the Convention,

Welcoming the progress made in the development of cooperative arrangements with relevant conventions, institutions and processes as reported by the Executive Secretary to its fourth meeting, while recognizing the need to further improve the method of work of the Conference of the Parties in terms of assessing work done in the context of these cooperative arrangements,

Noting that the Commission on Sustainable Development in its review of the implementation of Agenda 21, at the next comprehensive review of progress achieved in the implementation of Agenda 21 by the General Assembly in the year 2002, will require input on the status of implementation of the Convention on Biological Diversity,

1. *Expresses* its appreciation to those conventions and institutions that provided documentation and information to the Conference of the Parties at its fourth meeting;

2. *Endorses* the Joint Work Plan with the Convention on Wetlands of International Importance, especially as Waterfowl Habitat (Ramsar) contained in

UNEP/CBD/COP/4/Inf.8, as recommended by decisions III/21 and IV/4 as a framework for enhanced cooperation between these conventions and encourages its implementation;

3. *Also endorses* the memoranda of cooperation entered into by the Executive Secretary with: the Intergovernmental Oceanographic Commission, the World Bank, the Food and Agriculture Organization of the United Nations (FAO), the World Conservation Union (IUCN), the Cartagena Convention, the United Nations Educational, Scientific and Cultural Organization (UNESCO), and the United Nations Conference on Trade and Development (UNCTAD);

4. *Requests* that the Executive Secretary, on behalf of the Conference of the Parties, consider matters of liaison, cooperation and collaboration as a key responsibility;

5. *Requests* the Executive Secretary to continue to coordinate with the secretariats of relevant biodiversity-related conventions, institutions and processes, and to cooperate with related processes at regional and subregional levels, with a view to:

(a) Facilitating the exchange of information and experience;

(b) Exploring the possibility of procedures for promoting efficiencies between the reporting requirements of Parties under those instruments and conventions;

(c) Exploring the possibility of developing joint work programmes, similar to that between the Convention on Biological Diversity and the Convention on Wetlands referred to above, between the Convention on Biological Diversity and other relevant institutions and conventions;

(d) Exploring modalities, where appropriate, for suitable liaison arrangements in relevant centres, in particular Geneva and/or New York, for the purpose of enhancing linkages with relevant processes, which will assist in achieving greater coherence in these intergovernmental organizations and processes;

6. *Encourages* the Executive Secretary to develop relationships with other processes with a view to fostering good management practices in areas such as: methods and approaches to deal with protected areas; ecosystem and bioregional approaches to protected area management and sustainable use of biological diversity; mechanisms to enhance stakeholder involvement; methods for developing systems plans and integrating biological diversity considerations into sectoral strategies and plans; and transboundary protected areas;

7. *Takes note* of the Executive Secretary's observer status in the Committee on Trade and Environment of the World Trade Organization for the purpose of representing the Convention on Biological Diversity in meetings whose agendas have relevance to the Convention;

8. *Also notes* that some Parties to the Convention on Biological Diversity, particularly many developing countries, are not members of the World Trade Organization, and are therefore limited in their abilities to present their concerns regarding biological diversity at the World Trade Organization;

9. *Stresses* the need to ensure consistency in implementing the Convention on Biological Diversity and the World Trade Organization agreements, including the Agreement on Trade-Related Aspects of Intellectual Property Rights, with a view to promoting increased mutual supportiveness and integration of biological diversity concerns and the protection of intellectual property rights, and invites the World Trade Organization to consider how to achieve these objectives in the light of Article 16,

paragraph 5, of the Convention, taking into account the planned review of Article 27, paragraph 3 (b), of the Agreement on Trade-Related Aspects of Intellectual Property Rights in 1999;

10. *Emphasizes* that further work is required to help develop a common appreciation of the relationship between intellectual property rights and the relevant provisions of the Agreement on Trade-Related Aspects of Intellectual Property Rights and the Convention on Biological Diversity, in particular on issues relating to technology transfer and conservation and sustainable use of biological diversity and the fair and equitable sharing of benefits arising out of the use of genetic resources, including the protection of knowledge, innovations and practices of indigenous and local communities embodying traditional lifestyles relevant for the conservation and sustainable use of biological diversity.

11. *Requests* the Executive Secretary to enhance cooperation with the World Intellectual Property Organization with respect to the Organization's programme of work;

12. *Also requests* the Executive Secretary to prepare a report on the implementation of the Convention to assist the Conference of the Parties to contribute to the review of the implementation of Agenda 21 in the year 2002;

13. *Further requests* the Executive Secretary to strengthen relationships with, in particular, the United Nations Framework Convention on Climate Change and its Kyoto Protocol, and the United Nations Convention to Combat Desertification in those Countries Experiencing Serious Drought and/or Desertification, particularly in Africa, with a view to making implementation activities and institutional arrangements mutually supportive;

14. *Takes note* of the Programme for the further implementation of Agenda 21 and requests Parties to submit information to the Executive Secretary on, *inter alia*:

(a) Current threats to biological diversity from tourism activities;

(b) Basic approaches, strategies and instruments that demonstrate where tourism and the conservation and sustainable use of biological diversity are mutually supportive;

(c) The involvement of the private sector, local and indigenous communities in establishing sustainable tourism practices;

(d) Collaborative efforts at the regional and the subregional levels, including case studies of particular relevance;

(e) Infrastructure planning and regional and land-use planning for tourism that have incorporated consideration of the Convention on Biological Diversity; or

(f) Consideration of policies and activities which are supportive of its aims, in order to initiate a process of exchange of experiences, knowledge and best practices, under the Subsidiary Body on Scientific, Technical and Technological Advice, in particular at the national and regional levels on sustainable tourism and biological diversity within the framework of the Convention on Biological Diversity, including regarding protected areas;

15. *Further invites* Parties to provide information to the Executive Secretary on the biodiversity-related activities of the Commission on Sustainable Development, such as:

(a) Comprehensive review of the Programme of Action for the Sustainable Development of Small Island Developing States;

(b) Oceans and seas, and freshwater resources;

(c) Consumption and production patterns;

16. *Requests* the Executive Secretary to provide inputs based on the above submissions to the discussion at the Commission on Sustainable Development at its seventh session to ensure that any future work of the Commission on Sustainable Development in these areas fully incorporates biological diversity considerations and makes full use of existing materials and national guidelines;

17. *Requests* the Executive Secretary to report to the Conference of the Parties at its fifth meeting on the collaborative efforts with the Commission on Sustainable Development and with the Committee on Trade and Environment of the World Trade Organization, including suggestions for improving this relationship.

Decision IV/16: Institutional matters and the programme of work

The Conference of the Parties,

Recognizing the urgency of the effective and full implementation of the Convention,

Aware of the difficulties experienced in the operations of the Convention and in achieving its full and effective implementation,

Recalling the primacy of the role of the Conference of the Parties as provided for in Article 23, paragraph 4, of the Convention,

Conscious of the need to achieve the full participation of Parties in the implementation of the Convention and emphasising the need for open and transparent preparations for the Conference of the Parties,

Underscoring the need for the Subsidiary Body on Scientific, Technical and Technological Advice to focus on scientific, technical and technological aspects of the Convention in accordance with its Article 25,

1. *Decides* that the fifth meeting of the Conference of the Parties will take place in the second quarter of 2000 for a period of two weeks;

2. *Decides also* to hold an open-ended meeting to consider possible arrangements to improve preparations for and conduct of the meetings of the Conference of the Parties, taking into account proposals made at the fourth meeting of the Conference of the Parties, including a preparatory discussion of the item on access to genetic resources on the agenda of the fifth meeting of the Conference of the Parties. This meeting will be of three days duration and is to be held in conjunction with one of the meetings planned for 1999;

3. *Requests* the Executive Secretary to analyse for the meeting described in paragraph 2 of the present decision the development and experience of other conventions and agreements and their potential relevance to the work of the Convention;

4. *Decides* to consider at its fifth meeting the results of the meeting described in paragraph 2 of the present decision and the experience gained from the changes in the functioning of the Convention included in the present decision, with a view to taking a decision on the need for further measures to improve preparations for and conduct of meetings of the Conference of Parties;

5. *Requests* the Executive Secretary, subject to necessary voluntary contributions, to organize regional/subregional meetings to consider ways and means of implementing the Convention and the decisions of the Conference of the Parties;

6. *Requests* the Executive Secretary when preparing the provisional annotated agenda to clearly indicate whether matters are for information or for consideration and when preparing the supporting documentation to include suggestion of elements for draft decisions as appropriate;

7. *Invites* Parties to forward any proposed decisions to the Executive Secretary in sufficient time to enable him/her to circulate those draft decisions to all Parties at least three weeks before the commencement of meetings of the Conference of the Parties;

8. *Requests* the Executive Secretary to distribute the provisional annotated agenda for ordinary meetings of the Conference of the Parties as well as the principal documents for the meeting, in the official languages of the United Nations, as early as possible and in reasonable time for any regional preparatory meetings organized by the Executive Secretary and, in any event, preferably six months before the opening of its ordinary meetings;

9. *Invites* Parties to notify the Executive Secretary of any additional items they wish to add to the provisional agenda at least six weeks before the opening of the meeting;

10. *Requests* the Executive Secretary to prepare, in time for the next meeting of the Conference of the Parties, a handbook that relates the decisions of the Conference of the Parties, and other material relevant to the operation of the Convention, as well as to the text of the Convention;

11. *Adopts* the *modus operandi* of the Subsidiary Body on Scientific, Technical and Technological Advice as set out in annex I to the present decision;

12. *Decides* that the Subsidiary Body on Scientific, Technical and Technological Advice shall hold two meetings, each of five days duration, before next ordinary meeting of the Conference of the Parties;

13. *Decides* that, while the Subsidiary Body on Scientific, Technical and Technological Advice should consider the financial implications of its proposals, its recommendations will only include advice to the Conference of the Parties regarding financial matters, including guidance to the financial mechanism, when the Conference of the Parties has so requested;

14. *Decides also* that in future requests to the Subsidiary Body on Scientific, Technical and Technological Advice, the Conference of the Parties will make clear whether it expects to receive information for noting, recommendations for approval, or advice for decisions by the Conference of Parties, and that, likewise, the Subsidiary Body on Scientific, Technical and Technological Advice, when submitting recommendations to the Conference of the Parties, should indicate clearly whether it expects the Conference of the Parties to note, approve or decide on the matter in question;

15. *Requests* its Bureau to liaise on a regular basis with the bureaux of its subsidiary bodies, in particular the Bureau of the Subsidiary Body on Scientific, Technical and Technological Advice, and, to this end, *requests* the Executive Secretary to organize wherever possible back-to-back meetings of the bureaux of the Conference of the Parties and the Subsidiary Body on Scientific, Technical and Technological Advice;

16. *Adopts* the programme of work for the period from the fourth meeting of the Conference of the Parties until the seventh meeting of the Conference as contained in annex II to the present decision;

17. *Recognizes* that it may be necessary for the Executive Secretary, with the guidance of the Bureau of the Conference of the Parties, to adjust further the servicing of the programme of work in light of the resources available to the Secretariat;

18. *Decides* to review the programme of work at each ordinary meeting of the Conference, in the light of developments in the implementation of the Convention;

19. *Requests* the Executive Secretary to prepare the provisional agenda of the fifth meeting of the Conference of the Parties in agreement with the President within the framework of the programme of work contained in annex II to the present decision;

20. *Requests* the Subsidiary Body on Scientific, Technical and Technological Advice and other subsidiary bodies to prepare proposals for their programmes of work based on the priorities set out in annex II to the present decision, with a view to streamlining and focusing the agendas of their meetings;

21. *Requests* the Subsidiary Body on Scientific, Technical and Technological Advice, taking into account its proposals for the programme of work developed under paragraph 16 of the present decision, to advise the fifth meeting of the Conference of the Parties of the terms of reference for the ad hoc technical expert groups on thematic areas. The terms of reference should take into account the need, *inter alia*, to provide a peer-reviewed scientific and technical assessment of the status and trends of, and impacts on, biological diversity, including the effectiveness of the types of measures for conservation and sustainable use of biological diversity.

Annex I: *Modus operandi* of the Subsidiary Body on Scientific, Technical and Technological Advice[11]

ᗦ ᗦ ᗦ

11 The *modus operandi* of the Subsidiary Body on Scientific, Technical and Technological Advice as amended by decision V/20 has been reproduced in Section IV of this Handbook.

Annex II:
The programme of work

Meeting of the Conference of the Parties	*Items for in-depth consideration*
Fifth	Dryland, mediterranean, arid, semi-arid, grassland and savannah ecosystems Sustainable use, including tourism Access to genetic resources
Sixth	Forest ecosystems Alien species Benefit-sharing
Seventh	Mountain ecosystems Protected areas Transfer of technology and technology cooperation

Decision IV/17: Programme budget for the biennium 1999–2000

The Conference of the Parties,

Recalling paragraph 7 of the financial rules for the Conference of the Parties,

Recalling also decisions III/23 and III/24, adopted at its third session,

Having considered the proposed budget for the biennium 1999–2000 submitted by the Executive Secretary,

1. *Endorses* the administrative arrangements between the United Nations Environment Programme and the Secretariat of the Convention on Biological Diversity, contained in annex III of document UNEP/CBD/COP/4/24, which entered into force on 30 June 1997, and *requests* the Executive Secretary to report regularly to the Conference of the Parties, through its Bureau, on the implementation of its provisions;

2. *Approves* the programme budget for the biennium 1999–2000, amounting to US$17,301,600 for the purposes specified in table 1 below;

3. *Notes* the statement of the Trustee that there is an accumulated surplus in the amount of US$3,616,566 and decides to use this amount on an exceptional basis to offset the contributions from Parties during the biennium 1999–2000;

4. *Welcomes* the annual contribution of US$1,000,000 by the host Government to offset the contributions from Parties for the biennium 1999–2000;

5. *Approves* the staffing table for the programme budget as contained in table 2 below and *requests* that all staff positions be filled expeditiously;

6. *Decides* that the three Trust Funds (BY, BE, BZ) for the Convention shall be extended for the period of two years, beginning 1 January 2000 and ending 31 December 2001;

7. *Authorizes* the Executive Secretary to make transfers, between each of the main appropriation lines set out in table 1 below, up to an aggregate limit of 15 per cent of the total estimated for those appropriation lines, provided that a further limitation of up to a maximum 25 per cent of each such appropriation line shall apply;

8. *Invites* all Parties to the Convention to note that contributions to the core budget are due on 1 January of each year in accordance with paragraph 4 of the financial rules and to pay promptly and in full, for each of the years 1999 and 2000, the contributions required to finance expenditures approved under paragraph 2 above, as offset by surpluses noted in paragraph 3 and contributions noted under paragraph 4 of the present decision and, in this regard, *requests* the Executive Secretary to notify all Parties of the amount of their contributions by 1 October of the year preceding the year in which their contributions are due;

9. *Urges* ali Parties and States not Parties to the Convention, as well as governmental, intergovernmental and non-governmental organizations and other sources, to contribute to the special trust funds;

10. *Approves* the supplementary amount of US$542,400 to the 1998 budget for the additional activity related to the Biosafety Protocol, to be drawn from the surpluses in addition to those referred to in paragraph 3 above;

11. *Decides* that the amount of US$300,000 for servicing of the Working Group on Article 8 (j) shall be financed from the surpluses in addition to those referred to in paragraph 3 above;

12. *Takes note* of the funding estimates for the Special Voluntary Trust Fund (BE) for Additional Voluntary Contributions in Support of Approved Activities for the Biennium 1999–2000 specified by the Executive Secretary and included in Table 3 below, and invites Parties to make contributions to this fund;

13. *Takes note* of the funding estimates for the Special Voluntary Trust Fund (BZ) for Facilitating Participation of Parties in the Convention Process for the Biennium 1999–2000 specified by the Executive Secretary and included in Table 4 below, and *invites* Parties to make contributions to this fund;

14. *Authorizes* the Trustee to transfer the unspent balance of additional special voluntary contributions received prior to 1997 from the Trust Fund for the Convention (BY) to the Special Trust Fund (BE) for additional activities approved by the Conference of the Parties and *requests* the Executive Secretary to consult with the original donor country/countries on the use of these funds for additional activities approved by the Conference of the Parties;

15. *Requests* the Executive Secretary to report to the Conference of the Parties at its fifth session on income and budget performance, and to propose any adjustments that might be needed in the Convention budget for the biennium 1999–2000.

Table 1 Biennium budget of the Trust Fund for the Convention on Biological Diversity (1999–2000)

	1999 (US$ thousands)	*2000 (US$ thousands)*
EXPENDITURE		
I Programmes		
Executive direction and management and intergovernmental Affairs	813.5	1,839.1
Scientific, technical and technological matters	1,989.7	2,069.9
Implementation and communication	1,979.8	1,600.2
Biosafety Protocol	1,275.2	1,078.8
Support Service	1,289.6	1,375.4
Subtotal (I)	*7,347.8*	*7,963.4*
II Payments to the United Nations Environment Programme		
Programme support costs	955.2	1,035.2
Subtotal (II)	*955.2*	*1,035.2*
III Contingencies	**0.0**	**0.0**
Subtotal (III)	*0.0*	*0.0*
Total expenditure lines (I + II + III)	***8,303.0***	***8,998.6***
INCOME		
I Contribution from the host Government	**1,000.0**	**1,000.0**
II Savings from previous years (surplus)	**1,603.0**	**2,013.6**
Total income (I + II)	***2,603.0***	***3,013.6***
BUDGET TO BE SHARED BY PARTIES	**5,700.0**	**5,985.0**

Table 2 Staffing table (1999–2000)

		1998	*1999*	*2000*
A	**Professional category and above**			
	D-2	1	1	1
	D-1	3	3	3
	P-5	1	1	1
	P-4	7	10	10
	P-3	5	9	9
	P-2	5	3	3
	Total A	*22*	*27*	*27*

B General service category	**18**	**20**	**20**
Total B	*18*	*20*	*20*
TOTAL (A+B)	**40**	**47**	**47**

Table 3 Special Voluntary Trust Fund (BE) for additional voluntary contributions in support of approved activities for the biennium 1999–2000

	1999 (US$ thousands)	*2000 (US$ thousands)*
A *Servicing meetings*		
Regional meetings for the Conference of the Parties	186.2	0.0
Expert meetings and workshops	482.6	427.2
B Travel	1,847.5	1,673.4
C Consultants	15.0	15.8
D Printing of materials	60.0	0.0
Subtotal (I)	*2,591.3*	*2,116.4*
II Payments to the United Nations Environment Programme support costs	336.9	275.1
Subtotal (II)	*336.9*	*275.1*
Total Expenditure Lines (I + II)	**2,928.2**	**2,391.5**
Total Proposed Income	**0.0**	**0.0**
Budget to be financed from voluntary contributions	**2,928.2**	**2,391.5**

Table 4 Special Voluntary Trust Fund (BZ) for facilitating participation of parties in the Convention process for the biennium 1999–2000*

	1999 (US$ thousands)	*2000 (US$ thousands)*
Conference of the Parties	0	837.4
Regional meetings for the Conference of the Parties	525.6	0.0
Subsidiary Body on Scientific, Technical and Technological Advice	406.0	559.5
Working Group on Article 8 (j)	406.0	559.5
Inter-sessional meeting on *modus operandi* and access/benefit-sharing	319.0	0.0
Biosafety Working Group 6/COP	725.0	0.0

Intergovernmental Committee	0.0	685.1
Subtotal (I)	*2,381.6*	*2,641.5*
II Payments to the United Nations Environment Programme Programme support costs	309.6	343.4
Subtotal (II)	*309.6*	*343.4*
Total Expenditure Lines (I + II)	**2,691.2**	**2,984.9**
Total Income	**0.0**	**0.0**
Budget to be financed from voluntary contributions	**2,691.2**	**2,984.9**

* Developing Country Parties, in particular the least developed and small island developing States, and other Parties with economies in transition.

Table 5 Contributions to the Trust Fund for the Convention on Biological Diversity for the biennium 1999–2000

Party	*United Nations scale of assessments 1999*	*Scale with 25% ceiling, no LDC paying more than 0.01%*	*Contributions as per 1 January 1999*	*United Nations scale of assessments 2000*	*Scale with 25% ceiling, no LDC paying more than 0.01%*	*Contributions as per 1 January 2000*	*Total contributions 1999–2000*
	(%)	*(%)*	*(US$)*	*(%)*	*(%)*	*(US$)*	*(US$)*
Albania	0.003	0.004	226	0.003	0.004	240	466
Algeria	0.094	0.124	7,075	0.086	0.115	6,877	13,952
Angola	0.010	0.013	753	0.010	0.013	800	1,552
Antigua and Barbuda	0.002	0.003	151	0.002	0.003	160	310
Argentina	1.024	1.352	77,074	1.103	1.474	88,201	165,275
Armenia	0.011	0.015	828	0.006	0.008	480	1,308
Australia	1.482	1.957	111,547	1.483	1.981	118,588	230,134
Austria	0.941	1.243	70,827	0.942	1.259	75,327	146,154
Bahamas	0.015	0.020	1,129	0.015	0.020	1,199	2,328
Bahrain	0.017	0.022	1,280	0.017	0.023	1,359	2,639
Bangladesh	0.010	0.013	753	0.010	0.013	800	1,552
Barbados	0.008	0.011	602	0.008	0.011	640	1,242
Belarus	0.082	0.108	6,172	0.057	0.076	4,558	10,730
Belgium	1.103	1.456	83,020	1.104	1.475	88,281	171,301
Belize	0.001	0.001	75	0.001	0.001	80	155
Benin	0.002	0.003	151	0.002	0.003	160	310
Bhutan	0.001	0.001	75	0.001	0.001	80	155
Bolivia	0.007	0.009	527	0.007	0.009	560	1,087

Botswana	0.010	0.013	753	0.010	0.013	800	1,552
Brazil	1.470	1.941	110,644	1.471	1.965	117,628	228,272
Bulgaria	0.019	0.025	1,430	0.011	0.015	880	2,310
Burkina Faso	0.002	0.003	151	0.002	0.003	160	310
Burundi	0.001	0.001	75	0.001	0.001	80	155
Cambodia	0.001	0.001	75	0.001	0.001	80	155
Cameroon	0.013	0.017	978	0.013	0.017	1,040	2,018
Canada	2.754	3.637	207,287	2.732	3.650	218,464	425,751
Cape Verde	0.002	0.003	151	0.002	0.003	160	310
Central African Republic	0.001	0.001	75	0.001	0.001	80	155
Chad	0.001	0.001	75	0.001	0.001	80	155
Chile	0.131	0.173	9,860	0.036	0.048	2,879	12,739
China	0.973	1.285	73,236	0.995	1.329	79,565	152,800
Colombia	0.109	0.144	8,204	0.109	0.146	8,716	16,920
Comoros	0.001	0.001	75	0.001	0.001	80	155
Congo	0.003	0.004	226	0.003	0.004	240	466
Cook Islands	0.001	0.001	75	0.001	0.001	80	155
Costa Rica	0.016	0.021	1,204	0.016	0.021	1,279	2,484
Cote d'Ivoire	0.009	0.012	677	0.009	0.012	720	1,397
Croatia	0.036	0.048	2,710	0.030	0.040	2,399	5,109
Cuba	0.026	0.034	1,957	0.024	0.032	1,919	3,876
Cyprus	0.034	0.045	2,559	0.034	0.045	2,719	5,278
Czech Republic	0.121	0.160	9,107	0.107	0.143	8,556	17,664
Democratic People's Republic of Korea	0.019	0.025	1,430	0.015	0.020	1,199	2,630
Democratic Republic of the Congo	0.007	0.009	527	0.007	0.009	560	1,087
Denmark	0.691	0.912	52,010	0.692	0.925	55,336	107,346
Djibouti	0.001	0.001	75	0.001	0.001	80	155
Dominica	0.001	0.001	75	0.001	0.001	80	155
Dominican Republic	0.015	0.020	1,129	0.015	0.020	1,199	2,328
Ecuador	0.020	0.026	1,505	0.020	0.027	1,599	3,105
Egypt	0.065	0.086	4,892	0.065	0.087	5,198	10,090
El Salvador	0.012	0.016	903	0.012	0.016	960	1,863
Equatorial Guinea	0.001	0.001	75	0.001	0.001	80	155
Eritrea	0.001	0.001	75	0.001	0.001	80	155
Estonia	0.015	0.020	1,129	0.012	0.016	960	2,089
Ethiopia	0.006	0.008	452	0.006	0.008	480	931
European Community	2.500	2.500	142,500	2.500	2.500	149,625	292,125
Fiji	0.004	0.005	301	0.004	0.005	320	621
Finland	0.542	0.716	40,795	0.543	0.725	43,421	84,216
France	6.540	8.636	492,251	6.545	8.745	523,369	1,015,620
Gabon	0.015	0.020	1,129	0.015	0.020	1,199	2,328
Gambia	0.001	0.001	75	0.001	0.001	80	155
Georgia	0.019	0.025	1,430	0.007	0.009	560	1,990
Germany	9.808	12.951	738,226	9.857	13.170	788,212	1,526,438
Ghana	0.007	0.009	527	0.007	0.009	560	1,087
Greece	0.351	0.463	26,419	0.351	0.469	28,068	54,487
Grenada	0.001	0.001	75	0.001	0.001	80	155

Guatemala	0.018	0.024	1,355	0.018	0.024	1,439	2,794
Guinea	0.003	0.004	226	0.003	0.004	240	466
Guinea-Bissau	0.001	0.001	75	0.001	0.001	80	155
Guyana	0.001	0.001	75	0.001	0.001	80	155
Haiti	0.002	0.003	151	0.002	0.003	160	310
Honduras	0.003	0.004	226	0.003	0.004	240	466
Hungary	0.120	0.158	9,032	0.120	0.160	9,596	18,628
Iceland	0.032	0.042	2,409	0.032	0.043	2,559	4,967
India	0.299	0.395	22,505	0.299	0.399	23,909	46,415
Indonesia	0.184	0.243	13,849	0.188	0.251	15,033	28,883
Iran (Islamic Republic of)	0.193	0.255	14,527	0.161	0.215	12,874	27,401
Ireland	0.224	0.296	16,860	0.224	0.299	17,912	34,772
Israel	0.345	0.456	25,967	0.350	0.468	27,988	53,955
Italy	5.432	7.173	408,854	5.437	7.264	434,768	843,622
Jamaica	0.006	0.008	452	0.006	0.008	480	931
Japan	19.984	25.000	1,425,000	20.573	25.000	1,496,250	2,921,250
Jordan	0.006	0.008	452	0.006	0.008	480	931
Kazakstan	0.066	0.087	4,968	0.048	0.064	3,838	8,806
Kenya	0.007	0.009	527	0.007	0.009	560	1,087
Kiribati	0.001	0.001	75	0.001	0.001	80	155
Kyrgyzstan	0.008	0.011	602	0.006	0.008	480	1,082
Lao People's Democratic Republic	0.001	0.001	75	0.001	0.001	80	155
Latvia	0.024	0.032	1,806	0.017	0.023	1,359	3,166
Lebanon	0.016	0.021	1,204	0.016	0.021	1,279	2,484
Lesotho	0.002	0.003	151	0.002	0.003	160	310
Liechtenstein	0.006	0.008	452	0.006	0.008	480	931
Lithuania	0.022	0.029	1,656	0.015	0.020	1,199	2,855
Luxembourg	0.068	0.090	5,118	0.068	0.091	5,438	10,556
Madagascar	0.003	0.004	226	0.003	0.004	240	466
Malawi	0.002	0.003	151	0.002	0.003	160	310
Malaysia	0.180	0.238	13,548	0.183	0.245	14,634	28,182
Maldives	0.001	0.001	75	0.001	0.001	80	155
Mali	0.002	0.003	151	0.002	0.003	160	310
Marshall Islands	0.001	0.001	75	0.001	0.001	80	155
Mauritania	0.001	0.001	75	0.001	0.001	80	155
Mauritius	0.009	0.012	677	0.009	0.012	720	1,397
Mexico	0.980	1.294	73,762	0.995	1.329	79,565	153,327
Micronesia (Federated States of)	0.001	0.001	75	0.001	0.001	80	155
Monaco	0.004	0.005	301	0.004	0.005	320	621
Mongolia	0.002	0.003	151	0.002	0.003	160	310
Morocco	0.041	0.054	3,086	0.041	0.055	3,279	6,365
Mozambique	0.001	0.001	75	0.001	0.001	80	155
Myanmar	0.008	0.011	602	0.008	0.011	640	1,242
Namibia	0.007	0.009	527	0.007	0.009	560	1,087
Nauru	0.001	0.001	75	0.001	0.001	80	155
Nepal	0.004	0.005	301	0.004	0.005	320	621
Netherlands	1.631	2.154	122,762	1.632	2.180	130,502	253,264

New Zealand	0.221	0.292	16,634	0.221	0.295	17,672	34,306
Nicaragua	0.001	0.001	75	0.001	0.001	80	155
Niue	0.001	0.001	75	0.001	0.001	80	155
Niger	0.002	0.003	151	0.002	0.003	160	310
Nigeria	0.040	0.053	3,011	0.032	0.043	2,559	5,570
Norway	0.610	0.805	45,913	0.610	0.815	48,778	94,692
Oman	0.051	0.067	3,839	0.051	0.068	4,078	7,917
Pakistan	0.059	0.078	4,441	0.059	0.079	4,718	9,159
Panama	0.013	0.017	978	0.013	0.017	1,040	2,018
Papua New Guinea	0.007	0.009	527	0.007	0.009	560	1,087
Paraguay	0.014	0.018	1,054	0.014	0.019	1,120	2,173
Peru	0.095	0.125	7,150	0.099	0.132	7,917	15,067
Philippines	0.080	0.106	6,021	0.081	0.108	6,477	12,499
Poland	0.207	0.273	15,580	0.196	0.262	15,673	31,254
Portugal	0.417	0.551	31,387	0.431	0.576	34,465	65,851
Qatar	0.033	0.044	2,484	0.033	0.044	2,639	5,123
Republic of Korea	0.994	1.313	74,816	1.006	1.344	80,444	155,261
Republic of Moldova	0.018	0.024	1,355	0.010	0.013	800	2,154
Romania	0.067	0.088	5,043	0.056	0.075	4,478	9,521
Russian Federation	1.487	1.964	111,923	1.077	1.439	86,122	198,045
Rwanda	0.001	0.001	75	0.001	0.001	80	155
Saint Kitts and Nevis	0.001	0.001	75	0.001	0.001	80	155
Saint Lucia	0.001	0.001	75	0.001	0.001	80	155
Saint Vincent and the Grenadines	0.001	0.001	75	0.001	0.001	80	155
Samoa	0.001	0.001	75	0.001	0.001	80	155
San Marino	0.002	0.003	151	0.002	0.003	160	310
Senegal	0.006	0.008	452	0.006	0.008	480	931
Seychelles	0.002	0.003	151	0.002	0.003	160	310
Sierra Leone	0.001	0.001	75	0.001	0.001	80	155
Singapore	0.176	0.232	13,247	0.179	0.239	14,314	27,561
Slovakia	0.039	0.051	2,935	0.035	0.047	2,799	5,734
Slovenia	0.061	0.081	4,591	0.061	0.082	4,878	9,469
Solomon Islands	0.001	0.001	75	0.001	0.001	80	155
South Africa	0.366	0.483	27,548	0.366	0.489	29,267	56,815
Spain	2.589	3.419	194,868	2.591	3.462	207,189	402,057
Sri Lanka	0.012	0.016	903	0.012	0.016	960	1,863
Sudan	0.007	0.009	527	0.007	0.009	560	1,087
Suriname	0.004	0.005	301	0.004	0.005	320	621
Swaziland	0.002	0.003	151	0.002	0.003	160	310
Sweden	1.084	1.431	81,590	1.079	1.442	86,282	167,872
Switzerland	1.215	1.604	91,450	1.215	1.623	97,157	188,607
Syrian Arab Republic	0.064	0.085	4,817	0.064	0.086	5,118	9,935
Tajikistan	0.005	0.007	376	0.004	0.005	320	696
The Former Yugoslav Republic of Macedonia	0.004	0.005	301	0.004	0.005	320	621
Togo	0.001	0.001	75	0.001	0.001	80	155
Tonga	0.001	0.001	75	0.001	0.001	80	
Trinidad and Tobago	0.017	0.022	1,280	0.016	0.021	1,279	2,559

Tunisia	0.028	0.037	2,107	0.028	0.037	2,239	4,347
Turkey	0.440	0.581	33,118	0.440	0.588	35,184	68,302
Turkmenistan	0.008	0.011	602	0.006	0.008	480	1,082
Uganda	0.004	0.005	301	0.004	0.005	320	621
Ukraine	0.302	0.399	22,731	0.190	0.254	15,193	37,924
United Kingdom of Great Britain and Northern Ireland	5.090	6.721	383,113	5.090	6.801	407,020	790,133
United Republic of Tanzania	0.003	0.004	226	0.003	0.004	240	466
Uruguay	0.048	0.063	3,613	0.048	0.064	3,838	7,451
Uzbekistan	0.037	0.049	2,785	0.025	0.033	1,999	4,784
Vanuatu	0.001	0.001	75	0.001	0.001	80	155
Venezuela	0.176	0.232	13,247	0.160	0.214	12,794	26,041
Viet Nam	0.007	0.009	527	0.007	0.009	560	1,087
Yemen	0.010	0.013	753	0.010	0.013	800	1,552
Zambia	0.002	0.003	151	0.002	0.003	160	310
Zimbabwe	0.009	0.012	677	0.009	0.012	720	1,397
TOTAL	77.388	100.0	5.700m	77.336	100.0	5.985m	11.685m

Administrative arrangements between the United Nations Environment Programme (UNEP) and the Secretariat of the Convention on Biological Diversity (CBD)

Preamble

The Executive Director of the United Nations Environment Programme (UNEP) and the Executive Secretary of the Convention on Biological Diversity (CBD),

Pursuant to decision I/4 of the first meeting of the Conference of the Parties to the CBD which designated the UNEP to carry out the functions of the Secretariat of the Convention while ensuring its autonomy to discharge the functions referred to in Article 24;

Recalling decision 18/36 of the Eighteenth Session of the Governing Council of the UNEP which welcomed the designation of the UNEP to carry out the functions of the Secretariat of the Convention while ensuring its autonomy to discharge the functions referred to in Article 24;

Aware that decision II/19 of the second meeting of the Conference of the Parties accepted the offer of Canada to host the Permanent Secretariat of the CBD in Montreal;

Recalling decision III/23 of the third meeting of the Conference of the Parties invited the Executive Director of the UNEP and the Executive Secretary of the CBD to develop procedures, making an effort to conclude by 27 January 1997, with respect to the functioning of the Permanent Secretariat of the CBD, to clarify and make more effective their respective roles and responsibilities;

Cognizant that decision III/23 stressed further that the procedures must be in accordance with the United Nations financial and staff rules and regulations and with decision I/4 of the Conference of the Parties and should as far as possible, and where appropriate, follow the Personnel, Financial and Common Services arrangements agreed to between the United Nations and the Framework Convention on Climate Change;

Aware that some of the services required by the Secretariat of the CBD in accordance with Article 24 of the Convention and the appropriate decisions of the Conference of the Parties are provided by the United Nations Office at Nairobi;

Hereby decide to apply the following, effective immediately:

I Personnel arrangements

1. The Executive Secretary of the CBD will be appointed by the Executive Director of UNEP after consultation with the Conference of the Parties through its Bureau. The level and term of office of the appointment will be determined by the Conference of the Parties. The term of office may be extended by the Executive Director of UNEP after consultation with the Conference of the Parties. Consultations on these matters will be conducted through the Bureau of the Conference of the Parties. The Executive Director of UNEP will also consult the Bureau when appraising the performance of the Executive Secretary of the CBD and will provide the Bureau with the applicable performance criteria to be used in such appraisal. On an annual basis, the Bureau will submit its comments to the Executive Director of UNEP on the performance of the Executive Secretary of the CBD. The Executive Director of UNEP will reflect these comments in her/his performance evaluation of the Executive Secretary of the CBD. The Executive Director of UNEP will consult the Conference of the Parties, through its Bureau, on issues of concern to her/him in the performance of the Executive Secretary of the CBD.

2. In accordance with the relevant staff rules, the Executive Director of UNEP will, in full consultation with the Executive Secretary of the CBD, appoint CBD staff whose appointment will be limited to service with the Convention, unless mutually agreed otherwise and in accordance with United Nations Rules and Regulations.

3. Posts and their levels are established by the Conference of the Parties for classification and recruitment purposes in conformity with the principles laid down by the General Assembly of the United Nations.

4. The Executive Secretary of the CBD will make recommendations to the Executive Director of UNEP on the promotion of all staff up to D1 /L-6 level and on the (non) extensions of appointments of all staff of the Convention at or below the D1/L-6 level, except for terminations under article X of the Staff Regulations. The provisions of ST/SGT/213/Rev 1, concerning the designation of staff members performing significant functions in financial management, personnel management and General Services administration, shall be applicable to CBD. All appointments and promotions to posts above the D1/L-6 level, or termination of appointment above the D1/L-6 level, requires prior approval of the Secretary General of the United Nations

5. The Executive Director of UNEP will, in full consultation with, and on the recommendation of the Executive Secretary of the CBD, appoint, promote and terminate project personnel up to D1/L-6 level, except for terminations under article X of the Staff Regulations. In all cases, contracts will be offered by the Executive Director of UNEP for service of the Secretariat of the Convention, and their duration is subject to

availability of resources in the Trust Funds established by the Conference of the Parties to the CBD.

6. An Appointment and Promotion Board for CBD will be established at the seat of the Convention Secretariat by the Executive Director of UNEP in full consultation with the Executive Secretary of the CBD, to advise the Executive Director of UNEP on all matters related to appointments, promotions, and review of staff. The Board will consider all the appointments and promotions of staff in the General Service and related categories and in the Professional category up to D1/L-6 level.

7. The CBD Appointment and Promotion Board, which will make its recommendations to the Executive Director of UNEP for final approval, will follow the relevant UN Staff Regulations and Rules, the procedures of the Appointment and Promotion Board at UN Headquarters and the policies of the Secretary General of the United Nations in personnel questions. The Board will consist of four members and four alternates. Members and alternate members will be appointed by the Executive Director of UNEP in full consultation with the Executive Secretary of the CBD. A representative of the Human Resources Management Services of the United Nations Office in Nairobi (HRMS/UNON) will be an ex-officio member of the Board and will serve as its Secretary. The Executive Director of UNEP, in full consultation with the Executive Secretary of the CBD, will ensure that the other members and alternates are appointed after consultation with the CBD staff representative body referred to in paragraph 8 of this agreement. Such members and alternates will be appointed for fixed periods, normally of one year, subject to renewal.

8. Consistent with the Staff Regulations and Rules of the United Nations, a CBD staff representative body will be established, taking into account, as appropriate, the existing staff representative body (ies) at the seat of the Convention Secretariat and will be consulted on all matters related to staff.

9. Movements of staff between the Convention Secretariat and other parts of UNEP will be subject to the same conditions and arrangements as are applicable to staff serving with voluntarily funded programmes of the United Nations.

10. The principle of recruitment on as wide a geographical basis as possible will govern the Professional staff in accordance with the guidelines for voluntarily funded programmes.

11. Job descriptions are prepared and submitted to UNEP by the Executive Secretary for posts approved by the Conference of the Parties.

12. Once a post is classified, a recruitment process is carried out according to the following procedures:

(a) Vacancy announcements are issued to all Parties/signatories to the CBD, 'internally' to request candidates within UNEP and the UN system, and 'externally' to elicit applications worldwide;

(b) Upon completion of the time limit given for applications (which should not exceed six weeks), the HRMS/UNON submits the list of candidates and their detailed applications to the Executive Secretary;

(c) The Secretariat will constitute a panel to prepare a short list and advise the Executive Secretary on the most suitable candidate. The panel will normally follow agreed procedures for its selection including interviewing the short listed candidates;

(d) The Appointment and Promotion Board of the CBD, referred to in paragraphs 6 and 7 of this agreement, will review the recommendations and submit its advice to the Executive Director of UNEP for final approval;

(e) The selected candidate(s) will be offered appointment(s) by the Executive Director of UNEP after consultation with the Executive Secretary of the CBD, in accordance with paragraphs 3, 4 and 5 of this agreement.

13. As an 'external' recruitment process takes time, fixed-term appointments of short-term duration of less than one year (up to a maximum of eleven months) can be made as an interim solution, while the normal recruitment process is completed in accordance with the provisions of paragraphs 3, 4, 5, and 6 of this agreement.

14. The selection and terms of employment of consultants, within available allotments, will be decided by the Executive Secretary, in accordance with United Nations procedures.

15. Posts for General Services follow the International Civil Aviation Organization (ICAO) (the lead UN agency in Montreal) job classification standards. The procedure for selecting the most qualified candidate is also similar to that of the professional candidate. For these purposes, renewable contracts of up to but not exceeding eleven months for General Service staff may be offered by the Executive Secretary of the CBD.

16. The appropriate UN bodies, such as the Joint Appeal Board, the Joint Disciplinary Committee, the Claims Board and the Advisory Board on Compensation Claims, will have jurisdiction as regards all staff serving with the Convention.

17. Professional staff will normally be pay-rolled at UNEP Headquarters and their salaries deposited monthly in the individual bank accounts nominated by the staff unless agreed otherwise by UNEP and the CBD Secretariat.

18. For health insurance, Professional and General Services staff are enrolled in the Canadian Medicare which is a branch of Sunlife Medical Insurance. Enrollment is made once the staff member starts working and the staff member's portion of the premium is charged to his/her salary. The administration of this service is provided by ICAO.

19. Staff attendance, annual sick leave will be monitored by the Executive Secretary of the CBD or the person to whom he/she delegates this responsibility.

II Financial arrangements

General Provisions

20. The Financial Regulations and Rules of the United Nations will govern these financial and common services arrangements. These arrangements will also be consistent with the financial rules adopted by the Conference of the Parties.

21. Taking into account that the resources of CBD are constituted by contributions from the Parties to the CBD and are distinct from the United Nations resources, the financial transactions of the CBD Secretariat that utilize these resources will be exempted from such restrictions as the Secretary General of the United Nations may from time-to-time impose regarding the employment of staff and consultants and the use of funds for operational requirements, including the restrictions currently in force due to the financial situation of the United Nations.

22. The financial and common support services of the CBD Secretariat will be provided by UNEP, UNON or any other United Nations entity, as appropriate, and as agreed by the Executive Director of UNEP, in full cooperation with the Executive Secretary of the Convention.

III Contributions and funds

23. The Executive Director of UNEP, with approval of UNEP's Governing Council, has established the following trust funds to support the Convention process:

(a) Special account for the Core Administrative Budget of the CBD (General Trust Fund for the CBD-alpha code BY);

(b) Special fund for additional voluntary contributions to the core budget for approved activities under the CBD (General Trust Fund for additional voluntary contributions in support of approved activities under the CBD-alpha code BE);

(c) Special fund for voluntary contributions to facilitate the participation of Parties in the CBD process (General Trust Fund for voluntary contributions to facilitate the participation of Parties in the process of the CBD-alpha code BZ).

24. The trust funds, referred to in paragraph 21 above, will be subject to arrangements related to Appendix D of the Staff Regulations and Rules. The related resources and expenditures will be accounted for under a separate account to be established by the United Nations for this purpose.

25. For the purpose of recording funds and expenditures, the trust funds, referred to in paragraph 21 above, will be administered in accordance with UN Rules and Regulations with the following exception:

No operational reserve will be maintained under the Core Administrative Budget of the Convention account on the understanding that the CBD Working Capital Reserve will be maintained and administered under that account. No operational reserves will be maintained under the other trust fund accounts.

26. The CBD secretariat will be exempt from the requirement to submit cost plans and annual substantive and programme performance reports to the UNEP. It will, however, adopt appropriate financial planning and reporting practices corresponding to its own administrative needs and to such purposes as may be determined by the Conference of the Parties.

27. Notifications (invoices) of contributions due from parties to the Convention will be processed on the basis of the Executive Secretary's communication on approval of the CBD indicative scale of contribution amount for each Party, in cooperation with the Fund Management Branch of UNEP, as appropriate. Notifications (invoices) are to be sent by the CBD Secretariat to all Parties by 1 October of the year proceeding the year for which contributions are due. Pledged contributions will be recorded under the trust funds in accordance with the rules and regulations governing the acceptance of such pledges. Contributions of the CBD accounts shall be deposited in the following account:

UNEP Trust Funds Account No.015-002756
UNEP Bank Account
Chase Manhattan Bank
New York, N.Y. 10017

28. UNEP will promptly advise the Executive Secretary by facsimile or any other appropriate means of communication, of the receipt of the contributions and acknowledge receipt to the donors. On a monthly basis, UNEP will provide to the Executive Secretary an up-to-date report of the status of pledges, payments of contributions and expenditures.

IV Treasury

29. All contributions to the Convention are deposited in the Trust Funds referred to in paragraph 21 of this agreement, and in accordance with the terms of reference for such trust funds, it is the prerogative of the Secretary General of the United Nations to invest all available cash surpluses in the account to achieve the best possible investment returns. The Treasurer of the United Nations will therefore invest CBD monies that may not be immediately required. The interest earned on the Convention trust funds will be credited to the relevant trust funds.

V Budget

30. The budget of the Convention is approved by the Conference of the Parties. The Executive Secretary may commit resources only if such commitments are within the budget approved by the Conference of the Parties and within available resources.

31. The Executive Secretary will prepare draft allotments and staffing tables for activities under the Convention's budget, for final approval of the Executive Director of UNEP. These allotments constitute the authority to the Executive Secretary to enter into commitments and expend resources, including the extension of staff contracts. The Executive Secretary of the CBD has the responsibility to adhere to all applicable UN Regulations and Rules when exercising this authority.

32. Certification authority for expenditures from each of the Convention trust funds will reside with the Secretariat-based Fund and Administrative Officer, who will consult fully with the Executive Secretary of the CBD on such matters. The Secretariat-based Fund and Administrative Officer, in full consultation with the Executive Secretary, can delegate this authority to the responsible Fund Programme Management Officer in UNEP when necessary.

VI Accounting and reporting

33. UNEP/UNON will maintain, in full consultation with the Executive Secretary, the accounts for CBD, approve payments on behalf of the CBD Secretariat, provide payroll services, record obligations, disbursements and expenditures and provide a timely, up-to-date report of all accounts to the Executive Secretary in accordance with established procedures.

34. No disbursement will be made if funds are not available within the trust funds established for the Convention.

35. A bank account will be maintained in Montreal to support the day-to-day transactions of the Secretariat. This account shall be replenished as and when required. The Montreal Bank Account is not intended for the receipt of contributions, except in extraordinary circumstances and in accordance with United Nations Rules and Regulations. In such circumstances, the Executive Secretary will record the related reasons and provide them to UNEP.

36. On a monthly basis, UNEP/UNON will provide the Executive Secretary with up-to-date information on the status of allotments, trial balance and unliquidated obligations. The final accounts will be submitted to the Executive Secretary for certification and submissions to the Board of External Auditors and reporting to the Conference of the Parties in accordance with CBD Financial Procedures.

VII Procurement of goods and services

37. The Executive Secretary may approve procurement of goods and services up to a maximum of $70,000 for each transaction, provided that:

(a) except as provided in (c) below, contracts involving commitments in excess of $20,000 will be let only after competitive bidding or calling for proposals if proposals are called, a comparative analysis of such proposals shall be kept on record;

(b) contracts will be awarded to the lowest acceptable bidder, provided that where the interest of the Convention so required, all bids may be rejected. In such case the Executive Secretary will record the related reasons and provide them to UNEP;

(c) the Executive Secretary may award contracts without calling for proposals or formal invitations to bid, in the circumstances set out in paragraphs (b) to (h) to financial rule 110.19; in such cases, appropriate reasons will be recorded and provided to UNEP.

For any transaction in excess of $70,000, procurement will be handled under the procedures set out in financial rule: 111.17 (d), as applicable to UNEP.

Travel of the CBD Secretariat staff will be authorized by the Executive Secretary and will be at standards not higher than those which the United Nations may set from time to time. Travel of delegations under the terms of the Special Fund for Voluntary Contributions to Facilitate Participation of Parties in the CBD process will be governed by ST/SGB/107/Rev.6 and related legislative decisions of the Conference of the Parties, or donor requirements.

VIII Reimbursement for services provided to the Secretariat

39. All trust funds established for the CBD are subject to 13 per cent programme support reimbursement on actual recorded expenditures.

40. The above programme support funds will be used in part for financing the full and effective requirements of the administrative/personnel unit of the CBD Secretariat in Montreal. The remaining will be used for financing the services provided to the CBD Secretariat, including recruitment, services by UNEP/UNON to the APB

referred to in paragraphs 6, 7 and 12 (d) of this agreement, and the provision of human resources development staff by UNEP/UNON when required.

IX Conference and other services

41. UNEP/UNON will facilitate the coordination and provision of conference services to the sessions of the Conference of the Parties and its subsidiary bodies in full cooperation with the Executive Secretary of the CBD. The Executive Secretary of the CBD will consult with UNEP/UNON when subcontracting services to other institutions.

X Revision of this agreement

42. The provisions of this agreement or their application may, at the request of either party be reviewed at any time. Such a request will be made at least four months in advance, and will then be addressed at the next meeting of the Bureau of the Conference of the Parties or the next meeting of the Conference of the Parties, whichever comes first.

Signed:

Elizabeth Dowdeswell
Executive Director of UNEP

Date: 30 June 1997

Calestous Juma
Executive Secretary of CBD

Date: 30 June 1997

Decision IV/18: Date and venue of the fifth meeting of the Conference of the Parties

The Conference of the Parties,

1. *Welcomes* the kind offer of the Government of the Republic of Kenya to host the fifth meeting of the Conference of the Parties;

2. *Decides* that the fifth meeting of the Conference of the Parties will take place in Nairobi, Kenya, at a date to be specified by the Bureau, in accordance with paragraph 1 of decision IV/16, and communicated to all Parties.

Decision IV/19: Tribute to the Government and people of the Slovak Republic

The Conference of the Parties,

Having met in Bratislava from 4 to 15 May 1998, at the gracious invitation of the Government of the Slovak Republic,

Deeply appreciative of the special courtesy and the warm hospitality extended, and the excellent facilities provided, by the Government and people of the Slovak Republic to the Ministers, members of the delegations, observers and members of the Secretariat attending the Conference,

Expresses its sincere gratitude to the Government of the Slovak Republic and to its people for the cordial welcome which they accorded to the Conference and to those associated with its work and for their contribution to the success of the Conference.

DECISION IV/19

Decisions adopted by the first part of the first extraordinary meeting of the Conference of the Parties

Cartagena, Colombia, 22–24 February 1999

Decision EM-I/1: Decision on the continuation of the first extraordinary meeting of the Conference of the Parties to the Convention on Biological Diversity

The Conference of the Parties,

Recalling paragraph 3 of Article 19 of the Convention, by which the Parties are required to consider the need for and modalities of a protocol setting out appropriate procedures, including, in particular, advance informed agreement, in the field of the safe transfer, handling and use of any living modified organism resulting from biotechnology that may have adverse effect on the conservation and sustainable use of biological diversity,

Recalling also its decision II/5 of 17 November 1995 on consideration of the need for and modalities of a protocol setting out appropriate procedures, including, in particular, advance informed agreement, in the field of the safe transfer, handling and use of any living modified organisms, by which it agreed to begin a negotiation process to develop a protocol to address the concerns of Parties on those matters,

Recalling further its decision IV/3 of 15 May 1998, by which it agreed to hold an extraordinary meeting of the Conference of the Parties to address all matters relating to adoption of the protocol on biosafety and preparations for the first meeting of the Parties to the Protocol,

Noting the reports of the first five sessions of the Open-ended Ad Hoc Working Group on Biosafety,

Having considered with appreciation the report of the sixth session presented to it by the Chair of the Open-ended Ad Hoc Working Group on Biosafety,

Recognizing that a number of issues remain unresolved before the adoption of the protocol on biosafety,

1. *Decides* to suspend the first extraordinary meeting of the Conference of the Parties;

2. *Decides* to request the President of the first extraordinary meeting of the Conference of the Parties and the Bureau of the fourth meeting of the Conference of the Parties, in close consultation with the Executive Secretary, to decide on the date and venue of the resumed session of the first extraordinary meeting to be held as soon as practicable and, in any event, no later than the fifth meeting of the Conference of the Parties;

3. *Decides further* that the protocol on biosafety shall be called the Cartagena Protocol on Biosafety to the Convention on Biological Diversity;

4. *Decides further* to transmit the text of the draft protocol set out in appendix I to the report of the sixth meeting of the Open-ended Ad Hoc Working Group on Biosafety,[12] as well as the statements with respect to the text of the draft protocol contained in that report, to the Conference of the Parties at the resumed session of its extraordinary meeting;

5. *Stresses* the importance of concentrating at the resumed session on reaching a satisfactory resolution on the core issues and related issues as contained in the draft report of the first part of the meeting;[13]

6. *Affirms* its determination to complete the negotiation of the Cartagena Protocol on Biosafety for its adoption at the resumed session of the first extraordinary meeting of the Conference of the Parties;

7. *Approves* the amount of 480,000 United States dollars supplementary to the programme budget for the biennium 1999–2000 for the resumed session of the extraordinary meeting of the Conference of the Parties, to be funded from savings and surpluses from the BY Trust Fund;

8. *Calls upon* the Parties and States to provide voluntary contributions to the relevant trust funds of the Convention to cover the cost of the resumed session, including facilitation of participation in the resumed session by developing country Parties, in particular the least developed and small island developing States among them, and Parties with economies in transition.

Decision EM-I/2: Tribute to the Government and people of Colombia

The Conference of the Parties,

Having met in Cartagena de Indias from 22 to 24 February 1999, at the gracious invitation of the Government of the Republic of Colombia,

Deeply appreciative of the special courtesy and warm hospitality extended, and the excellent facilities provided, by the Government and people of the Republic of Colombia to the ministers, members of delegations, observers and members of the secretariat attending the meeting,

12 UNEP/CBD/ExCOP/1/2.
13 See UNEP/CBD/ExCOP/1/3 and Corr.1, Part One, paragraph 52.

Expresses its sincere gratitude to the Government of the Republic of Colombia and to its people for the cordial welcome which they accorded to the meeting and those associated with its work and for their contribution to the considerable progress achieved by the meeting.

Decision adopted by the resumed session of the first extraordinary meeting of the Conference of the Parties

Montreal, Canada, 24–29 January 2000

Decision EM-I/3: Adoption of the Cartagena Protocol and interim arrangements

The Conference of the Parties,

Recalling paragraph 3 of Article 19, by which the Parties are required to consider the need for and modalities of a protocol setting out appropriate procedures, including, in particular, advance informed agreement, in the field of the safe transfer, handling and use of any living modified organism resulting from biotechnology that may have adverse effects on the conservation and sustainable use of biological diversity,

Recalling its decision II/5 on consideration of the need for and modalities of a protocol for the safe transfer, handling and use of living modified organisms, by which it agreed to begin a negotiating process to develop a protocol to address the concerns of Parties on those matters,

Noting the reports of the six sessions of the Open-ended Ad Hoc Working Group on Biosafety,

Noting the valuable informal preparatory work carried out under the chairmanship of His Excellency Juan Mayr Maldonado in Montreal on 1 July 1999, in Vienna from 15 to 19 September 1999 and in Montreal from 20 to 22 January 2000,

Taking note of the UNEP International Technical Guidelines on Safety in Biotechnology,

Considering the needs of developing country Parties and Parties with economies in transition to evaluate the risks to their biodiversity and to make informed decisions associated with the transboundary movement of living modified organisms,

Considering also that arrangements are required pending the entry into force of the Cartagena Protocol on Biosafety to prepare for its effective operation once it enters into force,

I Adoption of the Cartagena Protocol

1. *Decides* to adopt the Cartagena Protocol on Biosafety to the Convention on Biological Diversity, as set out in the annex to the present decision;

2. *Requests* the Secretary-General of the United Nations to be the Depositary of the Protocol and to open it for signature at the United Nations Office at Nairobi during the fifth meeting of the Conference of the Parties from 15 May 2000 to 26 May 2000 and at the United Nations Headquarters in New York from 5 June 2000 to 4 June 2001;

3. *Calls upon* the Parties to the Convention on Biological Diversity to sign the Protocol from 15 May 2000 or at the earliest opportunity thereafter and to deposit instruments of ratification, acceptance or approval or instruments of accession, as appropriate, as soon as possible;

4. *Further calls upon* States that are not Parties to the Convention to ratify, accept, approve or accede to it, as appropriate, without delay, thereby enabling them also to become Parties to the Protocol;

II Intergovernmental Commmittee for the Cartagena Protocol (ICCP)

5. *Decides* to establish an open-ended ad hoc Intergovernmental Committee for the Cartagena Protocol on Biosafety (ICCP);

6. *Decides* that the Intergovernmental Committee shall undertake, with the support of the Executive Secretary, the preparations necessary for the first meeting of the Parties, at which time it will cease to exist, taking into account the budgetary provisions adopted by the Conference of the Parties;

7. *Notes* that the rules of procedure for the Conference of the Parties to the Convention shall apply, *mutatis mutandis*, to meetings of the Intergovernmental Committee;

8. *Decides* that the Chair of the Intergovernmental Committee shall be Ambassador Philemon Yang (Cameroon), and invites the Intergovernmental Committee to convene, at the present meeting of the Conference of the Parties, an organizational meeting for the purpose of electing its Bureau from among the representatives of the Parties present;

9. *Decides* that the Intergovernmental Committee shall hold its first meeting in late 2000;

10. *Requests* the Executive Secretary, in consultation with the Bureau of the Intergovernmental Committee to develop a work plan for the Committee for consideration and approval by the Conference of the Parties to the Convention on Biological Diversity at its fifth meeting;

11. *Calls upon* the Parties to the Convention and other States and regional economic integration organizations to designate a focal point for the Intergovernmental Committee and to inform the Executive Secretary accordingly;

12. *Encourages* Parties, States and regional economic integration organizations to provide the Intergovernmental Committee, through the Executive Secretary, infor-

mation on their existing programmes for regulating living modified organisms; and to provide related technical assistance, including training, to interested Parties and States;

13. *Requests* the Executive Secretary to commence preparatory work on the functioning of the biosafety clearing-house referred to in Article 20 of the Protocol, subject to the availability of resources referred to in the table following paragraph 20 of the present decision;

III Roster of experts

14. *Decides* to establish a regionally balanced roster of experts nominated by Governments, in fields relevant to risk assessment and risk management related to the Protocol, to provide advice and other support, as appropriate and upon request, to developing country Parties and Parties with economies in transition, to conduct risk assessment, make informed decisions, develop national human resources and promote institutional strengthening, associated with the transboundary movements of living modified organisms;

15. *Requests* the Executive Secretary to explore ways and means of obtaining financial resources to enable developing countries Parties and Parties with economies in transition to make full use of the roster of experts and to report thereon to the Conference of the Parties;

16. *Calls upon* Parties to promote regional cooperation for this initiative and invites international organizations, particularly those of the United Nations system, to also support within their mandates, this initiative;

IV Administrative and budgetary matters

17. *Reconfirms* the budget as approved in its decision IV/17, which includes an amount of US$1,078,800 for the Protocol on Biosafety for the year 2000 under the Trust Fund for the Convention on Biological Diversity (BY);

18. *Takes note* of the amounts supplementary to the funding estimates for the Special Voluntary Trust Fund (BE) for Additional Voluntary Contributions in Support of Approved Activities for the biennium 1999–2000 specified by the Executive Secretary and included in the table below and invites Parties and States to make contributions to that fund;

19. *Invites* the Executive Director of the United Nations Environment Programme, in cooperation with the Executive Secretary, to identify the necessary financial, technical and staff resources, which the United Nations Environment Programme can make available to the Executive Secretary to assist the latter in the organization of the expert and/or regional meetings;

20. *Decides* to consider the budget for the Protocol on Biosafety for the biennium 2001–2002 at the fifth meeting of the Conference of the Parties.

Table Supplementary budget for biosafety to the Special Voluntary Trust Fund (BE) for additional voluntary contributions in support of approved activities 1999–2000

		2000 (US$ thousands)
A	Meetings	
	ICCP Bureau meeting.	40
	Biosafety clearing-house common format meeting 30 participants	140
B	Biosafety clearing-house	41
C	Roster of experts	50
	Subtotal	271
D	Programme support costs (13 per cent)	35
	TOTAL	**306**

Annex: Cartagena Protocol on Biosafety to the Convention on Biological Diversity[14]

14 The Cartagena Protocol on Biosafety to the Convention on Biological Diversity has been reproduced in Section II of this Handbook.

Decisions adopted by the fifth meeting of the Conference of the Parties

Nairobi, Kenya, 15–26 May 2000

Decision V/1: Work plan of the Intergovernmental Committee for the Cartagena Protocol on Biosafety

The Conference of the Parties,

Welcoming the signatures of the Cartagena Protocol on Biosafety that have already taken place and reiterating the call of decision EM-I/3 to all Parties to the Convention on Biological Diversity to sign the Protocol at the earliest opportunity, and to deposit instruments of ratification, acceptance or approval, or instruments of accession, as appropriate, as soon as possible,

Reiterating also the call of decision EM-I/3 upon States that are not Parties to the Convention to ratify, accept, approve or accede to it, as appropriate, without delay, thereby enabling them also to become Parties to the Protocol,

Recalling the mandate given to the open-ended ad hoc Intergovernmental Committee for the Cartagena Protocol on Biosafety in decision EM-I/3 to undertake, with the support of the Executive Secretary, the preparations necessary for the first meeting of the Parties to the Protocol,

Reaffirming that the meeting of the Parties is the only sovereign body with regard to the implementation of the Protocol,

Emphasizing the preparatory character of the work to be undertaken by the Intergovernmental Committee in order to facilitate the work of the first meeting of the Parties to the Protocol,

Underscoring therefore that, without prejudice to the provisions of the Protocol, including time-frames, the meeting of the Parties is the only body entitled to decide on issues that are required to be addressed during its meetings, and to what extent and in which manner it wishes to use the preparatory work of the Intergovernmental Committee,

Noting that a work programme should reflect all issues that the meeting of the Parties to the Protocol might wish to address at its first meeting,

Emphasizing the necessity to complete as early as possible the preparations for the entry into force of the Protocol,

Emphasizing also the priority of launching the Biosafety Clearing-House no later than the entry into force of the Protocol, and also the need to engage in capacity-building as soon as possible,

Welcoming the decision taken by the Council of the Global Environment Facility at its fifteenth meeting with regard to supporting activities that will assist countries to prepare for the entry into force of the Protocol,

1. *Endorses* the work plan for the Intergovernmental Committee for the Cartagena Protocol on Biosafety as contained in the annex to the present decision;

2. *Requests* the Executive Secretary to invite all relevant stakeholders to contribute to the development and/or strengthening of capacities in biosafety for the purpose of the effective implementation of the Protocol, in particular in developing country Parties, and to report on progress made to the first meeting of the Parties;

3. *Requests also* the Executive Secretary to convene, prior to the first meeting of the Intergovernmental Committee for the Cartagena Protocol on Biosafety, the meeting of technical experts on the Biosafety Clearing-House referred to in the table at the end of decision EM-I/3, and reiterates its invitation to Parties and States to make contributions for the supplementary budget for biosafety to the Special Voluntary Trust Fund (BE) for Additional Voluntary Contributions in Support of Approved Activities for the biennium 1999–2000, as presented in the table at the end of decision EM-I/3;

4. *Welcomes* the generous offer made by the Government of France to host the first meeting of the Intergovernmental Committee for the Cartagena Protocol on Biosafety from 11 to 15 December 2000 in Montpellier.

Annex:
Work plan of the Intergovernmental Committee for the Cartagena Protocol on Biosafety

A Issues for consideration by the ICCP at its first meeting

1. *Decision-making (Article 10, paragraph 7)*

   Issue: Identification of basic elements for appropriate procedures and mechanisms to facilitate decision-making by Parties of import.

2. *Information-sharing (Article 20, Article 19)*

   Issues:

   - Determination of needs of Parties
   - Overview of existing activities/systems and possibilities for cooperation
   - Design of data-input systems
   - Development of common formats for reporting, eg, decisions, national legislations, points of contact, focal points, summaries of risk assessments, etc.
   - Development of operational systems, information-management policies and procedures for receiving and making information available, including quality-insurance procedures

- Means to ensure confidentiality of information
- Financial and technological resource requirements
- Other issues (such as Article 5)

3. *Capacity-building (Article 22, Article 28)*

   Issues:

   - Identification of the needs and involvement of Parties
   - Establishment and role of the roster of experts
   - Overview of completed activities in the field of biosafety (eg, capacity-building workshop in Mexico)
   - Overview of existing programmes/projects/activities and possibilities for cooperation (eg, UNEP activities and possible role)
   - Multilateral, regional and bilateral cooperation and the need for common understanding and harmonization
   - Involvement of the private sector
   - Elements of capacity-building with respect to risk assessment and management in accordance with Article 15, Article 16 and Annex III of the Protocol
   - Role of the Secretariat of the Convention
   - Financial and technological resource requirements
   - Other issues (such as Article 6)

4. *Handling, transport, packaging and identification (Article 18)*

   Issues:

   - Overview of relevant international rules and standards pertaining to handling, transport, packaging and identification
   - Consideration of modalities for developing standards with regard to handling, transport, packaging and identification

5. *Compliance (Article 34)*

   Issues:

   - Elements for a compliance regime
   - Options for a compliance regime

B Issues for consideration by the ICCP at its second meeting

1. *Liability and redress (Article 27)*

   Issue: Elaboration of a draft recommendation on the process for elaboration of international rules and procedures in the field of liability and redress for damage resulting from transboundary movements of living modified organisms, including, *inter alia*:

   - Review of existing relevant instruments
   - Identification of elements for liability and redress

2. *Monitoring and reporting (Article 33)*

   Issue: Format and timing for reporting.

3. *Secretariat (Article 31)*

   Issue: Development of a programme budget for the biennium following the entry into force of the Protocol.

4. *Guidance to the financial mechanism (Article 28, paragraph 5, Article 22)*

   Issue: Elaboration of guidance for the financial mechanism.

5. *Rules of procedure for the meeting of the Parties*

   Issue: Consideration of rules of procedure.

6. *Consideration of other issues necessary for effective implementation of the Protocol (eg, Article 29, paragraph 4)*

7. *Elaboration of a draft provisional agenda for the first meeting of the Parties*

Items for continued consideration from the first meeting of the ICCP

8. *Decision-making (Article 10, paragraph 7)*

9. *Information-sharing (Article 20)*

10. *Capacity-building (Article 22, Article 28, paragraph 28)*

11 *Handling, transport, packaging and identification (Article 18)*

   Issue: Modalities for a process for discussion on Article 18, paragraph 2 (a) by the first meeting of the Parties.

12. *Compliance (Article 34)*

Decision V/2: Progress report on the implementation of the programme of work on the biological diversity of inland water ecosystems (implementation of decision IV/4)

The Conference of the Parties,

Recognizing the need for continued cooperation between the Convention on Biological Diversity and other conventions and bodies dealing with different aspects of inland water biological diversity,

1. *Takes notes* of the various ways and means to implement the programme of work and obstacles in implementing some aspects of the work plan of the Subsidiary Body on Scientific, Technical and Technological Advice, as contained in the note by the Executive Secretary on the subject prepared for the fifth meeting of the Subsidiary Body (UNEP/CBD/SBSTTA/5/6), and *requests* the Executive Secretary to report to it on these matters before the seventh meeting of the Conference of Parties as part of the review of the programme of work on the biological diversity of inland water ecosystems by the Subsidiary Body at its eighth meeting;

2. *Endorses* the proposed joint work plan for the period 2000–2001 of the Convention on Biological Diversity and the Ramsar Convention on Wetlands of International Importance especially as Waterfowl Habitat (UNEP/CBD/SBSTTA/5/INF/12), which includes, *inter alia*, a River Basin Initiative, *encourages* Parties, other Governments and relevant bodies to support and participate in the Initiative, and *stresses* that Parties to the Convention on Biological Diversity that are not Parties to the Ramsar Convention shall not be disadvantaged in the workings and implementation of the joint work plan;

3. *Encourages* Parties to address the lack of information on the status of inland water biological diversity as a basis for future decisions on inland water at the national level and to include this information in their national reports;

4. *Requests* the Subsidiary Body on Scientific, Technical and Technological Advice to consider the recommendations contained in the forthcoming report of the World Commission on Dams, to be published in November 2000, and, as appropriate, to recommend to the Conference of the Parties at its sixth meeting the introduction of suitable elements into the programme of work on the biological diversity of inland water ecosystems;

5. *Further requests* the Subsidiary Body on Scientific, Technical and Technological Advice to include in its review before the seventh meeting of the Conference of Parties advice on the further elaboration and refinement of the programme of work on the biological diversity of inland water ecosystems, having due regard to the issues relating, *inter alia*, to water supply, land use and tenure, pollution, alien invasive species, the effects of El Niño, and environmental impact assessment;

6. *Requests* the Executive Secretary to compile systematically information on the implementation of the programme of work on the biological diversity of inland water ecosystems, including the report of the World Commission on Dams, for dissemination through the clearing-house mechanism, and to report on his efforts as part of the review of that programme of work that the Subsidiary Body on Scientific, Technical and Technological Advice will carry out before the seventh meeting of the Conference of Parties;

7. *Invites* relevant organizations and activities, in particular the Global International Waters Assessment, to contribute to the assessment of inland water biological diversity and to integrate a biological diversity component fully in their methodology protocols;

8. *Urges* the implementation of capacity-building measures for developing and implementing national and sectoral plans for the conservation and sustainable use of inland water ecosystems, including comprehensive assessments of the biological diversity of inland water ecosystems, and capacity-building programmes for monitoring the implementation of the programme of work and the trends in inland water biological diversity, and for information-gathering and dissemination among the riparian communities.

Decision V/3: Progress report on the implementation of the programme of work on marine and coastal biological diversity (implementation of decision IV/5)

The Conference of the Parties,

Recalling the need to implement the programme of work on marine and coastal biological diversity in a holistic manner, taking into account river basin issues, the effects of land-based activities (including pollution) and tourism plans,

Noting the relevance for the future implementation of the programme of work of the joint work plan 2000–2001 of the Convention on Biological Diversity and Ramsar Convention on Wetlands,

Stressing the importance of regional approaches to the implementation of the programme of work and therefore of cooperation with regional bodies,

1. *Takes note* of the tools that have been used for the implementation of the programme of work on the conservation and sustainable use of marine and coastal biological diversity, as set out in the note by the Executive Secretary on the subject prepared for the fifth meeting of the Subsidiary Body on Scientific, Technical and Technological Advice (UNEP/CBD/SBSTTA/5/7, annex I), *requests* the Executive Secretary to report to future meetings of the Subsidiary Body on Scientific, Technical and Technological Advice on the application of these tools, *encourages* the Secretariat and the Subsidiary Body to complete, as soon as possible, the implementation of decision IV/5 on the programme of work on marine and coastal biodiversity as adopted by the Conference of Parties at its fourth meeting, and *notes* that the work element on coral reefs was enabled at the fifth meeting of the Conference of the Parties, and will have a minimum three year time schedule;

I Coral reefs

2. *Endorses* the results of the Expert Consultation on Coral Bleaching, held in Manila from 11 to 13 October 1999, as contained in the annex to the present decision;

3. *Decides* to integrate coral reefs into programme element 2 (Marine and coastal living resources) of the programme of work;

4. *Requests* the Executive Secretary to integrate fully the issue of coral bleaching in the programme of work on the conservation and sustainable use of marine and coastal biological diversity and to develop and implement a specific work plan on coral bleaching, taking into account the recommendations set out in the annex to the present decision, as appropriate, and in cooperation with the United Nations Framework Convention on Climate Change, and *invites* Parties, other Governments and relevant bodies to contribute to its implementation. In conducting his work on coral bleaching, the Executive Secretary will also liaise with, *inter alia*, the Convention on Wetlands, the Convention on International Trade in Endangered Species of Wild Fauna and Flora, the United Nations Educational, Scientific and Cultural Organization (including the World Heritage Convention), the Food and Agriculture Organization of the United Nations, regional fisheries organizations, the Intergovernmental Panel on Climate Change and

the Global International Waters Assessment and will formally liaise with the Global Coral Reef Monitoring Network and the International Coral Reef Initiative;

5. *Notes* that there is significant evidence that climate change is a primary cause of the recent and severe extensive coral bleaching, and that this evidence is sufficient to warrant remedial measures being taken in line with the precautionary approach, *transmits* that view to the United Nations Framework Convention on Climate Change and *urges* the United Nations Framework Convention on Climate Change to take all possible actions to reduce the effect of climate change on water temperatures and to address the socio-economic impacts on the countries and communities most affected by coral bleaching;

6. *Urges* Parties, other Governments and relevant bodies to implement response measures to the phenomenon of coral bleaching by:

(a) Identifying and instituting additional and alternative measures for securing the livelihoods of people who directly depend on coral-reef services;

(b) Encouraging and supporting multidisciplinary approaches to action relating to coral-reef management, research and monitoring, including the use of early-warning systems for coral bleaching, and collaborating with the International Coral Reef Initiative and the Global Coral Reef Monitoring Network;

(c) Building stakeholder partnerships, community participation programmes and public education campaigns and information products that address the causes and consequences of coral bleaching;

(d) Using appropriate policy frameworks to implement integrated marine and coastal area management plans and programmes that supplement marine and coastal protected areas and the multiple conservation measures outlined in the Renewed Call to Action of the International Coral Reef Initiative;

(e) Supporting capacity-building measures, including training of and career opportunities for marine taxonomists, ecologists and members of other relevant disciplines, particularly at the national level;

(f) Implementing and coordinating targeted research programmes, including predictive modelling, in the context, as appropriate, of the ongoing activities referred to in paragraph 4 of the present decision;

7. *Invites* Parties, other Governments and relevant bodies to submit case-studies on the coral-bleaching phenomenon to the Executive Secretary, for dissemination through the clearing-house mechanism;

8. *Agrees* that physical degradation and destruction of coral reefs also pose a significant threat to the biological diversity of coral-reef ecosystems, and therefore *decides* to expand its request to the Subsidiary Body on Scientific, Technical and Technological Advice, as contained in section II, paragraph 1, of decision IV/5, so as to include the effects of such factors;

II Integrated marine and coastal area management

9. *Endorses* further work on developing guidelines for coastal areas, taking into account decision V/6, on the ecosystem approach;

10. *Encourages* the Subsidiary Body on Scientific, Technical and Technological Advice, with the assistance of the Executive Secretary, to continue work on ecosystem evaluation and assessment, *inter alia*, through guidelines on evaluation and indicators;

III Marine and coastal living resources

11. *Requests* the Executive Secretary to gather information on approaches to management of marine and coastal living resources in relation to those used by local and indigenous communities and to make the information available through the clearing-house mechanism;

12. *Takes note* of the work of the Executive Secretary on marine and coastal genetic resources, including bioprospecting, and *requests* the Subsidiary Body on Scientific, Technical and Technological Advice to analyse, and provide advice on scientific, technical and technological matters related to the issue of marine and coastal genetic resources;

13. *Suggests* that the Subsidiary Body on Scientific, Technical and Technological Advice consider the following issues and prioritize them as appropriate: the use of unsustainable fishing practices, including the effects on marine and coastal biological diversity of the discard of by-catch; the lack of use of marine and coastal protected areas in the context of management of marine and coastal living resources; and the economic value of marine and coastal resources, including sea grasses, mangroves and other coastal ecosystems; as well as capacity-building for undertaking stock assessments and for economic evaluations;

IV Alien species and genotypes

14. *Requests* the Executive Secretary to make use of existing information, expertise and best practices on alien species in the marine environment in the implementation of the work programme on alien species under decision IV/1 C;

V General

15. *Approves* the terms of reference and the duration of work specified for the ad hoc technical expert groups on marine and coastal protected areas and mariculture, as contained in annex II to recommendation V/14 of the Subsidiary Body on Scientific, Technical and Technological Advice, with the addition of 'Identification of best practices' for mariculture;

16. *Requests* the Executive Secretary to make further use of the roster of experts for peer-review and preparation of background documents;

VI Cooperation

17. *Invites* the United Nations Educational, Scientific and Cultural Organization to continue its strong involvement in the implementation of the programme of work, and *requests* the Executive Secretary to further strengthen cooperation with other global organizations;

18. *Requests* the Executive Secretary to coordinate with the secretariats of regional seas conventions and action plans with a view to exploring the possibility of further collaboration, including the development of joint work programmes, in the implementation of the Jakarta Mandate on Marine and Coastal Biological Diversity, paying particular attention to the identification of priorities for action at the regional level, the development of joint implementation strategies and identification of joint activities and the use of regional networks, and to report to the Conference of the Parties at its sixth meeting on collaboration with the regional seas conventions and action plans.

Annex: Priority areas for action on coral bleaching

A Information-gathering

Issue: Our ability to adequately project, and thus mitigate, the impacts of global warming on coral-reef ecosystems and the human communities which depend upon coral-reef services is limited by the paucity of information on:

(a) The taxonomic, genetic, physiological, spatial, and temporal factors governing the response of corals, zooxanthellae, the coral-zooxanthellae system, and other coral-reef-associated species to increases in sea-surface temperature;

(b) The role of coral reefs as critical habitat for marine species and natural resources for human communities;

(c) The current status of coral-reef health and threats to coral reefs; and

(d) The potential capacity of recovery[15] of corals and resilience of the ecosystem after mass mortality.

Response:

(a) Implement and coordinate targeted research programmes, including predictive modelling, that investigate: (1) the tolerance limits and adaptation capacity of coral-reef species to acute and chronic increases in sea-surface temperature; (2) the relationship among large-scale coral-bleaching events, global warming, and the more localized threats that already place reefs at risk; and (3) the frequency and extent of coral-bleaching and mortality events, as well as their impacts on ecological, social and economic systems;

(b) Implement and coordinate baseline assessments, long-term monitoring, and rapid response teams to measure the biological and meteorological variables relevant to coral bleaching, mortality and recovery, as well as the socio-economic parameters associated with coral-reef services. To this end, support and expand the Global Coral Reef Monitoring Network and regional networks, and data-repository and dissemination

15 Recovery is the return of a coral colony to a state of health, including a symbiotic relationship with zooxanthellae, after the health and/or symbiotic relationship has been disrupted by a stress or perturbation. Recovery may involve a change in the genetic composition of species of the zooxanthellae. Resilience is the return of a coral-reef ecosystem to a state in which living, reef-building corals play a prominent functional role, after this role has been disrupted by a stress or perturbation. A shift toward high dominance by frondose algae accompanied by a reduction in the functional role of coral would indicate a situation of low resilience.

systems including Reef Base – the Global Coral Reef Database. Also, the current combined Sida-SAREC and World Bank programme on coral-reef degradation in the Indian Ocean, as a response to the 1998 coral-bleaching event, could be used as an example;

(c) Develop a rapid response capability to document coral bleaching and mortality in developing countries and remote areas. This would involve the establishment of training programmes, survey protocols, availability of expert advice, and the establishment of a contingency fund or rapid release of special project funding;

(d) Encourage and support countries in the development and dissemination of status-of-the-reefs reports and case studies on the occurrence and impacts of coral bleaching.

Issue: The remoteness of many coral reefs and the paucity of funding and personnel to support on-site assessments of coral reefs require that remote-sensing technologies are developed and applied in the evaluation of coral-bleaching events.

Response: Extend the use of early-warning systems for coral bleaching by:

(a) Enhancing current NOAA AVHRR Hot Spot mapping by increasing resolution in targeted areas and carry out ground-truth validation exercises;

(b) Encouraging space agencies and private entities to maintain deployment of relevant sensors and to initiate design and deployment of specialized technology for shallow-oceans monitoring;

(c) Making the products of remote sensing readily accessible to coral reef scientists and managers worldwide with a view to those scientists and managers that are based in developing countries.

B Capacity-building

Issue: There is a substantial lack of trained personnel to investigate the causes and consequences of coral bleaching events.

Response: Support the training of and career opportunities for marine taxonomists, ecologists, and members of other relevant disciplines, particularly at the national and regional level.

Issue: Coral bleaching is a complex phenomenon. Understanding the causes and consequences of coral bleaching events requires the knowledge, skills, and technologies of a wide variety of disciplines. Any action aimed at addressing the issue should bear in mind the ecosystem approach, incorporating both the ecological and societal aspects of the problem.

Response: Encourage and support multidisciplinary approaches to coral-reef research, monitoring, socio-economics and management.

Issue: Public awareness and education are required to build support for effective research, monitoring, and management programmes, as well as policy measures.

Response: Build stakeholder partnerships, community participation programmes, and public education campaigns and information products that address the causes and consequences of coral bleaching.

C Policy development/implementation

Issue: Nearly 60 per cent of the world's coral reefs are threatened by localized, human activities that have the potential to exacerbate the impacts of coral-bleaching events. Evaluations of the 1998 coral-bleaching events suggest that marine protected areas alone may not provide adequate protection for at least some corals and other reef-associated species as sea-surface temperatures rise.

Response: Use existing policy frameworks to implement the multiple conservation measures outlined in the Renewed Call to Action of the International Coral Reef Initiative, and develop and implement comprehensive local-to-national-scale integrated marine and coastal area management plans that supplement marine protected areas.

Issue: Most coral reefs are located in developing countries, and the majority of the people living near coral reefs are often extremely poor. Thus, even minor declines in the productivity of coral-reef ecosystems as a result of coral bleaching events could have dramatic socio-economic consequences for local people who depend on coral-reef services.

Response: Identify and institute additional and alternative measures for securing the livelihoods of people who directly depend on coral-reef services.

Issue: Coral bleaching is relevant not only to the Convention on Biological Diversity but also the United Nations Framework Convention on Climate Change and the Convention on Wetlands. The ultimate objective of the United Nations Framework Convention on Climate Change is to reduce emissions in a manner that 'allows ecosystems to adapt naturally to climate change'. The United Nations Framework Convention on Climate Change calls upon Parties to take action in relation to funding, insurance, and technology transfer to address the adverse effects of climate change. The Convention on Wetlands provides guidance on the conservation and wise use of wetlands, including coral reefs.

Response: Initiate efforts to develop joint actions among the Convention on Biological Diversity, the United Nations Framework Convention on Climate Change, and the Convention on Wetlands to:

(a) Develop approaches for assessing the vulnerability of coral-reef species to global warming;

(b) Build capacity for predicting and monitoring the impacts of coral bleaching;

(c) Identify approaches for developing response measures to coral bleaching;

(d) Provide guidance to financial institutions, including the Global Environment Facility, to support such activities.

Issue: Coral bleaching has the potential to impact local fisheries, as well as certain high-value commercial pelagic fisheries and coastal ecosystems.

Response: Encourage the Food and Agriculture Organization of the United Nations and regional fisheries organizations to develop and implement measures to assess and mitigate the impacts of sea-surface temperature rise on fisheries.

Issue: Coral-bleaching events are a warning of even more severe impacts to marine systems. If anomalous sea-water temperatures continue to rise, become more frequent, or are prolonged, the physiological thresholds of other organisms will be surpassed. Not only will local fisheries be impacted, but certain high-value commercial pelagic fisheries and coastal ecosystems will be affected as well.

Response: Emphasize that coral bleaching can be monitored as an early warning of the impacts of global warming on marine ecosystems and that the collapse of coral-reef ecosystems could impact ecological processes of the larger marine system of which coral reefs are a part.

Issue: The observations of the 1998 coral-bleaching events suggest that coral-reef conservation can no longer be achieved without consideration of the global climate system and that it requires efforts to mitigate accelerated global climate change.

Response: Emphasize the interdependencies and uncertainties in the relationships among marine, terrestrial, and climatic systems.

D Financing

Issue: Because the issue of climate change is global and long-term in scale, Governments around the world need to work together to make funds available to implement initiatives to address the causes and consequences of coral bleaching.

Response: Mobilize international programmes and mechanisms for financial and technical development assistance, such as the World Bank, the United Nations Development Programme, regional development banks, as well as national and private sources to support implementation of these priority actions.

Recommendation V/14:

Annex II: Proposed terms of reference and duration of work for the ad hoc technical expert groups on marine and coastal protected areas, mariculture and forest biological diversity

A Ad hoc technical expert group on marine and coastal protected areas

Terms of reference[16]

1. Identify pilot research and monitoring projects, based on current proposals and ongoing projects aimed at assessing the value and effects of marine and coastal protected areas or similarly managed areas on sustainable use of marine and coastal living resources.

2. Review the desk-study called for in the operational objective 3.1, activity (c), of the programme of work on marine and coastal biological diversity (decision IV/5, annex). The desk-study to be conducted by the Executive Secretary consists of gathering and assimilating information relevant to the value and effect of marine and coastal protected areas on sustainable use of marine and coastal biodiversity.

3. Identify linkages between marine protected areas and sustainable use of marine and coastal biodiversity.

16 In accordance with programme element 3, operational objective 3.1, of the Jakarta Mandate programme of work.

4. Prepare recommendations on types of research to be carried out to understand the effects of marine and coastal protected or closed areas on population size and dynamics, subject to national legislation.

Duration of work

The ad hoc technical expert group on marine and coastal protected areas should start its work immediately after approval by the Conference of the Parties of the terms of reference and shall endeavour to complete the work not later than the eighth meeting of SBSTTA, at which 'protected areas' will be an item for in-depth consideration (see the SBSTTA programme of work in recommendation IV/1 C), and the seventh meeting of the Conference of the Parties at which 'protected areas' will be an item for in-depth consideration. Items 1, 3 and 4 can be undertaken immediately, but item 2 will start when the desk-study is complete.

B Ad hoc technical expert group on mariculture

Terms of reference[17]

1. Evaluate the current state of scientific and technological knowledge on the effects of mariculture on marine and coastal biodiversity.

2. Provide guidance on criteria, methods and techniques that avoid the adverse effects of mariculture, and also subsequent stock enhancement, on marine and coastal biological diversity and enhance the positive effects of mariculture on marine and coastal productivity.

Duration of work

The ad hoc expert group on mariculture should start immediately after the approval of the terms of reference by the Conference of the Parties. The time for the completion of these activities so that their output can be considered in depth by SBSTTA will depend on the time when SBSTTA might be requested by the Conference of the Parties at its fifth meeting to report or advise on aspects relating to sustainable use of biodiversity or when the Conference of the Parties might decide to review the Jakarta Mandate programme of work.

Decision V/4: Progress report on the implementation of the programme of work for forest biological diversity

The Conference of the Parties,

Stressing that, in the implementation of the programme of work for forest biological diversity, due consideration should be given to the role of all types of forests, including planted forests, and the restoration of forest ecosystems,

Noting the importance of supporting work on taxonomic, ecological and socio-economic issues for the restoration of forest ecosystems and conservation and sustainable use of forest biological diversity,

17 In accordance with programme element 4 of the Jakarta Mandate programme of work.

Noting the importance of forest ecosystems and forest resources (including wood and non-wood forest products and services) to indigenous and local communities and the need to ensure their participation in the assessment of status and trends of forest biodiversity for the conservation and sustainable use of forest biological diversity,

Noting the proposed establishment and coordinating role of the United Nations Forum on Forests,

Noting the potential impact of afforestation, reforestation, forest degradation and deforestation on forest biological diversity and on other ecosystems,

1. *Urges* the Parties, Governments and relevant organizations to advance the implementation of the work programme for forest biological diversity, as contained in decision IV/7;

2. *Decides* to consider expanding the focus of the work programme from research to practical action at its sixth meeting;

3. *Decides* to call upon Parties, Governments and organizations to take practical actions within the scope of the existing programme of work in order to address urgently the conservation and sustainable use of forest biological diversity, applying the ecosystem approach and taking into consideration the outcome of the fourth session of the Intergovernmental Forum on Forests (UNEP/CBD/COP/5/INF/16), and also contributing to the future work of the United Nations Forum on Forests;

4. *Decides* to establish an ad hoc technical expert group on forest biological diversity to assist the Subsidiary Body on Scientific, Technical and Technological Advice, on the basis of the terms specified in the annex, in its work on forest biological diversity;

5. *Requests* the Executive Secretary to nominate scientific and technical experts, including expertise in policy matters and traditional knowledge, to the ad hoc technical expert group mentioned in paragraph 4 above, with due regard to geographical representation;

6. *Requests* the Executive Secretary to prepare for the work of the ad hoc technical expert group by inviting various international organizations and institutions to contribute data and information relevant to the terms of reference;

7. *Invites* Parties, countries, international organizations, institutions and processes and other relevant bodies, as well as indigenous and local communities and non-governmental organizations to provide relevant information on the implementation of the work programme through, inter alia, case-studies, entries in national reports and other means, as appropriate;

8. *Encourages* Parties and other Governments to promote the integration of national forest programmes with national biodiversity strategies, applying the ecosystem approach and sustainable forest management;

9. *Further encourages* Parties and other Governments to ensure participation by the forest sector, private sector, indigenous and local communities and non-governmental organizations in the implementation of the programme of work;

10. *Recognizes* past efforts by different organizations and encourages Parties and other Governments to strengthen national capacities, including local capacities, to enhance the effectiveness and functions of forest protected area networks, as well as national and local capacities for implementation of sustainable forest management, including restoration, when needed;

11. *Requests* the Subsidiary Body on Scientific, Technical and Technological Advice to consider before the sixth meeting of the Conference of the Parties, where appropriate and feasible in collaboration with the appropriate bodies of the United Nations Framework Convention on Climate Change and the Intergovernmental Panel on Climate Change, the impact of climate change on forest biological diversity;

12. *Requests* the Subsidiary Body on Scientific, Technical and Technological Advice to consider the causes and effects of human induced uncontrolled forest fires on forest biological diversity and propose possible approaches to address negative impacts;

13. *Urges* Parties to consider without delay the proposals for action of the Intergovernmental Forum on Forests and the Intergovernmental Panel on Forests on programme element II.d (v), on valuation of forest goods and services;

14. *Requests* the Subsidiary Body on Scientific, Technical and Technological Advice to consider the impact of, and propose sustainable practices for, the harvesting of non-timber forest resources, including bush meat and living botanical resources;

15. *Requests* the Executive Secretary to invite relevant organizations and forest-related bodies, institutions and processes, including criteria and indicator processes, as well as indigenous and local communities, non-governmental organizations, and other relevant stakeholders to contribute to the assessment of status and trends, including gaps and priority actions needed to address threats to forest biological diversity;

16. *Urges* the United Nations Framework Convention on Climate Change, including its Kyoto Protocol, to ensure that future activities of the United Nations Framework Convention on Climate Change, including forest and carbon sequestration, are consistent with and supportive of the conservation and sustainable use of biological diversity;

17. *Requests* the Executive Secretary to assemble, in collaboration with the United Nations Framework Convention on Climate Change and the Intergovernmental Panel on Climate Change, existing information relating to the integration of biodiversity considerations, including biodiversity conservation, in the implementation of the United Nations Framework Convention on Climate Change and its Kyoto Protocol;

18. *Requests* the Subsidiary Body on Scientific, Technical and Technological Advice, prior to the sixth meeting of the Conference of Parties, to prepare scientific advice, where appropriate and feasible in collaboration with the appropriate bodies of the United Nations Framework Convention on Climate Change and the Intergovernmental Panel on Climate Change, in order to integrate biodiversity considerations, including biodiversity conservation, in the implementation of the United Nations Framework Convention on Climate Change and its Kyoto Protocol;

19. *Requests* the President of the fifth meeting of the Conference of the Parties of the Convention on Biological Diversity to transmit the present decision to the meeting of the Conference of the Parties of the United Nations Framework Convention on Climate Change at its sixth meeting;

20. *Invites* the Executive Secretary to strengthen cooperation with the United Nations Framework Convention on Climate Change, including its Kyoto Protocol, the United Nations Convention to Combat Desertification, the Convention on International Trade in Endangered Species of Wild Fauna and Flora (CITES), and the Ramsar Convention on Wetlands especially on issues relevant to forest biological diversity, taking into account the role of the United Nations Forum on Forests.

Annex:
Ad hoc technical expert group on forest biological diversity

Terms of reference

Taking into account the ecosystem approach and sustainable forest management, decisions of the Conference of the Parties on thematic and cross-cutting issues, in particular Article 8 (j), proposals for action agreed by the Intergovernmental Panel on Forests (IPF) and the Intergovernmental Forum on Forests (IFF), as well as the work of other relevant international processes and organizations including the Food and Agriculture Organization of the United Nations (FAO), processes related to criteria and indicators, the International Tropical Timber Organization (ITTO), and the Centre for International Forestry Research (CIFOR), the outcome of the Commission on Sustainable Development at its eighth meeting, and contributing to the future work of the United Nations Forum on Forests (UNFF) in the context of and in support of the programme of work for forest biological diversity, and making use of the information contained in available case-studies,

1. Provide advice on scientific programmes and international cooperation in research and development related to conservation and sustainable use of forest biological diversity in the context of the programme of work for forest biological diversity (decisions IV/7 and V/4);

2. (a) Carry out a review of available information on the status and trends of, and major threats to, forest biological biodiversity, to identify significant gaps in that information;

(b) Identify options and suggest priority actions, timeframes and relevant actors for the conservation and sustainable use of forest biological diversity for their implementation through activities such as:

(i) Identifying new measures and ways to improve the conservation of forest biological diversity in and outside existing protected areas;

(ii) Identifying practical measures to mitigate the direct and underlying causes of forest biodiversity loss;

(iii) Identifying tools and mechanisms to implement the identified measures and actions;

(iv) Identifying measures for the restoration of degraded forest; and

(v) Identifying strategies for enhancement of collaborative management with local and indigenous communities;

(c) To identify innovative, efficient and state-of-the-art technologies and know-how relating to assessment, planning, valuation, conservation and sustainable use of forest biodiversity and provide advice on ways and means of promoting the development and transfer of such technologies.

Duration of work

The work of the ad hoc technical expert group on forest biodiversity should be initiated immediately after approval by the Conference of the Parties at its fifth meeting of the terms of reference, and the nomination of experts, and completed not later than the seventh meeting of the Subsidiary Body on Scientific, Technical and Technological Advice, in time for the sixth meeting of the Conference of the Parties, which will consider forest biodiversity as one of the main priority issues.

Decision V/5: Agricultural biological diversity: Review of phase I of the programme of work and adoption of a multi-year work programme

The Conference of the Parties,

I Programme of work

1. *Welcomes* the assessment of ongoing activities and instruments (UNEP/CBD/SBSTTA/5/INF/10) and its main findings as presented in the note by the Executive Secretary on agricultural biological diversity: review of phase I of the programme of work and adoption of a multi-year programme of work (UNEP/CBD/COP/5/11);

2. *Takes note* of the decision on agriculture adopted by the Commission on Sustainable Development at its eighth session, held in New York from 24 April to 5 May 2000;

3. *Endorses* the programme of work on agricultural biological diversity contained in the annex to the present decision, contributing to the implementation of decision III/11;

4. *Urges* Parties, Governments, international and regional organizations, civil-society organizations and other relevant bodies to promote and, as appropriate, carry out the programme of work and to promote regional and thematic cooperation within this framework;

5. *Recognizes* the contribution of farmers, indigenous and local communities to the conservation and sustainable use of agricultural biodiversity and the importance of agricultural biodiversity to their livelihoods, *emphasizes* the importance of their participation in the implementation of the programme of work, and *recognizes* the need for incentives, in accordance with Article 11 of the Convention on Biological Diversity and consistent with its Article 22, and support for capacity-building and information exchange to benefit farmers, indigenous and local communities;

6. *Recalling* decision III/11, *requests* the Executive Secretary to invite the Food and Agriculture Organization of the United Nations to support the development and implementation of the programme of work, and also to expand cooperation by inviting other relevant organizations (such as the United Nations Development Programme, the United Nations Environment Programme, the World Bank, regional development banks, the centres of the Consultative Group on International Agricultural Research and other international agricultural research centres, and IUCN-The World Conservation Union), in supporting the implementation of the programme of work, and to avoid duplication of activities;

7. *Requests* the Executive Secretary to undertake the necessary steps for the full implementation of the programme of work;

8. *Requests* the Executive Secretary to prepare a progress report and proposals for the further implementation of this programme of work for consideration by the Subsidiary Body on Scientific, Technical and Technological Advice prior to the sixth meeting of the Conference of the Parties on the basis of which the Conference of the Parties may provide further guidance, for example, in the form of:

(a) A timetable for implementation of activities, including milestones;

(b) A schedule for reporting on further progress;

(c) Resource requirements; and

(d) Responsibilities of partners and collaborators;

9. *Invites* Parties, in accordance with Article 20 of the Convention, and bilateral and international funding agencies to provide support for the implementation of the activities of the programme of work on agricultural biological diversity, in particular, for capacity-building and case-studies in developing countries and countries with economies in transition;

10. *Invites* Parties, Governments and relevant organizations to support actions to raise public awareness in support of sustainable farming and food production systems that maintain agricultural biodiversity;

11. *Recognizes* the potential contribution that the revised International Undertaking on Plant Genetic Resources, in harmony with the Convention, would have to assist in the implementation of this programme of work;

12. While noting the report of the Chairman of the Commission on Genetic Resources for Food and Agriculture of the Food and Agriculture Organization of the United Nations (UNEP/CBD/COP/5/INF/12), *urges* the Commission to finalize its work as soon as possible. The International Undertaking is envisaged to play a crucial role in the implementation of the Convention on Biological Diversity. The Conference of the Parties *affirms* its willingness to consider a decision by the Conference of the Food and Agriculture Organization of the United Nations that the International Undertaking become a legally binding instrument with strong links to both the Food and Agriculture Organization of the United Nations and the Convention on Biological Diversity, and *calls upon* Parties to coordinate their positions in both forums;

13. *Welcomes* the adoption of the Rotterdam Convention on the Prior Informed Consent Procedure for Certain Hazardous Chemicals and Pesticides in International Trade, and *urges* Parties and Governments to ratify this Convention;

14. *Encourages* Parties and Governments to support the application of the Executive Secretary of the Convention on Biological Diversity for observer status in the Committee on Agriculture of the World Trade Organization, in line with paragraph 9 of decision IV/6 of the Conference of Parties;

II International initiative for the conservation and sustainable use of pollinators

Considering decision III/11, in which the Conference of the Parties established the programme of work on agricultural biodiversity, and called for priority attention to components of biological diversity responsible for the maintenance of ecosystem services important for the sustainability of agriculture, including pollinators,

Considering the recommendations of the Sao Paulo Declaration on Pollinators, based on the results of the Workshop on the Conservation and Sustainable Use of Pollinators in Agriculture, with an Emphasis on Bees, held in Sao Paulo, Brazil, from 7 to 9 October 1998, presented by the Brazilian Government at the fifth meeting of the Subsidiary Body on Scientific, Technical and Technological Advice,

Considering the urgent need to address the issue of worldwide decline of pollinator diversity, and considering recommendation V/9 of the Subsidiary Body on Scientific, Technical and Technological Advice,

15. *Decides* to establish an International Initiative for the Conservation and Sustainable Use of Pollinators as a cross-cutting initiative within the programme of work on agricultural biodiversity to promote coordinated action worldwide to:

(a) Monitor pollinator decline, its causes and its impact on pollination services;

(b) Address the lack of taxonomic information on pollinators;

(c) Assess the economic value of pollination and the economic impact of the decline of pollination services;

(d) Promote the conservation and the restoration and sustainable use of pollinator diversity in agriculture and related ecosystems;

16. *Requests* the Executive Secretary to invite the Food and Agriculture Organization of the United Nations to facilitate and coordinate the Initiative in close cooperation with other relevant organizations and to consider establishing a coordination mechanism, with geographical balance and with leading relevant organizations, to prepare a proposal for a plan of action taking into account the recommendations in the Sao Paulo Declaration on Pollinators, as well as on contributions submitted by countries and relevant organizations, for submission to and review by the Subsidiary Body on Scientific, Technical and Technological Advice and consideration by the Conference of the Parties at its sixth meeting;

17. *Invites* leading relevant organizations, such as IUCN-The World Conservation Union, the International Bee Research Association and the International Commission for Plant–Bee Relationships, the International Centre of Insect Physiology and Ecology, the international agriculture research centres of the Consultative Group on International Agricultural Research and other relevant regional and international bodies, to collaborate in supporting actions in Parties and countries subject to pollinator decline;

18. *Requests* the Executive Secretary, the Subsidiary Body on Scientific, Technical and Technological Advice and the financial mechanism to support the development and implementation of the Initiative and *invites* Parties and Governments to collaborate and compile case-studies and implement pilot projects, making use of the clearing-house mechanism, and to report to the Conference of the Parties at its sixth meeting.

III Genetic use restriction technologies

19. *Decides* to continue the work on genetic use restriction technologies under the umbrella of, and integrated into, each of the four elements of the programme of work on agricultural biological diversity and invites the Subsidiary Body on Scientific, Technical and Technological Advice to report to the Conference of the Parties at its sixth meeting;

20. Desiring to make the most efficient use of resources by avoiding duplication of effort and being cognizant of the work being undertaken and the expertise available in different forums, in particular, the Food and Agriculture Organization of the United Nations and its Commission on Genetic Resources for Food and Agriculture, *invites* the Food and Agriculture Organization of the United Nations, in close collaboration with the United Nations Educational, Scientific and Cultural Organization, the United Nations Environment Programme and other member organizations of the Ecosystem Conservation Group, and other competent organizations and research bodies, to further study the potential implications of genetic use restriction technologies for the conservation and sustainable use of agricultural biological diversity and the range of agricultural production systems in different countries, and identify relevant policy questions and socio-economic issues that may need to be addressed;

21. *Invites* the Food and Agriculture Organization of the United Nations and its Commission on Genetic Resources for Food and Agriculture and other competent organizations to inform the Conference of the Parties at its sixth meeting of their initiatives in this area;

22. *Recognizing* the need to better understand the intellectual-property-rights implications of genetic use restriction technologies, *invites* relevant organizations to study the impact of technologies on the protection of intellectual property in the agriculture sector, and its appropriateness for the agricultural sector, and to make assessments of the technologies concerned available through the clearing-house mechanism;

23. *Recommends* that, in the current absence of reliable data on genetic use restriction technologies, without which there is an inadequate basis on which to assess their potential risks, and in accordance with the precautionary approach, products incorporating such technologies should not be approved by Parties for field testing until appropriate scientific data can justify such testing, and for commercial use until appropriate, authorized and strictly controlled scientific assessments with regard to, *inter alia*, their ecological and socio-economic impacts and any adverse effects for biological diversity, food security and human health have been carried out in a transparent manner and the conditions for their safe and beneficial use validated. In order to enhance the capacity of all countries to address these issues, Parties should widely disseminate information on scientific assessments, including through the clearing-house mechanism, and share their expertise in this regard.

24. *Encourages* Parties and Governments to consider how to address generic concerns regarding such technologies as genetic use restriction technologies under international and national approaches to the safe and sustainable use of germplasm;

25. *Reaffirming* the need of Parties and Governments for additional information, and recalling Article 8 (g) of the Convention on Biological Diversity, which calls on Parties and Governments to establish or maintain procedures for regulating, managing or controlling risks associated with the use and release of living modified organisms resulting from biotechnology, *invites* Parties to carry out and disseminate the results through the clearing-house mechanism and submit scientific assessments on, *inter alia*, ecological, social and economic effects of genetic use restriction technologies taking into account such information, as available, as:

(a) The molecular biology information available;

(b) The genetic constructs and inducers used;

(c) Effects at the molecular level, such as site-specific effects, gene-silencing, epigenesis and recombination;

(d) Potential positive applications of the variety-specific genetic use restriction technologies on limiting gene flow, and possible negative impacts of genetic use restriction technologies on small populations of threatened wild relatives; and to make these assessments available through, *inter alia*, the clearing-house mechanism;

26. *Further encourages* Parties and Governments to identify ways and means to address the potential impacts of genetic use restriction technologies on the *in situ* and *ex situ* conservation and sustainable use, including food security, of agricultural biological diversity;

27. *Urges* Parties and Governments to assess whether there is a need to develop, and how to ensure the application of, effective regulations at national level which take into account, *inter alia*, the specific nature of variety-specific and trait-specific genetic use restriction technologies, in order to ensure the safety of human health, the environment, food security and the conservation and sustainable use of biological diversity and to make this information available through, *inter alia*, the clearing-house mechanism;

28. *Requests* the Executive Secretary to prepare a report, to be considered by the Subsidiary Body on Scientific, Technical and Technological Advice at a future meeting prior to the sixth meeting of the Conference of the Parties, on the status of development of genetic use restriction technologies and of relevant initiatives at international, regional and national levels on the basis of information provided by organizations, Parties and Governments;

29. *Recognizing* the importance of indigenous and local communities in the conservation and sustainable use of plant genetic resources according to Article 8 (j) of the Convention, and taking into account the revision of the International Undertaking on Plant Genetic Resources for Food and Agriculture, requests the Executive Secretary to discuss with those organizations with relevant expertise and representatives of indigenous and local communities on the potential impacts of the application of genetic use restriction technologies on those communities and on Farmers' Rights in keeping with the revision of the aforementioned International Undertaking to keep, use, exchange and sell seed or propagating material and to prepare a report to be considered by the Conference of the Parties.

Annex:
Programme of work on agricultural biodiversity

A Overall objectives, approach and guiding principles

1. The overall aim of the programme of work is to promote the objectives of the Convention in the area of agricultural biodiversity, in line with relevant decisions of the Conference of Parties, notably decisions II/15, III/11 and IV/6. This programme of work will also contribute to the implementation of chapter 14 of Agenda 21 (Sustainable agriculture and rural development). The scope of agricultural biodiversity is described in the appendix hereto.

2. More specifically, the objectives, as spelt out in paragraph 1 of decision III/11 of the Conference of the Parties to the Convention on Biological Diversity, are:

(a) To promote the positive effects and mitigate the negative impacts of agricultural systems and practices on biological diversity in agro-ecosystems and their interface with other ecosystems;

(b) To promote the conservation and sustainable use of genetic resources of actual and potential value for food and agriculture;

(c) To promote the fair and equitable sharing of benefits arising out of the use of genetic resources.

3. The proposed elements of the programme of work have been developed bearing in mind the need:

(a) To support the development of national strategies, programmes and action plans concerning agricultural biodiversity, in line with decision III/11 of the Conference of the Parties to the Convention on Biological Diversity, and to promote their integration in sectoral and cross-sectoral plans, programmes and policies;

(b) To build upon existing international plans of action, programmes and strategies that have been agreed by countries, in particular, the Global Plan of Action for the Conservation and Sustainable Utilization of Plant Genetic Resources for Food and Agriculture, the Global Strategy for the Management of Farm Animal Genetic Resources, and the International Plant Protection Convention (IPPC);

(c) To ensure harmony with the other relevant programmes of work under the Convention on Biological Diversity, including those relating to forest biological diversity, inland water biological diversity, marine and coastal biological diversity, and dry and sub-humid lands, as well as with cross-cutting issues such as access and benefit-sharing, sustainable use, indicators, alien species, the Global Taxonomy Initiative, and issues related to Article 8 (j);

(d) To promote synergy and coordination, and to avoid duplication, between relevant programmes of various international organizations and between programmes at the national and regional levels established under the auspices of international organizations, while respecting the mandates and existing programmes of work of each organization and the intergovernmental authority of the respective governing bodies, commissions and other forums.

4. In implementing the programme of work, the ecosystem approach adopted under the Convention on Biological Diversity will be applied. The application of this approach implies, *inter alia*, intersectoral cooperation, decentralization of management to the lowest level appropriate, equitable distribution of benefits, and the use of adaptive management policies that can deal with uncertainties and are modified in the light of experience and changing conditions. The implementation process will also build upon the knowledge, innovations and practices of local communities and thus complement Article 8 (j) of the Convention. A multi-disciplinary approach that takes into account scientific, social and economic issues is required.

5. The proposed programme of work has been developed in the light of the basis for action annexed to decision III/11. Its implementation, particularly the implementation of programme element 1, will shed further light on the status and trends of agricultural biodiversity.

B Proposed elements of a programme of work

6. Based on the above, the following elements for a programme of work agreed by the Conference of the Parties. It is important to note that the four programme elements are intended to be mutually reinforcing: outputs of certain elements would feed into others. Accordingly, the ordering of the elements does not imply sequential implementation. However prioritization of activities within each programme element will be necessary as set out in the sections on ways and means and timing of expected outputs. Within the framework of this programme of work, targeted cooperative initiatives may be launched.

Programme element 1. Assessments

Operational objective

To provide a comprehensive analysis of status and trends of the world's agricultural biodiversity and of their underlying causes (including a focus on the goods and services agricultural biodiversity provides), as well of local knowledge of its management.

Rationale

Processes for country-driven assessments are in place, or under development, for the crop and farm-animal genetic resources components. The assessments draw upon, and contribute to, comprehensive data and information systems. There is also much information about resources that provide the basis for agriculture (soil, water), and about land cover and use, climatic and agro-ecological zones. However, further assessments may be needed, for example, for microbial genetic resources, for the ecosystem services provided by agricultural biodiversity such as nutrient cycling, pest and disease regulation and pollination, and for social and economic aspects related to agricultural biodiversity. Assessments may also be needed for the interactions between agricultural practices, sustainable agriculture and the conservation and sustainable use of the components of biodiversity referred to in Annex I to the Convention. Understanding of the underlying causes of the loss of agricultural biodiversity is limited, as is understanding of the consequences of such loss for the functioning of agricultural ecosystems. Moreover, the assessments of the various components are conducted separately; there is no integrated assessment of agricultural biodiversity as a whole. There is also lack of widely accepted indicators of agricultural biodiversity. The further development and application of such indicators, as well as assessment methodologies, are necessary to allow an analysis of the status and trends of agricultural biodiversity and its various components and to facilitate the identification of biodiversity-friendly agricultural practices (see programme element 2).

Activities

1.1. Support the ongoing or planned assessments of different components of agricultural biodiversity, for example, the reports on the state of the world's plant genetic resources for food and agriculture,[18] and the state of the world's animal genetic resources for food and agriculture, as well as other relevant reports and assessments by FAO and other organizations, elaborated in a country-driven manner through consultative processes.

---

18 It should be noted that the FAO Commission on Genetic Resources for Food and Agriculture has decided that the second report on the state of the world's plant genetic resources will be prepared only once the negotiations for the revision of the International Undertaking have been completed.

1.2. Promote and develop specific assessments of additional components of agricultural biodiversity that provide ecological services, drawing upon the outputs of programme element 2. This might include targeted assessments on priority areas (for example, loss of pollinators, pest management and nutrient cycling).

1.3. Carry out an assessment of the knowledge, innovations and practices of farmers and indigenous and local communities in sustaining agricultural biodiversity and agro-ecosystem services for and in support of food production and food security.

1.4. Promote and develop assessments of the interactions between agricultural practices and the conservation and sustainable use of the components of biodiversity referred to in Annex I to the Convention.

1.5. Develop methods and techniques for assessing and monitoring the status and trends of agricultural biodiversity and other components of biodiversity in agricultural ecosystems, including:

(a) Criteria and guidelines for developing indicators to facilitate monitoring and assessment of the status and trends of biodiversity in different production systems and environments, and the impacts of various practices, building wherever possible on existing work, in accordance with decision V/7, on the development of indicators on biological diversity, in accordance to the particular characteristics and needs of Parties;

(b) An agreed terminology and classification for agro-ecosystems and production systems to facilitate the comparison and synthesis of various assessments and monitoring of different components of biodiversity in agricultural ecosystems, at all levels and scales, between countries, and regional and international partner organizations;[19]

(c) Data and information exchange on agricultural biodiversity (including available information on *ex situ* collections) in particular through the clearing-house mechanism under the Convention on Biological Diversity, building on existing networks, databases, and information systems;

(d) Methodology for analysis of the trends of agricultural biodiversity and its underlying causes, including socio-economic causes.

Ways and means

Exchange and use of experiences, information and findings from the assessments shall be facilitated by Parties, Governments and networks with consultation between countries and institutions, including use of existing networks.

Country-driven assessments of genetic resources of importance for food and agriculture (activity 1.1) shall be implemented, including through programmes of FAO and in close collaboration with other organizations, such as CGIAR. Resources may need to be identified to support additional assessments (activity 1.2), which would draw upon elements of existing programmes of international organizations, and the outputs of programme element 2.

19 This would draw upon, and not seek to replace, existing classification systems for ecosystems and farming systems (eg eco-region, agro-ecological zones, landscapes, land evaluation systems, production systems/environments, farming systems and farm typologies, etc.), taking into account physical resources (air, climate, land, water, vegetation types), human resource attributes (population intensity, land-use pressures, settlement patterns), and degree of market integration.

This programme element, particularly activity 1.5, will be supported through catalytic activities, building upon and bringing together existing programmes, in order to assist Parties to develop agricultural biodiversity indicators, agreed terminology, etc., through, *inter alia*, technical workshops, meetings and consultations, email conferences, preparation of discussion papers, and travel. Funding of these catalytic activities would be through the Secretariat, with in-kind contributions from participating organizations.

Timing of expected outputs

A key set of standard questions and a menu of potential indicators of agricultural biodiversity that may be used by Parties at their national level, and agreed terminology of production environments by 2002. Reports on the state of the world's genetic resources, as programmed, leading progressively towards a comprehensive assessment and understanding of agricultural biodiversity, with a focus on the goods and services it provides, by 2010.

Programme element 2. Adaptive management

Operational objective

To identify management practices, technologies and policies that promote the positive and mitigate the negative impacts of agriculture on biodiversity, and enhance productivity and the capacity to sustain livelihoods, by expanding knowledge, understanding and awareness of the multiple goods and services provided by the different levels and functions of agricultural biodiversity.

Rationale

There are large and fairly well-defined research agendas for genetic resources for food and agriculture. These include the development of complementary conservation and use strategies, and a focus on developing the conservation and use of under-utilized species. There are also an increasing number of case-studies on, for example, farm and *in situ* conservation of genetic resources, and community integrated pest management. However, far more understanding is needed of the multiple goods and services provided by the different levels and functions of agricultural biodiversity. Much more research is needed, for example, to examine the relationship between diversity, resilience and production in agro-ecosystems.

A blend of traditional and newer practices and technologies is used in agriculture, which utilize, or impact on, agricultural biodiversity in different ways, with particular consequences for biological diversity and for the sustainability and productivity of agricultural systems. A better understanding and application of these complex interactions could help to optimize the management of agricultural biodiversity in production systems.

Such work is essential in order to meet the objectives of decision III/11 of the Conference of the Parties to promote the positive and mitigate the negative impacts of agriculture on biological diversity, and enhance productivity and capacity to sustain livelihoods.

Activities

1.1. Carry out a series of case-studies, in a range of environments and production systems, and in each region:

(a) To identify key goods and services provided by agricultural biodiversity, needs for the conservation and sustainable use of components of this biological diversity in agricultural ecosystems, and threats to such diversity;

(b) To identify best management practices; and

(c) To monitor and assess the actual and potential impacts of existing and new agricultural technologies.

This activity would address the multiple goods and services provided by the different levels and functions of agricultural biodiversity and the interaction between its various components, as set out in the appendix hereto with a focus on certain specific and cross-cutting issues, such as:

(a) The role and potential of wild, under-utilized and neglected species, varieties and breeds, and products;

(b) The role of genetic diversity in providing resilience, reducing vulnerability, and enhancing adaptability of production systems to changing environments and needs;

(c) The synergies and interactions between different components of agricultural biodiversity;

(d) The role of pollinators, with particular reference to their economic benefits, and the effects of introduced species on indigenous pollinators and other aspects of biological diversity;

(e) The role of soil and other below-ground biodiversity in supporting agricultural production systems, especially in nutrient cycling;

(f) Pest and disease control mechanisms, including the role of natural enemies and other organisms at field and landscape levels, host plant resistance, and implications for agro-ecosystem management;

(g) The wider ecosystem services provided by agricultural biodiversity;

(h) The role of different temporal and spatial patterns in mosaics of land use, including complexes of different habitats;

(i) Possibilities of integrated landscape management as a means for the conservation and sustainable use of biodiversity.

2.2. Identify and promote the dissemination of information on cost-effective practices and technologies, and related policy and incentive measures that enhance the positive and mitigate the negative impacts of agriculture on biological diversity, productivity and capacity to sustain livelihoods, through:

(a) Comprehensive analyses in selected production systems of the costs and benefits of alternative management practices as identified from activity 2.1, and the valuation of the goods and services provided by agricultural biodiversity;

(b) Comprehensive analyses of the impacts of agricultural production, including their intensification and extensification, on the environment and identification of ways to mitigate negative and promote positive impacts;

(c) Identification, at international and national levels, in close collaboration with relevant international organizations, of appropriate marketing and trade policies, legal and economic measures which may support beneficial practices:

(i) Promotion of neglected and under-utilized species, varieties and breeds;

(ii) Promotion of local and indigenous knowledge;

(iii) Measures to add value to products of production systems that sustain biodiversity, and to diversify market opportunities;

(iv) Access and benefit-sharing measures and intellectual property issues;

(v) Economically and socially sound measures that act as incentives, in accordance with Article 11 and consistent with Article 22; and

(vi) Training and capacity-building in support of the above.

2.3. Promote methods of sustainable agriculture that employ management practices, technologies and policies that promote the positive and mitigate the negative impacts of agriculture on biodiversity, with particular focus on the needs of farmers and indigenous and local communities.

Ways and means

Case-studies will be carried out and provided by national institutions, civil-society organizations, and research institutes, with support from international organizations for catalysing preparation of studies, mobilizing funds, disseminating results, and facilitating feedback and lessons learned to case-study providers and policy makers. Inputs would be sought from all relevant stakeholders. Resources may need to be identified to promote such studies, to analyse the results and to provide necessary capacity-building and human-resource development, especially at the inter-community or district level. Where a need is identified, for example, through lessons learned from earlier case-studies, the Subsidiary Body on Technical, Technological Advice or the Conference of the Parties will be consulted to consider the promotion of regional or global programmes of case-studies, or focused research activities.

Timing of expected outputs

Thirty selected case-studies published, analysed and disseminated by 2005. The case-studies should be representative of regional issues and prioritize best practices and lessons learned that can be broadly applied.

Programme element 3. Capacity-building

Operational objective

To strengthen the capacities of farmers, indigenous and local communities, and their organizations and other stakeholders, to manage sustainably agricultural biodiversity so as to increase their benefits, and to promote awareness and responsible action.

Rationale

The management of agricultural biodiversity involves many stakeholders and often implies transfers of costs and benefits between stakeholder groups. It is therefore essential that mechanisms be developed not only to consult stakeholder groups, but also to facilitate their genuine participation in decision-making and in the sharing of benefits.

The sustainable management of agricultural biodiversity by farmers and their communities, in particular, is a prerequisite to achieving sustainable increases in food and livelihood security and to protecting natural resources. Decision III/11, paragraph 17 (c), of the Conference of the Parties encourages Parties to promote the 'mobilization of farming communities, including indigenous and local communities for the development, maintenance and use of their knowledge and practices in the conservation and sustainable use of biological diversity in the agricultural sector'. By paragraph 15 of the same decision, countries are encouraged 'to set up and maintain local-level forums for farmers, researchers, extension workers and other stakeholders to evolve genuine partnerships'. There is a largely unrealized potential to improve the management of various aspects of agricultural biodiversity at the level of the agro-ecosystem, through, for example, participatory breeding and selection strategies. Farmer groups, and other producer organizations, can be instrumental in furthering the interests of farmers in optimizing sustainable, diversified, production systems and consequently in promoting responsible actions concerning the conservation and sustainable use of agricultural biodiversity. Consumer organizations are also increasingly influential in this regard.

Activities

3.1. Promote enhanced capabilities to manage agricultural biodiversity by promoting partnerships among researchers, extension workers and farmers in research and development programmes for biological diversity conservation and sustainable use of biological diversity in agriculture. To achieve this, countries should be encouraged to set up and maintain, *inter alia*, local-level forums for farmers, including indigenous farmers using traditional knowledge, researchers, extension workers and other stakeholders to evolve genuine partnerships, including training and education programmes.

3.2. Enhance the capacity of indigenous and local communities for the development of strategies and methodologies for *in situ* conservation, sustainable use and management of agricultural biological diversity, building on indigenous knowledge systems.

3.3. Provide opportunities for farmers and local communities, and other stakeholder groups, to participate in the development and implementation of national strategies, plans and programmes for agricultural biodiversity, through decentralized policies and plans, and local government structures.

3.4. Identify and promote possible improvements in the policy environment, including benefit-sharing arrangements and incentive measures, to support local-level management of agricultural biodiversity.

3.5. Promote awareness about the value of agricultural biodiversity and the multiple goods and services provided by its different levels and functions, for sustainable productivity amongst producer organizations, agricultural cooperatives and enterprises, and consumers, with a view to promoting responsible practices

3.6. Promote networks of farmers and farmers' organizations at regional level for exchange of information and experiences.

Ways and means

This programme element is to be implemented primarily through initiatives within countries, including through extension services, local government, educational and civil-society organizations, including farmer/producer and consumer organizations and mechanisms emphasizing farmer–farmer exchange. This programme element would engage the widest possible range of civil-society organizations, including those not normally linked to biodiversity initiatives.

Funding is likely to be on a project or programme basis. Catalytic support may need to be provided through national, regional and global programmes, organizations, facilities and funding mechanisms, in particular to support capacity-building, exchange and feedback of policy and market information, and of lessons learned from this and programme element 2, between local organizations and policy makers, nationally, regionally and globally.

Timing of expected outputs

Progressive establishment of local-level forums and regional networks, with a coverage target of at least 1,000 communities by 2010.

Examples at country level of operational mechanisms for participation by a wide range of stakeholder groups including civil-society organizations, by 2002. Involvement of farmers and local communities in the majority of national programmes by 2010.

Programme element 4. Mainstreaming

Operational objective

To support the development of national plans or strategies for the conservation and sustainable use of agricultural biodiversity and to promote their mainstreaming and integration in sectoral and cross-sectoral plans and programmes.

Rationale

Many countries are now developing biodiversity strategies and action plans in the context of the Convention on Biological Diversity, and many also have a number of other policies, strategies and plans related to agriculture, the environment and national development.[20] Moreover, countries have agreed on global action plans for major components of biological diversity, such as plant genetic resources for food and agriculture, and, in Agenda 21 and the World Food Summit Plan of Action, on plans for sustainable development and food security in general.

In most countries, activities related to agricultural biodiversity are undertaken primarily by ministries responsible for agriculture. There is clearly a need to mainstream the action plans for components of agricultural biodiversity in sectoral development plans concerned with food, agriculture, forestry and fisheries, and to promote synergy and avoid duplication between the plans for the various components. Together with other thematic programmes of work, this could contribute to the integration of biodiversity considerations in national plans.

Development and implementation of action plans requires reliable and accessible information, but many countries do not have well developed information, communication or early-warning systems or the capacity to respond to identified threats.

20 These include agricultural sector plans, national environment action plans, national sustainable development strategies, national forestry action plans, World Bank plans for structural adjustment, etc.

Activities

4.1. Support the institutional framework and policy and planning mechanisms for the mainstreaming of agricultural biodiversity in agricultural strategies and action plans, and its integration into wider strategies and plans for biological diversity, through:

(a) Support for relevant institutions in the conduct of assessments on the status and trends of agricultural biodiversity within the context of ongoing biodiversity and sectoral assessments;

(b) Development of policy and planning guidelines, and training materials, and support for capacity-building initiatives at policy, technical and local levels in agricultural and environmental forums for the development, implementation, monitoring and evaluation of policies, programmes and actions for the conservation and sustainable use of agricultural biodiversity; and

(c) Improved consultation, coordination, and information-sharing within countries among respective focal points and lead institutions, relevant technical committees and coordinating bodies, to promote synergy in the implementation of agreed plans of action and between ongoing assessments and intergovernmental processes.

4.2. Support the development or adaptation of relevant systems of information, early warning and communication to enable effective assessment of the state of agricultural biodiversity and threats to it, in support of national strategies and action plans, and of appropriate response mechanisms.

4.3. Promote public awareness of the goods and services provided by agricultural biological diversity, and the value and importance of such diversity for agriculture and for society in general.

4.4. Promote ongoing and planned activities for the conservation, on farm, *in situ*, and *ex situ*, in particular, in the countries of origin, of the variability of genetic resources for food and agriculture, including their wild relatives.

Ways and means

Activities would be implemented primarily at national level through enhanced communication, coordination mechanisms and planning processes that involve all stakeholder groups, facilitated by international organizations, and by funding mechanisms.

This programme element should draw upon the experience of ongoing programmes (such as UNEP's support to national biodiversity strategies and action plans) and a critical analysis of existing practice.

National, regional and international projects and programmes that address policy and institutional development within specific sectors should make provision, as appropriate, for integration across sectors. Similarly, the development of guidelines should be carried out within the context of the objectives of this programme element.

Resources may need to be identified to further develop or adapt early-warning systems, including the capacity to identify thresholds and action needed, and for pilot examples of effective and sustainable response mechanisms to address threats at local, national and supranational levels.

Timing of expected outputs

Progressively increased capacity at national level for information management, assessment and communication. Over 100 countries to participate in various assessments under activities 1.1 and 1.2 by 2005.

Coordination between sectoral assessments and plans of action at national level in the majority of countries by 2005.

Range of guidelines published at the international level (on topics to be determined according to needs at national and regional levels).

Appendix:
The scope of agricultural biodiversity

1. Agricultural biodiversity is a broad term that includes all components of biological diversity of relevance to food and agriculture, and all components of biological diversity that constitute the agro-ecosystem: the variety and variability of animals, plants and micro-organisms, at the genetic, species and ecosystem levels, which are necessary to sustain key functions of the agro-ecosystem, its structure and processes, in accordance with annex I of decision III/11 of the Conference of the Parties to the Convention on Biological Diversity.

2. The Conference of Parties has recognized 'the special nature of agricultural biodiversity, its distinctive features, and problems needing distinctive solutions'.[21] The distinctive features include the following:

(a) Agricultural biodiversity is essential to satisfy basic human needs for food and livelihood security;

(b) Agricultural biodiversity is managed by farmers; many components of agricultural biodiversity depend on this human influence; indigenous knowledge and culture are integral parts of the management of agricultural biodiversity;

(c) There is a great interdependence between countries for the genetic resources for food and agriculture;

(d) For crops and domestic animals, diversity within species is at least as important as diversity between species and has been greatly expanded through agriculture;

(e) Because of the degree of human management of agricultural biodiversity, its conservation in production systems is inherently linked to sustainable use;

(f) Nonetheless, much biological diversity is now conserved ex situ in gene banks or breeders' materials;

(g) The interaction between the environment, genetic resources and management practices that occurs *in situ* within agro-ecosystems often contributes to maintaining a dynamic portfolio of agricultural biodiversity.

3. The following dimensions of agricultural biodiversity can be identified:

(a) Genetic resources for food and agriculture, including:

21 See decision II/15 of the Conference of the Parties to the Convention on Biological Diversity.

(i) Plant genetic resources, including pasture and rangeland species, genetic resources of trees that are an integral part of farming systems;

(ii) Animal genetic resources, including fishery genetic resources, in cases where fish production is part of the farming system, and insect genetic resources;

(iii) Microbial and fungal genetic resources.

These constitute the main units of production in agriculture, including cultivated species, domesticated species and managed wild plants and animals, as well as wild relatives of cultivated and domesticated species;

(b) Components of agricultural biodiversity that provide ecological services. These include a diverse range of organisms in agricultural production systems that contribute, at various scales to, *inter alia*:

(i) Nutrient cycling, decomposition of organic matter and maintenance of soil fertility;

(ii) Pest and disease regulation;

(iii) Pollination;

(iv) Maintenance and enhancement of local wildlife and habitats in their landscape,

(v) Maintenance of the hydrological cycle;

(vi) Erosion control;

(vii) Climate regulation and carbon sequestration;

(c) Abiotic factors, which have a determining effect on these aspects of agricultural biodiversity;

(d) Socio-economic and cultural dimensions since agricultural biodiversity is largely shaped by human activities and management practices. These include:

(i) Traditional and local knowledge of agricultural biodiversity, cultural factors and participatory processes;

(ii) Tourism associated with agricultural landscapes;

(iii) Other socio-economic factors.

Decision V/6: Ecosystem approach

The Conference of the Parties,

1. *Endorses* the description of the ecosystem approach and operational guidance contained in sections A and C of the annex to the present decision, recommends the application of the principles contained in section B of the annex, as reflecting the present level of common understanding, and *encourages* further conceptual elaboration, and practical verification;

2. *Calls upon* Parties, other Governments, and international organizations to apply, as appropriate, the ecosystem approach, giving consideration to the principles

and guidance contained in the annex to the present decision, and to develop practical expressions of the approach for national policies and legislation and for appropriate implementation activities, with adaptation to local, national, and, as appropriate, regional conditions, in particular in the context of activities developed within the thematic areas of the Convention;

3. *Invites* Parties, other Governments and relevant bodies to identify case-studies and implement pilot projects, and to organize, as appropriate, regional, national and local workshops, and consultations aiming to enhance awareness, share experiences, including through the clearing-house mechanism, and strengthen regional, national and local capacities on the ecosystem approach;

4. *Requests* the Executive Secretary to collect, analyse and compare the case-studies referred to in paragraph 3 above, and prepare a synthesis of case-studies and lessons learned for presentation to the Subsidiary Body on Scientific, Technical and Technological Advice prior to the seventh meeting of the Conference of the Parties;

5. *Requests* the Subsidiary Body on Scientific, Technical and Technological Advice, at a meeting prior to the seventh meeting of the Conference of the Parties, to review the principles and guidelines of the ecosystem approach, to prepare guidelines for its implementation, on the basis of case-studies and lessons learned, and to review the incorporation of the ecosystem approach into various programmes of work of the Convention;

6. Recognizes the need for support for capacity-building to implement the ecosystem approach, and invites Parties, Governments and relevant organizations to provide technical and financial support for this purpose;

7. *Encourages* Parties and Governments to promote regional cooperation, for example through the establishment of joint declarations or memoranda of understanding in applying the ecosystem approach across national borders.

Annex
A Description of the ecosystem approach

1. The ecosystem approach is a strategy for the integrated management of land, water and living resources that promotes conservation and sustainable use in an equitable way. Thus, the application of the ecosystem approach will help to reach a balance of the three objectives of the Convention: conservation; sustainable use; and the fair and equitable sharing of the benefits arising out of the utilization of genetic resources.

2. An ecosystem approach is based on the application of appropriate scientific methodologies focused on levels of biological organization, which encompass the essential structure, processes, functions and interactions among organisms and their environment. It recognizes that humans, with their cultural diversity, are an integral component of many ecosystems.

3. This focus on structure, processes, functions and interactions is consistent with the definition of 'ecosystem' provided in Article 2 of the Convention on Biological Diversity:

> '"*Ecosystem*" means a dynamic complex of plant, animal and micro-organism communities and their non-living environment interacting as a functional unit.'

This definition does not specify any particular spatial unit or scale, in contrast to the Convention definition of 'habitat'. Thus, the term 'ecosystem' does not, necessarily, correspond to the terms 'biome' or 'ecological zone', but can refer to any functioning unit at any scale. Indeed, the scale of analysis and action should be determined by the problem being addressed. It could, for example, be a grain of soil, a pond, a forest, a biome or the entire biosphere.

4. The ecosystem approach requires adaptive management to deal with the complex and dynamic nature of ecosystems and the absence of complete knowledge or understanding of their functioning. Ecosystem processes are often non-linear, and the outcome of such processes often shows time-lags. The result is discontinuities, leading to surprise and uncertainty. Management must be adaptive in order to be able to respond to such uncertainties and contain elements of 'learning-by-doing' or research feedback. Measures may need to be taken even when some cause-and-effect relationships are not yet fully established scientifically.

5. The ecosystem approach does not preclude other management and conservation approaches, such as biosphere reserves, protected areas, and single-species conservation programmes, as well as other approaches carried out under existing national policy and legislative frameworks, but could, rather, integrate all these approaches and other methodologies to deal with complex situations. There is no single way to implement the ecosystem approach, as it depends on local, provincial, national, regional or global conditions. Indeed, there are many ways in which ecosystem approaches may be used as the framework for delivering the objectives of the Convention in practice.

B Principles of the ecosystem approach

6. The following 12 principles are complementary and interlinked:

Principle 1: **The objectives of management of land, water and living resources are a matter of societal choice.**

Rationale: Different sectors of society view ecosystems in terms of their own economic, cultural and societal needs. Indigenous peoples and other local communities living on the land are important stakeholders and their rights and interests should be recognized. Both cultural and biological diversity are central components of the ecosystem approach, and management should take this into account. Societal choices should be expressed as clearly as possible. Ecosystems should be managed for their intrinsic values and for the tangible or intangible benefits for humans, in a fair and equitable way.

Principle 2: **Management should be decentralized to the lowest appropriate level.**

Rationale: Decentralized systems may lead to greater efficiency, effectiveness and equity. Management should involve all stakeholders and balance local interests with the wider public interest. The closer management is to the ecosystem, the greater the responsibility, ownership, accountability, participation, and use of local knowledge.

Principle 3: **Ecosystem managers should consider the effects (actual or potential) of their activities on adjacent and other ecosystems.**

Rationale: Management interventions in ecosystems often have unknown or unpredictable effects on other ecosystems; therefore, possible impacts need careful consideration and analysis. This may require new arrangements or ways of organization for institutions involved in decision-making to make, if necessary, appropriate compromises.

Principle 4: Recognizing potential gains from management, there is usually a need to understand and manage the ecosystem in an economic context. Any such ecosystem-management programme should:

(a) Reduce those market distortions that adversely affect biological diversity;

(b) Align incentives to promote biodiversity conservation and sustainable use;

(c) Internalize costs and benefits in the given ecosystem to the extent feasible.

Rationale: The greatest threat to biological diversity lies in its replacement by alternative systems of land use. This often arises through market distortions, which undervalue natural systems and populations and provide perverse incentives and subsidies to favour the conversion of land to less diverse systems.

Often those who benefit from conservation do not pay the costs associated with conservation and, similarly, those who generate environmental costs (eg pollution) escape responsibility. Alignment of incentives allows those who control the resource to benefit and ensures that those who generate environmental costs will pay.

Principle 5: Conservation of ecosystem structure and functioning, in order to maintain ecosystem services, should be a priority target of the ecosystem approach.

Rationale: Ecosystem functioning and resilience depends on a dynamic relationship within species, among species and between species and their abiotic environment, as well as the physical and chemical interactions within the environment. The conservation and, where appropriate, restoration of these interactions and processes is of greater significance for the long-term maintenance of biological diversity than simply protection of species.

Principle 6: Ecosystems must be managed within the limits of their functioning.

Rationale: In considering the likelihood or ease of attaining the management objectives, attention should be given to the environmental conditions that limit natural productivity, ecosystem structure, functioning and diversity. The limits to ecosystem functioning may be affected to different degrees by temporary, unpredictable or artificially maintained conditions and, accordingly, management should be appropriately cautious.

Principle 7: The ecosystem approach should be undertaken at the appropriate spatial and temporal scales.

Rationale: The approach should be bounded by spatial and temporal scales that are appropriate to the objectives. Boundaries for management will be defined operationally by users, managers, scientists and indigenous and local peoples. Connectivity between areas should be promoted where necessary. The ecosystem approach is based upon the hierarchical nature of biological diversity characterized by the interaction and integration of genes, species and ecosystems.

Principle 8: **Recognizing the varying temporal scales and lag-effects that characterize ecosystem processes, objectives for ecosystem management should be set for the long term.**

Rationale: Ecosystem processes are characterized by varying temporal scales and lag-effects. This inherently conflicts with the tendency of humans to favour short-term gains and immediate benefits over future ones.

Principle 9: **Management must recognize that change is inevitable.**

Rationale: Ecosystems change, including species composition and population abundance. Hence, management should adapt to the changes. Apart from their inherent dynamics of change, ecosystems are beset by a complex of uncertainties and potential 'surprises' in the human, biological and environmental realms. Traditional disturbance regimes may be important for ecosystem structure and functioning, and may need to be maintained or restored. The ecosystem approach must utilize adaptive management in order to anticipate and cater for such changes and events and should be cautious in making any decision that may foreclose options, but, at the same time, consider mitigating actions to cope with long-term changes such as climate change.

Principle 10: **The ecosystem approach should seek the appropriate balance between, and integration of, conservation and use of biological diversity.**

Rationale: Biological diversity is critical both for its intrinsic value and because of the key role it plays in providing the ecosystem and other services upon which we all ultimately depend. There has been a tendency in the past to manage components of biological diversity either as protected or non-protected. There is a need for a shift to more flexible situations, where conservation and use are seen in context and the full range of measures is applied in a continuum from strictly protected to human-made ecosystems.

Principle 11: **The ecosystem approach should consider all forms of relevant information, including scientific and indigenous and local knowledge, innovations and practices.**

Rationale: Information from all sources is critical to arriving at effective ecosystem management strategies. A much better knowledge of ecosystem functions and the impact of human use is desirable. All relevant information from any concerned area should be shared with all stakeholders and actors, taking into account, *inter alia*, any decision to be taken under Article 8 (j) of the Convention on Biological Diversity. Assumptions behind proposed management decisions should be made explicit and checked against available knowledge and views of stakeholders.

Principle 12: **The ecosystem approach should involve all relevant sectors of society and scientific disciplines.**

Rationale: Most problems of biological-diversity management are complex, with many interactions, side-effects and implications, and therefore should involve the necessary expertise and stakeholders at the local, national, regional and international level, as appropriate.

C Operational guidance for application of the ecosystem approach

7. In applying the 12 principles of the ecosystem approach, the following five points are proposed as operational guidance.

1 Focus on the functional relationships and processes within ecosystems

8. The many components of biodiversity control the stores and flows of energy, water and nutrients within ecosystems, and provide resistance to major perturbations. A much better knowledge of ecosystem functions and structure, and the roles of the components of biological diversity in ecosystems, is required, especially to understand: (i) ecosystem resilience and the effects of biodiversity loss (species and genetic levels) and habitat fragmentation; (ii) underlying causes of biodiversity loss; and (iii) determinants of local biological diversity in management decisions. Functional biodiversity in ecosystems provides many goods and services of economic and social importance. While there is a need to accelerate efforts to gain new knowledge about functional biodiversity, ecosystem management has to be carried out even in the absence of such knowledge. The ecosystem approach can facilitate practical management by ecosystem managers (whether local communities or national policy makers).

2 Enhance benefit-sharing

9. Benefits that flow from the array of functions provided by biological diversity at the ecosystem level provide the basis of human environmental security and sustainability. The ecosystem approach seeks that the benefits derived from these functions are maintained or restored. In particular, these functions should benefit the stakeholders responsible for their production and management. This requires, *inter alia*: capacity-building, especially at the level of local communities managing biological diversity in ecosystems; the proper valuation of ecosystem goods and services; the removal of perverse incentives that devalue ecosystem goods and services; and, consistent with the provisions of the Convention on Biological Diversity, where appropriate, their replacement with local incentives for good management practices.

3 Use adaptive management practices

10. Ecosystem processes and functions are complex and variable. Their level of uncertainty is increased by the interaction with social constructs, which need to be better understood. Therefore, ecosystem management must involve a learning process, which helps to adapt methodologies and practices to the ways in which these systems are being managed and monitored. Implementation programmes should be designed to adjust to the unexpected, rather than to act on the basis of a belief in certainties. Ecosystem management needs to recognize the diversity of social and cultural factors affecting natural-resource use. Similarly, there is a need for flexibility in policy-making and implementation. Long-term, inflexible decisions are likely to be inadequate or even destructive. Ecosystem management should be envisaged as a long-term experiment that builds on its results as it progresses. This 'learning-by-doing' will also serve as an important source of

information to gain knowledge of how best to monitor the results of management and evaluate whether established goals are being attained. In this respect, it would be desirable to establish or strengthen capacities of Parties for monitoring.

4 Carry out management actions at the scale appropriate for the issue being addressed, with decentralization to lowest level, as appropriate

11. As noted in section A above, an ecosystem is a functioning unit that can operate at any scale, depending upon the problem or issue being addressed. This understanding should define the appropriate level for management decisions and actions. Often, this approach will imply decentralization to the level of local communities. Effective decentralization requires proper empowerment, which implies that the stakeholder both has the opportunity to assume responsibility and the capacity to carry out the appropriate action, and needs to be supported by enabling policy and legislative frameworks. Where common property resources are involved, the most appropriate scale for management decisions and actions would necessarily be large enough to encompass the effects of practices by all the relevant stakeholders. Appropriate institutions would be required for such decision-making and, where necessary, for conflict resolution. Some problems and issues may require action at still higher levels, through, for example, transboundary cooperation, or even cooperation at global levels.

5 Ensure intersectoral cooperation

12. As the primary framework of action to be taken under the Convention, the ecosystem approach should be fully taken into account in developing and reviewing national biodiversity strategies and action plans. There is also a need to integrate the ecosystem approach into agriculture, fisheries, forestry and other production systems that have an effect on biodiversity. Management of natural resources, according to the ecosystem approach, calls for increased intersectoral communication and cooperation at a range of levels (government ministries, management agencies, etc.). This might be promoted through, for example, the formation of inter-ministerial bodies within the Government or the creation of networks for sharing information and experience.

Decision V/7: Identification, monitoring and assessment, and indicators

The Conference of the Parties,

1. *Requests* the Executive Secretary, in broad consultation with Parties, drawing on the roster of experts, and in collaboration with other relevant organizations, bodies and processes, to carry out the pending activities set out in the work programme on indicators of biological diversity as approved by decision IV/1 A of the Conference of the Parties and, in particular, to develop:

(a) A set of principles for designing national-level monitoring programmes and indicators;

(b) A key set of standard questions and a list of available and potential indicators, covering the ecosystem, species and genetic levels, taking into account the ecosystem approach, that may be used by Parties at their national level and in national reporting and that also allow for regional and global overviews on the state and trends of biodiversity and, if possible and appropriate, any responses from policy measures;

2. *Encourages* Parties and Governments to establish or increase regional cooperation in the field of indicators, monitoring and assessment and invites the Executive Secretary to establish a process through which the documents mentioned above are reviewed and broadly discussed at regional workshops on the basis of case-studies submitted by Parties, Governments and relevant organizations;

3. *Acknowledges* that the capacity of many countries, particularly least developed countries, to reliably and consistently monitor indicators is limited and that, therefore, indicators will need to be developed incrementally over time, based on national priorities;

4. *Invites* Parties, Governments and organizations to undertake appropriate actions to assist other Parties (particularly developing countries) to increase their capacity to develop and use indicators. Appropriate actions may include:

(a) Provision of training;

(b) Assisting in the development of national networks;

(c) Sharing experiences between and among countries, regions and organizations involved in the development and use of indicators;

5. *Requests* the Executive Secretary to produce an interim report on progress, including the ongoing work on indicators in the thematic and other work programmes, for review by the Subsidiary Body on Scientific, Technical and Technological Advice prior to the sixth meeting of the Conference of the Parties and to submit a final report on the conclusions of this initiative to the Conference of the Parties at its sixth meeting.

Decision V/8: Alien species that threaten ecosystems, habitats or species

The Conference of the Parties,

1. *Urges* Parties, Governments and relevant organizations to apply the interim guiding principles contained in annex I to the present decision, as appropriate, in the context of activities aimed at implementing Article 8 (h) of the Convention on Biological Diversity, and in the various sectors;

2. *Endorses* the outline for case-studies contained in annex II to the present decision;

3. *Urges* Parties, Governments and relevant organizations to submit case-studies to the Executive Secretary, particularly focusing on thematic assessments, on the basis of the outline contained in the annex to the present decision;

4. *Requests* the Convention's clearing-house mechanism to disseminate and compile these case-studies;

5. *Requests* Parties, other Governments, relevant bodies and other relevant international and regional binding and non-binding instruments, in the light of discussions by the Subsidiary Body on Scientific, Technical and Technological Advice at its fifth meeting, to submit to the Executive Secretary written comments on the interim guiding principles, to be taken into account, together with the case-studies, in the further elaboration of the interim guiding principles, to be considered by the Subsidiary

Body prior to the sixth meeting of the Conference of Parties, and requests the Executive Secretary to distribute those comments through the national focal points;

6. *Urges* Parties, other Governments and relevant bodies to give priority to the development and implementation of alien invasive species strategies and action plans;

7. *Strongly encourages* Parties to develop mechanisms for transboundary cooperation and regional and multilateral cooperation in order to deal with the issue, including the exchange of best practices;

8. *Urges* Parties, other Governments and relevant bodies, such as the Global Invasive Species Programme, in their work on alien invasive species, to give priority attention to geographically and evolutionarily isolated ecosystems, and to use the ecosystem approach and precautionary and biogeographical approaches, as appropriate;

9. *Encourages* Parties to develop effective education, training and public-awareness measures, as well as to inform the public about the different aspects of the issue, including the risks posed by alien invasive species;

10. *Requests* the Global Invasive Species Programme, in developing a global strategy to deal with alien invasive species, to ensure consistency with the provisions on alien invasive species in Article 8 (h) of the Convention and relevant provisions within other articles, including Article 14, taking into full account considerations on alien invasive species within relevant decisions of the Conference of the Parties on, for example, the conservation and sustainable use of inland-water, marine and coastal and forest biological diversity, and the biodiversity of dry and sub-humid lands;

11. *Requests* the Executive Secretary to cooperate with other international bodies and other relevant international and regional binding and non-binding instruments, such as the Convention on the Conservation of Migratory Species of Wild Animals, the Convention on International Trade in Endangered Species of Wild Fauna and Flora, the Convention on Wetlands of International Importance especially as Waterfowl Habitat (Ramsar), the Convention on the Conservation of European Wildlife and Natural Habitats, the International Plant Protection Convention and regional plant protection organizations, Codex Alimentarius, DIVERSITAS, the Office International des Epizooties, the United Nations Educational, Scientific and Cultural Organization, and the organizations mentioned in paragraph 14 of the present decision, with the aim of coordinating work on alien invasive species, and to report on potential joint programmes of work to the Subsidiary Body on Scientific, Technical and Technological Advice;

12. *Invites* the Parties, Governments, the Global Invasive Species Programme and other relevant bodies, to disseminate publicly available information which they hold or acquire, including databases of alien species, through the Convention's clearing-house mechanism;

13. *Invites* the Global Invasive Species Programme to report on its September 2000 meeting on the 'synthesis of GISP phase 1' to the Subsidiary Body on Scientific, Technical and Technological Advice prior to the sixth meeting of the Conference of Parties, recognizing the need to continue the work of the Global Invasive Species Programme through the prompt development of the second phase of the Global Invasive Species Programme, with emphasis on ecosystems vulnerable to alien species invasions;

14. *Requests* the Executive Secretary to collaborate with the Global Invasive Species Programme, the Food and Agriculture Organization of the United Nations, the International Maritime Organization, the World Health Organization and other relevant organizations, and other relevant internationally and regionally binding and non-binding instruments to assist the Parties to the Convention in:

(a) Developing standardized terminology on alien species;

(b) Developing criteria for assessing risks from introduction of alien species;

(c) Developing processes for assessing the socio-economic implications of alien invasive species, particularly the implications for indigenous and local communities;

(d) Furthering research on the impact of alien invasive species on biological diversity;

(e) Developing means to enhance the capacity of ecosystems to resist or recover from alien species invasions;

(f) Developing a system for reporting new invasions of alien species and the spread of alien species into new areas;

(g) Assessing priorities for taxonomic work;

15. *Requests* the Executive Secretary, in collaboration with the Global Invasive Species Programme, the Food and Agriculture Organization of the United Nations, the International Maritime Organization, the World Health Organization and other relevant organizations and instruments to develop a paper for consideration by the Subsidiary Body on Scientific, Technical and Technological Advice and the Conference of the Parties at its sixth meeting, comprising:

(a) A comprehensive review on the efficiency and efficacy of existing measures for prevention, early detection, eradication and control of alien invasive species and their impacts;

(b) A progress report on the matters listed in paragraphs 5 and 14 of the present decision;

(c) All options for future work on alien invasive species under the Convention on Biological Diversity, which would provide practical support to Parties, Governments and organizations in the implementation of Article 8 (h) of the Convention and lead to the full and effective implementation of Article 8 (h);

16. *Decides* that, at its sixth meeting, the Conference of the Parties, on the basis of the information referred to in paragraphs 5 and 15 of the present decision, will consider options for the full and effective implementation of Article 8 (h) including the possibilities of:

(a) Further developing the guiding principles on the prevention of introduction, and mitigation of the impacts, of alien invasive species;

(b) Developing an international instrument; and/or

(c) Other options;

17. *Invites* the Global Environment Facility, Parties, Governments and funding organizations to provide adequate and timely support to enable the Global Invasive Species Programme to fulfil the tasks outlined in the present decision.

DECISION V/8

Annex I:
Interim guiding principles for the prevention, introduction and mitigation of impacts of alien species

It should be noted that in the interim guiding principles below, terms are used for which a definition has not yet been developed, pending a decision by the Conference of Parties on the development of a standardized terminology on alien species, as mentioned in paragraph 5 of recommendation V/4. In the interim and for the purpose of these interim principles, to avoid confusion the following definitions are used: (i) 'alien' or 'alien species' refers to a species occurring outside its normal distribution; and (ii) 'alien invasive species' refers to those alien species which threaten ecosystems, habitats or species.

A General

Guiding principle 1: Precautionary approach

Given the unpredictability of the impacts on biological diversity of alien species, efforts to identify and prevent unintentional introductions as well as decisions concerning intentional introductions should be based on the precautionary approach. Lack of scientific certainty about the environmental, social and economic risk posed by a potentially invasive alien species or by a potential pathway should not be used as a reason for not taking preventative action against the introduction of potentially invasive alien species. Likewise, lack of certainty about the long-term implication of an invasion should not be used as a reason for postponing eradication, containment or control measures.

Guiding principle 2: Three-stage hierarchical approach

Prevention is generally far more cost effective and environmentally desirable than measures taken following introduction of an alien invasive species. Priority should be given to prevention of entry of alien invasive species (both between and within States). If entry has already taken place, actions should be undertaken to prevent the establishment and spread of alien species. The preferred response would be eradication at the earliest possible stage (principle 13). In the event that eradication is not feasible or is not cost-effective, containment (principle 14) and long-term control measures (principle 15) should be considered. Any examination of benefits and costs (both environmental and economic) should be done on a long-term basis.

Guiding principle 3: Ecosystem approach

All measures to deal with alien invasive species should be based on the ecosystem approach, in line with the relevant provisions of the Convention and the decisions of the Conference of the Parties.

Guiding principle 4: State responsibility

States should recognize the risk that they may pose to other States as a potential source of alien invasive species, and should take appropriate actions to minimize that risk. In accordance with Article 3 of the Convention on Biological Diversity, and principle 2 of the 1992 Rio Declaration on Environment and Development, States have the responsibility to ensure that activities within their jurisdiction or control do not cause damage to the environment of other States or of areas beyond the limits of national jurisdiction. In the context of alien invasive species, activities that could be a risk for another State include:

(a) The intentional or unintentional transfer of an alien invasive species to another State (even if it is harmless in the State of origin); and

(b) The intentional or unintentional introduction of an alien species into their own State if there is a risk of that species subsequently spreading (with or without a human vector) into another State and becoming invasive.

Guiding principle 5: Research and monitoring

In order to develop an adequate knowledge base to address the problem, States should undertake appropriate research on and monitoring of alien invasive species. This should document the history of invasions (origin, pathways and time-period), characteristics of the alien invasive species, ecology of the invasion, and the associated ecological and economic impacts and how they change over time. Monitoring is the key to early detection of new alien species. It requires targeted and general surveys, which can benefit from the involvement of local communities.

Guiding principle 6: Education and public awareness

States should facilitate education and public awareness of the risks associated with the introduction of alien species. When mitigation measures are required, education and public-awareness-oriented programmes should be set in motion so as to inform local communities and appropriate sector groups on how to support such measures.

B Prevention

Guiding principle 7: Border control and quarantine measures

1. States should implement border control and quarantine measures to ensure that:

(a) Intentional introductions are subject to appropriate authorization (principle 10);

(b) Unintentional or unauthorized introductions of alien species are minimized.

2. These measures should be based on an assessment of the risks posed by alien species and their potential pathways of entry. Existing appropriate governmental agencies or authorities should be strengthened and broadened as necessary, and staff should be properly trained to implement these measures. Early detection systems and regional coordination may be useful.

Guiding principle 8: Exchange of information

States should support the development of database(s), such as that currently under development by the Global Invasive Species Programme, for compilation and dissemination of information on alien species that threaten ecosystems, habitats or species, to be used in the context of any prevention, introduction and mitigation activities. This information should include incident lists, information on taxonomy and ecology of invasive species and on control methods, whenever available. The wide dissemination of this information, as well as national, regional and international guidelines, procedures and recommendations such as those being compiled by the Global Invasive Species Programme should also be facilitated through, *inter alia*, the clearing-house mechanism.

Guiding principle 9: Cooperation, including capacity-building

Depending on the situation, a State's response might be purely internal (within the country), or may require a cooperative effort between two or more countries, such as:

(a) Where a State of origin is aware that a species being exported has the potential to be invasive in the receiving State, the exporting State should provide information, as available, on the potential invasiveness of the species to the importing State. Particular attention should be paid where exporting Parties have similar environments;

(b) Agreements between countries, on a bilateral or multilateral basis, should be developed and used to regulate trade in certain alien species, with a focus on particularly damaging invasive species;

(c) States should support capacity-building programmes for States that lack the expertise and resources, including financial, to assess the risks of introducing alien species. Such capacity-building may involve technology transfer and the development of training programmes.

C Introduction of species

Guiding principle 10: Intentional introduction

No intentional introduction should take place without proper authorization from the relevant national authority or agency. A risk assessment, including environmental impact assessment, should be carried out as part of the evaluation process before coming to a decision on whether or not to authorize a proposed introduction. States should authorize the introduction of only those alien species that, based on this prior assessment, are unlikely to cause unacceptable harm to ecosystems, habitats or species, both within that State and in neighbouring States. The burden of proof that a proposed introduction is unlikely to cause such harm should be with the proposer of the introduction. Further, the anticipated benefits of such an introduction should strongly outweigh any actual and potential adverse effects and related costs. Authorization of an introduction may, where appropriate, be accompanied by conditions (eg, preparation of a mitigation plan, monitoring procedures, or containment requirements). The precautionary approach should be applied throughout all the above-mentioned measures.

Guiding principle 11: Unintentional introductions

1. All States should have in place provisions to address unintentional introductions (or intentional introductions that have established and become invasive). These include statutory and regulatory measures, institutions and agencies with appropriate responsibilities and with the operational resources required for rapid and effective action.

2. Common pathways leading to unintentional introductions need to be identified and appropriate provisions to minimize such introductions should be in place. Sectoral activities, such as fisheries, agriculture, forestry, horticulture, shipping (including the discharge of ballast waters), ground and air transportation, construction projects, landscaping, ornamental aquaculture, tourism and game-farming, are often pathways for unintentional introductions. Legislation requiring environmental impact assessment of

such activities should also require an assessment of the risks associated with unintentional introductions of alien invasive species.

D Mitigation of impacts

Guiding principle 12: Mitigation of impacts

Once the establishment of an alien invasive species has been detected, States should take steps such as eradication, containment and control, to mitigate the adverse effects. Techniques used for eradication, containment or control should be cost-effective, safe to the environment, humans and agriculture, as well as socially, culturally and ethically acceptable. Mitigation measures should take place in the earliest possible stage of invasion, on the basis of the precautionary approach. Hence, early detection of new introductions of potentially invasive or invasive species is important, and needs to be combined with the capacity to take rapid follow-up action.

Guiding principle 13: Eradication

Where it is feasible and cost-effective, eradication should be given priority over other measures to deal with established alien invasive species. The best opportunity for eradicating alien invasive species is in the early stages of invasion, when populations are small and localized; hence, early detection systems focused on high-risk entry points can be critically useful. Community support, built through comprehensive consultation, should be an integral part of eradication projects.

Guiding principle 14: Containment

When eradication is not appropriate, limitation of spread (containment) is an appropriate strategy only where the range of the invasive species is limited and containment within defined boundaries is possible. Regular monitoring outside the control boundaries is essential, with quick action to eradicate any new outbreaks.

Guiding principle 15: Control

Control measures should focus on reducing the damage caused rather than on merely reducing the numbers of the alien invasive species. Effective control will often rely on a range of integrated techniques. Most control measures will need to be regularly applied, resulting in a recurrent operating budget and the need for a long-term commitment to achieve and maintain results. In some instances, biological control may give long-term suppression of an alien invasive species without recurrent costs, but should always be implemented in line with existing national regulations, international codes and principle 10 above.

Annex II:
Outline for case-studies on alien species

To the extent possible, case-studies should be short and succinct summaries of experience on alien species at the country and regional levels. A case-study should focus on the prevention of introduction, control, and eradication of alien species that threaten ecosystems, habitats or species.

Case-studies should include the following sections (a summary of the information may be provided under each heading, and a more detailed paper may be attached; if the information were not available, this should be indicated in the appropriate section):

1. *Description of the problem*

   (a) Location of the case-study

   (b) History (origin, pathway and dates, including time-period between initial entry/first detection of alien species and development of impacts) of introduction(s)

   (c) Description of the alien species concerned: biology of the alien species (the scientific name of species should be indicated if possible) and ecology of the invasion(s) (type of and potential or actual impacts on biological diversity and ecosystem(s) invaded or threatened, and stakeholders involved)

   (d) Vector(s) of invasion(s) (eg of deliberate importation, contamination of imported goods, ballast water, hull-fouling and spread from adjacent area. It should be specified, if known, whether entry was deliberate and legal, deliberate and illegal, accidental, or natural.)

   (e) Assessment and monitoring activities conducted and methods applied, including difficulties encountered (eg uncertainties due to missing taxonomic knowledge)

2. *Options considered to address the problem*

   (a) Description of the decision-making process (stakeholders involved, consultation processes used, etc.)

   (b) Type of measures (research and monitoring; training of specialists; prevention, early detection, eradication, control/containment measures, habitat and/or natural community restoration; legal provisions; public education and awareness)

   (c) Options selected, time-frame and reasons for selecting the options

   (d) Institutions responsible for decisions and actions

3. *Implementation of measures, including assessment of effectiveness*

   (a) Ways and means set in place for implementation

   (b) Achievements (specify whether the action was fully successful, partially successful, or unsuccessful), including any adverse effects of the actions taken on the conservation and sustainable use of biodiversity

   (c) Costs of action

4. *Lessons learned from the operation and other conclusions*

   (a) Further measures needed, including transboundary, regional and multilateral cooperation

   (b) Replicability for other regions, ecosystems or groups of organisms

   (c) Information compilation and dissemination needed

Decision V/9: Global Taxonomy Initiative: Implementation and further advance of the suggestions for action

The Conference of the Parties,

1. *Establishes* a Global Taxonomy Initiative coordination mechanism to assist the Executive Secretary to facilitate international cooperation and coordinate activities under the Global Taxonomy Initiative in accordance with the terms of reference contained in the annex to this decision;

2. *Urges* Parties, Governments and relevant organizations to undertake the following priority activities to further the Global Taxonomy Initiative:

(a) The identification of national and regional priority taxonomic information requirements;

(b) Assessments of national taxonomic capacity to identify and, where possible, quantify national and regional-level taxonomic impediments and needs, including the identification of taxonomic tools, facilities and services required at all levels, and mechanisms to establish, support and maintain such tools, facilities and services;

(c) Establishment or consolidation of regional and national taxonomic reference centres;

(d) The building of taxonomic capacity, in particular in developing countries, including through partnerships between national, regional and international taxonomic reference centres, and through information networks;

(e) Communication to the Executive Secretary and Global Taxonomy Initiative coordination mechanism, by 31 December 2001, of suitable programmes, projects and initiatives for consideration as pilot projects under the Global Taxonomy Initiative;

3. *Requests* that the Executive Secretary, with the assistance of the Global Taxonomy Initiative coordination mechanism:

(a) Draft as a component of the strategic plan for the Convention on Biological Diversity a work programme for the Global Taxonomy Initiative defining timetables, goals, products and pilot projects, emphasizing its role in underpinning conservation, sustainable use and equitable sharing of benefits, for consideration by the Subsidiary Body on Scientific, Technical and Technological Advice;

(b) Initiate short-term activities, including regional meetings of scientists, managers and policy makers to prioritize the most urgent global taxonomic needs and facilitate the formulation of specific regional and national projects to meet the needs identified, and to report thereon to the Conference of the Parties at its sixth meeting;

(c) Synthesize the findings of previous meetings of experts on the Global Taxonomy Initiative (as contained in the note by the Executive Secretary on the review of the Global Taxonomy Initiative (UNEP/CBD/SBSTTA/5/4)), relevant sections of national reports submitted to the Conference of the Parties and recommendations of the Subsidiary Body on Scientific, Technical and Technological Advice on the Global Taxonomy Initiative, as advice for the proposed regional meetings;

(d) Use the Global Taxonomy Initiative as a forum to promote the importance of taxonomy and taxonomic tools in the implementation of the Convention;

4. *Requests* all Parties and Governments to designate a national Global Taxonomy Initiative focal point by 31 December 2000, linked to other national focal points, and participate in the development of regional networks to facilitate information-sharing for the Global Taxonomy Initiative;

5. *Invites* all interested international and regional conventions, initiatives and programmes to indicate their support for the Global Taxonomy Initiative and its coordination mechanism, through the Executive Secretary, and in so doing to specify their particular areas of interest and any support for the implementation of the Global Taxonomy Initiative that could be forthcoming;

6. *Urges* eligible Parties and consortia of eligible Parties to seek resources for the above priority actions through the financial mechanism, and requests the financial mechanism to continue promoting awareness of the Global Taxonomy Initiative in its outreach activities, such as the Capacity Development Initiative and the Country Dialogue Workshops, and to investigate ways both within and outside its operational programme structure to facilitate capacity-building in taxonomy, and the implementation of the short-term activities referred to in the annex to the present decision.

Annex:
Terms of reference for the coordination mechanism of the Global Taxonomy Initiative

Mandate

Building on the guidance contained in recommendation V/3 of the Subsidiary Body on Scientific, Technical and Technological Advice, the coordination mechanism shall assist the Executive Secretary to facilitate international cooperation and to coordinate activities on matters pertaining to the implementation and development of the Global Taxonomy Initiative (GTI). The Executive Secretary in carrying out this mandate will work closely with the clearing-house mechanism and report on progress of the Global Taxonomy Initiative to every other meeting of the Subsidiary Body on Scientific, Technical and Technological Advice, and, as appropriate, to the Conference of the Parties. The first meeting of the coordination mechanism shall take place no later than 30 November 2000. Meetings of the coordination mechanism can only take place with adequate representation from all regions, and subject to available resources.

Specific short-term activities to be undertaken prior to the sixth meeting of the Conference of the Parties

The Executive Secretary with the assistance of the Coordination Mechanism shall:

(a) Develop a work programme for the Global Taxonomy Initiative, consistent with the Convention strategic plan, for consideration by the Subsidiary Body on Scientific, Technical and Technological Advice;

(b) Convene regional meetings of scientists, managers and policy makers to prioritize the most urgent global taxonomic needs for consideration by the Subsidiary Body on Scientific, Technical and Technological Advice in finalizing the Global Taxonomy Initiative work programme;

(c) Establish mechanisms to use the Global Taxonomy Initiative as a forum to promote the importance of taxonomy and taxonomic tools in the implementation of the Convention's programmes of work.

Membership

The Executive Secretary, in consultation with the Bureau of the Subsidiary Body on Scientific, Technical and Technological Advice shall at the earliest opportunity select 10 members of the coordination mechanism, with due regard to geographical balance to allow two representatives from each region, on a rotational basis. The Executive Secretary shall invite a limited number of leading relevant organizations such as the United Nations Environment Programme, the United Nations Educational, Scientific and Cultural Organization, the Food and Agriculture Organization of the United Nations, the International Council of Scientific Unions, the Global Biodiversity Information Facility, the Global Environment Facility, and BioNET INTERNATIONAL to participate in the work of the coordination mechanism.

Decision V/10: Global strategy for plant conservation

The Conference of the Parties,

Recognizing that plant diversity is a common concern of humankind, and an essential resource for the planet,

Concerned that as many as two thirds of the world's plant species may be in danger of extinction in nature during the course of the twenty first century, and that this threatens humankind's expectation of using plant diversity to build sustainable, healthy and better lives for the future,

Taking note of the proposal contained in the Gran Canaria Declaration (UNEP/CBD/COP/5/INF/32), calling for the development of a Global Strategy for Plant Conservation, as well as the resolution of the XVI International Botanical Congress, held in St.Louis, Missouri, United States of America, in August 1999, and taking into account the International Agenda for Botanic Gardens in Conservation, the Global Invasive Species Programme, and the Plants Programme of the IUCN Species Survival Commission,

1. *Recognizes* that the Convention on Biological Diversity is a leading international convention for the conservation and sustainable use of biodiversity, and further recognizes the cross-cutting nature of plant conservation;

2. *Recognizes also* the important role of other existing initiatives, in particular the Global Plan of Action for the Conservation and Sustainable Utilization of Plant Genetic Resources for Food and Agriculture, and is aware of current efforts to revise the International Undertaking on Plant Genetic Resources for Food and Agriculture developed by the Food and Agriculture Organization of the United Nations;

3. *Decides* to consider, at its sixth meeting, the establishment of a global strategy for plant conservation;

4. *Requests* the Subsidiary Body on Scientific, Technical and Technological Advice to make recommendations to the Conference of the Parties, for consideration at its sixth meeting, regarding the development of a global strategy for plant conservation, which would be aimed at halting the current and continuing unacceptable loss of plant diversity;

5. In order to better enable the Subsidiary Body on Scientific, Technical and Technological Advice to carry out this task, *requests* the Executive Secretary to solicit the views of Parties, and to liaise with relevant organizations, including, *inter alia*, the Global Plan of Action of the Food and Agriculture Organization, the Man and the Biosphere Programme of the United Nations Educational, Scientific and Cultural Organization, Botanic Gardens Conservation International, and the Convention on International Trade in Endangered Species of Wild Fauna and Flora, in order to gather information regarding plant conservation, including information on existing international initiatives. This information is to be reported to the Subsidiary Body on Scientific, Technical and Technological Advice, together with advice on the relationship between plant conservation and the thematic work programmes.

Decision V/11: Additional financial resources

The Conference of the Parties,

Emphasizing the vital importance of adequate financial resources for the implementation of the Convention on Biological Diversity and *reaffirming* the importance of providing new and additional financial resources through the financial mechanism in accordance with Article 20 of the Convention,

Expressing its appreciation to those bilateral and regional funding institutions, United Nations institutions, intergovernmental organizations and nongovernmental organizations and convention secretariats that provided information regarding financial resources to the Conference of the Parties at its fifth meeting,

Noting that a number of funding institutions have increased financial support to biodiversity projects and activities or have taken this into account in their regular operations,

Also noting the lack of comprehensive information about financial support to biological diversity,

Welcoming the pilot study on aid targeting the objectives of the Rio conventions being carried out by the Development Assistance Committee of the Organisation for Economic Cooperation and Development,

1. *Requests* the Executive Secretary to further develop a database on biodiversity-related funding information, and make it available through the clearing-house mechanism and other means of communications, as appropriate;

2. *Invites* the Global Environment Facility to assist the Executive Secretary, in collaboration with the relevant international organizations and institutions, to convene a workshop on financing for biodiversity with a view to sharing knowledge and experi-

ence among funding institutions, and to explore the potential of the Global Environment Facility to act as a funding catalyst;

3. *Recognizes* the difficulties in developing a format for standardized information on financial support from developed country Parties for the objectives of the Convention and requests the workshop referred to in paragraph 2 of the present decision to provide further advice to the Executive Secretary on this matter;

4. *Urges* developed country Parties and encourages developing country Parties to establish a process to monitor financial support to biodiversity, and to provide further information in their national reports on financial support to biodiversity to the Conference of the Parties at its sixth meeting;

5. *Invites, inter alia,* funding institutions, United Nations bodies, intergovernmental organizations and non-governmental organizations to designate focal points, to develop a reporting relationship with the Convention, and to provide information to the Executive Secretary on their activities in support of the objectives of the Convention;

6. *Recognizes* that more complete information concerning the financial support, from all relevant sources, for the implementation of the objectives of the Convention, including the work programmes established by the Conference of the Parties, will assist it to develop further guidance to the financial mechanism and to better coordinate with other funding institutions;

7. *Requests* the Executive Secretary to explore further collaboration with the work on financial issues on Agenda 21 under the Commission on Sustainable Development, and to contribute to the High-Level Consultation on Financing for Development of the General Assembly in 2001;

8. *Also requests* the Executive Secretary to further develop collaboration with funding mechanisms of relevant conventions and agreements, and with relevant biodiversity-related programmes of international and regional organizations, and, as appropriate and upon request, to assist these in defining their funding strategies and programmes and in the promotion of capacity-building;

9. *Urges* developed country Parties to promote support for the implementation of the objectives of the Convention on Biological Diversity in the funding policy of their bilateral funding institutions and those of regional and multilateral funding institutions;

10. *Urges* developing country Parties to incorporate ways and means to support implementation of the objectives of the Convention on Biological Diversity into their dialogue with funding institutions;

11. *Emphasizes* the importance of financial support for the implementation of national biodiversity strategies and action plans and for capacity-building for implementation of the Cartagena Protocol;

12. *Notes* the cross-cutting nature of the involvement of the private sector, and resolves that the involvement of the private sector shall be included, as appropriate, on the agenda of the Conference of the Parties at its regular meetings and be integrated into the sectoral and thematic items under its programme of work;

13. *Notes also* that the involvement of all relevant stakeholders can contribute to the implementation of the Convention;

14. *Invites* Parties to include in their second national reports information on the involvement of the private sector;

15. *Invites* the United Nations Environment Programme, through its financial-sector initiatives, the World Bank and other financial institutions, to promote consideration of biological diversity by the financial sector;

16. *Urges* Parties, subject to their national legislation, to promote the consideration of tax exemptions in national taxation systems for biodiversity-related donations, and requests the Executive Secretary to encourage charitable institutions to support activities that promote the implementation of the Convention;

17. *Requests* the Executive Secretary to prepare a report on the implementation of the present decision for the consideration of the Conference of the Parties at its sixth meeting.

Decision V/12: Second review of the financial mechanism

The Conference of the Parties,

1. *Decides* to adopt the annex to the present decision, containing the objectives and criteria for the second review of the effectiveness of the financial mechanism to be conducted in time for the sixth meeting of the Conference of the Parties;

2. *Decides also* that this second review should be conducted under the authority of the Conference of the Parties;

3. *Decides further* that, based on the results of the review, the Conference of the Parties shall take appropriate action to improve the effectiveness of the mechanism if necessary.

Annex: Terms of reference for the second review of the effectiveness of the financial mechanism

A Objectives

1. In accordance with Article 21, paragraph 3, the Conference of the Parties will review the effectiveness of the mechanism, including the criteria and guidelines referred to in Article 21, paragraph 2, with a view to taking appropriate action to improve the effectiveness of the mechanism if necessary. For this purpose, effectiveness will include:

(a) The effectiveness of the financial mechanism and its institutional structure in providing and delivering financial resources, as well as in overseeing, monitoring and evaluating the activities financed by its resources;

(b) The conformity of the activities of the Global Environment Facility (GEF), as the institutional structure operating the financial mechanism, with the guidance of the Conference of the Parties; and

(c) The efficiency, effectiveness and sustainability of the GEF-funded activities on the implementation of the Convention and in the achievement of its three objectives.

B Methodology

2. The review will cover the activities of the financial mechanism for the period from November 1996 to June 2001, with special emphasis on those activities that have been concluded during the same period.

3. The review will cover all operational programmes of the financial mechanism relevant to the Convention on Biological Diversity.

4. The review should be carried out by an independent evaluator and shall draw upon, *inter alia*, the following sources of information:

(a) Information provided by the Parties and countries on their experiences regarding the financial mechanism;

(b) Reports prepared by the Global Environment Facility, including its reports to the Conference of the Parties, programme status reports, operational reports on GEF programmes and the GEF pipeline, reports of the GEF Monitoring and Evaluation Programme, in particular the second Overall Performance Study, operational reports on GEF programmes and the annual programme performance report;

(c) Project reviews and evaluation reports prepared by the Implementing Agencies;

(d) Information provided by other relevant stakeholders in GEF-financed biodiversity activities.

C Criteria

5. The effectiveness of the financial mechanism shall be assessed taking into account, *inter alia*:

(a) The steps and actions taken by the financial mechanism in response to the actions requested by the Conference of the Parties at its fourth meeting to improve the effectiveness of the financial mechanism, as set out in the annex to its decision IV/11;

(b) The actions taken by the financial mechanism in response to the guidance of the Conference of the Parties, as contained in decisions I/2, II/6, III/5, IV/13 and V/13;

(c) The findings and recommendations of the second Overall Performance Study of the GEF;

(d) Any other significant issue raised by the Parties.

D Procedures

6. Under the authority and with the support of the Conference of the Parties, the Executive Secretary shall contract an experienced independent evaluator to undertake the review, in accordance with the above objectives, methodology and criteria.

7. The Parties, countries and stakeholders, including relevant organizations, are invited to communicate to the Executive Secretary, by 30 September 2001, their detailed views on the effectiveness and efficiency of the financial mechanism on the basis of experience during the period under review.

8. The communications referred to above shall be structured along the lines of a questionnaire designed by the evaluator using the criteria adopted in the present terms of

reference, to be sent to the Parties as soon as practicable after the fifth meeting of the Conference of the Parties. The evaluator shall prepare a compilation and synthesis of the information received.

9. The evaluator will undertake such desk studies, interviews, field visits and collaboration with the GEF secretariat as may be required for the preparation of the study, subject to the availability of resources.

10. The compilation and synthesis of the information and recommendations for future improvements received in response to the questionnaire and the report of the evaluator shall be submitted to the Bureau for review and comments prior to their circulation.

11. The draft compilation and synthesis, and the report of the evaluator, will also be made available to GEF (the GEF secretariat and Implementing Agencies) for its review and comments. Such comments shall be included in the documentation and identified by source.

12. The Executive Secretary shall submit the documents to Parties at least three months prior to the sixth meeting of the Conference of the Parties.

Decision V/13: Further guidance to the financial mechanism

The Conference of the Parties,

Having examined the report of the Global Environment Facility (UNEP/CBD/COP/5/7),

Taking note of the note by the Executive Secretary (UNEP/CBD/COP/5/13/Add.1) with respect to previous guidance in relation to agenda items of the fifth meeting, in response to paragraph 4 of decision IV/11,

Taking note with appreciation of the efforts of the Global Environment Facility to provide additional funding for biodiversity enabling activities under expedited procedures, and urging it to continue to improve access to funding by developing country Parties and increase flexibility in its operational criteria,

1. *Welcomes* the decision of the Council of the Global Environment Facility requesting its secretariat, in consultation with the Implementing Agencies and the Secretariat of the Convention on Biological Diversity, to develop an initial strategy for assisting countries to prepare for the entry into force of the Cartagena Protocol on Biosafety;

2. *Decides* to provide the following additional guidance to the Global Environment Facility in the provision of financial resources, in conformity with decisions I/1, II/6, III/5 and IV/13 of the Conference of the Parties. In this regard, the Global Environment Facility shall provide financial resources to developing country Parties for country-driven activities and programmes, consistent with national priorities and objectives, recognizing that economic and social development and poverty eradication are the first and overriding priorities of developing countries. The Global Environment Facility, as the institutional structure operating the financial mechanism, should provide support:

(a) For projects utilizing the ecosystem approach, without prejudice to differing national needs and priorities which may require the application of approaches such as single-species conservation programmes, in accordance with decision V/6;

(b) As a priority, for projects which:

(i) Implement the Convention's programme of work on agricultural biodiversity, in accordance with decision V/5, through the timely finalization and implementation of its operational programme on agricultural biodiversity, and through the development and implementation of other relevant operational programmes;

(ii) Implement the Convention's programme of work on biodiversity of dry and sub-humid lands, in accordance with decision V/23, through the development, review and implementation of its operational programmes, in particular, the operational programme on arid and semi-arid ecosystems;

(iii) Assist in the implementation of the programme of work on forest biodiversity at the national, subregional and regional levels, and consider the operational objectives of the aforementioned programme of work as guidance for funding, in accordance with decision V/4;

(c) For projects which assist with the development and implementation of the International Initiative for the Conservation and Sustainable Use of Pollinators in Agriculture, in accordance with decision V/5;

(d) For capacity-building at the national, subregional and regional level to address the issue of coral bleaching within the context of implementation of the programme of work on marine and coastal biological diversity, in accordance with decision V/3;

(e) For the consultative processes referred to in paragraph 6 of decision V/19, which are aimed at assisting with the preparation of second national reports, taking into account the fact that the Conference of the Parties may develop guidelines for subsequent national reports;

(f) For participation in the clearing-house mechanism of the Convention, in accordance with decision V/14;

(g) For projects that will address the issue of access and benefit-sharing, in accordance with decision V/26;

(h) For projects that incorporate incentive measures that promote the development and implementation of social, economic and legal incentive measures for the conservation and sustainable use of biological diversity, in accordance with decision V/15;

(i) For the implementation of the priority activities identified in the programme of work on Article 8 (j) and related provisions, in accordance with decision V/16;

(j) To strengthen capabilities to develop monitoring programmes and suitable indicators for biological diversity, in accordance with decision V/7;

(k) To continue promoting awareness of the Global Taxonomy Initiative in the relevant activities of the Global Environment Facility, such as the Country Dialogue Workshops, and to facilitate capacity-building in taxonomy, including in its Capacity Development Initiative;

(l) For capacity development for education, public awareness and communication in biological diversity at the national and regional levels, in accordance with decision V/17;

(m) For activities to implement the Global Invasive Species Programme, in accordance with decision V/8;

(n) For the implementation of capacity-building measures for developing and implementing national and sectoral plans for the conservation and sustainable use of inland water ecosystems, including comprehensive assessments of the biological diversity of inland waters, and capacity-building programmes for monitoring the implementation of the programme of work and the trends in inland water biological diversity and for information gathering and dissemination among riparian communities.

Decision V/14: Scientific and technical cooperation and the clearing-house mechanism (Article 18)

The Conference of the Parties,

Reaffirming its previous requests to the Global Environment Facility, contained in decisions I/2, II/3, II/6, III/4, III/5, IV/2 and IV/13, to provide support for scientific and technical cooperation and capacity-building in relation to the clearing-house mechanism,

Recalling decision III/4, in which the Conference of the Parties established an informal advisory committee to be constituted and coordinated by the Executive Secretary in a transparent manner, to assist the clearing-house mechanism, and decision IV/2, in which the Conference of the Parties requested that the clearing-house mechanism be continuously assisted in its functioning by the informal advisory committee during and after the pilot phase,

1. *Notes* the report of the independent review of the pilot phase of the clearing-house mechanism (UNEP/CBD/COP/5/INF/2);

2. *Supports* the implementation of the strategic plan for the clearing-house mechanism (UNEP/CBD/COP/5/INF/3);

3. *Requests* the Executive Secretary, in consultation with the informal advisory committee, to monitor and review the operation of the clearing-house mechanism and report to the Conference of the Parties at its sixth meeting on any recommended adjustments to the operation of the clearing-house mechanism or to the strategic plan;

4. *Decides* that the strategic plan for the clearing-house mechanism shall become a component of the Strategic Plan of the Convention on Biological Diversity;

5. *Endorses* the longer-term programme of work for the clearing-house mechanism (UNEP/CBD/COP/5/INF/4), recognizing the important role that country partnerships can play in implementing this programme of work;

6. *Recommends* that Parties and Governments, subject to availability of resources and relevance, undertake as priorities for the biennium 2001–2002 the measures identified in annex I to the present decision;

7. *Decides* that the informal advisory committee referred to in decision III/4 shall have the following objectives:

(a) Provide advice on matters relating to the clearing-house mechanism and, in particular, on how to improve the effectiveness of the clearing-house mechanism as a mechanism to promote scientific and technical cooperation;

(b) Facilitate the implementation of guidance from the Conference of the Parties concerning the clearing-house mechanism;

(c) Facilitate greater input of Parties into the development of the clearing-house mechanism;

(d) Advise on ways and means to facilitate the development of the clearing-house mechanism network;

(e) Facilitate and encourage cooperation with other relevant international and regional information networks and initiatives;

8. *Decides* that the continuation and mandate of the informal advisory committee shall be reviewed at the seventh meeting of the Conference of the Parties;

9. *Calls upon* the Executive Secretary, in consultation with the informal advisory committee, to develop operational procedures for the informal advisory committee, for review at the seventh meeting of the Conference of the Parties, and to make these procedures, as well as the membership, available through the clearing-house mechanism;

10. *Requests* the Executive Secretary, in consultation with the informal advisory committee and other relevant bodies, and subject to available resources, to undertake the activities identified in annex II to the present decision.

Annex I:
Measures to be undertaken by Parties and Governments in the biennium 2001–2002, subject to availability of resources and relevance

(a) Establish national directories of scientific institutions and experts working on specific thematic areas of the Convention on Biological Diversity and make these available through the clearing-house mechanism.

(b) Conduct surveys to establish a national baseline of existing scientific and technical cooperation initiatives relevant to the implementation of the provisions of the Convention on Biological Diversity.

(c) Establish or strengthen clearing-house mechanism national focal points.

(d) Establish, through the national clearing-house mechanism focal points, links to non-governmental organizations and other institutions holding important relevant databases or undertaking significant work on biological diversity.

(e) Establish regional or subregional clearing-house mechanism focal points.

(f) Establish national, regional and subregional clearing-house mechanism thematic focal points.

(g) Further develop the clearing-house mechanism to assist developing country Parties and Parties with economies in transition to gain access to information in the field of scientific and technical cooperation, in particular on:

(i) Funding opportunities;

(ii) Access to and transfer of technologies;

(iii) Research cooperation facilities;

(iv) Repatriation of information;

(v) Training opportunities; and

(vi) Promoting and facilitating contact with relevant institutions, organizations, and the private sector, providing such services.

(h) Consider information providers as primary partners as a way of ensuring that a critical mass of scientific and technical information is made available.

(i) Consider the general public, the private sector, non-government organizations and all levels of government as important target audiences for the clearing-house mechanism.

(j) Develop initiatives to make information available through the clearing-house mechanism more useful for researchers and decision makers.

(k) Develop, provide and share services and tools for the purposes of enhancing and facilitating the implementation of the clearing-house mechanism and further improving synergies among the biodiversity-related and the Rio conventions.

(l) Undertake an analysis of the cost-effectiveness of the implementation of the clearing-house mechanism, taking into account investments in institutional, human, financial, technological and informational resources.

Annex II: Activities to be undertaken by the Executive Secretary, in consultation with the informal advisory committee and other relevant bodies, subject to available resources

(a) Develop ways and means to ensure a broader understanding of the role of, and the value added by, the clearing-house mechanism.

(b) Further develop non-Internet-based tools and training packages to assist Parties in their national implementation efforts.

(c) Identify and establish cooperative arrangements with those international thematic focal points that can provide relevant and appropriate thematic information, using the following criteria:

(i) Expertise on themes directly relevant to the Convention on Biological Diversity;

(ii) Experience and expertise at the international level;

(iii) Endorsement of the proposed cooperative arrangements by at least three national focal points;

(iv) Designation of a specific theme and a defined period of time;

(v) Selection of one or more thematic focal points for each theme;

(vi) Ability to leverage infrastructure;

(vii) Provision of relevant content;

(viii) Experience with specific issues;

(ix) Ability to advance the objectives of the clearing-house mechanism;

(x) Ability to advance the objectives of other partners;

(xi) Provision of open access to information;

(xii) Allowance for the custodianship to remain with the provider of information, as well as the provision of metadata in the public domain.

(d) Convene regional workshops to support capacity-building for clearing-house mechanism activities, training and awareness, with a focus on cooperation in biodiversity information for the implementation and management of the clearing-house mechanism at the national, subregional, bio-geographic and regional levels, as appropriate.

(e) Develop a pilot initiative to assist work on the thematic issues within the work programme of the Subsidiary Body on Scientific, Technical and Technological Advice, including:

(i) Identification by national focal points of national institutions and experts working on the specific theme, including through interlinkages with the rosters of experts in the relevant fields of the Convention on Biological Diversity;

(ii) Provision of relevant information to the Subsidiary Body on Scientific, Technical and Technological Advice by national focal points;

(iii) Use of the clearing-house mechanism to gather input to relevant assessments being undertaken by the Subsidiary Body on Scientific, Technical and Technological Advice;

(iv) Identification of scientific and technical cooperation needs at the national level for the implementation of pilot initiatives.

(f) Propose options for improving ways and means by which the clearing-house mechanism can facilitate access to and transfer of technology.

(g) Develop a list of best practices and identify potential functions to be recommended for implementation by clearing-house mechanism national focal points.

(h) Identify possible formats, protocols and standards for the improved exchange of biodiversity-related data, information and knowledge, including national reports, biodiversity assessments and Global Biodiversity Outlook reports, and convene an informal meeting on this issue.

(i) Identify options and explore cooperative arrangements to overcome language barriers affecting the use of the clearing-house mechanism, including the development or consolidation of tools and services.

(j) Develop a publicly accessible global electronic platform for scientific and technical cooperation in biodiversity on the Internet matching the demands and needs of Parties in accordance with Article 18 of the Convention.

(k) Encourage the establishment and maintenance of mirror sites of the Convention's website, within the other United Nations regions, as appropriate, in order to improve access to Internet-based information.

Longer-term programme of work of the clearing-house mechanism

Programme of work, schedule, roles and responsibilities, 1999–2004[22]

Section strategy in plan		*Tactics Strategy*	*Time frame (for bulk of work)* 99	00	01	02	03	04 to 09	*Roles and responsibilities*	*Costs*
I Scientific and technical cooperation										
5.2.1	Track best practices, needs and priorities for collaboration	• all parties post and prioritize the information							*Secretariat/IAC:* Facilitate and promote participation, *Regions, NFPs:* Add to on-line National Reports, assist countries unable to do so themselves	*All focal points:* Staff time
		• develop vehicle for automatically collecting, synthesizing and reporting the information • feature this information on CHM website, promote to users							*Secretariat/IAC:* Development a section of its websites to automatically collect, synthesize and report the information; promote its availability to global partners *Regions, NFPs:* Promote to local users	*Secretariat:* Development of the mechanism
		• additional methods of information sharing							*Secretariat/IAC:* Facilitate the organization of global and regional workshops, users' conferences, users'	*Secretariat:* Staff time, regional workshops, various communication materials such as CD

22 The CHM programme of work is intended to accompany the 1999–2004 strategic plan. The left-hand column provides the section number corresponding to the strategic plan.

Section strategy in plan	Tactics Strategy	Time frame (for bulk of work) 99	00	01	02	03	04 to 09	Roles and responsibilities	Costs
								groups, and *best practice* challenges, coordinate with related global initiatives, coordinate the development, updating and promotion of related documentation and training resources, provide a global mechanism for sending, and send targeted e-mails with short abstracts of best practices *Regions:* Coordinate and help organize regional/ thematic workshops and users' groups, coordinate with related regional/ thematic initiatives, send targeted e-mails with short abstracts of best practices *NFPs:* Host/participate in workshops, users' conferences, users' groups, and *best practice* challenges, coordinate with related national/local initiatives	ROMs and newsletters

5.2.2	Use funding to promote country involvement, partnering and progress in priority areas	• proactively work with GEF and other funders to support priority projects (see also 5.2.1)							*IAC:* Initiate and manage partnerships with international funders (such as GEF), develop proposed funding criteria, seek reserved funding, publish and promote *call for proposals* *Secretariat:* Provide mechanisms for sharing best practices resulting from the pilots (see 5.2.1) *GEF, Regions, TFPs and NFPs:* Help in setting up financial partnerships and obtaining reserved funding. Approve funding criteria and promote calls for proposals. Carry out/help fund strategic pilot projects, evaluations and sharing of results	*Secretariat:* Staff travel costs *GEF and other funders, Regions and countries:* Project funding
5.2.3	Provide a collaboration promotion mechanism for institutions and experts, and service and technology providers	• background research and guidelines							*Secretariat/IAC:* Facilitate development of the mechanism, coordinate development of minimum requirements and/or evaluation criteria *Regions, TFPs:* Develop minimum requirements and/or evaluation criteria	*Secretariat:* Staff time

Section strategy in plan	*Tactics Strategy*	*Time frame (for bulk of work)* 99	00	01	02	03	04 to 09	*Roles and responsibilities*	*Costs*
	• pilots							*IAC:* Initiate, help reserve GEF (and other) funding for pilots, attract and coordinate pilots *Secretariat:* Build corresponding section/ capabilities on its website, promote use of the mechanism among global actors; develop an inventory of initiatives and roster of experts *Regions, NFPs:* Initiate/fund/ carry out the pilots, promote use of the mechanism among regional/thematic actors, or by national/local actors	*Secretariat:* Staff time *GEF/Region/NFP funds:* Project funding
II Information exchange									
6.2.1 Ensure compatibility through standardization	• coordinate with standards organizations, identify best standards for CHM							*Secretariat/IAC:* Coordinate with related initiatives and standards organizations	Staff time + travel
	• document best standards and make accessible							*Secretariat/IAC:* Facilitate the setting of mutually agreed upon standards *Regions, NFPs:* Contribute	Staff time

										to the development of standards	
		• update and improve tools/ documents								*Secretariat/IAC:* Coordinate the development, updating and promotion of related documentation and training resources, follow the standards *Regions, NFPs:* Help coordinate the communication of and training in these standards, within their networks, follow the standards	Staff time
		• ensure that all CBD/CHM databases are Z39.50 protocol compliant								*Secretariat/IAC:* Ensure that Secretariat databases are compliant, facilitate other focal points in doing the same *Regions, NFPs:* Ensure that their databases are compliant	*Secretariat:* Time + consulting assistance (2001, 2002)
6.2.2	Track information needs, priorities and best practices	• develop and use multiple vehicles for enabling users to articulate individual and collective information needs and priorities (see also 5.2.1)								see 5.2.1	Staff time
6.2.3	Prioritize and promote expansion	• determine information gaps								*Secretariat/IAC:* Facilitate international prioritization	*Secretariat:* Time + assessments database

Section strategy in plan		Tactics Strategy	Time frame (for bulk of work) 99	00	01	02	03	04 to 09	Roles and responsibilities	Costs
		and priorities, and ensure that these are addressed • develop and maintain an assessments database of new technologies			■	■	■	■	process. Coordinate with related initiatives *Regions, NFPs:* Support and participate, identify and articulate needs	
6.2.4	Provide open, world-wide access to existing biodiversity information	• make existing information available through CHM nodes	■	■	■	■	■	■	*Secretariat/IAC:* Facilitate world-wide access, make global information available through the SCBD node *Regions, TFPs, NFPs:* Make relevant information available through their nodes	All focal points: Staff time
III Network development and organizational efficiency										
7.2.1	Provide start-up assistance and ongoing capacity building	• develop support materials and capacity building	■	■	■	■			*Secretariat/IAC:* Develop, publish and support startup materials; facilitate the development of regional workshop sessions; provide an operational model for implementation of CHM national, regional, sub-regional and thematic	*Secretariat:* Support materials

			focal points; monitor global capacity building needs and facilitate the development of required support	
			Regions, TFPs, NFPs: Install CHMs, follow startup guidelines; identify capacity building needs and make use of support offered; share best practices	*Regions, NFPs:* Project funding (through GEF), costs to develop and maintain their focal points
		• organize a meeting of CHM NFPs once a year	*Secretariat/IAC:* Organize the meetings *NFPs:* Attend the sessions (to be scheduled in conjunction with meetings they are already attending)	*Secretariat:* Staff time, insignificant incremental expenses
		• facilitate access to funding	*IAC:* Enhance accessibility to GEF and other funders	
		• provide partnering support	*Secretariat/IAC:* Publish partnering guidelines, initiate/support partnerships *Regions, TFPs:* Help initiate/support partnerships *NFPs:* Partner cooperatively	*Secretariat:* Staff time
7.2.2	Address obstacles to growth	• focus on developing countries, identify and remove obstacles	*Secretariat/IAC:* Coordinate international efforts to identify and eliminate barriers (including Independent Reviews and User Surveys)	*Secretariat/IAC*
			IAC: Liaise with GEF	*Funds:* Independent

Section strategy in plan		*Tactics Strategy*	*Time frame (for bulk of work)* 99	00	01	02	03	04 to 09	*Roles and responsibilities*	*Costs*
									Secretariat and Implementing Agencies to 'remove' barriers to access to GEF and other funding	reviews (2004) and additional user surveys (2001)
		• do the same at regional, subregional, and national levels							*Secretariat/IAC:* Capture learning, extrapolate to regional and subregional context *IAC:* Arrange for GEF and others to fund pilots *Regions, TFPs, NFPs:* Identify national/local barriers, seek solutions, pursue fuller CHM development	*Secretariat:* Staff time
7.2.3	Continue to maintain local ownership of information	• each level to post/ make available and maintain its own information							*Secretariat/IAC:* Post UN meeting and other global information, post and maintain generic guidelines, engines and program metrics *Regions, NFPs:* Encourage local posting and maintenance of appropriate information	*Secretariat:* Staff time
7.2.4	Rely on partnerships, and focus on facilitation	• identify and integrate new partners into CHM at every level, and build							*Secretariat/IAC:* Identify and attract CHM affiliates, request regions/NFPs to do the same, provide templates/guidelines for	*Secretariat:* Staff time + travel

		relationships • document agreements								documenting agreements *Regions, NFPs:* Identify and attract CHM affiliates, interconnect them with the CHM, document agreements, post on CHM	
7.2.5	Concentrate on value-added	• identify unique strengths and competencies of focal points, flesh out roles and identify value-added								*Secretariat/IAC:* Develop and promote concept and model, document and publish *Regions, NFPs:* Identify local value-added, post on local	*Secretariat/IAC:* Study value-added of all focal points (2002)
		• grow competence and promote value-added								*Secretariat/IAC:* Actively grow own core competence, promote CHM value-added *Regions, NFPs:* Promote CHM value-added locally	*Secretariat:* Staff time
7.2.6	Promote use of the CHM	• encourage development of country CHM promotion strategies, record and share learning, and expand to CHM focal points at all levels								*Secretariat/IAC:* Develop global CHM communication strategy and focus, develop planning template, facilitate development of national CHM strategies; provide promotional information to international partners, develop templates; develop a 'plain language' brochure that describes, demonstrates and communicates the role and value of the CHM	*Secretariat:* Staff time, promotional materials

Section strategy in plan		*Tactics Strategy*	*Time frame (for bulk of work)* 99	00	01	02	03	04 to 09	*Roles and responsibilities*	*Costs*
									Regions, TFPs, NFPs: Propose/carry out/help fund national/local CHM communication plans, share learning, provide promotional information to partners; develop templates	
7.2.7	Develop funding strategies for all focal points	• encourage development of funding strategies, record and share learning, and expand to CHM focal points at all levels							*IAC:* Develop long-term global funding strategy and facilitate development of national CHM funding strategies *Secretariat:* Develop planning template, develop 'plain language' materials that describe, demonstrate and communicate the role and value of the CHM *Regions, TFPs, NFPs:* Develop national/regional/thematic funding strategies; share learning	*Secretariat:* Staff time

Legend: IAC = Informal Advisory Committee; NFP = national focal point; TFP = thematic focal point. 13 October 1999

Decision V/15: Incentive measures

The Conference of the Parties,

Acknowledging the importance of incentive measures in achieving conservation and sustainable use of the components of biodiversity,

Recognizing that biodiversity provides global services to humankind that are not captured and adequately recognized by current economic relations, patterns and policies,

1. *Establishes* a programme of work that promotes the development and implementation of social, economic and legal incentive measures for the conservation and sustainable use of biological diversity, in synergy with specific programmes of work, in order to:

(a) Support Parties, Governments and organizations in developing practical policies and projects;

(b) Develop practical guidance to the financial mechanism for effective support and prioritization of these policies and projects;

2. *Decides* that the activities of the programme of work should result in the following:

(a) The assessment of representative existing incentive measures, review of case-studies, identification of new opportunities for incentive measures, and dissemination of information, through the clearing-house mechanism and other means, as appropriate;

(b) The development of methods to promote information on biodiversity in consumer decisions, for example through ecolabelling, if appropriate;

(c) The assessment, as appropriate and applicable to the circumstances of Parties, of the values of biodiversity, in order to internalize better these values in public policy initiatives and private-sector decisions;

(d) A consideration of biodiversity concerns in liability schemes;

(e) The creation of incentives for integration of biodiversity concerns in all sectors;

3. *Requests* the Executive Secretary to collaborate with relevant organizations, such as the Food and Agriculture Organization of the United Nations, the Organisation for Economic Cooperation and Development, the United Nations Conference on Trade and Development, the United Nations Development Programme, the United Nations Environment Programme, and IUCN-The World Conservation Union, in order to engage in a coordinated effort, and undertake through such an effort, as a first phase:

(a) To gather and disseminate additional information on instruments in support of positive incentives and their performance, and to develop a matrix identifying the range of instruments available, their purpose, interaction with other policy measures and effectiveness, with a view to identifying and designing relevant instruments, where appropriate, in support of positive measures;

(b) To continue gathering information on perverse incentive measures, and on ways and means to remove or mitigate their negative impacts on biological diversity, through case-studies and lessons learned, and consider how these ways and means may be applied;

(c) To elaborate proposals for the design and implementation of incentive measures, for consideration by the Subsidiary Body on Scientific, Technical and Technological Advice at its sixth or seventh meeting and by the Conference of the Parties at its sixth meeting;

4. *Decides* to integrate actions on incentives in thematic work programmes and ensure synergy with activities on sustainable use, noting that incentive measures are essential elements in developing effective approaches to conservation and sustainable use of biological diversity especially at the level of local communities;

5. *Requests* the Executive Secretary to promote coordinated action on incentives with other international biodiversity-related agreements and relevant organizations, noting specifically that the joint work plan of the Convention on Biological Diversity and the Convention on Wetlands for the period 2000–2001 (UNEP/CBD/SBSTTA/5/INF/12) includes consideration of incentive measures;

6. *Urges* Parties and other Governments to explore possible ways and means by which incentive measures promoted through the Kyoto Protocol under the United Nations Framework Convention on Climate Change can support the objectives of the Convention on Biological Diversity.

Decision V/16: Article 8 (j) and related provisions

The Conference of Parties,

Recalling its decision IV/9,

Recognizing the need to respect, preserve and maintain knowledge, innovations and practices of indigenous and local communities embodying traditional lifestyles relevant for the conservation and sustainable use of biological diversity and promote their wider application,

Noting the need for a long-term approach to the programme of work on implementation of Article 8 (j) and related provisions of the Convention on Biological Diversity, within a vision to be elaborated progressively, in line with the overall objectives set out in Article 8 (j) and related provisions,

Emphasizing the fundamental importance of ensuring the full and effective participation of indigenous and local communities in the implementation of Article 8 (j) and related provisions,

Noting the importance of integrating with the full and effective participation of indigenous and local communities the work on Article 8 (j) and related provisions into national, regional and international strategies, polices and action plans,

Recognizing the vital role that women play in the conservation and sustainable use of biodiversity, and emphasizing that greater attention should be given to strengthening this role and the participation of women of indigenous and local communities in the programme of work,

Further noting the linguistic and cultural diversity among indigenous and local communities as well as differences in their capacities,

Noting existing declarations by indigenous and local communities to the extent they relate to the conservation and sustainable use of biodiversity, including, *inter alia*, the Kari Oca Declaration, the Mataatua Declaration, the Santa Cruz Declaration, the Leticia Declaration and Plan of Action, the Treaty for Life Forms Patent Free Pacific, the Ukupseni Kuna Yala Declaration, the Heart of the Peoples Declaration on Biodiversity and Biological Ethics, the Jovel Declaration on Indigenous Communities, Indigenous Knowledge and Biodiversity, the Chiapas Declaration, other relevant declarations and statements of Indigenous Forums, as well as Convention 169 of the International Labour Organization, Agenda 21 and other relevant international conventions,

Recognizing the role that the International Indigenous Forum on Biodiversity has played since the third meeting of the Conference of the Parties in addressing the Conference of the Parties on the implementation of Article 8 (j) and related provisions,

Reaffirming the importance of making Article 8 (j) and related provisions of the Convention and provisions of international agreements related to intellectual property rights mutually supportive,

Further noting that there are existing international agreements, intellectual property rights, current laws and policies that may have influence on the implementation of Article 8 (j) and its related provisions,

Noting also that the methods of implementation of Article 8 (j) and related provisions differ among regions and countries in approach and capacity,

1. *Endorses* the programme of work as contained in the annex to the present decision, which shall be subject to periodic review during its implementation;

2 *Decides* to implement the programme of work giving priority to tasks 1, 2, 4, 5, 8, 9 and 11, as well as 7 and 12, which shall be initiated following completion of tasks 5, 9 and 11;

3. *Urges* Parties and Governments in collaboration with relevant organizations, subject to their national legislation, to promote and implement this programme of work, and to integrate the tasks identified into their ongoing programmes as appropriate to national circumstances, taking into account the identified collaboration opportunities;

4. *Requests* Parties, Governments and relevant organizations to take full account of existing instruments, guidelines, codes and other relevant activities in the implementation of the programme of work;

5. *Encourages* the participation of indigenous and local communities in the work of the Ad Hoc Open-ended Working Group on Access and Benefit-sharing on the development of guidelines and other approaches to ensure the respect, preservation and maintenance of knowledge, innovations and practices of indigenous and local communities embodying traditional lifestyles relevant for the conservation and sustainable use of biological diversity;

6. *Takes* into account the importance of the proposals for action on traditional forest-related knowledge of the Intergovernmental Panel on Forests/Intergovernmental Forum on Forests as an important part of this programme of work;

7. *Requests* Parties, Governments, and international, regional and national organizations to provide appropriate financial support for the implementation of the programme of work;

8. *Requests* the Executive Secretary to facilitate the integration of the relevant tasks of the programme of work in the future elaboration of the thematic programmes of the Convention on Biological Diversity and provide a report on the progress of the thematic programmes to the Ad Hoc Open-ended Inter-Sessional Working Group on Article 8 (j) and Related Provisions of the Convention on Biological Diversity;

9. *Decides* to extend the mandate of the Ad Hoc Open-ended Inter-Sessional Working Group on Article 8 (j) and Related Provisions of the Convention on Biological Diversity to review progress in the implementation of the priority tasks of its programme of work according to reports provided by the Executive Secretary, and the Parties to the meeting of the Working Group and recommend further action on the basis of this review. The Working Group should further explore ways for increased participation by indigenous and local communities in the thematic programmes of work of the Convention on Biological Diversity. The Working Group should report to the Conference of the Parties at its sixth meeting;

10. *Requests* Parties, Governments, subsidiary bodies of the Convention, the Executive Secretary and relevant organizations, including indigenous and local communities, when implementing the programme of work contained in the annex to the present decision and other relevant activities under the Convention, to fully incorporate women and women's organizations in the activities;

11. *Invites* Parties and Governments to support the participation of the International Indigenous Forum on Biodiversity, as well as relevant organizations representing indigenous and local communities, in advising the Conference of the Parties on the implementation of Article 8 (j) and related provisions;

12. *Urges* Parties and Governments and, as appropriate, international organizations, and organizations representing indigenous and local communities, to facilitate the full and effective participation of indigenous and local communities in the implementation of the Convention and, to this end:

(a) Provide opportunities for indigenous and local communities to identify their capacity needs, with the assistance of Governments and others, if they so require;

(b) Include, in proposals and plans for projects carried out in indigenous and local communities, funding requirements to build the communications capacity of indigenous and local communities to facilitate dissemination and exchange of information on issues related to traditional knowledge, innovations and practices;

(c) Provide for sufficient capacity in national institutions to respond to the needs of indigenous and local communities related to Article 8 (j) and related provisions;

(d) Strengthen and build capacity for communication among indigenous and local communities, and between indigenous and local communities and Governments, at local, national, regional and international levels, including with the Secretariat of the Convention on Biological Diversity, with direct participation and responsibility of indigenous and local communities through their appropriate focal points;

(e) Use other means of communication in addition to the Internet, such as newspapers, bulletins, and radio, and increasing the use of local languages;

(f) Provide case-studies on methods and approaches that contribute to the preservation of traditional knowledge, innovations and practices, including through their recording where appropriate, and that support control and decision-making by indigenous and local communities over the sharing of such knowledge, innovation and practices;

13. *Emphasizes once again* the need for case-studies developed in conjunction with indigenous and local communities requested in paragraphs 10 (b) and 15 of its decision IV/9, to enable a meaningful assessment of the effectiveness of existing legal and other appropriate forms of protection for the knowledge, innovations and practices of indigenous and local communities;

14. *Recognizes* the potential importance of *sui generis* and other appropriate systems for the protection of traditional knowledge of indigenous and local communities and the equitable sharing of benefits arising from its use to meet the provisions of the Convention on Biological Diversity, taking into account the ongoing work on Article 8 (j) and related provisions, and *transmits* its findings to the World Trade Organization and the World Intellectual Property Organization, as suggested in paragraph 6 (b) of recommendation 3 of the Inter-Sessional Meeting on the Operations of the Convention (UNEP/CBD/COP/5/4, annex);

15. *Invites* Parties and Governments to exchange information and share experiences regarding national legislation and other measures for the protection of the knowledge, innovations and practices of indigenous and local communities;

16. *Recognizes* that the maintenance of knowledge, innovations, and practices of indigenous and local communities is dependent on the maintenance of cultural identities and the material base that sustains them and *invites* Parties and Governments to take measures to promote the conservation and maintenance of such identities;

17. *Requests* Parties to support the development of registers of traditional knowledge, innovations and practices of indigenous and local communities embodying traditional lifestyles relevant for the conservation and sustainable use of biological diversity through participatory programmes and consultations with indigenous and local communities, taking into account strengthening legislation, customary practices and traditional systems of resource management, such as the protection of traditional knowledge against unauthorized use;

18. *Invites* Parties and Governments to increase the participation of representatives of indigenous and local community organizations in official delegations to meetings held under the Convention on Biological Diversity;

19. *Emphasizes* the need for arrangements controlled and determined by indigenous and local communities, to facilitate cooperation and information exchange among indigenous and local communities, for the purposes of, *inter alia*, helping to ensure that such communities are in a position to make informed decisions on whether or not to consent to the release of their knowledge, and, in this respect:

(a) *Requests* the Executive Secretary to fully utilize the clearing-house mechanism, to cooperate closely with indigenous and local communities to explore ways in which such needs may best be addressed;

(b) *Invites* Parties to consider ways and means of providing the necessary resources to enable the Secretariat to undertake the above-mentioned tasks;

20. *Further requests* Parties and international financial institutions to explore ways of providing the necessary funding for these activities.

Annex:
Programme of work on the implementation of Article 8 (j) and related provisions of the Convention on Biological Diveristy

Objectives

The objective of this programme of work is to promote within the framework of the Convention a just implementation of Article 8 (j) and related provisions, at local, national, regional and international levels and to ensure the full and effective participation of indigenous and local communities at all stages and levels of its implementation.

I General principles

1. Full and effective participation of indigenous and local communities in all stages of the identification and implementation of the elements of the programme of work. Full and effective participation of women of indigenous and local communities in all activities of the programme of work.

2. Traditional knowledge should be valued, given the same respect and considered as useful and necessary as other forms of knowledge.

3. A holistic approach consistent with the spiritual and cultural values and customary practices of the indigenous and local communities and their rights to have control over their traditional knowledge, innovations and practices.

4. The ecosystem approach is a strategy for the integrated management of land, water and living resources that promotes conservation and sustainable use of biological diversity in an equitable way.

5. Access to traditional knowledge, innovations and practices of indigenous and local communities should be subject to prior informed consent or prior informed approval from the holders of such knowledge, innovations and practices.

II Tasks of the first phase of the programme of work

Element 1. Participatory mechanisms for indigenous and local communities

Task 1. Parties to take measures to enhance and strengthen the capacity of indigenous and local communities to be effectively involved in decision-making related to the use of their traditional knowledge, innovations and practices relevant to the conservation and sustainable use of biological diversity subject to their prior informed approval and effective involvement.

Task 2. Parties to develop appropriate mechanisms, guidelines, legislation or other initiatives to foster and promote the effective participation of indigenous and local communities in decision-making, policy planning and development and implementation of the conservation and sustainable use of biological diversity at international, regional, subregional, national and local levels, including access and benefit-sharing and the designation and management of protected areas, taking into account the ecosystem approach.

Task 4. Parties to develop, as appropriate, mechanisms for promoting the full and effective participation of indigenous and local communities with specific provisions for the full, active and effective participation of women in all elements of the programme of work, taking into account the need to:

(a) Build on the basis of their knowledge,

(b) Strengthen their access to biological diversity;

(c) Strengthen their capacity on matters pertaining to the conservation, maintenance and protection of biological diversity;

(d) Promote the exchange of experiences and knowledge;

(e) Promote culturally appropriate and gender specific ways in which to document and preserve women's knowledge of biological diversity

Element 2. Status and trends in relation to Article 8 (j) and related provisions

Task 5. The Executive Secretary to prepare, for the next meeting of the Ad Hoc Working Group, an outline of a composite report on the status and trends regarding the knowledge, innovations and practices of indigenous and local communities, a plan and a timetable for its preparation, based, *inter alia*, on advice submitted by Parties, Governments, indigenous and local communities and other relevant organizations regarding sources and availability of information on these matters. Parties, Governments and indigenous and local communities and other relevant organizations to submit the information and advice to address the requirements of this task and Parties to include in their national reports the current state of implementation of Article 8 (j).

Element 4. Equitable sharing of benefits

Task 7. Based on tasks 1, 2 and 4, the Working Group to develop guidelines for the development of mechanisms, legislation or other appropriate initiatives to ensure: (i) that indigenous and local communities obtain a fair and equitable share of benefits arising from the use and application of their knowledge, innovations and practices; (ii) that private and public institutions interested in using such knowledge, practices and innovations obtain the prior informed approval of the indigenous and local communities; (iii) advancement of the identification of the obligations of countries of origin, as well as Parties and Governments where such knowledge, innovations and practices and the associated genetic resources are used.

Element 5. Exchange and dissemination of information

Task 8. Identification of a focal point within the clearing-house mechanism to liaise with indigenous and local communities.

Element 6. Monitoring elements

Task 9. The Working Group to develop, in cooperation with indigenous and local communities, guidelines or recommendations for the conduct of cultural, environmental and social impact assessments regarding any development proposed to take place on sacred sites and on lands or waters occupied or used by indigenous and local communities. The guidelines and recommendations should ensure the participation of indigenous and local communities in the assessment and review.

Element 7. Legal elements

Task 11. The Working Group to assess existing subnational, as appropriate, national and international instruments, particularly intellectual property rights instruments, that may have implications on the protection of the knowledge, innovations and practices of indigenous and local communities with a view to identifying synergies between these instruments and the objectives of Article 8 (j).

Task 12. The Working Group to develop guidelines that will assist Parties and Governments in the development of legislation or other mechanisms, as appropriate, to implement Article 8 (j) and its related provisions (which could include *sui generis* systems), and definitions of relevant key terms and concepts in Article 8 (j) and related provisions at international, regional and national levels, that recognize, safeguard and fully guarantee the rights of indigenous and local communities over their traditional knowledge, innovations and practices, within the context of the Convention.

III Tasks of the second phase of the programme of work

Element 1. Participatory mechanisms for indigenous and local communities

Task 3. On the request of the Executive Secretary, Parties and Governments, with the full participation of indigenous and local communities, would establish a roster of experts based on the methodologies used by the Conference of Parties, to allow the experts to support the implementation of this programme of work.

Element 3. Traditional cultural practices for conservation and sustainable use

Task 6. The Ad Hoc Working Group to develop guidelines for the respect, preservation and maintenance of traditional knowledge, innovations and practices and their wider application in accordance with Article 8 (j).

Task 13. The Ad Hoc Working Group to develop a set of guiding principles and standards to strengthen the use of traditional knowledge and other forms of knowledge for the conservation and sustainable use of biological diversity, taking into account the role that traditional knowledge can play with respect to the ecosystem approach, *in situ* conservation, taxonomy, biodiversity monitoring and environmental impact assessments in all biodiversity sectors.

Task 14. The Ad Hoc Working Group to develop guidelines and proposals for the establishment of national incentive schemes for indigenous and local communities to preserve and maintain their traditional knowledge, innovations and practices and for the application of such knowledge, innovations and practices in national strategies and programmes for the conservation and sustainable use of biological diversity.

Task 15. The Ad Hoc Working Group to develop guidelines that would facilitate repatriation of information, including cultural property, in accordance with Article 17, paragraph 2, of the Convention on Biological Diversity in order to facilitate the recovery of traditional knowledge of biological diversity.

Element 5. Exchange and dissemination of information

Task 16. The Executive Secretary to identify, compile and analyse, with the participation of indigenous and local communities, existing and customary codes of ethical conduct to guide the development of models for codes of ethical conduct for research, access to, use, exchange and management of information concerning traditional knowledge, innovations and practices for the conservation and sustainable use of biological diversity.

Element 6. Monitoring elements

Task 10. The Ad Hoc Working Group to develop standards and guidelines for the reporting and prevention of unlawful appropriation of traditional knowledge and related genetic resources.

Task 17. The Executive Secretary to develop, in cooperation with Governments and indigenous and local communities, methods and criteria to assist in assessing the implementation of Article 8 (j) and related provisions at the international, regional, national and local levels, and reporting of such in national reports in conformity with Article 26.

IV Ways and means

In developing and implementing the programme of work, the Executive Secretary shall solicit information from Parties, Governments, indigenous and local communities and other relevant organizations, and consult with the liaison group on Article 8 (j) and related provisions.

The Executive Secretary to develop, in consultation with indigenous and local communities, Parties, Governments, and relevant international organizations, a questionnaire, as a basis for the provision of information concerning: (i) existing instruments and activities relevant to the tasks of the programme of work; (ii) gaps and needs concerning the guidelines referred to in task 6 above; and (iii) priorities for the further development of the programme of work.

The Executive Secretary to consult with and invite relevant international organizations to contribute to the implementation of this programme of work, also with a view to avoiding duplication and to encouraging synergies.

This programme of work shall, as relevant, take into account the work of the Ad Hoc Open-ended Working Group on Access and Benefit-sharing, and, as far as possible, be carried out in collaboration with other relevant organizations, including the World Intellectual Property Organization (WIPO).

Parties, Governments, and international, regional and national organizations to provide appropriate financial support for the implementation of the programme of work.

Decision V/17: Education and public awareness

The Conference of the Parties,

1. *Takes note* of the information provided by the Executive Secretary with regard to education and public awareness (UNEP/CBD/COP/5/13, section IV);

2. *Requests* the Executive Secretary, in cooperation with the United Nations Educational, Cultural and Scientific Organization, to convene a consultative working group of experts, including the United Nations Environment Programme, the World

Bank, the United Nations Institute for Training and Research, the Commission for Education and Communication of IUCN, the World-Wide Fund for Nature, representatives of Parties and other relevant bodies to further advance and, in particular, to identify priority activities for the proposed global initiative on biological diversity education and public awareness;

3. *Decides* that the working group should take into account priorities developed by the Conference of the Parties for its work programme, and, when approved by the Conference of the Parties, priorities identified in the strategic plan for the Convention;

4. *Invites* the United Nations Educational, Scientific and Cultural Organization, through its education programmes, to actively integrate biological diversity into all levels of formal education systems as a component of the development of the global initiative;

5. *Endorses* paragraph 7 of recommendation IV/1 A of the Subsidiary Body on Scientific, Technical and Technological Advice, which states that education and public awareness be included in the discussions on the work programmes on thematic issues;

6. *Invites* Parties, Governments, organizations and institutions to support capacity-building for education and communication in biological diversity as part of their national biodiversity strategies and action plans, taking into account the global initiative;

7. *Requests* the Executive Secretary to:

(a) Further develop the public information and outreach activities of the Secretariat, including through the use of the clearing-house mechanism to raise awareness of biological diversity issues amongst all sectors of society, including indigenous and local communities;

(b) Designate a theme each year for the International Day for Biological Diversity and prepare background information to be placed on the clearing-house mechanism;

(c) Consult the United Nations Secretariat on the feasibility of changing the designated date of the International Day for Biological Diversity to 22 May and provide advice on this matter to the Parties by February 2001;

(d) Report on progress achieved in developing the global initiative to the Conference of the Parties at its sixth meeting.

Decision V/18: Impact assessment, liability and redress

The Conference of the Parties,

I Impact assessment

1. *Invites* Parties, Governments and other relevant organizations:

(a) To implement paragraph 1 of Article 14 of the Convention on Biological

Diversity in conjunction with other components of the Convention and to integrate environmental impact assessment into the work programmes on thematic areas, including the biological diversity of inland water ecosystems, marine and coastal biological diversity, forest biological diversity, agricultural biological diversity, and the biological diversity of dry and sub-humid lands, and on alien species and tourism;

(b) To address loss of biological diversity and the interrelated socio-economic, cultural and human-health aspects relevant to biological diversity when carrying out environmental impact assessments;

(c) To consider biological diversity concerns from the early stages of the drafting process, when developing new legislative and regulatory frameworks;

(d) To ensure the involvement of interested and affected stakeholders in a participatory approach to all stages of the assessment process, including governmental bodies, the private sector, research and scientific institutions, indigenous and local communities and non-governmental organizations, including by using appropriate mechanisms, such as the establishment of committees, at the appropriate level;

(e) To organize expert meetings, workshops and seminars, as well as training, educational and public awareness programmes and exchange programmes, and carry out pilot environmental impact assessment projects, in order to promote the development of local expertise in methodologies, techniques and procedures;

2. *Encourages* Parties, Governments and relevant organizations:

(a) To use strategic environmental assessments to assess not only the impact of individual projects, but also their cumulative and global effects, incorporating biological diversity considerations at the decision-making and/or environmental planning level;

(b) To include the development of alternatives, mitigation measures and consideration of the elaboration of compensation measures in environmental impact assessment;

3. *Requests* Parties to include in their national reports information on practices, systems, mechanisms and experiences in the area of strategic environmental assessment and impact assessment;

4. *Requests* the Subsidiary Body on Scientific, Technical and Technological Advice to further develop guidelines for incorporating biodiversity-related issues into legislation and/or processes on strategic environmental assessment impact assessment, in collaboration with the scientific community, the private sector, indigenous and local communities, non-governmental organizations and relevant organizations at the international, regional, subregional and national levels, such as the Scientific and Technical Review Panel of the Convention on Wetlands, the Scientific Council of the Convention on Migratory Species, DIVERSITAS, IUCN-The World Conservation Union, the International Association for Impact Assessment and the United Nations Environment Programme, as well as the Parties, and further elaborate the application of the precautionary approach and the ecosystem approach, taking into account needs for capacity-building, with a view to completion by the sixth meeting of the Conference of the Parties;

5. *Also requests* the Executive Secretary:

(a) To disseminate case-studies received;

(b) To renew the call for further case-studies, including case-studies on negative impacts and, in particular, on impact assessments that take the ecosystem approach into account;

(c) To compile and evaluate existing guidelines, procedures and provisions for environmental impact assessment;

(d) To make this information available, together with information on existing guidelines on incorporating biological diversity considerations into environmental impact assessment, through, *inter alia*, the clearing-house mechanism in order to facilitate sharing of information and exchange of experiences at the regional, national and local levels;

II Liability and redress

6. *Renews the invitation* to Parties, Governments, and relevant international organizations, contained in its decision IV/10 C, paragraph 8, to provide the Executive Secretary with information on national, international and regional measures and agreements on liability and redress applicable to damage to biological diversity, acknowledging that some Parties, Governments and organizations have already provided the Executive Secretary with such information;

7. *Requests* the Executive Secretary to update the synthesis report submitted to the fifth meeting of the Conference of the Parties (UNEP/CBD/COP/5/16) to include information contained in further submissions by Parties, Governments and relevant international organizations, taking into account other relevant information including, in particular, information on the work of the International Law Commission and on the development and application of liability regimes under other multilateral instruments, including the Antarctic Treaty, the Basel Convention on the Control of Transboundary Movements of Hazardous Wastes and Their Disposal, and the Cartagena Protocol on Biosafety, for the consideration of the Conference of the Parties at its sixth meeting;

8. *Welcomes* the offer of the Government of France to organize a workshop on liability and redress in the context of the Convention on Biological Diversity;

9. *Decides* to consider at its sixth meeting a process for reviewing paragraph 2 of Article 14, including the establishment of an ad hoc technical expert group, taking into account consideration of these issues within the framework of the Cartagena Protocol on Biosafety, and the outcome of the workshop referred to in paragraph 8 of the present decision.

Decision V/19: National reporting

The Conference of the Parties,

1. *Takes note* of recommendation V/13 of the Subsidiary Body for Scientific, Technical and Technological Advice on guidelines for national reports;

2. *Endorses* the format contained in annex I of the note by the Executive Secretary on national reporting (UNEP/CBD/COP/5/13/Add.2) as the recommended format for future national reports to be submitted by Parties in accordance with Article 26 of the Convention;

3. *Requests* the Executive Secretary to further develop this format to incorporate the views expressed by Parties and further questions arising from the decisions of its fifth meeting and to make the revised format available to Parties by September 2000;

4. *Is of the view* that national reports developed in this format will help Parties to measure the state of national implementation of the Convention and to review national priorities and actions;

5. *Requests* Parties to submit their next national report:

(a) By 15 May 2001;

(b) In an official language of the Conference of the Parties;

(c) In both hard copy and electronic format; and thereafter for consideration at alternate ordinary meetings of the Conference of the Parties, and include them in their clearing-house mechanism national focal point where feasible;

6. *Recommends* that Parties prepare their national reports through a consultative process involving all relevant stakeholders, as appropriate, or by drawing upon information developed through other consultative processes;

7. *Also invites* Parties to prepare detailed thematic reports on one or more of the items for in-depth consideration at its ordinary meetings, thereby providing national contributions to the work of the Conference of Parties and its subsidiary bodies;

8. Accordingly, *invites* Parties to submit to the Executive Secretary, reports on forest ecosystems, alien species and benefit-sharing for consideration at its sixth meeting:

(a) In accordance with the formats contained, respectively, in annexes II, III and IV of the note by the Executive Secretary on national reporting;

(b) By, respectively, 15 May 2001, 30 September 2000, and 30 December 2000;

(c) In an official language of the Conference of the Parties;

(d) In both hard copy and electronic format;

9. *Requests* the Executive Secretary to:

(a) Prepare reports based on information contained in national reports for consideration by the Conference of the Parties at its meetings, and make them available through the clearing-house mechanism;

(b) Keep the format of national reports under review, and provide further advice to the Conference of Parties on its revision;

(c) Proceed with the further development and implementation of the proposals for streamlining national reporting contained in section 5.2 of the 'Feasibility study for a harmonized information management infrastructure for biodiversity-related treaties', in collaboration with the secretariats of the other biodiversity-related conventions, with a view to simplifying reporting procedures and reducing the burden of reporting on Parties, and report on progress to the Conference of the Parties at its sixth meeting;

10. *Invites* organizations, such as the United Nations Development Programme and the United Nations Environment Programme, undertaking regional or global programmes providing support to Parties in biodiversity planning, including capacity development, to provide the Executive Secretary with information on programme activities and lessons learned.

Decision V/20: Operations of the Convention

The Conference of the Parties,

I The Conference of the Parties

1. *Decides* to amend rule 4 of its rules of procedure by replacing paragraph 1 with the following paragraph:

> '1. Ordinary meetings of the Conference of the Parties shall be held every two years. The Conference of the Parties shall from time to time review the periodicity of its ordinary meetings in the light of the progress achieved in the implementation of the Convention.'

2. *Decides* that its provisional agenda should include the following standing items:

(a) Organizational matters;

(b) Reports from subsidiary bodies, the financial mechanism and the Executive Secretary;

(c) Review of the implementation of the programme of work;

(d) Priority issues for review and guidance; and

(e) Other matters;

3. *Decides* that, to the extent possible, its decisions should identify expected outcomes, activities to achieve those outcomes, those to whom the decisions are directed and timetables for action and follow-up;

4. *Decides* to review its previous decisions periodically in order to assess their status of implementation;

5. *Decides* to amend its rules of procedure:

(a) By replacing the first two sentences of paragraph 1 of rule 21 with the following sentences:

> 'At the commencement of the first session of each ordinary meeting a President and ten Vice-Presidents, one of whom shall act as Rapporteur, are to be elected from among the representatives of the Parties. They shall serve as the bureau of the Conference of the Parties. The term of office of the President shall commence straight away and the terms of office of the Vice-Presidents shall commence upon the closure of the meeting at which they are elected.'; and

(b) By replacing the first two sentences of paragraph 2 of rule 21 with the following sentences:

> 'The President shall remain in office until a new President is elected at the commencement of the next ordinary meeting and the Vice-Presidents shall remain in office until the closure of the next ordinary meeting. They shall serve as the bureau of any extraordinary meeting held during their term of office and provide guidance to the Secretariat with regard to preparations for, and conduct of, meetings of the Conference of the Parties.'; and

(c) By replacing the words 'a President for the meeting' in rule 25 with 'a new President';

6. *Decides* to review the effectiveness of the changes referred to in paragraph 5 of the present decision, in the light of experience, at its seventh meeting;

7. *Decides* to revise its procedures for decision-making regarding administrative and financial matters with a view to ensuring:

(a) Transparency;

(b) Participation; and

(c) Full consideration of its other decisions;

8. *Decides* that guidance to the financial mechanism should be incorporated into a single decision, including the identification of priority issues which will provide support for cross-cutting issues and capacity-building, especially for developing countries, in a manner that:

(a) Is transparent;

(b) Allows participation; and

(c) Allows full consideration of its other decisions;

9. *Requests* the Executive Secretary to limit the number of pre-session documents for any of its meetings, to keep them as short as feasible, if possible less than 15 pages, and to include an executive summary in each;

II Strategic Plan for the Convention

10. *Decides* to prepare and develop a Strategic Plan for the Convention, with a view to considering and adopting the Strategic Plan at its sixth meeting;

11. *Decides* that the Strategic Plan shall be based on the longer-term programmes of work of the Conference of the Parties and of the Subsidiary Body on Scientific, Technical and Technological Advice, and that the Strategic Plan shall provide strategic and operational guidance for the implementation of these programmes of work;

12. *Decides* that the Strategic Plan will initially cover the period 2002–2010;

13. *Decides* that the Strategic Plan shall contain a set of operational goals that the Conference of the Parties has decided that it wishes to be achieved in the period covered by the Strategic Plan, and that these operational goals shall relate to the following three main areas of work:

(a) The thematic programmes;

(b) Cross-cutting issues and initiatives; and

(c) The implementation of the provisions of the Convention;

14. *Decides* that these operational goals shall reflect levels of elaboration, progress of development, stages of implementation, state of knowledge and capacities, and degrees of cooperation, with respect to the three main areas of work;

15. *Decides* that within each of these goals, the Strategic Plan shall identify, as far as possible, the following parameters:

(a) Planned activities;

(b) The expected products;

(c) The timing of each of these activities and products;

(d) The actors carrying out these activities and cooperation with relevant organizations;

(e) The mechanisms used to realize and/or support the goals and activities, or to generate the expected products; and

(f) Financial, human-resource and other capacity requirements;

16. *Requests* the Executive Secretary to develop the Strategic Plan, in accordance with the above parameters, and including options where appropriate, and to engage in a participatory process that ensures:

(a) Incorporation of the views of Parties and the Bureau of the Conference of the Parties;

(b) Consideration by the Subsidiary Body on Scientific, Technical and Technological Advice and its Bureau, and other relevant subsidiary bodies of the Convention on matters relevant to their mandates; and

(c) Input from other interested countries and organizations; with a view to preparing a full draft Strategic Plan in time for consideration and adoption by the Conference of the Parties at its sixth meeting;

III Operations of the Subsidiary Body on Scientific, Technical and Technological Advice

17. *Decides* that meetings of the Subsidiary Body on Scientific Technical and Technological Advice should take place every year;

18. *Decides* that the Chair of the Subsidiary Body on Scientific, Technical and Technological Advice or other members of the Bureau authorized by him or her may represent the Subsidiary Body at meetings of the scientific bodies of other conventions and relevant biological-diversity-related conventions, institutions and processes;

19. *Encourages* the Bureau of the Subsidiary Body on Scientific, Technical and Technological Advice to hold meetings with equivalent bodies of other relevant biological-diversity-related conventions, institutions and processes;

20. *Recognizes* that in certain cases it will be appropriate for the Subsidiary Body on Scientific, Technical and Technological Advice to make recommendations that include options or alternatives;

21. *Decides* that the Subsidiary Body on Scientific, Technical and Technological Advice may establish ad hoc technical expert groups and adopt terms of reference for them, and shall seek ways to ensure transparency in the choice of experts and the rationalization of meetings, and decides to give effect to this by amending paragraph 12 (c) of the *modus operandi* of the Subsidiary Body (decision IV/16, annex I) to read:

'(c) Within the available budgetary resources, the Subsidiary Body on Scientific, Technical and Technological Advice will determine the exact duration and specific terms of reference when establishing such expert groups under the guidance of the Conference of the Parties;'

22. *Confirms* that the Subsidiary Body on Scientific, Technical and Technological Advice, within the available budgetary resources for matters related to its mandate, may make requests to the Executive Secretary and utilize the clearing-house mechanism, and other appropriate means, to assist in the preparation of its meetings;

23. *Decides* to make an assessment at its sixth meeting of the recommendations made to it by the Subsidiary Body on Scientific, Technical and Technological Advice with a view to providing guidance to the Subsidiary Body on ways to improve its inputs;

24. *Decides* that the guidance to the Subsidiary Body on Scientific, Technical and Technological Advice contained in specific decisions of a meeting of the Conference of the Parties should take into account the need for a coherent and realistic programme of work for the Subsidiary Body, including the identification of priority issues, allowing flexibility in timing, and *agrees* that the Subsidiary Body on Scientific, Technical and Technological Advice may, if necessary, adjust the timing of its consideration of issues;

25. *Recognizes* that there is a need to improve the quality of the scientific, technical and technological advice provided to the Conference of the Parties, and to undertake sound scientific and technical assessments, including in-depth assessments of the state of knowledge on issues critical for the implementation of the Convention;

26. *Requests* the Subsidiary Body on Scientific, Technical and Technological Advice to continue to improve the way it conducts its scientific, technical and technological work in order to improve the quality of its advice to the Conference of the Parties;

27. *Decides* that, in its scientific, technical and technological work and, in particular, scientific assessments, the Convention should make use of existing programmes and activities of the Convention or of other bodies and of expertise made available by Parties;

28. *Notes* the report of the brainstorming meeting on scientific assessment (UNEP/CBD/COP/5/INF/1), and refers it to the Subsidiary Body on Scientific, Technical and Technological Advice for consideration and, where appropriate, use in its work;

29. *Requests* the Subsidiary Body on Scientific, Technical and Technological Advice:

(a) To identify and, where needed, further develop, procedures and methods to undertake or participate in scientific assessments, or make use of existing ones, taking into account considerations of participation, effectiveness and costs;

(b) To undertake a limited number of pilot scientific assessment projects, in preparation for the sixth meeting of the Conference of the Parties, and to invite, among others, the Millennium Ecosystem Assessment to work closely together with the Subsidiary Body in this area; and to facilitate and support the implementation of these projects; and, at an appropriate stage, to carry out an evaluation of them;

(c) To develop further its methodologies for scientific assessment, and to provide advice to Parties on scientific assessment design and implementation;

(d) To identify and regularly update, within the context of its programme of work, assessment priorities and information needs;

(e) To review the implementation of decision II/1 relating to the Global Biodiversity Outlook and provide the results of that review to the Conference of the Parties at its sixth meeting, together with advice on means to enhance implementation and/or any desirable amendments to the decision;

30. *Notes* the proposed uniform methodology for the use of the roster of experts, set out in annex I to recommendation V/14 of the Subsidiary Body on Scientific, Technical and Technological Advice, and refers this to the Subsidiary Body and the Executive Secretary for consideration and, where appropriate, use in their work;

31. *Encourages* Parties, other Governments and relevant bodies when nominating their experts for inclusion in the roster to consider:

(a) Gender balance;

(b) Involvement of indigenous people and members of local communities;

(c) Range of relevant disciplines and expertise, including, *inter alia*, biological, legal, social and economic sciences, and traditional knowledge;

IV Other matters

32. *Decides* that every effort should be made to promote the development of the clearing-house mechanism with respect to its role in facilitating the transfer of technology and know-how through exchanging and disseminating information, and in enhancing capacity-building, especially at the national level, taking into account the review of the mechanism;

33. *Recognizes* that activities at the subregional and regional levels, including existing regional processes established for other biological-diversity-related purposes, have an important role to play in preparing for Convention meetings and enhancing implementation of the Convention, and *calls on* Parties to participate actively in suitable subregional and regional activities, as well as on the Executive Secretary, subject to necessary voluntary contributions, to facilitate the involvement in such subregional and regional activities of developing country Parties, in particular the least developed and small island developing States, and other Parties with economies in transition;

34. *Requests* the Executive Secretary to continue enhancing communication with the Parties through the notification system for the Convention with respect to inter-sessional activities, documents received, selection of experts for technical panels, peer-review processes initiated by the Executive Secretary, and liaison groups and other expert bodies, and to make such information available through the clearing-house mechanism save to the extent that an expert objects to the release of information concerning him or her;

35. *Decides* to improve the functioning of the existing operational procedures for the conduct of meetings under the Convention, particularly to allow small delegations to participate more effectively, including in relation to the scheduling of agenda items and dealing with timetable changes;

36. *Calls on* the Executive Secretary to use national reports, as appropriate, to gather focused information as part of the preparatory process for issues in the work

programme, and decides to reflect this approach in its decisions on national reports arising from work agreed to in decision IV/14, on national reports by Parties;

V Implementation

37. *Decides* that it is necessary to enhance the review and facilitation of implementation of the Convention;

38. *Decides* to hold an open-ended inter-sessional meeting, to assist with preparations for the sixth meeting of the Conference of the Parties. The meeting will be of three days duration and is to be held in conjunction with an existing meeting. The meeting will consider, and to the extent possible develop draft elements of decisions on, the following topics:

(a) Preparation of the Strategic Plan for the Convention;

(b) The second national reports; and

(c) Means to support implementation of the Convention, in particular, implementation of priority actions in national biodiversity strategies and action plans;

39. *Decides* to review at its sixth meeting, in the light of this experience, the role of inter-sessional processes in enhancing implementation of the Convention;

40. *Decides* to enhance further the functions of subregional and regional processes in preparing for meetings under the Convention and in promoting the implementation of the Convention at the regional, subregional and national levels;

41. *Requests* the Executive Secretary to provide an overview of existing mechanisms and processes for review of national implementation of environmental instruments, and *invites* Parties to undertake, on a voluntary basis, a review of national programmes and needs related to the implementation of the Convention and, if appropriate, to inform the Executive Secretary accordingly.

Decision V/21: Cooperation with other bodies

The Conference of the Parties,

1. *Takes note* of ongoing cooperation activities;

2. *Invites* the Executive Secretary to strengthen cooperation, particularly in the area of scientific and technical assessment of biodiversity, bearing in mind the importance of biodiversity assessments in identifying emerging issues and reviewing the programmes of work and the impact of measures taken under the Convention;

3. *Invites* the Executive Secretary to strengthen the cooperation with the United Nations Framework Convention on Climate Change, including its Kyoto Protocol, on relevant issues such as dry and sub-humid lands, forest biological diversity, coral reefs, and incentive measures;

4. *Welcomes and endorses* the second joint work plan (2000–2001) between the Convention on Biological Diversity and the Ramsar Convention on Wetlands (UNEP/CBD/SBSTTA/5/INF/12), and *commends* it as a useful example of future cooperation between the Convention on Biological Diversity and other environmental conventions;

5. *Notes* that the second joint work plan between the Convention on Biological Diversity and the Ramsar Convention on Wetlands includes a range of cooperative actions in relation to several ecosystem themes and cross-cutting issues of the Convention on Biological Diversity, as well as proposing actions to harmonize institutional processes, and requests the Subsidiary Body on Scientific, Technical and Technological Advice and the Executive Secretary to take these actions fully into consideration in furthering the respective programmes of work for these areas;

6. Recalling decision III/21, *takes note* of the United Nations Environment Programme/Convention on Migratory Species study on the complementarities between the Convention on Migratory Species and the Convention on Biological Diversity (UNEP/CBD/COP/5/INF/28);

7. *Requests* the Executive Secretary to take the study into consideration and, in collaboration with the Secretariat of the Convention on Migratory Species, to develop a proposal on how migratory species could be integrated into the work programme of the Convention on Biological Diversity, and the role the Convention on Migratory Species could play in the implementation of the Convention on Biological Diversity with regard to, *inter alia*, the ecosystem approach, the Global Taxonomy Initiative, indicators, assessments and monitoring, protected areas, public education and awareness, and sustainable use, including tourism;

8. *Requests* the Executive Secretary to submit the proposal referred to in paragraph 7 above for review by the Subsidiary Body on Scientific, Technical and Technological Advice prior to the sixth meeting of the Conference of the Parties and *requests* the Subsidiary Body to provide advice to the Conference of the Parties at its sixth meeting;

9. *Takes note* of the International Biodiversity Observation Year of DIVERSITAS, to take place from 2001 to 2002, and *requests* the Executive Secretary and *invites* Parties, to find ways and means of collaborating with this initiative and ensure complementarity with the initiative foreseen to be undertaken by the United Nations Educational, Scientific and Cultural Organization and the Secretariat of the Convention on Biological Diversity to increase scientific knowledge and public awareness of the crucial role of biodiversity for sustainable development;

10. *Requests* the Subsidiary Body on Scientific, Technical and Technological Advice to identify opportunities for collaboration with the Millennium Ecosystem Assessment in contributing to the assessment needs of the Convention, in particular through the pilot scientific assessment projects referred to in paragraph 29 (b) of decision V/20;

11. *Decides* to accept the invitation of the Millennium Ecosystem Assessment to be represented in the Executive Committee, *nominates* for this purpose the Chair of the Subsidiary Body on Scientific, Technical and Technological Advice and the Executive Secretary, and *directs* that the Subsidiary Body on Scientific, Technical and Technological Advice be kept informed on developments and progress;

12. *Recognizes* the importance of the Global Biodiversity Forum as a mechanism for building understanding and capacity in implementing the Convention, and encourages support of the Global Biodiversity Forum process.

DECISION V/21

Decision V/22: Budget for the programme of work for the biennium 2001–2002

The Conference of the Parties,

Having considered the proposed budget for the biennium 2001–2002 submitted by the Executive Secretary (UNEP/CBD/COP/5/18 and Add.1),

Noting the commendable work done by the Executive Secretary and his staff in the delivery of the programme of work for biennium 1999–2000,

Noting with appreciation the annual contribution to the rental of the premises of the Secretariat, as well as the annual contribution of US$1 million, by the host Government for the period 1996–2000, which was used to offset planned expenditures and *urging* that this be continued for the biennium 2001–2002,

Noting also that there is wide support for the implementation of the Convention's work programme among Governments, international organizations, non-governmental organizations, and the private sector, through the provision of expertise, information and human and financial resources,

1. *Approves* a programme budget of US$8,594,000 for the year 2001 and of US$10,049,900 for the year 2002, for the purposes listed in table 1 below;

2. *Adopts* the indicative scale of contributions for 2001 and 2002 contained in the annex to the present decision;

3. *Approves* the staffing table for the programme budget contained in table 2 below and *requests* that all staff positions be filled expeditiously;

4. *Approves* a drawing of US$5,203,200 from the unspent balances or contributions ('carry-over') from previous financial periods to cover part of the 2001–2002 budget;

5. *Authorizes* the Executive Secretary to transfer resources among the programmes within the limits agreed to in decisions IV/17 and III/23, namely the ability to transfer between each of the main appropriation lines set out in table 1 up to an aggregate of 15 per cent of the total programme budget, provided that a further limitation of up to a maximum of 25 per cent of each such appropriation line shall apply;

6. *Notes with concern* that a number of Parties have not paid their contributions to the core budget (BY Trust Fund) for previous years, which are due on 1 January of each year in accordance with paragraph 4 of the financial rules, and the late payment of contributions to the core budget by Parties during each calendar year of a biennium, which have contributed to the significant carry-over from one biennium to the next, and, in the event that there is no improvement in the payment of contributions by Parties, *invites* the Executive Secretary to submit proposals for promoting full and timely payment of contributions by Parties for the consideration and review of the seventh meeting of the Conference of the Parties;

7. *Urges* Parties that have still not paid their contributions to the core budget (BY Trust Fund) to do so without delay, and *requests* the Executive Secretary to publish and regularly update information on the status of contributions of Parties to the Convention's trust funds (BY, BE, BZ);

8. *Decides*, with regard to contributions due from 1 January 2001 onwards, that Parties whose contributions are in arrears for two or more years will be allowed to attend the meetings of the Convention's bodies with a maximum of two delegates until their arrears have been cleared;

9. *Further decides* that, with regard to contributions due from 1 January 2001 onwards, Parties that are not least developed countries or small island developing States whose contributions are in arrears for two or more years, will not receive funding from the Secretariat to attend meetings of the Convention's bodies until their arrears have been cleared;

10. *Authorizes* the Executive Secretary to enter into commitments up to the level of the approved budget, drawing on available cash resources, including unspent balances, contributions from previous financial periods and miscellaneous income;

11. *Decides also* to fund, upon request, from the core budget (BY) the participation of members of the bureaux of the Conference of the Parties, Subsidiary Body on Scientific, Technical and Technological Advice and the Intergovernmental Committee on the Cartagena Protocol on Biosafety at the inter-sessional meetings of the respective bureaux;

12. *Takes note* of the decisions of the Bureau of the fourth meeting of the Conference of the Parties authorizing the Executive Secretary to utilize savings, unspent balances from previous financial periods and miscellaneous income in the amount of US$1,565,000 from the BY Trust Fund to fund the participation of developing country Parties, in particular the least developed and small island developing States, and other Parties with economies in transition, in the meetings of the Convention and *requests* the Executive Secretary, in consultation with the Bureau, to monitor the availability of voluntary contributions to the BZ Trust Fund in the event of any shortfall;

13. *Decides* that the trust funds (BY, BE, BZ) for the Convention shall be extended for the period of two years, beginning 1 January 2002 and ending 31 December 2003;

14. *Invites* all Parties to the Convention to note that contributions to the core budget (BY) are due on 1 January of the year in which these contributions have been budgeted for, and to pay them promptly, and *urges* Parties, in a position to do so, to pay by 1 October 2000 for the calendar year 2001 and by 1 October 2001 for the calendar year 2002 the contributions required to finance expenditures approved under paragraph 1 above, as offset by the amount in paragraph 4, and, in this regard, *requests* that Parties be notified of the amount of their contributions by 1 August of the year preceding the year in which the contributions are due;

15. *Urges* all Parties and States not Parties to the Convention, as well as governmental, intergovernmental and non-governmental organizations and other sources, to contribute to the trust funds (BY, BE, BZ) of the Convention;

16. *Takes note* of the funding estimates for the Special Voluntary Trust Fund (BE) for Additional Voluntary Contributions in Support of Approved Activities for the Biennium 2001–2002 specified by the Executive Secretary and included in table 3 below, and *urges* Parties to make contributions to this Fund;

17. *Takes note* of the funding estimates for the special voluntary Trust Fund (BZ) for facilitating participation of developing country Parties, in particular the least developed and the small island developing States amongst them, and other Parties with

economies in transition, for the biennium 2001–2002, as specified by the Executive Secretary and included in table 4 below, and urges Parties to make contributions to this Fund;

18. *Authorizes* the Executive Secretary, in consultation with the Bureau of the Conference of the Parties, to adjust the servicing of the programme of the work, including postponement of meetings, if sufficient resources are not available to the Secretariat in a timely fashion;

19. *Requests* the Executive Secretary to prepare and submit a budget for the programme of work for the biennium 2003–2004 for the sixth meeting of the Conference of the Parties, and report on income and budget performance as well as any adjustments made to the Convention budget for the biennium 2001–2002;

20. *Instructs* the Executive Secretary, in an effort to improve the efficiency of the Secretariat and to attract highly qualified staff to the Secretariat, to enter into direct administrative and contractual arrangements with Parties and organizations – in response to offers of human resources and other support to the Secretariat – as may be necessary for the effective discharge of the functions of the Secretariat, while ensuring the efficient use of available competencies, resources and services, and taking into account United Nations rules and regulations. Special attention should be given to possibilities of creating synergies with relevant, existing work programmes or activities that are being implemented within the framework of other international organizations;

21. *Requests* the President of the Conference of the Parties to consult with the Secretary-General of the United Nations on an assessment of the level of the post of the Executive Secretary of the Convention and report to the Bureau of the Conference of the Parties, taking into account paragraph 1 of the Administrative Arrangements endorsed in decision IV/17.

Table 1 Biennium budget of the Trust Fund for the Convention on Biological Diversity 2001–2002

	Expenditures	*2001 (US$ thousands)*	*2002 (US$ thousands)*
I	**Programmes**		
	Executive direction and management	529.7	547.6
	Scientific, technical and technological matters	963.9	1,014.1
	Social, economic and legal matters	850.7	1,178.2
	Implementation and outreach	1,527.7	1,587.5
	Biosafety	830.6	870.9
	Resource management and conference services	2,902.7	3,695.4
	Subtotal (I)	*7,605.3*	*8,893.7*
II	**Programme support charge 13%**	**988.7**	**1,156.2**
	Total budget (I + II)	*8,594.0*	*10,049.9*
	Savings from previous years (surplus)	2,000.0	3,203.2
	NET TOTAL (Amount to be paid by the Parties)	**6,594.0**	**6,846.7**

Table 2 Secretariat-wide staffing requirements from the core budget*

		2001	2002
A	**Professional category**		
	D-2	1	1
	D-1	3	3
	P-5	3	3
	P-4	11	11
	P-3	13	13
	P-2	2	2
	Total professional category	*33*	*33*
B	**Total general service category**	**23**	**23**
TOTAL (A+B)		**56**	**56**

* The P-4 Fund management post funded from the OTL will be subject to reclassification to P-5 in 2001–2002.

Table 3 Special Voluntary Trust Fund (BE) for additional voluntary contributions in support of approved activities for the biennium 2001–2002 (thousands of United States dollars)

	Description	*2001 (US$ thousands)*	*2002 (US$ thousands)*
I			
A	**Meetings/workshops**		
	Executive direction and management		
	Regional meetings for COP 6 (4)	0.0	100.0
	Scientific, technical and technological matters		
	Regional workshops (5)	200.0	300.0
	Advisory group meetings	30.0	30.0
	Meetings of ad hoc technical expert groups (6)	210.0	210.0
	Implementation and outreach		
	Workshops on additional financial resources	100.0	100.0
	Regional workshops on the clearing-house mechanism	100.0	100.0
	CHM advisory committee	30.0	30.0
	Biosafety		
	Regional meetings for the Biosafety Protocol	100.0	100.0
	ICCP technical expert meetings (4)	140.0	140.0
	Social, economic and legal matters		
	Workshop on sustainable use and tourism	100.0	100.0

	Panel of Experts on Access and Benefit-sharing	230.0	0.0
B	**Staff**		
	Taxonomy Programme Officer (Australia/Sweden)	100.0	100.0
	Agricultural Biodiversity Programme Officer (FAO)	110.0	110.0
	Senior Programme Officer (Netherlands)	127.4	120.0
C	**Travel**		
	Travel of COP President	7.0	7.0
	Travel of SBSTTA Chair	7.0	7.0
D	**Consultants**		
	Ecosystem evaluation and assessment guidelines	15.0	15.0
	Clearing-house mechanism	15.0	15.0
E	**Sub-contracts**		
	Financial resources database and commissioned studies	33.0	0.0
	Independent review of the financial mechanism	150.0	0.0
	Global Biodiversity Outlook	100.0	100.0
	Global Taxonomy Initiative	100.0	50.0
	Pilot phase – assessments	100.0	0.0
	Clearing-house mechanism	50.0	50.0
F	**Fellowships**	**100.0**	**100.0**
Subtotal I		*2,254.4*	*1,884.0*
II	**PROGRAMME SUPPORT COSTS (13%)**	**293.1**	**244.9**
TOTAL (I+II)		**2,547.5**	**2,128.9**

Table 4 Special Voluntary Trust Fund (BZ) for facilitating participation of Parties in the Convention process for the biennium 2001–2002*

		2001 (US$ thousands)	2002 (US$ thousands)
I	Meetings		
	Sixth meeting of the Conference of the Parties	0.0	761.8
	Regional meetings for the Conference of the Parties	0.0	329.4
	Subsidiary Body on Scientific, Technical and Technological Advice	483.6	483.6
	Inter-Sessional Meeting on the Operations of the Convention	483.6	0.0
	Intergovernmental Committee on the Cartagena Protocol on Biosafety	483.6	483.6
	Ad Hoc Working Group on Access and Benefit-sharing	0.0	105.8
	Ad Hoc Working Group on Article 8 (j)	0.0	480.7

	Regional meetings for the Biosafety Protocol	329.4	0.0
	Subtotal I	*1,780.2*	*2,644.9*
II	**Programme support costs (13%)**	**231.4**	**343.8**
TOTAL (I+II)		**2,011.6**	**2,988.7**

* Developing country Parties, in particular the least developed and small island developing States among them, and other Parties with economies in transition.

Annex:
Scale of contributions to the Trust Fund for the Convention on Biological Diversity for 2001–2002

Member country	*UN scale of assessments 2000 (%)*	*Scale with 25 per cent ceiling, no LDC paying more than 0.01 % (%)*	*Contributions as per 1 January 2001 (US$)*	*UN scale of assessments 2000 (%)*	*Scale with 25 per cent ceiling, no LDC paying more than 0.01 % (%)*	*Contributions as per 1 January 2002 (US$)*	*Total contributions 2001–2002 (US$)*
Albania	0.003	0.00400	263	0.003	0.00400	274	537
Algeria	0.086	0.11452	7,552	0.086	0.11452	7,841	15,393
Angola	0.010	0.01332	878	0.010	0.01332	912	1,790
Antigua and Barbuda	0.002	0.00266	176	0.002	0.00266	182	358
Argentina	1.103	1.46883	96,855	1.103	1.46883	100,566	197,421
Armenia	0.006	0.00799	527	0.006	0.00799	547	1,074
Australia	1.483	1.97486	130,223	1.483	1.97486	135,213	265,435
Austria	0.942	1.25443	82,717	0.942	1.25443	85,887	168,604
Bahamas	0.015	0.01998	1,317	0.015	0.01998	1,368	2,685
Bahrain	0.017	0.02264	1,493	0.017	0.02264	1,550	3,043
Bangladesh	0.010	0.01332	878	0.010	0.01332	912	1,790
Barbados	0.008	0.01065	702	0.008	0.01065	729	1,432
Belarus	0.057	0.07591	5,005	0.057	0.07591	5,197	10,202
Belgium	1.104	1.47016	96,942	1.104	1.47016	100,658	197,600
Belize	0.001	0.00133	88	0.001	0.00133	91	179
Benin	0.002	0.00266	176	0.002	0.00266	182	358
Bhutan	0.001	0.00133	88	0.001	0.00133	91	179
Bolivia	0.007	0.00932	615	0.007	0.00932	638	1,253
Botswana	0.010	0.01332	878	0.010	0.01332	912	1,790
Brazil	1.471	1.95888	129,169	1.471	1.95888	134,119	263,288
Bulgaria	0.011	0.01465	966	0.011	0.01465	1,003	1,969
Burkina Faso	0.002	0.00266	176	0.002	0.00266	182	358

Burundi	0.001	0.00133	88	0.001	0.00133	91	179
Cambodia	0.001	0.00133	88	0.001	0.00133	91	179
Cameroon	0.013	0.01731	1,142	0.013	0.01731	1,185	2,327
Canada	2.732	3.63812	239,897	2.732	3.63812	249,091	488,988
Cape Verde	0.002	0.00266	176	0.002	0.00266	182	358
Central African Republic	0.001	0.00133	88	0.001	0.00133	91	179
Chad	0.001	0.00133	88	0.001	0.00133	91	179
Chile	0.036	0.04794	3,161	0.036	0.04794	3,282	6,443
China	0.995	1.32501	87,371	0.995	1.32501	90,719	178,091
Colombia	0.109	0.14515	9,571	0.109	0.14515	9,938	19,509
Comoros	0.001	0.00133	88	0.001	0.00133	91	179
Congo	0.003	0.00400	263	0.003	0.00400	274	537
Cook Islands	0.001	0.00133	88	0.001	0.00133	91	179
Costa Rica	0.016	0.02131	1,405	0.016	0.02131	1,459	2,864
Cote d'Ivoire	0.009	0.01199	790	0.009	0.01199	821	1,611
Croatia	0.030	0.03995	2,634	0.030	0.03995	2,735	5,370
Cuba	0.024	0.03196	2,107	0.024	0.03196	2,188	4,296
Cyprus	0.034	0.04528	2,986	0.034	0.04528	3,100	6,086
Czech Republic	0.107	0.14249	9,396	0.107	0.14249	9,756	19,151
Democratic People's Republic of Korea	0.015	0.01998	1,317	0.015	0.01998	1,368	2,685
Democratic Republic of the Congo	0.007	0.00932	615	0.007	0.00932	638	1,253
Denmark	0.692	0.92151	60,765	0.692	0.92151	63,093	123,858
Djibouti	0.001	0.00133	88	0.001	0.00133	91	179
Dominica	0.001	0.00133	88	0.001	0.00133	91	179
Dominican Republic	0.015	0.01998	1,317	0.015	0.01998	1,368	2,685
Ecuador	0.020	0.02663	1,756	0.020	0.02663	1,824	3,580
Egypt	0.065	0.08656	5,708	0.065	0.08656	5,926	11,634
El Salvador	0.012	0.01598	1,054	0.012	0.01598	1,094	2,148
Equatorial Guinea	0.001	0.00133	88	0.001	0.00133	91	179
Eritrea	0.001	0.00133	88	0.001	0.00133	91	179
Estonia	0.012	0.01598	1,054	0.012	0.01598	1,094	2,148
Ethiopia	0.006	0.00799	527	0.006	0.00799	547	1,074
European Community	2.500	2.50000	164,850	2.500	2.50000	171,168	336,018
Fiji	0.004	0.00533	351	0.004	0.00533	365	716
Finland	0.543	0.72310	47,681	0.543	0.72310	49,508	97,189
France	6.545	8.71577	574,718	6.545	8.71577	596,742	1,171,460
Gabon	0.015	0.01998	1,317	0.015	0.01998	1,368	2,685
Gambia	0.001	0.00133	88	0.001	0.00133	91	179
Georgia	0.007	0.00932	615	0.007	0.00932	638	1,253
Germany	9.857	13.12625	865,545	9.857	13.12625	898,715	1,764,260
Ghana	0.007	0.00932	615	0.007	0.00932	638	1,253
Greece	0.351	0.46742	30,821	0.351	0.46742	32,003	62,824
Grenada	0.001	0.00133	88	0.001	0.00133	91	179
Guatemala	0.018	0.02397	1,581	0.018	0.02397	1,641	3,222
Guinea	0.003	0.00400	263	0.003	0.00400	274	537
Guinea-Bissau	0.001	0.00133	88	0.001	0.00133	91	179
Guyana	0.001	0.00133	88	0.001	0.00133	91	179

Haiti	0.002	0.00266	176	0.002	0.00266	182	358
Honduras	0.003	0.00400	263	0.003	0.00400	274	537
Hungary	0.120	0.15980	10,537	0.120	0.15980	10,941	21,478
Iceland	0.032	0.04261	2,810	0.032	0.04261	2,918	5,728
India	0.299	0.39817	26,255	0.299	0.39817	27,261	53,517
Indonesia	0.188	0.25035	16,508	0.188	0.25035	17,141	33,649
Iran (Islamic Republic of)	0.161	0.21440	14,137	0.161	0.21440	14,679	28,817
Ireland	0.224	0.29829	19,669	0.224	0.29829	20,423	40,093
Israel	0.350	0.46608	30,734	0.350	0.46608	31,911	62,645
Italy	5.437	7.24028	477,424	5.437	7.24028	495,720	973,144
Jamaica	0.006	0.00799	527	0.006	0.00799	547	1,074
Japan	20.573	25.00000	1,648,500	20.573	25.00000	1,711,675	3,360,175
Jordan	0.006	0.00799	527	0.006	0.00799	547	1,074
Kazakhstan	0.048	0.06392	4,215	0.048	0.06392	4,376	8,591
Kenya	0.007	0.00932	615	0.007	0.00932	638	1,253
Kiribati	0.001	0.00133	88	0.001	0.00133	91	179
Kyrgyzstan	0.006	0.00799	527	0.006	0.00799	547	1,074
Lao People's Democratic Republic	0.001	0.00133	88	0.001	0.00133	91	179
Latvia	0.017	0.02264	1,493	0.017	0.02264	1,550	3,043
Lebanon	0.016	0.02131	1,405	0.016	0.02131	1,459	2,864
Lesotho	0.002	0.00266	176	0.002	0.00266	182	358
Liechtenstein	0.006	0.00799	527	0.006	0.00799	547	1,074
Lithuania	0.015	0.01998	1,317	0.015	0.01998	1,368	2,685
Luxembourg	0.068	0.09055	5,971	0.068	0.09055	6,200	12,171
Madagascar	0.003	0.00400	263	0.003	0.00400	274	537
Malawi	0.002	0.00266	176	0.002	0.00266	182	358
Malaysia	0.183	0.24370	16,069	0.183	0.24370	16,685	32,754
Maldives	0.001	0.00133	88	0.001	0.00133	91	179
Mali	0.002	0.00266	176	0.002	0.00266	182	358
Marshall Islands	0.001	0.00133	88	0.001	0.00133	91	179
Mauritania	0.001	0.00133	88	0.001	0.00133	91	179
Mauritius	0.009	0.01199	790	0.009	0.01199	821	1,611
Mexico	0.995	1.32501	87,371	0.995	1.32501	90,719	178,091
Micronesia (Federated States of)	0.001	0.00133	88	0.001	0.00133	91	179
Monaco	0.004	0.00533	351	0.004	0.00533	365	716
Mongolia	0.002	0.00266	176	0.002	0.00266	182	358
Morocco	0.041	0.05460	3,600	0.041	0.05460	3,738	7,338
Mozambique	0.001	0.00133	88	0.001	0.00133	91	179
Myanmar	0.008	0.01065	702	0.008	0.01065	729	1,432
Namibia	0.007	0.00932	615	0.007	0.00932	638	1,253
Nauru	0.001	0.00133	88	0.001	0.00133	91	179
Nepal	0.004	0.00533	351	0.004	0.00533	365	716
Netherlands	1.632	2.17328	143,306	1.632	2.17328	148,798	292,104
New Zealand	0.221	0.29430	19,406	0.221	0.29430	20,150	39,556
Nicaragua	0.001	0.00133	88	0.001	0.00133	91	179
Niue	0.001	0.00133	88	0.001	0.00133	91	179
Niger	0.002	0.00266	176	0.002	0.00266	182	358

Nigeria	0.032	0.04261	2,810	0.032	0.04261	2,918	5,728
Norway	0.610	0.81232	53,564	0.610	0.81232	55,617	109,181
Oman	0.051	0.06792	4,478	0.051	0.06792	4,650	9,128
Pakistan	0.059	0.07857	5,181	0.059	0.07857	5,379	10,560
Palau	0.001	0.00133	88	0.001	0.00133	91	179
Panama	0.013	0.01731	1,142	0.013	0.01731	1,185	2,327
Papua New Guinea	0.007	0.00932	615	0.007	0.00932	638	1,253
Paraguay	0.014	0.01864	1,229	0.014	0.01864	1,276	2,506
Peru	0.099	0.13184	8,693	0.099	0.13184	9,026	17,720
Philippines	0.081	0.10787	7,113	0.081	0.10787	7,385	14,498
Poland	0.196	0.26101	17,211	0.196	0.26101	17,870	35,081
Portugal	0.431	0.57395	37,846	0.431	0.57395	39,297	77,143
Qatar	0.033	0.04395	2,898	0.033	0.04395	3,009	5,907
Republic of Korea	1.006	1.33966	88,337	1.006	1.33966	91,722	180,059
Republic of Moldova	0.010	0.01332	878	0.010	0.01332	912	1,790
Romania	0.056	0.07457	4,917	0.056	0.07457	5,106	10,023
Russian Federation	1.077	1.43421	94,572	1.077	1.43421	98,196	192,767
Rwanda	0.001	0.00133	88	0.001	0.00133	91	179
Saint Kitts and Nevis	0.001	0.00133	88	0.001	0.00133	91	179
Saint Lucia	0.001	0.00133	88	0.001	0.00133	91	179
Saint Vincent and the Grenadines	0.001	0.00133	88	0.001	0.00133	91	179
Samoa	0.001	0.00133	88	0.001	0.00133	91	179
San Marino	0.002	0.00266	176	0.002	0.00266	182	358
Sao Tome and Principe	0.001	0.00133	88	0.001	0.00133	91	179
Senegal	0.006	0.00799	527	0.006	0.00799	547	1,074
Seychelles	0.002	0.00266	176	0.002	0.00266	182	358
Sierra Leone	0.001	0.00133	88	0.001	0.00133	91	179
Singapore	0.179	0.23837	15,718	0.179	0.23837	16,320	32,038
Slovakia	0.035	0.04661	3,073	0.035	0.04661	3,191	6,264
Slovenia	0.061	0.08123	5,356	0.061	0.08123	5,562	10,918
Solomon Islands	0.001	0.00133	88	0.001	0.00133	91	179
South Africa	0.366	0.48739	32,139	0.366	0.48739	33,370	65,509
Spain	2.591	3.45035	227,516	2.591	3.45035	236,235	463,751
Sri Lanka	0.012	0.01598	1,054	0.012	0.01598	1,094	2,148
Sudan	0.007	0.00932	615	0.007	0.00932	638	1,253
Suriname	0.004	0.00533	351	0.004	0.00533	365	716
Swaziland	0.002	0.00266	176	0.002	0.00266	182	358
Sweden	1.079	1.43687	94,747	1.079	1.43687	98,378	193,125
Switzerland	1.215	1.61798	106,689	1.215	1.61798	110,778	217,467
Syrian Arab Republic	0.064	0.08523	5,620	0.064	0.08523	5,835	11,455
Tajikistan	0.004	0.00533	351	0.004	0.00533	365	716
The former Yugoslav Republic of Macedonia	0.004	0.00533	351	0.004	0.00533	365	716
Togo	0.001	0.00133	88	0.001	0.00133	91	179
Tonga	0.001	0.00133	88	0.001	0.00133	91	179
Trinidad and Tobago	0.016	0.02131	1,405	0.016	0.02131	1,459	2,864
Tunisia	0.028	0.03729	2,459	0.028	0.03729	2,553	5,012
Turkey	0.440	0.58593	38,636	0.440	0.58593	40,117	78,754

Turkmenistan	0.006	0.00799	527	0.006	0.00799	547	1,074
Uganda	0.004	0.00533	351	0.004	0.00533	365	716
Ukraine	0.190	0.25302	16,684	0.190	0.25302	17,323	34,007
United Arab Emirates	0.178	0.23704	15,630	0.178	0.23704	16,229	31,859
United Kingdom of Great Britain and Northern Ireland	5.090	6.77819	446,954	5.090	6.77819	464,082	911,036
United Republic of Tanzania	0.003	0.00400	263	0.003	0.00400	274	537
Uruguay	0.048	0.06392	4,215	0.048	0.06392	4,376	8,591
Uzbekistan	0.025	0.03329	2,195	0.025	0.03329	2,279	4,475
Vanuatu	0.001	0.00133	88	0.001	0.00133	91	179
Venezuela	0.160	0.21307	14,050	0.160	0.21307	14,588	28,638
Viet Nam	0.007	0.00932	615	0.007	0.00932	638	1,253
Yemen	0.010	0.01332	878	0.010	0.01332	912	1,790
Zambia	0.002	0.00266	176	0.002	0.00266	182	358
Zimbabwe	0.009	0.01199	790	0.009	0.01199	821	1,611
TOTAL	**77.516**	**100.000**	**6.594m**	**77.516**	**100.000**	**6.847m**	**13.441m**

Decision V/23: Consideration of options for conservation and sustainable use of biological diversity in dryland, Mediterranean, arid, semi-arid, grassland and savannah ecosystems

The Conference of the Parties,

1. *Establishes* a programme of work on the biological diversity of dryland, Mediterranean, arid, semi-arid, grassland, and savannah ecosystems, which may also be known as the programme on 'dry and sub-humid lands', bearing in mind the close linkages between poverty and loss of biological diversity in these areas;

2. *Endorses* the programme of work contained in annex I to the present decision;

3. *Urges* Parties, countries, international and regional organizations, major groups and other relevant bodies to implement it, to support scientifically, technically and financially its activities at the national and regional levels and to foster cooperation among countries within regions and subregions sharing similar biomes;

4. *Endorses* the indicative list of levels of implementation and coordination for the various activities which are proposed in annex II, and the process described in the paragraphs 5, 6 and 7 below, and illustrated in annex III;

5. *Requests* the Subsidiary Body on Scientific, Technical and Technological Advice to review and assess periodically the status and trends of the biological diversity of dry and sub-humid lands on the basis of the outputs of the activities of the programme of work, and make recommendations for the further prioritization, refinement and scheduling of the programme of work based on the review by the Executive Secretary referred to in paragraph 8 below;

6. *Requests* the Executive Secretary to review this programme of work and identify expected outcomes, further activities to achieve these outcomes, those who should implement these activities, and timetables for action and follow-up, taking into account the suggestions of the technical group of experts, and to present these to the Subsidiary Body on Scientific, Technical and Technological Advice for consideration at a following meeting. This process should be carried out in close collaboration with the Executive Secretary of the United Nations Convention to Combat Desertification and other relevant bodies to provide synergy and avoid duplication;

7. *Requests* the Subsidiary Body on Scientific, Technical and Technological Advice to establish an ad hoc technical group of experts with the following tasks:

(a) Consolidate and assess information on the status and trends of biodiversity of dry and sub-humid lands, on the possible establishment of an international network of dry and sub-humid areas of particular value for biodiversity, on indicators, on processes affecting biodiversity, on global benefits derived from biodiversity, and on the socio-economic impacts of its loss, including the interrelationship between biodiversity and poverty;

(b) Assess the progress and the effects of the specific measures that have been taken for the conservation and sustainable use of biodiversity, for resource management and for the support of sustainable livelihoods;

(c) Assess international priorities set up at the regional and global levels and make proposals for expected outcomes, further activities, possible actors that may implement them, and timetables for action;

8. *Requests* the Executive Secretary to collaborate with the Secretariat of the Convention to Combat Desertification, including through the development of a joint work programme, drawing upon the elements contained in the note by the Executive Secretary on coordination between the Convention on Biological diversity and the Convention to Combat Desertification (UNEP/CBD/COP/5/INF/15), as well as with other relevant bodies, in the implementation and further elaboration of the programme of work and further requests the Executive Secretary to seek inputs from and collaborate with countries with sub-humid lands, and with other bodies relevant to sub-humid lands;

9. *Requests* the Executive Secretary to establish a roster of experts on the biological diversity of dry and sub-humid lands. This should be carried out in close collaboration with the Executive Secretary of the Convention to Combat Desertification and other relevant bodies to provide synergy and avoid duplication;

10. *Requests* the Executive Secretary to make available relevant information on the biological diversity of dry and sub-humid lands through various means, including the development in the clearing-house mechanism of a database on dry and sub-humid lands;

11. *Invites* bilateral and international funding agencies to provide support for the implementation of the activities of the programme of work on the biodiversity of dry and sub-humid lands, in particular for capacity-building in developing countries and countries with economies in transition.

Annex I:
Draft programme of work on dry and sub-humid lands

I Introduction

1. The overall aim of the programme of work is to promote the three objectives of the Convention in dry and sub-humid lands.[23]

2. The elaboration and implementation of the programme of work should:

(a) Build upon existing knowledge and ongoing activities and management practices, and promote a concerted response to fill knowledge gaps while supporting best management practices through partnership among countries and institutions;

(b) Ensure harmony with the other relevant thematic programmes of work under the Convention on Biological Diversity, as well as the work on cross-cutting issue;

(c) Promote synergy and coordination, and avoid unnecessary duplication, between related conventions, particularly the United Nations Convention to Combat Desertification, and the programmes of various international organizations, while respecting the mandates and existing programmes of work of each organization and the intergovernmental authority of the respective governing bodies;

(d) Promote effective stakeholder participation, including the identification of priorities, in planning, in research and in monitoring and evaluating research;

(e) Respond to national priorities through the implementation of specific activities in a flexible and demand-driven manner;

(f) Support the development of national strategies and programmes and promote the integration of biological-diversity concerns in sectoral and cross-sectoral plans, programmes and policies, in furtherance of Article 6 of the Convention on Biological Diversity, in seeking harmonization and avoiding duplication when undertaking activities relevant to other related conventions, in particular the United Nations Convention to Combat Desertification.

3. The elaboration and implementation of the programme of work should aim at applying the ecosystem approach adopted under the Convention on Biological Diversity. Implementation of the programme of work will also build upon the knowledge, innovations and practices of indigenous and local communities consistent with Article 8 (j) of the Convention.

II Programme of work

4. The programme of work is divided in two parts, 'Assessments' and 'Targeted actions in response to identified needs', to be implemented in parallel. Knowledge gained through the assessments will help guide the responses needed, while lessons learned from activities will feed back into the assessments.

23 The programme of work does not apply to polar and tundra regions.

Part A: Assessments

Operational objective

5. To assemble and analyse information on the state of the biological diversity of dry and sub-humid lands and the pressures on it, to disseminate existing knowledge and best practices, and to fill knowledge gaps, in order to determine adequate activities.

Rationale

6. Ecosystems of dry and sub-humid lands tend to be naturally highly dynamic systems. Assessment of the status and trends of the biological diversity of dry and sub-humid lands is therefore particularly challenging. A better understanding of the biological diversity of dry and sub-humid lands, their dynamics, their socio-economic value and the consequences of their loss and change is needed. This also includes the merits of short-term adaptive management practices compared with long-term management planning. This should not, however, be seen as a prerequisite for targeted actions for the conservation and sustainable use of the biological diversity of dry and sub-humid lands. Indeed, lessons learned from practices, including indigenous and local community practices, contribute to the knowledge base. Since water constraints are a defining characteristic of dry and sub-humid lands, effective water management strategies underpin their successful management. This requires an appropriate balance between the immediate water requirements of humans, their livestock and crops, and water required to maintain biodiversity and ecosystem integrity.

Activities

Activity 1. Assessment of the status and trends of the biological diversity of dry and sub-humid lands, including landraces, and the effectiveness of conservation measures.

Activity 2. Identification of specific areas within dry and sub-humid lands of particular value for biological diversity and/or under particular threat, such as, *inter alia*, endemic species and low lying wetlands, with reference to the criteria in Annex I to the Convention on Biological Diversity.

Activity 3. Further development of indicators of the biological diversity of dry and sub-humid lands and its loss, for the various ecosystem types, for use in the assessment of status and trends of this biological diversity.

Activity 4. Building knowledge on ecological, physical and social processes that affect the biological diversity of dry and sub-humid lands, especially ecosystem structure and functioning (eg, grazing, droughts, floods, fires, tourism, agricultural conversion or abandonment).

Activity 5. Identification of the local and global benefits, including soil and water conservation, derived from the biological diversity of dry and sub-humid lands, assessment of the socio-economic impact of its loss, and the undertaking of studies on the interrelationship between biodiversity and poverty, including analysis of: (i) the benefits from biodiversity for poverty alleviation; and (ii) the impact of biodiversity conservation on the poorest.

Activity 6. Identification and dissemination of best management practices, including knowledge, innovations and practices of indigenous and local communities that can be broadly applied, consistent with the programme of work under the Convention on Article 8 (j) and related provisions.

Ways and means

7. The activities of part A are to be carried out through:

(a) Consolidation of information from various ongoing sources, including those under other international conventions, the Global Observing Systems, and other programmes. This process would draw upon ongoing work of these existing programmes, with additional catalytic activities, such as workshops, further use of the clearing-house mechanism under the Convention on Biological Diversity, and partnerships between organizations, including, where appropriate, joint activities of the secretariats of the Convention on Biological Diversity and of the Convention to Combat Desertification, drawing upon the elements contained in the note by the Executive Secretary on possible elements of a joint work programme between the two secretariats on the biological diversity of dry and sub-humid lands (UNEP/CBD/COP/5/INF/15) in determining priorities for these activities;

Targeted research, including existing programmes of international and national research centres and research systems and other relevant international or regional programmes, with additional funding for priority work needed to overcome barriers to the conservation and sustainable use of the biological diversity of dry and sub-humid lands;

Multidisciplinary and interdisciplinary case-studies on management practices, carried out primarily by national and regional institutions, including civil-society organizations and research institutions, with support from international organizations for catalysing the preparation of studies, mobilizing funds, disseminating results, and facilitating feedback and lessons learned to case-study providers and policy makers. New resources could be needed to promote such studies to analyse the results and to provide necessary capacity-building and human-resource development;

(d) Dissemination of information and capacity-building required by assessment activities.

Part B: Targeted actions in response to identified needs

Operational objective

8. To promote the conservation of the biological diversity of dry and sub-humid lands, the sustainable use of its components and the fair and equitable sharing of the benefits arising out of the utilization of its genetic resources, and to combat the loss of biological diversity in dry and sub-humid lands and its socio-economic consequences.

Rationale

9. The activity needed to promote the conservation and sustainable use of the biological diversity of dry and sub-humid lands will depend on the state of the dry and sub-humid lands resources and the nature of the threats. Hence, a range of options needs to be considered, from sustainable use to *in situ* and *ex situ* conservation.

10. Many dry and sub-humid land resources must be managed at the level of watersheds, or at higher spatial levels, implying community or inter-community, rather than individual, management. This is often further complicated by multiple user groups (eg, agriculturalists, pastoralists and fisherfolk) and the migratory habits of some animal species and users of biological diversity. Institutions need to be developed or strengthened to provide for biological diversity management at the appropriate scale and for conflict resolution.

11. Sustainable use of biological diversity in dry and sub-humid lands may require the development of alternative livelihoods, and the creation of markets and other incentives to enable and promote responsible use.

Activities

Activity 7. Promotion of specific measures for the conservation and sustainable use of the biological diversity of dry and sub-humid lands, through, *inter alia*:

(a) The use and the establishment of additional protected areas and the development of further specific measures for the conservation of the biological diversity of dry and sub-humid lands, including the strengthening of measures in existing protected areas; investments in the development and promotion of sustainable livelihoods, including alternative livelihoods; and conservation measures;

(b) The rehabilitation or restoration of the biological diversity of degraded dry and sub-humid lands, with the associated benefits arising thereof, such as soil and water conservation;

(c) The management of invasive alien species;

(d) The sustainable management of dry and sub-humid land production systems;

(e) The appropriate management and sustainable use of water resources;

(f) Where necessary, the conservation *in situ* as well as *ex situ*, as a complement to the latter, of the biological diversity of dry and sub-humid lands, taking due account of better understanding of climate variability in developing effective *in situ* biological conservation strategies;

(g) The economic valuation of the biological diversity of dry and sub-humid lands, as well as the development and the use of economic instruments and the promotion of the introduction of adaptive technologies that enhance productivity of dry and sub-humid lands ecosystems;

(h) The sustainable use or husbandry of plant and animal biomass, through adaptive management, bearing in mind the potential population fluctuation in dry and sub-humid lands, and the support by Parties of national policies, legislation and land-use practices, which promote effective biodiversity conservation and sustainable use;

(i) The establishment and promotion of training, education and public awareness;

(j) The facilitation and improvement of the availability, the accessibility and exchange of information on sustainable use of the biological diversity of dry and sub-humid lands;

(k) The establishment and promotion of research and development programmes with a focus on, *inter alia*, building local capacity for effective conservation and sustainable use of the biological diversity of dry and sub-humid lands;

(l) Cooperation with the Ramsar Convention on Wetlands and the Convention on the Conservation of Migratory Species with regard to, *inter alia*, integrated catchment management incorporating wetlands ecosystems as integral parts of dry and sub-humid lands, and the creation of migratory-species corridors across dry and sub-humid lands during seasonal periods, as well as with the Convention on International Trade in Endangered Species (CITES) with regard to rare and endangered species in dry and sub-humid lands;

(m) Cooperation with all relevant conventions, in particular with the Convention to Combat Desertification with respect to, *inter alia*, the sustainable use of the biological diversity of dry and sub-humid lands, the application of the ecosystem approach, the assessment of the status and trends of this biological diversity as well as to its threats.

Activity 8. Promotion of responsible resource management, at appropriate levels, applying the ecosystem approach, through an enabling policy environment, including, *inter alia*:

(a) Strengthening of appropriate local institutional structures for resource management, supporting indigenous and local techniques of resource use that enable conservation and sustainable use in the long term, and/or combining appropriate existing institutions and techniques with innovative approaches to enable synergies;

(b) Decentralization of management to the lowest level, as appropriate, keeping in mind the need for common resource management and with due consideration to, *inter alia*, involving indigenous and local communities in planning and managing projects;

(c) Creating or strengthening appropriate institutions for land tenure and conflict resolution;

(d) Encouraging bilateral and subregional cooperation to address transboundary issues (such as facilitating access to transboundary rangelands), as appropriate, and in accordance with national legislation and international agreements;

(e) Harmonizing sectoral policies and instruments to promote the conservation and the sustainable use of biological diversity of dry and sub-humid lands, including by, *inter alia*, taking advantage of the existing national action programmes under the Convention to Combat Desertification frameworks at the country level, as well as, as appropriate, other existing and relevant sectoral plans and policies.

Activity 9. Support for sustainable livelihoods through, *inter alia*:

(a) Diversifying sources of income to reduce the negative pressures on the biological diversity of dry and sub-humid lands;

(b) Promoting sustainable harvesting including of wildlife, as well as ranching, including game-ranching;

(c) Exploring innovative sustainable uses of the biological diversity of dry and sub-humid lands for local income generation, and promoting their wider application;

(d) Developing markets for products derived from the sustainable use of biological diversity in dry and sub-humid lands, adding value to harvested produce; and

(e) Establishing mechanisms and frameworks for promoting fair and equitable sharing of the benefits arising out of the utilization of the genetic resources of dry and sub-humid lands, including bioprospecting.

Ways and means

The activities of part B to be carried out through:

(a) Capacity-building, particularly at the national and local levels, as well as investments in the development and promotion of sustainable livelihoods, including alternative livelihoods, and conservation measures, through participatory and bottom-up processes, with funding from bilateral and multilateral sources, and catalytic support from international organizations;

(b) Establishment of an international network of designated demonstration sites to facilitate the sharing of information and experience in implementing the programme of work, as well as to demonstrate and to promote conservation and sustainable use integration on the context of dry and sub-humid lands;

(c) Case-studies on successful management of dry and sub-humid lands that could be disseminated through, *inter alia*, the clearing-house mechanism;

(d) Improved consultation, coordination and information-sharing, including, *inter alia*, documentation on knowledge and practices of indigenous and local communities, within countries among respective focal points and lead institutions relevant to the implementation of the Convention to Combat Desertification, the Convention on Biological Diversity and other relevant global conventions and programmes, facilitated by the secretariats of the various conventions and other international organizations;

(e) Enhanced interaction between the work programmes of the Convention on Biological Diversity and the Convention to Combat Desertification, through, *inter alia*, the regional networks and action plans of the latter, drawing upon the elements contained in the note by the Executive Secretary on possible elements of a joint work programme between the two secretariats on the biological diversity of dry and sub-humid lands (UNEP/CBD/COP/5/INF/15) in determining priorities for this interaction; and

(f) Partnerships between all relevant stakeholders at all levels, including international organizations and programmes, as well as national and local partners, scientists and land users.

III Reporting framework

12. It is proposed that Parties and other bodies be requested to report on the implementation of the programme of work through, *inter alia*:

(a) Appropriate sections of the national reports on biological diversity prepared for the Conference of the Parties under Article 26 of the Convention on Biological Diversity; and/or

(b) Reports made in the context of the Convention to Combat Desertification and other relevant conventions, with due regard to, *inter alia*, promoting harmonization, avoiding duplication, and enhancing transparency.

13. The Subsidiary Body on Scientific, Technical and Technological Advice is to review such reports and make recommendation for the further prioritization and refinement of the programme of work at that time. Thereafter, the implementation of the programme is to be reviewed as determined by the Conference of the Parties.

Annex II: Indicative list of levels of implementation of the programme of work on dry and sub-humid lands

Activity	*Level of implementation*	*Level of coordination*
1	National	Ecoregional
2	National	Ecoregional
3	Ecoregional	
5	National, ecoregional, international	
6	Ecoregional	
7 a	National, ecoregional	
7 b	National	
7 c	National, ecoregional	
7 d	National	Ecoregional
7 e	National, ecoregional	
7 f	National, international	
7 g	National	Ecoregional
7 h	National	Ecoregional
7 i	National	Ecoregional
7 j	Ecoregional, international	
7 k	National, ecoregional	
7 l	International	
7 m	International	
8 a	National	Ecoregional
8 b	National	Ecoregional
8 c	Ecoregional	
8 d	National, ecoregional	
8 e	National	Ecoregional
9 a	National	Ecoregional
9 b	National	Ecoregional
9 c	National	Ecoregional
9 d	National	Ecoregional
9 e	National, international	

Annex III:
Illustration of the process outlined in paragraphs 5, 6 and 7 of decision V/23

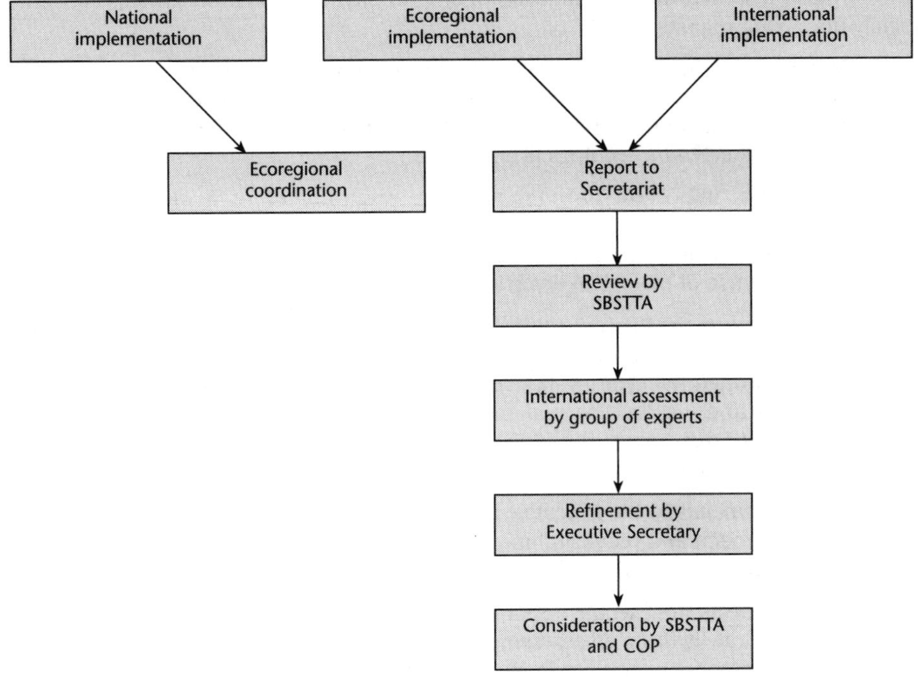

Decision V/24: Sustainable use as a cross-cutting issue

The Conference of the Parties,

Recognizing that conservation of biodiversity is a global service to humankind and is not captured and adequately recognized by current economic relations and patterns,

Recognizing also that conservation and sustainable use of biological diversity is essential to the survival of species and also benefits humankind particularly those people who are dependent on biological resources for their livelihoods,

Further recognizing the importance of integrating, as far as possible and as appropriate, the conservation and sustainable use of biological diversity into sectoral or cross-sectoral plans, programmes and policies, and recognizing the importance of addressing this issue in national biodiversity strategies and action plans, in accordance with Articles 6 and 10 of the Convention on Biological Diversity,

Taking into account the decisions of the Conference of the Parties and the ecosystem approach,

Noting the synergies between the conservation and sustainable use of biological diversity,

Noting also that the highest levels of biodiversity often occur in the less economically developed regions,

Recognizing the harmful effects of war and poverty on the conservation and sustainable use of biological diversity especially in regions rich in endemic species, and the need for mobilization of financial and technical resources for the rehabilitation and restoration of affected bio-ecological zones,

Noting the important linkages with the programmes of work on indicators (decision V/7) and incentive measures (decision V/15), and that appropriate indicators and incentive measures are essential elements in developing effective approaches to the sustainable use of biological diversity,

1. *Requests* the Executive Secretary to invite organizations involved in sustainable-use initiatives, and other relevant organizations, to gather, compile and disseminate through the clearing-house mechanism and other means, case-studies on best practices and lessons learned from the use of biological diversity under the thematic areas of the Convention, drawing on the experience of Parties, Governments, relevant organizations, the private sector and indigenous and local communities;

2. *Commends* to the Executive Secretary the process being used to develop the ecosystem approach and requests him, together with relevant organizations, to adapt and immediately initiate that process for relevant work on sustainable use;

3. *Requests* the Executive Secretary to assemble, in collaboration with relevant organizations, drawing from an assessment of the case-studies referred to in paragraph 1 above, and the process referred to in paragraph 2 above, practical principles, operational guidelines and associated instruments, and guidance specific to sectors and biomes, which would assist Parties and Governments to develop ways to achieve the sustainable use of biological diversity, within the framework of the ecosystem approach, and to present a progress report for consideration by the Subsidiary Body on Scientific, Technical and Technological Advice prior to the sixth meeting of the Conference of the Parties;

4 *Invites* Parties and Governments to identify indicators and incentive measures for sectors relevant to the conservation and sustainable use of biodiversity;

5. *Invites* Parties, Governments and relevant organizations to undertake appropriate actions to assist other Parties, especially developing countries and countries with economies in transition, to increase their capacity to implement sustainable-use practices, programmes and policies at regional, national and local levels, especially in pursuit of poverty alleviation. Appropriate actions may include:

(a) Workshops;

(b) Assistance to Parties in the identification of sectors where priority action is required;

(c) Assistance to Parties in the development of appropriate action plans;

(d) Information dissemination and appropriate technology transfer under mutually agreed terms;

6. *Urges* Parties, Governments and organizations to develop or explore mechanisms to involve the private sector and indigenous and local communities in initiatives on the sustainable use of biological diversity, and in mechanisms to ensure that indigenous and local communities benefit from such sustainable use;

7. *Recognizes* that sustainable use can be an effective tool in imbuing value to biodiversity, and *invites* Parties to identify areas for conservation that would benefit through the sustainable use of biological diversity, and to communicate this information to the Executive Secretary.

Decision V/25: Biological diversity and tourism

The Conference of the Parties,

Recognizing the increasing importance of tourism for social and economic development at local, national and regional levels,

Recognizing also that sustainable tourism depends on community involvement and participation,

Recognizing further that communities should benefit from sustainable tourism,

Recognizing also that tourism is closely linked to the preservation of a healthy environment, which in turn is an essential element of tourism development and helps to raise public awareness on some biodiversity issues.

1. *Endorses* the assessment of the interlinkages between biological diversity and tourism contained in the annex to the present decision, which includes:

(a) The economic importance of tourism and its interrelationship with the conservation and sustainable use of biological diversity;

(b) The potential impacts of tourism on biological diversity, including economic, social and environmental impacts;

2. *Accepts* the invitation to participate in the international work programme on sustainable tourism development under the Commission on Sustainable Development process with regard to biological diversity, in particular, with a view to contributing to international guidelines for activities related to sustainable tourism development in vulnerable terrestrial, marine and coastal ecosystems and habitats of major importance for biological diversity and protected areas, including fragile riparian and mountain ecosystems, bearing in mind the need for such guidelines to apply to activities both within and outside protected areas, and taking into account existing guidelines, and requests the Executive Secretary to prepare a proposal for the contribution on guidelines, for example by convening an international workshop;

3. *Decides* to transmit the assessment of the interlinkages between tourism and biological diversity to the Commission on Sustainable Development, with the recommendation to the Commission on Sustainable Development to incorporate the assessment in the international work programme on sustainable tourism development;

4. *Recommends* to Parties, Governments, the tourism industry and relevant international organizations, in particular the World Tourism Organization, to consider this assessment as a basis for their policies, programmes and activities in the field of sustainable tourism, and *encourages* them to pay particular attention to:

(a) The unique role of ecotourism – that is, tourism that relies on the existence and maintenance of biological diversity and habitats – and the need to develop clear strategies to develop sustainable ecotourism sectors which provides for full and effective participation and viable income-generating opportunities for indigenous and local communities;

(b) The need to develop, with all the potential stakeholders, strategies and plans, based on the ecosystem approach and aiming at a balance between economic, social, cultural and environmental concerns, while maximizing opportunities for the conservation and sustainable use of biological diversity, the equitable sharing of benefits and the recognition of traditional knowledge, in accordance with Article 8 (j) of the Convention, and seeking to minimize risks to biological diversity;

(c) The need for long-term monitoring and assessment, including the development and use of indicators to measure impacts of tourism on biological diversity and consequently to improve strategies and plans for tourism activities;

(d) Tangible benefits to the local economies, such as job creation and the sharing of benefits arising from the sustainable use of biological diversity for tourism purposes. In this regard, small and medium-sized enterprises can play a major role;

(e) The need to develop sustainable tourism which is an important mechanism for the conservation and sustainable use of biological diversity, and to meet the expectations of all stakeholders, while encouraging responsible behaviour on the part of tourists and the tourist industry, tourism enterprises and the local population;

(f) Awareness-raising, information-sharing, education and training of tourism operators and their staff and sensitization of tourists on biological diversity issues and technical and capacity-building at the local level, which enhance the goal of the respect and the conservation of biological diversity and its sustainable use;

(g) The fact that in order to contribute to the sustainable use of biological diversity through tourism, there is a need to implement a flexible mix of instruments, such as integrated planning, multi-stakeholder dialogue that includes indigenous peoples, zoning in land-use planning, environmental impact assessment, strategic environmental assessment, standards, industry performance-recognition programmes, recognized accreditation bodies, ecolabelling, codes of good practice, environmental management and audit systems, economic instruments, indicators and limits regarding the carrying capacity of the natural areas;

(h) The importance of the involvement and the need for the participation of indigenous and local communities and their interface with other sectors in the development and management of tourism, as well as their monitoring and assessment, including of cultural and spiritual impacts;

(i) The importance of the understanding of the values and knowledge of use of biological diversity held by the indigenous and local communities and the opportunities these offer for sustainable tourism and the support of local tourism;

5. *Endorses* the work of the Subsidiary Body on Scientific, Technical and Technological Advice on tourism as an example of sustainable use of biological diversity by exchanging experiences, knowledge and best practices through the clearing-house mechanism, and *encourages* Parties, Governments and relevant organizations to continue to submit to the Executive Secretary case-studies in this regard;

6. In order to contribute further to the international work programme on sustainable tourism development under the Commission on Sustainable Development process with regard to biological diversity, and, in particular, to the review of its implementation, which will be carried out in 2002, *requests* the Subsidiary Body on Scientific, Technical and Technological Advice to transmit its findings, through the Executive Secretary, to the Commission on Sustainable Development at its tenth session;

7. *Encourages* Parties, Governments, the tourism industry and relevant organizations to undertake activities including local capacity-building, that would be supportive of the preparations for both the International Year of Ecotourism and the International Year of Mountains, as well as activities of the International Coral Reef Initiative, and, in particular:

(a) *Urges* the tourism industry to work in partnership with all stakeholders and to commit to work within principles and guidelines for sustainable tourism development;

(b) *Encourages* Parties and Governments to complement voluntary efforts by establishing enabling policies and legal frameworks for the effective implementation of sustainable tourism.

Annex:
Assessment of the interlinkages between tourism and biological diversity

I The role of tourism in the sustainable use of biological resources

1. The sustainable use of the components of biological diversity is one of the three objectives of the Convention on Biological Diversity. For the purposes of the Convention, 'sustainable use' means 'the use of components of biological diversity in a way and at a rate that does not lead to the long-term decline of biological diversity, thereby maintaining its potential to meet the needs and aspirations of present and future generations' (Article 2). This definition of sustainable use is consistent with the concept of sustainable development as elaborated in the Rio Declaration on Environment and Development and Agenda 21, whereby 'sustainable development' meets the needs and aspirations of the current generations without compromising the ability to meet those of future generations. Sustainable development cannot be achieved without the sustainable use of the world's biological resources. The concept of sustainable use is grounded in Article 10 of the Convention on Biological Diversity, on sustainable use of components of biological diversity, and in Article 6, on general measures for conservation and sustainable use of biological diversity.

2. Sustainable tourism is developed and managed in a manner that is consistent with Agenda 21 and the ongoing work on this matter as promoted by the Commission on Sustainable Development. As such, sustainable tourism includes such aspects as sustainable use of resources, including biological resources, and minimizes environmental, ecological, cultural and social impacts, and maximizes benefits. For sustainable patterns of consumption and production in the tourism sector, it is essential to strengthen national policy development and enhance capacity in the areas of physical planning, impact assessment, and the use of economic and regulatory instruments, as well as in the areas of information, education and marketing. Particular attention should be paid to the degra-

dation of biological diversity and fragile ecosystems, such as coral reefs, mountains, coastal areas and wetlands. Ecotourism is a new, growing sector of tourism, which relies on the existence and maintenance of biological diversity and habitats. While it may require less infrastructure construction and facility-building than conventional tourism, proper planning and management are important to the sustainable development of ecotourism and to prevent threats to biological diversity on which it is intrinsically dependent.

A *Economic importance of tourism*

3. Tourism is one of the world's fastest growing industries and the major source of foreign exchange earnings for many developing countries. The receipts from international tourism grew at an average annual rate of 9 per cent for the ten-year period from 1988 to 1997, reaching $443 billion in 1997. Tourist arrivals worldwide increased by 5 per cent per annum on average during the same period.[24] According to WTO, tourism receipts accounted for a little over 8 per cent of total world exports of goods and almost 35 per cent of the total world exports of services in 1997. The breakdown of the travel account balance shows that the industrialized countries as a whole are the net importers of such services, while the developing countries as a whole have been increasing their surplus. The surplus for the latter group of countries widened steadily from $4.6 billion in 1980 to $65.9 billion in 1996, offsetting more than two thirds of their current account deficit in 1996. The travel surplus has widened steadily in all developing regions in the past decade. Economies in transition recorded a deficit of $3.5 billion in 1995, which swung back to a surplus of $1.5 billion in 1996.

4. From the production point of view, tourism contributes around 1.5 per cent of world gross national product (GNP).[25] Tourism is also a major source of employment, the hotel accommodation sector alone employing around 11.3 million people worldwide.[26] Furthermore, tourism based on the natural environment is a vital and growing segment of the tourism industry, accounting for $260 billion in 1995.[27] In a number of developing countries, tourism has already overtaken cash-crop agriculture or mineral extraction as their major source of national income.[28]

B *Tourism and environment*

5. The global social, economic and environmental impacts of tourism are immense and highly complex. Given that a high percentage of tourism involves visits to naturally and culturally distinguished sites, generating large amounts of revenue, there are clearly major opportunities for investing in the maintenance and sustainable use of biological resources. At the same time, efforts must be made to minimize the adverse impacts of the tourism industry on biological diversity.

---

24 World Tourism Organization, Tourism Highlights 1997.

25 Report of the Secretary-General on tourism and sustainable development, addendum: Tourism and economic development, Commission on Sustainable Development, seventh session, January 1999 (Advance unedited copy).

26 Ibid.

27 Jeffrey McNeely, 'Tourism and Biodiversity: a natural partnership', presented at the Symposium on Tourism and Biodiversity, Utrecht, 17 April 1997.

28 Report of the Secretary-General on tourism and sustainable development, addendum: Tourism and economic development, Commission on Sustainable Development, seventh session, January 1999 (Advance unedited copy).

6. Historical observation indicates that self-regulation of the tourism industry for sustainable use of biological resources has only rarely been successful. This is due to a number of factors. First, as there are many individual operators, local environmental conditions may be viewed as a type of common property resource. It will not be in the interests of any individual operator to invest more than his or her competitors in maintaining the general environmental standards in the resort. Similarly, operators are very likely to 'export' their adverse environmental impacts, such as refuse, waste water and sewage, to parts of the surrounding area unlikely to be visited by tourists. This reaches its most extreme form in so-called 'enclave' tourism, where tourists may remain for their entire stay in an artificially maintained environment isolated from its surroundings.

7. Second, international tourism operates in an increasingly global market in which investors and tourists have an ever-widening choice of destinations. Indeed the search for new and novel areas and experiences is one of the major engines driving the tourism life-cycle. Moreover, much of the tourism industry is controlled by financial interests located away from tourist destinations. When environmental conditions begin to deteriorate in a given location, operators are likely to shift to alternative locations rather than to invest in improving those conditions.

8. Finally, the international tourism market is fiercely competitive, much of it operating on low profit margins. Operators are therefore often extremely reluctant to absorb any additional costs associated with improving environmental conditions, and instead will often find it economically expedient to shift their area of operation rather than face such costs.

C Potential benefits of tourism for the conservation of biological diversity and the sustainable use of its components

9. Despite the potential negative impacts, and given the fact that tourism generates a large proportion of income and that a growing percentage of tourism is nature-based, tourism does present a significant potential for realizing benefits in terms of the conservation of biological diversity and the sustainable use of its components. This section addresses the potential benefits of tourism. Among the benefits are direct revenues generated by fees and taxes incurred and voluntary payments for the use of biological resources. These revenues can be used for the maintenance of natural areas and the contribution of tourism to economic development, including linkage effects to other related sectors and job-creation.

10. *Revenue creation for the maintenance of natural areas.* The most direct means of exploiting tourism for the sustainable use of biological resources is through the harnessing of some proportion of tourism revenues for that end. This may be achieved either through a generalized environmental tax on tourists or particular tourism activities or by charging fees for access to biological resources, the revenue from which can then be used for their maintenance. The latter procedure generally means charging entrance fees to national parks and other protected areas, but also includes fees for activities such as fishing, hunting and diving. Voluntary payment from visitors can also assist in conservation and management of places they visit. It may include donation, membership, sponsorship, merchandise and practical tasks.

11. There are several notable, and evidently expanding, specialist tourism sectors, where participants may be willing to pay such fees. There is growing interest in tourism programmes that involve tourists in biodiversity observation and monitoring to support conservation programmes. The largest single specialist sector at present is probably bird-

watching, although it is not clear whether bird-watchers as a group are in fact any more willing to pay than less-specialized tourists. In marine-based wildlife tourism, scuba-diving represents an important specialist sector. The specialist sector which appears to show the highest willingness to pay is sport hunting, where very large licence fees can be charged under some circumstances. It must also be recognized that these fees and taxes can also be used as measures to regulate the level of access to concerned sites and biological resources. In addition, the prospect of their continued revenue generation provides a direct incentive for the maintenance of the populations or ecosystems. One potential negative aspect of specialist tourism, however, can be the relatively low level of local community involvement since relatively few local people will be involved as specialist guides or park managers.

12. *The contribution of tourism to economic development.* Whether tourists are paying access fees or not, they have a major economic impact on the areas that they visit. Tourist expenditures, in net terms, generate income to the host communities by, for example:

(a) *Funding the development of infrastructure and services.* Tourism also stimulates infrastructure investment, such as construction of buildings, roads, railroads, airports, sewage systems, water-treatment facilities and other tourism-related facilities. Existing infrastructure may also be used in a manner which benefits local communities, where the tourist is using the facility in one way, while the community uses it in another. For example, a school may gain revenue from its use as a campground or conference venue. Improved and cheap transport services might also be brought to local communities by increased tourism;

(b) *Providing jobs.* Tourism generates job opportunities in the sector and offers various related business opportunities derived from tourism. People involved in tourism activities may become more conscious of the value of conserving their natural areas;

(c) *Providing funds for development or maintenance of sustainable practices.* Increasing revenue flows in a region may also allow development of more sustainable land-use practices, by allowing, for example, farmers to use improved rotations and some level of fertilizer input, rather than relying on slash-and-burn cultivation to restore soil fertility through fallow periods;

(d) *Providing alternative and supplementary ways for communities to receive revenue from biological diversity.* Tourism can also provide a viable economic alternative to unsustainable production or harvesting practices or other activities deleterious to the environment, particularly in marginal areas, helping to eradicate poverty;

(e) *Generating incomes.* In some areas, low-input and small-scale agricultural activities that result in both an attractive environment and the maintenance of high levels of biological diversity can also offer an opportunity for tourism. Sale of products (souvenirs, crafts and arts) derived from sustainably harvested natural resources may also provide significant opportunities for income-generation and employment. Tourists who have experienced a country associated with clean and green values may be encouraged to select products from that country.

13. Sustainable tourism can make positive improvements to biological diversity conservation especially when local communities are directly involved with operators. If such local communities receive income directly from a tourist enterprise, they, in turn, increase their evaluation of the resources around them. This is followed by greater protection and conservation of those resources as they are recognized as the source of income.

14. *Public education and awareness.* Tourism can serve as a major educational opportunity, increasing knowledge of natural ecosystems and local communities amongst a broad range of people, in particular by tour operators and guides with specialized training in biological diversity conservation, indigenous and local communities. Such education may be reciprocal. In some parts of the world, local people have become more aware of the uniqueness of their local biological resources, for example the presence of endemic species, through the advent of tourism. Better-informed tourists are more willing to pay for the access to natural sites. Tourism can also provide incentives to maintain traditional arts and crafts and opportunities to learn about different cultures. Furthermore, tourism may, under some circumstances, encourage the maintenance or revitalization of traditional practices that are favourable to the sustainable use of biological resources and that would otherwise be in danger of being lost.

II Potential impacts on biological diversity of tourism

15. In considering the role of tourism in the sustainable use of biological resources and their diversity, it is important that the potential adverse impacts of tourism are fully considered. These are roughly divided into environmental impacts and socio-economic impacts, the latter generally being those imposed on local and indigenous communities. Although such impacts on biological resources may be less easy to quantify and analyse systematically, they may be at least as important as, if not more important than, environmental impacts in the long term. Section A below addresses the potential adverse impacts on environment, while section B contains the potential socio-economic impacts.

A *Environmental impacts*

16. *Use of land and resources.* Direct use of natural resources, both renewable and non-renewable, in the provision of tourist facilities is one of the most significant direct impacts of tourism in a given area. Such use may be one-off or may be recurring. The most important are: (i) the use of land for accommodation and other infrastructure provision, including road networks; and (ii) the use of building materials. Strong competition for the use of land between tourism and other sectors results in rising prices, which increase the pressures on, for example, agricultural land. The choice of site is also an important factor. Generally preferred 'attractive landscape sites', such as sandy beaches, lakes and riversides, and mountain tops and slopes, are often transitional zones, normally characterized by species-rich ecosystems. As a result of the construction of buildings in these areas, they are often either destroyed or severely impaired.[29] Deforestation and intensified or unsustainable use of land also cause erosion and loss of biological diversity. Due to lack of more suitable sites for construction of buildings and other infrastructure, coastal wetlands are often drained and filled. Construction of marinas in certain sites and water-based tourist activities can also impact on ecosystems and even coastal coral reefs. In addition, building materials are often extracted in an unsustainable manner from ecosystems. Excessive use of fine sand of beaches, reef limestone and wood can cause severe erosion.[30] Furthermore, creation of congenial conditions for tourists may often entail various forms of environmental manipulation that may have consequences for biological resources beyond the limits of acceptable change.

29 Biodiversity and Tourism: Conflicts on the world's seacoasts and strategies for their solution, German Federal Agency for Nature and Conservation ed., 1997.
30 Ibid.

17. *Impacts on vegetation.* Direct impact on the species composition of vegetation on the ground layer can be caused by trampling and off-road driving. Off-road driving is often carried out in ecosystems perceived as a low value, such as deserts. Deserts are fragile ecosystems which can be seriously damaged by a single passage of a motor vehicle. Plant-picking and uprooting by plant collectors and casual flower-pickers can also lead to loss of individual species. Passage of tourism vehicles, particularly in high volumes along popular routes, and associated vehicle pollution also have adverse effects on vegetation, resulting in a loss of vegetation cover. Furthermore, forest fires may be caused by the careless use of campfires. The choice of sites for construction facilities can also affect vegetation patterns and species diversity.[31]

18. *Impacts on wildlife.* Wildlife tourism and other types of nature-oriented tourism may have a number of direct impacts on natural resources. The severity of these impacts is variable and has rarely been quantified for any specific cases. Actual or potential impacts include: (i) damage caused by tourism activities and equipment; (ii) increased risk of the spread of pathogens from humans or companion animals to wild species; (iii) increased risk of introduction of alien species; (iv) disturbance of wild species, thereby disrupting normal behaviour and conceivably affecting mortality and reproductive success; (v) alterations in habitats; and (vi) unsustainable consumption of wildlife by tourists.

19. One of the direct effects on wildlife of unregulated tourism may be the depletion of local populations of certain species caused by unregulated hunting, shooting and fishing. Uneducated divers and tour operators can cause extensive damage to coral reefs through trampling and anchoring. Tourists and tourist transportation means can increase the risk of introducing alien species. In addition, the manner and frequency of human presence can cause disturbance to the behaviour of animals, in particular, noise caused by radios, motorboat engines and motor vehicles. Even without much noise, some waterfowl can be agitated by canoes and rowing boats. Construction activities related to tourism can cause enormous alteration to wildlife habitats and ecosystems. Furthermore, increased consumption of wildlife by tourists can affect local wildlife populations and local fisheries as well as the amount available for consumption by local people. Souvenir manufacturing using wildlife, in particular such endangered species as corals and turtle shells, can also seriously affect those populations.

20. *Impacts on mountain environments.* Tourism has for many years been focused on mountain areas, which provide opportunities for hiking, white-water rafting, fly fishing, para-gliding and winter sports, especially skiing and related activities. Pressures from these activities on biological resources and their diversity are enormous and include: erosion and pollution from the construction of hiking trails, bridges in high mountains, camp sites, chalets and hotels. There has been increasing awareness of and publicity on the negative effects of tourism on mountains. The Kathmandu Declaration on Mountain Activities was adopted as long ago as 1982 by the International Union of Alpine Associations, in order to address these pressures on the fragile mountain ecosystems and to call for improved practices. The Convention on the Protection of the Alps, signed in 1991, and its Protocol on Tourism are the first international legal instruments addressing the potential risks associated with mountain tourism. The case-study on the Annapurna Conservation Area project also points out the difficulty in managing increased tourism activities in the fragile mountain ecosystems.

21. *Impacts on the marine and coastal environment.* Tourism activities may have major impacts on the marine and coastal environment, the resources they host and the diversity

31 Ibid.

of those resources. Most often, those impacts are due to inappropriate planning, irresponsible behaviour by tourists and operators and/or lack of education and awareness of the impacts by, for example, tourist resorts along the coastal zones. But sometimes decisions for tourism development are based only on the potential economic benefit, in spite of the known potential damage to the environment, as in the case of various coral reef resorts. Coastal erosion often affects many coastal infrastructures that have been built for tourism purposes. However, it is often those very infrastructures that have altered dune-replenishment processes (causing beach erosion), modified local currents by building harbour-like structures (causing, for example, the smothering of superficial corals), and led to eutrophication through inappropriate positioning of the resort sewage systems and the often absent treatment of the water discharged. In open waters, shipping for tourism purposes has sometimes been found to cause pollution due to intentional release, and to carry alien invasive species into new environments.

22. While the impact of tourism on coastal resources may already be a serious issue, the degradation of these resources may cause the impoverishment of their diversity, as in the case of mangrove ecosystems adjacent to tourist resorts. This may have significant ecological and economic implications for and displacement of local populations.

23. *Impacts on water resources.* Freshwater, in general, is already facing growing demand from agriculture, industry and households in many parts of the world. In some locations, such as in many small island developing States, additional demand from tourism, which is extremely water-intensive, is an acute problem.[32] The extraction of groundwater by some tourism activities can cause desiccation, resulting in loss of biological diversity. For the quality of water, some activities are potentially more damaging than others. For example, use of motorboats can lead to beach and shoreline erosion, dissemination of aquatic weed nuisances, chemical contamination, and turbulence and turbidity in shallow waters.[33] The disposal of untreated effluents into surrounding rivers and seas can cause eutrophication. It can also introduce a large amount of pathogens into the water body, making it dangerous for swimming. Naturally nutrient-rich ecosystems, such as mangroves, can perform buffer and filtering functions to a certain extent.[34]

24. *Waste management.* Disposal of waste produced by the tourism industry may cause major environmental problems. Such waste can generally be divided into: sewage and waste-water; chemical wastes, toxic substances and pollutants; and solid waste (garbage or rubbish). The effect of direct discharge of untreated sewage leading to eutrophication, oxygen deficit and algal blooms has already been pointed out.

25. *Environmental impact of travel.* Travel to and from international tourist destinations causes significant environmental impacts through pollution and production of 'greenhouse' gases. A high proportion of international tourist travel is by air. Such travel is believed to be the most environmentally costly per passenger-kilometre, although the true costs are difficult to assess accurately, as are the impacts on biological resources and their diversity.

32 Report of the Secretary-General on sustainable tourism development in small island developing States (E/CN.17/1996/20/Add.3), submitted to the Commission on Sustainable Development at its fourth session, held in 1996,

33 *Tourism, ecotourism, and protected areas,* Hector Ceballos-Lascurain, IUCN, 1996.

34 *Biodiversity and Tourism: Conflicts on the world's seacoasts and strategies for their solution,* German Federal Agency for Nature and Conservation ed., 1997.

B *Socio-economic and cultural impacts of tourism*

26. *Influx of people and related social degradation.* Increased tourism activities can cause an influx of people seeking employment or entrepreneurial opportunities, but who may not be able to find suitable employment. This may cause social degradation, such as local prostitution, drug abuse and so forth.[35] In addition, due to the unstable nature of international tourism, communities that come to rely heavily on tourism in economic terms are vulnerable to the changes in the flow of tourist arrivals and may face sudden loss of income and jobs in times of downturn.

27. *Impacts on local communities.* When tourism development occurs, economic benefits are usually unequally distributed amongst members of local communities. There is evidence suggesting that those who benefit are often limited in number and that those who benefit most are often those who were at an economic advantage to begin with, particularly landowners who can afford the investment. Specialist tourism can also involve a relatively small segment of a local community, possibly removing contact of the larger community with the resources in question. In the case of foreign direct investment, much of the profit may be transferred back to the home country. Therefore, tourism can actually increase inequalities in communities, and thus relative poverty. In addition, tourism increases local demand for goods and services, including food, resulting in higher prices and potentially decreased availability for local people. Such trends are often more prevalent where there is a lack of consultation with the peoples and communities involved in tourism.

28. A more direct example of where tourism may conflict directly with the needs and aspirations of local peoples is where the latter are excluded from particular areas given over to tourism, or at least have their rights of access severely curtailed. This is most likely to occur in protected areas created to conserve wildlife. In most cases, however, the designation of such areas as protected, and the exclusion of local people from them, have preceded the development of tourism in such areas, rather than having been a product of it. On the other hand, as in the case of the Maldives, direct conflict can be avoided by isolating the tourism industry from the bulk of the indigenous population. This isolation has been possible in the Maldives because of the availability of a large number of uninhabited islands that can be developed into tourist-resort islands.[36]

29. *Impacts on cultural values.* Tourism has a highly complex impact on cultural values. Tourism activities may lead to inter-generational conflicts through changing aspirations of younger members of communities who may have more contact with, and are more likely to be affected by, the behaviour of tourists. Furthermore, they may affect gender relationships through, for example, offering different employment opportunities to men and women. Traditional practices and events may also be influenced by the tourist preferences. This may lead to erosion of traditional practices, including cultural erosion and disruption of traditional lifestyles. Additionally, tourism development can lead to the loss of access by indigenous and local communities to their land and resources as well as sacred sites, which are integral to the maintenance of traditional knowledge systems and traditional lifestyles.

---

35 For further elaboration, see the addendum to the report of the Secretary-General on tourism and sustainable development entitled 'Tourism and social development', submitted to the Commission on Sustainable Development at its seventh session, held in 1999.

36 *Tourism and the Environment Case Studies on Goa, India, and the Maldives*, Kalidas Sawkar, Ligia Noronha, Antonio Mascarenhas, O.S. Chauhan, and Simad Saeed, Economic Development Institute of the World Bank, 1998.

Decision V/26: Access to genetic resources

A Access and benefit-sharing arrangements

The Conference of the Parties,

1. *Requests* Parties to designate a national focal point and one or more competent national authorities, as appropriate, to be responsible for access and benefit-sharing arrangements or to provide information on such arrangements within its jurisdiction;

2. *Requests* Parties to notify the Executive Secretary of the names and addresses of its focal points and competent authorities;

3. *Urges* Parties to ensure that national biodiversity strategies as well as legislative, administrative or policy measures on access and benefit-sharing contribute to conservation and sustainable-use objectives;

4. *Recognizing* the importance for Parties to promote trust-building and transparency in order to facilitate the exchange of genetic resources, particularly with regard to the implementation of Article 15 of the Convention:

(a) *Urges* Parties to pay particular attention to their obligations under Articles 15, 16 and 19 of the Convention, and *requests* them to report to the Conference of the Parties on the measures they have taken to this effect;

(b) *Notes* that legislative, administrative or policy measures for access and benefit-sharing need to promote flexibility, while recognizing the need for sufficient regulation of access to genetic resources to promote the objectives of the Convention;

(c) *Notes* that all countries are providers and recipients of genetic resources, and *urges* recipient countries to adopt, appropriate to national circumstances, legislative, administrative or policy measures consistent with the objectives of the Convention that are supportive of efforts made by provider countries to ensure that access to their genetic resources for scientific, commercial and other uses, and associated knowledge, innovations and practices of indigenous and local communities embodying traditional lifestyles relevant to the conservation and sustainable use of biological diversity, as appropriate, is subject to Articles 15, 16 and 19 of the Convention, unless otherwise determined by that provider country;

(d) *Recognizing* the complexity of this issue, with particular consideration of the multiplicity of prior informed consent considerations, *invites* Parties to cooperate further to find practical and equitable solutions to this issue;

5. *Notes* that the promotion of a comprehensive legal and administrative system may facilitate access to and use of genetic resources and contribute to mutually agreed terms in line with the aims of the Convention;

6. *Notes* that, in the absence of comprehensive legislation and national strategies for access and benefit-sharing, voluntary measures, including guidelines, may help ensure realization of the objectives of the Convention, and to that end invites the Parties to consider promotion of their use;

7. *Stresses* that it is important that, in developing national legislation on access, Parties take into account and allow for the development of a multilateral system to facilitate access and benefit-sharing in the context of the International Undertaking on Plant Genetic Resources, which is currently being revised;

8. *Notes* the report of the Chairman of the Commission on Genetic Resources for Food and Agriculture of the Food and Agriculture Organization of the United Nations (UNEP/CBD/COP/5/INF/12) and *urges* the Commission to finalize its work as soon as possible. The International Undertaking is envisaged to play a crucial role in the implementation of the Convention on Biological Diversity. The Conference of the Parties *affirms* its willingness to consider a decision by the Conference of the Food and Agriculture Organization of the United Nations that the International Undertaking become a legally binding instrument with strong links to both the Food and Agriculture Organization of the United Nations and the Convention on Biological Diversity, and *calls upon* Parties to coordinate their positions in both forums;

9. *Notes* the common understandings of the Panel of Experts on Access and Benefit-sharing with respect to prior informed consent and mutually agreed terms as contained in paragraphs 156 to 165 of its report (UNEP/CBD/COP/5/8);

10. *Decides* to reconvene the Panel of Experts on Access and Benefit-sharing with a concrete mandate and agenda. The Panel will conduct further work on outstanding issues from its first meeting, especially:

(a) Assessment of user and provider experience in access to genetic resources and benefit-sharing and study of complementary options;

(b) Identification of approaches to involvement of stakeholders in access to genetic resources and benefit-sharing processes; and will include additional expertise. The Panel will submit its report to the Ad Hoc Open-ended Working Group on Access and Benefit-sharing referred to in paragraph 11 below;

11. *Decides* to establish an Ad Hoc Open-ended Working Group, composed of representatives, including experts, nominated by Governments and regional economic integration organizations, with the mandate to develop guidelines and other approaches for submission to the Conference of the Parties and to assist Parties and stakeholders in addressing the following elements as relevant to access to genetic resources and benefit-sharing, *inter alia*: terms for prior informed consent and mutually agreed terms; roles, responsibilities and participation of stakeholders; relevant aspects relating to *in situ* and *ex situ* conservation and sustainable use; mechanisms for benefit-sharing, for example through technology transfer and joint research and development; and means to ensure the respect, preservation and maintenance of knowledge, innovations and practices of indigenous and local communities embodying traditional lifestyles relevant for the conservation and sustainable use of biological diversity, taking into account, *inter alia*, work by the World Intellectual Property Organization on intellectual property rights issues.

The above-mentioned elements should, in particular, serve as inputs when developing and drafting:

(a) Legislative, administrative or policy measures on access and benefit-sharing; and

(b) Contracts or other arrangements under mutually agreed terms for access and benefit-sharing.

The results of the deliberations of the Working Group, including draft guidelines and other approaches, shall be submitted for consideration by the Conference of the Parties at its sixth meeting.

The work of the Working Group shall take into account the reports of the Panel of Experts on Access and Benefit-sharing and other relevant information.

The Working Group will be open to the participation of indigenous and local communities, non-governmental organizations, industry and scientific and academic institutions, as well as intergovernmental organizations.

The Working Group shall maintain communication and exchange of information with the Working Group on Article 8 (j) and Related Provisions of the Convention on Biological Diversity.

In order to build capacity for access and benefit-sharing, the Open-ended Working Group shall consider issues of capacity-building, including those needs identified in paragraphs 14 (a), (b), (c) and (d) below;

12. *Notes* that information is a critical aspect of providing the necessary parity of bargaining power for stakeholders in access and benefit-sharing arrangements, and that, in this respect, there is a particular need for more information regarding:

(a) User institutions;

(b) The market for genetic resources;

(c) Non-monetary benefits;

(d) New and emerging mechanisms for benefit-sharing;

(e) Incentive measures;

(f) Clarification of definitions;

(g) *Sui generis* systems; and

(h) 'Intermediaries';

13. *Requests* the Executive Secretary to compile the information referred to in paragraph 12 above and disseminate it through the clearing-house mechanism and relevant meetings, and requests Parties and organizations to provide such information to assist the Executive Secretary;

14. *Notes* that further development of capacities regarding all aspects of access and benefit-sharing arrangements is required for all stakeholders, including local governments, academic institutions, and indigenous and local communities, and that key capacity-building needs include:

(a) Assessment and inventory of biological resources as well as information management;

(b) Contract negotiation skills;

(c) Legal drafting skills for development of access and benefit-sharing measures;

(d) Means for the protection of traditional knowledge associated with genetic resources;

15. *Noting* that the Panel of Experts on Access and Benefit-sharing was not able to come to any conclusions about the role of intellectual property rights in the implementation of access and benefit-sharing arrangements, and that the Panel developed a list of specific issues that require further study (UNEP/CBD/COP/5/8, paragraphs 127–138):

(a) *Invites* Parties and relevant organizations to submit to the Executive Secretary information on these issues by 31 December 2000;

(b) *Requests* the Executive Secretary, on the basis of these submissions and other relevant material, to make available for the second meeting of the Panel, or the first meeting of the Ad Hoc Open-ended Working Group, a report on these specific issues;

(c) *Recalls* recommendation 3 of the Inter-Sessional Meeting on the Operations of the Convention, and *requests* the Executive Secretary to prepare his report in consultation with, *inter alia*, the Secretariat of the World Intellectual Property Organization;

(d) *Invites* relevant international organizations, including the World Intellectual Property Organization, to analyse issues of intellectual property rights as they relate to access to genetic resources and benefit-sharing, including the provision of information on the origin of genetic resources, if known, when submitting applications for intellectual property rights, including patents;

(e) *Requests* relevant international organizations, for example, the World Intellectual Property Organization and the International Union for the Protection of New Varieties of Plants, in their work on intellectual property rights issues, to take due account of relevant provisions of the Convention on Biological Diversity, including the impact of intellectual property rights on the conservation and sustainable use of biological diversity, and in particular the value of knowledge, innovations and practices of indigenous and local communities embodying traditional lifestyles relevant for the conservation and sustainable use of biological diversity;

(f) *Requests* the Executive Secretary to explore experience and possibilities for synergistic interactions resulting from collaboration in research, joint development and the transfer of technology following access to genetic resources.

B The relationship between intellectual property rights and the relevant provisions of the Agreement on Trade-related Aspects of Intellectual Property Rights and the Convention on Biological Diversity

The Conference of the Parties,

Noting recommendation 3 of the Inter-Sessional Meeting on the Operations of the Convention, concerning the relationship between intellectual property rights and the relevant provisions of the Agreement on Trade-related Aspects of Intellectual Property Rights and the Convention,

1. *Reaffirms* the importance of systems such as *sui generis* and others for the protection of traditional knowledge of indigenous and local communities and the equitable sharing of benefits arising from its use to meet the provisions of the Convention, taking into account the ongoing work on Article 8 (j) and related provisions;

2. *Invites* the World Trade Organization to acknowledge relevant provisions of the Convention and to take into account the fact that the provisions of the Agreement on Trade-related Aspects of Intellectual Property Rights and the Convention on Biological Diversity are interrelated and to further explore this interrelationship;

3. *Requests* the Executive Secretary to transmit the present decision to the secretariats of the World Trade Organization and the World Intellectual Property

Organization, for use by appropriate bodies of these organizations, and to endeavour to undertake further cooperation and consultation with these organizations;

4. *Renews* its request to the Executive Secretary of the Convention to apply for observer status on the Council for the Trade-related Aspects of Intellectual Property Rights, and requests him to report back to the Conference of the Parties on his efforts.

C *Ex situ* collections acquired prior to the entry into force of the Convention and not addressed by the Commission on Genetic Resources for Food and Agriculture

The Conference of the Parties,

1. *Decides* to continue the information-gathering exercise on *ex situ* collections acquired prior to the entry into force of the Convention and not addressed by the Commission on Genetic Resources for Food and Agriculture of the Food and Agriculture Organization of the United Nations initiated by decision IV/8;

2. *Requests* the Executive Secretary to gather available information of the type described in the annexes to the present decision, as appropriate, from Parties, Governments and relevant organizations and forums through questionnaires;

3. *Invites* relevant organizations and forums already involved in consideration of these issues to provide this information to the Executive Secretary;

4. *Invites* Parties, Governments and other organizations to provide capacity-building and technology development and transfer for the maintenance and utilization of *ex situ* collections;

5. *Requests* the Executive Secretary to report to the Conference of the Parties at its sixth meeting on the implementation of the present decision.

Annex I: Elements for a questionnaire on *ex situ* collections

A questionnaire to solicit the relevant information may contain the following elements:

1. Number, types and status, including legal status and institutional links, of relevant collections;

2. Approximate number of accessions acquired prior to the entry into force of, or not in accordance with, the Convention on Biological Diversity (<100; >100; >1000; other);

3. Whether the following information is likely to be available: country of origin; name of depositor; date of deposit; terms of access under which the material is available (All available; Some available; None available);

4. Any relevant policies regarding collections that are not addressed by the FAO Commission on Genetic Resources for Food and Agriculture, where appropriate, in particular those addressing the issue of access to the relevant collections, including matters relating to repatriation of information and repatriation of duplicates of germplasm collections;

5. Information regarding the number of requests for information and the exchange of germplasm;

6. Details of the benefits from shared germplasm and information on costs of maintaining such collections;

7. Any other relevant information.

Annex II: Questionnaire on *ex situ* collections

Objective

To inform consideration of the implementation of the Convention on Biological Diversity by *ex situ* collections.

1 Information on collections

	Number of accessions			
	Pre-Convention on Biological Diversity		Post-Convention on Biological Diversity	
	Public	Private	Public	Private
PLANT GENETIC RESOURCES seed gene banks: field collections: (eg botanic gardens and arboreta) other: (eg DNA, pollen in cold storage, tissue cultures, herbaria)				
ANIMAL GENETIC RESOURCES whole animal collections: (eg zoological gardens; rare breed collections) other: (eg DNA, semen, ova in cold storage)				
MICROBIAL GENETIC RESOURCES culture collections: other:				

2 Information on pre-Convention on Biological Diversity collections

(Information to be differentiated between plant genetic resources, animal genetic resources and microbial genetic resources.)

Is information available on:	For all accessions	For most accessions	For some accessions	For few accessions	For no accessions
country of origin					
name of depositor					
date of deposit					
user institution/ country					

3 Conditions/restrictions on access and use

(Information to be differentiated between plant genetic resources, animal genetic resources and microbial genetic resources.)

(a) Description of the main conditions/restrictions (including those contained in national law, those set by the collections themselves and those set by depositors) on access to and use of genetic resources identified separately, if appropriate, for pre-Convention on Biological Diversity and post-Convention on Biological Diversity material.

(b) What limitations, if any (legal or practical), are there on applying the provisions of the Convention on Biological Diversity to the supply of pre-Convention on Biological Diversity materials for collections in your country?

4 Use of collections

(Information to be differentiated between plant genetic resources, animal genetic resources and microbial genetic resources.)

Information on the number of requests for genetic resources and for information differentiated by type of collection (public/private) and by the source of the request (national/foreign; public/private).

5 Additional information

(Information to be differentiated between plant genetic resources, animal genetic resources and microbial genetic resources.)

Any additional relevant information on other key characteristics of collections, for example:

- Focus on medicinal plants, certain families/genera/species, emphasis on economic importance, certain ecosystems (eg drylands);
- Whether the accessions are duplicated elsewhere (for conservation purposes and to determine the genetic diversity of collections world-wide).

Decision V/27: Contribution of the Convention on Biological Diversity to the ten-year review of progress achieved since the United Nations Conference on Environment and Development

The Conference of the Parties,

Recognizing the importance of the forthcoming ten-year review of progress achieved in the implementation of the outcome of the United Nations Conference on Environment and Development, scheduled for the year 2002,

1. *Welcomes* General Assembly resolution 54/218, in which the General Assembly, *inter alia*, invited the secretariat of the Convention to provide reports on how its activities are contributing to the implementation of Agenda 21 and the Programme for the Further Implementation of Agenda 21, for the consideration of the General Assembly at its fifty-fifth session,

2. *Also welcomes* the invitation of the Commission on Sustainable Development extended to secretariats of UNCED-related conventions to support preparatory activities of the ten-year review, and to review and assess their respective programmes of work since United Nations Conference on Environment and Development;

3. *Requests* the Executive Secretary to support such preparatory activities and, in particular, to report to the Commission on Sustainable Development on progress made in the implementation of the Convention;

4. *Encourages* Parties, Governments and countries to highlight and emphasize biological diversity considerations in their contributions to the ten-year review.

Decision V/28: Tribute to the Government and people of Kenya

The Conference of the Parties,

Having met in Nairobi from 15 to 26 May 2000, at the gracious invitation of the Government of Kenya,

Deeply appreciative of the special courtesy and the warm hospitality extended by the Government and people of Kenya to the Ministers, members of the delegations, observers and members of the Secretariat attending the meeting,

Expresses its sincere gratitude to the Government of Kenya and to its people for the cordial welcome that they accorded to the meeting and to those associated with its work, and for their contribution to the success of the meeting.

Decision V/29: Date and venue of the sixth meeting of the Conference of the Parties

The Conference of the Parties,

1. *Welcomes* the kind offer of the Government of the Netherlands to host the sixth meeting of the Conference of the Parties;

2. *Decides* that the sixth meeting of the Conference of the Parties will take place in The Hague, the Netherlands, at a date to be specified by the Bureau, in the second quarter of 2002, and communicated to all Parties.

Index of key terms

Article numbers are listed in **bold** for Articles of the Convention and in *italics* for Articles of the Cartagena Protocol

Index of Articles, decisions and recommendations

Page numbers in **bold** indicate the page or pages where the text of each Article, decision or recommendation is to be found

Articles of the Convention on Biological Diversity

Articles of the Cartagena Protocol on Biosafety

Decisions of the Conference of the Parties

Recommendations of the Subsidiary Body on Scientific, Technical and Technological Advice